STRANGE
FRUIT

STRANGE

PLAYS ON
LYNCHING
BY
AMERICAN
WOMEN

FRUIT

edited by

Kathy A. Perkins and Judith L. Stephens

INDIANA UNIVERSITY PRESS   BLOOMINGTON AND INDIANAPOLIS

Library of Congress Cataloging-in-Publication Data

Strange Fruit : plays on lynching by American women /
edited by Kathy A. Perkins and Judith L. Stephens.
p.   cm.
Includes bibliographical references (p.   ).
ISBN 0-253-33356-3 (cl : alk. paper). —
ISBN 0-253-21163-8 (pa : alk. paper)
1. Lynching—United States—Drama. 2. American drama—
Women authors. 3. American drama—Afro-American authors.
4. Afro-Americans—Drama.   I. Perkins, Kathy A., date.
II. Stephens, Judith L. (Judith Louise), date.
PS627.L95S73   1997
812'.5080355—dc21   97-29605

1   2   3   4   5   02   01   00   99   98   97

THE EDITORS DEDICATE THIS ANTHOLOGY
TO OUR FAMILIES AND TO THE FAMILIES
OF ALL LYNCHING VICTIMS.

◆

TO MARION PERKINS, SR., AND TO THE
MEMORY OF MARY MORRIS STEPHENS AND
RICHARD A. STEPHENS.

CONTENTS

◆
INTRODUCTION

◆
THE PLAYS AND PLAYWRIGHTS

FOREWORD
SANDRA L. RICHARDS

The haunting sound of Billie Holiday ever so slowly singing, "Black bodies swinging in the southern breeze. . . . Strange fruit hanging from the poplar trees," evokes a mental image of a charred, dismembered black body hanging from a tree while white men, women, and children look up at it in apparent satisfaction. Why revisit such a scene of horror? Why read a book of plays dealing with the subject of lynching?

The Billie Holiday song also speaks of blood at the roots of a tree that is metonymically characteristic of the American landscape, blood that has seeped into the soil that nourishes us all—black and white especially, but finally all who claim the United States as home. We read in order to chart a future. That is, this anthology is a challenge to a collective, historical amnesia that would forget the late nineteenth and twentieth century social ritual wherein white men brutally maintained their power by terrorizing black communities through the periodic, public maiming, burning, and quartering of people who had refused to accept their subservient role in society or who had simply been in the wrong place at the wrong time and fallen victim to mob rule. Blacks, perhaps, don't want to remember the utter degradation and helplessness of those moments. Whites, understandably, don't want to remember the dastardly acts of their grandparents, uncles, aunts, and other relatives but do, perhaps, want to enjoy the legacy of privilege that those forebears have passed on. And so for our different reasons, we would will to forget, we would collectively struggle to remove from our consciousness the knowledge that this peculiarly American tree continues to bear strange fruit. Admittedly, the very public social ritual of which Holiday sang for the most part no longer occurs. But even a cursory perusal of reports on hate crimes statistics, produced by the United States Attorney General's Office, or of *Klanwatch,* published by the Southern Poverty Law Center, reveals the extent to which rabid racism—sometimes clothed in the garb of church burnings, internet postings, individual acts of murder, or militia movements—flourishes.

But this anthology, *Strange Fruit: Plays on Lynching by American Women,* also tells another story. It is an inspiring narrative of resistance on the part of black and white women. Women who through their dramatizations of the effects of lynching on self, family, and community resisted racist, sexist constructions, women who believed that they could make a difference. These artists challenge us to similarly stare history in the face and reject the harvest of hatred and fear with which we presently live. Thus hopefully we read and, in so doing, use this tradition of struggle to orient ourselves towards contemporary battles. The women whose work is included in this anthology knew, as we must come to accept, that our very lives depend on this remembering and resistance.

ACKNOWLEDGMENTS

We would like to thank the following individuals for their advice and guidance in the preparation of this anthology: James V. Hatch, Toni L. Barton, Barbara Mollett, Trudier Harris, James Cameron, Lois Malou Jones, Victor Leo Walker, Winona L. Fletcher, Esme Bhan, the late May Miller, Dennis Gouran, Sandra L. Richards, and the late Joseph Lacy.

To the staff at the following research centers and libraries: Moorland-Spingarn Research Center, Fisk University Special Collections, Schomburg Center for Research in Black Culture, New York Public Library for the Performing Arts, The Library of Congress, The Penn State Schuylkill Campus.

Special thanks to the Black Theatre Network (BTN), Association for Theatre in Higher Education (ATHE), the National Conference of African American Theatre (NCAAT), the Women and Theatre Program (WTP), and the Black Theatre Association (BTA).

Also to those individuals who assisted with research, editing, and manuscript preparation: Wendy Barber, Diane Evans, Meg Greco, Ann Haugo, Rita Disroe, Siona Benjamin-Kruge, Ah-Jeong Kim, Eileen Smith, and Ann Snyder.

From the University of Illinois: The Research Board, Joseph Smith; from Penn State University: The College of the Liberal Arts, The Institute for the Arts and Humanistic Studies, Women's Studies, the Department of Theatre Arts, the Department of Speech Communications, the Schuylkill Campus.

Others who have offered personal support: Nancy M. Davis, Linda Perkins, Vincent Wimbush, Marion and Minerva Perkins, Jane White, Esther Smith, Helen Hendy, Danielle Richards, Nora Lea Garay, Mary Jane Stephens, and Louise Morris.

INTRODUCTION

Lynching Dramas and Women: History and Critical Context

JUDITH L. STEPHENS

> We have a terrible history that should be told.
>
> —James Cameron, *Founder, America's Black Holocaust Museum*

The brutal history of lynching in the United States and its legacy are recurring themes in the work of American artists. As a uniquely American form of racial violence in which thousands of individuals, primarily black men, were killed by white mobs, lynching exerts a powerful force in the configuration of a national racial consciousness. The term lynching has had different meanings at different times. A person who was lynched was a victim of mob violence but was not always killed and both men and women from various ethnic and racial groups have been lynched. For the purposes of this study, lynching means the murder of black individuals, primarily black men, by a white mob with no repercussions for the perpetrators. This is the particular form of lynching that became a systematic feature of black/white race relations in the United States after 1865 and which lynching dramas address.[1]

Although all forms of racial violence are reflected in the work of both black and white artists, the most persistent focus on lynching is found in the work of African American artists. Studies on lynching and its representation in the arts can reveal the cultural impact of this legacy and provide insight into a history that simultaneously unites and divides black and white Americans.

This anthology's focus on lynching and its representation in theatre offers a perspective of "lynching drama" as a unique genre and a valuable source for exploring women's contribution to the American stage. A lynching drama is *a play in which the threat or occurrence of a lynching, past or present, has major impact on the dramatic action.* Each playwright's treatment of lynching is different, reflecting the time period as well as the artist's individual perspective and style, but the focus on a lynching incident and its impact form the hallmark of the genre.

Lynching plays can be recognized as a distinct genre of American drama because: (1) they are based on lynching as a manifestation of black/white race relations *specifically* in the United States; (2) they reflect the philosophy of both white supremacists, who supported lynching, and the historical anti-lynching movement, which originated in the African American community; (3) they are written almost exclusively by American playwrights (one known exception is Jean-Paul Sartre's *The Respectful Prostitute*) and portray American settings and characters; and (4) they have been produced in all regions of the United States throughout the twentieth century. Lynching plays encompass both one-act and full-length dramas as well as a variety of production styles. All currently known lynching dramas are listed in the table at the end of this volume.

Although lynching plays have existed as a form of American theatre for at least ninety years, they have remained a largely unrecognized and unexamined genre in theatre history and dramatic criticism. Articles by Winona Fletcher, Judith L. Stephens, and Gloria T. Hull focus on lynching plays and play-wrights, but no full-length study has existed on these dramas and their place in American theatre history.[2] These plays represent a distinctly American experience shaped by the African American struggle for survival and the simultaneous existence of interracial conflict and cooperation that has characterized black/white relations throughout American history. As a form of racial violence, lynching was fostered by an ideology of white supremacy, which developed and flourished within the United States after the abolition of slavery.[3] Lynching plays are both a dramatic record of racial history in the United States and a continuously evolving dramatic form that preserves the knowledge of this particular form of racial violence and the memory of its victims.

Although references to lynching appear in early African American dramas, such as William Wells Brown's *The Escape; Or, A Leap for Freedom* (1858), lynching drama developed as a form when playwrights moved beyond brief references and focused on a specific lynching incident. One of the earliest dramas by a white playwright to include a lynching incident is Thomas Dixon's *The Clansman* (1906) which gave sanction to lynching as protection for whites from the so-called black threat and as necessary punishment for black men who allegedly raped white women.[4] Plays by Angelina Weld Grimké (*Rachel*, 1916) and Ridgely Torrence (*Granny Maumee,* 1914) clearly portrayed the injustice of lynching and its impact on families and communities. As such they not only reflect the philosophy and interracial nature of the anti-lynching movement but also mark the beginning of an anti-lynching tradition in theatre.[5]

This anthology reflects the branch of lynching drama pioneered by Grimké and Torrence, which records the injustice of lynching and its impact on families and communities. The tradition continues to evolve in the works of contemporary playwrights, represented in this volume by Endesha Ida Mae Holland, Sandra Seaton, and Michon Boston. As a body of work, plays written in the anti-lynching tradition represent an important community of consciousness between black and white Americans and reveal an artistic tradition that both preserves and transcends black/white racial separation in the unity of dramatic form.

The editors have chosen to limit this volume of plays to dramas written by women because women played a unique role in the anti-lynching movement and in the development of lynching drama. Given this particular history, these plays can be seen as a source of womanist/feminist drama.[6] The compound "womanist/feminist" is used here to represent black women's leadership in the anti-lynching movement and to recognize the tradition of black and white American women working together toward common goals, but also to signify white women's frequent reproduction of the racist attitudes of white supremacy.

The criteria for inclusion were that the play be written by a woman and exhibit dramatic quality in the construction of plot and characters. The collection includes examples of both one-act and full-length lynching dramas written over a time span of approximately eighty years. A variety of production styles are represented, ranging from the early realism of *Rachel* (1916) to the experimental techniques of bifurcated characters and multiple narratives found in *Miss Ida B. Wells* (1983). The dialogue in many of the early one-act plays reflects the folk drama tradition in which playwrights attempted to artistically represent the rhythms and patterns of speech common to a particular people, culture, or region. The several selections representing the 1930s reflect that decade's increase in the number of reported lynchings.

WOMEN AND THE ANTI-LYNCHING TRADITION

Historians agree that the organized campaign against lynching was marked by extensive interracial cooperation among women under the leadership of black women. Ida B. Wells's first annual report and public speech on lynching in 1892, Mary Church Terrell's 1904 essay, "Lynching from a Negro's Point of View," Mary B. Talbert's Anti-Lynching Crusade in 1922, and Mary McLeod Bethune's 1930 statement urging southern white women to assume responsibility for halting the rise in racial violence all testify to the leadership of black women in the fight against lynching.

African American women, such as Ida B. Wells, were the first to articulate the connection between the lynching of black men, the sexual exploitation of black and white women, and the role white women played in maintaining the system of racial oppression. According to Hazel Carby, Wells had argued as early as 1892 that white men used the ownership of the body of the white female as a terrain on which to lynch the black male. Black women, who were positioned outside the protection of the ideology of true womanhood, could clearly see the compromised role of white women; that is, that lynchings were being carried out on their behalf.[7] Bettina Aptheker has documented the importance of this insight, which linked lynching to the triple oppression of black men and women and white women. "In defending the racial integrity of Black manhood, Wells simultaneously affirmed the virtue of Black woman-hood and the independence of white womanhood. For the dialectics of the lynch mentality required the dehumanization of Black men (as rapists), Black women (as prostitutes), and white women (as property) whose honor was to be avenged by the men who possessed them."[8] But white women were apparently reluctant to adopt this view of lynching. Not until the 1930s did white women begin to realize that southern male chivalry was largely a means of control and repression and that lynching was an extension of that control, as much over white women as over African Americans.

According to Rosalyn Terborg-Penn, "The Anti-Lynching Crusade was perhaps the most influential link in the drive for interracial cooperation among women's groups. As a result of its efforts, the 1922 National Council of Women, representing thirteen million American women, resolved to 'endorse the Anti-Lynching Crusade recently launched by the colored women of this country.'"[9] The continued impact of black women's leadership is seen in the 1930s with the formation of the (white) Association of Southern Women for the Prevention of Lynching (ASWPL). Terborg-Penn states, "Without a doubt, it was the leadership of black women, many of whom had been active in the late 19th century women's club movement, who motivated white women in 1930 to organize the Association of Southern Women for the Prevention of Lynching."[10] Gerda Lerner has also cited lynching as "the issue above all others which prompted black and white women to seek interracial cooperation, with black women taking the leadership and coaxing, prodding, and shaming white women into action."[11] In her definitive history of the ASWPL, Jacquelyn Dowd Hall notes the enthusiasm with which both the white and black press greeted the formation of ASWPL but emphasizes the importance of earlier anti-lynching activities carried out by the African American community which "shaped the social and political climate that made the founding of ASWPL possible."[12]

Black women's leadership in the drive for interracial cooperation among women in the anti-lynching movement is reflected in this volume by the fact that they wrote the earliest plays and the largest number of plays. Kathy Perkins notes, "When black women first picked up the pen as playwrights they chose to speak out against the atrocities of lynching."[13] Playwrights such as Angelina Grimké and Georgia Douglas Johnson had contributed their time to the anti-lynching movement. Reflecting the interracial cooperation of the movement, plays by May Miller and Ann Seymour were submitted to a contest for one-act plays on the theme of lynching that was sponsored by the ASWPL. This is the only known organization to have sponsored a contest for plays specifically focusing on lynching and aiming to "promote an anti-lynching spirit through-out the South."[14] Black theatre pioneers Randolph Edmonds and Anne Cooke were among the contest judges.

When the ASWPL was formed, the worst years of mob violence were over;

but after years of steady decline, lynchings started to increase again in the 1930s, an effect of the economic disasters of the Great Depression and the increased idleness and irritability among whites.[15] Stirred by the "increase in the number and viciousness of lynchings," the Writers' League Against Lynching was formed in 1934 "to help formulate public opinion against such lawlessness" (see letter to Annie Nathan Meyer, Appendix 1). The response of playwrights is seen in the fact that the editors have, thus far, identified the 1930s as the most prolific decade for lynching dramas.

A crucial area of common ground between black and white women working in the anti-lynching movement centered on combating the mythology of the black male rapist. Ida B. Wells had clearly articulated white women's role in supporting this mythology in 1892, but white women did not take organized action until the ASWPL was formed in 1930. The primary aim of the ASWPL was to drive home the point that black men did not provoke lynching by raping white women and that white women did not want this murder carried out under the myth that it was for their protection. According to Hall, the importance of the ASWPL was that no one could drive this point home with such "dramatic force" as a group of southern white women.[16] Finally, white women were publicly accepting the responsibility that black women had been pointing out to them for decades. This crucial area of mutual understanding for black and white women is reflected in this collection of plays; eight out of fifteen include a lynching victim unjustly accused of attacking a white woman. Even though statistics refuted the myth that black men were raping white women, this myth persisted throughout the South as the so-called primary reason for lynching. According to Fletcher, "The use of the black male–white female rape argument is the basis for most of the dramas on the lynching theme written in the thirties and also continued to be the argument most frequently heard in society."[17]

AN INTERRACIAL WOMANIST/FEMINIST DRAMA

Current language usage seems inadequate to express the perspective represented by these plays. What do we call a collection of plays by black and white women addressing an area that has not been previously explored in drama? As a historical source of womanist/feminist drama, the plays in this volume represent a site of struggle against dominant racial and gender ideologies of nineteenth and early twentieth century America. "Dominant racial ideology" means those prevalent views of the white culture that work to maintain a belief in white supremacy; "dominant gender ideology" means those perspectives of the white culture which support male superiority. Lynching plays represent a challenge to the social order of white male supremacy by revealing how the exploitation of black men and women and white women was interdependent and vital to such an order. Additionally, the plays expose the role of white women in maintaining a system of racial oppression.

Historians have documented the religious, economic, anthropological, and social philosophies used in the development of an ideology of white supremacy. For white supremacists, the necessity for such an ideology was brought about by the Civil War and the racial equality implied by the passage of the Fourteenth and Fifteenth Amendments. Lynching was a manifestation of this ideology and became an indicator of black/white race relations in the United States during the late nineteenth and early twentieth centuries. Lynchings reached their peak in 1892 when 255 individuals (155 black victims, 100 white) were killed by lynch mobs. As the years progressed, the number of lynchings decreased, but the ratio of black to white victims increased. Of the 100 lynchings recorded from 1924 to 1928, 91 of the victims were black and 9 were white.[18]

The developing racism against African Americans after the Civil War became welded to notions of gender in the white community. Black men were increasingly lynched because they were no longer valuable property as slaves and because as free men they began to pose an economic and political threat to notions of white manhood. According to some historians, lynching a black male was seen as a rite of passage for young white males, a ritual in which they asserted their so-called manhood by the public display of vengeful force.[19] The ideology of white supremacy relegated both black and white women to the status of sexual property for white males: black women were sexually exploited and deemed unworthy of protection; white women were controlled by the mask of chivalry and the myth that their honor was in need of protection from the sexual advances of black males. Although white male supremacist views are most commonly associated with the Ku Klux Klan, Nancy MacLean's recent study concludes that "core elements of Klan ideology," such as those based on race and gender, found acceptance in the wider American culture, including the sanctioning of "extralegal violence in defense of prevailing relations of power."[20]

Lynching plays by women challenged at the deepest level the hierarchical power relationships based on gender and race. The strength of their indictment lay in their representation of how these structures of domination were played out in everyday life. Because lynching drama was developing simultaneously with social realism and folk drama in American theatre, these plays involve particularized characters (meaning the playwright had attempted to represent true-to-life individuals instead of type characters) who speak and act in localized settings of daily routine.[21] The plays further reflect the theatre's developing realism by presenting lynching as a serious social problem that is not given resolution or closure.[22] A significant source of the dramatic power of these plays is that they bring the brutality of lynching directly into the everyday, common environments of the home, school, church, and workplace. Lynching plays gave artistic form to a brutal reality for African Americans and theatrically created an empathic common reality for white audiences. Incorporating the ideas of literary social protest, folk drama, and stage realism, lynching dramas represent an important intersection of contemporary social and artistic developments for early twentieth-century theatre in the United States.

As women's writing, these plays connect lynching to the experiences of women. *Rachel* by Angelina Grimké, *Aftermath* by Mary Burrill, and *Iola's Letter* by Michon Boston portray how the lynching of black men affected their families and communities. Georgia Douglas Johnson (*Safe*) and Ann Seymour (*Lawd, Does You Undahstan'?*) portray the grief of black women who make the extreme sacrifice of killing their offspring as a form of escape from the violence of a lynch mob. Johnson's *Blue-Eyed Black Boy* (c. 1930) and Annie Nathan Meyer's *Black Souls* (1924, 1932) address the ironies surrounding the unrestricted *actual* sexual exploitation of black women by white men and the lynching of black men for *alleged* attacks on white women. Other shared views are seen in dramas by May Miller, Sandra Seaton, and Evelyn Keller, which all expose the ineffectiveness of turning to the American judicial system as a recourse to lynching. Plays by Burrill, Regina Andrews, and Meyer each question the effectiveness of prayer or the wisdom of practicing nonviolence in the face of lynching.

CHARACTERISTICS OF LYNCHING DRAMAS BY WOMEN

All lynching plays include a focus on the threat or occurrence of a lynching incident and the impact of this incident on the characters. The plays by women share additional commonalities; for example, the home is the most common setting, and dialogue is interspersed with alternative discourse in the form of music, poetry, or prayer. A distinct heritage is reflected in the plays by black women in that the lynching incident is described, most commonly by a woman, to other characters, and this verbal re-creation or telling of events plays a prominent role in the drama.

1. An Environment of Daily Routine: Most of the plays written by black women are set in the black home. In these domestic settings, the skills and tools of sewing, ironing, cleaning, and food preparation are prominently displayed and become an integral part of the plays' action. By giving their plays domestic settings and by creating characters who are family members and neighbors, these playwrights record a view of the black home as an important place of education and resistance. Jacqueline Jones has provided insight into how black women have historically seen the "duties of domestic nurture" as a means to protect the family from white society and challenge the system of economic exploitation.[23] These lynching dramas reflect the high value black women have always placed on home maintenance and family life. Furthermore, the juxtaposition of the brutal public act of lynching with the private, intimate atmosphere of the home creates a theatre of jarring contrasts and incongruity for those who idealize the "American home" by equating it with an atmosphere of safety and peace. Within this context, the repetition of the domestic routine is seen not as a reflection of women's limited life experience, but as an aesthetic component that imparts strong dramatic contrast and contributes to the emotional power of the plays. Although a wider variety of community locations such as the home, church, school, and public workplace are seen in plays by white women, the home is the most commonly portrayed setting in all lynching plays by women.

2. An Alternative Medium: Music, Poetry, Prayer: By including poetry, prayer, and music, these plays reveal an aesthetic tradition in which such forms become an essential element of the drama, or an alternative medium for women playwrights. These elements provide counterpoints to the rhythm created by the dialogue, and, as Margaret Wilkerson explains, "help to express the rage, irony, and profundity of Black American life in tonalities and colorations absent from conventional western speech."[24]

This alternative medium takes the form of complete songs, such as "Slumber Boat" in *Rachel;* segments of songs, such as the hymns from the neighboring church in *A Sunday Morning in the South;* or background music such as "Take the A-Train" in *The Bridge Party.* Prayer emerges in the form of a prologue, or as part of the dramatic action in *Climbing Jacob's Ladder,* or as the brief supplications ("Do Lord, do Lord! Help us this night") of Hester, Mandy, or Annabel in *Blue-Eyed Black Boy, Safe,* and *Nails and Thorns.* In *Iola's Letter,* Ida B. Wells is pictured saying grace at the Moss family dinner table and a Mourner sings a solo/prayer after Thomas Moss is lynched. Similarly, the poetry of Claude McKay and Paul Lawrence Dunbar becomes an essential element of *Miss Ida B. Wells* as part of the playwright's attempt to express, artistically, the atrocities of lynching.

Lynching plays by white women also employ these techniques of an alternative medium. *Black Souls* by Annie Nathan Meyer includes poetry, prayer, and spirituals that were selected by Zora Neale Hurston. Ann Seymour incorporates poetry, music, and prayer in *Lawd, Does You Undahstan'?,* and Lillian Smith's *Strange Fruit* includes the music of a Southern revival meeting.

Props and sound effects chosen for their emotional or spiritual qualities—such as the Bible, religious paintings, and sounds of birds—are also common to many of the plays. Influences of Christianity such as the revival meeting in *Strange Fruit* and the church services in *A Sunday Morning in the South* and *Climbing Jacob's Ladder* pervade these plays and serve to emphasize religious hypocrisy in the white community and deep religious faith in the black community. This common spiritual dimension reflects the religious nature of much of the women's anti-lynching movement. The letterhead for Mary Talbert's Anti-Lynching Crusaders proclaimed, "To Your Knees, and Don't Stop Praying," and women's church groups were the staunchest supporters of ASWPL.[25]

3. A Woman's Telling of Events: All lynching plays by black women in this volume, with the exception of Regina Andrews's *Climbing Jacob's Ladder,* involve a black woman describing, or re-creating through her words, a lynching incident that has taken place in the past or is presently occurring. From Mrs. Loving's long, detailed, and painful speech in *Rachel* to Matilda's terse and halting, but equally painful, "They—they done lynched him," in *A Sunday Morning in the South,* it is women who serve as messengers relaying the tragic news, or as mediums through which the lynching is revealed or re-created. Burrill's *Aftermath* employs the power of dialogue between brother and sister as the sister responds to her brother's questions about the lynching of their father. In *Iola's Letter,* Ida B. Wells leads a group of men and women from the Memphis community as they recount the events surrounding the lynching of Thomas Moss, Calvin McDowell, and Henry Stewart. Johnson's *Safe* and *Blue-Eyed Black Boy* employ three women (mother, daughter, and friend/ neighbor) as a chorus reacting from inside the home to the sights and sounds of a lynching occurring outside. In *Nails and Thorns,* Annabel accurately fore-tells the events of a lynching despite the fact that the white law officer in charge refuses to heed her warnings. Holland's *Miss Ida B. Wells* employs two actresses (WELLS ONE and WELLS TWO) who re-create a collage of lynching incidents combined with reactions of witnesses. In Seaton's *The Bridge Party,* a group of women speaking separately produce a unified, choral effect by reciting the incidents surrounding the lynching of fourteen-year-old Cordie Cheek. This esthetic quality reinforces recognition of the important role black women play in passing on vital knowledge through an oral tradition and honors the pioneer-ing efforts of Ida B. Wells who, through her speeches, was "possibly the first person to publicly recite the horrors of lynching."[26]

White women playwrights frequently focus on a lynching by using the verbal re-creation technique but only one of their plays portrays a black woman re-creating the events of a past lynching. In Ann Seymour's *Lawd, Does You Undahstan'?,* the character of Aunt Doady recounts the vivid memories of her son's lynching as she fears for the life of her grandson. Evelyn Keller's *Voice in the Wilderness* and Annie Nathan Meyer's *Black Souls* both focus on a white woman recounting the events of a lynching. Meyer's play, like Andrews's *Climbing Jacob's Ladder,* also portrays a black man recounting, in brutal detail, the events of a lynching. In Smith's *Strange Fruit* the events of a lynching are re-created through brief, restrained exchanges between a white father and son and a white brother and sister.

CONCLUSION

Anti-lynching ideology clearly created a common aesthetic ground for black and white women playwrights, which can be recognized in the reciprocity of ideas and frequent repetition of dramatic techniques chosen to represent the brutality and injustice of lynching. These plays are complementary and recip-rocal, both womanist and feminist, in that they reflect commonalities and differences between and among black and white women. Dramas written in the anti-lynching tradition reveal a distinct heritage of black culture as well as an ideology that forms a community of consciousness for black and white women.

This first collection of lynching dramas will, we hope, promote a recognition of their importance to the American theatre and women's unique contribution to the tradition. The volume's focus on plays by women suggests their value as a historical source of womanist/feminist drama but the growing list of play titles recorded in the Table of Lynching Dramas suggests the need for a more comprehensive study. Such a study would permit a broader investigation into the origins, development, and variety of the genre.

Lynching dramas provide fertile ground for creating a new approach to the study of American theatre and culture. They offer us a fuller picture of how theatre reflects the intersection of artistic and social movements. As a distinctly American genre, they help us see ways in which theatre functions as a site for analyzing how black and white Americans have been complicit and/or resistant to racial and sexual domination.

NOTES

1. The history of this particular form of lynching is well documented. For general studies, see: Arthur Raper, *The Tragedy of Lynching* (Chapel Hill: University of North Carolina Press, 1933); Stewart E. Tolnay and E. M. Beck, *A Festival of Violence: An Analysis of Southern Lynchings* (Chicago: University of Illinois Press, 1995); Ralph Ginzburg, *100 Years of Lynching* (New York: Lancer Books, 1976); Ida B. Wells-Barnett, *On Lynchings: Southern Horrors, a Red Record, and Mob Rule in New Orleans* (New York: Arno Press and the New York Times, 1969); Walter White, *Rope and Faggot: A Biography of Judge Lynch* (New York: Arno Press, 1969); James E. Cutler, *Lynch Law: An Investigation into the History of Lynching in the United States* (Montclair: Patterson Smith, 1969); and Robert Zangrando, *The NAACP Crusade against Lynching, 1909–1950* (Philadelphia: Temple University Press, 1980). For contemporary newspaper commentary see W. E. B. Du Bois, "We are a Nation of Murderers," in Daniel Walden, ed., *W. E. B. Du Bois: The Crisis Writings* (Greenwich, Conn.: Fawcett, 1972). For an examination of lynching and its impact on African American literature see Trudier Harris, *Exorcising Blackness: Historical and Literary Lynching and Burning Rituals* (Bloomington: Indiana University Press, 1984).

2. Winona Fletcher, "From Genteel Poet to Revolutionary Playwright: Georgia Douglas Johnson," *Theatre Annual*, 30 (1985): 41–64. Judith Stephens, "The Anti-Lynch Play: Toward an Interracial Feminist Dialogue in Theatre," *Journal of American Drama and Theatre* 2 (Fall 1990): 59–69; and "Anti-Lynch Plays by African American Women: Race, Gender, and Social Protest in American Drama," *African American Review* 26 (Summer 1992): 329–339; "Lynching, American Theatre and the Preservation of a Tradition," *Journal of American Drama and Theatre* 9 (Winter 1997): 54–65. Gloria T. Hull discusses the lynching dramas of Grimké, Nelson, and Johnson in her book, *Color, Sex, and Poetry: Three Women Writers of the Harlem Renaissance* (Bloomington: Indiana University Press, 1987).

3. See, for example, Guion Griffis Johnson, "The Ideology of White Supremacy, 1876–1910," in *Essays in Southern History: The James Sprunt Studies in History and Political Science*, ed. Fletcher Melvin Green, vol. 31 (Chapel Hill: University of North Carolina, 1949), 124–156; and Joel Williamson, *The Crucible of Race: Black–*

White Relations in the American South Since Emancipation (New York: Oxford, 1984).

4. For a critical analysis of *The Clansman* and its espousal of the central myths of white supremacy, see Samuel Arthur Hay, "The Image of the Black Man as Projected by Representative White American Dramatists, 1900–1963" (Ph.D. diss., Cornell University, 1971). D. W. Griffith's film *Birth of a Nation* (1915) was based on Dixon's play.

5. A range of terminology has been used to refer to plays with a lynching theme. The phrase "anti-lynching play" has been used by recent writers such as Hatch, Brown-Guillory, and Stephens to describe dramas written to protest lynching. Scholars Winona Fletcher and Kathy Perkins have pointed out that the phrase is redundant from a black perspective because only white playwrights (such as Dixon) ever wrote plays that supported lynching, and that Georgia Douglas Johnson specifically referred to her lynching dramas as simply "plays on lynching." See Perkins, *Black Female Playwrights,* 123.

6. The term womanist is taken from Alice Walker's *In Search of Our Mother's Gardens* (New York: Harcourt Brace Jovanovich, 1983): "Womanist: **1.** . . . A black feminist or feminist of color; from the black folk expression, 'you acting womanish,' i.e., like a woman, usually referring to outrageous, audacious, courageous, or *willful* behavior . . . **2.** Also, a woman who loves other women, sexually and/or nonsexually . . . Sometimes loves individual men, sexually and/or nonsexually . . . **3.** Loves music, loves dance, loves the moon, loves the Spirit . . . **4.** Womanist is to feminist as purple is to lavender."

7. Hazel Carby, "'On the Threshold of Women's Era': Lynching, Empire and Sexuality," in *Black Feminist Theory: "Race," Writing, and Difference,* ed. Henry Louis Gates, Jr. (Chicago: University of Chicago Press, 1985), 301–616. Also see Glenda Dickerson, "The Cult of True Womanhood: Toward a Womanist Attitude in African-American Theatre," in *Performing Feminisms: Feminist Critical Theory and Theatre,* ed. Sue Ellen Case (Baltimore: Johns Hopkins University Press, 1990), 109–118.

8. Bettina Aptheker, *Women's Legacy: Essays on Race, Sex, and Class in American History* (Amherst: University of Massachusetts Press, 1982), 62.

9. Rosalyn Terborg-Penn, "Discontented Black Feminists: Prelude and Post-script to the Passage of the Nineteenth Amendment," in *Decades of Discontent: The Women's Movement, 1920–1940,* ed. Lois Scharf and Joan Jensen (Westport, Conn.: Greenwood, 1983). Also see "African American Women's Networks in the Anti-Lynching Crusade," in *Gender, Class, Race, and Reform in the Progressive Era,* ed. Noralee Frankel and Nancy S. Dye (Lexington: University of Kentucky Press, 1991).

10. Terborg-Penn, "Discontented Black Feminists," 272–273.

11. Gerda Lerner, ed., *Black Women in White America* (New York: Vintage Books, 1973), 212.

12. Jacquelyn Dowd Hall, *Revolt Against Chivalry: Jessie Daniel Ames and the Women's Campaign Against Lynching* (New York: Columbia University Press, 1979), 164–165.

13. Kathy A. Perkins, "Lynching Plays by Mary P. Burrill and Angelina Weld Grimké," paper presented for Association for Theatre in Higher Education (ATHE) panel, Atlanta, 1992.

14. ASWPL Papers, 1936.

15. Arthur Raper, *The Tragedy of Lynching*, 1933, 6; Trudier Harris, *Exorcising Blackness: Historical and Literary Lynching and Burning Rituals*, 1984, 96.

16. Hall, *Revolt Against Chivalry*, 167.

17. Fletcher, "Genteel Poet," 51.

18. See tables in Hall, *Revolt Against Chivalry*, 134–135. According to statistics from Tuskegee Institute, a total of 4,743 lynchings occurred from 1882 to 1968. Of that total, 1,297 were white victims and 3,446 were black (Zangrando, 3). Mary Talbert's Anti-Lynching Crusaders reported that 83 women were lynched between 1889 and 1922. Of that total, 17 were white and 66 were black (from Mary Talbert's file at the Beinecke Rare Book and Manuscript Library, Yale University).

19. Dennis Downey and Raymond Hyser, *No Crooked Death: The Lynching of Zachariah Walker* (Chicago: University of Chicago Press, 1991), 144–145.

20. Nancy MacLean, *Behind the Mask of Chivalry: The Making of the Second Ku Klux Klan* (New York: Oxford, 1994), 187.

21. According to Randolph Edmonds, after 1910 the movements of realism and folk drama converged to give American drama more significant plays and playwrights (385). Individuals such as Frederick Koch, Alexander Drummond, Montgomery Gregory, and Alain Locke championed a folk drama that valued authentic reproduction of common life and attempted the artistic representation of the speech, characters, manners, and incidents of a particular people, culture, or region. See Locke, "The Drama of Negro Life," in Alain Locke and Montgomery Gregory, eds. *Plays of Negro Life: A Source-Book of Native American Drama* (Westport, Conn.: Negro Universities Press, 1927), 1970.

22. Brenda Murphy, *American Realism and American Drama, 1880–1940* (New York: Cambridge University Press, 1987), xii.

23. Jacqueline Jones, *Labor of Love, Labor of Sorrow: Black Women, Work, and the Family, from Slavery to the Present* (New York: Vintage, 1985), 323.

24. Margaret Wilkerson, "Music as Metaphor: New Plays By Black Women," in Lynda Hart, ed., *Making a Spectacle: Feminist Essays on Contemporary Women's Theatre* (Ann Arbor: University of Michigan Press, 1989), 62.

25. Hall, *Revolt Against Chivalry*, 165 and 175.

26. Alfreda M. Duster, ed., *Crusade for Justice: The Autobiography of Ida B. Wells* (Chicago: University of Chicago Press, 1970), ix.

The Impact of Lynching on the Art of African American Women

✺

KATHY A. PERKINS

In May, 1918, a white plantation owner in Brooks County, Georgia, got into a quarrel with one of his colored tenants and the tenant killed him. A mob sought to avenge his death but could not find the suspected man. They therefore lynched another colored man named Hayes Turner. His wife, Mary Turner, threatened to have members of the mob arrested. The mob therefore started after her. She fled home and was found there the next morning. She was in the eighth month of pregnancy, but the mob of several hundred took her to a small stream, tied her ankles together and hung her on a tree head downwards. Gasoline was thrown on her clothes and she was set on fire. One of the members of the mob took a knife and split her abdomen open so that the unborn child fell from her womb to the ground and the child's head was crushed under the heel of another member of the mob; Mary Turner's body was finally riddled with bullets.[1]

Throughout the latter half of the nineteenth century and early part of the twentieth, such accounts were common in American newspapers, particularly among African American presses. Well into the 1950s, lynching remained one of the most pressing issues within the African American community.

America heard of the horrors of lynching, not only from women playwrights in substantial numbers, but also from women in all areas of the arts. Visual artists, musicians, and choreographers such as Meta Vaux Warrick Fuller, Lois Malou Jones, Billie Holiday, Nina Simone, Katherine Dunham, and Pearl Primus all contributed to exposing the brutality of lynching through their individual talents. Although white women, such as choreographer Helen Tamaris, in the 1920s and 1930s have used their art to address the issue of lynching, African American women have maintained a consistent tradition in expressing their sentiments on lynching through the arts. These women were participating in the larger social movement initiated in 1892 by Ida B. Wells, who documented the horrors of lynching through her newspaper editorials and publications, arguing, "No other nation, civilized or savage, burns its criminals; only under the stars and stripes is the human holocaust possible. . . . Why is mob murder permitted by a Christian nation?"[2] Joining her in protests were such black organizations as the Woman's Loyal Union (1892), the Colored Woman's League of Washington, D.C. (1892), the National Federation of Afro-American Women (1895), and the National Association of Colored Women (1896).

Meta Vaux Warrick Fuller, one of the most prominent sculptors of the Harlem Renaissance, became one of the earliest visual artists to protest the horrors of lynching with her sculpture *Mary Turner (A Silent Protest)* in 1919. So moved was Fuller by Turner's death, she felt the need to create something significant. The painted plaster sculpture, measuring 15 x 5¼ x 4½", shows a woman, clutching her pregnant stomach, looking down into the faces of the mob. Historian Benjamin Brawley, a contemporary of Fuller, contended, "Her early work is not delicate or pretty; it is gruesome and terrible; but it is also intense and vital, and from it speaks the very tragedy of the Negro race."[3] "Fuller became a powerful symbol of artistic determination for a generation of Black Artists who came after her."[4] *Mary Turner,* currently housed in the Museum of Afro-American History in Boston, is one of Fuller's most noted works. Fuller is one of few known artists—visual or literary—to produce a work centered around the lynching of a woman, although many black women were lynched.

Playwright Angelina Grimké responded to the Mary Turner lynching in a short story, "The Creaking" (1920), later retitled "Goldie." It would be nearly a half century before another artist depicted the lynching of black women. Margaret Walker in her 1966 novel *Jubilee* includes an incident in which two black women are lynched for allegedly poisoning their masters' families. Every slave in the county is forced to attend the event, which is held on the Fourth of July. Walker characterizes the white people present as being in a holiday mood, while the slaves keep silent.

The lack of representation of women as direct victims of lynching is remarkable when one recognizes that women were consistently subjected to the same brutality as men. Mary Talbert, organizer and national director of the Anti-Lynching Crusade, documented in "A Detailed List of Known Lynchings of Women in the United States: 1889–1922" that during that period eighty-three women were lynched, several of whom were white. It is interesting to note that of all the known plays by women—both black and white—none focuses on the lynching of a woman.

When the sound of the blues arrived on the American scene during the second decade of the twentieth century, singers such as Ma Rainey, Bessie Smith, and Victoria Spivey would render songs about atrocities in the South, although few of these songs were recorded. "Strange Fruit," made famous by vocalist Billie Holiday in 1939, would come to exemplify the horrors of lynching and was one of the earliest protest recordings to receive national attention:

Southern trees bear a strange fruit
Blood on the leaves and blood at the root
Black body swingin in the Southern breeze
Strange fruit hanging from the poplar trees

Pastoral scene of the gallant South
The bulging eyes and the twisted mouth
Scent of magnolia sweet and fresh
And the sudden smell of burning flesh

Here is a fruit for the crows to pluck
For the rain to gather, for the wind to suck
For the sun to rot, for the tree to drop
Here is a strange and bitter crop.

Holiday introduced the controversial song, written by white poet Lewis Allan, which she performed at Cafe Society, New York City's first interracial club. Never before had a vocal artist been so direct with the issue of lynching. Because of the untimely death of Holiday's father, "Strange Fruit" had special meaning to her, often leaving her in a severe state of depression after rendering the song. Clarence Holiday died because, given segregation laws in Texas in 1937, he could not be admitted to the local white hospital. "Strange Fruit" reminded her that her father had been lynched by the South's racism.[5] So controversial was the song that Holiday's label, Columbia Records, refused to record it. Instead, it was recorded by Holiday on Commodore Records in 1939, and it propelled her to stardom.

In 1943, at the same Cafe Society, choreographer Pearl Primus premiered a ballet in protest of lynching performed to the spoken poem "Strange Fruit." Primus, struck by the vivid images in Lewis Allen's poem, "created the dance as a solo and interpreted the poem, psychologically, from two perspectives. First she extracted the emotional reactions of one individual following the lynching. Next, she interpreted those emotional reactions through the feelings of a woman; a white woman."[6] As Primus has stated, "It dawned on me that if I could isolate a person from a lynch mob, I would have a different character from the brute who participated in the crime. People don't commit horrible crimes like this when they are alone and sober."[7]

During the 1920s through the 1940s, prominent scholar Alain Locke encouraged African American visual artists who had studied in Europe to document "Negro" life. Painter Lois Malou Jones, a long-time friend of sculptor Meta Fuller, responded to Locke's challenge by producing such works as *Meditation (Mob Victim)* in 1944. Unlike most works, which displayed the victim struggling for freedom, Jones's painting reveals an elderly African American male, bound by the hands, passively looking up to the heavens. In a 1993 interview Jones explained why she chose such a passive image. She said she had met a curious-looking man on U Street in Washington, D.C., and asked him to come and pose as a man about to be lynched. When the man arrived, she instructed him to "take the look" of a struggling man with a rope around his neck. But, telling her that he had witnessed an actual lynching as a young man in the South, the gentleman produced the resigned expression in *Mob Victim.*

Using the song "Strange Fruit," the renowned choreographer and dancer Katherine Dunham created the 1953 ballet *Southland,* in which the lynching of a man is dramatized on stage. It was performed in Santiago, Chile, primarily to show the world the injustices of the United States. In the prologue to the ballet Dunham wrote:

> And although I have not smelled the smell of burning flesh, and have never seen a black body swaying from a southern tree, I have felt these things in spirit, and finally through the creative artist comes the need of the person to show this thing to the world, hoping that by so exposing the ill the conscience of the many will protest and save further destruction and humiliation. . . . This is not all of America, it is not all of the south, but it is a living, present part.[8]

The State Department instructed her to remove the scene, but Dunham replied that she would remove it when lynching ceased in the United States. The continued performance of the piece contributed to the demise of her company later in 1965, for she was hounded by the State Department and the FBI. In a May 14, 1994, interview Ms. Dunham indicated that she was aware of the consequences of presenting such a piece, but it was important for her to expose *Southland* to the world. She expressed a desire to have *Southland* performed in the United States, where it has never been staged.

Even after the decrease in lynching atrocities in the 1950s, representation of lynching in the arts did not cease within the African American community. Lynching continued to be a topic in the works of many African American artists. Playwright Lorraine Hansberry wrote the poem *Lynchsong* in 1951:

> I can hear Rosalee
> See the eyes of Willie McGee
> My mother told me about
> Lynchings
> My mother told me about
> The dark nights
> And dirt roads
> And torch lights
> And lynch robes
> . . . . .
>
> The
> faces of men
> Laughing white

> Faces of men
> Dead in the night
> sorrow night
> and a
> sorrow night

Against the background of the 1955 murder of fourteen-year-old Emmett Till for allegedly whistling at a white woman in Mississippi and the murder of civil rights workers like James Chaney, Michael Schwerner, and Andrew Goodman, Nina Simone recorded the famous "Mississippi Goddam." Although the song does not directly speak of lynching, Simone implicitly alludes to it when she protests:

> Alabama's got me so upset, Tennessee made me lose my rest,
> And everybody knows about Mississippi, goddam.
> Can't you see it, can't you feel it, it's all in the air;
> I can't stand the pressure much longer, someone say a prayer.
> Alabama's got me so upset, Tennessee made me lose my rest,
> And everybody knows about Mississippi, goddam.
> —(Nina Simone, 1964, Fox)

Lynching is also a prevalent topic in contemporary works by African American visual artists such as Elizabeth Catlett and Pat Ward Williams. Catlett's 1992 color lithograph *To Marry* juxtaposes a struggling lynch victim with the kiss of a marrying couple. Williams's most famous piece, *Accused/Blowtorch/Padlock* (1986) uses a series of close-up shots from an actual lynching which appeared in *Life Magazine*. "Williams' photographic constructions are concerned with a personal response to history. She investigates imagery dealing with race, and family. She combines narrative and appropriate images from magazines to create her photographic constructions."[9]

In the 1990s, rap artists like X-Clan, De Lench Mob, Ice T, Sister Solja, and Public Enemy focused on the subject of lynching in order to remind a younger generation of America's horrible past. New renditions of the song "Strange Fruit," such as the one by young R&B singer Cassandra Wilson, are being recorded. Lynching as a topic in the arts is as controversial in the 1990s as it was during the early part of the century. For example, at the University of Oklahoma, an unidentified young woman created a series of quilts that included images of Ku Klux Klan lynchings of black men. The young woman was quoted as saying that she included the pictures of the lynchings "to acknowledge a history of social injustice between races." The quilts were removed from a public foyer at the university to another room because "students could not learn in a setting where they had to pass on their way to class and see how their forefathers had been lynched."[10]

African American women continue to carry on the tradition begun by women such as Angelina Grimké, Mary Burrill, Meta Fuller, and Billie Holiday. Within the African American community art is still viewed as a vehicle to connect social and political conditions. It is hoped that this collection of plays will bring to light an area of history that has been previously ignored by the larger society.

NOTES

1. October 11, 1922, Talbert Correspondence. Beinecke Rare Book and Manuscript Library, Yale University.

2. Mildred I. Thompson, *Ida B. Wells-Barnett: An Exploratory Study of an American Black Woman, 1893–1930* (Brooklyn: Carlson Publishing, Inc., 1990), 262. From a speech delivered at the National Negro Conference and published in the proceedings in 1909.

3. Benjamin Brawley, *The Negro in Literature and Art (in the United States)* (New York: Duffield & Company, 1921), 124.

4. Introduction by Mary Schmidt Campbell, Studio Museum of Harlem, *Harlem Renaissance: Art of Black America* (New York: Harry N. Abrams, 1987), 27.

5. Robert O'Meally, *Lady Day: The Many Faces of Billie Holiday* (New York: Arcade Publishing, 1991).

6. Jean Ruth Glover, "Pearl Primus: Cross-Cultural Pioneer of American Dance" (M.A. thesis, American University, 1989), 60.

7. Glover, "Pearl Primus," 60–61.

8. Katherine Dunham Papers, Southern Illinois University Archives, Carbondale, Illinois.

9. Deborah Willis and Howard Dodson, *Black Photographers Bear Witness: 100 Years of Social Protest* (Williamstown, Mass.: Williams College Museum of Art, 1989).

10. "Pictures of Lynchings Prompt Complaints," *Chronicle of Higher Education*, March 30, 1994, A6.

THE PLAYS AND
PLAYWRIGHTS

Angelina Weld Grimké
(1880–1958)

Upon learning that her father and brother were lynched, Angelina Grimké's heroine, Rachel, considers the fear black mothers must feel for their newborn sons and states, "Why it would be more merciful to strangle the little things at birth."[1] Because Grimké's unflinching approach to portraying racism resulted in such dialogue, *Rachel* encountered immediate controversy as a stage production. The play was first produced in 1916 by the Drama Committee of the Washington, D.C., branch of the NAACP and is recognized as "the first attempt to use the stage for race propaganda in order to enlighten the American people relative to the lamentable condition of ten million colored citizens in this free republic."[2] A minority section of this committee dissented from the use of the stage as a propaganda platform and formed the Howard Players organization which favored "folk plays" and a more artistic approach.

Rachel was also criticized for promoting race suicide, a criticism Grimké felt compelled to answer. In her published response, Grimké stated her purpose was to show how "a highly strung girl, a dreamer and an idealist" reacts to "race prejudice."[3] She directed the play toward whites, but primarily toward the white women whom she viewed as "one of the most conservative elements of society" and "about the worst enemies with which the colored race has to contend." Grimké believed that "if anything can make all women sisters underneath their skins, it is motherhood."[4] Focusing on motherhood as the most "vulnerable point" in white women's armor, Grimké hoped that her drama might serve as an arena for interracial communication: "If, then, the white women of this country could see, feel, understand just what effect their prejudice and the prejudice of their fathers, brothers, husbands, and sons were having on the souls of the colored mothers everywhere, and upon the mothers that are to be, a great power to affect public opinion would be set free and the battle would be half won."[5]

Present-day readers may find the play's sense of futility objectionable, but, according to Brenda Murphy, leaving problems unresolved was the predominant characteristic of early realism as it developed on the American stage.[6] The appeal to white women is only one of the many dimensions of this play. Grimké appropriated the current dominant gender ideology of the period, which idealized motherhood, in order to demonstrate how that ideology did not apply to black women.[7]

Angelina Grimké's *Rachel* is the earliest known example of a full-length drama written in the anti-lynching tradition. *Rachel* and Ridgely Torrence's one-act play *Granny Maumee* (first produced in 1914) share the distinction of beginning the anti-lynching tradition. Grimké's play is a family-centered drama, in which the past lynching of the father and son is re-created through the speech of the mother, producing a profound effect on the lives of all family members and especially on Rachel, the daughter.

The play was first produced in 1916; but, according to Gloria T. Hull, Grimké had started to work on it at least as early as 1914 and was circulating the manuscript for critical response in 1915.[8] The traditional historical importance of the play is that it is the first non-musical written, produced, and publicly performed by African Americans for which we have an extant script. According to Hull, most of the contemporary reviews were favorable, but over the years critical reaction has been extremely varied. Descriptions range from "a play with no conflict and little characterization" to "a play whose central conflict is waged in the arena of religious doubt and faith" with a "main character who approaches an authentically tragic identity."[9] Contemporary readers are usually reminded to consider the play in its historical context, and terms such as sentimental and melodramatic are commonly used to describe its language and style. But theatre scholars, critics, and artists have continued to read, interpret, and produce Grimké's drama. Kathy Perkins has suggested that Grimké and her pioneer play deserve a special place in American theatre history for revealing the psychological impact of racism on the lives of black Americans, and Margaret Wilkerson has noted the play's "striking sensitivity to the special way racism and sexism affect the black woman."[10]

The conditions of Grimké's early life influenced her writing and directed her energies toward work which combined artistic expression and social consciousness. She was born in Boston on February 27, 1880, to a white mother (Sarah Stanley) and a black father (Archibald Grimké). Grimké's father was a nephew of the famous abolitionists and women's-rights advocates Sarah Grimké and Angelina Grimké Weld. Hull suggests that the playwright's heritage of social activism helps account for the propagandistic nature of her fiction and drama. Grimké was raised in an atmosphere of religious, feminist, political, and racial liberalism. An overwhelming need to please her father may have placed restraints on Grimké's covert lesbian sexuality and, ultimately, on her creativity as a writer. Archibald Grimké, her father, was a prominent lawyer and journalist, served as U.S. Consul in Santo Domingo, and was vice-president of the NAACP. Her mother left the family when Grimké was still quite young. Information on Sarah Stanley is scant. Both Hull and Herron report that some correspondence took place between mother and daughter, and that as late as 1914 Grimké noted a date as the sixteenth anniversary of her mother's death. The estrangement from her mother may explain why motherhood is a major theme in her literary works and why all of her female characters have loving mothers or mother surrogates.[11]

Grimké attended a variety of upper-class, liberal schools, and graduated from the Boston Normal School of Gymnastics in 1902. She taught physical education and, later, English in various schools in Washington, D.C. Her shyness and quiet melancholy became more pronounced, especially after the death of her father in 1930, and she lived in retirement in New York until her death in 1958. Critics have speculated that her sexuality might have been a motivating factor in creating a protagonist who rejects the social imperative of motherhood.[12] Looking back over Grimké's life, Gloria Hull concludes, "She leaves the impression of a talented writer whose potential was never realized."[13]

Grimké's outrage over the lynching of African Americans in the United States is reflected in her early activism as well as in her drama, fiction, and poetry. At the age of nineteen, she collected signatures on a petition for an anti-lynching campaign. Her unpublished play *Mara* is similar to *Rachel* in its focus on the destructive effects of racism and the lynching of a black family. *Blackness, The Closing Door,* and *Goldie* are all short stories dealing with lynching and include graphic descriptions of mob violence that were "unknown in African American fictional literature prior to the work of Richard Wright."[14]

Rachel is traditionally considered a drama of new beginnings. Samuel Hay notes that drama depicting the horrors of lynching began with Grimké, and Claudia Tate identifies Grimké's work as the location of "a new point in African American literature," where depictions of racial protest start satisfying the expectations of twentieth-century black readers.[15] As this study reveals, Grimké's *Rachel* represents the foundation of a unique American dramatic genre which continues to develop on the contemporary stage.

NOTES

1. See Rachel's speech at the end of Act One. The first production took place March 3–4, 1916, at the Myrtilla Miner Normal School in Washington, D.C. According to Gloria T. Hull, all actors were amateurs or semiprofessionals and under the direction of Nathaniel Guy. Cast members included Zita Dyson and Rachel Guy. Subsequent productions were held at The Neighborhood Playhouse, New York City (April 1917), and in Cambridge, Mass. (May 1917, sponsored by St. Bartholomew's Church). Hull also records that the New Castle, Pennsylvania, Colored Branch of the YMCA requested permission to stage the play in 1924 (119). Professor Tish Jones directed a production at Spelman College in 1991.

2. Montgomery Gregory, "A Chronology of Negro Theatre," Alain Locke and

Montgomery Gregory, eds., *Plays of Negro Life: A Source Book of Native American Drama* (New York: Harper and Brothers, 1927), 414.

3. Angelina Grimké, "'Rachel' The Play of the Month: The Reason and Synopsis by the Author," *The Competitor,* Vol. 1, No. 1, 1920, 51–52.

4. Grimké, "'Rachel' The Play of the Month," 52.

5. Ibid.

6. Michael Greene, "Angelina Weld Grimké," *Dictionary of Literary Biography,* 153, and Brenda Murphy, *American Realism and American Drama, 1880–1940* (New York: Cambridge University Press, 1987), xii.

7. See Judith Stephens, "Anti-Lynch Plays by African American Women: Race, Gender, and Social Protest in American Drama," *African American Review* 26 (1992): 329–339.

8. Gloria T. Hull, *Color, Sex, and Poetry: Three Women Writers of the Harlem Renaissance* (Bloomington: Indiana University Press, 1987), 119.

9. Sterling Brown, *Negro Poetry and Drama and the Negro in American Fiction* (New York: Atheneum, 1978), 129; and William Storm, "Reactions of a 'Highly Strung Girl': Psychology and Dramatic Representation in Angelina W. Grimké's *Rachel,*" *African American Review,* 27 (Fall 1993): 463.

10. Kathy A. Perkins, ed., *Black Female Playwrights: An Anthology of Plays before 1950* (Bloomington: Indiana University Press, 1989), 8; and Margaret Wilkerson, ed., *9 Plays by Black Women* (New York: Mentor Press, 1986), xvi.

11. Hull, *Color, Sex, and Poetry,* 110.

12. See, for example, Carolivia Herron, ed., *Selected Works of Angelina Grimké* (New York: Oxford University Press, 1991), 17.

13. Hull, *Color, Sex, and Poetry,* 26.

14. Herron, *Selected Works of Angelina Grimké,* 21.

15. Claudia Tate, *Allegories of Political Desire: The Black Heroine's Text at the Turn of the Century* (New York: Oxford University Press, 1992), 210; and Samuel A. Hay, *African American Theatre: An Historical and Critical Analysis* (New York: Cambridge University Press, 1994), 132.

Rachel

1916

❦

Angelina Weld Grimké

CHARACTERS

MRS. LOVING, *mother*
RACHEL LOVING, *her daughter*
TOM LOVING, *her son*
JOHN STRONG, *Tom's friend*
JIMMY, *the neighbor's small boy*
MRS. LANE, *a black woman*
ETHEL, *her daughter*
EDITH, LOUISE, NANCY, MARY, MARTHA, JENNY, *children*

ACT ONE

The scene is a room scrupulously neat and clean and plainly furnished. The walls are painted green, the woodwork, white. In the rear at the left [left and right are from the spectator's point of view], an open doorway leads into a hall. Its bare, green wall and white baseboard are all that can be seen of it. It leads into the other rooms of the flat. In the center of the rear wall of the room is a window. It is shut. The white sash curtains are pushed to right and left as far as they will go. The green shade is rolled up to the top. Through the window can be seen the red bricks of a house wall, and the tops of a couple of trees moving now and then in the wind. Within the window, and just below the sill, is a shelf upon which are a few potted plants. Between the window and the door is a bookcase full of books and above it, hanging on the wall, a simply framed, inexpensive copy of Millet's The Reapers. *There is a run extending from the right center to just below the right upper entrance. It is the vestibule of the flat. Its open doorway faces the left wall. In the right wall near the front is another window. Here the sash curtains are drawn together and the green shade is partly lowered. The window is up from the bottom. Through it street noises can be heard. In front of this window is an open, threaded sewing machine. Some fabric, white fabric, is lying upon it. There is a chair in front of the machine and at the machine's left a small table covered with a green cloth. In the rear of the left wall and directly opposite to the entrance to the flat is the doorway leading into the kitchenette, dishes on shelves can be seen behind glass doors.*

In the center of the left wall is a fireplace with a grate in it for coals; over this is a wooden mantel painted white. In the center is a small clock. A pair of vases, green and white in coloring, one at each end, complete the ornaments. Over the mantel is a narrow mirror; and over this, hanging on the wall, Burne-Jones's Golden Stairs, *simply framed. Against the front end of the left wall is an upright piano with a stool in front of it. On top is music neatly piled. Hanging over the piano is Raphael's* Sistine Madonna. *In the center of the floor is a green rug, and in the center of this, a rectangular dining room table, the long side facing front. It is covered with a green tablecloth. Three dining room chairs are at the table, one at either end and one at the rear facing front. Above the table is a chandelier with four gas jets enclosed by glass globes. At the right front center is a rather shabby armchair upholstered in green.*

Before the sewing machine, MRS. LOVING *is seated. She looks worried. She is sewing swiftly and deftly by hand upon a waist in her lap. It is a white, beautiful thing and she sews upon it delicately. It is about half-past four in the afternoon; and the light is failing. Mrs. Loving pauses in her sewing, rises and lets the window shade near her go up to the top. She pushes the sash curtains to either side, the corner of a red brick house wall being thus brought into view. She shivers slightly, then pushes the window down at the bottom and lowers it a trifle from the top. The street noises become less distinct. She takes off her thimble, rubs her hands gently, puts the thimble on again, and looks at the clock on the mantel. She then reseats herself, with her chair as close to the window as possible and begins to sew. Presently a key is heard, and the door opens and shuts noisily.* RACHEL *comes in from the vestibule. In her left arm she carries four or five books strapped together; under her right, a roll of music. Her hat is twisted over her left ear and her hair is falling in tendrils about her face. She brings into the room with her the spirit of abounding life, health, joy, youth. Mrs. Loving pauses, needle in hand, as soon as she hears the turning key and the banging door. There is a smile on her face. For a second, mother and daughter smile at each other. Then Rachel throws her books upon the dining room table, places the music there also, but with care, and rushing to her mother, gives her a bear hug and a kiss.*

RACHEL: Ma dear! dear, old Ma dear!

MRS. LOVING: Look out for the needle, Rachel! The waist! Oh, Rachel!

RACHEL: (*on her knees and shaking her finger directly under her mother's nose*) You old, old fraud! You know you adore being hugged. I've a good mind . . .

MRS. LOVING: Now, Rachel, please! Besides, I know your tricks. You think you can make me forget you are late. What time is it?

RACHEL: (*looking at the clock and expressing surprise*) Jiminy Xmas! (*whistles*) Why, it's five o'clock!

MRS. LOVING: (*severely*) Well!

RACHEL: (*plaintively*) Now, Ma dear, you're going to be horrid and cross.

MRS. LOVING: (*laughing*) Really, Rachel, that expression is not particularly affecting, when your hat is over your ear, and you look, with your hair over your eyes, exactly like someone's pet poodle. I wonder if you are ever going to grow up and be ladylike.

RACHEL: Oh! Ma dear, I hope not, not for the longest time, two long, long, years at least. I just want to be silly and irresponsible, and have you to love and torment, and, of course, Tom, too.

MRS. LOVING: (*smiling down at Rachel*) You'll not make me forget, young lady. Why are you late, Rachel?

RACHEL: Well, Ma dear, I'm your pet poodle, and my hat is over my ear, and I'm late, for the loveliest reason.

MRS. LOVING: Don't be silly, Rachel.

RACHEL: That may sound silly, but it isn't. And please don't "Rachel" me so much. It was honestly one whole hour ago when I opened the front door downstairs. I know it was, because I heard the postman telling someone it was four o'clock. Well, I climbed the first flight, and was just starting up the second, when a little shrill voice said, "Lo!" I raised my eyes, and there, half-way up the stairs, sitting in the middle of a step, was just the dearest, cutest, darlingest little brown baby boy you ever saw. "Lo! yourself," I said. "What are you doing and who are you anyway?" "I'm Jimmy; and I'm widing to New York on the choo-choo tars." As he looked entirely too young to be going such a distance by himself, I asked him if I might go too. For a minute or two he considered the question and me very seriously, and then he said, "Es," and made room for me on the step beside him. We've been everywhere: New York, Chicago, Boston, London, Paris and Oshkosh. I wish you could have heard him say that last place. I suggested going there just to hear him. Now, Ma dear, is it any wonder I am late? See all the places we have been in one "teeny, weeny" hour? We would have been traveling yet, but his horrid, little mother came out and called him in. They're in the flat below, the new people. But before he went, Ma dear, he said the "cunningest" thing. He said, "Will you turn out an' p'ay wif me aden in two minutes?" I nearly hugged him to death, and it's a wonder my hat is on my head at all. Hats are such unimportant nuisances anyway!

MRS. LOVING: Unimportant nuisances! What ridiculous language you do use, Rachel! Well, I'm no prophet, but I see very distinctly what is going to happen. This little brown baby will be living here night and day. You're not happy unless some child is trailing along in your rear.

RACHEL: (*mischievously*) Now, Ma dear, who's a hypocrite? What? I suppose you don't like children! I can tell you one thing, though, it won't be my fault if he isn't here night and day. Oh, I wish he were all mine, every bit of him! Ma dear, do you suppose that "she woman" he calls mother would let him come up here until it is time for him to go to bed? I'm going down there this minute. (*rises impetuously*)

MRS. LOVING: Rachel, for Heaven's sake! No! I am entirely too busy and tired today without being bothered with a child romping around in here.

RACHEL: (*reluctantly and a trifle petulantly*) Very well, then. (*for several moments she watches her mother, who has begun to sew again. The displeasure vanishes from her face*) Ma dear!

MRS. LOVING: Well.

RACHEL: Is there anything wrong today?

MRS. LOVING: I'm just tired, chickabiddy, that's all.

RACHEL: (*moves over to the table. Mechanically takes off her hat and coat and carries them out into the entryway of the flat. She returns and goes to the looking glass over the fireplace and tucks in the tendrils of her hair in rather a preoccupied manner. The electric doorbell rings. She returns to the speaking tube in the vestibule. Her voice is heard answering*) Yes!—Yes!—No, I'm not Mrs. Loving. She's here, yes!—What? Oh! come right up! (*appearing in the doorway*) Ma dear, it's some man, who is coming for Mrs. Strong's waist.

MRS. LOVING: (*pausing and looking at Rachel*) It is probably her son. She said she would send for it this afternoon. (*Rachel disappears. A door is heard opening and closing. There is the sound of a man's voice. Rachel ushers in* MR. JOHN STRONG.)

STRONG: (*bowing pleasantly to Mrs. Loving*) Mrs. Loving? (*Mrs. Loving bows, puts down her sewing, rises and goes toward Strong.*) My name is Strong. My mother asked me to come by and get her waist this afternoon. She hoped it would be finished.

MRS. LOVING: Yes, Mr. Strong, it is all ready. If you'll sit down a minute, I'll wrap it up for you. (*She goes into hallway leading to other rooms in flat.*)

RACHEL: (*manifestly ill at ease at being left alone with a stranger; attempting, however, to be the polite hostess*) Do sit down, Mr. Strong. (*They both sit.*)

RACHEL: (*nervously after a pause*) It's a very pleasant day, isn't it, Mr. Strong?

STRONG: Yes, very. (*He leans back composedly, his hat on his knee, the faintest expression of amusement in his eyes.*)

RACHEL: (*after a pause*) It's quite a climb up to our flat, don't you think?

STRONG: Why, no! It didn't strike me so. I'm not old enough yet to mind stairs.

RACHEL: (*nervously*) Oh! I didn't mean that you are old! Anyone can see you are quite young, that is, of course, not too young, but,— (*Strong laughs quietly*) There! I don't blame you for laughing. I'm always clumsy just like that.

MRS. LOVING: (*calling from the other room*) Rachel, bring me a needle and the sixty cotton, please.

RACHEL: All right, Ma dear! (*rummages for the cotton in the machine drawer, and upsets several spools upon the floor. To Strong*) You see! I can't even get a spool of cotton without spilling things all over the floor. (*Strong smiles, Rachel picks up the spools and finally gets the cotton and needle*) Excuse me! (*goes out door leading to other rooms. Strong, left to himself, looks around casually. The* Golden Stairs *interests him and the* Sistine Madonna.)

RACHEL: (*reenters, evidently continuing her function of hostess*) We were talking about the climb to our flat, weren't we? You see, when you're poor, you have to live in a top flat. There is always a compensation, though; we have bully—

I mean nice air, better light, a lovely view, and nobody "thud-thudding" up and down over our heads night and day. The people below have our "thud-thudding," and it must be something awful, especially when Tom and I play "Ivanhoe" and have a tournament up here. We're entirely too old, but we still play. Ma dear rather dreads the climb up three flights so Tom and I do all the errands. We don't mind climbing the stairs, particularly when we go up two or three at a time,—that is—Tom still does. I can't, Ma dear stopped me. (*sighs*) I've got to grow up it seems.

STRONG: (*evidently amused*) It is rather hard being a girl, isn't it?

RACHEL: Oh, no! It's not hard at all. That's the trouble; they won't let me be a girl. I'd love to be.

MRS. LOVING: (*reentering with parcel. She smiles*) My chatterbox, I see, is entertaining you, Mr. Strong. I'm sorry to have kept you waiting, but I forgot, I found, to sew the ruching in the neck. I hope everything is satisfactory. If it isn't, I'll be glad to make any changes.

STRONG: (*who has risen upon her entrance*) Thank you, Mrs. Loving, I'm sure everything is all right.

(*He takes the package and bows to her and Rachel. He moves towards the vestibule, Mrs. Loving following him. She passes through the doorway first. Before leaving, Strong turns for a second and looks back quietly at Rachel. He goes out too. Rachel returns to the mirror, looks at her face for a second, and then begins to touch and pat her hair lightly and delicately here and there. Mrs. Loving returns.*)

RACHEL: (*still at the glass*) He was rather nice, wasn't he Ma dear?—for a man? (*laughs*) I guess my reason's a vain one,—he let me do all the talking. (*pauses*) Strong? Strong? Ma dear, is his mother the little woman with the sad, black eyes?

MRS. LOVING: (*resuming her sewing; sitting before the machine*) Yes. I was rather curious, I confess, to see this son of hers. The whole time I'm fitting her she talks of nothing else. She worships him. (*pauses*) It's rather a sad case, I believe. She is a widow. Her husband was a doctor and left her a little money. She came up from the South to educate this boy. Both of them worked hard and the boy got through college. Three months he hunted for work that a college man might expect to get. You see he had the tremendous handicap of being colored. As the two of them had to live, one day, without her knowing it, he hired himself out as a waiter. He has been one now for two years. He is evidently goodness itself to his mother.

RACHEL: (*slowly and thoughtfully*) Just because he is colored! (*pauses*) We sing a song at school, I believe, about "The land of the free and the home of the brave." What an amusing nation it is.

MRS. LOVING: (*watching Rachel anxiously*) Come, Rachel, you haven't time for "amusing nations." Remember, you haven't practiced any this afternoon. And put your books away; don't leave them on the table. You didn't practice any this morning either, did you?

RACHEL: No, Ma dear,—didn't wake up in time. (*goes to the table and in an abstracted manner puts books on the bookcase; returns to the table; picks up the roll of sheet music she has brought home with her; brightens; impulsively*) Ma dear, just listen to this lullaby. It's the sweetest thing. I was so "daffy" over it, one of the girls at school lent it to me. (*She rushes to the piano with the music and plays the accompaniment through softly and then sings, still softly and with great expression, Jessie Gaynor's "Slumber Boat"*)

> Baby's boat's the silver moon;
> Sailing in the sky,
> Sailing o'er the sea of sleep,
> While the clouds float by.
> Sail, baby, sail,
> Out upon that sea,
> Only don't forget to sail
> Back again to me.
> Baby's fishing for a dream,
> Fishing near and far,
> His line a silver moonbeam is,
> His bait a silver star.
> Sail, baby, sail,
> Out upon that sea,

Listen, Ma dear, right here. Isn't it lovely?

(*plays and sings very softly and slowly*)

> Only don't forget to sail
> Back again to me.

(*pauses; in hushed tones*) Ma dear, it's so beautiful—it—it hurts.

MRS. LOVING: (*quietly*) Yes, dear, it is pretty.

RACHEL: (*for several minutes watches her mother's profile from the piano stool. Her expression is rather wistful*) Ma dear!

MRS. LOVING: Yes, Rachel.

RACHEL: What's the matter?

MRS. LOVING: (*without turning*) Matter! What do you mean?

RACHEL: I don't know. I just feel something is not quite right with you.

MRS. LOVING: I'm only tired—that's all.

RACHEL: Perhaps. But— (*watches her mother a moment or two longer; shakes her head; turns back to the piano. She is thoughtful; looks at her hands in her lap*) Ma dear, wouldn't it be nice if we could keep all the babies in the world—always little babies? Then they'd be always little, and cunning, and lovable; and they could never grow up, then, and—and—be bad. I'm so sorry for mothers whose little babies—grow up—and—are bad.

MRS. LOVING: (*startled; controlling herself, looks at Rachel anxiously, perplexedly.*

Rachel's eyes are still on her hands. Attempting a light tone) Come, Rachel, what experience have you had with mothers whose babies have grown up to be bad? You—you talk like an old, old woman.

RACHEL: (*without raising her eyes, quietly*) I know I'm not old; but, just the same I know that is true. (*softly*) And I'm sorry for the mothers.

MRS. LOVING: (*with a forced laugh*) Well, Miss Methuselah, how do you happen to know all this? Mothers whose babies grow up to be bad don't, as a rule, parade their faults before the world.

RACHEL: That's just it—that's how you know. They don't talk at all.

MRS. LOVING: (*involuntarily*) Oh! (*ceases to sew; looks at Rachel sharply; she is plainly worried. There is a long silence. Presently Rachel raises her eyes to Raphael's* Madonna *over the piano. Her expression becomes rapt; then very softly, her eyes still on the picture, she plays and sings Nevin's "Mighty Lak' A Rose"*)

> Sweetest li'l feller,
> Ev'rybody knows;
> Dunno what to call him,
> But he mighty lak' a rose!
> Lookin' at his Mammy
> Wid eyes so shiny blue,
> Mek' you think that heav'n
> Is comin' clost ter you!
> W'en his dar a sleepin'
> In his li'l place
> Think I see de angels
> Lookin' thro' de lace.
> W'en de dark is fallin',
> W'en de shadders creep,
> Den dey comes on tip-toe,
> Ter kiss him in his sleep.
> Sweetest li'l feller, etc.

(*With head still raised, after she has finished, she closes her eyes. Half to herself and slowly*) I think the loveliest thing of all the lovely things in this world is just (*almost in a whisper*) being a mother!

MRS. LOVING: (*turns and laughs*) Well, of all the startling children, Rachel! I am getting to feel, when you're around, as though I'm shut up with dynamite. What next? (*Rachel rises, goes slowly to her mother, and kneels down beside her. She does not touch her mother.*) Why so serious, chickabiddy?

RACHEL: (*slowly and quietly*) It is not kind to laugh at sacred things. When you laughed, it was as though you laughed—at God!

MRS. LOVING: (*startled*) Rachel!

RACHEL: (*still quietly*) It's true. It was the best in me that said that—it was God! (*pauses*) And, Ma dear, if I believed that I should grow up and not be a mother, I'd pray to die now. I've thought about it a lot, Ma dear, and once I dreamed, and a voice said to me—oh! it was so real—"Rachel, you are to be a mother to little children." Wasn't that beautiful? Ever since I have known how Mary felt at the Annunciation. (*almost in a whisper*) God spoke to me through someone, and I believe. And it has explained so much to me. I know now why I just can't resist any child. I have to love it—it calls me—it—draws me. I want to take care of it, wash it, dress it, live for it. I want the feel of its little warm body against me, its breath on my neck, its hands against my face. (*pauses thoughtfully for a few moments*) Ma dear, here's something I don't understand: I love the little black and brown babies best of all. There is something about them that—that—clutches at my heart. Why—why—should they be—oh!—pathetic? I don't understand. It's dim. More than the other babies, I feel that I must protect them. They're in danger, but from what? I don't know. I've tried so hard to understand, but I can't. (*her face radiant and beautiful*) Ma dear, I think their white teeth and the clear whites of their big black eyes and their dimples everywhere—are—are— (*breaks off*) And, Ma dear, because I love them best, I pray God every night to give me, when I grow up, little black and brown babies—to protect and guard. (*wistfully*) Now, Ma dear, don't you see why you must never laugh at me again? Dear, dear, Ma dear? (*buries her head in her mother's lap and sobs*)

Mrs. Loving: (*for a few seconds, sits as though dazed, and then instinctively begins to caress the head in her lap. To herself*) And I suppose my experience is every mother's. Sooner or later—[all] of a sudden she finds her own child a stranger to her. (*to Rachel, very tenderly*) Poor little girl! Poor little chickabiddy!

Rachel: (*raising her head*) Why do you say, "Poor little girl," like that? I don't understand. Why, Ma dear, I never saw tears in your eyes before. Is it—is it—because you know the things I do not understand? Oh! it is that.

Mrs. Loving: (*simply*) Yes, Rachel, and I cannot save you.

Rachel: Ma dear, you frighten me. Save me from what?

Mrs. Loving: Just life, my little chickabiddy!

Rachel: Is life so terrible? I had found it mostly beautiful. How can life be terrible, when the world is full of little children?

Mrs. Loving: (*very sadly*) Oh, Rachel! Rachel!

Rachel: Ma dear, what have I said?

Mrs. Loving: (*forcing a smile*) Why, the truth, of course, Rachel. Life is not terrible when there are little children—and you—and Tom—and a roof over our heads—and work—and food—and clothes—and sleep at night. (*pauses*) Rachel, I am not myself today. I'm tired. Forget what I've said. Come, chickabiddy, wipe your eyes and smile. That's only an imitation smile, but it's better than none. Jump up now, and light the lamp for me, will you? Tom's late, isn't he? I shall want you to go, too, for the rolls and pie for supper.

Rachel: (*rises rather wearily and goes into the kitchenette. While she is out of the room Mrs. Loving does not move. She sits staring in front of her. Mrs. Loving can just be seen when Rachel reenters with the lamp. She places it on the small table near her mother, adjusts it, so the light falls on her mother's work, and then lowers the window shades at the windows. She still droops. Mrs. Loving, while Rachel is in the room, is industrious. Rachel puts on her hat and coat listlessly. She does not look in the glass)* Where is the money, Ma dear? I'm ready.

MRS. LOVING: Before you go, Rachel, just give a look at the meat and see if it is cooking all right, will you dearie?

RACHEL: (*goes out into the kitchenette and presently returns*) It's all right, Ma dear.

MRS. LOVING: (*while Rachel is out of the room, she takes her pocketbook out of the machine drawer, opens it, takes out money and gives it to Rachel upon her return*) A dozen brown rolls, Rachel. Be sure they're brown! And, I guess,—an apple pie. As you and Tom never seem to get enough apple pie, get the largest she has. And here is a quarter. Get some candy—any kind you like, chickabiddy. Let's have a party tonight, I feel extravagant. Why, Rachel! why are you crying?

RACHEL: Nothing, dear Ma dear. I'll be all right when I get in the air. Good-bye! (*rushes out of the flat. Mrs. Loving sits idle. Presently the outer door of the flat opens and shuts with a bang, and* TOM *appears. Mrs. Loving begins to work as soon as she hears the banging door.*)

TOM: 'Lo, Ma! Where's Sis,—out? The door's off the latch. (*kisses his mother and hangs hat in entryway*)

MRS. LOVING: (*greeting him with the same beautiful smile with which she greeted Rachel*) Rachel just went after the rolls and pie. She'll be back in a few minutes. You're late, Tommy.

TOM: No, Ma—you forget—it's pay day. (*with decided shyness and awkwardness he hands her his wages*) Here, Ma!

MRS. LOVING: (*proudly counting it*) But, Tommy, this is every bit of it. You'll need some.

TOM: Not yet! (*constrainedly*) I only wish—Say, Ma, I hate to see you work so hard. (*fiercely*) Some day—some day— (*breaks off*)

MRS. LOVING: Son, I'm as proud as though you had given me a million dollars.

TOM: (*emphatically*) I may some day,—you see. (*abruptly changing the subject*) Gee! Ma, I'm hungry. What's for dinner? Smells good.

MRS. LOVING: Lamb and dumplings and rice.

TOM: Gee! I'm glad I'm living—and a pie too?

MRS. LOVING: Apple pie, Tommy.

TOM: Say, Ma, don't wake me up. And shall "muzzer's" own little boy set the table?

MRS. LOVING: Thank you, Son.

TOM: (*folds the green cloth, hangs it over the back of the armchair, gets white tablecloth from kitchenette and sets the table. The whole time he is whistling blithely a popular air. He lights one of the gas jets over the table*) Ma!

MRS. LOVING: Yes, Son?

TOM: I made "squad" today,—I'm quarterback. Five other fellows tried to make it. We'll all have to buy new hats, now.

MRS. LOVING: (*with surprise*) Buy new hats! Why?

Tom: (*makes a ridiculous gesture to show that his head and hers are both swelling*) Honest, Ma, I had to carry my hat in my hand tonight,—couldn't even get it to perch aloft.

Mrs. Loving: (*smiling*) Well, I for one, Son, am not going to say anything to make you more conceited.

Tom: You don't have to say anything. Why, Ma, ever since I told you, you can almost look down your own back your head is so high. What? (*Mrs. Loving laughs. The outer door of the flat opens and shuts. Rachel's voice is heard.*)

Rachel: (*without*) My! that was a "dreful" climb, wasn't it? Ma, I've got something here for you. (*appears in the doorway carrying packages and leading a little boy by the hand. The little fellow is shy but smiling.*) Hello, Tommy! Here, take these things for me. This is Jimmy. Isn't he a dear? Come, Jimmy. (*Tom carries the packages into the kitchenette. Rachel leads* Jimmy *to Mrs. Loving*) Ma dear, this is my brown baby. I'm going to take him right downstairs again. His mother is as sweet as can be, and let me bring him up just to see you. Jimmy, this is Ma dear. (*Mrs. Loving turns expectantly to see the child. Standing before her, he raises his face to hers with an engaging smile. Suddenly, without word or warning, her body stiffens; her hands grip her sewing convulsively; her eyes stare. She makes no sound.*)

Rachel: (*frightened*) Ma dear! What is the matter? Tom! Quick! (*Tom reenters and goes to them.*)

Mrs. Loving: (*controlling herself with an effort and breathing hard*) Nothing, dears, nothing. I must be—I—am—nervous tonight. (*with a forced smile*) How do-you-do, Jimmy? Now, Rachel—perhaps—don't you think—you had better take him back to his mother? Good night, Jimmy! (*eyes the child in a fascinated way the whole time he is in the room. Rachel, very much perturbed, takes the child out*) Tom, open that window, please! There! That's better! (*still breathing deeply*) What a fool I am!

Tom: (*patting his mother awkwardly on the back*) You're all pegged out, that's the trouble—working entirely too hard. Can't you stop for the night and go to bed right after supper?

Mrs. Loving: I'll see, Tommy dear. Now I must look after the supper.

Tom: Huh! Well, I guess not. How old do you think Rachel and I are anyway? I see; you think we'll break some of this be-au-tiful Hav-i-land china we bought at the "Five and Ten Cent Store." (*to Rachel who has just reentered wearing a puzzled and worried expression. She is without hat and coat*) Say, Rachel, do you think you're old enough?

Rachel: Old enough for what, Tommy?

Tom: To dish up the supper for Ma.

Rachel: (*with attempted sprightliness*) Ma dear thinks nothing can go on in this little flat unless she does it. Let's show her a thing or two. (*They bring in the dinner. Mrs. Loving with trembling hands tries to sew. Tom and Rachel watch her covertly. Presently she gets up.*)

Mrs. Loving: I'll be back in a minute, children. (*goes out the door that leads to the other rooms of the flat. Tom and Rachel look at each other.*)

RACHEL: (*in a low voice, keeping her eyes on the door*) Why do you suppose she acted so strangely about Jimmy?

TOM: Don't know—nervous, I guess,—worn out. I wish— (*breaks off*)

RACHEL: (*slowly*) It may be that; but she hasn't been herself this afternoon. I wonder—Look out! Here she comes!

TOM: (*in a whisper*) Liven her up. (*Rachel nods. Mrs. Loving reenters. Both rush to her and lead her to her place at right end of the table. She smiles and tries to appear cheerful. They sit down, Tom opposite Mrs. Loving and Rachel at the side facing front. Mrs. Loving asks grace. Her voice trembles. She helps the children bountifully, herself sparingly. Every once in a while she stops eating and stares blankly into her plate; then, remembering where she is suddenly, looks around with a start and goes on eating. Tom and Rachel appear not to notice her.*)

TOM: Ma's "some" cook, isn't she?

RACHEL: Is she! Delmonico's isn't in it.

TOM: (*presently*) Say, Rachel, do you remember that Reynolds boy in the fourth year?

RACHEL: Yes. You mean the one who is flat-nosed, freckled, and who squints and sneers?

TOM: (*looking at Rachel admiringly*) The same.

RACHEL: (*vehemently*) I hate him!

MRS. LOVING: Rachel, you do use such violent language. Why hate him?

RACHEL: I do—that's all.

TOM: Ma, if you saw him just once, you'd understand. No one likes him. But, then, what can you expect? His father's in "quod" doing time for something, I don't know just what. One of the fellows says he has a real decent mother, though. She never mentions him in any way, shape or form, he says. Hard on her, isn't it? Bet I'd keep my head shut too;—you'd never get a yap out of me. (*Rachel looks up quickly at her mother; Mrs. Loving stiffens perceptibly, but keeps her eyes on her plate. Rachel catches Tom's eye; silently draws his attention to their mother; and shakes her head warningly at him.*)

TOM: (*continuing hastily and clumsily*) Well, anyway, he called me "Nigger" today. If his face isn't black, his eye is.

RACHEL: Good! Oh! Why did you let the other one go?

TOM: (*grinning*) I knew he said things behind my back; but today he was hopping mad, because I made quarterback. He didn't!

RACHEL: Oh, Tommy! How lovely! Ma dear, did you hear that? (*chants*) Our Tommy's on the team! Our Tommy's on the team!

TOM: (*trying not to appear pleased*) Ma dear, what did I say about er—er "capital" enlargements?

MRS. LOVING: (*smiling*) You're right, Son.

TOM: I hope you got that "capital," Rachel. How's that for Latin knowledge? Eh?

RACHEL: I don't think much of your knowledge, Tommy dear; but (*continuing to chant*) Our Tommy's on the team! Our Tommy's on the team! Our— (*breaks off*) I've a good mind to kiss you.

TOM: (*threateningly*) Don't you dare.

RACHEL: (*rising and going toward him*) I will! I will! I will!

TOM: (*rising, too, and dodging her*) No, you don't, young lady. (*a tremendous tussle and scuffle ensues*)

MRS. LOVING: (*laughing*) For Heaven's sake! children, do stop playing and eat your supper. (*they nod brightly at each other behind her back and return smiling to the table*)

RACHEL: (*sticking out her tongue at Tom*) I will!

TOM: (*mimicking her*) You won't!

MRS. LOVING: Children! (*they eat for a time in silence*)

RACHEL: Ma dear, have you noticed Mary Shaw doesn't come here much these days?

MRS. LOVING: Why, that's so, she doesn't. Have you two quarreled?

RACHEL: No, Ma dear. (*uncomfortably*) I—think I know the reason—but I don't like to say, unless I'm certain.

TOM: Well, I know. I've seen her lately with those two girls who have just come from the South. Twice she bowed stiffly, and the last time made believe she didn't see me.

RACHEL: Then you think—? Oh! I was afraid it was that.

TOM: (*bitterly*) Yes—we're "niggers"—that's why.

MRS. LOVING: (*slowly and sadly*) Rachel, that's one of the things I can't save you from. I worried considerably about Mary, at first—you do take your friend-ships so seriously. I knew exactly how it would end. (*pauses*) And then I saw that if Mary Shaw didn't teach you the lesson—someone else would. They don't want you, dearies, when you and they grow up. You may have every-thing in your favor—but they don't dare to like you.

RACHEL: I know all that is generally true—but I had hoped that Mary— (*breaks off*)

TOM: Well, I guess we can still go on living even if people don't speak to us. I'll never bow to her again—that's certain.

MRS. LOVING: But, Son, that wouldn't be polite, if she bowed to you first.

TOM: Can't help it. I guess I can be blind, too.

MRS. LOVING: (*wearily*) Well—perhaps you are right—I don't know. It's the way I feel about it too—but—I wish my son always to be a gentleman.

TOM: If being a gentleman means not being a man—I don't wish to be one.

RACHEL: Oh! well, perhaps we're wrong about Mary—I hope we are. (*sighs*) Anyway, let's forget it. Tommy, guess what I've got. (*rises, goes out into entryway swiftly, and returns holding up a small bag*) Ma dear treated. Guess!

TOM: Ma, you're a thoroughbred. Well, let's see—it's—a dozen dill pickles?

RACHEL: Oh! stop fooling.

TOM: I'm not. Tripe?

RACHEL: Silly!

TOM: Hog's jowl?

RACHEL: Ugh! Give it up—quarterback.

Tom: Pig's feet?

Rachel: (*in pretended disgust*) Oh! Ma dear—send him from the table. It's CANDY!

Tom: Candy? Funny, I never thought of that! And I was just about to say some nice, delicious chitlings. Candy! Well! Well! (*Rachel disdainfully carries the candy to her mother, returns to her own seat with the bag and helps herself. She ignores Tom.*)

Tom: (*in an aggrieved voice*) You see, Ma, how she treats me. (*in affected tones*) I have a good mind, young lady, to punish you, er—er corporally speaking. Tut! Tut! I have a mind to master thee—I mean—you. Methinks that if I should advance upon you, apply, perchance, two or three digits to your glossy locks and extract—aha!—say, a strand—you would no more defy me. (*he starts to rise*)

Mrs. Loving: (*quickly and sharply*) Rachel! give Tom the candy and stop playing. (*Rachel obeys. They eat in silence. The old depression returns. When the candy is all gone, Rachel pushes her chair back, and is just about to rise, when her mother, who is very evidently nerving herself for something, stops her.*) Just a moment, Rachel. (*pauses, continuing slowly and very seriously*) Tom and Rachel! I have been trying to make up my mind for some time whether a certain thing is my duty or not. Today—I have decided it is. You are old enough, now,—and I see you ought to be told. Do you know what day this is? (*both Tom and Rachel have been watching their mother intently*) It's the sixteenth of October. Does that mean anything to either of you?

Tom and Rachel: (*wonderingly*) No.

Mrs. Loving: (*looking at both of them thoughtfully, half to herself*) No—I don't know why it should. (*slowly*) Ten years ago—today—your father and your half-brother died.

Tom: I do remember, now, that you told us it was in October.

Rachel: (*with a sigh*) That explains—today.

Mrs. Loving: Yes, Rachel. (*pauses*) Do you know—how they—died?

Tom and Rachel: Why, no.

Mrs. Loving: Did it ever strike you as strange—that they—died—the same day?

Tom: Well, yes.

Rachel: We often wondered, Tom and I; but—but somehow we never quite dared to ask you. You—you—always refused to talk about them, you know, Ma dear.

Mrs. Loving: Did you think—that—perhaps—the reason—I—I wouldn't talk about them—was—because, because—I was ashamed—of them? (*Tom and Rachel look uncomfortable.*)

Rachel: Well, Ma dear—we—we—did—wonder.

Mrs. Loving: (*questioningly*) And you thought?

Rachel: (*haltingly*) W-e-l-l—

Mrs. Loving: (*sharply*) Yes?

Tom: Oh! come, now, Rachel, you know we haven't bothered about it at all. Why should we? We've been happy.

Mrs. Loving: But when you have thought—you've been ashamed? (*intensely*) Have you?

Tom: Now, Ma, aren't you making a lot out of nothing?

Mrs. Loving: (*slowly*) No. (*half to herself*) You evade—both—of you. You have been ashamed. And I never dreamed until today you could take it this way. How blind—how almost criminally blind, I have been.

Rachel: (*tremulously*) Oh! Ma dear, don't! (*Tom and Rachel watch their mother anxiously and uncomfortably. Mrs. Loving is very evidently nerving herself for something.*)

Mrs. Loving: (*very slowly, with restrained emotion*) Tom—and Rachel!

Tom: Ma!

Rachel: Ma dear! (*a tense, breathless pause*)

Mrs. Loving: (*bracing herself*) They—they—were lynched!!

Tom and Rachel: (*in a whisper*) Lynched!

Mrs. Loving: (*slowly, laboring under strong but restrained emotion*) Yes—by Christian people—in a Christian land. We found out afterwards they were all church members in good standing—the best people. (*a silence*) Your father was a man among men. He was a fanatic. He was a Saint!

Tom: (*breathing with difficulty*) Ma—can you—will you—tell us—about it?

Mrs. Loving: I believe it to be my duty. (*a silence*) When I married your father I was a widow. My little George was seven years old. From the very beginning he worshiped your father. He followed him around—just like a little dog. All children were like that with him. I myself have never seen anybody like him. "Big" seems to fit him better than any other word. He was big-bodied—big-souled. His loves were big and his hates. You can imagine, then, how the wrongs of the Negro—ate into his soul. (*pauses*) He was utterly fearless. (*a silence*) He edited and owned, for several years, a small Negro paper. In it he said a great many daring things. I used to plead with him to be more careful. I was always afraid for him. For a long time, nothing happened—he was too important to the community. And then—one night—ten years ago—a mob made up of the respectable people in the town lynched an innocent black man—and what was worse—they knew him to be innocent. A white man was guilty. I never saw your father so wrought up over anything: he couldn't eat; he couldn't sleep; he brooded night and day over it. And then—realizing fully the great risk he was running, although I begged him not to—and all his friends also—he deliberately and calmly went to work and published a most terrific denunciation of that mob. The old prophets in the Bible were not more terrible than he. A day or two later, he received an anonymous letter, very evidently from an educated man, calling upon him to retract his words in the next issue. If he refused his life was threatened. The next week's issue contained an arraignment as frightful, if not more so, than the previous one. Each word was white-hot, searing. That night, some dozen masked men came to our house.

RACHEL: (*moaning*) Oh, Ma dear! Ma dear!

MRS. LOVING: (*too absorbed to hear*) We were not asleep—your father and I. They broke down the front door and made their way to our bedroom. Your father kissed me—and took up his revolver. It was always loaded. They broke down the door. (*a silence. She continues slowly and quietly*) I tried to shut my eyes—I could not. Four masked men fell—they did not move any more—after a little. (*pauses*) Your father was finally overpowered and dragged out. In the hall—my little seventeen-year-old George tried to rescue him. Your father begged him not to interfere. He paid no attention. It ended in their dragging them both out. (*pauses*) My little George—was—a man! (*controls herself with an effort*) He never made an outcry. His last words to me were: "Ma, I am glad to go with Father." I could only nod to him. (*pauses*) While they were dragging them down the steps, I crept into the room where you were. You were both asleep. Rachel, I remember, was smiling. I knelt down by you—and covered my ears with my hands—and waited. I could not pray—I couldn't for a long time—afterwards. (*a silence*) It was very still when I finally uncovered my ears. The only sounds were the faint rustle of leaves and the "tap-tapping of the twig of a tree" against the window. I hear it still—sometimes in my dreams. It was the tree—where they were. (*a silence*) While I had knelt there waiting—I had made up my mind what to do. I dressed myself and then I woke you both up and dressed you. (*pauses*) We set forth. It was a black, still night. Alternately dragging you along and carrying you—I walked five miles to the house of some friends. They took us in, and we remained there until I had seen my dead laid comfortably at rest. They lent me money to come North—I couldn't bring you up—in the South. (*a silence*) Always remember this: There never lived anywhere—or at any time—any two whiter or more beautiful souls. God gave me one for a husband and one for a son and I am proud. (*brokenly*) You—must—be—proud—too. (*a long silence. Mrs. Loving bows her head in her hands. Tom controls himself with an effort. Rachel creeps softly to her mother, kneels beside her and lifts the hem of her dress to her lips. She does not dare touch her. She adores her with her eyes.*)

MRS. LOVING: (*presently raising her head and glancing at the clock*) Tom, it's time, now, for you to go to work. Rachel and I will finish up here.

TOM: (*still laboring under great emotion, goes out into the entryway and comes back and stands in the doorway with his cap. He twirls it around and around nervously*) I want you to know, Ma, before I go—how—how proud I am. Why, I didn't believe two people could be like that—and live. And then to find out that one—was your own father—and one—your own brother.—It's wonderful! I'm—not much yet, Ma, but—I've—just got to be something now. (*breaks off. His face becomes distorted with passion and hatred*) When I think—when I think—of those devils with white skins—living somewhere today—living and happy—I—see—red! I—I—good-bye! (*rushes out, the door bangs*)

MRS. LOVING: (*half to herself*) I was afraid—of just that. I wonder—if I did the wise thing—after all.

RACHEL: (*with a gesture infinitely tender, puts her arm around her mother*) Yes, Ma dear, you did. And, hereafter, Tom and I share and share alike with you. To think, Ma dear, of ten years of this—all alone. It's wicked! (*a short silence*)

MRS. LOVING: And, Rachel, about that dear, little boy, Jimmy.

RACHEL: Now, Ma dear, tell me tomorrow. You've stood enough for one day.

MRS. LOVING: No, it's better over and done with—all at once. If I had seen that dear child suddenly any other day than this—I might have borne it better. When he lifted his little face to me—and smiled—for a moment—I thought it was the end—of all things. Rachel, he is the image of my boy—my George!

RACHEL: Ma dear!

MRS. LOVING: And, Rachel—it will hurt—to see him again.

RACHEL: I understand, Ma dear. (*a silence. Suddenly*) Ma, dear, I am beginning to see—to understand—so much. (*slowly and thoughtfully*) Ten years ago, all things being equal, Jimmy might have been—George? Isn't that so?

MRS. LOVING: Why—yes, if I understand you.

RACHEL: I guess that doesn't sound very clear. It's only getting clear to me, little by little. Do you mind my thinking out loud to you?

MRS. LOVING: No, chickabiddy.

RACHEL: If Jimmy went South now—and grew up—he might be—a George?

MRS. LOVING: Yes.

RACHEL: Then, the South is full of tens, hundreds, thousands of little boys, who, one day may be—and some of them with certainty—Georges?

MRS. LOVING: Yes, Rachel.

RACHEL: And the little babies, the dear, little, helpless babies, being born today—now—and those who will be, tomorrow, and all the tomorrows to come—have that sooner or later to look forward to? They will laugh and play and sing and be happy and grow up, perhaps, and be ambitious—just for that?

MRS. LOVING: Yes, Rachel.

RACHEL: Then, everywhere, everywhere, throughout the South, there are hundreds of dark mothers who live in fear, terrible, suffocating fear, whose rest by night is broken, and whose joy by day in their babies on their hearts is three parts—pain. Oh, I know this is true—for this is the way I should feel, if I were little Jimmy's mother. How horrible! Why—it would be more merciful—to strangle the little things at birth. And so this nation—this white Christian nation—has deliberately set its curse upon the most beautiful—the most holy thing in life—motherhood! Why—it—makes—you doubt—God!

MRS. LOVING: Oh, hush! little girl. Hush!

RACHEL: (*suddenly with a great cry*) Why, Ma dear, you know. You were a mother, George's mother. So, this is what it means. Oh, Ma dear! Ma dear! (*faints in her mother's arms*)

ACT TWO

Time: *October 16, four years later; seven o'clock in the morning.*

Scene: The same room. There have been very evident improvements made. The room is not so bare; it is cosier. On the shelf, before each window, are potted red geraniums. At the windows are green denim drapery curtains covering fresh white dotted Swiss inner curtains. At each doorway are green denim portieres. On the wall between the kitchenette and the entrance to the outer rooms of the flat, a new picture is hanging, Millet's The Man With the Hoe. *Hanging against the side of the run that faces front is Watts's* Hope. *There is another easy-chair at the left front. The table in the center is covered with a white tablecloth. A small asparagus fern is in the middle of this. When the curtain rises there is the clatter of dishes in the kitchenette. Presently Rachel enters with dishes and silver in her hands. She is clad in a bungalow apron. She is noticeably all of four years older. She frowns as she sets the table. There is a set expression about the mouth. A child's voice is heard from the rooms within.*)

JIMMY: (*still unseen*) Ma Rachel!

RACHEL: (*pauses and smiles*) What is it, Jimmy boy?

JIMMY: (*appearing in rear doorway, half-dressed, breathless, and tremendously excited over something. Rushes toward Rachel*) Three guesses! Three guesses! Ma Rachel!

RACHEL: (*her whole face softening*) Well, let's see—maybe there is a circus in town.

JIMMY: No siree! (*in a sing-song*) You're not right! You're not right!

RACHEL: Well, maybe Ma Loving's going to take you somewhere.

JIMMY: No! (*vigorously shaking his head*) It's—

RACHEL: (*interrupting quickly*) You said I could have three guesses, honey. I've only had two.

JIMMY: I thought you had three. How many are three!

RACHEL: (*counting on her fingers*) One! Two! Three! I've only had one! two!—See? Perhaps Uncle Tom is going to give you some candy.

JIMMY: (*dancing up and down*) No! No! No! (*catches his breath*) I leaned over the bathtub, way over, and got hold of the chain with the button on the end, and dropped it into the little round place in the bottom. And then I runned lots of water in the tub and climbed over and fell in splash! just like a big stone: (*loudly*) and took a bath all by myself alone.

RACHEL: (*laughing and hugging him*) All by yourself, honey? You ran the water, too, boy, not "runned" it. What I want to know is, where was Ma Loving all this time?

JIMMY: I stole in "creepy-creep" and looked at Ma Loving and she was awful fast asleep. (*proudly*) Ma Rachel, I'm a "nawful" big boy now, aren't I? I are almost a man, aren't I?

RACHEL: Oh! Boy, I'm getting tired of correcting you—"I am almost a man, am I not?" Jimmy, boy, what will Ma Rachel do, if you grow up? Why, I won't have a little boy any more! Honey, you mustn't grow up, do you hear? You mustn't.

JIMMY: Oh, yes, I must; and you'll have me just the same. Ma Rachel. I'm going to be a policeman and make lots of money for you and Ma Loving and Uncle Tom, and I'm going to buy you some trains and fire engines, and little, cunning ponies, and some rabbits, and some great 'normous banks full of money—lots of it. And then, we are going to live in a great, big castle and eat lots of ice cream, all the time, and drink lots and lots of nice pink lemonade.

RACHEL: What a generous Jimmy boy! (*hugs him*) Before I give you "morning kiss," I must see how clean my boy is. (*inspects teeth, ears and neck*) Jimmy, you're sweet and clean enough to eat. (*kisses him; he tries to strangle her with hugs*) Now the hands. Oh! Jimmy, look at those nails! Oh! Jimmy! (*Jimmy wriggles and tries to get his hands away*) Honey, get my file off of my bureau and go to Ma Loving; she must be awake by this time. Why, honey, what's the matter with your feet?

JIMMY: I don't know. I thought they looked kind of queer, myself. What's the matter with them?

RACHEL: (*laughing*) You have your shoes on the wrong feet.

JIMMY: (*bursts out laughing*) Isn't that most 'normously funny? I'm a case, aren't I— (*pauses thoughtfully*) I mean—am I not, Ma Rachel?

RACHEL: Yes, honey, a great big case of molasses. Come, you must hurry now, and get dressed. You don't want to be late for school, you know.

JIMMY: Ma Rachel! (*shyly*) I—I have been making something for you all the morning—ever since I waked up. It's awful nice. It's—stoop down, Ma Rachel, please—a great, big— (*puts both arms about her neck and gives her a noisy kiss. Rachel kisses him in return, then pushes his head back. For a long moment they look at each other; and, then, laughing joyously, he makes believe he is a horse, and goes prancing out of the room. Rachel, with a softer, gentler expression, continues setting the table. Presently, Mrs. Loving, bent and worn-looking, appears in the doorway in the rear. She limps a trifle.*)

MRS. LOVING: Good morning, dearie. How's my little girl, this morning? (*looks around the room*) Why, where's Tom? I was certain I heard him running the water in the tub, some time ago. (*limps into the room*)

RACHEL: (*laughing*) Tom isn't up yet. Have you seen Jimmy?

MRS. LOVING: Jimmy? No. I didn't know he was awake, even.

RACHEL: (*going to her mother and kissing her*) Well! What do you think of that! I sent the young gentleman to you, a few minutes ago, for help with his nails. He is very much grown up this morning, so I suppose that explains why he didn't come to you. Yesterday, all day, you know, he was a puppy. No one knows what he will be by tomorrow. All of this, Ma dear, is preliminary to telling you that Jimmy boy has stolen a march on you, this morning.

MRS. LOVING: Stolen a march! How?

RACHEL: It appears that he took his bath all by himself and, as a result, he is so conceited, peacocks aren't in it with him.

MRS. LOVING: I heard the water running and thought, of course, it was Tom. Why, the little rascal! I must go and see how he has left things. I was just about to wake him up.

RACHEL: Rheumatism's not much better this morning, Ma dear. (*confronting her mother*) Tell me the truth, now, did you or you not try that liniment I bought you yesterday?

MRS. LOVING: (*guiltily*) Well, Rachel, you see—it was this way, I was—I was so tired, last night,—I—I really forgot it.

RACHEL: I thought as much. Shame on you!

MRS. LOVING: As soon as I walk around a bit it will be all right. It always is. It's bad, when I first get up—that's all. I'll be spry enough in a few minutes. (*limps to the door; pauses*) Rachel, I don't know why the thought should strike me, but how very strangely things turn out. If any one had told me four years ago that Jimmy would be living with us, I should have laughed at him. Then it hurt to see him; now it would hurt not to. (*softly*) Rachel, sometimes—I wonder—if, perhaps, God—hasn't relented a little—and given me back my boy,—my George.

RACHEL: The whole thing was strange, wasn't it?

MRS. LOVING: Yes, God's ways are strange and often very beautiful; perhaps all would be beautiful—if we only understood.

RACHEL: God's ways are certainly very mysterious. Why, of all the people in this apartment house, should Jimmy's father and mother be the only two to take the smallpox, and the only two to die. It's queer!

MRS. LOVING: It doesn't seem like two years ago, does it?

RACHEL: Two years, Ma dear! Why it's three the third of January.

MRS. LOVING: Are you sure, Rachel?

RACHEL: (*gently*) I don't believe I could ever forget that, Ma dear.

MRS. LOVING: No, I suppose not. That is one of the differences between youth and old age—youth attaches tremendous importance to dates—old age does not.

RACHEL: (*quickly*) Ma dear, don't talk like that. You're not old.

MRS. LOVING: Oh! yes, I am, dearie. It's sixty long years since I was born; and I am much older than that, much older.

RACHEL: Please, Ma dear, please!

MRS. LOVING: (*smiling*) Very well, dearie, I won't say it any more. (*a pause*) By the way,—how—does Tom strike you, these days?

RACHEL: (*avoiding her mother's eye*) The same old, bantering, cheerful Tom. Why?

MRS. LOVING: I know he's all that, dearie, but it isn't possible for him to be really cheerful. (*pauses; goes on wistfully*) When you are little, we mothers can kiss away all the trouble, but when you grow up—and go out—into the world—and get hurt—we are helpless. There is nothing we can do.

RACHEL: Don't worry about Tom, Ma dear, he's game. He doesn't show the white feather.

MRS. LOVING: Did you see him, when he came in, last night?

RACHEL: Yes.

MRS. LOVING: Had he had—any luck?

RACHEL: No. (*firmly*) Ma dear, we may as well face it—it's hopeless, I'm afraid.

MRS. LOVING: I'm afraid—you are right. (*shakes her head sadly*) Well, I'll go and see how Jimmy has left things and wake up Tom, if he isn't awake yet. It's the waking up in the mornings that's hard. (*goes limping out rear door. Rachel frowns as she continues going back and forth between the kitchenette and the table. Presently Tom appears in the door at the rear. He watches Rachel several moments before he speaks or enters. Rachel looks grim enough.*)

TOM: (*entering and smiling*) Good morning, "Merry Sunshine"! Have you, perhaps, been taking a—er—prolonged draught of that very delightful beverage—vinegar? (*Rachel, with a knife in her hand, looks up unsmiling. In pretended fright*) I take it all back, I'm sure. May I request, humbly, that before I press my chaste, morning salute upon your forbidding lips, that you—that you—that you—er—in some way rid yourself of that—er—knife? (*bows as Rachel puts it down*) I thank you. (*he comes to her and tips her head back; gently*) What's the matter with my little Sis?

RACHEL: (*her face softening*) Tommy dear, don't mind me. I'm getting wicked, I guess. At present I feel just like—like curdled milk. Once upon a time, I used to have quite a nice disposition, didn't I, Tommy?

TOM: (*smiling*) Did you, indeed! I'm not going to flatter you. Well, brace yourself, old lady. Ready, One! Two! Three! Go! (*kisses her, then puts his hands on either side of her face, and raising it, looks down into it*) You're a pretty decent little sister, Sis, that's what T. Loving thinks about it; and he knows a thing or two. (*abruptly looking around*) Has the paper come yet?

RACHEL: I haven't looked, it must have, though, by this time. (*Tom, hands in his pockets, goes into the vestibule. He whistles. The outer door opens and closes, and presently he saunters back, newspaper in hand. He lounges carelessly in the armchair and looks at Rachel.*)

TOM: May T. Loving be of any service to you?

RACHEL: Service! How?

TOM: May he run, say any errands, set the table, cook the breakfast? Anything?

RACHEL: (*watching the lazy figure*) You look like working.

TOM: (*grinning*) It's at least—polite—to offer.

RACHEL: You can't do anything; I don't trust you to do it right. You may just sit there, and read your paper—and try to behave yourself.

TOM: (*in affectedly meek tones*) Thank you, ma'am. (*opens the paper, but does not read. Jimmy presently enters riding around the table on a cane. Rachel peeps in from the kitchenette and smiles. Tom puts down his paper*) 'Lo! Big Fellow, what's this?

JIMMY: (*disgustedly*) How can I hear? I'm miles and miles away yet. (*prances around and around the room; presently stops near Tom, attempting a gruff voice*) Good morning!

TOM: (*lowering his paper again*) Bless my stars! Who's this? Well, if it isn't Mr. Mason! How-do-you-do, Mr. Mason? That's a beautiful horse you have there. He limps a trifle in his left, hind, front foot, though.

JIMMY: He doesn't!

Tom: He does!

Jimmy: (*fiercely*) He doesn't!

Tom: (*as fiercely*) I say he does!

Mrs. Loving: (*appearing in the doorway in the rear*) For Heaven's sake! What is this? Good morning, Tommy.

Tom: (*rising and going toward his mother, Jimmy following astride of the cane in his rear*) Good morning, Ma. (*kisses her; lays his head on her shoulder and makes believe he is crying; in a high falsetto*) Ma! Jimmy says his horse doesn't limp in his hind, front right leg, and I says he does.

Jimmy: (*throws his cane aside, rolls on the floor and kicks up his heels. He roars with laughter*) I think Uncle Tom is funnier than any clown in the "kickus."

Tom: (*raising his head and looking down at Jimmy; Rachel stands in the kitchenette doorway*) In the what, Jimmy?

Jimmy: In the "kickus," of course.

Tom: "Kickus"! "Kickus"! Oh, Lordy! (*Tom and Rachel shriek with laughter; Mrs. Loving looks amused; Jimmy, very much affronted, gets upon his feet again. Tom leans over and swings Jimmy high in the air*) Boy, you'll be the death of me yet. Circus, Son! Circus!

Jimmy: (*from on high, soberly and with injured dignity*) Well, I thinks "kickus" and circus are very much alike. Please put me down.

Rachel: (*from the doorway*) We laugh, honey, because we love you so much.

Jimmy: (*somewhat mollified, to Tom*) Is that so, Uncle Tom?

Tom: Surest thing in the world! (*severely*) Come, get down, young man. Don't you know you'll wear my arms out? Besides, there is something in my lower vest pocket, that's just dying to come to you. Get down, I say.

Jimmy: (*laughing*) How can I get down? (*wriggles around*)

Tom: How should I know? Just get down, of course. (*very suddenly puts Jimmy down on his feet. Jimmy tries to climb up over him.*)

Jimmy: Please sit down, Uncle Tom.

Tom: (*in feigned surprise*) Sit down! What for?

Jimmy: (*pummeling him with his little fists, loudly*) Why, you said there was something for me in your pocket.

Tom: (*sitting down*) So I did. How forgetful I am!

Jimmy: (*finding a bright, shiny penny, shrieks*) Oh! Oh! OH! (*climbs up and kisses Tom noisily*)

Tom: Why, Jimmy! You embarrass me. My! My!

Jimmy: What is 'barrass?

Tom: You make me blush.

Jimmy: What's that?

Mrs. Loving: Come, come, children! Rachel has the breakfast on the table. (*Tom sits in Jimmy's place and Jimmy tries to drag him out.*)

Tom: What's the matter, now?

Jimmy: You're in *my* place.

Tom: Well, can't you sit in mine?

JIMMY: (*wistfully*) I wants to sit by my Ma Rachel.

TOM: Well, so do I.

RACHEL: Tom, stop teasing Jimmy. Honey, don't you let him bother you; ask him please prettily.

JIMMY: Please prettily, Uncle Tom.

TOM: Oh! well then. (*gets up and takes his own place. They sit as they did in Act One only Jimmy sits between Tom, at the end, and Rachel.*)

JIMMY: (*loudly*) Oh, goody! goody! goody! We've got sau-sa-ges.

MRS. LOVING: Sh!

JIMMY: (*silenced for a few moments; Rachel ties a big napkin around his neck, and prepares his breakfast. He breaks forth again suddenly and excitedly*) Uncle Tom!

TOM: Sir?

JIMMY: I took a bath this morning, all by myself alone, in the bathtub, and I ranned, no (*doubtfully*) I runned, I think—the water all in it, and got in it all by myself; and Ma Loving thought it was you; but it was me.

TOM: (*in feignedly severe tones*) See here, young man, this won't do. Don't you know I'm the only one who is allowed to do that here? It's a perfect waste of water—that's what it is.

JIMMY: (*undaunted*) Oh! no, you're not the ony one, 'cause Ma Loving and Ma Rachel and me—alls takes baths every single morning. So, there!

TOM: You 'barrass me. (*Jimmy opens his mouth to ask a question; Tom quickly*) Young gentleman, your mouth is open. Close it, sir; close it.

MRS. LOVING: Tom, you're as big a child exactly as Jimmy.

TOM: (*bowing to right and left*) You compliment me. I thank you, I am sure. (*They finish in silence.*)

JIMMY: (*sighing with contentment*) I'm through, Ma Rachel.

MRS. LOVING: Jimmy, you're a big boy, now, aren't you? (*Jimmy nods his head vigorously and looks proud.*) I wonder if you're big enough to wash your own hands, this morning?

JIMMY: (*shrilly*) Yes, ma'am.

MRS. LOVING: Well, if they're beautifully clean, I'll give you another penny.

JIMMY: (*excitedly to Rachel*) Please untie my napkin, Ma Rachel! (*Rachel does so*) "Excoose" me, please.

MRS. LOVING AND RACHEL: Certainly. (*Jimmy climbs down and rushes out at the rear doorway*)

MRS. LOVING: (*solemnly and slowly; breaking the silence*) Rachel, do you know what day this is?

RACHEL: (*looking at her plate; slowly*) Yes, Ma dear.

MRS. LOVING: Tom.

TOM: (*grimly and slowly*) Yes, Ma. (*A silence*)

MRS. LOVING: (*impressively*) We must never—as long—as we live—forget this day.

RACHEL: No, Ma dear.

TOM: No, Ma. (*Another silence*)

Tom: (*slowly; as though thinking aloud*) I hear people talk about God's justice—and I wonder. There, are you, Ma. There isn't a sacrifice—that you haven't made. You're still working your fingers to the bone—sewing—just so all of us may keep on living. Rachel is a graduate in Domestic Science; she was high in her class; most of the girls below her in rank have positions in the schools. I'm an electrical engineer—and I've tried steadily for several months—to practice my profession. It seems our educations aren't of much use to us: we aren't allowed to make good—because our skins are dark. (*pauses*) And, in the South today, there are white men— (*controls himself*) They have everything; they're well-dressed, well-fed, well-housed; they're prosperous in business; they're important politically; they're pillars in the church. I know all this is true—I've inquired. Their children (our ages, some of them) are growing up around them; and they are having a square deal handed out to them—college, position, wealth, and best of all, freedom, without galling restrictions, to work out their own salvations. With ability, they may become anything; and all this will be true of their children's children after them. (*a pause*) Look at us—and look at them. We are destined to failure—they, to success. Their children shall grow up in hope; ours, in despair. Our hands are clean;—theirs are red with blood—red with the blood of a noble man—and a boy. They're nothing but low, cowardly, bestial murderers. The scum of the earth shall succeed.—God's justice, I suppose.

Mrs. Loving: (*rising and going to Tom; brokenly*) Tom, promise me—one thing.

Tom: (*rises gently*) What is it, Ma?

Mrs. Loving: That—you'll try—not to lose faith—in God. I've been where you are now—and it's black. Tom, we don't understand God's ways. My son, I know, now—He is beautiful. Tom, won't you try to believe, again?

Tom: (*slowly, but not convincingly*) I'll try, Ma.

Mrs. Loving: (*sighs*) Each one, I suppose, has to work out his own salvation. (*after a pause*) Rachel, if you'll get Jimmy ready, I'll take him to school. I've got to go downtown shopping for a customer, this morning. (*Rachel rises and goes out the rear doorway; Mrs. Loving, limping very slightly now, follows. She turns and looks back yearningly at Tom, who has seated himself again, and is staring unseeingly at his plate. She goes out. Tom sits without moving until he hears Mrs. Loving's voice within and Rachel's faintly; then he gets the paper, sits in the armchair and pretends to read.*)

Mrs. Loving: (*from within*) A yard, you say, Rachel? You're sure that will be enough. Oh! you've measured it. Anything else?—What?—Oh! all right. I'll be back by one o'clock, anyway. Good-bye. (*enters with Jimmy. Both are dressed for the street. Tom looks up brightly at Jimmy.*)

Tom: Hello! Big Fellow, where are you taking my mother, I'd like to know? This is a pretty kettle of fish.

Jimmy: (*laughing*) Aren't you funny, Uncle Tom! Why, I'm not taking her anywhere. She's taking me. (*importantly*) I'm going to school.

Tom: Big Fellow, come here. (*Jimmy comes with a rush*) Now, where's that penny

I gave you? No, I don't want to see it. All right. Did Ma Loving give you another? (*vigorous noddings of the head from Jimmy*) I wish you to promise me solemnly—Now, listen! Here, don't wriggle so! not to buy—Listen! too many pints of ice cream with my penny. Understand?

JIMMY: (*very seriously*) Yes, Uncle Tom, cross my "tummy"! I promise.

TOM: Well, then, you may go. I guess that will be all for the present. (*Jimmy loiters around looking up wistfully into his face*) Well?

JIMMY: Haven't you—aren't you—isn't you—forgetting something?

TOM: (*grabbing at his pockets*) Bless my stars! what now?

JIMMY: If you could kind of lean over this way. (*Tom leans forward*) No, not that way. (*Tom leans toward the side away from Jimmy*) No, this way, this way! (*laughs and pummels him with his little fists*) This way!

TOM: (*leaning toward Jimmy*) Well, why didn't you say so, at first?

JIMMY: (*puts his arms around Tom's neck and kisses him*) Good-bye, dear old Uncle Tom. (*Tom catches him and hugs him hard*) I likes to be hugged like that—I can taste—sau-sa-ges.

TOM: You 'barrass me, Son. Here, Ma, take your boy. Now remember all I told you, Jimmy.

JIMMY: I 'members.

MRS. LOVING: God bless you, Tom. Good luck.

TOM: (*much affected, but with restraint, rising*) Thank you—Good-bye. (*Mrs. Loving and Jimmy go out through the vestibule. Tom lights a cigarette and tries to read the paper. He soon sinks into a brown study. Presently Rachel enters humming. Tom relights his cigarette; and Rachel proceeds to clear the table. In the midst of this, the bell rings three distinct times.*)

RACHEL AND TOM: John!

TOM: I wonder what's up—It's rather early for him.—I'll go. (*rises leisurely and goes out into the vestibule. The outer door opens and shuts. Men's voices are heard. Tom and John Strong enter. During the ensuing conversation Rachel finishes clearing the table, takes the fern off, puts on the green tablecloth, places a doily carefully in the centre, and replaces the fern. She apparently pays no attention to the conversation between her brother and Strong. After she has finished, she goes to the kitchenette. The rattle of dishes can be heard now and then.*)

RACHEL: (*brightly*) Well, stranger, how does it happen you're out so early in the morning?

STRONG: I hadn't seen any of you for a week, and I thought I'd come by, on my way to work, and find out how things are going. There is no need of asking how you are, Rachel. And the mother and the boy?

RACHEL: Ma dear's rheumatism still holds on.—Jimmy's fine.

STRONG: I'm sorry to hear that your mother is not well. There isn't a remedy going that my mother doesn't know about. I'll get her advice and let you know. (*turning to Tom*) Well, Tom, how goes it? (*Strong and Tom sit.*)

TOM: (*smiling grimly*) There's plenty of "go," but no "git there." (*There is a pause.*)

STRONG: I was hoping for better news.

TOM: If I remember rightly, not so many years ago, you tried—and failed. Then, a colored man had hardly a ghost of a show;—now he hasn't even the ghost of a ghost.

STRONG: That's true enough. (*a pause*) What are you going to do?

TOM: (*slowly*) I'll do this little "going act" of mine the rest of the week; (*pauses*) and then, I'll do anything I can get to do. If necessary, I suppose, I can be a "white-wing."

STRONG: Tom, I came— (*breaks off; continuing slowly*) Six years ago, I found I was up against a stone wall—your experience, you see, to the letter. I couldn't let my mother starve, so I became a waiter. (*pauses*) I studied waiting; I made a science of it, an art. In a comparatively short time, I'm a headwaiter and I'm up against another stone wall. I've reached my limit. I'm thirty-two now, and I'll die a headwaiter. (*a pause*) College friends, so-called, and acquaintances used to come into the restaurant. One or two at first—attempted to commiserate with me. They didn't do it again. I waited upon them—I did my best. Many of them tipped me. (*pauses and smiles grimly*) I can remember my first tip, still. They come in yet; many of them are already powers, not only in this city, but in the country. Some of them make a personal request that I wait upon them. I am an artist, now, in my proper sphere. They tip me well, extremely well—the larger the tip, the more pleased they are with me. Because of me, in their own eyes, they're philanthropists. Amusing, isn't it? I can stand their attitude now. My philosophy—learned hard, is to make the best of everything you can, and go on. At best, life isn't so very long. You're wondering why I'm telling you all this. I wish you to see things exactly as they are. There are many disadvantages and some advantages in being a waiter. My mother can live comfortably; I am able, even, to see that she gets some of the luxuries. Tom, it's this way—I can always get you a job as a waiter; I'll teach you the art. If you care to begin the end of the week—all right. And remember this, as long as I keep my job—this offer holds good.

TOM: I—I— (*breaks off*) Thank you. (*a pause; then smiling wryly*) I guess it's safe enough to say, you'll see me at the end of the week. John, you're— (*breaking off again. A silence interrupted presently by the sound of much vigorous rapping on the outer door of the flat. Rachel appears and crosses over toward the vestibule.*)

RACHEL: Hear the racket! My kiddies gently begging for admittance. It's about twenty minutes of nine, isn't it? (*Tom nods*) I thought so. (*Goes into the entryway; presently reappears with a group of six little girls ranging in age from five to about nine. All are fighting to be close to her; and all are talking at once. There is one exception: the smallest tot is self-possessed and self-sufficient. She carries a red geranium in her hand and gives it her full attention.*)

LITTLE MARY: It's my turn to get "Morning kiss" first, this morning, Miss Rachel. You kissed Louise first yesterday. You said you'd kiss us "alphebetically." (*ending in a shriek*) You promised! (*Rachel kisses* MARY, *who subsides.*)

LITTLE NANCY: (*imperiously*) Now, me. (*Rachel kisses her, and then amid shrieks, recriminations, pulling of hair, jostling, etc., she kisses the rest. The small tot is still oblivious to everything that is going on.*)

RACHEL: (*laughing*) You children will pull me limb from limb; and then I'll be all dead; and you'll be sorry—see, if you aren't. (*they fall back immediately. Tom and Strong watch in amused silence. Rachel loses all self-consciousness, and seems to bloom in the children's midst*) Edith! come here this minute, and let me tie your hair-ribbon again. Nancy, I'm ashamed of you, I saw you trying to pull it off. (NANCY *looks abashed but mischievous*) Louise, you look as sweet as sweet, this morning; and Jenny, where did you get the pretty, pretty dress?

LITTLE JENNY: (*snuffling, but proud*) My mother made it. (*pauses with more snuffles*) My mother says I have a very bad cold. (*there is a brief silence interrupted by the small tot with the geranium*)

LITTLE MARTHA: (*in a sweet, little voice*) I—have—a—pitty—'ittle flower.

RACHEL: Honey, it's beautiful. Don't you want "Morning kiss" too?

LITTLE MARTHA: Yes, I do.

RACHEL: Come, honey. (*Rachel kisses her*) Are you going to give the pretty flower to Jenny's teacher? (*vigorous shakings of the head in denial*) Is it for— Mother? (*more shakings of the head*) Is it for—let's see—Daddy? (*more shakings of the head*) I give up. To whom are you going to give the pretty flower, honey?

LITTLE MARTHA: (*Shyly*) "Oo."

RACHEL: You darling!

LITTLE MARTHA: Muzzer and I picked it—for "oo." Here 't is. (*puts her finger in her mouth, and gives it shyly*)

RACHEL: Well, I'm going to pay you with three big kisses. One! Two! Three!

LITTLE MARTHA: I can count, One! Two! Free! Tan't I? I am going to school soon; and wants to put the flower in your hair.

RACHEL: (*kneels*) All right, baby. (LITTLE MARTHA *fumbles and Rachel helps her.*)

LITTLE MARTHA: (*dreamily*) Miss Rachel, the 'ittle flower loves you. It told me so. It said it wanted to lie in your hair. It is going to tell you a pitty 'ittle secret. You listen awful hard—and you'll hear. I wish I were a fairy and had a little wand, I'd turn everything into flowers. Wouldn't that be nice, Miss Rachel?

RACHEL: Lovely, honey!

LITTLE JENNY: (*snuffling loudly*) If I were a fairy and had a wand, I'd turn you, Miss Rachel, into a queen—and then I'd always be near you and see that you were happy.

RACHEL: Honey, how beautiful!

LITTLE LOUISE: I'd make my mother happy—if I were a fairy. She cries all the time. My father can't get anything to do.

LITTLE NANCY: If I were a fairy, I'd turn a boy in my school into a spider. I hate him.

RACHEL: Honey, why?

LITTLE NANCY: I'll tell you sometime—I hate him.

LITTLE EDITH: Where's Jimmy, Miss Rachel?

RACHEL: He went long ago; and chickies, you'll have to clear out, all of you, now, or you'll be late. Shoo! Shoo! (*she drives them out prettily before her. They laugh merrily. They all go into the vestibule.*)

TOM: (*slowly*) Does it ever strike you—how pathetic and tragic a thing—a little colored child is?

STRONG: Yes.

TOM: Today, we colored men and women, everywhere—are up against it. Every year, we are having a harder time of it. In the South, they make it as impossible as they can for us to get an education. We're hemmed in on all sides. Our one safeguard—the ballot—in most states, is taken away already, or is being taken away. Economically, in a few lines, we have a slight show— but at what a cost! In the North, they make a pretense of liberality: they give us the ballot and a good education, and then—snuff us out. Each year, the problem just to live, gets more difficult to solve. How about these children— if we're fools enough to have any. (*Rachel reenters. Her face is drawn and pale. She returns to the kitchenette.*)

STRONG: (*slowly, with emphasis*) That part—is damnable! (*a silence*)

TOM: (*suddenly looking at the clock*) It's later than I thought. I'll have to be pulling out of here now, if you don't mind. (*raising his voice*) Rachel! (*Rachel, still drawn and pale, appears in the doorway of the kitchenette. She is without her apron*) I've got to go now, Sis. I leave John in your hands.

STRONG: I've got to go, myself, in a few minutes.

TOM: Nonsense, man! Sit still. I'll begin to think, in a minute, you're afraid of the ladies.

STRONG: I am.

TOM: What! And not ashamed to acknowledge it?

STRONG: No.

TOM: You're lots wiser than I dreamed. So long! (*gets hat out in the entryway and returns; smiles wryly*) "Morituri Salutamus." (*they nod at him—Rachel wistfully. He goes out. There is the sound of an opening and closing door. Rachel sits down. A rather uncomfortable silence, on the part of Rachel, ensues. Strong is imperturbable.*)

RACHEL: (*nervously*) John!

STRONG: Well?

RACHEL: I—I listened.

STRONG: Listened! To what?

RACHEL: To you and Tom.

STRONG: Well,—what of it ?

RACHEL: I didn't think it was quite fair not to tell you. It—it seemed, well, like eavesdropping.

STRONG: Don't worry about it. Nonsense!

RACHEL: I'm glad—I want to thank you for what you did for Tom. He needs you, and will need you. You'll help him.

STRONG: (*thoughtfully*) Rachel, each one—has his own little battles. I'll do what I can. After all, an outsider doesn't help much.

RACHEL: But friendship—just friendship—helps.

STRONG: Yes. (*a silence*) Rachel, do you hear anything encouraging from the schools? Any hope for you yet?

RACHEL: No, nor ever will be. I know that now. There's no more chance for me than there is for Tom,—or than there was for you—or for any of us with dark skins. It's lucky for me that I love to keep house, and cook, and sew. I'll never get anything else. Ma dear's sewing, the little work Tom has been able to get, and the little sewing I sometimes get to do—keep us from the poorhouse. We live. According to your philosophy, I suppose, make the best of it—it might be worse.

STRONG: (*quietly*) You don't want to get morbid over these things, you know.

RACHEL: (*scornfully*) That's it. If you see things as they are, you're either pessimistic or morbid.

STRONG: In the long run, do you believe, that attitude of mind—will be—beneficial to you? I'm ten years older than you. I tried your way. I know. Mine is the only sane one. (*goes over to her slowly; deliberately puts his hands on her hair, and tips her head back. He looks down into her face quietly without saying anything.*)

RACHEL: (*nervous and startled*) Why, John, don't! (*he pays no attention, but continues to look down into her face.*)

STRONG: (*half to himself*) Perhaps—if you had—a little more fun in your life, your point of view would be—more normal. I'll arrange it so I can take you to some theatre, one night this week.

RACHEL: (*irritably*) You talk as though I were a—a jellyfish. You'll take me, how do you know I'll go?

STRONG: You will.

RACHEL: (*sarcastically*) Indeed! (*Strong makes no reply*) I wonder if you know how—how—maddening you are. Why, you talk as though my will counts for nothing. It's as if you're trying to master me. I think a domineering man is detestable.

STRONG: (*softly*) If he's, perhaps, the man?

RACHEL: (*hurriedly, as though she had not heard*) Besides, some of these theatres put you off by yourself as though you had leprosy. I'm not going.

STRONG: (*smiling at her*) You know I wouldn't ask you to go, under those circumstances. (*a silence*) Well, I must be going now. (*he takes her hand, and looks at it reverently. Rachel, at first resists; but he refuses to let go. When she finds it is useless, she ceases to resist. He turns his head and smiles down into her face*) Rachel, I am coming back to see you, this evening.

RACHEL: I'm sure we'll all be very glad to see you.

STRONG: (*looking at her calmly*) I said— you. (*very deliberately, he turns her hand palm upwards, leans over and kisses it; then he puts it back into her lap. He touches her cheek lightly*) Good-bye—little Rachel. (*turns in the vestibule door and looks back, smiling*) Until tonight. (*He goes out. Rachel sits for some time without moving. She is lost in a beautiful daydream. Presently she sighs happily, and after looking furtively around the room, lifts the palm Strong has kissed to her lips. She laughs shyly and jumping up, begins to hum. She opens the widow at the rear of the room and then commences to thread the sewing machine. She hums happily the whole time. A light rapping is heard at the outer door. Rachel listens. It stops, and begins again. There is something insistent and yet hopeless in the sound. Rachel, looking puzzled, goes out into the vestibule. . . . The door closes. Rachel, a black woman, poorly dressed, and a little ugly, black child come in. There is the stoniness of despair in the woman's face. The child is thin, nervous, suspicious, frightened.*)

MRS. LANE: (*in a sharp, but toneless voice*) May I sit down? I'm tired.

RACHEL: (*puzzled, but gracious; draws up a chair for her*) Why, certainly.

MRS. LANE: No, you don't know me—never even heard of me—nor I of you. I was looking at the vacant flat on this floor—and saw your name—on your door,—"Loving!" It's a strange name to come across—in this world.—I thought, perhaps, you might give me some information. (*The child hides behind her mother and looks around at Rachel in a frightened way.*)

RACHEL: (*smiling at the woman and child in a kindly manner*) I'll be glad to tell you anything I am able, Mrs.—

MRS. LANE: Lane. What I want to know is, how do they treat the colored children in the school I noticed around the corner? (*The child clutches at her mother's dress.*)

RACHEL: (*perplexed*) Very well—I'm sure.

MRS. LANE: (*bluntly*) What reason have you for being sure?

RACHEL: Why, the little boy I've adopted goes there; and he's very happy. All the children in this apartment house go there too; and I know they're happy.

MRS. LANE: Do you know how many colored children there are in the school?

RACHEL: Why, I should guess around thirty.

MRS. LANE: I see. (*pauses*) What color is this little adopted boy of yours?

RACHEL: (*gently*) Why—he's brown.

MRS. LANE: Any black children there?

RACHEL: (*nervously*) Why—yes.

MRS. LANE: Do you mind if I send Ethel over by the piano to sit?

RACHEL: N—no, certainly not. (*places a chair by the piano and goes to the little girl holding out her hand. She smiles beautifully. The child gets farther behind her mother.*)

MRS. LANE: She won't go to you—she's afraid of everybody now but her father and me. Come, Ethel. (MRS. LANE *takes the little girl by the hand and leads her to the chair. In a gentler voice*) Sit down, Ethel. (*Ethel obeys. When her mother starts back again toward Rachel, she holds out her hands pitifully. She makes no sound.*) I'm not going to leave you, Ethel. I'll be right over here. You can see me. (*The look of agony on the child's face, as her mother leaves her, makes Rachel shudder.*) Do you mind if we sit over here by the sewing machine? Thank you. (*They move their chairs.*)

RACHEL: (*looking at the little, pitiful figure watching its mother almost unblinkingly*) Does Ethel like apples, Mrs. Lane?

MRS. LANE: Yes.

RACHEL: Do you mind if I give her one?

MRS. LANE: No. Thank you, very much.

RACHEL: (*goes into the kitchenette and returns with a fringed napkin, a plate, and a big red apple, cut into quarters. She goes to the little girl, who cowers away from her; very gently*) Here, dear, little girl, is a beautiful apple for you. (*The gentle tones have no appeal for the trembling child before her.*)

MRS. LANE: (*coming forward*) I'm sorry, but I'm afraid she won't take it from you. Ethel, the kind lady has given you an apple. Thank her nicely. Here! I'll spread the napkin for you, and put the plate in your lap. Thank the lady like a good little girl.

ETHEL: (*very low*) Thank you. (*they return to their seats. Ethel with difficulty holds the plate in her lap. During the rest of the interview between Rachel and her mother, she divides her attention between the apple on the plate and her mother's face. She makes no attempt to eat the apple, but holds the plate in her lap with a care that is painful to watch. Often, too, she looks over her shoulder fearfully. The conversation between Rachel and her mother is carried on in low tones.*)

MRS. LANE: I've got to move—it's Ethel.

RACHEL: What is the matter with that child? It's—it's heartbreaking to see her.

MRS. LANE: I understand how you feel,—I don't feel anything, myself, any more. (*a pause*) My husband and I are poor, and we're ugly and we're black. Ethel looks like her father more than she does like me. We live in 55th Street—near the railroad. It's a poor neighborhood, but the rent's cheap. My husband is a porter in a store and, to help out, I'm a caretaker. (*pauses*) I don't know why I'm telling you all this. We had a nice little home—and the three of us were happy. Now we've got to move.

RACHEL: Move! Why?

MRS. LANE: It's Ethel. I put her in school this September. She stayed two weeks. (*pointing to Ethel*) That's the result.

RACHEL: (*in horror*) You mean—that just two weeks—in school—did that?

MRS. LANE: Yes. Ethel never had a sick day in her life—before. (*a brief pause*) I took her to the doctor at the end of the two weeks. He say's she's a nervous wreck.

RACHEL: But what could they have done to her?

MRS. LANE: (*laughs grimly and mirthlessly*) I'll tell you what they did the first day. Ethel is naturally sensitive and backward. She's not assertive. The teacher saw that, and, after I had left, told her to sit in a seat in the rear of the class. She was alone there—in a corner. The children, immediately feeling there was something wrong with Ethel because of the teacher's attitude, turned and stared at her. When the teacher's back was turned they whispered about her, pointed their fingers at her and tittered. The teacher divided the class into two parts, divisions, I believe, they are called. She forgot all about Ethel, of course, until the last minute, and then, looking back, said sharply:

"That little girl there may join this division," meaning the group of pupils standing around her. Ethel naturally moved slowly. The teacher called her sulky and told her to lose a part of her recess. When Ethel came up—the children drew away from her in every direction. She was left standing alone. The teacher then proceeded to give a lesson about kindness to animals. Funny, isn't it, kindness to animals? The children forgot Ethel in the excitement of talking about their pets. Presently, the teacher turned to Ethel and said disagreeably: "Have you a pet?" Ethel said, "Yes," very low. "Come, speak up, you sulky child, what is it?" Ethel said: "A blind puppy." They all laughed, the teacher and all. Strange, isn't it, but Ethel loves that puppy. She spoke up: "It's mean to laugh at a little blind puppy. I'm glad he's blind." This remark brought forth more laughter. "Why are you glad," the teacher asked curiously. Ethel refused to say. (*pauses*) When I asked her why, do you know what she told me? "If he saw me, he might not love me any more." (*a pause*) Did I tell you that Ethel is only seven years old?

RACHEL: (*drawing her breath sharply*) Oh! I didn't believe any one could be as cruel as that—to a little child.

MRS. LANE: It isn't very pleasant, is it? When the teacher found out that Ethel wouldn't answer, she said severely: "Take your seat!" At recess, all the children went out. Ethel could hear them playing and laughing and shrieking. Even the teacher went too. She was made to sit there alone—in that big room—because God there made her ugly—and black. (*pauses*) When the recess was half over the teacher came back. "You may go now," she said coldly. Ethel didn't stir. "Did you hear me!" "Yes'm." "Why don't you obey?" "I don't want to go out, please." "You don't, don't you, you stubborn child! Go immediately!" Ethel went. She stood by the school steps. No one spoke to her. The children near her moved away in every direction. They stopped playing, many of them, and watched her. They stared as only children can stare. Some began whispering about her. Presently one child came up and ran her hand roughly over Ethel's face. She looked at her hand and Ethel's face and ran screaming back to the others, "It won't come off! See!" Other children followed the first child's example. Then one boy spoke up loudly: "I know what she is, she's a nigger!" Many took up the cry. God or the devil interfered—the bell rang. The children filed in. One boy boldly called her "Nigger!" before the teacher. She said, "That isn't nice,"—but she smiled at the boy. Things went on about the same for the rest of the day. At the end of school, Ethel put on her hat and coat—the teacher made her hang them at a distance from the other pupils' wraps; and started for home. Quite a crowd escorted her. They called her "Nigger!" all the way. I made Ethel go the next day. I complained to the authorities. They treated me lightly. I was determined not to let them force my child out of school. At the end of two weeks—I had to take her out.

RACHEL: (*brokenly*) Why,—I never—in all my life—heard anything—so—pitiful.

MRS. LANE: Did you ever go to school here?

RACHEL: Yes. I was made to feel my color—but I never had an experience like that.

MRS. LANE: How many years ago were you in the graded schools?

RACHEL: Oh!—around ten.

MRS. LANE: (*laughs grimly*) Ten years! Every year things are getting worse. Last year wasn't as bad as this. (*pauses*) So they treat the children all right in this school?

RACHEL: Yes! Yes! I know that.

MRS. LANE: I can't afford to take this flat here, but I'll take it. I'm going to have Ethel educated. Although, when you think of it,—it's all rather useless—this education! What are our children going to do with it, when they get it? We strive and save and sacrifice to educate them—and the whole time—down underneath, we know—they'll have no chance.

RACHEL: (*sadly*) Yes, that's true, all right, God seems to have forgotten us.

MRS. LANE: God! It's all a lie about God. I know.—This fall I sent Ethel to a white Sunday school near us. She received the same treatment there she did in the day school. Her being there, nearly broke up the school. At the end, the superintendent called her to him and asked her if she didn't know of some nice colored Sunday school. He told her she must feel out of place and uncomfortable there. That's your Church of God!

RACHEL: Oh! how unspeakably brutal. (*controls herself with an effort; after a pause*) Have you any other children?

MRS. LANE: (*dryly*) Hardly! If I had another—I'd kill it. It's kinder. (*rising presently*) Well, I must go now. Thank you for your information—and for listening. (*suddenly*) You aren't married, are you?

RACHEL: No.

MRS. LANE: Don't marry,—that's my advice. Come, Ethel. (*Ethel gets up and puts down the things in her lap, carefully upon her chair. She goes in a hurried, timid way to her mother and clutches her hand*) Say good-bye to the lady.

ETHEL: (*faintly*) Good-bye.

RACHEL: (*kneeling by the little girl—a beautiful smile on her face*) Dear little girl, won't you let me kiss you good-bye? I love little girls. (*the child hides behind her mother; continuing brokenly*) Oh!—no child—ever did—that to me—before!

MRS. LANE: (*in a gentler voice*) Perhaps, when we move in here, the first of the month, things may be better. Thank you, again. Good morning! You don't belie your name.

(*All three go into the vestibule. The outside door opens and closes. Rachel as though dazed and striken returns. She sits in a chair, leans forward, and clasping her hands loosely between her knees, stares at the chair with the apple on it where Ethel Lane has sat. She does not move for some time. Then she gets up, goes to the window in the rear center and sits there. She breathes in the air deeply and then goes to the sewing machine and begins to sew on something she is making. Presently her feet slow down on the pedals; she stops, and begins brooding again. After a short pause, she gets up and begins to pace up and down slowly, mechanically, her head bent forward. The sharp ringing of the electric bell breaks in upon this. Rachel starts and goes slowly into the vestibule. She is heard speaking dully through the tube.)*

RACHEL: Yes!—All right! Bring it up! (*presently she returns with a long flower box. She opens it listlessly at the table. Within are six beautiful crimson rosebuds with long stems. Rachel looks at the name on the card. She sinks down slowly on her knees and leans her head against the table. She sighs wearily*) Oh! John! John!— What are we to do?—I'm—I'm afraid! Everywhere—it is the same thing. My mother! My little brother! Little, black, crushed Ethel! (*in a whisper*) Oh! God! You who I have been taught to believe are so good, so beautiful, how could—You permit—these things? (*pauses, raises her head and sees the rosebuds. Her face softens and grows beautiful, very sweetly*) Dear little rosebuds— you—make me think—of sleeping, curled up, happy babies. Dear beautiful, little rosebuds! (*pauses; goes on thoughtfully to the rosebuds*) When—I look—at you—I believe—God is beautiful. He who can make a little exquisite thing like this, and this, can't be cruel. Oh! He can't mean me—to give up—love— and the hope of little children. (*there is the sound of a small hand knocking at the outer door. Rachel smiles*) My Jimmy! It must be twelve o'clock. (*rises*) I didn't dream it was so late. (*starts for the vestibule*) Oh! the world can't be so bad. I don't believe it. I won't. I must forget that little girl. My little Jimmy is happy—and today John—sent me beautiful rosebuds. Oh, there are lovely things, yet. (*goes into the vestibule. A child's eager cry is heard; and Rachel, carrying Jimmy in her arms, comes in. He has both about her neck and is hugging her. With him in her arms, she sits down in the armchair at the right front.*)

RACHEL: Well, honey, how was school today?

JIMMY: (*sobering a trifle*) All right, Ma Rachel. (*suddenly sees the roses*) Oh! look at the pretty flowers. Why, Ma Rachel, you forgot to put them in water. They'll die.

RACHEL: Well, so they will. Hop down this minute, and I'll put them in right away. (*gathers up the box and flowers and goes into the kitchenette. Jimmy climbs back into the chair. He looks thoughtful and serious. Rachel comes back with the buds in a tall glass vase. She puts the fern on top of the piano, and places the vase in the center of the table.*) There, honey, that's better, isn't it? Aren't they lovely?

JIMMY: Yes, that's lots better. Now they won't die, will they? Rosebuds are just like little "chilyun," aren't they, Ma Rachel? If you are good to them, they'll grow up into lovely roses, won't they? And if you hurt them, they'll die. Ma Rachel do you think all peoples are kind to little rosebuds?

RACHEL: (*watching Jimmy shortly*) Why, of course. Who could hurt little children? Who would have the heart to do such a thing?

JIMMY: If you hurt them, it would be lots kinder, wouldn't it, to kill them all at once, and not a little bit and a little bit?

RACHEL: (*sharply*) Why, honey boy, why are you talking like this?

JIMMY: Ma Rachel, what is a "Nigger?"

(*Rachel recoils as though she had been struck.*)

RACHEL: Honey boy, why—why do you ask that?

JIMMY: Some big boys called me that when I came out of school just now. They said: "Look at the little nigger!" And they laughed. One of them runned, no ranned, after me and threw stones; and they all kept calling "Nigger! Nigger! Nigger!" One stone struck me hard in the back, and it hurt awful bad; but I didn't cry, Ma Rachel. I wouldn't let them make me cry. The stone hurts me there, Ma Rachel; but what they called me hurts and hurts here. What is a "Nigger," Ma Rachel?

RACHEL: (*controlling herself with a tremendous effort. At last she sweeps down upon him and hugs and kisses him*) Why, honey boy, those boys didn't mean anything. Silly, little, honey boy! They're rough, that's all. How could they mean anything?

JIMMY: You're only saying that, Ma Rachel, so I won't be hurt. I know. It wouldn't ache here like it does—if they didn't mean something.

RACHEL: (*abruptly*) Where's Mary, honey?

JIMMY: She's in her flat. She came in just after I did.

RACHEL: Well, honey, I'm going to give you two big cookies, and two to take to Mary; and you may stay in there and play with her, till I get your lunch ready. Won't that be jolly?

JIMMY: (*brightening a little*) Why, you never give me but one at a time. You'll give me two?—One? Two?

RACHEL: (*gets the cookies and brings them to him. Jimmy climbs down from the chair.*) Shoo! now, little honey boy. See how many laughs you can make for me, before I come after you. Hear? Have a good time, now.

(*Jimmy starts for the door quickly; but he begins to slow down. His face gets long and serious again. Rachel watches him.*)

RACHEL: (*jumping at him*) Shoo! Shoo! Get out of here quickly, little chicken. (*she follows him out. The outer door opens and shuts. Presently she returns. She looks old and worn and grey. Calmly. Pauses*) First, it's little, black Ethel and then it's Jimmy. Tomorrow, it will be some other little child. The blight— sooner or later—strikes all. My little Jimmy, only seven years old, poisoned! (*through the open window comes the laughter of little children at play. Rachel shuddering, covers her ears*) And once I said, centuries ago, it must have been: "How can life be so terrible, when there are little children in the world?" Terrible! Terrible! (*in a whisper, slowly*) That's the reason it is so terrible. (*the laughter reaches her again; this time she listens*) And, suddenly, some day, from out of the black, the blight shall descend, and shall still forever—the laughter on those little lips, and in those little hearts. (*pauses thoughtfully*) And the loveliest thing—almost, that ever happened to me, that beautiful voice, in my dream, those beautiful words: "Rachel, you are to be the mother to little children." (*pauses, then slowly and with dawning surprise*) Why, God, you were making a mock of me; you were laughing at me. I didn't believe God could laugh at our sufferings, but He can. We are accursed, accursed! We have nothing, absolutely nothing. (*Strong's rosebuds attract her attention. She goes over to them, puts her hands out as if to touch them, and then shakes her head, very sweetly.*) No, little rosebuds, I may not touch you. Dear, little, baby rosebuds,—I am accursed. (*gradually her whole form stiffens; she breathes deeply; at last slowly*) You God!—You terrible, laughing God! Listen! I swear—and may my soul be damned to all eternity, if I do break this oath— I swear—that no child of mine shall ever lie upon my breast, for I will not have it rise up, in the terrible days that are to be—and call me cursed. (*a pause, very wistfully; questioningly*) Never to know the loveliest thing in all the world—the feel of a little head, the touch of little hands, the beautiful utter dependence—of a little child? (*with sudden frenzy*) You can laugh, O God! Well, so can I. (*bursts into terrible, racking laughter*) But I can be kinder than You. (*Fiercely she snatches the rosebuds from the vase, grasps them roughly, tears each head from the stem, and grinds it under her feet. The vase goes over with a crash; the water drips unheeded over the tablecloth and floor.*) If I kill, You Mighty God, I kill at once—I do not torture. (*falls face downward on the floor. The laughter of the children shrills loudly through the window.*)

ACT THREE

Time: *Seven o'clock in the evening, one week later.*

Place: *The same room. There is a coal fire in the grate. The curtains are drawn. A lighted oil lamp with dark green porcelain shade is in the center of the table. Mrs. Loving and Tom are sitting by the table, Mrs. Loving sewing, Tom reading. There is the sound of much laughter and the shrill screaming of a child from the bedrooms. Presently Jimmy clad in a flannelette sleeping suit, covering all of him but his head and hands, chases a pillow, which has come flying through the doorway at the rear. He struggles with it, finally gets it in his arms, and rushes as fast as he can through the doorway again. Rachel jumps at him with a cry. He drops the pillow and shrieks. There is a tussle for possession of it, and they disappear. The noise grows louder and merrier. Tom puts down his paper and grins. He looks at his mother.*

Tom: Well, who's the giddy one in this family now?

Mrs. Loving: (*shaking her head in troubled manner*) I don't like it. It worries me. Rachel— (*breaks off*)

Tom: Have you found out, yet—

Mrs. Loving: (*turning and looking toward the rear doorway, quickly interrupting him*) Sh! (*Rachel, laughing, her hair tumbling over her shoulders, comes rushing into the room. Jimmy is in close pursuit. He tries to catch her, but she dodges him. They are both breathless.*)

Mrs. Loving: (*deprecatingly*) Really, Rachel, Jimmy will be so excited he won't be able to sleep. It's after his bedtime, now. Don't you think you had better stop?

RACHEL: All right, Ma dear. Come on, Jimmy; let's play "Old Folks" and sit by the fire. (*she begins to push the big armchair over to the fire. Tom jumps up, moves her aside, and pushes it himself. Jimmy renders assistance.*)

TOM: Thanks, Big Fellow, you are "sure some" strong. I'll remember you when these people around here come for me to move pianos and such things around. Shake! (*They shake hands.*)

JIMMY: (*proudly*) I am awful strong, am I not?

TOM: You "sure" are a Hercules. (*hurriedly, as Jimmy's mouth and eyes open wide*) And see here! Don't ask me tonight who that was. I'll tell you the first thing tomorrow morning. Hear? (*returns to his chair and paper*)

RACHEL: (*sitting down*) Come on, honey boy, and sit in my lap.

JIMMY: (*doubtfully*) I thought we were going to play "Old Folks."

RACHEL: We are.

JIMMY: Do old folks sit in each other's laps?

RACHEL: Old folks do anything. Come on.

JIMMY: (*hesitatingly climbs into her lap, but presently snuggles down and sighs audibly from sheer content; Rachel starts to bind up her hair*) Ma Rachel, don't please! I like your hair like that. You're—you're pretty. I like to feel of it; and it smells like—like—oh!—like a barn.

RACHEL: My! how complimentary! I like that. Like a barn, indeed!

JIMMY: What's "complimentary"?

RACHEL: Oh! saying nice things about me. (*pinching his cheek and laughing*) That my hair is like a barn, for instance.

JIMMY: (*stoutly*) Well, that is "complimentary." It smells like hay—like the hay in the barn you took me to, one day, last summer. 'Member?

RACHEL: Yes honey.

JIMMY: (*after a brief pause*) Ma Rachel!

RACHEL: Well?

JIMMY: Tell me a story, please. It's "storytime," now, isn't it?

RACHEL: Well, let's see. (*they both look into the fire for a space; beginning softly*) Once upon a time, there were two, dear, little boys, and they were all alone in the world. They lived with a cruel, old man and woman, who made them work hard, very hard—all day, and beat them when they did not move fast enough, and always, every night, before they went to bed. They slept in an attic on a rickety, narrow bed, that went screech! screech! whenever they moved. And, in summer, they nearly died with the heat up there, and in winter, with the cold. One wintry night, when they were both weeping very bitterly after a particularly hard beating, they suddenly heard a pleasant voice saying: "Why are you crying, little boys?" They looked up, and there, in the moonlight, by their bed, was the dearest, little old lady. She was dressed all in grey, from the peak of her little pointed hat to her little, buckled shoes. She held a black cane much taller than her little self. Her hair fell about her ears in tiny, grey corkscrew curls, and they bobbed about as she moved. Her eyes were black and bright—as bright as—well, as that lovely, white light there. No, there! And her cheeks were as red as the apple I gave you yesterday. Do you remember?

JIMMY: (*dreamily*) Yes.

RACHEL: "Why are you crying, little boys?" she asked again, in a lovely, low, little voice. "Because we are tired and sore and hungry and cold; and we are all alone in the world; and we don't know how to laugh any more. We should so like to laugh again." "Why, that's easy," she said, "it's just like this." And she laughed a little, joyous, musical laugh. "Try!" she commanded. They tried, but their laughing boxes were very rusty, and they made horrid sounds. "Well," she said, "I advise you to pack up, and go away, as soon as you can, to the Land of Laughter. You'll soon learn there, I can tell you." "Is there such a land?" they asked doubtfully. "To be sure there is," she answered the least bit sharply. "We never heard of it," they said. "Well, I'm sure there must be plenty of things you never heard about," she said just the "leastest" bit more sharply. "In a moment you'll be telling me flowers don't talk together, and the birds." "We never heard of such a thing," they said in surprise, their eyes like saucers. "There!" she said, bobbing her little curls. "What did I tell you? You have much to learn." "How do you get to the Land of Laughter?" they asked. "You go out of the eastern gate of the town, just as the sun is rising; and you take the highway there, and follow it; and if you go with it long enough, it will bring you to the very gates of the Land of Laughter. It's a long, long way from here; and it will take you many days." The words had scarcely left her mouth, when, lo! the little lady disappeared, and where she had stood was the white square of moonlight—nothing else. And without more ado these two little boys put their arms around each other and fell fast asleep. And in the grey, just before daybreak, they awoke and dressed; and, putting on their ragged caps and mittens, for it was a wintry day, they stole out of the house and made for the eastern gate. And just as they reached it, and passed through, the whole east leapt into fire. All day they walked, and many days thereafter, and kindly people, by the way, took them in and gave them food and drink and sometimes a bed at night. Often they slept by the roadside, but they didn't mind that for the climate was delightful—not too hot, and not too cold. They soon threw away their ragged little mittens. They walked for many days, and there was no Land of Laughter. Once they met an old man, richly dressed, with shining jewels on his fingers, and he stopped them and asked: "Where are you going so fast, little boys?" "We are going to the Land of Laughter," they said together gravely. "That," said the old man, "is a very foolish thing to do. Come with me, and I will take you to the Land of Riches. I will cover you with garments of beauty, and give you jewels and a castle to live in and servants and horses and many things besides." And they said to him: "No, we wish to learn how to laugh again; we have forgotten how, and we are going to the Land of Laughter." "You will regret not going with me. See if you don't," he said and he left them in quite a huff. And they walked again, many days, and again they met an old man. He was tall and imposing looking and very dignified. And he said: "Where are you going so fast, little boys?" "We are going to the Land of Laughter," they said together very seriously. "What!" he said, "that is an extremely foolish thing to do. Come with me, and I will give you power. I will make you great men: generals, kings, emperors. Whatever you desire to accomplish will be permitted you." And they smiled politely: "Thank you very much, but we have forgotten how to laugh, and we are going there to learn how." He looked upon them haughtily, without speaking, and disappeared. And they walked and walked more days; and they met another old man. And he was clad in rags, and his face was thin, and his eyes were unhappy. And he whispered to them: "Where are you going so fast, little boys?" "We are going to the Land of Laughter," they answered, without a smile. "Laughter! Laughter! that is useless. Come with me and I will show you the beauty of life through sacrifice, suffering for others. That is the only life. I come from the Land of Sacrifice." And they thanked him kindly, but said: "We have suffered long enough. We have forgotten how to laugh. We would learn again." And they went on; and he looked after them very wistfully. They walked more days, and at last they came to the Land of Laughter. And how do you suppose they knew this? Because they could hear, over the wall, the sound of joyous laughter,—the laughter of men, women, and children. And one sat guarding the gate, and they went to her. "We have come a long, long distance; and we would enter the Land of Laughter." "Let me see you smile, first," she said gently. "I sit at the gate; and no one who does not know how to smile may enter the Land of Laughter." And they tried to smile, but could not. "Go away and practice," she said kindly, "and come back tomorrow." And they went away, and practiced all night how to smile; and in the morning they returned, and the gentle lady at the gate said: "Dear little boys, have you learned how to smile?" And they said: "We have tried. How is this?" "Better," she said, "much better. Practice some more, and come back tomorrow." And they went away obediently and practiced. And they came the third day. And she said: "Now try again." And tears of delight came into her lovely eyes. "Those were very beautiful smiles," she said. "Now, you may enter." And she unlocked the gate, and kissed them both, and they entered the Land—the beautiful Land of Laughter. Never had they seen such blue skies, such green trees and grass; never had they heard such birds' songs. And people, men, women and children, laughing softly, came to meet them, and took them in and made them at home; and soon, very soon, they learned to sleep. And they grew up here, and married, and had laughing, happy children. And sometimes they thought of the Land of Riches, and said: "Ah! well!" and sometimes of the Land of Power, and sighed a little; and sometimes of the Land of Sacrifice—and their eyes were wistful. But they soon forgot, and laughed again. And they grew old, laughing. And then when they died—a laugh was on their lips. Thus are things in the beautiful Land of Laughter. (*There is a long pause.*)

JIMMY: I like that story, Ma Rachel. It's nice to laugh, isn't it? Is there such a land?

RACHEL: (*softly*) What do you think, honey?

JIMMY: I thinks it would be awful nice if there was. Don't you?

RACHEL: (*wistfully*) If there only were! If there only were!

JIMMY: Ma Rachel.

RACHEL: Well?

JIMMY: It makes you think—kind of—doesn't it—of sunshine medicine?

RACHEL: Yes, honey,—but it isn't medicine there. It's always there—just like—well—like our air here. It's always sunshine there.

JIMMY: Always sunshine? Never any dark?

RACHEL: No, honey.

JIMMY: You'd—never—be—afraid there, then, would you? Never afraid of nothing?

RACHEL: No, honey.

JIMMY: (*with a big sigh*) Oh!—Oh! I wish it was here—not there. (*puts his hand up to Rachel's face; suddenly sits up and looks at her*) Why, Ma Rachel dear, you're crying. Your face is all wet. Why! Don't cry! Don't cry!

RACHEL: (*gently*) Do you remember that I told you the lady at the gate had tears of joy in her eyes, when the two dear little boys smiled that beautiful smile?

JIMMY: Yes.

RACHEL: Well, these are tears of joy, honey, that's all—tears of joy.

JIMMY: It must be awful queer to have tears of joy, 'cause you're happy. I never did. (*with a sigh*) But, if you say they are, dear Ma Rachel, they must be. You knows everything, don't you?

RACHEL: (*sadly*) Some things, honey, some things. (*a silence*)

JIMMY: (*sighing happily*) This is the beautiful-est night I ever knew. If you would do just one more thing, it would be lots more beautiful. Will you, Ma Rachel?

RACHEL: Well, what, honey?

JIMMY: Will you sing—at the piano, I mean, it's lots prettier that way—the little song you used to rock me to sleep by? You know, the one about the "Slumber Boat"?

RACHEL: Oh! honey, not tonight. You're too tired. It's bedtime now.

JIMMY: (*patting her face with his little hand; wheedlingly*) Please! Ma Rachel, please! pretty please!

RACHEL: Well, honey boy, this once, then. Tonight, you shall have the little song—I used to sing you to sleep by (*half to herself*) perhaps for the last time.

JIMMY: Why, Ma Rachel, why the last time?

RACHEL: (*shaking her head sadly, goes to the piano; in a whisper*) The last time. (*She twists up her hair into a knot at the back of her head and looks at the keys for a few moments; then she plays the accompaniment of the "Slumber Boat" through softly, and, after a moment, sings. Her voice is full of pent-up longing, and heartbreak, and hopelessness. She ends in a little sob, but attempts to cover it by singing, lightly and daintily, the chorus of "The Owl and the Moon."* . . . *Then softly and with infinite tenderness, almost against her will, she plays and sings again the refrain of "Slumber Boat.")*

> Sail, baby, sail
> Out from that sea,
> Only don't forget to sail
> Back again to me.

(Presently she rises and goes to Jimmy who is lolling back happily in the big chair. During the singing, Tom and Mrs. Loving apparently do not listen; when she sobs, however, Tom's hand on his paper tightens; Mrs. Loving's needle poises for a moment in mid-air. Neither looks at Rachel. Jimmy evidently has not noticed the sob.)

RACHEL: *(kneeling by Jimmy)* Well, honey, how did you like it?

JIMMY: *(proceeding to pull down her hair from the twist)* It was lovely, Ma Rachel. *(yawns audibly)* Now, Ma Rachel, I'm just beautifully sleepy. *(dreamily)* I think that p'r'aps I'll go to the Land of Laughter tonight in my dreams. I'll go in the "Slumber Boat" and come back in the morning and tell you all about it. Shall I?

RACHEL: Yes, honey. *(whispers)*

> Only don't forget to sail
> Back again to me.

TOM: *(suddenly)* Rachel! *(Rachel starts slightly)* I nearly forgot. John is coming here tonight to see how you are. He told me to tell you so.

RACHEL: *(stiffens perceptibly, then in different tones)* Very well. Thank you. *(suddenly with a little cry she puts her arms around Jimmy)* Jimmy! honey! don't go tonight. Don't go without Ma Rachel. Wait for me, honey. I do so wish to go, too, to the Land of Laughter. Think of it, Jimmy; nothing but birds always singing, and flowers always blooming, and skies always blue—and people, all of them, always laughing, laughing. You'll wait for Ma Rachel, won't you, honey?

JIMMY: Is there really and truly, Ma Rachel, a Land of Laughter?

RACHEL: Oh! Jimmy, let's hope so; let's pray so.

JIMMY: *(frowns)* I've been thinking— *(pauses)* You have to smile at the gate, don't you, to get in?

RACHEL: Yes, honey.

JIMMY: Well, I guess I couldn't smile if my Ma Rachel wasn't somewhere close to me. So I couldn't get in after all, could I? Tonight, I'll go somewhere else, and tell you all about it. And then, some day, we'll go together, won't we ?

RACHEL: *(sadly)* Yes, honey, some day—some day. *(a short silence)* Well, this isn't going to "sleepy-sleep," is it? Go, now, and say good night to Ma Loving and Uncle Tom.

JIMMY: *(gets down obediently, and goes first to Mrs. Loving. She leans over, and he puts his little arms around her neck. They kiss; very sweetly*) Sweet dreams! God keep you all the night!

MRS. LOVING: The sweetest of sweet dreams to you, dear little boy! Good night! (*Rachel watches, unwatched, the scene. Her eyes are full of yearning.*)

JIMMY: (*going to Tom, who makes believe he does not see him*) Uncle Tom!

TOM: (*jumps as though tremendously startled; Jimmy laughs*) My! how you frightened me. You'll put my gizzard out of commission, if you do that often. Well, sir, what can I do for you?

JIMMY: I came to say good night.

TOM: (*gathering Jimmy up in his arms and kissing him; gently and with emotion*) Good night, dear little Big Fellow! Good night!

JIMMY: Sweet dreams! God keep you all the night! (*goes sedately to Rachel, and holds out his little hand*) I'm ready, Ma Rachel. (*yawns*) I'm so nice and sleepy.

RACHEL: (*with Jimmy's hand in hers, she hesitates a moment, and then approaches Tom slowly. For a short time she stands looking down at him; suddenly leaning over him*) Why, Tom, what a pretty tie! Is it new?

TOM: Well, no, not exactly. I've had it about a month. It is rather a beauty, isn't it?

RACHEL: Why, I never remember seeing it.

TOM: (*laughing*) I guess not. I saw to that.

RACHEL: Stingy!

TOM: Well, I am—where my ties are concerned. I've had experience.

RACHEL: (*tentatively*) Tom!

TOM: Well?

RACHEL: (*nervously and wistfully*) Are you—will you—I mean, won't you be home this evening?

TOM: You've got a long memory, Sis. I've that engagement, you know. Why?

RACHEL: (*hastily*) I forgot; so you have.

TOM: Why?

RACHEL: (*hastily*) Oh! nothing—nothing. Come on, Jimmy boy, you can hardly keep those little peepers open, can you? Come on, honey. (*Rachel and Jimmy go out the rear doorway. There is a silence.*)

MRS. LOVING: (*slowly, as though thinking aloud*) I try to make out what could have happened; but it's no use—I can't. Those four days, she lay in bed hardly moving, scarcely speaking. Only her eyes seemed alive. I never saw such a wide, tragic look in my life. It was as though her soul had been mortally wounded. But how? how? What could have happened?

TOM: (*quietly*) I don't know. She generally tells me everything; but she avoids me now. If we are alone in a room—she gets out. I don't know what it means.

MRS. LOVING: She will hardly let Jimmy out of her sight. While he's at school, she's nervous and excited. She seems always to be listening, but for what? When he returns, she nearly devours him. And she always asks him in a frightened sort of way, her face as pale and tense as can be: "Well, honey boy, how was school today?" And he always answers, "Fine, Ma Rachel, fine! I learned—"; and then he goes on to tell her everything that has happened. And when he has finished, she says in an uneasy sort of way: "Is—is that all?" And when he says "Yes," she relaxes and becomes limp. After a little while she becomes feverishly happy. She plays with Jimmy and the children more than ever she did—and she played a good deal, as you know. They're here, or she's with them. Yesterday, I said in remonstrance, when she came in, her face pale and haggard and black hollows under her eyes: "Rachel, remember you're just out of a sick-bed. You're not well enough to go on like this." "I know," was all she would say, "but I've got to. I can't help myself. This part of their little lives must be happy—it just must be." (*pauses*) The last couple of nights, Jimmy has awakened and cried most pitfully. She wouldn't let me go to him; said I had enough trouble, and she could quiet him. She never will let me know why he cries; but she stays with him, and soothes him until, at last, he falls asleep again. Every time she has come out like a rag; and her face is like a dead woman's. Strange isn't it, this is the first time we have ever been able to talk it over? Tom, what could have happened?

Tom: I don't know, Ma, but I feel as you do; something terrible and sudden has hurt her soul; and, poor little thing, she's trying bravely to readjust herself to life again. (*pauses, looks at his watch, and then rises and goes to her. He pats her back awkwardly*) Well, Ma, I'm going now. Don't worry too much. Youth, you know, gets over things finally. It takes them hard, that's all—. At least, that's what the older heads tell us. (*gets his hat and stands in the vestibule doorway*) Ma, you know, I begin with John tomorrow. (*with emotion*) I don't believe we'll ever forget John. Good night! (*exit. Mrs. Loving continues to sew. Rachel, her hair arranged, reenters through the rear doorway. She is humming.*)

Rachel: He's sleeping like a top. Aren't little children, Ma dear, the sweetest things, when they're all helpless and asleep? One little hand is under his cheek; and he's smiling. (*stops suddenly, biting her lips. A pause*) Where's Tom?

Mrs. Loving: He went out a few minutes ago.

Rachel: (*sitting in Tom's chair and picking up his paper. She is exceedingly nervous. She looks the paper over rapidly; presently trying to make her tone casual*) Ma,—you—you—aren't going anywhere tonight, are you?

Mrs. Loving: I've got to go out for a short time about half-past eight. Mrs. Jordan, you know. I'll not be gone very long, though. Why?

Rachel: Oh! nothing particular. I just thought it would be cosy if we could sit here together the rest of the evening. Can't you go tomorrow?

Mrs. Loving: Why, I don't see how I can. I've made the engagement. It's about a new reception gown; and she's exceedingly exacting, as you know. I can't afford to lose her.

Rachel: No, I suppose not. All right, Ma dear. (*presently, paper in hand, she laughs, but not quite naturally*) Look! Ma dear! How is that for fashion, anyway? Isn't it the "limit"? (*rises and shows her mother a picture in the paper. As she is in the act, the bell rings. With a startled cry*) Oh! (*drops the paper, and grips her mother's hand*)

MRS. LOVING: (*anxiously*) Rachel, your nerves are right on edge; and your hand feels like fire. I'll have to see a doctor about you; and that's all there is to it.

RACHEL: (*laughing nervously and moving toward the vestibule*) Nonsense, Ma dear! Just because I let out a whoop now and then, and have nice warm hands? (*goes out, is heard talking through the tube*) Yes! (*her voice emitting tremendous relief*) Oh! bring it right up! (*appearing in the doorway*) Ma dear, did you buy anything at Goddard's today?

MRS. LOVING: Yes; and I've been wondering why they were so late in delivering it. I bought it early this morning. (*Rachel goes out again. A door opens and shuts. She reappears with a bundle.*)

MRS. LOVING: Put it on my bed, Rachel, please. (*exit Rachel rear doorway; presently returns empty-handed; sits down again at the table with the paper between herself and mother; sinks in a deep revery. Suddenly there is the sound of many loud knocks made by numerous small fists. Rachel drops the paper, and comes to a sitting posture, tense again. Her mother looks at her, but says nothing. Almost immediately Rachel relaxes.*)

RACHEL: My kiddies! They're late, this evening. (*goes out into the vestibule. A door opens and shuts. There is the shrill, excited sound of childish voices. Rachel comes in surrounded by the children, all trying to say something to her at once. Rachel puts her finger on her lip and points toward the doorway in the rear. They all quiet down. She sits on the floor in the front of the stage, and the children all cluster around her. Their conversation takes place in a half-whisper. As they enter they nod brightly at Mrs. Loving, who smiles in return*) Why so late, kiddies? It's long past "sleepy-time."

LITTLE NANCY: We've been playing "Hide and Seek," and having the mostest fun. We promised, all of us, that if we could play until half-past seven tonight we "wouldn't make any fuss about going to bed at seven o'clock the rest of the week. It's awful hard to go. I hate to go to bed!

LITTLE MARY, LOUISE, AND EDITH: So do I! So do I! So do I!

LITTLE MARTHA: I don't. I love bed. My bed, after my muzzer tucks me all in, is like a nice warm bag. I just stick my nose out. When I lifts my head up I can see the light from the dining room come in the door. I can hear my muzzer and fazzer talking nice and low; and then, before I know it, I'm fast asleep, and I dream pretty things, and in about a minute its morning again. I love my little bed, and I love to dream.

Little MARY: (*aggressively*) Well, I guess I love to dream too. I wish I could dream, though, without going to bed.

LITTLE NANCY: When I grow up, I'm never going to bed at night! (*darkly*) You see.

LITTLE LOUISE: "Grown-ups" just love to poke their heads out of windows and cry, "Child'run, it's time for bed now; and you'd better hurry, too, I can tell you." They "sure" are queer, for sometimes when I wake up, it must be about twelve o'clock, I can hear my big sister giggling and talking to some silly man. If it's good for me to go to bed early—I should think—

RACHEL: (*interrupting suddenly*) Why, where is my little Jenny? Excuse me, Louise dear.

LITTLE MARTHA: Her cold is awful bad. She coughs like this (*giving a distressing imitation*) and snuffles all the time. She can't talk out loud, and she can't go to sleep. Muzzer says she's fev'rish—I thinks that's what she says. Jenny says she knows she could go to sleep, if you would come and sit with her a little while.

RACHEL: I certainly will. I'll go when you do, honey.

LITTLE MARTHA: (*softly stroking Rachel's arm*) You're the very nicest "grown-up," (*loyally*) exept my muzzer, of course, I ever knew. You knows all about little chil'run and you can be one, although you're all grown up. I think you would make a lovely muzzer. (*to the rest of the children*) Don't you?

ALL: (*in excited whispers*) Yes, I do.

RACHEL: (*winces, then says gently*) Come, kiddies, you must go now, or your mothers will blame me for keeping you. (*rises, as do the rest. Little Martha puts her hand into Rachel's*) Ma dear, I'm going down to sit a little while with Jenny. I'll be back before you go, though. Come, kiddies, say good night to my mother.

ALL: (*gravely*) Good night! Sweet dreams! God keep you all the night.

MRS. LOVING: Good night dears! Sweet dreams, all!

(*Exeunt Rachel and the children. Mrs. Loving continues to sew. The bell presently rings three distinct times. In a few moments, Mrs. Loving gets up and goes out into the vestibule. A door opens and closes. Mrs. Loving and John Strong come in. He is a trifle pale but his imperturbable self. Mrs. Loving, somewhat nervous, takes her seat and resumes her sewing. She motions Strong to a chair. He returns to the vestibule, leaves his hat, returns, and sits down.*)

STRONG: Well, how is everything?

MRS. LOVING: Oh! about the same, I guess. Tom's out. John, we'll never forget you—and your kindness.

STRONG: That was nothing. And Rachel?

MRS. LOVING: She'll be back presently. She went to sit with a sick child for a little while.

STRONG: And how is she?

MRS. LOVING: She's not herself yet, but I think she is better.

STRONG: (*after a short pause*) Well, what did happen—exactly?

MRS. LOVING: That's just what I don't know.

STRONG: When you came home—you couldn't get in—was that it?

MRS. LOVING: Yes. (*pauses*) It was just a week ago today. I was downtown all the morning. It was about one o'clock when I got back. I had forgotten my key. I rapped on the door and then called. There was no answer. A window was open, and I could feel the air under the door, and I could hear it as the draught sucked it through. There was no other sound. Presently I made such a noise the people began to come out into the hall. Jimmy was in one of the flats playing with a little girl named Mary. He told me he had left Rachel here a short time before. She had given him four cookies, two for him and two for Mary, and had told him he could play with her until she came to tell him his lunch was ready. I saw he was getting frightened, so I got the little girl and her mother to keep him in their flat. Then, as no man was at home, I sent out for help. Three men broke the door down. (*pauses*) We found Rachel unconscious, lying on her face. For a few minutes I thought she was dead. (*pauses*) A vase had fallen over on the table and the water had dripped through the cloth and onto the floor. There had been flowers in it. When I left, there were no flowers here. What she could have done to them, I can't say. The long stems were lying everywhere, and the flowers had been ground into the floor. I could tell that they must have been roses from the stems. After we had put her to bed and called the doctor, and she had finally regained consciousness, I very naturally asked her what had happened. All she would say was, "Ma dear, I'm too—tired—please." For four days she lay in bed scarcely moving, speaking only when spoken to. That first day, when Jimmy came in to see her, she shrank away from him. We had to take him out, and comfort him as best we could. We kept him away, almost by force, until she got up. And, then, she was utterly miserable when he was out of her sight. What happened, I don't know. She avoids Tom, and she won't tell me. (*pauses*) Tom and I both believe her soul has been hurt. The trouble isn't with her body. You'll find her highly nervous. Sometimes she is very much depressed; again she is feverishly gay— almost reckless. What do you think about it, John?

STRONG: (*who has listened quietly*) Had anybody been here, do you know?

MRS. LOVING: No, I don't. I don't like to ask Rachel; and I can't ask the neighbors.

STRONG: No, of course not. (*pauses*) You say there were some flowers?

MRS. LOVING: Yes.

STRONG: And the flowers were ground into the carpet?

MRS. LOVING: Yes.

STRONG: Did you happen to notice the box? They must have come in a box, don't you think?

MRS. LOVING: Yes, there was a box in the kitchenette. It was from "Marcy's." I saw no card.

STRONG: (*slowly*) It is rather strange. (*a long silence during which the outer door opens and shuts. Rachel is heard singing. She stops abruptly. In a second or two she appears in the door. There is an air of suppressed excitement about her*)

RACHEL: Hello! John. (*Strong rises, nods at her, and brings forward for her the big armchair near the fire*) I thought that was your hat in the hall. It's brand new, I know—but it looks "John like." How are you? Ma! Jenny went to sleep like a little lamb. I don't like her breathing, though. (*looks from one to the other; flippantly*) Who's dead? (*nods her thanks to Strong for the chair and sits down*)

MRS. LOVING: Dead, Rachel?

RACHEL: Yes. The atmosphere here is so funereal,—it's positively "crapey."

STRONG: I don't know why it should be—I was just asking how you are.

RACHEL: Heavens! Does the mere inquiry into my health precipitate such an atmosphere? Your two faces were as long—as long— (*breaks off*) Kind sir, let me assure you, I am in the very best of health. And how are you, John?

STRONG: Oh! I'm always well. (*sits down*)

MRS. LOVING: Rachel, I'll have to get ready to go now. John, don't hurry. I'll be back shortly, probably in three-quarters of an hour—maybe less.

RACHEL: And maybe more, if I remember Mrs. Jordan. However, Ma dear, I'll do the best I can—while you are away. I'll try to be a credit to your training. (*Mrs. Loving smiles and goes out the rear doorway.*) Now, let's see—in the books of etiquette, I believe, the properly reared young lady always asks the young gentleman caller—you're young enough, aren't you, to be classed still as a "young gentleman caller"? (*no answer*) Well, anyway, she always asks the young gentleman caller sweetly something about the weather. (*primly*) This has been an exceedingly beautiful day, hasn't it, Mr. Strong? (*No answer from Strong, who, with his head resting against the back of the chair and his knees crossed is watching her in an amused, quizzical manner*) Well, really, every properly brought up young gentleman, I'm sure, ought to know, that it's exceedingly rude not to answer a civil question.

STRONG: (*lazily*) Tell me what to answer, Rachel.

RACHEL: Say, "Yes, very"; and look interested and pleased when you say it.

STRONG: (*with a half-smile*) Yes, very.

RACHEL: Well, I certainly wouldn't characterize that as a particularly animated remark. Besides, when you look at me through half-closed lids like that— and kind of smile—what are you thinking? (*no answer*) John Strong, are you deaf or—just plain stupid?

STRONG: Plain stupid, I guess.

RACHEL: (*in wheedling tones*) What were you thinking, John?

STRONG: (*slowly*) I was thinking— (*breaks off*)

RACHEL: (*irritably*) Well?

STRONG: I've changed my mind.

RACHEL: You're not going to tell me?

STRONG: No.

(*Mrs. Loving, dressed for the street, comes in.*)

MRS. LOVING: Good-bye, children. Rachel, don't quarrel so much with John. Let me see—if I have my key. (*feels in her bag*) Yes, I have it. I'll be back shortly. Good-bye. (*Strong and Rachel rise. He bows.*)

RACHEL: Good-bye, Ma dear. Hurry back as soon as you can, won't you? (*exit Mrs. Loving through the vestibule. Strong leans back, again in his chair, and watches Rachel through half-closed eyes. Rachel sits in her chair nervously*)

STRONG: Do you mind if I smoke?

RACHEL: You know I don't.

STRONG: I am trying to behave like—Reginald—"the properly reared young gentleman caller." (*lights a cigar; goes over to the fire, and throws his match away. Rachel goes into the kitchenette, and brings him a saucer for his ashes. She places it on the table near him*) Thank you. (*they both sit again, Strong very evidently enjoying his cigar and Rachel*) Now this is what I call cosy.

RACHEL: Cosy! Why?

STRONG: A nice warm room—shut in—curtains drawn—a cheerful fire crackling at my back—a lamp, not an electric or gas one, but one of your plain, old-fashioned kerosene ones—

RACHEL: (*interrupting*) Ma dear would like to catch you, I am sure, talking about her lamp like that. "Old-fashioned! plain!"—You have nerve.

STRONG: (*continuing as though he had not been interrupted*) A comfortable chair—a good cigar—and not very far away, a little lady, who is looking charming, so near, that if I reached over, I could touch her. You there—and I here.—It's living.

RACHEL: Well of all things! A compliment—and from you! How did it slip out, pray? (*no answer*) I suppose that you realize that a conversation between two persons is absolutely impossible, if one has to do her share all alone. Soon my ingenuity for introducing interesting subjects will be exhausted; and then will follow what, I believe, the story books call, "an uncomfortable silence."

STRONG: (*slowly*) Silence—between friends—isn't such a bad thing.

RACHEL: Thanks awfully. (*leans back; cups her cheek in her hand, and makes no pretense at further conversation. The old look of introspection returns to her eyes. She does not move.*)

STRONG: (*quietly*) Rachel! (*Rachel starts perceptibly.*) You must remember I'm here. I don't like looking into your soul—when you forget you're not alone.

RACHEL: I hadn't forgotten.

STRONG: Wouldn't it be easier for you, little girl, if you could tell—someone?

RACHEL: No. (*a silence*)

STRONG: Rachel,—you're fond of flowers,—aren't you?

RACHEL: Yes.

STRONG: Rosebuds—red rosebuds—particularly?

RACHEL: (*nervously*) Yes.

STRONG: Did you—dislike—the giver?

RACHEL: (*more nervously; bracing herself*) No, of course not.

STRONG: Rachel,—why—why—did you—kill the roses—then?

RACHEL: (*twisting her hands*) Oh, John! I'm so sorry, Ma dear told you that. She didn't know you sent them.

STRONG: So I gathered. (*pauses and then leans forward; quietly*) Rachel, little girl, why—did you kill them?

RACHEL: (*breathing quickly*) Don't you believe—it—a—a—kindness—sometimes—to kill?

STRONG: (*after a pause*) You—considered—it—a—kindness—to kill them?

RACHEL: Yes. (*another pause*)

STRONG: Do you mean—just—the roses?

RACHEL: (*breathing more quickly*) John!— Oh! must I say?

STRONG: Yes, little Rachel.

RACHEL: (*in a whisper*) No. (*there is a long pause. Rachel leans back limply, and closes her eyes. Presently Strong rises, and moves his chair very close to hers. She does not stir. He puts his cigar on the saucer.*)

STRONG: (*leaning forward; very gently*) Little girl, little girl, can't you tell me why?

RACHEL: (*wearily*) I can't.—It hurts—too much—to talk about it yet,—please.

STRONG: (*takes her hand; looks at it a few minutes and then at her quietly*) You— don't—care, then? (*she winces*) Rachel!—Look at me, little girl! (*as if against her will, she looks at him. Her eyes are fearful, hunted. She tries to look away, to draw away her hand; but he holds her gaze and her hand steadily*) Do you?

RACHEL: (*almost sobbing*) John! John! don't ask me. You are drawing my very soul out of my body with your eyes. You must not talk this way. You mustn't look—John, don't! (*tries to shield her eyes*)

STRONG: (*quietly takes both of her hands, and kisses the backs and the palms slowly. A look of horror creeps into her face. He deliberately raises his eyes and looks at her mouth. She recoils as though she expected him to strike her. He resumes slowly*) If— you—do—care, and I know now—that you do—nothing else, nothing should count.

RACHEL: (*wrenching herself from his grasp and rising. She covers her ears; she breathes rapidly.*) No! No! No!—You must stop. (*laughs nervously; continues feverishly*) I'm not behaving very well as a hostess, am I? Let's see. What shall I do? I'll play you something, John. How will that do? Or I'll sing to you. You used to like to hear me sing; you said my voice, I remember, was sympathetic, didn't you? (*moves quickly to the piano*) I'll sing you a pretty little song. I think it's beautiful. You've never heard it, I know. I've never sung it to you before. It's Nevin's "At Twilight." (*pauses, looks down, before she begins, then turns toward him and says quietly and sweetly*) Sometimes—in the coming years— I want—you to remember—I sang you this little song.—Will you?—I think it will make it easier for me—when I—when I— (*breaks off and begins the first chords. Strong goes slowly to the piano. He leans there watching intently. Rachel sings:*)

> The roses of yester-year
> Were all of them white and red;
> It fills my heart with silent fear
> To find all their beauty fled.
> The roses of white are sere,
> All faded the roses red,
> And one who loves me is not here
> And one that I love is dead.

(*A long pause. Then Strong goes to her and lifts her from the piano stool. He puts one arm around her very tenderly and pushes her head back so he can look into her eyes. She shuts them, but is passive.*)

STRONG: (*gently*) Little girl, little girl, don't you know that suggestions—suggestions—like those you are sending yourself constantly—are wicked things? You, who are so gentle, so loving, so warm— (*breaks off and crushes her to him. He kisses her many times. She does not resist, but in the midst of his caresses she breaks suddenly into convulsive laughter. He tries to hush the terrible sound with his mouth; then brokenly*) Little girl—don't laugh—like that.

RACHEL: (*interrupted throughout by her laughter*) I have to.—God is laughing.—We're his puppets.—He pulls the wires,—and we're so funny to Him.—I'm laughing too—because I can hear—my little children—weeping. They come to me generally while I'm asleep,—but I can hear them now.—They've begged me—do you understand?—begged me—not to bring them here;—and I've promised them—not to.—I've promised. I can't stand the sound of their crying.—I have to laugh—Oh! John! laugh!—laugh too!—I can't drown their weeping.

(*Strong picks her up bodily and carries her to the armchair.*)

STRONG: (*harshly*) Now, stop that!

RACHEL: (*in sheer surprise*) W-h-a-t?

STRONG: (*still harshly*) Stop that!—You've lost your self-control.— Find yourself again!

(*He leaves her and goes over to the fireplace, and stands looking down into it for some little time. Rachel, little by little, becomes calmer. Strong returns and sits beside her again. She doesn't move. He smoothes her hair back gently, and kisses her forehead—and then, slowly, her mouth. She does not resist; simply sits there, with shut eyes, inert, limp.*)

STRONG: Rachel! (*pauses*) There is a little flat on 43rd Street. It faces south and overlooks a little park. Do you remember it?—it's on the top floor.—Once I remember your saying—you liked it. That was over a year ago. That same day—I rented it. I've never lived there. No one knows about it—not even my mother. It's completely furnished now—and waiting—do you know for whom? Every single thing in it, I've bought myself—even to the pins on the little bird's-eye maple dresser. It has been the happiest year I have ever known. I furnished it—one room at a time. It's the prettiest, the most homelike little flat I've ever seen. (*very low*) Everything there—breathes love. Do you know for whom it is waiting? On the sitting room floor is a beautiful Turkish rug—red, and blue and gold. It's soft—and rich—and do you know for whose little feet it is waiting? There are delicate curtains at the windows and a bookcase full of friendly, eager, little books.—Do you know for whom they are waiting? There are comfortable leather chairs, just the right size, and a beautiful piano—that I leave open—sometimes, and lovely pictures of Madonnas. Do you know for whom they are waiting? There is an open fireplace with logs of wood, all carefully piled on gleaming andirons—and waiting. There is a bellows and a pair of shining tongs—waiting. And in the kitchenette painted blue and white, and smelling sweet with paint, is everything: bright pots and pans and kettles, and blue and white enamelware, and all kinds of knives and forks and spoons—and on the door—a roller-towel. Little girl, do you know for whom they are all waiting? And somewhere—there's a big, strong man—with broad shoulders. And he's willing and anxious to do anything—everything, and he's waiting very patiently. Little girl, is it to be—yes or no ?

RACHEL: (*during Strong's speech life has come flooding back to her. Her eyes are shining; her face, eager. For a moment she is beautifully happy*) Oh! you're too good to me and mine, John. I—didn't dream any one—could be—so good. (*leans forward and puts his big hand against her cheek and kisses it shyly*)

STRONG: (*quietly*) Is it—yes—or no, little girl?

RACHEL: (*feverishly, gripping his hands*) Oh, yes! yes! yes! and take me quickly, John. Take me before I can think any more. You mustn't let me think, John. And you'll be good to me, won't you? Every second of every minute, of every hour, of every day, you'll have me in your thoughts won't you? And you'll be with me every minute that you can? And, John, John!—you'll keep away the weeping of my little children. You won't let me hear it, will you? You'll make me forget everything everything—won't you?—Life is so short, John. (*shivers and then fearfully and slowly*) And eternity so—long. (*feverishly again*) And, John, after I am dead—promise me, promise me you'll love me more. (*shivers again*) I'll need love then. Oh! I'll need it. (*suddenly there comes to their ears the sound of a child's weeping. It is monotonous, hopeless, terribly afraid. Rachel recoils*) Oh! John!—Listen!—It's my boy, again.—I—John—I'll be back in a little while. (*goes swiftly to the door in the rear, pauses and looks back. The weeping continues. Her eyes are tragic. Slowly she kisses her hand to him and disappears. Strong stands where she has left him looking down. The weeping stops. Presently Rachel appears in the doorway. She is haggard and grey. She does not enter the room. She speaks as one dead might speak—tonelessly, slowly.*)

RACHEL: Do you wish to know why Jimmy is crying?

STRONG: Yes.

RACHEL: I am twenty-two—and I'm old; you're thirty-two—and you're old; Tom's twenty-three—and he is old. Ma dear's sixty—and she said once she is much older than that. She is. We are all blighted; we are all accursed—all of us—, everywhere, we whose skins are dark—our lives blasted by the white man's prejudice. (*pauses*) And my little Jimmy—seven years old, that's all— is blighted too. In a year or two, at best, he will be made old by suffering. (*pauses*) One week ago, today, some white boys, older and larger than my little Jimmy, as he was leaving the school—called him "Nigger"! They chased him through the streets calling him, "Nigger! Nigger! Nigger!" One boy threw stones at him. There is still a bruise on his little back where one struck him. That will get well; but they bruised his soul—and that will never—get well. He asked me what "Nigger" meant. I made light of the whole thing, laughed it off. He went to his little playmates, and very naturally asked them. The oldest of them is nine!—and they knew, poor little things—and they told him. (*pauses*) For the last couple of nights he has been dreaming—about these boys. And he always awakes—in the dark—afraid—afraid—of the now—and the future—I have seen that look of deadly fear—in the eyes—of other little children. I know what it is myself.—I was twelve—when some big boys chased me and called me names.—I never left the house afterwards—without being afraid. I was afraid, in the streets—in the school—in the church, everywhere, always, afraid of being hurt. And I—was not—afraid in vain. (*the weeping begins again*) He's only a baby—and he's blighted. (*to Jimmy*) Honey, I'm right here. I'm coming in just a minute. Don't cry. (*to Strong*) If it nearly kills me to hear my Jimmy's crying, do you think I could stand it, when my own child, flesh of my flesh, blood of my blood—learned the same reason for weeping? Do you? (*pauses*) Ever since I fell here—a week ago—I am afraid—to go—to sleep, for every time I do—my children come—and beg me—weeping—not to—bring them here—to suffer. Tonight, they came—when I was awake. (*pauses*) I have promised them again, now—by Jimmy's bed. (*in a whisper*) I have damned—my soul to all eternity—if I do. (*to Jimmy*) Honey, don't! I'm coming. (*to Strong*) And John,—dear John— you see—it can never be—all the beautiful, beautiful, things—you have— told me about. (*wistfully*) No—they—can never be—now. (*Strong comes toward her*) No,—John dear,—you—must not—touch me—any more. (*pauses*) Dear, this—is—"Good-bye."

STRONG: (*quietly*) It's not fair—to you, Rachel, to take you—at your word— tonight. You're sick; you've brooded so long, so continuously,—you've lost— your perspective. Don't answer, yet. Think it over for another week and I'll come back.

RACHEL: (*wearily*) No,—I can't think—any more.

STRONG: You realize—fully—you're sending me—for always?

RACHEL: Yes.

STRONG: And you care?

RACHEL: Yes.

STRONG: It's settled, then, for all time—"Good-bye!"

RACHEL: (*after a pause*) Yes.

STRONG: (*stands looking at her steadily a long time, and then moves to the door and turns, facing her; with infinite tenderness*) Good-bye, dear, little Rachel—God bless you.

RACHEL: Good-bye, John! (*Strong goes out. A door opens and shuts, There is finality in the sound. The weeping continues. Suddenly, with a great cry*) John! John! (*runs out into the vestibule. She presently returns. She is calm again. Slowly*) No! No! John. Not for us. (*a pause; with infinite yearning*) Oh! John,—if it only—if it only— (*breaks off, controls herself. Slowly again; thoughtfully*) No— No sunshine—no laughter—always—darkness. That is it. Even our little flat— (*in a whisper*) John's and mine—the little flat—that calls, calls us— through darkness. It shall wait—and wait—in vain—in darkness. Oh, John! (*pauses*) And my little children! my little children! (*the weeping ceases; pauses*) I shall never—see—you—now. Your little, brown, beautiful bodies—I shall never see.—Your dimples—everywhere—your laughter—your tears—the beautiful, lovely feel of you here. (*puts her hands against her heart*) Never— never—to be. (*a pause, fiercely*) But you are somewhere—and wherever you are you are mine! You are mine! All of you! Every bit of you! Even God can't take you away. (*a pause; very sweetly; pathetically*) Little children! My little children!—No more need you come to me—weeping—weeping. You may be happy now—you are safe. Little weeping voices, hush! hush! (*the weeping begins again. To Jimmy, her whole soul in her voice*) Jimmy! My little Jimmy! Honey! I'm coming.—Ma Rachel loves you so. (*sobs and goes blindly, unsteadily to the rear doorway; she leans her head there one second against the door; and then stumbles through and disappears. The light in the lamp flickers and goes out. . . . It is black. The terrible, heartbreaking weeping continues.*)

Mary Powell Burrill
(1884–1946)

Mary P. Burrill was one of the earliest playwrights to dramatize African Americans taking up arms against whites for the injustices of lynching. Like her close friend and contemporary, Angelina Grimké, Burrill was vocal about the rights of black women. Although she is known to have written other works, only two plays survive. Her first published work, *Aftermath*, appeared in the April 1919 *Liberator*. *Aftermath* is an example of the many lynching plays by black women in which characters are lynched for crimes other than the assault of a white woman. In September of that year, her second play, *They That Sit in Darkness*, was published in *Birth Control Review*, a periodical advocating birth control rights of women. *Birth Control Review* dedicated this issue on "The Negroes' Need for Birth Control, as Seen by Themselves." This issue included a short story by Grimké.

There is no known performance record for *They That Sit in Darkness. Aftermath*, however, competed in the David Belasco Sixth Annual Little Theatre Tournament on May 7, 1928, at the Frolic Theatre in New York City. Produced under the auspices of the Krigwa Players and the Workers' Drama League, the production left Burrill devastated:

> I feel that the ending which the players, without my knowledge or consent, appended to the play was not only an unwarranted violation of the rights of an author, but a serious artistic blunder as well. . . . The ending tacked on by the players changed what might otherwise have been an effective dramatic close into cheap melodramatic claptrap.[1]

The review in the May 19 issue of *Billboard* states that the "white trash theme is too offensive," and that the Krigwa Players took a prize in the previous year's tournament with a "more plausible tale of contemporary negro life, which did not deal with a race problem." He continues by describing the changed ending which the players presented: "Shots are heard off stage, the soldier staggers in, almost carrying the badly put together scenery with him and dies melodramatically."[2] Speculation is that the producers (white) of the tournament feared that using Burrill's version of the play would cause controversy. The other possibility was that Charles Burroughs, the director, changed the ending to guarantee acceptance in the tournament. There are no records of subsequent productions of *Aftermath*.

The daughter of Clara and John Burrill, Mary Burrill was born and educated in Washington, D.C. She graduated in 1901 from the famous M Street School (later known as Dunbar High). When her family moved to Boston, Burrill attended Emerson College of Oratory, which later became Emerson College, and received a diploma in 1904. In 1929 Burrill returned to Emerson and earned a Bachelor of Literary Interpretation (BLI). During this period, she revised *They That Sit in Darkness* and retitled it *Unto the Third and Fourth Generations*; it was published in the 1930 *Emersonian* yearbook and awarded "Best Junior Play of the Year."

In 1905 she began her teaching career at her alma mater, the M Street School, and from that year to around 1920, she alternated teaching English between M Street and Armstrong Technical High School until she was permanently assigned to M Street (Dunbar High by then). Burrill also served as director of the School of Expression, part of the Washington, D.C., Conservatory of Music, headed by Harriet Gibbs Marshall. As director from 1907 to 1911, she taught elocution, public speaking, and dramatics. Burrill enjoyed an outstanding reputation both as a teacher and as a director for the numerous dramatic productions she staged throughout the capitol city. Very little is known about Burrill's activities outside of her teaching and directing career. The only other record of Burrill's interest in lynching is displayed in a scrapbook, located at Dunbar High School, which contains a 1942 radio program highlighting Burrill reading *And They Lynched Him on a Tree,* by Katherine Chapin.[3]

Starting in the 1920s and continuing for nearly fifteen years, Burrill became known throughout the city for her narration with the Howard University Choir in its Christmas production of *The Other Wise Men,* drawing large crowds. She was also popular for her productions of Maeterlinck's *The Blue Bird* and J. M. Barrie's *Quality Street.* Burrill's colleague Elsie Brown Smith notes that "People anticipated her plays and knew they would be a success."[4]

Gloria Johnson's November 1944 Dunbar High School article on Burrill's retirement states:

> The plays which have been given by Miss Burrill were always finished productions and artistic. The student actors were more like professionals than amateurs. . . .
>
> If you saw Ernest Anderson in the movie, "In This Our Life," or Richard Huey on Broadway in "Bloomer Girl," you should know that these stars formerly occupied seats in room 57, and it was here that they admit, they received their first inspiration to try the stage.

Burrill inspired many of her students to perform and pursue playwriting. Two of her prize students were Willis Richardson and May Miller. Richardson went on to become the first black dramatist on Broadway with *The Chip Woman's Fortune* (1923). Miller was encouraged by Burrill to write her first play, *Pandora's Box*, winning Miller a fifty-cent cash prize as well as publication in the 1914 *School's Progress* magazine. (Miller's play *Nails and Thorns* appears in this anthology.) Burrill was so well respected that the Dunbar Class of 1945 dedicated their yearbook to her.

Burrill's friends included playwrights Georgia Douglas Johnson and Alice Dunbar Nelson. For nearly 25 years she was a close companion of Lucy Diggs Slowe, who was the first Dean of Women at Howard University. When Burrill retired from Dunbar High School in 1944, she moved to New York City, where she died in 1946.

NOTES

1. Letter from Mary P. Burrill to W. E. B. Du Bois, 22 May 1928. W. E. B. Du Bois Collection, University of Massachusetts Library Special Collections, Amherst.

2. *Billboard,* May 19, 1928. Vol. 40, pg. 7.

3. From Mary P. Burrill's scrapbook, library of the Dunbar High School, Washington, D.C.

4. Telephone interview with Elsie Brown Smith, February 23, 1988.

Aftermath

1919

❧❧❧

Mary Powell Burrill

CHARACTERS

MILLIE, *a young woman*
MAM SUE, *an old woman*
REV. LUKE MOSEBY, *a clergyman*
LONNIE, *a young man*
MRS. HAWKINS, *a friend*
JOHN, *a soldier*

Time: *The present.*
Place: *The Thornton cabin in South Carolina.*
It is late afternoon of a cool day in early spring. A soft afterglow pours in at the little window of the Thornton cabin. The light falls on MILLIE, *a slender brown girl of sixteen, who stands near the window, ironing. She wears a black dress and a big gingham apron. A clothes-horse weighted down with freshly ironed garments is nearby. In the rear there is a door leading out to the road. To the left, another door leads into the other room of the cabin. To the right there is a great stone hearth blackened by age. A Bible rests on the mantel over the hearth. An old armchair and a small table on which is a kerosene lamp are near the hearth. In the center of the room sits a well-scrubbed kitchen table and a substantial wooden chair. In front of the hearth, in a low rocking chair drawn close to the smouldering woodfire, sits* MAM SUE *busily sewing. The many colors in the old patchwork quilt that she is mending, together with the faded red of the bandanna on her head, contrast strangely with her black dress. Mam Sue is very old. Her ebony face is seamed with wrinkles; and in her bleared, watery eyes there is a world-old sorrow. A service flag containing one star hangs in the little window of the cabin.*

MAM SUE: (*crooning the old melody*)

> O, yes, yonder comes mah Lawd,
> He is comin' dis way
> Wid his sword in his han'
> O, yes, yonder comes—

(*A burning log falls apart, and Mam Sue suddenly stops singing and gazes intently at the fire. She speaks in deep mysterious tones to Millie, who has finished her task and has come to the hearth to put up her irons.*) See dat log dah, Millie? De one fallin' tuh de side dah wid de big flame lappin' 'round hit? Dat means big doin's 'round heah tonight!

MILLIE: (*with a start*) Oh, Mam Sue, don' you go proph'sying no mo'! You seen big doin's in dat fire de night befo' them w'ite devuls come in heah an' tuk'n po' dad out and bu'nt him!

MAM SUE: (*calmly*) No, Millie, Ah didn' see no big doin's dat night—Ah see'd evul doin's an' Ah tole yo' po' daddy to keep erway f'om town de nex' day wid his cotton. Ah jes knowed dat he wuz gwine to git in a row wid dem w'ite debbils—but he wou'd'n lis'n tuh his ole mammy—De good Lawd sen' me dese warnin's in dis fiah, jes lak He sen' His messiges in de fiah to Moses. Yo' chillun bettah lis'n to—

MILLIE: (*nervously*) Oh, Mam Sue, you skeers me when you talks erbout seein' all them things in de fire—

MAM SUE: Yuh gits skeered cause yuh don' put yo' trus' in de good Lawd! He kin tek keer o' yuh no mattuh whut com'!

MILLIE: (*bitterly*) Sometimes I thinks that Gawd's done fu'got us po' cullud people. Gawd didn' tek no keer o' po' dad and *he* put *his* trus' in Him! He uster set evah night by dis fire at dis here table and read his Bible an' pray—but jes look whut happen' to dad! That don' look like Gawd wuz tekin' keer—

MAM SUE: (*sharply*) Heish yo' mouf, Millie! Ah ain't a-gwine to 'ave dat sinner-talk 'roun' hyeah! (*derisively*) Gawd don't tek no keer o' yuh? Ain't yuh bin prayin' night an' mawnin' fo' Gawd to sen' yo' brudder back f'om de war 'live an' whole? An' ain't yuh git dat lettah no longer'n yistiddy sayin' dat de fightin's all done stopp't an' dat de blessid Lawd's done brung yo' brudder thoo all dem battuls live an' whole? Don' dat look lak de Lawd's done 'membered yuh?

MILLIE: (*thoughtfully*) I reckon youse right, Mam Sue. But ef anything had a-happen' to John I wuz' nevah goin' to pray no mo'!

(*Millie goes to the clothes-horse and folds the garments and lays them carefully into a large basket. Mam Sue falls again to her crooning.*)

MAM SUE:

> O, yes, yonder comes mah Lawd,
> He's comin' dis way-a.

MILLIE: Lonnie's so late gittin' home tonight; I guess I'd bettah tek Mis' Hart's wash home tonight myse'f.

MAM SUE: Yas, Lonnie's mighty late. Ah reckons you'd bettah slip erlon' wid hit. (*Millie gets her hat from the adjoining room and is about to leave with the basket when Mam Sue calls significantly*) Millie?

MILLIE: Yas, Mam Sue.

MAM SUE: (*firmly*) Don' yo' fu'git to drap dat lettah fu' John in de Pos' Awfus ez yuh goes by. Whah's de lettah?

MILLIE: (*reluctantly*) But, Mam Sue, please don' lets—

(*A knock is heard. Millie opens the door and* REV. LUKE MOSEBY *enters. Moseby is a wiry little old man with a black, kindly face, and bright, searching eyes; his woolly hair and beard are snow-white. He is dressed in a rusty black suit with a coat of clerical cut that comes to his knees. In one hand he carries a large Bible, and in the other, a stout walking stick.*)

MILLIE: Good evenin', Brother Moseby, come right in.

MOSEBY: Good eben', Millie. Good eben', Mam Sue. Ah jes drap't in to see ef you-all is still trus'in de good Lawd an'—

MAM SUE: Lor', Brudder Moseby, ain't Ah bin trus'n' de good Lawd nigh onter dese eighty yeah! Whut fu' yuh think Ah's agwine to quit w'en Ah'm in sight o' de Promis' Lan'? Millie, fetch Brudder Moseby dat cheer.

MOSEBY: (*drawing his chair to the fire*) Dat's right, Mam Sue, you jes a-keep on trus'n an' prayin' an evahthing's gwine to come aw-right. (*observing Millie is about to leave*) Don' lemme 'tain yuh, Millie, but whut's all dis good news wese bin heahin' bout yo' brudder John? Dey say he's done won some kind o' medal ober dah in France?

MILLIE: (*brightening up*) Oh, yes, we got a lettah day befo' yestiddy f'om John tellin' us all erbout it. He's won de War Cross! He fought off twenty Germuns all erlone an' saved his whole comp'ny an' the gret French Gen'rul come an' pinned de medal on him, hisse'f!

MOSEBY: De Lawd bles' his soul! Ah know'd dat boy wud mek good!

MILLIE: (*excited by the glory of it all*) An' he's been to Paris, an' the fines' people stopp't him when they seen his medal, an' shook his han' an' smiled at him— an' he kin go evahwhere, an' dey ain't nobody all the time a-lookin'down on him, an' a-sneerin' at him 'cause he's black; but evahwhere they's jes gran' to him! An' he sez it's the firs' time evah in his life he's felt lak a real, sho-nuf man!

MOSEBY: Well, honey don't de Holy Book say, "De fust shill be las' and the las' shill be fust"?

MAM SUE: (*fervently*) Dat hit do! An' de Holy Book ain't nebber tole no lie!

MOSEBY: Folks ober in Char'ston is sayin' dat some sojers is gwine to lan' dah today or tomorrer. Ah reckons day'll all be comin' 'long soon now dat de war's done stopp't.

MILLIE: I jes hates the thought of John comin' home an' hearin' 'bout dad!

MOSEBY: (*in astonishment*) Whut! Yuh mean to say yuh ain't 'rite him 'bout yo' daddy, yit?

MAM SUE: Dat she ain't! Millie mus' 'ave huh way! She 'lowed huh brudder ough'n be tole, an 'dat huh could keep on writin' to him jes lak huh dad wuz livin'—Millie allus done de writin'—An' Ah lets huh 'ave huh way—

MOSEBY: (*shaking his head in disapproval*) Yuh mean tuh say—

MILLIE: (*pleading*) But, Brother Moseby, I couldn't write John no bad news w'ilst he wuz way over there by hisse'f. He had 'nuf to worry him with death a'-starin' him in the face evah day!

MAM SUE: Yas, Brudder Moseby, Millie's bin carryin' on dem lies in huh lettahs fu' de las' six months; but today Ah jes sez to huh—Dis war done stopp't now, an' John he gwine to be comin' home soon, an' he ain't agwine to come hyeah an' fin' me wid no lie on mah soul! An' Ah med huh set down an' tell him de whole truf. She's gwine out to pos' dat lettah dis minute.

MOSEBY: (*still disapproving*) No good nebber come—

(*The door is pushed violently open, and* LONNIE, *a sturdy black boy of eighteen, rushes in breathlessly.*)

LONNIE: Mam Sue! Millie! Whut'da yuh think? John's come home!

MILLIE: (*speechless with astonishment*) John? Home? Where's he at?

MAM SUE: (*incredulously*) Whut yuh sayin'? John done come home? Bles de Lawd! Bles' de Lawd! Millie, didn' Ah tell yuh sumpin wuz gwine tuh happen?

LONNIE: (*excitedly*) I wuz sweepin' up de sto' jes befo' leavin' an' de phone rung—it wuz John—he wuz at Char'ston—jes landid! His comp'ny's waitin' to git de ten o'clock train fu' Camp Reed, whah dey's goin' to be mustered out.

MOSEBY: But how's he gwine to get erway?

LONNIE: Oh, good evenin', Brother Moseby, Ise jes so 'cited I didn' see yuh— Why his Cap'n done give him leave to run over heah 'tell de train's ready. He ought tuh be heah now 'cause it's mos' two hours sence he wuz talkin'—

MAM SUE: Whuffo yuh so long comin' home an' tellin' us?

LONNIE: (*hesitatingly*) I did start right out but when I git to Sherley's corner I seen a whole lot of them w'ite hoodlums hangin' 'round de feed sto'—I jes felt like dey wuz jes waitin' dah to start sumpin, so I dodged 'em by tekin' de long way home.

MILLIE: Po' Lonnie! He's allus dodgin' po' w'ite trash!

LONNIE: (*sullenly*) Well, yuh see whut dad got by not dodgin' 'em.

MOSEBY: (*rising to go*) Ah mus' be steppin' long now. Ah got to stop in to see ole man Hawkins; he's mighty sick. Ah'll drap in on mah way back fu' a word o' prayer wid John.

MAM SUE: Lonnie, yu'd bettah run erlon' as Brudder Moseby go an' tote dat wash tuh Mis' Ha't. An' drap in Mis' Hawkins' sto' an' git some soap an' starch; an' Ah reckons yu'd bettah bring me a bottle o' linimint—dis ole pain done come back in mah knee. (*to Moseby*) Good eben, Brudder Moseby.

MOSEBY: Good eben, Mam Sue; Good eben, Millie, an' Gawd bles' yuh.

LONNIE: (*as he is leaving*) Tell John I'll git back fo' he leaves.

(*Lonnie and Moseby leave. Millie closes the door behind them and then goes to the window and looks out anxiously.*)

MILLIE: (*musingly*) Po' John! Po' John! (*turning to Mam Sue*) Mam Sue?

MAM SUE: Yas, Millie.

MILLIE: (*hesitatingly*) Who's goin' to tell John 'bout dad?

MAM SUE: (*realizing for the first time that the task must fall to someone*) Dunno. Ah reckons yu'd bettah.

MILLIE: (*going to Mam Sue and kneeling softly at her side*) Mam Sue, don' let's tell him now! He's got only a li'l hour to spen' with us—an' it's the firs' time fu' so long! John loved daddy so! Let 'im be happy jes a li'l longer—we kin tell 'im the truth when he comes back fu' good. Please, Mam Sue!

MAM SUE: (*softened by Millie's pleading*) Honey chile, John gwine to be askin' for his daddy fust thing—dey ain't no way—

MILLIE: (*gaining courage*) Oh, yes, 'tis! We kin tell 'im dad's gone to town—anything, jes so's he kin spen' these few li'l minutes in peace! I'll fix the Bible jes like dad's been in an' been a-readin' in it! He won't know no bettah!

(*Millie takes the Bible from the mantel and opening it at random lays it on the table; she draws the old armchair close to the table as her father had been wont to do every evening when he read his Bible.*)

MAM SUE: (*shaking her head doubtfully*) Ah ain't much on actin' dis lie, Millie.

(*The soft afterglow fades and the little cabin is filled with shadows. Millie goes again to the window and peers out. Mam Sue falls again to her crooning.*)

MAM SUE: (*crooning*):

> O, yes, yonder comes mah Lawd,
> He's comin' dis way
> Wid his sword in his han'—

(*to Millie*) Millie, bettah light de lamp, it's gittin' dark.

> He's gwine ter hew dem sinners down
> Right lebbal to de groun'
> O, yes, yonder comes mah Lawd—

(*As Millie is lighting the lamp, whistling is heard in the distance. Millie listens intently, then rushes to the window. The whistling comes nearer; it rings out clear and familiar—"Though the boys are far away, they dream of home."*)

MILLIE: (*excitedly*) That's him! That's John, Mam Sue!

(*Millie rushes out of doors. The voices of* JOHN *and Millie are heard from without in greetings. Presently, John and Millie enter the cabin. John is tall and straight—a good soldier and a strong man. He wears the uniform of a private in the American Army. One hand is clasped in both of Millie's. In the other, he carries an old-fashioned valise. The War Cross is pinned on his breast. On his sleeve three chevrons tell mutely of wounds suffered in the cause of freedom. His brown face is aglow with life and the joy of homecoming.*)

JOHN: (*eagerly*) Where's Dad? Where's Mam Sue?

MAM SUE: (*hobbling painfully to meet him*) Heah's ole Mam Sue! (*John takes her tenderly in his arms*) Bles' yo' heart, chile, bles' yo' heart! Tuh think dat de good Lawd's done lemme live to see dis day!

JOHN: Dear old Mam Sue! Gee, but I'm glad to see you an' Millie again!

MAM SUE: Didn' Ah say dat yuh wuz comin' back hyeah?

JOHN: (*smiling*) Same old Mam Sue with huh faith an' huh prayers! But where's dad? (*he glances toward the open Bible*) He's been in from de field, ain't he?

MILLIE: (*without lifting her eyes*) Yes, he's come in but he had to go out ag'in— to Sherley's feed sto'.

JOHN: (*reaching for his cap that he has tossed upon the table*) That ain't far. I've jes a few minutes so I'd bettah run down there an' hunt him up. Won't he be surprised!

MILLIE: (*confused*) No—no, John—I fu'got; he ain't gone to Sherley's, he's gone to town.

JOHN:(*disappointed*) To town? I hope he'll git in befo I'm leavin'. There's no tellin' how long they'll keep me at Camp Reed. Where's Lonnie?

MAM SUE: Lonnie's done gone to Mis' Ha't's wid de wash. He'll be back to-reckly.

MILLIE: (*admiring the medal on his breast*) An' this is the medal? Tell us all erbout it, John.

JOHN: Oh, Sis, it's an awful story—wait 'til I git back fu' good. Let's see whut I've got in dis bag fu' you. (*he places the worn valise on the table and opens it. He takes out a bright-colored dress pattern*) That's fu' you, Millie, and quit wearin' them black clothes.

(*Millie takes the silk and hugs it eagerly to her breast; suddenly there sweeps into her mind the realization that she cannot wear it, and the silk falls to the floor.*)

MILLIE: (*trying to be brave*) Oh, John, it's jes lovely! (*as she shows it to Mam Sue*) Look, Mam Sue!

JOHN: (*flourishing a bright shawl*) An' this is fu' Mam Sue. Mam Sue'll be so gay!

MAM SUE: (*admiring the gift*) Who'd evah b'lieved dat yo' ole Mam Sue would live to be wearin' clo'es whut huh gran'chile done brung huh f'om Eu'ope!

JOHN: Never you mind, Mam Sue, one of these days I'm goin' to tek you an' Millie over there, so's you kin breathe free jes once befo' yuh die.

MAM SUE: It's got tuh be soon, 'cause dis ole body's mos' wo'e out; an' de good Lawd's gwine to be callin' me to pay mah debt 'fo' long.

JOHN: (*showing some handkerchiefs, with gay borders*) These are fu' Lonnie. (*He next takes out a tiny box that might contain a bit of jewelry*) An' this is fu' dad. Sum'pin he's been wantin' fu' years. I ain't goin' to open it 'till he comes.

(*Millie walks into the shadows and furtively wipes a tear from her eyes.*)

JOHN: (*taking two army pistols from his bag and placing them on the table*) An' these las' are fu' youahs truly.

MILLIE: (*looking at them, fearfully*) Oh, John, are them youahs?

JOHN: One of 'em's mine; the other's my Lieutenant's. I've been cleanin' it fu' him. Don' tech 'em—'cause mine's loaded.

MILLIE: (*still looking at them in fearful wonder*) Did they learn yuh how to shoot 'em?

JOHN: Yep, an' I kin evah mo' pick 'em off!

MILLIE: (*reproachfully*) Oh, John!

JOHN: Nevah you worry, li'l Sis, John's nevah goin' to use 'em less it's right fu' him to. (*He places the pistols on the mantel—on the very spot where the Bible has lain.*) My! but it's good to be home! I've been erway only two years but it seems like two cent'ries. All that life ovah there seems like some awful dream!

MAM SUE: (*fervently*) Ah know it do! Many's de day yo'ole Mam Sue set in dis cheer an' prayed fu' yuh.

JOHN: Lots of times, too, in the trenches when I wuz dog-tired, an' sick, an' achin' wid the cold I uster say: well, if we're sufferin' all this for the oppressed, like they tell us, then Mam Sue, an' Dad, an Millie come in on that—they'll git some good ou'n it if I don't! An' I'd shet my eyes an' fu'git the cold, an' the pain, an' them old guns spittin' death all 'round us; an' see you folks settin' here by this fire—Mam Sue, noddin', an' singin'; dad a spellin' out his Bible—(*He glances toward the open book.*) Let's see whut he's been readin'—(*John takes up the Bible and reads the first passage upon which his eye falls.*) "But I say unto you, love your enemies, bless them that curse you, an' do good to them that hate you"—(*He lets the Bible fall to the table.*) That ain't the dope they been feedin' us soljers on! "Love your enemies?" It's been—git a good aim at 'em, an' let huh go!

MAM SUE: (*surprised*) Honey, Ah hates to hyeah yuh talkin' lak dat! It sound lak yuh done fu'git yuh Gawd!

JOHN: No, Mam Sue, I ain't fu'got God, but I've quit thinkin' that prayers kin do ever'thing. I've seen a whole lot sence I've been erway from here. I've seen some men go into battle with a curse on their lips, and I've seen them same men come back with never a scratch; an' I've seen men whut read their Bibles befo' battle, an' prayed to live, left dead on the field. Yes, Mam Sue, I've seen a heap an' I've done a tall lot o' thinkin' sence I've been erway from here. An' I b'lieve it's jes like this—beyon' a certain point prayers ain't no good! The Lawd does jes so much for you, then it's up to you to do the res' fu' yourse'f. The Lawd's done His part when He's done give me strength an' courage; I got tuh do the res' fu' myse'f!

MAM SUE: (*shaking her head*) Ah don' lak dat kin' o' talk—it don' bode no good!

(*The door opens and Lonnie enters with packages. He slips the bolt across the door.*)

JOHN:(*rushing to Lonnie and seizing his hand*) Hello, Lonnie, ole man!

LONNIE: Hello, John, Gee, but Ah'm glad tuh see yuh!

JOHN: Boy, you should 'ave been with me! It would 'ave taken some of the skeeriness out o' yuh, an' done yuh a worl' o' good.

LONNIE: (*ignoring John's remark*) Here's the soap an' starch, Millie.

MAM SUE: Has yuh brung mah linimint?

LONNIE: Yassum, it's in de packige.

MILLIE: (*unwrapping the package*) No, it ain't, Lonnie.

LONNIE: Mis' Hawkins give it tuh me. Ah mus' a lef'it on de counter. Ah'll git it w'en Ah goes to de train wid John.

MILLIE: (*showing him the handkerchief*) See whut John done brought you! An' look on de mantel! (*pointing to the pistols*)

LONNIE: (*drawing back in fear as he glances at the pistols*) You'd bettah hide them things! No cullud man bettah be seen wid dem things down heah!

JOHN: That's all right, Lonnie, nevah you fear. I'm goin' to keep 'em an' I ain't a-goin' to hide 'em either. See them. (*pointing to the wound chevrons on his arm*) Well, when I got them wounds, I let out all the rabbit-blood 'at wuz in me! (*defiantly*) Ef I kin be trusted with a gun in France, I kin be trusted with one in South Car'lina.

MAM SUE: (*sensing trouble*) Millie, yu'd bettah fix some suppah fu' John.

JOHN: (*looking at his watch*) I don' want a thing. I've got to be leavin' in a little while. I'm 'fraid I'm goin' to miss dad after all.

(*The knob of the door is turned as though someone is trying to enter. Then there is a loud knock on the door.*)

JOHN: (*excitedly*) That's dad! Don't tell him I'm here!

(*John tips hurriedly into the adjoining room. Lonnie unbolts the door and* MRS. SELENA HAWKINS *enters.*)

MRS. HAWKINS: Lonnie fu'got de liniment so I thought I' bettah run ovah wid hit, 'cause when Mam Sue sen' fu' dis stuff she sho'needs hit. Brudder Moseby's been tellin' me dat John's done come home.

JOHN: (*coming from his hiding place and trying to conceal his disappointment*) Yes, I'm here. Good eve-nin', Mis' Hawkins. Glad to see you.

MRS. HAWKINS:(*shaking hands with John*) Well, lan' sakes alive! Ef it ain't John sho'nuf! An' ain't he lookin' gran'! Jes look at dat medal a-shining' on his coat! Put on yuh cap, boy, an' lemme see how yuh look!

JOHN: Sure! (*John puts on his overseas cap and, smiling, stands at attention a few paces off, while Mam Sue, Lonnie, and Millie form an admiring circle around him.*)

MRS. HAWKINS: Now don' he sholy look gran'! I knows yo' sistah an' gran' mammy's proud o' yuh! (*A note of sadness creeps into her voice.*) Ef only yuh po' daddy had a-lived to see dis day!

(*John looks at her in amazement. Millie and Mam Sue stand transfixed with terror over the sudden betrayal.*)

JOHN: (*looking from one to the other and repeating her words as though he can scarcely realize their meaning*) "Ef your po' daddy had lived—" (*to Millie*) Whut does this mean?

(*Millie sinks sobbing into the chair at the table and buries her face in her hands.*)

MRS. HAWKINS: Lor', Millie, I thought you'd tole him!

(*Bewildered by the catastrophe that she has precipitated, Mrs. Hawkins slips out of the cabin.*)

JOHN: (*shaking Millie almost roughly*) Come, Millie, have you been lyin' to me? Is dad gone?

MILLIE: (*through her sobs*) I jes hated to tell you—you wuz so far erway—

JOHN: (*nervously*) Come, Millie, for God's sake don' keep me in this su'pense! I'm a brave soldier—I kin stan' it—did he suffer much? Wuz he sick long?

MILLIE: He wuzn't sick no time—them w'ite devuls come in heah an' dragged him—

JOHN: (*desperately*) My God! You mean they lynched dad?

MILLIE: (*sobbing piteously*) They burnt him down by the big gum tree!

JOHN: (*desperately*) Whut fu', Millie? What fu'?

MILLIE: He got in a row wid ole Mister Withrow 'bout the price of cotton—an' he called dad a liar an' struck him—an' dad he up an' struck him back—

JOHN: (*brokenly*) Didn' they try him? Didn' they give him a chance? Whut'd the Sheriff do? An' the Gov-nur?

MILLIE: (*through her sobs*) They didn't do nothin'.

JOHN: Oh, God! Oh, God! (*then recovering first bitter anguish and speaking*) So they've come into ouah home, have they! (*He strides over to Lonnie and seizes him by the collar.*) An' whut wuz you doin' when them hounds come in here after dad?

LONNIE: (*hopelessly*) They wuz so many of 'em come an' git 'im—whut could Ah do?

JOHN: Do? You could 'ave fought 'em like a man!

MAM SUE: (*pleadingly*) Don't be too hard on 'im, John, we'se ain't got no gun 'round heah!

JOHN: Then he should 'ave burnt their damn kennels ovah their heads! Who was it leadin' em?

MILLIE: Old man Withrow and the Sherley boys, they started it all.

(*Gradually assuming the look of a man who has determined to do some terrible work that must be done, John walks deliberately toward the mantel where the revolvers are lying.*)

JOHN: (*bitterly*) I've been helpin' the w'ite man git his freedom, I reckon I'd bettah try now to get my own!

MAM SUE: (*terrified*) Whut yuh gwine ter do?

JOHN: (*with bitterness growing in his voice*) I'm sick o' these w'ite folks doin's—we're "fine, trus'worthy feller citizuns" when they're handin' us out guns, an' Liberty Bonds, an' chuckin' us off to die; but we ain't a damn thing when it comes to handin' us the rights we done fought an' bled fu'! I'm sick o' this sort o' life—an' I'm goin' to put an end to it!

MILLIE: (*rushing to the mantel, and covering the revolvers with her hands*) Oh, no, no, John! Mam Sue, John's gwine to kill hisse'f!

MAM SUE: (*piteously*) Oh, mah honey, don' yuh go do nothin' to bring sin on yo' soul! Pray to de good Lawd to tek all dis fiery feelin' out'n yo' heart! Wait 'tel Brudder Moseby come back—he's gwine to pray—

JOHN: (*his speech growing more impassioned and bitter*) This ain't no time fu' preachers or prayers! You mean to tell me I mus' let them w'ite devuls send me miles erway to suffer an' be shot up fu' the freedom of people I ain't nevah seen, while they're burnin' an' killin' my folks here at home! To Hell with 'em!

(*He pushes Millie aside, and, seizing the revolvers, thrusts the loaded one into his pocket and begins deliberately to load the other.*)

MILLIE: (*throwing her arms about his neck*) Oh, John, they'll kill yuh!

JOHN: (*defiantly*) Whut ef they do! I ain't skeered o' none of 'em! I've faced worse guns than any sneakin' hounds kin show me! To Hell with 'em! (*He thrusts the revolver that he has just loaded into Lonnie's hands.*) Take this, an' come on here, boy, an' we'll see what Withrow an' his gang have got to say!

(*Followed by Lonnie, who is bewildered and speechless, John rushes out of the cabin and disappears in the gathering darkness.*)

CURTAIN

Corrie Crandall Howell
(dates unknown)

The *Forfeit* is a prime example of a one-act lynching drama written in the anti-lynching tradition. It is unique among lynching dramas by women because it shows a white woman's active participation in lynching. The play registers a strong protest against the injustice of lynching by portraying a white woman, Fanny Clark, who actively supports the lynching of an innocent black man for a crime her own son has committed. Fanny delivers the innocent black victim, Jeff Sparks, into the hands of a lynch mob in order to shield her own son, who is guilty of raping and beating the local school teacher in a small rural southern community. *The Forfeit* reveals the depth and viciousness of racism by portraying how the bigotry of a white mother makes her an accomplice to the brutal murder of an innocent man.

The Forfeit is in some ways a common play for the early twentieth century American stage. It reflects the combined influence of the developing stage realism and folk drama tradition. But the approach to the lynching incident makes the writing and publishing of this play in 1925 a courageous act. It presents an uncommon dramatic portrayal of white motherhood that unmasks the racist and gendered assumptions of white male dominance and lynch mob mentality. Perhaps this uncommon and undoubtedly unpopular perspective helps to account for the obscurity of the play and playwright.

The Forfeit was published in the literary journal *Poet Lore* in 1925. The play is cited in Ina Ten Eyck Firkins's *Index to Plays, 1800 to 1926* (1927), Hannah Logassa's *Index to One-Act Plays, 1924–31* (1932), and Frances Diodato Bzowski's *American Women Playwrights, 1900–1930* (1992). The editors have been unable to locate any other reference to Howell or her play. Some of the sources consulted in an extensive research effort were: The New York Public Library at Lincoln Center, The Federal Theatre Project, The Frederick Koch Papers and Records of the Department of Dramatic Arts (*Carolina Playmakers*), University of North Carolina at Chapel Hill, Hatch-Billops Collection, Library of Congress, Moorland-Springarn Research Center at Howard University, Association of Southern Women for the Prevention of Lynching Papers, the current editors of *Poet Lore,* Boston Public Library, Schomburg Center for Research in Black Culture, Penn State University Libraries, and Harvard Theatre Collection. A notice asking librarians throughout the country for any information on Howell or her play was placed in *Reference Quarterly.*

The obscurity of the play and of Corrie Crandall Howell—a name that could be a pseudonym—point to the neglect of the genre and the need for further research. The editors are hopeful that the publication of this anthology will help us locate information concerning the play and its playwright.

The Forfeit
1925

❦

Corrie Crandall Howell

CHARACTERS

Tom Clark, *a farmer*
Fanny, *Tom's wife*
Woodrow Jenkins, *a neighbor's son*
Bud Clark, *Tom's son*
Jeff Sparks, *a Negro farm hand*
Two Neighbors

Time: *an early evening in winter.*
Place: *a Southern rural community.*

The scene is the bedroom in Tom's house. At center back is a door leading into front yard. On either side of door is a window with torn shades pulled down to within an inch or so of window ledge. On right center a recessed door leads into the kitchen; when this door is open a hiding place is formed. At right front a fireplace; on mantel are a clock, medicine bottles, and small lamp. Over the mantel Tom's gun is hung. Across corner, left back, a cottage organ, forming another hiding place. In center front a table with large lamp and Fanny's sewing on it. A bed and a dresser and chairs are the other furniture in set, lithographs of a religious nature are hung on the walls. As curtain rises, Tom and Fanny are found seated on either side of table, center front. Tom, a middle-aged man with a querulous expression, is whittling an ax handle and whistling softly to himself. Fanny is piecing a quilt. She is rather pretty, of a gentle nervous type, but with a hint of hidden depths of force.

Tom: (*spitting into fire*) Whar yer reckon Bud is all this yere time?

Fanny: (*slowly*) I reckon he went (*pausing to match quilt pieces*) over to Dobbses Mill, he likes ter hear ole man Dobbs talk.

Tom: Huh, I reckon hit aint ole man Dobbs he goes ter see. He goes ter play craps up in ther loft. (*rising*) And he gwine ter quit hit or us'll hev trouble. (*angrily*) Hows I gwine ter make er crop with him er layin off all ther time. (*shaking his fist at Fanny*) Hit aint right. And hits all yer fault. Er petting him, and er makin over him all ther time. Whuts yer got ter show fer hit? (*Fanny tries to interrupt*) Yer listen ter me. A lazy, good fer nuthin lout! He gwine ter change his ways or us'll—

(*A loud knock is heard at center back. Tom and Fanny are still for a moment, then as knock is repeated, Tom goes to door and exits. A subdued murmur of voices is heard and the glow of lighted torches shines through the torn window shades. Fanny stands listening, her hands at her throat and a look of apprehension on her face. Tom enters. Throws ax handle in corner. Goes to mantel, takes down gun, examines it and starts toward door center back.*)

FANNY: (*intercepting him*) Whuts ther matter, Tom? Whar yer gwine?

TOM: (*pushing her aside*) Thars gwine ter be a hangin in Hell, ternight. (*exits*)

FANNY: (*goes slowly toward her chair*) I wish Bud—

(*The door at center is pushed violently open and* WOODROW *enters, a freckle-faced wide-mouthed boy of about thirteen, barefoot, in overalls and farm hat, an unlighted torch in his hands.*)

FANNY: (*startled*) Woodrow!

WOODROW: Yas'm Mis Fanny. Kin I light this yer torch, hit jes wont stay lit. (*He lights torch at fire and starts toward door.*)

FANNY: (*catching him by his arm*) Jes hold yer hosses a minit. Whuts all this yer gwines on about?

WOODROW: (*excitedly*) Thars gwine ter be a hangin! (*pausing in wonderment*) Haint yer heared about hit?

FANNY: (*shaking her head*) I haint heared nuthin. Tell me, Woodrow.

WOODROW: (*remembering*) I haint got time. I gotter go. Lemme go I tel yer!

FANNY: (*holding him tighter*) Yer got plenty time. Tell me. Wuz hit a killin?

WOODROW: (*looking longingly toward door*) Naw, hit warnt no killin, hit was— (*lowering his voice*) 'Twas teacher.

FANNY: Teacher? (*understanding*) Oh, my God! Yer mean she was— was—?

WOODROW: (*nodding his head*) Yep. Ole man Berry found her jest before dark, as he wuz comin home from Dobbeses Mill. He brung her ter ther Doctor's and then he cum over ter ther store ter tell Paw and ther rest.

FANNY: (*wonderingly*) Who done hit?

WOODROW: Dunno. They done been huntin sence, but they caint ketch no buddy tel they gits aholt of Jason's bloodhounds. He haint got home yit.

FANNY: Wuz she ded?

WOODROW: Naw. But she caint talk none. Her throat's all swelled up (*he drops torch and circles his throat with his hands*) and her close is all tore offen her. I reckon he drug her round considerable. (*suddenly remembering what her death will mean to him*) Hot dog! If she dies, thar wont be no school this yere again. (*begins scuffling, his feet for pure joyousness*)

FANNY: (*paying no attention to him*) Whar did yer say he found her?

WOODROW: Jest this side of the Mill. Down in ther bottom by ther little branch.

FANNY: Whut wuz she adoin down thar alone?

WOODROW: Maw sez she tole her this mornin thet she wuz agoin ter git sum ferns fer ther school yard this afternoon. I reckon thet wuz whut she wuz adoin. (*pausing and looking intently at Fanny*) Why, yer orto ter go ter ther Doctor's house and see her, she shore looks turrible.

FANNY: (*shuddering*) I dont want ter.

WOODROW: (*pulling away from Fanny, gently*) Maw and all ther wimen er thar, agoin on like forty. Yer orto go.

A VOICE: (*at center back*) Woodrow— Yer paw sez ef yer cumin with us, yer better come on.

WOODROW: I'm comin. (*picks up torch, goes to fire, lights it*) Did yer'll git ther hounds?

VOICE: Yep. Cum on, ef yer cumin.

FANNY: (*quickly*) Wait er minit, Woodrow. I got sumthin fer yer. (*goes to mantel and from behind clock takes down an old snuff box from which she gets a half dollar, goes to Woodrow*) Here, take this and tell me jest as soon as she dies ef she sed ennythin and dont let on I give hit ter yer or Tom'll git us both.

WOODROW: (*taking money*) Wellum. But I'se gwine to help ketch him fust. (*goes out center back*)

FANNY: (*sits and tries to sew, but her hands tremble so, she is obliged to stop. Softly*) She wuz a pretty gal, fer a city gal. (*listens for a moment as if she hears a noise*) I wish Bud wud cum (*listens again with her hand at her throat as door center back is pushed softly open and* BUD *comes quietly into room. He is a heavy-set, sullen-looking youth in the early twenties, with the appearance of having just emerged from a catastrophic state*)

FANNY: (*eagerly*) Buddy! Honey, whar hev her been so long? (*then noticing his disheveled appearance*) Whut hev yer been adoin?

BUD: (*sullenly*) Jest wrasslin with ther fellers. Got ennythin ter eat?

FANNY: I kept yer supper fer yer. Hits warmin on ther stove. (*takes lamp from mantel and goes out right*)

(*Bud sits in Fanny's chair by table. Fanny enters right with supper. Arranges supper on table in front of Bud. Exits right. Re-enters with lamp.*)

FANNY: Wud yer ruther hev sum coffee, Bud?

BUD: Naw, I kin make out with milk. (*eats supper slowly, while Fanny watches him anxiously*) Whars Paw?

FANNY: He's— (*a sound of hounds baying is faintly heard*)

BUD: (*starting to his feet*) Whuts that? Sounds like Jason's hounds.

FANNY: Hits— Hits them.

BUD: (*hoarsely*) Whut fer?

FANNY: They found teacher. (*an exclamation from Bud makes her look at him with alarm*) Bud, Buddy! Whuts ther matter? Is yer sick? (*goes to him and for a moment stands staring at him, then gaspingly*) Bud! Buddy?! Yer didn't! Tell yer Maw yer didn't do hit! (*then as she reads the truth in his face she stands stricken, horror of things unimaginable in her face, her hands at her throat as if choking*)

(*Bud gropes as if blinded for his chair. The baying of the hounds is clearer now and the shouts of the men are heard.*)

FANNY: (*arousing herself with difficulty*) Bud! We gotter do sumthin, quick. Them hounds will track yer right ter ther door.

(*Bud tries to speak. Gives up the attempt. Drops his head into his hand and mutters to himself.*)

FANNY: (*beating her hands softly together*) We gotter do sumthin, we gotter do sumthin, quick. (*goes to window center back, looks out. Comes back to Bud and leaning over him touches his hair softly, then as he jerks away from her, she walks around the room, aimlessly, touching the furniture as she passes. A knock is heard at center back.*)

FANNY: (*tremulously*) Who's thar?

VOICE: Hits me, Mis Fanny. Hits Jeff.

FANNY: Whut yer want?

VOICE: I done brung yer them taters yer wanted.

FANNY: (*a look of understanding on her face*) Jest wait er minit. (*goes to Bud and shaking him points to door, right, whispers*) Git behind thar so's he caint see yer.

BUD: (*half rising then dropping back into chair mutters something she cannot hear*) Let me erlone caint yer?

FANNY: (*grasps Bud by the arm and drags him to door right, pushes him behind it, props a chair in front and calls out*) Cum in Jeff.

(*Enter* JEFF, *a slight negro with a stupid, good-natured face. He is dragging a heavy sack and grumbling as he walks.*)

JEFF: These yere taters sure is heavy. (*drops sack in front of fireplace*)

FANNY: I warnt in no hurry fer them. Yer needn't hev cum so soon. (*The hounds are heard clearly now. They both listen.*)

JEFF: How cum ther hounds is out ternight?

FANNY: (*hesitating*) Rabbit huntin, I reckon.

JEFF: (*laughing*) Why, Mis Fanny, yer knows they haint no rabbits out ternight. Nohow, Jason dont never let ther hounds out fer jest rabbits.

FANNY: (*staring at Jeff as if he were an apparition*) I reckon not.

JEFF: (*noticing Fanny's expression*) Whuts ter matter, Mis Fanny? Yer shore looks powerful funny. (*then seeing the remains of supper on the table*) Is yer got enny cold bread I cud hev, I'se mighty hongry.

FANNY: (*eagerly*) Thars a heap of cold vit'els in the kitchen on ther stove. Jest take ther lamp in thar and hep yerself.

JEFF: (*taking lamp and sack goes toward door right*) Whar'll I put ther taters?

FANNY: Put 'im in ther corner by ther safe. (*Jeff exits right.*)

(*Fanny softly closes door after Jeff and bolts it. Grasps Bud firmly by arm and pushes him across room to organ and motions him to hide behind it.*)

BUD: (*thickly*) Whut yer agoin ter do Maw?

FANNY: (*pushes him behind organ, shoves it in place again*) Stay thar til I tell yer ter move. (*Takes dinner bell from organ and exits center back. She is heard ringing bell. Fanny enters center back. Goes to mantel and leans against it as the baying of the hounds and the shouts of the men are heard near at hand through the open door.*)

JEFF: (*Knocking on door right*) Mis Fanny! this yere door is stuck, hit wont open. Cum let me out. Mis Fanny!

FANNY: Jest a minit. I'm cumin.

(*Tom enters from door center back, followed by two neighbors.*)

TOM: (*excitedly*) Whar is he? Who is hit?

FANNY: (*pointing to door right*) He's in thar. Hits nigger Jeff. (*goes to organ as men rush out door right*)

(*Loud wails from Jeff and sounds of scuffing and blows are heard. Fanny leans against organ twisting her hands together, a look of agony on her face. Tom enters from right with lamp, followed by the two neighbors, holding Jeff between them.*)

JEFF: (*frantic with fear*) I haint done nuthin! I haint done nuthin at all. Miss Fanny done tole me I cud hev sum supper. Oh, Lordy! White folks lemme go!

TOM: (*striking Jeff from rear*) Shet up, yer black devil, yer is gwine ter find out whut yer's done fore long. Yer'll wish yer never been born fore ther night's over. (*to the men*) Whut yer waitin on. Take him out of yere I tel yer. (*kicking Jeff as men drag him toward door center back*) We's gwine ter teach allyer black niggers to leave white wimen alone, ef us have to burn every every black ape one of yer ter do it.

JEFF: (*his body limp between the two men, continues to shriek*) White folks, I haint done nuthin. I'se a pore ole nigger living in ther fear of ther Lord. Please, white folks lemme go. Lemme, Lemme go! Before ther Lord I haint done nuthin. Lordy! Lordy! Hep me ter git out of this yere. (*collapses*)

TOM: (*angrily*) Git him out of yere. Whut yer hangin back fer?

(*Woodrow enters from center back.*)

WOODROW: (*in high excitement*) She's ded, Mis Fanny! Maw sez she never sed nuthin at all.

(*Fanny sways, catches hold of organ, as* CURTAIN *falls.*)

Georgia Douglas Johnson
(1877?-1966)

Georgia Douglas Johnson was the most prolific of all playwrights who wrote dramas on lynching. Her six known lynching plays are *Safe, Blue-Eyed Black Boy*, two versions of *A Sunday Morning in the South*, and two lost plays—*And Still They Paused*, and *A Bill to Be Passed*. Unlike her plays on non-lynching themes, none of her lynching dramas was published or produced in her lifetime. This irony speaks loudly to the genre and its critical reception.[1]

When the American theatre is studied from the perspective of the anti-lynching tradition, Johnson clearly emerges as a central figure. With *A Sunday Morning in the South* (1925), she became the first playwright to deal truthfully with the issue of alleged interracial rape of white women and to dramatize white women's complicity in the lynching ritual. She was also a pioneer in writing plays in the anti-lynching tradition in which a lynching incident occurs during the dramatic action. Understanding the nature of theatre and its power to make offstage events as powerful as those occurring on stage, she paved the way (with *Blue-Eyed Black Boy* and *Safe*) for the use of sound and lighting effects, vivid oral description, and audience imagination to convey the horrors of lynching and its impact on families.

Winona Fletcher notes the economy of Johnson's artistic technique in creating "tightly structured dramas," which Margaret Wilkerson describes as "taut and spare in dialogue and action based on the very real drama of terrorist acts directed at the Southern black community."[2] Judith Barlow cites Johnson's "believable characters that sharply differed from the comic, bumbling, black figures so often created by white dramatists" and, Joycelyn Donlon notes, Johnson's dialogue represented "authentic folk speech rather than the stereotypical mutilated English."[3] Drawing on the historical tradition of social protest drama and the contemporary developments of "stage realism" and "folk drama," Johnson's plays reflect the universal human struggle for survival within the specific context of black southern families resisting the brutality and injustice of lynching.

According to Winona Fletcher and Kathy Perkins, Johnson had already won recognition as a poet when she was encouraged by friends to try her talents as a dramatist in the early 1920s. Fletcher and Perkins establish important connections between Johnson's contributions to the anti-lynching campaign of the period, her growing awareness of the impact drama could have on effecting social change, and her submission of four "plays on lynching" to the Federal Theatre Project (FTP), 1935–1939.[4] Fletcher notes that none of Johnson's plays was produced by FTP and reveals the barriers faced by playwrights who write social protest drama from a black perspective. In examining the comments of FTP readers on Johnson's plays, Fletcher reports that one reader noted, "It would appeal to many audiences composed of men and women who have feverish ideas about the lynching 'Down South.' Its rather unhealthful matter would interest and delight many loose thinking, race baiting persons both black and white."[5]

Safe received more favorable comments, but FTP readers were "aghast at the notion that a lynching could take place for no obvious 'good reason'" and criticized Johnson for suggesting so in the play.[6] The response of one FTP reader was that "*In fact* the crime that produces lynching is vastly fouler," prompting Fletcher to observe, "Clearly, this reader has fallen victim to the myth that 'only rape produced lynching down South' and expects the playwright to protect this myth by ignoring the truth."[7] Fletcher's valuable study provides insight into how racial attitudes and myths surrounding the atrocity of lynching became barriers to the production of lynching dramas. *A Sunday Morning in the South* was judged as "not offensive" to either blacks or whites and accepted by FTP readers but, as mentioned earlier, there is no record of either its publication or production in Johnson's lifetime.

Gloria T. Hull notes that most of Johnson's plays focus on female characters, a trait seen in her lynching dramas, which serve as an expression of the "unique horror" black women felt about lynching.[8] Elizabeth Brown-Guillory sees the stand against lynching expressed in *A Sunday Morning in the South, Blue-Eyed Black Boy,* and *Safe* as an indication that Johnson was "preoccupied with pointing to the atrocities faced by many blacks at the hands of the lynch mob."[9] The two lost plays, *A Bill to Be Passed* and *And Still They Paused,* apparently expressed support for the passage of the Dyer anti-lynching bill in the 1920s.

Plays by Johnson that did not deal with lynching were more likely to win recognition through production or publication. *Blue Blood,* in which a young mulatto couple about to marry discover that they have the same white father, won honorable mention in the 1926 *Opportunity* play contest. The play was produced by the W. E. B. Du Bois Krigwa Players and published in Frank Shay's *Fifty More Contemporary One-Act Plays,* 1928. *Plumes,* which treats the struggle of a black mother to deal with poverty and her daughter's illness, was awarded *Opportunity*'s first place in 1927 and was produced the same year by the Harlem Experimental Theatre. Johnson's historical dramas, *Frederick Douglass* and *William and Ellen Craft,* were published and produced in her lifetime.[10]

Throughout her life Johnson worked as a file clerk, teacher, and librarian. After the death of her husband, Lincoln, in 1925, she worked for the Department of Labor as Commissioner of Conciliation. She saw that her two sons received quality educations while she continued to work and write.[11] Known as "an individual with a big heart," Johnson took in stray dogs and cats and ran a correspondence club "for lonely people all over the world."[12] Her home on S Street in Washington, D.C., became a regular meeting place for writers, artists, and public figures, as well as for former prison inmates with whom she had corresponded. Donlon writes:

> Johnson named her house "Half Way Home" in part because she saw herself as half way between everybody and everything and trying to bring them together, and also because she wanted to make her home a place where anyone who would fight half way to survive could do so.[13]

Although Brown-Guillory reports that many of Johnson's non-lynching plays were produced in church halls, lofts, and schools in the Washington, D.C., area, this multitalented artist ultimately found more success as a poet than a playwright. Johnson was awarded an honorary doctorate from Atlanta University in 1965 and continued to publish poetry until her death at the age of eighty. Documentation of barriers to the production of her plays on lynching, coupled with the fact that much of what she wrote is lost, serves to emphasize her position as a leading figure in a largely unrecognized and unexamined dramatic genre. Her position as the most prolific (but unproduced) playwright of lynching drama testifies to her vision of theatre as "art for life's sake" and her struggle to help bring such a theatre into being.

NOTES

1. Fannie E. Hicklen credits Johnson with ten lynching plays in her 1965 dissertation, "The American Negro Playwright, 1920–1964."

2. Winona Fletcher, "From Genteel Poet to Revolutionary Playwright: Georgia Douglas Johnson," *Theatre Annual*, 40 (1985), 41; Margaret B. Wilkerson, ed., *9 Plays by Black Women* (New York: Mentor Books, 1986), xviii.

3. Judith E. Barlow, ed., *Plays by American Women: 1900–1930* (New York: Applause Theatre Books, 1985), xxvi; and Jocelyn Hazelwood Donlon, "Georgia Douglas Johnson" in Darlene Clark Hine, ed., *Black Women in America: A Historical Encyclopedia* (Brooklyn: Carlson, 1993), 641.

4. Winona Fletcher, "Georgia Douglas Johnson," in Trudier Harris, ed., *Dictionary of Literary Biography (Vol. 51): Afro-American Writers from the Harlem Renaissance to 1940* (Detroit: Gale Research Company, 1987), 159; and Fletcher, "Georgia Douglas Johnson" in Alice Robinson, Vera Mowry Roberts, and Milly Barranger, eds. *Notable Women in the American Theatre: A Biographical Dictionary* (New York: Greenwood Press, 1989), 475; and Kathy A. Perkins ed., *Black Female*

Playwrights: An Anthology of Plays before 1950 (Bloomington: Indiana University Press), 22.

5. Fletcher, *Theatre Annual,* 53.

6. Fletcher, *Theatre Annual,* 54–55.

7. Fletcher, *Theatre Annual,* 55.

8. Gloria T. Hull, *Color, Sex, and Poetry: Three Women Writers of the Harlem Renaissance* (Bloomington: Indiana University Press, 1987), 229, n. 19.

9. Elizabeth Brown Guillory, ed., *Wines in the Wilderness: Plays by African American Women from the Harlem Renaissance to the Present* (New York: Praeger, 1990), 15, and *Their Place on the Stage: Black Women Playwrights in America* (New York: Praeger, 1990), 7.

10. Both are published in Willis Richardson and May Miller, eds., *Negro History in Thirteen Plays* (Washington, D.C.: Associated Publishers), 1935.

11. James V. Hatch and Ted Shine, "Georgia Douglas Johnson," *Black Theatre USA: The Early Period, 1847–1938* (New York: The Free Press, 1996), 640–642.

12. Perkins, 22.

13. Donlon, 13.

A Sunday Morning in the South
1925

Georgia Douglas Johnson

CHARACTERS

SUE JONES, *grandmother, aged seventy*
TOM GRIGGS, *her grandson, aged nineteen*
BOSSIE GRIGGS, *her grandson, aged seven*
LIZA TWIGGS, *a friend, aged sixty*
MATILDA BROWN, *a friend, aged fifty*
WHITE GIRL
FIRST OFFICER
SECOND OFFICER

Place: *A town in the South.*
Time: *1924.*
Scene: *Kitchen in* SUE JONES's *two-room house. A window on left, a door leading to back yard and another leading to front room. A stove against the back wall, a table near it, four chairs, an old-time pie safe with dishes and two bottles—one clear and one dark—a wooden water bucket with shiny brass bales, and a tin dipper hanging near it on a nail.*

As the curtain rises Sue Jones is seen putting the breakfast on the kitchen table. She wears a red bandanna handkerchief on her grey head, a big blue gingham apron tied around her waist, and big wide old lady comfort shoes. She uses a stick as she has a sore leg, and moves about with a stoop and a limp as she goes back and forth from the stove to the table.

SUE: (*calling*) Tom, Tom, you and Bossie better come on out here and git your breakfast before it gits cold; I got good hot rolls this mornin!
TOM: (*from next room*) All right grannie, we're coming.
SUE: You better ef you know whut's good for you. (*opens stove door, looks at rolls, then begins humming and singing*)

Eugh . . . eu . . . eugh . . .
Jes look at the morning star

Eugh . . . eu . . . eugh . . .
We'll all git home bye and bye . . .

(*As she finishes the song* Tom *and* Bossie *come hurrying into the kitchen, placing their chairs at the table; there is one already at the table for Sue. Sue takes rolls out of stove with her apron and brings them to the table.*) It's as hard to git yawll out of the bed on Sunday morning as it is to pull hen's teeth.

Tom: (*eating. The church bell next door is heard ringing*) Eugh—there's the church bell. I sho meant to git out to meeting this morning but my back still hurts me. Remember I told you last night how I sprained it lifting them heavy boxes for Mr. John?

Sue: (*giving Bossie a roll and a piece of sausage*) You hadn't oughter done it; you oughter ast him to let somebody hep you—you aint no hoss!

Tom: I reckin I oughter had but I didn't know how heavy they was till I started and then he was gone.

Sue: You oughter had some of my snake oil linament on it last night, that's whut!

Tom: I wish I hader but I was so dead tired I got outer my clothes and went straight to bed. I muster been sleep by nine er clock I reckin.

Sue: Nine er clock! You is crazy! Twant no moren eight when I called you to go to the store and git me a yeast cake fur my light rolls and you was sleeping like a log of wood; I had to send Bossie fur it.

Bossie: Yes, and you snored so loud I thought you would a choked. (*holding out his plate and licking his lips*) Grannie kin I have some more?

Sue: Whut? Where is all thot I jest give you?

Bossie: (*rubbing his stomach with his other hand and smiling broadly*) It's gone down the red lane struttin'.

Sue: Well this is all you gointer git this mornin. (*helping him to more rolls and sausage*) When you git big and work like Tom you kin stuff all you wants to.

Bossie: I aint never gointer break my back like Tom working hard— a gointer be a—a preacher that's whut and . . .

Sue: (*catching sight of someone passing the window as she approached the back door*) I bleve that's Liza Twiggs must be on her way to church and smelled these light rolls and coffee. (*a knock is heard at the back door*) Let her in, Bossie!

(*Bossie jumps up from the table, hurries to the door and opens it.*)

Liza: (*enters sniffing*) Mawning yawll.

Sue: Morning Liza—on your way to church?

Liza: Yes the first bell just rung and I thought I'd drop in a minute. (*whiffs again*) Coffee sho smells good!

Sue: Tastes better'n it smells—Pull up a cheer and swaller a cupful with one of these light rolls.

Liza: (*drawing up a chair*) Dont keer if I do. (*she is helped to coffee and rolls while Bossie looks at her disapprovingly. To Sue*) How is your leg gitting on?

Sue: Well as I kin expect. I won't never walk on it good no mo. It eats and eats.

Sho is lucky I'm right here next door to church. (*to Tom*) Open that winder, Tom, so I kin hear the singing. (*Tom opens window. To Liza*) Folks don't like to set next to me in church no mo. Tinks its ketching—a cancer or somethin'. (*then brightly*) Whut you know good?

(*From the church next door is heard the hymn, drifting through the window: "Amazing grace how sweet the sound / That saves a wretch like me . . ."*)

LIZA: (*listening*) They done started "Amazing grace." (*music continues as a background for their talk. Still eating*) That music she is sweet but I got to finish eatin first, then I'll go . . .

SUE: I ast you whut you know good.

LIZA: Well, I don't know nothin tall good, but I did hear as how the police is all over now trying to run down some po Nigger they say that's tacked a white woman last night right up here near the Pine Street market. They says as how the white folks is shonuff mad too, and if they ketch him they gointer make short work of him.

SUE: (*still drinking coffee*) Eugh, eugh, eugh, you don't say. I don't hold wid no rascality and I bleves in meting out punishment to the guilty but they fust ought to fine out who done it tho and then let the law hanel 'em. That's what I says.

LIZA: Me too, I thinks the law oughter hanel 'em too, but you know a sight of times they gits the wrong man and goes and strings him up and don't fin out who done it till it's too late!

SUE: That's so. And sometimes the white uns been knowed to blackin they faces and make you bleve some po Nigger done it.

TOM: They lynch you bout anything too, not jest women. They say Zeb Brooks was strung up because he and his boss had er argiment.

LIZA: Sho did. I says the law's the law and it ought er be er ark uv safty to pertect the weak and not some little old flimsy shack that a puff of wind can blow down.

TOM: I been thinking a whole lot about these things and I mean to go to night school and git a little book learning so as I can do something to help—help change the laws . . . make em strong . . . I sometimes get right upset and wonder whut would I do if they ever tried to put something on me . . .

LIZA: Pshaw . . . everybody knows you . . . nobody would bother you . . .

SUE: No sonnie, you won't never hafter worry bout sich like that but you kin hep to save them po devels that they do git after.

(*Singing comes from the church next door.*)

> Shine on me, shine on me.
> Let the light from the lighthouse shine on me,
> Shine on me, shine on me,
> Let the light from the lighthouse shine on me.

TOM: It takes a sight of learning to understand the law and I'm a gointer . . . (*a *quick rap is heard at the door and it is almost immediately pushed open and an* OFFICER *enters as the four at table look up at him in open-mouthed amazement)*

FIRST OFFICER: Tom Griggs live here?

SUE: (*starting up excitedly*) Yes sir. (*stammering*)

FIRST OFFICER: (*looking at Tom*) You Tom Griggs?

TOM: (*puzzled*) Yes sir.

FIRST OFFICER: (*roughly*) Where were you last night at ten o'clock?

SUE: (*answering quickly for Tom*) Right here sir, he was right here at home. Whut you want to know fer?

FIRST OFFICER: (*to Sue*) You keep quiet, old woman. (*to Tom*) Say, you answer up. Can't you talk? Where were you last night at ten o'clock.

TOM: (*uneasily*) Gramma told you. I was right here at home—in bed at eight o'clock.

FIRST OFFICER: That sounds fishy to me—in bed at eight o'clock! And who else knows you were here?

SUE: Say Mr. Officer, whut you tryin to do to my granson. Shore as God Amighty is up in them heabens he was right here in bed. I seed him and his little brother Bossie there saw him, didn't you Bossie?

BOSSIE: (*in a frightened whisper*) Yessum, I seed him and I heered him!

FIRST OFFICER: (*to Bossie*) Shut up. Your word's nothing. (*looking at Sue*) Nor yours either. Both of you'd lie for him. (*steps to back door and makes a sign to someone outside, then comes back into the room taking a piece of paper from his vest pocket and reads slowly, looking at Tom critically as he checks each item*) Age around twenty, five feet five or six, brown skin . . . (*he folds up the paper and puts it back into his vest*) Yep! fits like a glove. (*Sue, Liza, and Tom look from one to the other with growing amazement and terror as* SECOND OFFICER *pushes open the door and stands there supporting a young* WHITE GIRL *on his arm.*)

SECOND OFFICER: (*to girl*) Is this the man?

WHITE GIRL: (*hesitatingly*) I—I'm not sure . . . but . . . but he looks something like him . . . (*holding back*)

FIRST OFFICER: (*encouragingly*) Take a good look, Miss. He fits our description perfect. Color, size, age, everything. Pine Street Market ain't no where from here, and he surely did pass that way last night. He was there all right, all right! We got it figgered all out. (*to Girl, who looks down at her feet*) You say he looks like him?

WHITE GIRL: (*looking at him again quickly*) Y-e-s (*slowly and undecidedly*) I think so. I . . . I . . . (*then she covers her face with her arm and turns quickly and moves away from the door, supported by Second Officer. First Officer makes a step toward Tom and slips handcuffs on him before any one is aware what is happening*)

SUE: (*holding on to her chair and shaking her cane at the officer, while Bossie comes up close to her and snivels in her apron*) Whut you doing? What you doing? You can't rest my granson—he ain't done nothing—you can't rest him!

FIRST OFFICER: Be quiet, old woman. I'm just going to take him along to the sheriff to question him and if he's telling the truth he'll be right back home here in no time.

SUE: But you can't rest him; he don't know no mo bout that po little white chile than I do—You can't take him!

TOM: (*utterly bewildered*) Granma, don't take on so. I'll go long with him to the sheriff. I'll splain to him how I couldn't a done it when I was here sleep all the time—I never laid eyes on that white lady before in all my life.

SUE: (*to Tom*) Course you ain't. (*to officer*) Mr. Officer, that white chile ain't never seed my granson before—All Niggers looks alike to her; she so upset she don't know whut she's saying.

FIRST OFFICER: (*to Sue as he pulls Tom along*) You just keep cool Grannie, he'll be right back—if he's innocent. (*to Tom*) And the quieter you comes along the better it will be for you.

TOM: (*looking back at his grandma from the doorway with terror in his eyes*) I'll be right back granny—don't cry—don't cry—Jest as soon as I see— (*The officer pulls him out of the doorway.*)

LIZA: (*standing with her hands clasped together, her head bowed and swaying from side to side with emotion. She prays*) Sweet Jesus, do come down and hep us this mornin. You knows our hearts and you knows this po boy ain't done nothing wrong. You said you would hep the fatherless and the motherless; do Jesus bring this po orphan back to his ole cripple grannie safe and sound, do Jesus!

BOSSIE: (*crying and pulling at his grandma's apron*) Grannie, grannie, whut they gointer do to my brother? Whut they gointer do to him?

SUE: (*brokenly*) The good Jesus only knows, but I'm a talking to the Lord now asting Him to . . . (*a rap is heard at the door; it is almost immediately pushed open and* MATILDA BROWN *enters hurriedly and excitedly.*)

MATILDA: (*breathlessly*) Miss Liza, as I was coming long I seed Tom wid the police and there was some white mens wid guns a trying to take him away from the police—said he'd done been dentified and they want gointer be cheated outen they Nigger this time. I, I flew on down here to tell you, you better do somethin'.

SUE: (*shaking nervously from side to side as she leans on her cane for support*) Oh my God, whut kin I do?

LIZA: (*alertly*) You got to git word to some of your good white folks, that's whut and git em to save him.

SUE: Yes . . . That's whut . . . Lemme see . . . (*she stands tense thinking a moment*) I got it . . . Miss Vilet . . . I got to git to Miss Vilet . . . I nused her when she was a baby and she'll do it . . . Her pa's the Jedge.

LIZA: That's right! I'll go. You can't go quick.

MATILDA: No. Lemme go; I kin move in a hurry, lemme go!

SUE: All right Tildy. Tell Miss Vilet her ole nuse Sue is callin on her and don't fail me; tell her they done took Tom and he is perfect innercent, and they gointer take him away from the police, and ax her to ax her pa the Jedge to go git Tom and save him fur God's sake. Now hurry, Tildy, fly!

BOSSIE: (*to Sue*) Lemme go long; I knows how to git there quick cutting through the ole field.

LIZA: Yes they knows Bossie and he kin hep tell.

SUE: Yes Bossie, gone, yawll hurry, hurry! (*Matilda and Bossie hurry out of the back door and Sue sinks down into a chair exhausted while Liza comes over to her and pats her on the back.*)

LIZA: Now, now evrything's gointer be all right . . . Miss Vilet'll fix it . . . she ain't gointer let her ole mammy call on her for nothing . . . she'll make her pa save him.

SUE: Yes, she's a good chile . . . I knows she'll save him.

(*Sue moves her lips in prayer. From the church next door comes the sound of singing; the two women listen to the words with emotion.*)

> Alas, and did my savior bleed
> And did my sovereign die
> Would he devote his sacred head
> For such a worm as I.
> Must Jesus bear the cross alone
> And all the world go free,
> No, there's a cross for every one
> And there's a cross for me.

(*Sue rocks back and forth in chair, head buried in her apron. Liza walks up and down the floor, throws her hands up imploringly now and then.*)

LIZA: Oh Lord, hep us to bear our cross! Hep us!

SUE: (*drooping*) Liza, I'm feeling sorter fainty lack; git me my bottle of camphor out of the safe yonder.

LIZA: (*going to safe*) Yes chile, I'll git it. You done gone through a whole lot this mornin, God knows. (*takes up a bottle and holds it up for Sue to see*) This it?

SUE: (*shaking her head*) Eugh eugh, that's my sweet oil. It's the yuther one in the black bottle . . . see it?

LIZA: (*taking out bottle and smelling it*) Yes, here it is. Strong too. It'll do you good. I has them sinking spells too sometimes. (*comes over to Sue with stopper out of bottle and holds it to her nose*) There, draw a deep bref of it; feel better?

SUE: I'll feel better tereckly. My old heart is gittin weak.

LIZA: Set back comfortable in your cheer and listen to the singin; they also sho talkin to the Lord fur you in that church this mornin. Listen! (*the church is singing*)

> I must tell Jesus, I cannot bear my burdens alone
> In my distress he surely will help me
> I cannot bear my burdens alone.
>
> I must tell Jesus, I cannot bear my burdens alone
> Jesus my Lord he surely will help me
> Jesus will help me, Jesus alone.

LIZA: That's all, that's all we kin do jes tell Jesus! Jesus! Jesus please bow down your ear! (*walks up and down mumbling a soft prayer as the singing continues mournfully*)

SUE: I reckin Tildy's bout on her way back now. I knows Miss Vilet done got her pa by now, don't you reckin, Liza.

LIZA: (*sympathetically*) Course; I spects Tom'll be coming back too any minit now. Everybody knows he ain't done no harm.

SUE: (*listening to running feet at the door and sitting up straight in chair*) Who dat coming? (*Matilda pushes open the door and comes in all excited and panting while Bossie follows her crying*) Whut's the matter? Didn't you find Miss Vilet?

MATILDA: (*reluctantly*) It want no use.

SUE: No use?

LIZA: Whut you mean?

MATILDA: I mean—I mean—

LIZA: For God's sake Tildy, whut's happened?

MATILDA: They—they done lynched him.

SUE: (*screams*) Jesus! (*gasps and falls limp in her chair. Singing from church begins. Bossie runs to her, crying afresh. Liza puts the camphor bottle to her nose again as Matilda feels her heart; they work over her a few minutes, shake their heads and with drooping shoulders, wring their hands. While this action takes place the words of this song pour forth from church:*)

Lord have mercy.
Lord have mercy,
Lord have mercy over me.

(*Sung first time with words and repeated in a low hum as curtain slowly falls.*)

Safe

c. 1929

❧

Georgia Douglas Johnson

CHARACTERS

LIZA PETTIGREW, *the wife*
JOHN PETTIGREW, *the husband*
MANDY GRIMES, *Liza's mother*
DR. JENKINS, *physician*
HANNAH WIGGINS, *neighbor*

SETTING

Place: *Southern town*
Time: *1893*

Scene: Front room of a three-room cottage. Back door leading to kitchen. Door to left leading to Liza's room. A front door and a cot along the wall. A table and oil lamp, three chairs, baby garments, a basket of socks, newspapers, etc.

Scene Opens: LIZA *is discovered sewing on some small white garments.* JOHN *is reading the evening paper by an oil lamp on the table.*

LIZA: (*lifting her voice*) Ma, come on outer that kitchen—jest stack up them supper dishes and come on and set down and rest, you hear?

MANDY: (*from kitchen*) All right, Liza, I'm coming out in a minute now.

LIZA: (*to John*) Ma's been on her feet all day long. She don't know how to rest herself.

JOHN: (*absently*) Eughhu. She sho don't. (*continues reading*)

LIZA: (*calling again*) Come on, Ma.

MANDY: (*appearing in the kitchen doorway*) I hate to leave them dishes all dirty overnight, but if I must, I must. (*She looks about the room for something to do.*) I reckon I will jest mend John's socks while I'm setting here. (*She brings a basket with socks, needle and thread in it over near the table light with a chair.*)

LIZA: No, Ma, you lay down on your cot and stretch out a while and rest. First thing you know I'll be down and then you got to be up and around waiting on me—so rest while you kin.

MANDY: (*obediently putting up the sewing basket*) All right, honey. I'll stretch out a minute or so if you wants me to. (*She goes over to her cot against the wall and falls down heavily with a sigh upon it.*) My, this feels good to my old bones.

LIZA: Of course, it do—you're plum wore out; you done a sight of washing today.

MANDY: (*yawning*) Yes, I been going pretty steady today. What you making on now?

LIZA: Just hemming some little flannel belly bands. (*She holds up one for her mother to see.*) I got all the night gowns ready now. My time's pretty nigh near.

MANDY: Yes, it's jest about time—nine months I count it.

JOHN: (*lowering the paper*) Well, well, well. I see they done caught Sam Hosea and put him in jail.

MANDY: When they ketch him?

JOHN: Paper says this morning. I reckon his ma is plum crazy if she's heered they got him.

LIZA: I knows her. She's a little skinny brown-skinned woman. Belong to our church. She use to bring Sam along pretty regular all the time. He was a nice motherly sort of boy, not mor'n seventeen I'd say. Lemme see. 'Twant no woman mixed up in it, was it?

JOHN: No, seems like he and his boss had some sort of dispute about wages—the boss slapped him and Sam up and hit him back they says.

MANDY: Eugh eugh—that's mighty unhealthy sounding business for this part of the country. Hittin a white man, he better hadder made tracks far away from here I'm er thinking.

(*Just then there's a soft knock at the door.*)

JOHN: I wonder who that is.

LIZA: Go see!

(*John goes to the door.* HANNAH WIGGINS *enters.*)

JOHN: Howdy, Miss Wiggins, come in and take a cheer.

HANNAH: (*still standing and excited-like*) Howdy! I jest thought I'd drop over here, being as Liza was so near her time and, and—

MANDY: (*sitting up on the cot*) Go on Hannah; what's the matter, you look all flusterated—what's up?

LIZA: Set down, Miss Hannah, there's a cheer.

HANNAH: (*sitting down on the edge of the chair uneasily*) I, I come over here to see how Liza was most special—then I wanted to see if yaw'll knowed about the trouble—

MANDY: Liza's fine. But what trouble is it you're talking 'bout? We ain't heered nothing 'tall!

JOHN: I saw in the papers they done caught Sam Hosea—we all thought he'd got out of town. I jest read 'bout it.

HANNAH: Yes, but that ain't all. (*shakes her head*)

LIZA: What else is it? Tell us!

HANNAH: (*looks around the room again, floundering*) You see I heered they done formed a mob downtown and it mout be there'll be hell to pay tonight!

JOHN: (*excitedly*) Who told you that?

HANNAH: Jim Brown told me 'bout it. He dropped in our house jest now and said as how things didn't look good at all downtown. So I thought I better run over and tell yaw'll.

JOHN: Ain't they gointer call out the soldiers, did he say?

HANNAH: No, he jest said the crowds was gathering and it didn't look good in town.

LIZA: (*in awed tones*) You don't reckon they'll take Sam out of the jail, do you, John?

JOHN: I don't know. (*he gets up and goes to the door*) I think I'll step down the streets and see what they knows by Briggze's store.

MANDY: (*to John*) You think you oughter go out?

LIZA: Be keerful and don't stay long.

JOHN: I'll be right back. Don't yaw'll worry. (*goes out*)

LIZA: I been setting here thinking 'bout that poor boy Sam—him working hard to take kere of his widder mother, doing the best he kin, trying to be a man and stan up for hissef, and what do he git? A slap in the face.

HANNAH: Chile, that ain't nothing—if he gits off with a slap. These white folks is mad—mad—he done hit a white man back.

MANDY: They ain't gointer stan for it. I done seen it happen before.

LIZA: What's little nigger boys born for anyhow? I sho hopes mine will be a girl. I don't want no boy baby to be hounded down and kicked 'round. No, I don't want to ever have no boy chile!

MANDY: Hush, honey, that's a sin. God sends what he wants us to have—we can't pick and choose.

HANNAH: No, we sho can't. We got to swaller the bitter with the sweet. (*just then a shot is heard*)

MANDY: (*jumping up*) What's that?

HANNAH: Sho sounded like a shot to me. I b'lieve them white folks is up to something this night.

LIZA: Listen, ain't that noise coming this a way?

HANNAH: It sho sounds like it. (*goes over to the door, cracks it, peeps out and listens*) They's coming—big crowd headed this way.

MANDY: (*excitedly*) We better put out the light and pull that curtain way down.

HANNAH: Yes, that's right, you can't tell what them devils might git it in they heads to do.

(*There is an increasing sound.*)

LIZA: (*in awed tones*) They wouldn't come in here? Would they?

MANDY: (*consolingly*) No, they wouldn't, but then we better keep it dark.

(*Another shot rings out. The women jump and look at each other in fear.*)

Liza: (*plaintively*) I wonder where John is—

Mandy: He oughter been back here before now. (*she goes to the window and peeps cautiously out from behind [the] shade. Hannah follows and then Liza.*)

Hannah: You stay back, Liza. You oughtenter see sich things—not in your delicate state.

Liza: But what they doing? Where they goin to?

Mandy: Yes, go back, Liza, and set down. Let us watch. (*a confusion of many footsteps and tramping horses as the roar becomes louder*)

Liza: (*beginning to walk up and down the room restlessly*) Ma, Ma, do you think they got him—do you think they'll hang him . . . ?

Mandy: (*patting Liza on the shoulder*) I don't know. You try and kep quiet. You hadn't ought to hear all this screeching hell—God help you! (*goes back to window*)

Hannah: She sho oughten. It's a sin and a shame! Coming right by here, too . . .

(*Then a voice rises above the men outside shouting, "Don't hang me, don't hang me! I don't want to die! Mother! Mother!"*)

Liza: (*jumping up*) That's him! That's Sam! They got him. (*she runs to the door and looks out. Hannah and Mandy follow her quickly and drag her back, shutting the door quickly*)

Mandy: They'll shoot you! You can't do that! They're mad—mad!

Liza: (*crumpling up on the chair shivering, her teeth chattering*) Oh my God, did you hear that poor boy crying for his mother? He's jest a boy—jest a boy—jest a little boy! (*the roar outside continues*)

Hannah: (*to Mandy*) This is mighty bad for her, mighty bad—

Mandy: (*looking at Liza critically*) Yes, it sho is. (*she thinks a minute*) I hates to ast you, but John ain't got back and we ought to git a doctor. Could you steal out the back and git him?

Hannah: Yes, I'll go, I kin steal out the back ways.

Mandy: Better hurry, Hannah. I don't like the looks of her. (*Hannah goes out through back*)

Liza: (*continues to shiver and shake*) Oh, where is John? Where is John? What you reckon has happened? Oh, that poor boy—poor little nigger boy!

Mandy: Try not to worry so, honey. We's in the Lord's hands. (*shaking her head*) My poor, poor chile. I'll heat a kettle of water, then I'm gointer fix your bed so you can lay down when you feel like it.

(*Hoarse laughter is heard outside as the noise grows less and less. Mandy goes into small bedroom adjoining kitchen for a moment, then comes back, looks at Liza, shakes her head. Then Liza begins walking up and down the floor all doubled over as if in pain. She goes to the window occasionally and looks out from behind the shade. The noise of countless passing feet is heard and an occasional curse or laugh. She trembles slightly every time she looks and begins pacing up and down again.*)

MANDY: (*coming over from the bedroom*) Come on and lay down now, chile; the doctor'll be here to reckly. I'll git all your little things together for you. (*goes over and begins to gather up the little white garments Liza had been sewing on*)

LIZA: (*stands stooped over in the opening of her bedroom door*) Did you hear him cry for his mother? Did you?

MANDY: Yes, honey chile, I heard him, but you musn't think about that now. Fergit it. Remember your own little baby—you got him to think about. You got to born him safe!

LIZA: (*looks at Mandy wild-eyed*) What you say?

MANDY: Born him safe! Born him safe! That's what you got to do.

LIZA: (*turning her head from side to side as she stands half stooped in the doorway, she repeats*) Born him safe! . . . Safe . . . (*she hysterically disappears into the next room*)

MANDY: (*sighs and continues picking up the little garments, smoothing them out nervously. Just then the door opens and John enters*) Oh, where you been, John? Why didn't you come back before now?

JOHN: I tried to but I got headed off—they come right by here too. It was terrible, terrible . . . Where's she?

MANDY: In the room. I done sent fur the doctor; he'll be here any minute.

JOHN: (*nervously going toward Liza's bedroom*) I'll go in and see her. Poor little Liza. (*enters room*)

MANDY: (*goes to the window and peers out and listens as scattering footsteps sound outside on the sidewalk. Then she busies herself about the room, turns down her bed, lights the lamp and turns it down low. Just then there is a knock at the kitchen door. Calling*) John! John! (*John comes to the door.*) See if that ain't Hannah at the back door with the doctor.

JOHN: (*hurrying*) All right. (*he goes through the kitchen and returns with* DR. JENKINS)

MANDY: I'm sho glad you come, Doctor; she's right in there. Please hurry.

DR. JENKINS: (*to Mandy*) Get me some hot water.

MANDY: I got it ready for you. John, git the kettle! (*John goes in kitchen*) She's terrible upset, Doctor, terrible . . .

DR. JENKINS: I know—Hannah told me all about it; she stopped at her house a minute or two, but said tell you she'd be here to help.

JOHN: (*returning with kettle*) Here 'tis.

MANDY: Set it in the room.

(*The doctor goes into the room with his bag and John comes out.*)

MANDY: How is she?

JOHN:Mighty upset.

MANDY: She ain't never seen no lynching not before, and it was terrible—her being so nigh her time too.

JOHN: Do you think she'll git through all right?

MANDY: I pray God she do. But she's shook to pieces.

JOHN: I oughter been here myself, but I didn't know I was gointer be cut off . . .

MANDY: Course you didn't. We's all in the hands of the Lawd.

JOHN: (*drops his hands helplessly on his knees*) What a terrible night.

MANDY: I wish Hannah would come on back. I'm that nervish.

JOHN: She was right brave to go for the doctor.

MANDY: Want she?

(*Just then a baby's cry is heard from the next room and both of them jump up and look toward the closed door. They take a step forward and wait.*)

JOHN: You reckon she's all right?

MANDY: I hope so, but . . .

JOHN: But what?

MANDY: I don't know zactly; I never did see her look like she looked tonight.

JOHN: (*groaning*) I wish the Lord this night was over.

MANDY: God knows I do too—my poor, poor chile.

(*They wait for what seems like an eternity listening to the muffled sounds in the next room. Then the doctor appears at the door, closing it behind him. His face looks distressed.*)

MANDY: (*nervously*) How is she? Can I go in?

JOHN: (*agitatedly*) How is she, Doc?

DR. JENKINS: (*holding up one hand*) Wait a minute, calm yourselves. I've got something to tell you, and I don't hardly know how . . .

MANDY: (*bursting into tears*) She ain't dead, is she? Doc, my poor chile ain't dead?

JOHN: (*biting his lips*) Tell us, Doc, tell us! What is it?

DR. JENKINS: She's all right and the baby was born all right—big and fine. You heard him cry . . .

JOHN: Yes . . .

MANDY: Yes, we heard.

DR. JENKINS: And she asked me right away, "Is it a girl?"

JOHN, MANDY: (*stretching their necks out further to listen*) Yes, yes, Doc! Go on!

DR. JENKINS: And I said, "No, child, it's a fine boy," and then I turned my back a minute to wash in the basin. When I looked around again she had her hands about the baby's throat choking it. I tried to stop her, but its little tongue was already hanging from its mouth. It was dead! Then she began, she kept muttering over and over again: "Now he's safe—safe from the lynchers! Safe!"

(*John falls down on a chair sobbing, his face in his hands, as Mandy, stooped with misery, drags her feet heavily toward the closed door. She opens it softly and goes in. The doctor stands, a picture of helplessness as he looks at them in their grief.*)

CURTAIN

Blue-Eyed Black Boy

c. 1930

❧

Georgia Douglas Johnson

CHARACTERS

Pauline Waters, *mother*
Rebecca Waters, *daughter*
Dr. Thomas Grey, *fiancé of Rebecca*
Hester Grant, *Pauline's best friend*

Scene: A kitchen in Mrs. Waters's *cottage. A stove with food keeping warm and an ironing board in the corner, a table with a lighted oil lamp and two chairs. Door, slightly ajar, leads to the front room and window opening on to a side street.*

Scene Opens: Pauline *is discovered seated in a large rocker with her left foot bandaged and resting on a low stool.*

Pauline: (*calling to the other room*) Rebecca, come on. Your iron is hot now, I know.

Rebecca: (*answers from the front room*) I'm coming now, Ma. (*She enters holding a lacy garment in her hands.*) I had to tack these bows on. How you like it now?

Pauline: (*scanning the long night dress set off with little pink bows that Rebecca is holding up for her inspection*) Eugh-hu, it shore is pretty. I don't believe anybody ever had as fine a wedding gown in this whole town.

Rebecca: Humph! (*shrugs her shoulders proudly as she tests the iron to see if it is hot and then takes it over to the board and begins to press the gown*) That's to be expected, ain't it? Everybody in the Baptist Church looks up to us, don't they?

Pauline: Shore they do. I ain't carried myself straight all these years for nothing. Your father was shore one proud man; he put us on a pinnacle!

Rebecca: Well, I sure have tried to walk straight all my life.

Pauline: Yes, and I'm shore proud. Now here you is getting ready to marry a young doctor. My my! (*then she suddenly says*) Ouch! I wish he would come on over here to change the dressing on my foot. Hope I ain't going to have lock jaw.

REBECCA: You won't. Tom knows his business. (*She tosses her head proudly. She looks over to the stove and goes on.*) Wish Jack would come on home and eat his supper so's I could clean up the dishes.

PAULINE: What time is it?

REBECCA: (*goes to the middle door and peeps in the next room*) The clock in position to exactly five minutes after seven. He oughter been here a whole hour ago.

PAULINE: I wonder what's keeping him?

REBECCA: Well, there's one thing sure and certain: he's not running after girls.

PAULINE: No, he shore don't. Just give him a book and he's happy. Says he's going to quit running that crane and learn engineering soons you get married. He's been mighty tied down since your father died taking care of us.

REBECCA: Everybody says he's the smartest and the finest looking black boy in the whole town.

PAULINE: Yes, he is good looking even if he is mine. Some of 'em lay it to his eyes. (*She looks far off thoughtfully.*)

REBECCA: Yes, they do set him off. It's funny that he's the only one in our family's got blue eyes though. Pa's was black, and yours and mine are black too. It certainly is strange; wish I'd had 'em.

PAULINE: Oh, you be satisfied. You're pretty enough. Hush, there's the doctor's buggy stopping now. Go let him in. (*Rebecca goes to the door while Pauline bends over, grunting and touching her foot. DR. GREY enters, bag in hand, with Rebecca.*)

DR. GREY: Well, how's my patient feeling? Better, I know.

PAULINE: Now don't you be kidding me, Doctor. My foot's been paining me terrible, I'm scared to death I'm going to have the lock jaw. For God's sake don't let me . . . (*Rebecca places chair for him near her mother.*)

DR. GREY: (*unwinds the bandages, looks at foot and opens his bag*) Fine, it's doing fine. You'll have to keep off it for a week more, and then you'll be all right.

PAULINE: Can't walk on it for a week?

DR. GREY: Not unless you want to die of blood poisoning—lock jaw, I mean! (*He touches the foot with iodine and puts on new bandage.*) That was an old, rusty nail you stuck in your foot. A pretty close call. (*He looks lovingly at Rebecca.*)

PAULINE: Well, I'm tickled to have such a good doctor for my new son.

DR. GREY: You bet. (*then thoughtfully*) I saw some mighty rough looking hoodlums gathering on the streets as I came in. Looks like there might be some trouble somewhere.

REBECCA: Oh, they're always having a squabble on these streets. You get used to 'em—and you will too after a while.

PAULINE: Yes, there's always something stirring everyday. I just go on and on and don't pay 'em no mind myself.

DR. GREY: (*patting the foot tenderly*) Now that's all right. You keep off of it, hear me? Or I won't vouch for the outcome.

PAULINE: It's so sore; I can't stand up even if I was a kind to. (*A knock is heard.*) See who's at the back door, Rebecca. (*She peeps out.*)

REBECCA: (*goes to the door and cracks it*) Who there?

HESTER: Me, me, it's Hester—Hester Grant. Lemme in. (*Rebecca opens the door and* HESTER *comes panting in. She looks around as if hating to speak before the others then blurts out*) Pauline, it's Jack. Your son Jack has been 'rested . . . 'rested and put in jail.

PAULINE: 'Rested?

REBECCA: Good Lord.

DR. GREY: What for? (*moves about restlessly*)

HESTER: They say he done brushed against a white woman on the street. They had er argument and she hollowed out he's attacking her. A crew of white men come up and started beating on him and the policeman, when he was coming home from work, dragged him to the jailhouse.

PAULINE: My God, my God! It ain't so! He ain't brushed up against no lady. My boy ain't! He's, he's a gentleman, that's what he is.

HESTER: (*moves about restlessly. She has something else to say*) And, and Pauline, that ain't the worse, that ain't the worse. They, they say there's gointer to be a lynching tonight. They gointer break open the jail and string him up! (*She finishes desperately.*)

PAULINE: String him up? My son? They can't do that—not to my son, not him!

DR. GREY: (*excitedly*) I'll drive over and see the Judge. He'll do something to stop it.

HESTER: (*sarcastically*) Him? Not him! He's a lyncher his own self. Don't put no trust in him. Ain't he done let 'em lynch six niggers in the last year jes' gone? Him! (*She scoffs again.*)

REBECCA: (*wringing her hands*) We got to do something. (*goes up to Dr. Grey*) Do you know anybody else, anybody at all, who could save him?

PAULINE: Wait, wait. I know what I'll do. I don't care what it costs. (*to Rebecca*) Fly in yonder (*points to the next room*) and get me that little tin box out of the left hand side of the tray in my trunk. Hurry. Fly! (*Rebecca hurries out while Dr. Grey and Hester look on in bewilderment*) Lynch my son? My son? (*she yells to Rebecca in the next room*) Get it? You got it?

REBECCA: (*from next room*) Yes, Ma, I got it. (*hurries in with a small tin box in her hand and hands it to her mother*)

PAULINE: (*feverishly tossing out the odd bits of jewelry in the box, finally coming up with a small ring. She turns to Dr. Grey*): Here, Tom, take this. Run, jump on your horse and buggy and fly over to Governor Tinkham's house and don't you let nobody—nobody—stop you. Just give him this ring and say, "Pauline sent this. She says they goin to lynch her son born 21 years ago." Mind you, say 21 years ago. Then say, listen close. "Look in his eyes and you'll save him."

DR. GREY: (*listens in amazement but grasps the small ring in his hand and hastens toward the door saying*) Don't worry. I'll put it in his hands and tell him what you said just as quick as my horse can make it. (*When he leaves the room, Rebecca and Hester look at Pauline in astonishment.*)

HESTER: (*starting as if from a dream*) Well, well, well, I don't git what you mean, but I reckon you knows what you is doing. (*She and Rebecca watch Dr. Grey from the front window as he drives away.*)

PAULINE: I shorely do!

REBECCA: (*comes over and throws her arms around her mother's neck*) Mother, what does it all mean? Can you really save him?

PAULINE: (*confidently*) Wait and see. I'll tell you more about it after a while. Don't ask me now.

HESTER: (*going over to the window*) I hope he'll git over to the Governor's in time. (*looking out*) Ump! There goes a bunch of men with guns now and here comes another all slouched over and pushing on the same way.

REBECCA: (*joining her at the window, with bated breath*) And look, look! Here come wagons full. (*The rumble of wagon wheels is heard.*) See 'em, Hester? All piled in with their guns, too.

(*Pauline's lips move in prayer; her head is turned deliberately away from the window. She sighs deeply now and then.*)

HESTER: Do Lord, do Lord! Help us this night.

REBECCA: (with trembling voice) Hussies! Look at them men on horses! (Horses' hooves are heard in the street outside. Rebecca cries lightly.)

HESTER: Jesus, Jesus! Please come down and help us this night!

REBECCA: (*running over to her mother and flinging her arms about her neck*) Oh, mother, mother! What will we do? Do you hear 'em? Do you hear all them men on horses and wagons going up to the jail? Poor brother! Poor boy.

PAULINE: Trust in God, daughter. I've got faith in Him, faith in . . . in the Governor. He won't fail. (*She continues to move her lips in prayer.*)

(*Rebecca rushes back to the window as new sounds of wagon wheels are heard.*)

HESTER: (*at window*) Still coming!

REBECCA: Why don't Tom come back? Why don't he hurry?

HESTER: Hush, chile! He ain't had time yet.

PAULINE: (*breaks out in an audible prayer*) Lord Jesus, I know I've sinned against your holy law, but you did forgive me and let me hold up my head again. Help me again, dear Jesus. Help me to save my innocent child, him who never done no wrong. Save him, Lord. Let his father . . . (*she stops and looks around at the two women, then cautiously speaks*) You understand all I mean, sweet Jesus. Come down and rise with this wild mob tonight. Pour your love into their wicked hearts. Lord, Lord, hear my prayer.

HESTER: (*at window*) Do Lord, hear.

PAULINE: (*restlessly looking toward the others*) Any sight of Tom yet?

REBECCA: No, Ma. I don't see him no where yet.

HESTER: Give him time.

PAULINE: Time! Time! It'll be too late reckly. Too late . . . (*she sobs, her head lifted, listening*) What that?

HESTER: (*peers out and listens*) What?

PAULINE: The sound of many feet I hear?

REBECCA: (*looks out interested*) I see 'em, I see 'em! Wait! Wait! Ma! Ma! (*hysterically*) It's the state troops! It's the Guards, it's the Guards, Ma! They's coming. Look, Miss Hester!

HESTER: They shore is, Jesus. Shore as I'm born—them military. They's come—come to save him.

REBECCA: And yonders Tom at the gate—he's coming.

DR. GREY: (*rushing in as the others look at him in amazement*) He's saved, Miss Waters! Saved! Did the Governor send the troops?

CURTAIN

Regina M. Anderson Andrews
(1901–1993)

Before coming to New York, I had been very much influenced by
Ida B. Wells Barnett of Chicago.... When I was a child in Chicago
and first heard of lynchings, they were incomprehensible. It's under-
standable that in my twenties I would have to write a play about
lynching.[1]

egina Anderson Andrews, quoted above, wrote her first play, *Climbing
Jacob's Ladder*, in 1930. The play is significant because it is one of the
earliest produced lynching plays by an African American woman.
Given her lack of access to a tradition, Andrews makes interesting and
unique choices. The action takes place outside of the home, which was
unusual for a work written by African American women during this
period, and it does not feature a female lead character. An interesting aspect of
Andrews's play is that the action occurs in the church. Another unique feature
is the detailed description by a young boy of the lynching event.

Because she had probably never seen an actual production focusing on
lynching by an African American, unless she had seen Mary Burrill's *Aftermath*
in 1928, Andrews had very few role models to follow. She found herself in a
situation that many playwrights of her era faced—an issue of social urgency, but
no models for how to dramatize it.

Climbing Jacob's Ladder was produced by the Harlem Experimental Theatre
April 24, 1931, at St. Philips Parish House, where the group was housed.
Although there are no known reviews of the play, a photo of the production is
featured in the July 1931 issue of the NAACP's *Crisis* magazine. In Loften
Mitchell's *Voices of the Black Theatre*, Andrews recalls taking her early version of
the play to W. E. B. Du Bois. According to Andrews, Du Bois suggested she
rewrite the play. "Take it back and write it over and be very careful of what you
are doing. You can do better than this, and I urge you to do better. Then, bring
it back to me."[2] After seeing the production, Du Bois wrote Andrews: "Your

play was thrilling. I enjoyed it immensely, and it gripped the audience."[3] There is no complete extant copy of *Climbing Jacob's Ladder,* nor is it known whether the script published here is an earlier or later draft. Because of the numerous markings, revisions, and deletions, and also due to the stereotypical characters and melodramatic incidents, the editors of this anthology believe that this version is the early draft presented to Du Bois. Du Bois was possibly disturbed by the use of the word "nigger" in the church and the argument over finances during such a horrifying event. The script in its present state is clear enough to follow, but the play is missing three pages that include a speech by Mrs. Townsend, one of the educated leaders of the community, and possibly a speech from the lynching victim's family. The missing pages might also mention the crime the young man has allegedly committed, because it is not clear why he is lynched.

Andrews published very little during her lifetime. Her other plays include *Underground* (1933), about a slave's escape through the Underground Railroad, which was produced in 1932 at the New School for Social Research and then again at St. Philips Parish House. She also wrote *Matilda* (n.d.) and *The Man Who Passed* (n.d.). *Matilda* also deals with the Underground Railroad, and is possibly another version of *Underground.*

Regina M. Anderson was born May 21, 1901, in Chicago, the daughter of William Grant Anderson, an attorney, and Margaret Anderson. Andrews was educated at the Normal Training School in Chicago and continued her studies at Wilberforce University in Ohio and at the University of Chicago. Relocating to New York City, she studied at City College and completed her Masters of Library Science from Columbia University. While a student, she was employed by several branches of the New York Public Library, including the 115th Street Branch and the 135th Street Branch (now the Schomburg Center for Research in Black Culture). Her position at the 135th Street Branch put her in close contact with prominent as well as emerging artists and intellectuals of Harlem. In the basement of the 135th Street Branch, Andrews assisted in the organization of the Krigwa Players, established under the leadership of W. E. B. Du Bois in 1926. During this period Andrews became caught up in the activities of the Harlem Renaissance, especially theatre. She supported the philosophy of Du Bois and Krigwa that black theatre should be exclusively about, by, for, and near blacks. Andrews was instrumental in helping to nurture the Little Negro Theatre Movement in Harlem.

Prior to her marriage in 1926 to attorney and later New York assemblyman William T. Andrews, Regina Andrews shared an apartment with Ethel Ray Nance and Louella Tucker at 580 St. Nicholas Avenue on Sugar Hill. The apartment, known as "580," functioned as a salon for artists and intellectuals of the period, very much like Georgia Douglas Johnson's S Street salon in Washington, D.C.

When the Krigwa Theatre disbanded around 1928 because of financial difficulties, Andrews and others of the Harlem community decided to organize the Harlem Experimental Theatre. Andrews explains:

When Dorothy Peterson, Harold Jackman, and one or two others sat with me and discussed how we could recreate the little theatre Dr. Du Bois had established with Krigwa, we met in the 135th Street Library. . . . What do we want to do? What is our goal? What are we going to achieve? These were the questions. . . . And so the Harlem Experimental Theatre was born.[4]

The Harlem Experimental Theatre began producing in 1928, at the 135th Street Library basement, with Mary Cass Canfield's *The Duchess Says Her Prayers* and Paul Green's *The No' Count Boy.* The group did not limit themselves to black plays until they could produce their own. Later they would produce such black-authored plays as *Plumes* by Georgia Douglas Johnson, *Get Thee Behind Me, Satan* by Robert Dorsey, and the works by Andrews. While the Harlem Experimental Theatre was housed in the 135th Street Library, Andrews worked under a pseudonym. According to Andrews, "I wrote the play *Climbing Jacob's Ladder* under an assumed name, Ursala Trelling, because of my professional association with the library."[5]

In 1931, the group moved to St. Philips Parish House and continued producing many original works by black authors, as well as those by several white authors. Broadway actress Rose McClendon joined the group later as a director to give some professional guidance and expertise. The group continued until the mid 1930s. When the Federal Theatre Project (FTP) came to New York City, many of the members of the Harlem Experimental Theatre were sought after to join the FTP. After the demise of her own group, Andrews continued to encourage other little theatre groups such as the Harlem Suitcase Theatre and the American Negro Theatre.

Andrews retired as chief librarian in 1967 from the 135th Street Library. After retirement, she continued to be active in social organizations such as the National Urban League and the National Council of Women. She also worked with the State Commission for Human Rights. In 1971, Andrews and former roommate Ethel Ray Nance coedited *Chronology of African-Americans in New York, 1621–1966.* Regina Andrews died February 5, 1993, at the Bethel Nursing Home in Ossining, New York.

NOTES

1. Loften Mitchell, ed., *Voices of the Black Theatre* (Clifton, N.J.: James T. White, 1975), 78.
2. Ibid., 79.
3. Ibid., 79.
4. Ibid., 73.
5. Ibid., 76.

Climbing Jacob's Ladder

A TRAGEDY OF NEGRO LIFE 1931

❧

Regina M. Anderson Andrews

PRAYER

Dear Father who art in Heaven, we come before you this evening with bowed down heads and heavy hearts, asking for mercy and compassion for one of thy children.

Oh Lord, let the light of thy spirit shine in our hearts tonight and please help this lamb from thy fold. Lord give him strength to go on, give him courage to fight his battle.

Now dear Lord touch the hearts of thy children here tonight that they may be generous in their efforts to do good.

Help us to realize that we don't know when nor where the hand of fate is going to strike next, but oh Lord we do know that when and where-so-never it may strike our faith in Thee is able to carry us on—yes able to carry us on from one good degree o' grace to another.

Lord, let us remember the words of the poet that "Faith is like a mighty rock in the time of storm. Faith will help in despair and save us from all alarm."

Lord, when we've done drunk our last cup of sorrow and when the hell-hounds is through chasing us 'round this weary world help us to land way up—way up when trouble can't find us no more. We asks in thy name.

AMEN.

CAST

REV. LUMPKIN, *pastor of the Haven of Rest Baptist Church*
JOHN GADDIE, *master of ceremonies*
ETHEL RANDOLPH TOWNSEND (AND HUSBAND), *an "influence" in the community*
GEORGE CHIPPIE (AND A FRIEND)

Reprinted by permission of the Manuscripts, Archives and Rare Books Division, Schomburg Center for Research in Black Culture, The New York Public Library, Astor, Lenox and Tilden Foundations.

Dr. Gerald Loving
Mother of Prisoner
Two Daughters
Rev. Sampson
Sammy
A Man
Spectators who have come to the Mass Meeting

Time: *Present, Wednesday evening.*

Scene: *Interior of the Haven of Rest Baptist Church, a shabby little place of worship in an outlying Negro district in the South.*

On the walls are class banners and one or two large embossed mottoes and pictures such as the Shepherd guiding his flock, etc. A pulpit has been erected on the stage and is being used as a speakers' platform, with the speakers' table in the center and chairs for ten people. A group of spectators who have come to the Mass Meeting are seating facing the pulpit.

Minister enters left. He is a middle-aged, dark-complexioned, God-fearing soul, with sufficient intelligence to have gained the confidence, love, and respect of his flock. The evening is warm and he wipes his face several times as he takes his seat and fans with a large palm-leaf fan. A sister of the church comes up and puts a usual pitcher of water on the table.

Rev. Lumpkin: Thank you sister. (*swallows a generous glassful of water*)

(John Gaddie, *a very serious-minded young man who acts as master of ceremonies, enters right.*)

John Gaddie: How do you do, Rev. Lumpkin?

Rev. Lumpkin: (*waving him to a seat at right of table*) Good evening Bro. Gaddie. Well, son, we have a grave mission before us tonight, but the Lord is with us.

(*Enter* Mrs. Ethel Randolph Townsend *and her husband; the latter is a quiet, modest, homely person, quite overshadowed by a prepossessing and important wife. Mrs. Townsend is obviously the upper-class Negro woman, interested in the welfare of the people in the community in which she has chosen to live. Both* Rev. Lumpkin *and Bro. Gaddie rise and bow with deference. Enter* George Chippie *and his friend. Chippie is black in color, obviously ignorant but well meaning; his face beams with the knowledge of his sudden rise into the limelight. Enter* Dr. Gerald Loving, *a person of some importance in the community. Handshaking and conversation aside, they all take seats on the platform.*

([*In the meantime the empty front seats in the church are being filled: poor people, old people and working people, the interested, the curious. Different groups of friends and factions are finding seats together, Sister Jones is calling to Sister Mirandi, etc.*] *The* Mother of the Prisoner *and her* Two Daughters *enter, one about 15, the other about 25. They take seats in the audience. Someone goes up and tells Bro. Gaddie of their presence; he consults with Rev. Lumpkin and they agree that the mother and her two daughters should be invited to sit on the platform in the seats reserved for them. When they are called, the youngest daughter grumblingly objects but the eldest helps the mother to her feet, and all three go to the platform and take their seats without a word, the mother with care-worn face and bowed head, the two daughters with a blank numbed expression which they retain throughout the entire evening, as they look directly out into and through the audience. Brother Gaddie looks at the minister, who nods.)*

JOHN GADDIE: As our meeting was called for 8: 30, and it is now nine . . .

REV. SAMPSON: (*from the Pilgrim Baptist Mission, seated left, obviously an irritable and quarrelsome contender*) Now listen heah Mistah Chairman, jes' let me start you off right, ain't no usin you makin' any back han' remarks about dis meetin' being late. Colored folks is busy people! We're busy arnin' a libin' an getten our white folks off to dere meetins and pleasures, de Lord knows dat. Dats jes why, when old Gabe blows de horn on Jedgment day, de Lawds gwine to say "Gabriel lebe de pearly gates open a haf howah longer for mah black chillun, de'll be late, but deys on der way. (*sits*)

JOHN GADDIE: And as I was about to say, since all of our speakers of the evening have arrived I think it best that we proceed with our business which is of grave importance. I need not go into the seriousness of what is ahead of us, we have been hearing about the matter now for several months, and these other good people are here to bring the details to your attention. The first speaker of the evening needs no introduction, our good Rev. Lumpkin, who has so generously given over his church, and regular evening for prayer to our meeting, and who has acted as spiritual advisor for our friend Wash Thomas during these many weeks of his imprisonment—Rev. Lumpkin.

REV. LUMPKIN: (*rising and standing behind the speakers' table, speaks with the Negro minister's usual ponderousness tempered with sincerity—bowing slowly*) Speakers of the evening, Brothers and Sisters and friends, I haven't much to say this evening, I am too filled with the thought of the terrible fate overhanging our boy, Wash Thomas, who has been pining his heart out in Eaton County Jail for nearly six months. I won't tell you about his case, others can do that better than I, but let me leave this message with you. I have bowed my head in prayer with this boy for many days. I know that he is innocent, and then besides, I have known Wash since he was a little codger,—just ten years ago he was running in that door ahead of his mother, comin to prayer meeting on a Wednesday night just like this. Just yesterday he put his big hand in mine and said, "Rev. Mah time is gettin short, say a little prayer." I knew then when I looked into his eyes, that boy was innocent. (*louder*) Are we going to let this terrible crime be committed in the name of justice? Are we going to let an innocent black man be crucified? (*shouts of no*) He needs your help. His mother and sisters add their silent plea to mine for help. His mother's heart is bleeding. She needs her boy. As I look over this eager audience tonight, I know that the Lord is with us, and we are going to save him. (*sits*)

(*Murmurs of "Yes Lord, we gwine ter save him."*)

JOHN GADDIE: (*rising to introduce Dr. Loving*) Dr. Loving has lived in our little community for a good many years, where he has ministered to rich and poor alike: you all know him and his famliar horse and buggy.—Dr. Loving.

DR. LOVING: (*substantial-looking professional man*) Mr. Chairman, Rev. Lumpkin, friends, there is really very little for me to say to you on this occasion. You all know that I am with you, and that my heart is with this boy in prison, I know without misgiving that he has been unfairly sentenced. Let's all pull together and do what we can to help him. (*sits. Applause*)

DR. LOVING: (*rising again*) Incidentally, Rev. Lumpkin, we heard yesterday that he had been returned here to Yancyville Jail, is that true?

REV. LUMPKIN: Yes, it is true: it might spur all of his friends on who are trying to help him to know that Wash is here in Yancyville Jail again. (*murmured cries of surprise and pleasure in audience*) When I talked with the Warden yesterday, he said the Mayor thought they could bring him back now for awhile, as he is needed as an important witness in another case. Its been so long now—and the white folks aint feelin so bitter toward Wash. Yes, he's been in the town jail since yesterday. I saw him last night. He's lookin fine, fine! Said even though the folks over there in the county seat had been mighty good to him, he was glad to get back here to Yancyville Jail house. He seems to feel nearer to us. And how that boy did straighten up when I told him about the meeting here tonight. Yes, Wash sure was one happy boy last night.

JOHN GADDIE: (*rising to introduce Mrs. Ethel Randolph Townsend*) We have all known for years that when we were in trouble of any kind that there was one woman to whom we could go for advice and counsel. She has never been too busy to listen. When Wash Thomas's case came up months ago, Mrs. Ethel Randolph Townsend was one of the first to offer her services. She has done everything that could be done from interviewing the Mayor and the Governor, to personally getting up petitions and having them signed. For the benefit of the few here who do not know what we have been trying to do, she has consented to tell us about it tonight.

[Two Pages Missing. *George Chippie is speaking:*]

generous in his remarks—sho makes me feel good, makes me feel better to see you all heah, and know dat you is doing you bes ter help. You know, Wash Thomas an I was kids togedder, an no one knows bettern me, dat he wouldn't kill a little ant, why, we all know Wash Thomas. Why he's one ob de boys. If you don know him you've heard about him, he never was one of dem modest kind of quiet folks to hide his light under no bushel,—allus makin noise and gitten in trowble but he was'n bad—no he never was real bad. He's in de pen now. Ah knows bettern you do dat he wouldn' hurt nobody. We all gotta hep now and get him free. We reads in de papers all about how de Negroes up north organizes and does things, now why caint we oganize right heah in Mississippi and do somthin too. Dats what we needs to do—*organize.*

MRS. TOWNSEND: (*officiously*) Mr. Chippie has done a greal deal more good than he is willing to tell you about, but we won't talk about that now.

REV. LUMPKIN: The Lord knows, Mrs. Townsend.

JOHN GADDIE: We all realize what an important role our young Brother Chippie has played in helping with the affairs of our sorely tried friend beyond the prison walls. Friends, we must save this boy! Which brings us down to the most important part of our meeting here tonight. The Governor of the state has promised us through an intermediary, whom we interviewed on Monday, that if we can raise $300 to cover the cost of defending Wash Thomas, we stand every chance of saving him and we are here tonight for that purpose. First we must have a committee to handle the money. That we must have! Suppose I name the members subject to your approval. (*nods and murmurs of approval*) Then, (*adjusts his glasses and reads from notes*) Mr. Chippie, Chairman, Mrs. Townsend, Rev. Lumpkin, Dr. Loving and my-self. Does that meet with your approval? (*approval expressed through the audience, "yes suh suits me," "jus as you say mistah," etc.*)

(*At this time a clanging of bells is heard outside of the church, running of many feet, barking of dogs, etc. One boy in the audience, SAMMY, slips out almost unnoticed. He is about 18 or 20 years old. Movement in the audience, children try to slip out but are restrained, murmurs of "mus be a fire, she must be a whopper, lissen at dat noise," etc. As the noises near and pass the church, they gain in intensity, dying slowly away in the distance.*)

JOHN GADDIE: (*rising and knocking for order impatiently*) We must ask for your attention and interest friends—fires occur every day, but the days in which we can save Wash Thomas are numbered. We will now turn the meeting over to Rev. Lumpkin, who has so kindly consented to help us raise—

REV. SAMPSON: (*interrupts from left corner of church. He has just prior to this time been fidgeting and consulting with members of his flock who sit near him. He is obviously a jealous minister from another Baptist church.*) Before dis heah meetin an money raisin goes any fudder, me an membahs of mah church, heah in dis corner wants to know in just whose pants pockets is dis money gwinta res', dat is, who's gwinta handle de money, an jes what is you'll gwinta do wid it? Now! jes scusin us fer interruptin, but dat is what we wants to know. Dese heah committee sounds mighty fine, but dere ain't no us'n dat word causin' any mystery bout which puhson actually has de money. (*cat-calls and hisses from rear. "Sit down, who wants you to talk," etc., etc.*)

JOHN GADDIE: (*irritated*) Well, Rev. Sampson, why didn't you express your dissatisfaction before? *We're* going to hold the money.

REV. SAMPSON: (*ruffled*) Dat's alright Mistah Chairman, Ise spressin' it now, right now. As mah Gran Pop ustah say, "it aint what yah usta was, its what yah now am is!" So is'e spressin' it now—des's is mah chillun from mah church, and dey looks to me fer guidance. Yes sah! looks to me! Wer'e gibbin' our money, and we wants to know whose gwinta handle dat money. You say *We*—who is *We*?

JOHN GADDIE: (*face clearing up and obviously a bit relieved*) Oh, I see, Rev. Sampson, well this money will be in the hands of two members of the Committee—Mr. Chippie and Mrs. Townsend.

REV. SAMPSON: Well, den what is you gwinta do wid de money when you gits it?

JOHN GADDIE: We are going to hire the best lawyer in the State of Mississippi to make a fight for Wash Thomas's life. Tell your church members we're going to do the very best we can.

REV. SAMPSON: Pears to me like one of mah members from de Pilgrim Baptist Church might be on dat dere committee—jest seems data way to me.

JOHN GADDIE: Won't you work on the Committee with us, Rev. Sampson?

REV. SAMPSON: (*hesitating but eager*) Well, now Brudder—

JOHN GADDIE: That's alright, Rev. Sampson, don't be modest on this occasion, we need your help.

REV. SAMPSON: Well, in dat case, Mr. Chairman, Ah might consent to give you some of mah time, pears to me like ah might. (*turns hurriedly to his little flock*) It's all right, brudders and sisters, gib all you got and keep on gibben; de committees done been organized.

JOHN GADDIE: (*turning to minister*) Alright Rev. Lumpkin.

REV. LUMPKIN: (*rising*) I'm simply going to put the money raised in the hands of de Lord. Tonight is our last chance to raise enough money to save Wash Thomas. We need $300. His dear mother here is silently praying for your help. (*rising inflection in voice*) Are we going to save her son? (*cries of* "yes suh, yes Rev. we'se all gwine to hep") Your pennies will help—dimes, nickles and dollars. Remember that we are banding together to save this boy from meeting his maker with a rope around his neck on the scaffold. As Mr. Chippie says—let's all organize like they do up north and do this work together. (*cries of* "Ahmen, De Lord's wid us Rev.") Are we going to save him—let us pray . . . (*kneels*)

"Dear Lord in Heaven we come before you this evening with heavy hearts, asking for mercy and compassion for one of thy children. Dear Father let the light of thy spirit shine in our hearts tonight to help this lamb from Thy fold. Give him strength to go on, give him courage to fight his battle. Now dear Lord touch the hearts of Thy children here tonight that they may be generous in this effort to do good. Make them realise that we do not know where the hand of fate is going to strike next but Heavenly Father, we all know that when friends turn their backs on us and we're up against the wall, our faith in thee will carry us on. Let us remember the words of the poet: " . . . when we done run around this world of sorrow." *[missing sentence]* Now I'm going to ask Sister Green to act as Secretary at left side of this table with Bro. Chippie on the right to help her call out the names of the folks as they give their money. Now my friends, do your best, as our good friend Rev. Sampson says, give all you've got and keep giving. Brother Cole, start us up a little song, not too loud now, just enough to keep the spirit moving.

(*Brother Cole starts softly*—"Get on Board Little Children." *The audience joins in, there is a little emotional patting of feet, lines begin to form in the aisle, going to each table, with the people joking and chatting among themselves. Names are being called out loudly from each table—*"Mother Mattie Johnson $1.00, Brother Taylor $5.00, what's your name Sister? Oh yes, Sister Whiters, $2.00"—*loud voice*— "Dr. Loving $10.00, The Lord will bless you Brother." *Applause from the audience and murmurs of* "sho is a good man," *etc.* Sam White $2.00. *At this point Bro. Gaddie instructs the secretaries to count the money.*)

JOHN GADDIE: Ninety-one dollars and fifty cents at the table on the left and one hundred and eight dollars and twenty-five cents at the table on the right. One hundred and ninety-nine dollars and seventy-five cents, Reverend.

REV. LUMPKIN: Now my children we're doing fine—fine (*rubbing hands together*) The Lord *will* provide. Let me see now, we just need one hundred dollars and twenty-five cents. Why my friends, that is such a small amount, such a small amount to us and so much to that boy behind those grey walls. Now I know there are some of us here who want to give 50 cents or a dime, a nickle or even a few pennies, every bit helps—another little song now— (*someone begins* "Tis Me, Tis Me," *several more straggle down the aisle— children with pennies, old ladies, etc.*)

REV. LUMPKIN: (*quietly counting money*) Now my friends we need $70 more.

(*There is silence and no one moves. After several moments a flashily dressed man in a grey checked suit, large linked gold watch chain, and cane comes down the aisle. He places $15 on the table with great gusto. They ask his name.*)

MAN: No suh! don't need to be axin mah name. Is'e from de Cotton Plant Pool Room down de road a piece. You knows all about it cause your's allus preachin an yapping bout how wese sinnin' down dere, but dis little scription is from me and de boys, dey nominated me to come up heah and bring it to yall to hep dat boy Wash. Naw, he ain't one of us but hes'e colored just like we is—so, (*embarrassed*) Have a cigar Rev? No? (*twirls cane and goes jauntily down the aisle*)

(*At this point a storm can be seen coming up outside, with intermittent flashes of lightning*)

REV. LUMPKIN: This is certainly mighty good of the boys down at the Cotton Plant. How much do we need now, Bro. Gaddie?

JOHN GADDIE: Fifty-five dollars, Reverend.

REV. LUMPKIN: Ah my children we can give thanks to our Maker, We're going to succeed in our mission. Wash Thomas is going to be saved.

(*Interrupted by a spontaneous burst of song—and shouting—they all sing,* 'I Love Jesus, So Do I," *etc.*)

(*Congregation rises as one person and begins a general circling around, and handshaking of good fellowship. One or two are audibly moved by the spirit. One sister, spurred on by uncontrolled emotion, shouts her thankfulness,* "So happy Ah can't hep it! So happy caint hep it!" *Tears of joy stream down her face, others in different parts of the church take up the cry—a general current of religious fervor is felt throughout the group as they shout praising the Lord. A sudden commotion is heard at the rear. In reality the front entrance of the church. Sammy, who disappeared earlier during the evening, staggers in. His eyes are bloodshot, his clothes are torn, and his face and hands bruised. He stares wildly about and hesitantly stumbles down the aisle. One or two terrified cries of surprise are heard throughout the audience)*

SAMMY: Stop it! Fer Gawd's sake, stop it! Deys got im!

REV. LUMPKIN: Quiet Sammy, quiet, what's the matter?

SAMMY: Yes, dey got him! All de time you niggers is been a raising dis money— *(hurls some of it to floor)* deys been stringin Wash Thomas up a tree *(words fail as he gurgles in throat)*

MR. CHIPPIE: Stop your slobberin boy; tell us what dey done to my pal! *(flashes of lightning outside)*

SAMMY: *(falling heavily against the table as he tells his story, the dollars and the pennies clink unnoticed, falling to the floor)* I slipped out a here about an hour ago while you niggahs was doin' what de *white folks* telled yo to do—while yo was doing dat, dey was breaking open de jail door digging out po Wash— God, dey brought him right by heah,—dat's when de bells was ringin, and de dogs a yappin. You heard 'em. [*The remainder of this speech is marked for deletion from the script:*] I slipped out! Dey had him tied to a car naked, full of blood an sweat. Dey dragged him about a mile or so, me sneakin behin. Den, I saw em doublin' back—I climb up a tree, dey stopped across de road almost in front of me, and cut his body loose. God, he stood up somehow! An all de time dos white folks was jumpin roun like niggers at a feast in Africa— buildin a fire an cuttin switches, an yellin' and screamin. *(sobs)* Dey made him stan, and Wash, he stood dere somehow wif his head up, wild 'n' proud. Dey all beat him, yelling, "Say dat you did it nigger, say dat you did it," even de wimmen and chillun. *(sobs)*

MOTHER: *(with shining eyes)* What did Wash say? What did mah boy say?

SAMMY: Hump! He held de head back somehow, threw it back and laughed, jest laughed, jes like,—oh, sort of proud like ah'll allus hear him.

MR. CHIPPIE: *(strained)* an—an den!

SAMMY: Dey whipped out dat rope, n' put it round his neck, shoutin', "Las chance nigger." An Wash laughed again, long an loud, an, Oh I can't tell . . . *(breaks down sobbing)*

(Cries of "Lawd is yah dere? Is yah still sittin in Hebben? Mercy Lawd, mercy!" *A wild movement throughout audience—to draw knives and razors.* "Let's get em folks." *Great commotion in the aisle as they surround the boy—*"Which way did dey go, Dey talk about organizing, Let's organize now and fight! Hell, Wash is gone boys, what yo gwine to do? Damn de organization"—*this is said all together. Same man dressed in checked suit with a cigar in his mouth comes down the aisle. He is sharpening a razor on his thumb.)*

MAN: Pears to me like you needs de boys from de Cotton Plant now. Wash's daid, is he? Don't worry Parson, go ahaid n' pray. We'll get eben somehow—in de words of your text, "De good Lord will provide a way."

REV. LUMPKIN: Brothers and Sisters, think what you are doing. You are right! Wash's gone! Will more bloodshed bring him back? Remember the words of the Sufferer of old, "Father forgive them for they know not what they do." (*cries of Ahmen from those sitting, wild cries of rage and protest from those standing*)

(*Rev. Lumpkin's attempt to restrain proves of no avail, and a group of men join the man from the Cotton Plant; they start down the aisle plotting noisily among themselves. As they rush the door and hurl it open, a terrific crash of thunder is heard, and flashes of lightning pierce the heavens. They huddle back into the room, cowed by superstition and fear.*)

REV. SAMPSON: (*jumping up on bench*) Buck Collins, put away dat knife. Dat's de hand ob God flashin across de Hebbens warnin you not to sin no mo. Did knives ever hep Niggahs? What heped yo when dey whipped yo out a Africa? Prayah! what heped yo when dey beat yo in de cotton field and picked black babies from dere muddahs' breasts? Prayah! What heped cha when black boys was herded like dumb dribben cattle from de cotton fields to be cannon foddah in de white man's war? Git down on yo knees brudders 'n sisters 'n pray. (*They all slowly sit, kneel or stand, some huddled against the wall.*)

REV. LUMPKIN: (*kneeling*) "Oh Lord, we're troubled in mind, troubled in mind, Lord! The stars have gone out and the moon has hid its face. Heavenly Father give me strength to pray for this black soul on its way to your pearly gates. He's climbin, Lord, climbin' Jacob's Ladder to an everlasting home not made with hands. Help him, Lord!

(*A few sobbing murmers are heard. The storm has abated. Quietly from the rear a mellow sorrowful voice is raised in song*)

"Were you there when they crucified my Lord?"

(*The curtain is slowly lowered.*)

"Oh!—sometimes it causes me to tremble, tremble!"

(*At first Sammy stares wildly in broken protest against this final silent resignation—slowly his body relaxes, his head falls slowly in his arms.*)

CURTAIN

Annie Nathan Meyer
(1867–1951)

lack Souls, written in 1924 but not produced until 1932, is one of the earliest known lynching dramas by a white woman. The play confronts many of the issues surrounding lynching, such as white women's desire for black men and the sexual exploitation of black women by white men. *Black Souls* also portrays the contrasting ideas among black Americans on the most effective ways to work against the forces of repression and for self-affirmation. Finally, Meyer's play underscores the hypocrisy of a nation which sends black soldiers overseas to fight for the freedom of other countries but, at the same time, permits lynchings to continue here at home. The point is made that mob violence will continue as long as a corrupt system of government is led by officials who condone lynching or look the other way when it happens.

Letters from Meyer's file at the American Jewish Archives document her persistence in a long struggle to have her play produced. In 1924, producer Winthrop Ames rejected the play, explaining,

> I am afraid I should be a bad market for the play about the colored people. Some years ago I did one (a very good play it was, by Ned Sheldon, called "The Nigger") and the difficulties with the public over it were too great to make me want to attempt another.[1]

The production, opening on March 30, 1932, at the Provincetown Playhouse, ran only for twelve performances, with New York critics praising the acting but disparaging the play. One reviewer wrote, "What the authoress lacked in dramatic power was successfully supplied by the players," while another concluded, "Despite clever staging and earnest performances, the play fails to become either an exciting bit of theatre or a convincing treatise."[2] Rose McClendon's acting was the most highly acclaimed aspect of the production. A critic for *Billboard* wrote of "a particularly inept and strikingly undramatic play saved by a stirring performance of Rose McClendon who deserves better material for her brilliant talents."[3] Apparently stung by the critical reviews and

resentful of the unanimous high praise for McClendon, Meyer bitterly recorded her own disappointment in the actress, complaining that she played her
"big scene" with her back toward the audience.[4]

In spite of the brief New York run and negative reviews, *Black Souls* is of value
to the anti-lynching dramatic tradition because it exemplifies simultaneous
conflict and cohesion of black and white women within the specific context of
lynching drama. Although the play reflects a vital area of common understanding shared by contemporary black and white women in combating the mythology of the black male rapist, it simultaneously provokes racial division surrounding the ability of white playwrights to create authentic black characters in
convincing situations. Both black and white critics noted the unconvincing
character of David Lewis, the "sentimental poet" who is lynched after his
"gallant gesture" of sacrificing his life to save a white woman's "good name."[5]
Meyer held that the most original element in her play was the dramatization of
a white woman's attraction to a black man, or the southern white man's dread
of what lay beneath the lynching of the Negro and the cry of rape.[6] The
possibility of white women desiring black men suggested they were no longer
content with their role as property of white men. Most critics avoided com-
menting on this issue.

Meyer drew on the help of African American artists in writing *Black Souls*.
James Weldon Johnson edited the dialogue for authenticity of expression while
Zora Neale Hurston selected the spirituals, which were sung by members of her
choral group in the New York production. Both Hurston and Johnson responded to various drafts of the play, and Meyer noted that one of "many
satisfactions" connected with writing *Black Souls* was the acceptance it found
among black Americans.[7] Perhaps it was Johnson or Hurston who advised
Meyer to omit from the 1932 version a tableau depicting the aftermath of a
lynching. Meyer's stage directions in the 1924 manuscript are a rare example of
stage realism employed to represent the actual visual effects of the aftermath of
a lynching:

> *Scene 6: A Tableau*
> The details must be left to the director. The effect must be a picture of
> a lynching. David's body tied to a stake—charred. Heavy shadows, the
> flaring up and dying down of the fire in front of the body. Without too
> much emphasis there must be a suggestion of the Christ figure,
> crucified. The emotional effect of martyrdom, of patient suffering, of
> terrible agony, of helplessness of the victim in the face of the mob
> spirit. . . . (1924 manuscript, Library of Congress)

While both black and white artists produced works that expressed a connection
between the crucified Christ figure and lynching victims, this unpublished
scene prompts consideration of the power and limitations of realism as a style
of production in the representation of lynching.

Black theatre critics were not as unanimously disparaging of Meyer's play as the New York reviewers had been, but they were clearly not enthusiastic. Sterling Brown compared the play to Grimké's *Rachel* in that "it deals with educated Negroes for propaganda purposes," but he concluded:

> The plot remains unconvincing and the dialogue is too often stilted and heavy with direct propaganda, especially when the sentimental poet, David, speaks. The play does have a striking situation and much understanding of the truckling that Negro educators are forced to do.[8]

A contemporary review in *Crisis* described the play as "overladen with racial propaganda, awkward, and unimpressive," but publisher George Schuyler saw it as an example of drama that was "getting away from old stereotypes of the Negro" which had "enabled America to rationalize color discrimination and justify persecution." Schuyler concluded, "If this trend continues, our nation may in time emerge from its present savage state."[9] In two more recent histories of black theatre, Loften Mitchell pays *Black Souls* the dreaded compliment of being "a well intentioned play" while Randolph Edmonds acknowledges the drama as "an attack on lynching" but includes it in a listing of selected titles that exemplify the various problems connected with white playwrights creating black characters and addressing racial themes.[10]

Abram Hill of the American Negro Theatre was not interested in producing *Black Souls*, but director Venzuella Jones was. Jones secured backing from the WPA, only to have the support withdrawn after six weeks of rehearsals. Meyer writes of this incident in her autobiography:

> Suddenly I received a letter from the heads of the WPA. They felt that my play was worthy of a far better production than the rehearsals had warranted them to expect. Therefore, for my sake they were withdrawing the play. Well I know this was not a sincere, or even truthful statement. There had been rife for some time rumors of dissatisfaction on the part of the authorities with the radical flavor of the plays which the WPA had put on. The WPA became alarmed. It was not time to put on a play which showed up so nakedly what lay behind the persecution of the Negro.[11]

Black Souls is a significant lynching drama because it foregrounds the issues created by the historical matrix of racial ideology and the esthetics of lynching drama. Dramatizing anti-lynching philosophy was often problematic for both black and white playwrights. Critics charged Grimké's *Rachel* with promoting race suicide, while Meyer claimed that she was condemned for "daring to write a play about Negroes when she had never lived in the South."[12]

Annie Nathan Meyer was born in New York City to a prominent Jewish family that dated to the revolutionary era. In 1885 she was admitted to a course of study at Columbia University where women, who were not permitted to attend classes, could study independently for the same examinations taken by men. Meyer was told by her father that she should never expect to marry because men hate intelligent wives. She subsequently devoted her energies to the struggle for women in higher education and became a founder of Barnard College, serving on its board of trustees for many years. She married Dr. Alfred Meyer in 1887 and pursued her own literary career, writing novels, plays, short stories, and numerous articles on education, art, and feminism. Meyer's work reflects her contradictory convictions about the issues of her day. Although she clearly supported higher education for women and the acceptance of women in all professions, her writing reflects her antisuffrage views and her resistance to the idea that women could successfully combine marriage and a career.[13]

The inclusion of *Black Souls* in this anthology suggests a new consideration of what has traditionally been called "feminist drama" for the historical period. The dramas by white playwrights usually considered "feminist" for the 1920s and 1930s are those works by Rachel Crothers, Zona Gale, Susan Glaspell, and Sophie Treadwell in which white women struggle with their circumscribed roles, changing status, or striving for independence. *Black Souls,* which has never been discussed as feminist drama, suggests the possibilities and problems of a womanist/feminist drama because it represents the views of white women who joined with black women in taking a stand against lynching.

NOTES

1. Letter from Winthrop Ames to Meyer, June 27, 1924. Annie Nathan Meyer file, American Jewish Archives.

2. "Rose McClendon Rises to Heights in *Black Souls,*" *New York American,* March 31, 1932; Howard Barnes, "Black Souls," *New York Herald Tribune,* March 31, 1932.

3. Jack Mehler, "The New Plays on Broadway," *The Billboard,* April 16, 1932.

4. Meyer's autobiography, *It's Been Fun* (New York: Henry Schuman, 1954), 267, and letter to James Weldon Johnson, July 14, 1932, from Meyer's file at the American Jewish Archives. Rose McClendon was frequently cast as the female lead in lynching dramas written by white playwrights. In 1929 she played Goldie in Paul Green's Pulitzer Prize–winning *In Abraham's Bosom* and, before being cast in *Black Souls,* she played the role of Mammy in James Knox Miller's *Never No More* in which her character refuses to shelter her son, who is accused of murder, from a lynch mob but who threatens the same mob with a dynamite bomb when they try to burn out her entire family.

5. Sterling Brown, *Negro Poetry and Drama and the Negro in American Fiction* (New York: Atheneum, 1978), 129; and John Chapman, "Black Man's Burden, White Dominance at Provincetown," *New York News,* March 31, 1932.

6. Meyer, *It's Been Fun,* 271.

7. Meyer, *It's Been Fun,* 268.

8. Brown, *Negro Poetry and Drama and the Negro in American Fiction,* 129.

9. "Black Souls," *The Crisis,* May 1932, p. 163, and George S. Schuyler, "Redrawing the Color Line," Black Souls programme, 1932.

10. Loften Mitchell, *Black Drama: The Story of the American Negro in the Theatre* (New York: Hawthorne Books, 1967), 96; and Randolph Edmonds, "Black Drama in the American Theatre: 1700–1970," in *The American Theatre: A Sum of Its Parts* (New York: Samuel French, 1971), 396.

11. Meyer, *It's Been Fun,* 271.

12. Meyer, *It's Been Fun,* 268.

13. For further information on Meyer's life see Jean Carwile Masteller, "Annie Nathan Meyer," in Lina Mainiero, ed., *American Women Writers: A Critical Reference Guide* (New York: Frederick Ungar, 1981), 166–168, and Meyer's autobiography, *It's Been Fun.* For Meyer's association with Barnard College see Lynn D. Gorden, "Annie Nathan Meyer and Barnard College: Mission and Identity in Women's Higher Education, 1889–1950," *History of Education Quarterly,* 26 (Winter, 1986): 503–522.

Black Souls

A PLAY IN SIX SCENES   1932

❧

Annie Nathan Meyer

PERSONS OF THE PLAY

(IN ORDER OF THEIR APPEARANCE)

ANDREW MORGAN, *Principal of Magnolia, a School for Colored People in the Black Belt*

PHYLLIS MORGAN, *his wife, Lady Principal of the school*

ETTIE, JAMIE, *their children*

DAVID LEWIS, *Phyllis's brother. A poet. Professor of Belles Lettres*

CORINNE THOMPSON, *a young teacher*

ULYSSES CLARK, *another young teacher*

SENATOR VERNE, *State Senator*

LUELLA VERNE, *his daughter*

JUNIUS AUGUSTUS, *a small boy*

THE GOVERNOR OF THE STATE

A QUARTETTE OF COLORED SINGERS

The entire action of the play takes place within eight hours, a few years after the World War.

Scene 1: The study of the Principal of Magnolia. Morning.
Scene 2: The same. Noon.
Scene 3: In the neighboring woods. Two hours later.
Scene 4: The same as Scene 1. Shortly after.
Scene 5: The platform in the school Assembly Room immediately following Scene 4.
Scene 6: The same as Scene 1. Sunset.

SCENE I

The study of the Principal of Magnolia, a school for colored people in the Black Belt. The furniture of the room is simple, yet in good taste. The walls are well lined with books; sunshine floods the room. Through the two French windows there is glimpsed a suggestion of the lovely Spring of the far South. The door at back leads into the hall—and so into the auditorium of the School. The door at the left leads into the bedroom.

ANDREW MORGAN *is seated at his desk which is covered with an orderly array of wire baskets filled with papers, reports, etc. Some students are rehearsing the lovely spiritual* "Steal Away" *in the Assembly Room across the hall.*

As the singing proceeds, PHYLLIS *opens the door of her bedroom and stands there, listening quietly. Phyllis is dressed very daintily, though simply, in a summer gown. Andrew smiles at his wife as she enters and she smiles back at him.*

PHYLLIS: (*as the singing ceases*) How beautiful! There's nothing lovelier in the world!

ANDREW: The boys have been practicing hard. I hope the guests will be pleased.

PHYLLIS: (*smiling*) Isn't that typical! I was thinking of their sheer beauty—you of what they could accomplish for the school.

ANDREW: Yes. I was thinking it might open their purses.

PHYLLIS: (*shaking her finger at him mockingly*) Andrew! Andrew!

ANDREW: (*as she comes near to him, he catches her hand and plays with her fingers*) It's all very well for you and Davey to laugh at me, but it's up to me to pay the bills.

PHYLLIS: I know. I know. It hasn't been easy.

ANDREW: There have been times when I almost lost faith.

PHYLLIS: You! No, I can't believe that.

ANDREW: (*gently, smiling*) I said—almost. (*continuing reminiscently*) The hardest thing was when I had no money for my teachers. Do you know, Phyllis, I think our school has been blessed with the most wonderful, self-sacrificing men and women in the world.

PHYLLIS: They do work hard. And now getting ready for the visitors the past few weeks on top of their regular work—I wonder if we really had the right to ask it of them!

ANDREW: They're glad and proud to do it. They know what all this means to us. It's the first time the visitors from the North have included Magnolia in their tour. Just think, besides the Governor, we're expecting the Chairman of the General Education Board, the Treasurer of the Slater Fund, a Harvard Professor and the President of Oberlin. Why, there isn't a teacher in the whole school who isn't as pleased as I am.

PHYLLIS: They *are* dears. Well, it's you who inspire them!

ANDREW: And who inspires me? My dear, my dear, it doesn't seem quite respectable to be so fond of each other after eight years of married life!

PHYLLIS: Dear Andrew!

ANDREW: (*rises, tucks her arm under his and goes to the window*) It makes me feel pretty proud to look out there. (*quietly, but with deep feeling*) Guess I know every stick and stone on the place.

PHYLLIS: And love it!

ANDREW: And love it! There's nothing I wouldn't do for it. You can't help loving what you've suffered for. When I think of those old days, trudging from door to door, like a beggar, not knowing where I was to lay my head, without decent food for days—

PHYLLIS: (*sympathetically*) I know! (*after a pause*) Remember the night the girl students came to you and said they couldn't stand the cold rooms any longer? And you told them stories about Booker Washington and the hardships he endured to get an education, until they were ashamed of themselves!

ANDREW: And that very night, after they'd gone to bed, the mail brought me a check for fifty dollars. (*chuckling*) And I harnessed up and roused old Jackson out of his bed and made him sell me twenty-five comforters.

PHYLLIS: And in the morning when the girls woke up and found them on the beds, they thought a miracle had happened.

ANDREW: (*simply*) It had. (*after a pause*) And it wasn't the only miracle. Look what's grown from one ramshackle log cabin. It'll look nice to see the new dormitory there, won't it? I tell you Phyllis, Senator Verne's been a mighty good friend to Magnolia. And now taking the Chairmanship of the Board of Trustees. (*as Phyllis moves off and begins to finger things on Andrew's desk*) You still don't like him after all he's done for us?

PHYLLIS: I still don't like him. I wish he weren't coming.

ANDREW: (*amused*) If your old grandmother was alive, she'd give you fits. Why the Senator is quality—he's from one of the finest old families in the state.

PHYLLIS: (*with suppressed passion*) When will we colored folk stop being over-awed by Quality? Quality should mean Character.

ANDREW: (*following her over to her desk*) Oh, but my dear, the Senator's been pushing that bill to pay better salaries to the colored teachers. He'll be in Washington next, you'll see.

PHYLLIS: (*troubled*) You think he'll be a United States Senator?

ANDREW: (*jovial, oblivious to his wife's nervous dread, he seats himself again at his desk*) Yes. It'll be mighty handy to have a real friend of our people in the Senate.

PHYLLIS: (*below her breath*) "A real friend!" (*She looks at him as if hesitating whether or not to confide her troubles to him. Finally she decides in the negative. He is absorbed in something on his desk and does not look up. Phyllis goes to him and passes her hand gently over his hair. She is embarrassed and feels for words*) Would you be terribly disappointed, Andrew, if Senator Verne didn't give us that new dormitory after all?

ANDREW: (*looking up, surprised*) Disappointed? Well, I should say so. Why the bottom would drop out of all my plans. I'm fitting up the old dormitory for the new electrical courses. The boys are just wild to be electrical engineers. Why do you say such things?

PHYLLIS: Oh, I don't know—just so's you wouldn't be too much disappointed if he changes his mind—if—he sort of loses interest in the school—

ANDREW: (*heartily*) He's more interested than ever. And he isn't a man to go back on his word. (*this Phyllis finds very disturbing*) He's already told me it's going to be a Memorial to his late wife.

PHYLLIS: Here! (*suddenly breaks out into hysterical laughter*)

ANDREW: (*jumping up*) Why Phyllis! What's the matter? Sit down. You're overtired. I've let you do too much.

PHYLLIS: (*sitting down in his chair*) No, I'm all right. (*but she laughs some more, though not so violently*)

ANDREW: Coming again so soon after the Easter visit can only mean one thing—

PHYLLIS: (*with a meaning which he fails utterly to read*) Yes, only one thing.

ETTIE: (*running in with her little brother. Both are dressed in white, she with a beautiful pink ribbon bow in her hair*) Oh, Mother, Mother, are we all right? Will we do for the parade?

JAMIE: (*also running up to his mother*) Are we all right? When does the parade begin?

PHYLLIS: (*looking them over*) Yes, you look fine. But how on earth am I going to keep you like that until the guests arrive! (*looks out of the window*) Here comes Uncle Davey, he'll help me out. (*The children run to the window and wave their little hands frantically, jumping up and down.*)

DAVID: (*enters through the window. The children are evidently very fond of their uncle and greet him vociferously to the great danger of their clothes. David hugs Ettie and pats Jamie on the head. He greets his sister affectionately*) You look as fresh and lovely as the Spring morning.

PHYLLIS: For goodness' sake, Davey, don't crush her dress. I'm wondering how on earth I'm going to keep them clean 'til the procession is over.

DAVID: (*admonishing Ettie not to be so wild*) Do you hear now? And what is Jamie going to be? Captain? Drum Major?

ETTIE: (*dancing up and down*) We're going to throw flowers on the path.

JAMIE: (*proudly*) We're the head of the procession.

DAVID: My!

PHYLLIS: We're all so busy—around here—had to get them dressed early. But now I don't know what on earth to do with them.

DAVID: (*smiling*) So you want me to keep them right side up. Come on chickabiddies! (*as they come on him with considerable enthusiasm*) Hey there! Didn't you hear your mother say I've got to return you in all your starched elegance? Slowly, now, slowly! (*He takes their hands and soberly, very gradually walks to the window with them.*) I'll take them to watch the May pole being decorated. (*to the children*) Now, I'm going to be your little boy, and you're my father and mother, and fathers and mothers always walk along nicely and show their little boy how to behave. (*He disappears with his charges, who walk before him very sedately.*)

PHYLLIS: (*looking after him and sighing*) Andrew, Davey isn't happy here.

ANDREW: (*worried*) You've noticed it, too?

PHYLLIS: Davey'll never be contented here. Ever since he came back he's been eating his heart out for those evenings in Paris at the café—writers, poets, painters—

ANDREW: Paris! His work lies here with his own people who need him.

PHYLLIS: No, it won't work with Davey. He's always craved to be with beautiful things. When he was a little fellow, he was always running to the Great House. Mama tried beatings to stop him. They taunted him with wanting to go White. I can see him now, sobbing his little heart out: "It isn't the white folks—it's because they got all the pretty things." He used to trudge two miles every day—not to the back door for cookies, but to hang about the front to get a peep at the lovely things inside. Once he'd been hiding in the bushes for hours just to watch the fountains playing.

ANDREW: Yes, it isn't an easy world for black men. It's hell for black poets. (*Laughter is heard outside and* CORINNE *and* ULYSSES *enter through the window. Corinne carries some spring blossoms in her hand. Ulysses is crazy about her and watches her every moment.*)

PHYLLIS: (*taking the spray from Corinne that she offers her*) Oh thanks. How lovely! Have you finished decorating the Assembly Room?

CORINNE: Yes ma'am, we thought maybe you'd like some in here.

PHYLLIS: (*smelling her spray*) How sweet they are!

CORINNE: No sweeter'n you.

ANDREW: Good for you, Miss Thompson.

ULYSSES: There won't be a sweeter-looking woman here—not one. (*He looks embarrassed at Corinne who laughs*)

PHYLLIS: (*looking at him mockingly*) Now you've gone and done it! (*Ulysses looks crushed*)

CORINNE: He hasn't done anything at all. Don't I know this mahogany blonde ain't much on looks? I have to be appreciated for solider qualities.

ULYSSES: (*to hide his embarrassment*) I'll go get the basket.

CORINNE: I'll help you carry it.

PHYLLIS: Have you thought of the guests' rooms?

CORINNE: Oh yes, Mrs. Morgan, the whole place smiles a welcome.

ULYSSES: (*to Corinne as the two leave by the window*) I know where there are some fine boughs.

DAVID: (*entering from the door to the hall. He holds up his hands comically as Phyllis looks inquiringly at him.*) It's all right! I left them quietly watching the rehearsal of the May dances. Miss Nutting has them in tow and swears she'd guard their immaculateness.

PHYLLIS: Thank you, Davey.

ANDREW: You weren't at breakfast, Davey. Feeling all right?

DAVID: Oh yes, perfectly, thank you. I took a long walk in the woods. Nature is the only thing around here that isn't upset over the coming of the great folks. The pines stood up as straight and unbending as ever.

ANDREW: (*very gently*) I don't think you need any lessons, my boy, in standing up straight and unbending.

DAVID: (*at right looking out window*) You'd rather see me truckle to my Lords and Masters?

ANDREW: (*at table; hurt*) The coming of these distinguished visitors means a great deal to me. I had hoped to all of us.

DAVID: (*instantly his usual charming self. His smile has rare charm*) Sorry! Of course they do. I get in these black moods. (*crosses left*)

ANDREW: They don't do any good.

PHYLLIS: Well, if you two will excuse me, I've a couple of things to attend to. (*leaves through the hall door*)

DAVID: (*looking after her*) Phyllis is a saint!

ANDREW: She is the sunshine of the place. She was in town all day yesterday. Did you know? They wanted her to confer about the Day Nurseries.

DAVID: (*downstage left; ironically*) The white women beginning to take the colored women seriously, eh? (*looking as if he'd like to say something else, but thinks the better of it*) Good! And I suppose you expect lots more wonderful things to happen from the distinguished visitors being here, eh?

ANDREW: Yes, it puts us definitely on the educational map—besides Senator Verne—

DAVID: (*ironic*) There's a man who seems no end interested in the school—no end—

ANDREW: What do you mean?

DAVID: (*uncomfortable*) I think he's interested in Phyllis.

ANDREW: Nonsense!

DAVID: The Vernes were the big people down our way when we were children. Did the Senator show the slightest interest in the school until his visit here at Easter?

ANDREW: (*heartily*) No, his interest started when he saw for himself what splendid work we were doing. Had a hard time persuading him to come, but once here, just like any number of others, his interest was aroused. You see how soon he comes again.

DAVID: (*drily*) Yes, I see! That daughter of his coming, too, I suppose?

ANDREW: Yes, pretty little thing!

DAVID: (*below his breath*) Damn sight too pretty. (*Andrew looks at him in astonishment*)

ANDREW: What do you mean? Do you know her?

DAVID: Yes, she was over there.

ANDREW: In France?

DAVID: Yes, you know my regiment was attached to the Fourth French Army. That was when they didn't know what to do with us—before they had got up their nerve to start persecuting us—

ANDREW: I know—I know.

DAVID: She'd been in school there and joined the French women at once.

ANDREW: You saw much of her?

DAVID: (*hesitates a second*) She was mighty decent. Think of a southern girl asked to wait on niggers! Another American girl said she'd see them starve first!

ANDREW: It was a great thing for her to learn that a man may be a brave soldier even if his skin is black.—And you haven't seen her since?

DAVID: (*passionately*) You don't think for a minute any friendship between us would be possible here!

ANDREW: What are you going to do? Avoid her?

DAVID: (*bitterly*) Take my cue from the young lady—just as any gentleman would. (*sits on chair alongside of desk*) But look here, I didn't come here to chatter—I came to ask you to look at the blackboard I've fixed up. I'm afraid I can't impress your distinguished visitors as easily with improvements in the teaching of literature as you can with improvements in ears of corn.

ANDREW: (*gets up; putting his arms affectionately about David's shoulder*) I'm proud of my corn, and I'm proud of my lumber mills, and my blacksmith shop, but I'm proudest of all of having the poet David Lewis on my faculty. (*David laughs and makes some sound of skepticism, but he is pleased. Andrew continuing with a little chuckle*) Maybe I do boast a little more to the white folks of my new tractor. They're more interested in our potatoes than our poetry.

DAVID: (*quoting with amusement*)

> "What deeds have sprung from plow and pick
> What bank notes from tomatoes!
> No dainty crop of rhetoric
> Can match one of potatoes!"

ANDREW: You know, it isn't easy to get the best scholars to an Industrial School. Once I get them here, I can knock some good, hard sense into them about the dignity of Labor. But it's the fact that you are here to teach them that brings me my best men and women.

DAVID: (*as the two go out together through the door to the hall*) You're absurdly generous, old man, tho' I don't say it isn't easy to listen to! (*exit both*)

ULYSSES: (*peeping in from the window*) I tell you there's no one here.

CORINNE: (*entering*) They've gone? Come, we must hurry. The grand folks will be here soon.

(*All during this scene they place boughs of spring blossoms about the room.*)

ULYSSES: (*hugging her*) You've certainly made me one happy man. Honey! Honey! I don't deserve it.

CORINNE: Now you quit running yourself down! President Morgan said he'd trust you quicker than anyone else to go out and bring the tradition of Magnolia to the people.

ULYSSES: That's honey to my ears all right. For that's just what I'm going to do.

CORINNE: (*her face falling*) Oh, 'Lysses, are we going to leave here? (*he nods*) I love it so!

ULYSSES: So do I love it, but you know our education's only loaned us so we can lend it to others.

CORINNE: (*overwhelmed at the thought of leaving the place she loves so*) Oh, 'Lysses! Have we got to go away from here?

(*It may be suggested to the Director to have some of the students rehearsing spirituals outdoors. Very low while Ulysses speaks.*)

ULYSSES: Yes, Honey-love. Leave all the comforts. Leave the nice, clean, white beds, and the warm coverings at night. And the sweet-smelling rooms. Leave all the good food, and the people who know you and like you and think like you do. Leave Magnolia and go out into the dirt and the misery, and hunger and cold. And no decent place to lay your head when night comes. But we go out in His name. Are you afraid, Honey? Will you refuse to help your people who need you so bitterly?

CORINNE: (*looking at him proudly*) Of course, I won't refuse. You'll be at the head of your own school.

ULYSSES: Plenty of hard work before that will come.

CORINNE: Pshaw! It won't take you long—I know! That will be fine! You'll be a big man—like Dr. Morgan and Booker Washington.

ULYSSES: Well, anyway, I'm not going to take you away until I've got a little place all fixed up for you.

CORINNE: You go away from here, without me! No, I'm going with you when you go.

ULYSSES: I'll just go ahead a little bit and find the best place to settle down.

CORINNE: No. I want to share all your hardships.

ULYSSES: There'll be plenty left for you to share. Don't you worry! But I've got to see where we'd be welcomed. There's white folks with guns loaded for Negroes who want to put up schools. They're afraid we're going to fill them full of conceit and not knowing their place. Why, Honey-love, there's plenty places where you wouldn't be safe.

CORINNE: I'd not be afraid with you!

ULYSSES: (*earnestly*) No, Corinne, I couldn't protect you. There are white men who think nothing of taking a colored woman away from her husband.

CORINNE: (*shrinking and grabbing his arm*) Oh, 'Lysses!

ULYSSES: Yes, I'm not taking any chances. If a fellow can't protect his own wife from another fellow—there ain't no use calling yourself a man.

CORINNE: We'll be married before you go?

ULYSSES: Yes, indeedy! Not taking any chances that way, either. (*she laughs*) And I'm coming back for you just as soon as ever I can. You bet your life on that, I won't need any urging.

ANDREW: (*entering with David*) So! You two've settled it. Good!

DAVID: (*putting out his hand to Ulysses*) Congratulations, old man!

ULYSSES: We're going to start a school, Professor, down where I came from.

ANDREW: That's fine!

ULYSSES: I'm going to go down first and have a look around.

DAVID: (*stage left; jokingly*) Good! Never had half a chance with you hanging around.

CORINNE: We're going to be married first. Isn't it wonderful?

ANDREW: (*gravely*) Yes, Miss Thompson, it's just that. We'll miss you, but every one of us will be willing to work harder, because that's what our school was founded for—for its graduates to go out and found more Magnolias where they are most needed.

CORINNE: I know I'll work for two while he's gone.

ULYSSES: Well, I'm not gone yet. Maybe I'll be coming back again defeated like old Please Williams.

DAVID: Poor old Please! He was some discouraged. But Ulysses, just you let the white folks think you're going to educate the Negroes away from the cotton fields, and you'll come back all right—in a pine box.

CORINNE: (*grabbing Ulysses's arm*) Oh, Professor Lewis!

DAVID: That's all right. I was only fooling. (*but they all know there is much grim truth in what he said*)

ANDREW: I guess Ulysses and Miss Thompson know the hard struggle that lies before them. But they'll not flinch from it. They aren't the flinching kind.

ULYSSES: Thank you, Professor Morgan. I've got it all thought out. I won't take any books with me at first. I'll say I'm going to teach the poor colored folks to patch their roofs and mend their fences. The white folks won't mind that.

CORINNE: (*anxiously*) Yes, 'Lysses, don't you go getting the white folks down on you. Getting cocky just don't get you anywhere. (*Andrew exchanges an appreciative glance with David.*)

PHYLLIS: (*entering and sizing up what has happened between Ulysses and Corinne*) Well, well, what's all this? (*as Corinne rushes up to her, and lifts her face eagerly to her. Phyllis kisses her*) I'm so glad. She'll make you a wonderful wife, Mr. Clarke.

ULYSSES: I know she will, Mrs. Morgan. Thank you.

CORINNE: Thank you all very much. Well, we must be going.

ULYSSES: Yes. Thank you all for your good wishes.

ANDREW: (*as the two leave through the window*) You certainly have them. (*turning to Phyllis*) You'll miss her in your work. She's admirable with youngsters.

PHYLLIS: (*smiling mischievously*) Almost as good as David is. I'll miss her, but I'm so glad for them both. Only there's something so pathetic about all colored couples. It does seem as if they marry into such a terrible struggle. Indeed, they don't wait for trouble to come. They go out half way to meet it.

ANDREW: Yes, they are starting out to found another Magnolia that will be a torch to the ignorant. (*sits at desk*)

DAVID: (*at a shelf of books picking out a book*) Lucky if it doesn't prove to be a torch to their own oil-soaked bodies.

PHYLLIS: Oh, Davey, don't!

DAVID: (*as he glances through the pages of the book*) My dear girl, the South says it is afraid of Negro dishonesty and ignorance, but it's more afraid of Negro knowledge and efficiency.

ANDREW: Isn't that a little harsh?

DAVID: (*shutting the book and crossing to Andrew*) There's no good shutting your eyes to the truth. They want things to remain as they are. They don't want them to improve. They'll look on Ulysses as a trouble maker.

PHYLLIS: Oh, Andrew, maybe we shouldn't let them go!

ANDREW: (*with a sad smile*) If a black man begins to run away from trouble, he'd have to run clear off the earth.

DAVID: (*crosses to window*) No, only off these "benighted States!"

PHYLLIS: Well, I can't stay and listen to you both bang away at each other—I've got work to do. (*leaves through hall door*)

ANDREW: Davey, you're unjust. More and more men of the South are ashamed of the way we've been treated. They're going to see to it we get a square deal.

DAVID: (*at window*) Ha! We've scared them by so many going North. They're beginning to be afraid they won't get the crops in. They're full of talk just now about the South loving the Negro, understanding him better! They're actually beginning to advertise in the papers "The land of the citron and the magnolia calls to you." Blah!

ANDREW: You can't deny that our school has powerful friends.

DAVID: (*crosses to Andrew*) Of course, it has. It keeps colored people in their place. You acknowledge the dominance of the white race. All your life, Andy, you've been counselling patience instead of defiance.

ANDREW: I've tried hard to follow Christ's way.

DAVID: How they do love to stress Christ's meekness—when it suits their purpose! How about Jesus the rebel, denouncer of hypocrisy and injustice? We hear precious little of him!

ANDREW: Love accomplishes where hate defeats. We are slowly gaining ground.

DAVID: There speaks the "slave mind" in you. Haven't you realized yet all the boasted "loyalty" of the Negro was just his "Slave-mindedness"?

ANDREW: They were splendidly loyal to their trust.

DAVID: Loyal to whom? To their friends or their enemies? If they'd had the souls of free men, they'd have told the white men to stay at home and take care of their own crops and their own women folks. They'd have risen as one man to fight with the North that was trying to set them free. And it's just the same slave mind the South is trying to keep in us today. Are you blind? Didn't they resent it when in France we were being treated like men? Didn't they circulate all sorts of lying stories? Were we allowed to march with the other American soldiers on Armistice Day? And when we returned to our grateful country, did they cheer us? No, they were too busy seeing we were kept in our place! Did they think of our blood—as red as theirs—spilled on Flanders Field? No, they jeered and hooted at us because we held ourselves up straight as men. Uncle Sam's uniform was no protection for black men. The authorities even took away our guns and our pistols for fear we'd resent the insult to our country's soldiers. And they clapped our men into jail and murdered some in cold blood because with our bare hands we succeeded in showing a bit of the indignation that was seething and boiling within us!

ANDREW: I know. I know. There have been grave injustices. But things are improving all the time. There are not near so many lynchings—

DAVID: —Because the Negro has learned to shoot back. Nigger hunting isn't the safe sport it was before the War.

ANDREW: (*turning and pacing the floor*) I wish I could make you see the importance of this work we're doing—see it with my eyes, love it with my heart. It doesn't seem to me there is anything—anything it would ask of me that I wouldn't give it—cheerfully. Did I ever tell you how near I came to dying for it down at Misgah?

DAVID: No.

ANDREW: (*sits on desk*) No, I never even told Phyllis. I didn't want to worry her. When the colored people heard I was trying to start a school, they came trudging in for miles about. The pathetic eagerness of those poor people for an education! It was a warm day and the Church windows where I spoke were open. A couple of lads riding by misunderstood what I was saying about fighting the battle of ignorance, and rode off spreading the news that I was egging them on to rise up and massacre all the white folks. Davey, never again do I want to see such abject fear as was on the faces of those poor people when the mob rode up to get me.

DAVID: I can imagine.

ANDREW: Without giving me a chance to say a word, a rope was flung about my neck and I was dragged along. . . . When I regained consciousness I was lying on a pile of wood, and I smelled gasoline.

DAVID: Andy!

ANDREW: Hundreds of faces looked down on me and not one look of pity—not one. The boys climbed a tree with the end of the rope in their hands. (*David groans*) Suddenly, an old man—drunk—held up his hand—"You're so good with the gab" says he "go on and talk!" They loosened the rope—I tumbled to my knees—too dizzy to stand. So I closed my eyes and prayed. Lord how I prayed! Then I talked as I never had before—I knew it was my one chance for my life. I told them I was only trying to teach the darkies how to live decently. I promised them I wouldn't educate them above their position— that I'd make them better farmers, better carpenters, better neighbors.

DAVID: Well, what happened?

ANDREW: The old drunk cut the rope about my neck and they took up a collection then and there. They pressed into my hand more than three hundred dollars—the biggest sum I'd received yet.

DAVID: A narrow shave!

PHYLLIS: (*rushes in, opens door upstage*) They're here! They're here!

ANDREW: So early? (*Looks at his watch. He also goes to the door upstage. David goes to the window and stands looking out with his back to the door.*)

(SENATOR VERNE *enters with his daughter,* LUELLA, *a pretty girl of seventeen. Verne shakes hands with Andrew and quickly turns to Phyllis and shakes her hand.*)

VERNE: Motored over from the junction. The Governor bet me he'd get here as quick by train. But you see he was wrong!

ANDREW: (*smiling*) Our trains don't put themselves out hurrying any.

VERNE: (*to Phyllis*) My daughter.

PHYLLIS: Glad to meet you.

LUELLA: I'm glad to meet Davey's sister. (*Crosses to David*)

PHYLLIS: You know my brother?

VERNE: Met him I understand over there. You see Luella was in school in France.

PHYLLIS: (*quietly as she watches Luella greet David*) I see. I see!

ANDREW: If you'll excuse me I'll run down to the Guest House and welcome the Governor when he comes.

VERNE: Then I'll go with you—I want to collect my bet. (*to Phyllis*) Won't you come with us?

PHYLLIS: Certainly.

(*All three exit.*)

LUELLA: (*at window*) Well, aren't you glad to see me?

DAVID: (*trying to stand on his dignity, and be a bit offish, but it is not easy with bright eyes and challenging red lips smiling at you*) I am always glad to welcome friends of Magnolia.

LUELLA: "Friends of Magnolia." I thought I was your friend.

DAVID: You were—in France.

LUELLA: Well?

DAVID: This is not France—it is Dixie Land—

LUELLA: No, it isn't France, but you and I are the same—no, I believe you are different—you have changed.

DAVID: (*passionately*) No, the change was over there—when for the first time in my life I found myself treated like a man.

LUELLA: You taught me to respect the man—do you wish me to unlearn it all?

DAVID: It would be wiser—you are no longer in a land where a man is a man "for a' that."

LUELLA: You make it very difficult for me.

DAVID: It is difficult. Why pretend it is anything else?

LUELLA: I like doing difficult things.

DAVID: So long as you don't attempt the impossible.

LUELLA: (*with a coquettish toss of her pretty head*) Who knows what's impossible 'til one tries?

DAVID: There are some schools that teach one.

LUELLA: I've never been there, and I refuse to be frightened. I am still your friend and I want to know all about your life—everything.

DAVID: (*bitterly*) At your service. Until something more amusing turns up!

LUELLA: Do you think that's quite fair?

DAVID: Forgive me! I don't mean to hurt you, but—oh, how can I make you understand? Do you realize if you and I should go into town together in a motor as we did in France, the mob would drag me from my seat?

LUELLA: Nonsense! I don't believe you.

DAVID: Oh, I don't mean, of course, if I were your chauffeur—they'd permit me to drive your car if I were in the front seat and you in the back.

LUELLA: The South then has learned nothing from the War? Nothing?

DAVID: No, but the Negro has. (*Luella laughs, a little light laugh.*)

LUELLA: You are going to show me the place. I'm crazy to see everything.

DAVID: I shall be only too glad to show you through the grounds.

LUELLA: Oh, but the woods, too, they looked so attractive as we drove here.

DAVID: No, you must get another guide for the woods.

LUELLA: Nonsense. I remember you know all the flowers, and the bird notes. Do you remember that day in the woods near Main-de-Massige?

DAVID: Must I remind you again that this is not the Champagne sector of France?

LUELLA: And you've got to show me the old shack where you wrote your poems.

DAVID: (*touched*) You remember that?

LUELLA:

> "I had forgot wide fields and clear brown streams
> And now unwillingly you've made me dream."

DAVID: You can still quote it? You haven't forgotten!

LUELLA: (*meaningfully*) I've forgotten nothing. Tell me, do you still use it? Or do you do your work here?

DAVID: (*with a quick reaction as if he does not care for the atmosphere of the school*) Here! No, I couldn't write here.

LUELLA: (*understandingly*) I know—too much the professor.

DAVID: (*crosses to sit at desk*) Yes, I can lecture about poetry—talk about it for hours at a stretch but when it comes to writing it—creating— (*leaves it go with a gesture*)

LUELLA: I know.

DAVID: I suppose I've got used to the feeling of being all alone—cut off by myself—no one knowing where I am—used to the sound of whispering winds that go searching by—

LUELLA: (*crosses to desk*) I just can't wait to see it. Let's cut as much of the ceremonies as we can, and—

DAVID: (*gets up*) No. I can't take you out there.

LUELLA: (*hurt*) You don't want me to see it? Your Holy of Holies!

DAVID: It isn't that!

LUELLA: (*skeptical*) Oh, isn't it!

DAVID: It's outside the grounds of the school.

LUELLA: Well, what of it?

DAVID: (*smiling*) That remark shows how long you've been away from here.

LUELLA: (*impatiently*) Well, I'm here now—and I do ask.

DAVID: (*as if half to himself—anyway it slips out*) God! You are beautiful!

LUELLA: Ah, now you're more like your old self!

DAVID: Miss Verne, believe me, it would be much better for both of us if you would forget those beautiful—those wonderful days together in France.

LUELLA: (*tauntingly*) The Captain Lewis I knew then was a very brave man.

DAVID: Even he would be afraid for you now—and here.

LUELLA: You and I have faced danger before—do you remember when you saved my life?

DAVID: Miss Verne, I beg you to believe that the hellishness of your white aristocrat is worse than that of the enemy we knew.

LUELLA: (*turns away*) The War that was to make the world safe for Democracy!

DAVID: Not for the black world. (*They stand talking to one another.*)

PHYLLIS: (*enters with the Senator, crosses to Luella*) I'll show you over to your room, Miss Verne. You might like to freshen up after your trip.

VERNE: (*crossing over after Phyllis*) Nonsense! You needn't make any compliments with Luella. She'll find her way all right.

LUELLA: Of course! Or Professor Lewis can show me the way across the campus. Won't you?

(*David bows stiffly.*)

PHYLLIS: (*uncertainly to David*) You don't know her room.

VERNE: (*draws Luella to him. Looks at her adoringly*) What do you think, Mrs. Morgan, this young rascal refused to be left behind! Gave up a dance, and all sorts of things to come here with her Dad. (*Luella looks slyly at David who looks annoyed.*) What do you think of that, eh?

LUELLA: Well I knew they were going to make a lot of you and the gift of Verne Hall and I always like to be on hand to see you get what's coming to you.

VERNE: (*amused and looking significantly at Phyllis*) H'm! Is that a compliment or a threat?

LUELLA: (*pertly*) A threat if you don't behave.

VERNE: Well, perhaps, Professor Lewis, you will be good enough to show my daughter the way?

DAVID: (*stiffly*) Certainly, Sir.

PHYLLIS: (*greatly distressed at the tete-a-tete Verne is forcing on her; to her brother*) You know the South Guest Room?

DAVID: Of course. (*he passes through the window with Luella*)

VERNE: (*at window*) So now that I've come back as I said I would, you haven't much of a welcome for me after all!

PHYLLIS: (*center, trying to speak very conventionally to cover both his real meaning and her own embarrassment*) Yes, indeed, we all appreciate so much your coming. It was very good of you.

VERNE: I don't care a hang about what you "all" thought. Are you going to be good to me?

PHYLLIS: Why certainly! We'll do everything in our power to make your stay pleasant.

VERNE: (*crosses to Phyllis*) You will, will you? You know what I want. There's no use running away from me as you did last Easter. I'm going to see you don't run away from me this time.

PHYLLIS: (*crosses to window; formally*) You've made my husband so happy, Senator Verne, over your gift. It is most generous of you.

VERNE: That's nothing to what I can do. That's only a beginning. Think of all I can do for the School and for your husband.

PHYLLIS: (*going to the window*) Have you seen yet the site for Verne Hall? (*as he comes behind her and grasps her by the arm, she gives a little frightened gasp*) Maria Verne Hall in memory of your late wife.

VERNE: (*close to her, amused*) You needn't think you can switch me off that way! (*laughs*) If she were alive right now, it wouldn't make any difference. Why should it? (*gloating over her*) I haven't had a woman weave a spell like this over me for years. What is it? You're handsome. But it isn't that. I've known plenty of handsome women. There's something about you—

PHYLLIS: Senator Verne, please!

VERNE: You're afraid of someone coming?

PHYLLIS: Please! Please! I've told you you have no right—

VERNE: You weren't so stand-offish when you were a girl.

PHYLLIS: You had me in your power then.

VERNE: I have you in my power now.

PHYLLIS: No!

VERNE: I can tell your husband.

PHYLLIS: (*indignantly*) What can you tell him?

VERNE: (*slyly*) You know.

PHYLLIS: Yes, you can tell him that you took advantage of me when I was sixteen years old—coming to your house to sew—I saved every penny I could lay my hands on to get an education. I was afraid of you—you told me if I complained I'd be put in jail—I was all alone—my brother was away at school. I knew no one would believe me anyway.

VERNE: You were a damned attractive little thing—but by Jove! You're even more attractive now. I never was so surprised as when I came here last Easter. Your husband had been bothering me for years to come. Why didn't I come sooner?

PHYLLIS: Senator Verne, you don't seem to understand. I don't love you—never have—I love my husband—I adore him. (*The Senator continues to look at her, smiling cynically.*) You think I'm making a ridiculous fuss for a colored woman! But let me tell you, I'm just as proud of my honor as a white woman is of hers—

VERNE: I know too many colored women.

PHYLLIS: (*walks right*) You know easy-going black women and you know plenty of easy-going white women. I tell you there's hundreds of black women like me who love our husbands and are faithful to them. We are mothers—don't you think we want our children to respect us and look up to us? (*looks at him as he stands there, a cold sneer on his face*) Oh, what's the use! I'm only wasting my breath. But God knows—if it's hard for the black man to rise—it's been harder still for the black woman. You dare to talk about the black man's lust. Good God! You—the kings of the earth! You—the superior white man! What do you think when God looks into your souls, and into the souls of my people—don't you think He sees which are really white and which are black?

VERNE: (*crosses to her*) All very fine—but I want you— (*He tries to grab her in his arms and kiss her. They struggle.*)

VOICE OF GOVERNOR OUTSIDE: Where are you, Senator?

VERNE: (*who was following Phyllis, turns and rushes to the hall door*) Coming Governor, coming! (*Alone, Phyllis sinks to a chair, panting, distressed.*)

CURTAIN

(*to indicate passing of a short time*)

SCENE 2

Scene: Same as Scene 1.

Phyllis discovered on a low seat with her two children leaning against her knee. The proud bow is somewhat crushed and the starched immaculateness of both children's clothes is somewhat dimmed—yet they must not look at all unkempt.

PHYLLIS: (*finishing the story she has been reading them*) "Thus died that brave and noble soul Crispus Attucks. Never forget, boys and girls, that it was one of your own race who was first to fall in the great Cause of the American Revolution. Always cherish the proud fact that the blood of a Negro was the very first blood to be shed for the freedom of America." (*She closes the book.*)

ETTIE: Is that all?

PHYLLIS: Yes, that's all.

JAMIE: (*with a long sigh*) When I grow up I'm going to be a Crispus Attucks.

PHYLLIS: I'm sure my boy will grow up to be a fine, brave man, like his father.

JAMIE: Yes, but I'd like to give my blood for my country. (*Phyllis hugs him*)

ETTIE: Isn't there any more at all?

JAMIE: Tell us another, Mummie.

PHYLLIS: No, Jamie-Boy, Mother has to attend to something. You can both sit over there in the corner and look at the pictures. Remember, you promised if I let you sit here in Father's study, you'd be very good. (*She rises, goes to her bedroom. At the door she turns and watches the children tenderly. They have seated themselves in the corner and are turning over the pages of the book.*)

ETTIE: (*eagerly putting her forefinger on a page*) Cris— Crismus—

JAMIE: (*laughing at her*) Crispus, Goosie!

PHYLLIS: That's right. Crispus Attucks. Think of him and always be proud of your colored blood. (*goes into the bedroom*)

DAVID: (*entering*) Hulloa, kids!

(*Both children spring up excitedly. Ettie clasps her little hands about Unkie's knees and clamors for a kiss which he gives her. Jamie tugs at his coattails.*)

ETTIE: Unkie, Unkie, you tell us a story!

JAMIE: (*jigging with delight*) A story! A story!

DAVID: (*catching Ettie up and swinging her to his shoulder whence she looks down on Jamie, swinging her legs in triumph*) So you want a story, eh? I don't know any new ones.

ETTIE: Tell us 'bout Queen Ethiopia.

JAMIE: No, no, bout General Toussaint l'Ouverture.

DAVID: (*swinging Ettie down and placing her carefully on his knee as he seats himself. Jamie stands expectantly leaning against his other knee*) Let me see, let me see—oh, I know! (*begins very solemnly*)

> "Bridle up er rat,
> Saddle up er cat, And han' me down my big straw hat.
> In come de cat,
> Out go de rat
> Down go the baby wid 'is big straw hat."

(*He carefully spills laughing Ettie from his knee, holding on to her hands.*)

JAMIE: (*eagerly*) Do it to me!

PHYLLIS: (*poking her head in from the bedroom door, and smiling as she watches her brother, whom she adores, playing with her children*) Now children, it's time for lunch.

(*Jamie turns obediently toward his mother while Ettie does not budge. Possibly Jamie's stomach asks more clamorously for its food.*)

ETTIE: (*clapping her hands*) Oh, Unkie give us the scarey one! Mummy, can't he just tell us the scarey one?

PHYLLIS: Well, just that one, and then come in and wash your hands. (*She stands and watches David turn up his coat collar and crouch toward the children while they stand in fascinated, wide-eyed terror.*)

DAVID: (*speaking in a deep, hoarse voice*)

> "W'en de big owl whoops
> An' de screech owl screeks
> An' de win' makes a howlin' sound,
> You liddle woolly heads

Had better kiver up
'Case the hants is comin' 'round."

(*The children scream in mock—and half real—terror as he grabs them. He escorts them to their mother. Phyllis takes Ettie's hands. As he approaches the door, Jamie holds out his hands.*)

JAMIE: My hands ain't dirty. (*starts to go back to his uncle*)
PHYLLIS: Let's see those wonderful hands. (*after an inspection of them*) Humph!
    I thought so. (*she grabs him by the arm and the three disappear into the bedroom*)

(*The moment David is alone his expression changes. He looks anxious and upset. Andrew enters. For an instant the two men look at each other. Andrew looks grieved, David a bit surly.*)

ANDREW: So, you couldn't stick it out! It was only a few minutes more.
DAVID: I couldn't stand their damnable smugness—all the empty, meaningless
    flattery. How you could endure it! You were actually purring.
ANDREW: They've gone to a great deal of expense and trouble to come all the
    way down here.
DAVID: (*ironic*) "You're the most wonderful teacher the South has seen, white
    or black." "The most eloquent orator." "The wisest leader your people have
    known." Oh, I grant you they know how to fling their compliments! But you
    mustn't break bread with the white folks. You're doing more to help the
    South than any two other men, but the luncheon table musn't be polluted by
    your black skin!
ANDREW: (*trying to pass it off as a matter of course, but his heart is wounded, deep
    down*) Glad to have a moment's breathing space.
DAVID: If it was Hampton, the Principal would be eating with the distin-
    guished guests.
ANDREW: (*quietly*) You forget the Principal of Hampton is a white man. (*he
    turns to David affectionately*) I know you suffer. But, it's better to be the one
    who suffers than the one who inflicts suffering. You haven't forgot what
    Booker Washington said: "The man who is down, looking up, can catch a
    glimpse now and then of Heaven, but the man who can only look down is
    quite likely to see another and quite different place." Why man, you yourself
    wrote: "It's from the trodden flower true fragrance springs."
DAVID: Well, your distinguished guests having gazed their fill at a nigger shoe
    a horse and another roof a house, they think possibly the Negro is worth
    saving.
ANDREW: I also showed them one of America's greatest poets.
DAVID: (*with one of his rare smiles*) That's taking an unfair advantage of me. But
    how on earth could you be so polite to that old freak who asked you if you
    weren't afraid of educating the colored women away from domestic service!
    And to that sharpnosed Yankee who comes buzzing around here every year
    for cheap scab labor!

ANDREW: Well, anyway, you showed both of them where they get off.

DAVID: I know it. I've probably offended them and they won't come again.

ANDREW: (*with a wry smile*) That "old freak" as you call her—was good for two hundred and fifty dollars a year.

DAVID: I'm awfully sorry, Andy. I'm no good here. Doing you no good and no good to myself. You'd better let me go.

ANDREW: (*his face falling*) Go? You?

DAVID: Yes, I've made up my mind. I wasn't going to say anything to you, but I'm sailing day after tomorrow—you mustn't try to persuade me this time.

ANDREW: (*reproachfully*) You were going away without saying a word to me?

DAVID: We've been over it all so often. Why, Andy, I realize I'll never amount to anything 'til I can get away from here. In Paris I can hold up my head— live where I choose—walk where I choose—eat where I choose.

ANDREW: (*bewildered*) You are sailing day after tomorrow?

DAVID: (*imploringly*) Yes, Andy, old man, don't try to stop me. I can just make the four ten at the junction.

ANDREW: Davey, is there any special reason for leaving just now? Are you running away from anyone?

DAVID: Maybe I am! But what's the difference? You know it's nothing new with me. I want to feel free!

ANDREW: (*scornfully*) Free! You want to feel free? But how about the other twelve million you leave behind—will they feel free? You want to get away from the petty injustices—from the hatreds and the torture of being despised and trampled on!—I know. But it'll go on just the same. And if you're doing nothing to stop it, you can't get away from it no matter how many thousand miles you go. You may escape physical lynching, but let me tell you, you will be morally lynched.

DAVID: (*much moved*) Andy!

ANDREW: (*implacable*) That's what the Negro is who turns his back on his own people, morally lynched! (*David is tortured*) You say you can't live here. Well you won't be living there—you'll be dead. (*David starts*) Yes, dead at the heart—the worst kind of death. You want to go away from all the terrible things that happen here—You want to forget. But there are some things a man can't forget. There are some things a man has no right to forget. Can you forget how your little home was burned to the ground, the home your father was so proud of, the home he worked so hard to build? Can you forget how he was shot down in cold blood for doing what any man would do who calls himself a man?—for protecting a young girl from drunken white beasts? And your mother. Do you want to forget how she was killed for passing a gun to your father? And how your little sister Carrie's head was smashed in because she clung to her mother's skirts? Do you want to forget how you ran in the night, stumbling and falling, until you came to old Zeb's house, with your sister Phyllis in your arms? And how you swore you'd always stay by her and protect her? And do you dare to forget that you dedicated your life to educating the colored people so they'd know how to protect themselves? Forget! Why, man, you might as well try to tell me you can forget that your heart beats as to tell me you can forget the past that throbs in your veins!

DAVID: (*in crushed, dull tones*) Very well Andy, I'll stay! (*with a sudden flash of his old spirit*) I think it's a mistake. I honestly do. (*again hopeless*) But I'll stay.

(*With an exclamation of delight, Andrew clasps David's hand. David snaps his jaws determinedly. His eyes seem to read into the future the Tragedy that lies inevitably there. But he has given his word. He squares his shoulders to meet whatever Fate holds in store for him.*)

CURTAIN

INTERMISSION

SCENE 3

2 P.M. Deep in the woods, the interior of an old, broken-down shack is seen. It must give the impression of being surrounded with trees and bushes. Possibly something of this is seen on one side of the shack, or if necessary, the undergrowth may be seen at back through door and window. It should be broken down just enough to give picturesqueness.

Luella and David enter. Luella is enormously interested and looks about and examines various things with glee.

LUELLA: So this is where you wrote all those wonderful poems?

DAVID: (*at door; amazed at her enthusiasm and curiosity, but nervous at having weakened and brought her here so far from the school grounds*) Yes, this is the old shack.

LUELLA: (*reading from script on a table where stands a typewriter*)

> "How came your lips to touch the sacred fire?
> How, in your darkness, did you come to know
> The power and the beauty of the minstrel's lyre?"

DAVID: Now we'd better go.

LUELLA: Go! Why, I've just come.

DAVID: I know it, but you'd very much better not have come at all. (*Luella makes a little face at him and examines his desk.*) Please come!

LUELLA: (*looks at the script*) I want to see what you're writing now.

DAVID: (*takes paper from her; suddenly realizing what is there, tries to hide it from her. She struggles laughingly and manages to glance at it—suddenly cries "Oh!" and lets him take it from her. He places the paper in the drawer of the desk.*) It's not finished. Now then—you know we have a long walk back.

LUELLA: Yes, that's why I want to rest now. (*seats herself on couch*) Give me a cigarette.

DAVID: (*after he has handed her a cigarette and lit it for her*) It's only half a mile to the school grounds, we can rest there.

LUELLA: Young man, I prefer to rest here.

DAVID: (*edging to door*) Miss Verne, I begged you not to come here. Really, you must go back at once. I had no right to weaken. You don't understand what you're doing—and I do. Do you think you could find your way back alone?

LUELLA: Brrr!—you can't frighten me with all the bogies you're trying to stir up—but I'd be scared to death to walk through all those woods alone—

DAVID: Then I'll go and send Corinne back for you.

LUELLA: I must say, you're not treating me at all nicely. I'm surprised at you, Lieutenant David Lewis!

DAVID: I did as you asked me.

LUELLA: Pooh! You walked through the woods sulking.

DAVID: (*quickly*) Sulking? (*He looks as if he wants to say a lot more, but suppresses it.*)

LUELLA: Yes, you used to promise to teach me the bird notes.

DAVID: The birds seemed so absurdly happy—I'm out of tune with them.

LUELLA: I begin to think that as clever a poet as I have always thought you— you're even cleverer at making excuses—and running away. When you left for here you thought I was safe at the luncheon, didn't you? (*as David does not answer at once*) Didn't you?

DAVID: Yes—I did.

LUELLA: And you say you're not clever at running away!

DAVID: (*smiling*) Not clever—wise! (*Luella tosses her head.*) Also a true Spartan—give me credit for that, please.

LUELLA: You have given me no reason to think that you have been denying yourself anything.

DAVID: No Spartan wears his heart upon his sleeve.

LUELLA: (*lightly*) Have you a heart?

DAVID: (*a spasm of pain crosses his face*) I was permitted the luxury of one in France.—Why didn't you stay at the luncheon?

LUELLA: I hate listening to speeches. You are angry that I followed you?

DAVID: Come, we really must turn back now.

LUELLA: I'm not going back yet.

DAVID: (*gravely*) It is far safer to talk in the grounds of the school.

LUELLA: I don't want to be safe. Why do you treat me like a child?

DAVID: You've lived in tolerant France—you can't believe what the South is.

LUELLA: I can't believe any sane man or woman could see any harm in our remaining friends.

DAVID: Sane? But I tell you on the subject of black and white the South isn't sane.

LUELLA: Oh forget it! Forget it like we used to forget Big Bertha booming away—When I first arrived at the hut I was like that other southern girl. But the French girls made me ashamed of myself. I fed your soldiers, and I read to them and played to them and sang to them, you remember?

DAVID: (*with deep feeling*) Yes, I remember.

LUELLA: I danced with you—and nothing happened.

DAVID: Did nothing happen to you?—It did to me!

LUELLA: (*embarrassed for a moment by his meaning*) Well, anyway you've warned me now and done your best to frighten me off. Sit down.

DAVID: (*sits beside her and enters into her mood*) What is your wish, Madame Princess—a slice of the moon?

LUELLA: I want you to tell me some more of those wonderful folk tales you used to tell me—they're fascinating.

DAVID: What is new—and strange—is apt to be fascinating.

LUELLA: (*with a little shiver*) Yes.

DAVID: But there is one story you ought to hear.

LUELLA: (*with raised eyebrows*) Ought?

DAVID: (*quietly persistent*) Ought!

LUELLA: You won't ever let yourself forget you are a schoolmaster.

DAVID: There is so much I won't let myself forget.

LUELLA: Won't?

DAVID: Won't!

LUELLA: Go on, I hate cocksureness.

DAVID: May you never lose yours! Well, once there was a fairy princess who walked in a fairy woods with an old, old man—

LUELLA: I don't like stories about old men.

DAVID: Well, he wasn't really so very old in years, but in experience, in knowledge of evil, and suffering, he was, oh, immeasurably older than she.

LUELLA: Go on!

DAVID: And as they walked in the fairy woods, the fairy princess dangled before the poor man's eyes all the most beautiful things of life, all he had ever cherished, all he had ever longed for, all he had ever dreamed.

LUELLA: She did that?

DAVID: Yes, oh yes! All this wonderful, wonderful treasure, she held out to him, dazzling him with its splendour.

LUELLA: And yet, dazzled as he was, he spurned what she offered him?

DAVID: He did not spurn it. He was afraid to touch it—for her sake.

LUELLA: For her sake?

DAVID: Yes, for he alone of the two knew the danger. The inevitable tragedy, the heartbreak.

LUELLA: I think your old man was a very foolish man.

DAVID: Foolish? Or full of wisdom?

LUELLA: Foolish to turn away from what his princess offered him. How could she ever learn, save through experience?

DAVID: There are some things it is better not to learn.

LUELLA: No. I want to know everything. (*rises, stretching out her arms passionately*) To feel everything, to experience everything!

DAVID: (*also rising and looking at her*) Greedy children are always punished.

LUELLA: I have never been punished in my whole life.

DAVID: I wonder what life will do to you!

LUELLA: I'm not afraid of life.

DAVID: Youth unafraid!

LUELLA: I want life—I want it—bubbling over the brim. (*looks into his eyes challengingly*)

DAVID: (*looks at her*) You are not afraid? You are such a child!

LUELLA: I'm not a child! . . . I am a woman—with the feelings of a woman.

DAVID: (*his face near hers*) And you are not afraid?

LUELLA: I am afraid of nothing. You hear? Nothing!

DAVID: (*stands regarding her passionately. He struggles with a desire to take her into his arms. Suddenly he catches sight of a white face peering in at the window*) God! (*this is murmured below his breath. Swiftly he makes up his mind to do what he can to save her. He would rather be killed for the usual cause than have her encounter the scorn and possible violence that would be aimed against her if white men suspected her of actually inviting him to bring her to this lonely place in the woods. Therefore, he seizes her by the arm and drags her to the old sofa in the corner*)

LUELLA: (*astounded*) What are you doing? Are you crazy?

DAVID: (*pulling her to couch. Speaking in a thick strange voice, but very loud*) What am I doing? Just what I intended doing when I forced you to come out here with me, against your will.

LUELLA: Why, David—

DAVID: (*hisses in her ear*) Don't deny it! Your good name—your very life depends on it. (*continues to drag her roughly*)

LUELLA: Stop! Stop, I say!

(*At the open door two men stand. They say nothing, but each holds a gun in his hands.*)

QUICK CURTAIN

SCENE 4

4 P.M. Scene the same as Scenes 1 and 2.

The stage is empty. JUNIUS AUGUSTUS, *a very small and very black boy, enters through one of the windows. He looks behind him fearfully, then about the room.*)

JUNIUS AUGUSTUS: (*calling in a husky whisper*) Missy Morgan! Missy Morgan! Is you dere, Missy Morgan?

PHYLLIS: (*calling from her bedroom*) Yes, want me?

JUNIUS AUGUSTUS: Missy Morgan! Missy Morgan!

PHYLLIS: (*entering*) Yes, what is it? Why, Junius Augustus, what is the matter?

JUNIUS AUGUSTUS: (*his eyes rolling as if they will roll out of their sockets*) Is all you alone, by yourself?

PHYLLIS: (*amused*) Yes, I'm all alone. (*then disturbed by the boy's evident fear*) Why, what's the matter with you? (*tries to be severe, but the boy's appearance is more conducive to laughter*) Now why do you want to know whether I'm alone or not? Junius Augustus, you've been getting into mischief again!

JUNIUS AUGUSTUS: No'm I ain't done been gettin' into no mischief.

PHYLLIS: You've been doing something naughty, or you wouldn't be so scared.

JUNIUS AUGUSTUS: (*in an agony of fear*) I—ain't skeered o' nothin'.

PHYLLIS: (*smiling*) No, you're only frightened out of your wits. (*sits down, takes him by the arms, tries to get him to confide in her*) Now, tell me all about it. (*There is a slight scraping sound outside. Phyllis turns her head, but does not place the sound as coming from the window. But Junius Augustus gives a shivery, hopeless glance in the right direction. He cowers as he looks back to the window through which he entered the room.*)

JUNIUS AUGUSTUS: Yas'm.

PHYLLIS: Who sent you here?

JUNIUS AUGUSTUS: (*swallowing hard*) Mr. Davey sent me.

PHYLLIS: David? My brother David—nonsense!

JUNIUS AUGUSTUS: Yas'm, Miss Morgan.

PHYLLIS: You don't mean to tell me he scared you like that?

JUNIUS AUGUSTUS: No'm. (*chuckling*) Mr. Davey, he never scared no one. (*Then remembering his errand, he sobers up.*)

PHYLLIS: Well, somebody did. What did Mr. David send you for?

JUNIUS AUGUSTUS: (*speaking very deliberately, as if repeating a lesson*) He done send me for his coat.

PHYLLIS: (*puzzled*) His coat? What coat? Look here, Junius Augustus, are you trying to steal a coat from me?

JUNIUS AUGUSTUS: No'm, I ain't trying to steal nothin'.

PHYLLIS: After all I've done for you!

JUNIUS AUGUSTUS: No'm. No'm. I ain't stealin no coat. My Pappy he don' need none now.

PHYLLIS: (*laughing*) A good reason for not stealing one! Sonny, why on earth does my brother want a coat? Why does he send you for it? And what kind of a coat does he want?

JUNIUS AUGUSTUS: I don't know—jus' some kin' of a coat he's been wearin'.

PHYLLIS: (*suddenly struck with a thought*) Has he gone horsebacking? Has he fallen from his horse? Is that it? Is he hurt?

JUNIUS AUGUSTUS: Yas'm. No'm.

PHYLLIS: (*exasperated*) Well, which is it?

JUNIUS AUGUSTUS: (*confused*) Yas'm, he done fall off'n his horse. No'm, he ain't hurt.

PHYLLIS: You're hiding something from me. Is he seriously hurt? Where is he? I'll go to him.

JUNIUS AUGUSTUS: (*earnestly*) Oh, no'm, don't you do dat. He—he ain't hurt—he jes' done fall off'n his horse—an'—an' tore his coat.

PHYLLIS: Then why doesn't he come home himself and get another one? Oh, well— (*sees her husband's coat hanging on the back of his desk chair*) Here, take this one of my husband's. 'That'll do.

JUNIUS AUGUSTUS: (*very much upset*) Oh, no'm, dat won't do at all!

PHYLLIS: Why not? (*Junius Augustus shakes his head vigorously*) Of course, it will! My husband and my brother are much the same size.

JUNIUS AUGUSTUS: Oh no'm. He said mos' partickly it must be one of his own coats.

PHYLLIS: (*she throws Andrew's coat down again*) Well, wait here, I'll go upstairs. No, I've got a coat of his right there—I was mending it. (*As she goes into bedroom, a shadow falls on the window and a hoarse voice threatens the boy who is thrown nearly into a fit.*)

VOICE: Hurry! You little devil! Hurry! Don't you try any monkey tricks with me. (*The shadow disappears as Phyllis enters the room again carrying a coat.*)

PHYLLIS: (*handing the boy the coat*) Here. Tell Mr. David to hurry home. The big meeting's going to begin.

JUNIUS AUGUSTUS: Yas'm. (*scoots off with the coat through the window. Phyllis arranges something on Andrew's desk. She fondles his coat, lays her cheek against it.*)

PHYLLIS: Dear old Andy! Shabby and worn like him! (*She takes the coat into her bedroom. Returns without it. Hears the voice of her husband talking to the Senator. Leaves quickly by the window*)

ANDREW: (*outside the door*) It's mighty good of you, Senator.

VERNE: (*outside the door*) We'll step in a second before it begins—you can put it in your desk. (*enters just ahead of Andrew. Turns and hands him a folded document*) Here's the deed for the farm, duly registered. I've just returned from the Court House.

ANDREW: (*taking the document from the Senator*) It's wonderful, Senator. I don't know how to thank you. (*He unlocks a drawer in his desk, places the paper there, locks up the drawer again.*)

VERNE: (*who has been looking about the room eagerly*) Good! I thought you said your wife was here?

ANDREW: She was a minute ago. (*goes to the bedroom, opens the door*) Phyllis! Oh, Phyllis! She must have gone to get a seat, it's getting pretty crowded. Great occasion! I tell you, Senator, that was a splendid thing to do for us—after all you've already done, too.

VERNE: Oh that's all right. The land wasn't doing me any good. And I knew you could farm it to good purpose.

ANDREW: (*happy*) It gives me just the acreage I wanted for an experiment in crop rotation.

VERNE: Fine! You're becoming a real power in the community. I bet you a lot of the white farmers come to you for advice.

ANDREW: Oh well, I do what I can.

VERNE: Yes, you've built up a wonderful position for yourself—it redounds to the credit of your whole race. Everyone looks up to you as a true leader of your people.

ANDREW: (*glowing*) That's mighty nice of you Senator. What did you think of our Pageant showing the progress we have made?

VERNE: Beautiful! Beautiful! I had to slip off, though, to run down to the County Seat and get this fixed up. But what I saw was admirable! We've got used to expecting things from you—but I'm mighty sorry to see you haven't got all your Negroes around here in hand yet.

ANDREW: Oh, they're loyal—devoted to the school—seem to think I can do anything—but— (*anxiously*) Just what do you mean? Nothing wrong?

VERNE: Oh, some trouble down at the County Seat.

ANDREW: Trouble? Not—

VERNE: Yes.

ANDREW: Good heavens! Impossible!

VERNE: (*carelessly*) Some black beast.

ANDREW: Don't tell me a lynching!

VERNE: Yes, he got away somehow, but they'll catch him. They've sent for Ed Reilly.

ANDREW: The bloodhounds!

VERNE: The best in the State. They've sent for the man's coat to give the dogs the scent.

ANDREW: I must stop it.

VERNE: Pretty well out of hand by now, I imagine.

ANDREW: (*pacing up and down*) You don't know what it means. We haven't had any trouble like that since I came—it's terrible. I've got to stop it somehow.

VERNE: And lose all the popularity you've got?

ANDREW: I can't stop to think of myself. (*goes toward the window*)

VERNE: (*putting his hand on Andrew's arm*) But think of your people. See here, Morgan, you've worked up considerable goodwill for yourself and your school around here—I wouldn't like to see you lose it by acting foolishly—or rashly.

ANDREW: Very well. Then you must put a stop to it, Senator.

VERNE: I? I'm not trying to commit political suicide. (*Andrew groans a protest*) It's a pretty serious thing trying to stop a lynching in these parts—especially if it's for cause!

ANDREW: (*bitterly*) "For cause"! Some poor devil becoming too insistent for the money that's due him!

VERNE: Don't you believe it!

ANDREW: You don't believe me? I assure you it's the way it goes—the Negro becomes unwisely persistent for his money—the white man starts a rumor— oh, it isn't difficult after that!

VERNE: Well, anyway, you may be sure it wasn't that this time—I heard something about a nigger and a white girl.

ANDREW: They always say that!

VERNE: (*angrily*) I tell you the girl was found with him.

ANDREW: I know every Negro for miles around. There isn't one capable of such a thing. Maybe some half-witted fellow's come here who ought to be put into an asylum—

VERNE: (*severely*) Look here Morgan, this won't do! I've always liked you—thought you different from the rest of the educated niggers—got some common sense about you—I'm all the more sorry to see you taking it like this.

ANDREW: But Senator, I'm only trying to save the good name of our State.

VERNE: You're too damned reluctant to admit a nigger's guilt.

ANDREW: But why not try him? Your juries are white, your Judges white, the whole machinery of the Law is in white hands. Why, you don't even allow colored people to testify. Surely you can't be afraid of a miscarriage of justice.

VERNE: (*stiffly*) There are some things a man of red blood refuses to subject his women to.

ANDREW: But you subject them to killing innocent men!

VERNE: There you go again with your "innocent" men! Don't you ever admit that a nigger is guilty? That's the matter with the whole of you— I'm forced to realize you're no different from the rest— This shielding and protecting of your own people has got to stop. You hang a damn sight too close together. We white folks won't stand for it. We white men are banded together in the most sacred Cause in the world—the Supremacy of the White Race. And we mean to maintain it—at all costs—you hear? At all costs!

ANDREW: But Senator, you know President Wilson said lynching was a blow at the heart of the nation. I appeal to you—I appeal to you in his name to use your authority and stop this lynching.

VERNE: No man in his senses would stop a lynching that had gone as far as this.

ANDREW: You'd be honored for it—from one end of the country to the other.

VERNE: I'd live on the front page for a day—then total oblivion.

ANDREW: (*going toward the door*) I'll appeal to the Governor.

VERNE: (*barring his way*) Are you mad? The Governor will do nothing. I know him better than you do.

ANDREW: I can't believe it. I tell you the people of the South are beginning to wake up to this national disgrace.

VERNE: (*quietly but significantly*) Not the people who nominate for second terms.

ANDREW: (*crushed*) God!

VERNE: (*not unkindly*) Tell you what you do—I'll send you down in my car— (*Andrew goes to thank him*) After you've finished your speech. (*Andrew looks crushed*) Why man, you've got in there the greatest audience you've ever had. You can't afford to make a rumpus. They'd never come again. After it's all over you can go down there, find out what you can—keep my car as long as you like. Why, for goodness' sake, man, what's one nigger against all you can do right here and now for hundreds—thousands of them? Pull yourself together, Morgan. Remember how long and how hard you've worked just for this chance. (*pulling out his watch*) I'll go in and tell them you'll be with us in a minute. (*He leaves swiftly through the hall door. As he reaches the Assembly Room, faint applause is heard. Andrew, alone, looks after the Senator for an instant, tries to control himself. His face works. Finally he beats his clenched hand on his desk.*)

ANDREW: Hypocrite! Pharisee! Damn your smug soul! Damn you! Damn you!

PHYLLIS: (*she has entered just in time to hear him.*) Why Andrew! (*rushes over to him*) What's happened?

ANDREW: (*stands an instant looking at her, gradually recovers his composure, though his breast still heaves*) I don't wonder you're surprised at your smooth, truckling husband. (*suddenly sits down bewildered, with his head in his hands*)

PHYLLIS: What upset you so?

ANDREW: (*rising unsteadily and looking at her*) He told me—that man just told me—

PHYLLIS: (EVA ZOE:*frightened*) Who? The Senator? (*Andrew nods his head. Phyllis can barely control her terror.*) What's he told you?

ANDREW: He told me there's a lynching—a lynching— (*Phyllis had expected to hear something quite different. She claps her hand over her mouth to hide her feelings, for she realizes she can't afford to show her relief.*) A lynching going on right now as we're talking. And I can do nothing. Davey's right. I've bowed and scraped, and kowtowed till I have no manhood left.

PHYLLIS: What are you going to do? They're waiting in there for you.

ANDREW: (*bitterly ironic*) What am I going to do? I'm going in there to make my Annual Address. I'm going in there to make a speech while five miles away one of my own people is being done to death. Am I going in there to tell them they're cowards? Lip servers? False Christians? No. I'm going to tell them what splendid citizens they are. How noble, how generous! Am I going to tell them they're making the constitution of the United States the laughing stock of the whole world? No. I'm going to tell them what a wonderful people they are—so much better than all the rest of the world put together. "Protectors of Democracy" for the whole of civilization. And we can't even abide by the laws we make for ourselves.

PHYLLIS: Andrew! You must control yourself.

ANDREW: (*sardonic*) Oh, don't be afraid! Do you think I'm going to tell them the truth? Oh, dear me, no! That wouldn't do at all. I'm going to tell them how well the black people and the dear, kind white people get on here. Hypocrite! Truckler! Liar! (*He squares his shoulders and goes to the door. Then he turns around to his wife, and just before he disappears, he says:*) They've sent for Ed Reilly's bloodhounds.

(*Alone, Phyllis gradually recalls Junius Augustus' terror—his request for David's coat—his refusal to accept Andrew's coat instead. With a terrible cry she springs up and runs after Andrew.*)

PHYLLIS: Andrew! Andrew! Don't go in there! Don't go in there! (*loud applause from the Assembly Room. She realizes it is too late.*)

CURTAIN

INTERMISSION

SCENE 5

The platform in the Assembly Room.

Note: This scene may be given effectively and inexpensively by means of black drapes. The stage becomes the platform of the school auditorium. The audience becomes the school audience. On the platform are seated Andrew, Senator Verne, the Governor, Ulysses and Corinne, and the quartette of singers. It would be well to have some of the other distinguished visitors if it can be arranged.

As the curtain rises, the spiritual "Holy unto the Lord" is being sung. When it is over, there is applause.

VERNE: (*who is Chairman, rising*) And now, we are to have the great pleasure and honor of listening to the Governor of this State. (*applause*) An upright man, sensitive to the fair name of our beloved Commonwealth, fearless in the performance of his duties, unmoved by Clamor or Vituperation. His Excellency, the Governor.

THE GOVERNOR: (*a large man who speaks ponderously and in the deep voice and insincere tones of the politician*) My friends:

It is a great pleasure for me to be with you today. I have long heard of and admired this wonderful school, of yours, and since coming here and seeing it for myself, my admiration and wonder have grown by leaps and bounds. I only wish that my own son and daughter could have the inestimable privilege of getting their education at such a splendid institution. (*much applause. Andrew, who has seemed listless, his mind far away, now smiles ironically at the Governor, a smile, however, which is quickly suppressed.*) Fortunate indeed are you young men and young women who are today leaving the shelter of your loving Alma Mater so magnificently equipped for the battle of life. For our good friend here, the Principal of Magnolia, I have long held the greatest possible esteem. He is a sincere and honest worker in the Lord's Vineyard who has rightly looked upon Education as a tool to be used rather than a jewel to be treasured. Without putting foolish ideas of equality or of false grandeur into the heads of his people, he has, on the contrary, taught them to become better farmers, willing and able tillers of the soil, workingmen, self respecting, God-fearing laborers, knowing their place and keeping it.

The problem of the South, ladies and gentlemen, is not an easy one; it is to carry on within her body politic two separate races nearly equal in numbers. She must carry these races in peace, for discord means ruin. She must carry them separately, for assimilation means debasement. She must carry them in equal justice, for to this she is pledged in honor and gratitude. (*loud applause, led by Verne*) It is not easy, but it is possible—we must each and all of us make it possible—for these two races, white and black,—to show without embarrassment to either that the two races can live together, peacefully, helpfully, honorably and harmoniously here in the South, each making its own contribution to the glory of our great country. In all your high endeavors to reach this goal you may be assured of the unstinted sympathy and cooperation of every good man and woman in the South. We are not only willing, but eager to help. We most earnestly deplore the occasional outbreaks of ill wind between white men and black men. We realize that both black and white must exercise self-control, a spirit of tolerance, and a deep-seated desire to accord to each other absolute justice and fair play. (*The Governor sits down amid applause. Andrew springs up as if to speak to the Governor. Verne motions him to sit down and steps to the front of the platform.*)

VERNE: We shall now listen to some more singing. (*A spiritual, "Every Time I Feel the Spirit," is now sung.*)

VERNE: The Principal of this School—the utterly fearless, indomitable man who has built up Magnolia from a single log-cabin—needs no introduction from me. (*applause*) Andrew Morgan is the outstanding Negro of this generation. His sturdy, forthright nature hasn't the slightest conception of the meaning of the word defeat. I really believe that never in his whole life has he compromised with what he believed to be the Right. I present to you Andrew Morgan, leader of his people, Educator, Orator, and Founder of the greatest institution in the world for creating and preserving the self-respect of the Negro. (*applause*)

ANDREW: (*rising and coming to the front. Verne seats himself*) Friends from far and near, I am glad to welcome you to Magnolia. You have spent the day seeing the outside of our School. I would like in a few minutes to give you some idea of its inner Spirit. For it is not so important that my pupils go through Magnolia, as it is that the spirit of Magnolia should go through them. (*applause*) When you are dealing with men and women, you are dealing with forces where the spirit is the master. You can not conquer a human being until you have first conquered his spirit. And the spirit is often unconquerable. We Negroes must keep an unconquerable spirit in the face of discouragement. Remember, if you white people find the riddle of life too hard to read, we black people find it just a little harder. If it is difficult for you white people to find and face your duty, it is even more difficult for us. If your heart sickens in the blood and dust of the battle of life, remember for us the dust is thicker and the battle fiercer. I have been accused of thinking only of my own people, of forgetting the larger problems of the South. But this is not so. It could not be, for the problem of the Negro is the problem of the South. The South can never rise to its full spiritual or material status until it has broken off the curse of intolerance and mob violence. You know it was said that the great Lincoln, in taking the shackles off the slave, did not only free the slave, but the white slave-owner. Never was anything truer. The doctrine that some men are less than human brothers, dwarfs the man or the race that holds it, as well as it humiliates the men or the race toward whom it is directed. The supreme test of a nation lies in its attitude to dependent races. Are we Americans engaged in raising up these people who look to us for guidance? Or are we concerned only in keeping them in their place? It is not for me to make answer. But I want to plunge those questions into your hearts. In one respect at least we can all agree there has been distinct progress. There has been in the past year encouraging lessenings in the number of lynchings. (*The sound of hounds baying is heard, at first faintly. Andrew starts, but quickly recovers himself.*) Last year there were half as many as disgraced the South the year before. (*The baying grows nearer. Those behind him show signs of restlessness. The quartette leaves in excitement*) There were fifty-seven lynchings in 1922—and only twenty-eight in 1923— (*His voice is drowned out in the nearer approach of the hounds. Confusion*)

CURTAIN

SCENE 6

7 p.m. Same as Scene I. Dusk.

The afterglow of a passionate sunset comes through the window. At rise, the stage is empty.

Andrew enters from the hall—a pathetic figure utterly crushed in his grief. He crosses heavily to his desk and sits down. In a low solemn voice he recites as if to himself.

ANDREW:

> "Come!
> Let us go unto our God.
> And when we stand before Him
> I shall say—
> 'Lord I do not hate.
> I am hated.
> I scourge no one.
> I am scourged.
> I covet no lands.
> My lands are coveted.
> I mock no peoples.
> My peoples are mocked!'
> And white man, what will you say?"

(*A sob bursts from him. He buries his face in his hands.*)

PHYLLIS: (*heard from outside through the window*) Leave me be! Leave me be! Leave me be! I tell you! You think you've got me frightened like the poor little thing you took advantage of fifteen years ago. I'm not afraid of you, I'll show you up.

VERNE: (*also outside*) Who'd believe you?

PHYLLIS: I'll pull the mask from you so the whole world shall see what you really are!

VERNE: Who'll take a nigger woman's word against a white man's? I'll say you were my mistress and are furious because I won't take you on again. (*The moment Phyllis's voice is heard Andrew raises his head. He sits motionless in the shadow and is not seen at once by either Phyllis or Verne, until they enter.*)

PHYLLIS: (*as she sees Andrew*) Andrew! Kill that man—kill him!

VERNE: (*coolly but watching Andrew closely*) Returned a little sooner than you expected, didn't you?

ANDREW: (*rushing toward him*) You scoundrel! I'm going to kill you!

VERNE: Oh no, you're not!

ANDREW: What's going to stop me? I can kill you with my bare hands.

VERNE: You know what's going to stop you just as well as I do. You lay a hand on me and you'll start the biggest race riot the South has had yet.

PHYLLIS: (*noting that Andrew falters*) It was Davey, our Davey who was being lynched. I ran and ran through the woods. I couldn't find out anything. I fell down. I think I fainted. He found me—tried to take me there—you heard— as a child he had me—kill him! He's no good anyway. Kill him!

ANDREW: (*rushing toward Verne*) You damned cur!

VERNE: Look out what you're doing!

ANDREW: Doing? I'm going to kill you. (*Andrew gets his hands on Verne. The two struggle. Verne manages to free himself long enough to pant.*)

VERNE: There won't be a nigger left alive in the whole state.

PHYLLIS: He won't care! S'long as you're dead!

VERNE: (*seeing that Andrew clenches his hands, his face tortured with indecision, pressing his advantage*) But you care! You'll set the Negroes back two genera-tions. You, their leader—you'll destroy them worse than their worst enemy would. How do you like that, eh?

PHYLLIS: (*to her husband, scornfully*) Are you afraid?

ANDREW: For my body? No! For my people? Yes—horribly afraid!

PHYLLIS: (*impatiently stamping her foot*) Are you a man?

ANDREW: (*from the depth of his soul*) How in God's name can a Negro be a man?

PHYLLIS: (*contemptuously*) Truckler!

(*During this scene Andrew prays fervently, oblivious to what the others say. He is struggling for self control, praying for strength to conquer his desire for vengeance.*)

ANDREW: Oh dear God! Must I think of my people even now? He's shamed her, violated her. God! Do you care only for the purity of white women? I've got to kill him—I've just got to kill him.

PHYLLIS: Go on—kill him!

VERNE: What you do to me will be avenged on your people a thousand fold. You've just seen one lynching. Do you want to see hundreds— thousands?

ANDREW: Oh God! Give me the strength to keep my hands off him! Give me the courage to think only of my duty to my poor, persecuted people.

VERNE: You'll be lighting the torch that won't leave a nigger's cabin standing! Nothing but blackened stumps!

PHYLLIS: Don't listen to him!

ANDREW: Dear Lord, fill me with the spirit of the Master. "No man can drag me down to his level by making me hate him!" (*He opens his eyes, shows he has conquered himself—speaks after a pause with great sadness and immense dignity.*) After all—it is only one more sacrifice. I thought I had given my all—I was mistaken—I still had my manhood. (*He now has himself thoroughly in command. He straightens up, goes toward Verne and speaks in ringing, commanding tones.*) Sit down! (*Verne hesitates*) Sit down! (*Verne sits down wonderingly.*)

ANDREW: (*after a pause—while the two men watch each other and Phyllis watches both*) I'm not going to kill you.

PHYLLIS: Coward!

ANDREW: (*with quiet dignity*) No. A coward would have killed. I'm not going to touch you. But in a few minutes, you'll be begging me to kill you. (*to Phyllis in a lower voice*) Go get her. (*nods in direction of bedroom. Phyllis exits*)

VERNE: (*impatiently*) You bragged you're going to make me whimper. Try it! And be damned to you!

ANDREW: You'll whimper all right. Don't fool yourself. I'm not saving your life from any pity for you. Death would have been more merciful.

VERNE: (*his nerves growing taut under the strain*) Stop your boasting!

ANDREW: (*very gently*) It's not boasting. I've watched you. I know you. You're wrong-headed and evil-minded, and self-indulgent—

VERNE: (*ironic*) Go on!

ANDREW: You think nothing of forcing a colored woman, you don't think twice about breaking a colored man's home—or his heart—but there's one ideal in your pig-headed egoism you cling to—that your white women must be guarded against the black man.

VERNE: (*snarling*) And they'll continue to be guarded!

ANDREW: (*imperturbably*) You talk about "insuperable barriers" between the races, yet with five or six million mulattos it looks as if the barrier wasn't so great after all. You white conquerors stalk about as you choose among our coloured women—our sisters and our daughters and our wives, as free as you like. You don't see any harm in it. But once let a single black man retaliate among your white women—

VERNE: I'll get you for this!

ANDREW: (*scornfully*) Then your boasted Nordic supremacy really seems threatened. That man you stopped me from saving was my brother David.

VERNE: Huh! Do you think I'm going to beg you to kill me out of grief for him?

ANDREW: (*proceeding unmoved*) For this particular crime for which David was killed, it takes two— (*Phyllis leads in Luella. Her gown is disarranged, her hair down—she looks utterly wretched and distraught. Seeing her father, she puts out her arms to him. As he shrinks from her, she shudders and drops her face in her hands.*)

VERNE: (*beside himself*) He should have been cut in small pieces while he was alive ... I'd have wielded the knife myself. I'll have every nigger in this county boiled in oil—I'll—

ANDREW: (*his voice rising above Verne's scream*) I tell you David was killed for attacking your daughter. But that isn't the worst of it. It isn't even what you're going to think the worst of it. David was innocent.

VERNE: Like hell he was!

ANDREW: David Lewis was innocent. But he was guilty of being too complaisant to your daughter's wooing.

VERNE: You black devil! It's a lie—an infernal lie!

PHYLLIS: Why a lie? Weren't you crazy about me?

ANDREW: I congratulate you. Your daughter takes after you.

VERNE: No child of mine could so disgrace her white womanhood.

PHYLLIS: Not if you had first disgraced your white manhood?

VERNE: (*almost incoherent with rage*) No, no, no! You just want to see me suffer. I'll never believe it, I tell you, never, never, never! Luella, tell him he lies!

LUELLA: But it's not a lie—it's the truth!

VERNE: You slut!

LUELLA: Calling names won't do any good. What do you want of me? Why are you bringing me in here? (*looks about her*) This is the very room I saw him in a few hours ago, alive. (*wails*) Oh what have I done? What have I done!

ANDREW: (*crossing over to her*) One moment, please. I won't distress you longer than I have to—but I want your father to hear from your lips just what happened. Did you go walking through the woods with my brother this afternoon?

LUELLA: (*moaning*) Oh I did! I did! Why didn't I listen to him? Why didn't I listen to him!

VERNE: Do you mean to say that damned nigger didn't entice you there?

LUELLA: Oh no no! He warned me that it was dangerous. And when we were there he tried to get me to go back.

ANDREW: You mean to say my brother warned you not to go there, yet you persisted?

LUELLA: Yes. I wouldn't listen to him. I didn't believe him. I thought it was just his pride. I didn't know—I didn't understand—oh my God! How could I know? How could I understand? He told me I didn't know the South—but I wouldn't listen to him. I thought I knew better—I just wanted to be with him—

VERNE: (*beside himself*) My daughter beg for a nigger's favors! Is there no shame in you?

LUELLA: Yes I'm bitterly ashamed—bitterly. (*with a sudden flare-up*) Not for what you think—but because I was yellow—I couldn't stand up and face those men. I hadn't the courage to say it was all my fault—it isn't so easy with a gun stuck in your face—but they knew—they knew all right—they called me "Nigger-Lover."

VERNE: (*passionately*) That's what you are—damn you! Nigger-lover! Nigger-lover!

PHYLLIS: (*with intense scorn*) You dare call her that!

VERNE: I'm going to kill you—I tell you—I'm going to kill you. (*springs up. Andrew holds him, makes him seat himself again*)

PHYLLIS: (*scornfully*) You weren't thinking any of killing yourself, were you? What's she done I'd like to know that's made her not fit to live?

LUELLA: (*contemptuously*) You can kill me if you want to—do you imagine I want to live? You don't know—you can't realize—they cut off his hands and feet before they burned him alive—I didn't know men could be such fiends. They forced me to watch it. I tried to shut my eyes. I couldn't—his lips were bitten clear through in his agony—but he never let out a groan. I tried to call to him but not a sound came—there was a tree behind him—a bough like a cross—I prayed to him—to forgive me. But I can't forgive myself. I can never forgive myself—never! (*suddenly pleading to Phyllis*) Oh, don't look at me like that! Don't look at me like that! I didn't mean to—I didn't know—honestly I didn't!

ANDREW: Poor child! You couldn't have saved him—no matter what you'd have said.

LUELLA: What's that?

ANDREW: If you'd had the courage to tell the truth, it would have made it only worse.

LUELLA: Oh you think so? You really think so? You aren't just saying that to relieve me? Then I'm not guilty of his death? But I must be. He didn't want me to leave the school grounds—oh what have I done! What have I done! If only I'd have had the courage to tell the truth—if only I hadn't been ashamed to say I loved him.

VERNE: (*in disgust*) Love! You dare to call it love!

LUELLA: Yes, I know now father—

VERNE: Don't dare call me father—I disown you—I never want to set eyes on you again. You can go back to your beloved France where you can be as shameless as you like. From now on remember, you are no child of mine!

PHYLLIS: (*putting her arms about Luella protectively*) Yes, she is your child! That's just what she is! Blood of your blood and flesh of your flesh. How dare you think you can take us black women into your arms without your lusts getting into the blood of your children? If you want your women to stay clean, you've got to stay clean yourselves.

LUELLA: You can't think me unclean because I loved your brother!

PHYLLIS: No—but the whole world will.

VERNE: Every decent man will. (*His voice suddenly breaks. His rage leaves him. Utterly broken, he slumps in the chair and cries despairingly*) Oh kill me kill me, I ask it!

PHYLLIS: No! You'll live for this poor child. Live to protect her from herself. Now I know why you white men go out of your senses when a black man attacks your women. You call it by high-sounding names—"preserving the purity of the white race"—but it's just plain jealous fear. You know it isn't always the black man who runs after the white woman, sometimes it's the other way around. That's why you become wild beasts and burn and slay and cut up living bodies—you're afraid the truth will out—you're afraid your saintly, white women will be known for what they are!

THE GOVERNOR: (*speaking from outside in the hall*) Where are you, Senator? We've just got time to make the junction.

VERNE: (*rising and pulling himself together. Phyllis' terrific arraignment has made him writhe, physically and mentally. He has to control himself and rush out before the Governor will enter*) Coming Governor, coming! (*He puts his arm about Luella and helps her out as he continues talking*) Luella had a slight accident— (*The Senator and Luella leave. Phyllis sinks into a chair. Andrew remains near the window on the other side of the room. The stage is slowly darkening*)

PHYLLIS: I'll go away until you can forget.

ANDREW: But you can never forget that I failed you.

PHYLLIS: (*crosses swiftly over to him*) You! Fail me!

ANDREW: (*somberly*) You asked me to kill him.

PHYLLIS: (*looking into his face tenderly*) I was wrong to ask it. I should have known you'd put your people's heartbreak above your own.

ANDREW: (*in a voice vibrant with agony—all the more so because of all he has had to suppress*) No! A man would have let nothing, nothing come before his own wife! Oh God! No human being has the right to rob another of his manhood.

(*Outside the students are singing that lovely spiritual "Your Soul and Mine." Phyllis clings to Andrew. Together they stand there, her head on his shoulder. The spiritual stops.*)

SLOW CURTAIN

May Miller

(1899–1995)

In a 1987 interview, May Miller discussed her concern for the survival of humankind, a subject often reflected in her plays and much of her poetry. In her works, Miller deals with humanism and social and political issues, continually questioning the morality and humanity of the society in which we all live. Recognized as one of the most celebrated and prolific black playwrights of the 1920s and 1930s, along with her close friend Georgia Douglas Johnson, Miller wrote fifteen plays, eleven of which were published; many were staged by numerous little theatre groups and at colleges. The uniqueness of Miller's works during the 1920s and 1930s lies in her daring to venture from the home and to incorporate white characters in key roles. The inclusion of white characters in many of her works expanded the methods through which she could deal with racial issues of the time. Unlike most of her contemporaries, who contained the action of the play primarily to the American home, Miller set the action of her plays as far away as Africa and Haiti.

Miller was born January 26, 1899, to Kelly and Annie Mae Miller in Washington, D.C., on the campus of Howard University, where her father was a dean and prominent professor. Miller was greatly influenced by her father, an excellent orator who would recite the lines of many poems. Miller's creative life was also enriched by her attending the noted M Street School (later known as Dunbar High), where she studied under playwrights Mary Burrill and Angelina Grimké. Burrill encouraged Miller to write her first play, *Pandora's Box*, in 1914. The play was published that same year in the *School Progress Magazine*.

After graduating in 1916, Miller enrolled at Howard University, where she received further encouragement to write under the direction of professors Alain Locke and Montgomery T. Gregory. Academically at the helm of her class, she earned a B.A. in 1920, and at her graduation she won the first playwriting award for her one-act drama *Within the Shadows*.

After graduation, Miller taught drama, speech, and dance at the Frederick

Douglass High School in Baltimore. Her years at Douglass were both prolific and active. She wrote plays in order to educate her students about black history. Miller, along with many of the black writers of the time, also saw drama as a vehicle for effecting social change. While in Baltimore, Miller joined W. E. B. Du Bois's Krigwa Players, which was an early Negro Little Theatre group dedicated to promoting black playwrights. Miller performed as well as directed for the Krigwa Players. During the 1920s and 1930s, Miller submitted her plays to various literary contests. In 1925 *The Bog Guide* placed third in the *Opportunity* playwriting contest. *The Cussed Thing* received an honorable mention in the 1926 contest. During her summer months, Miller studied playwriting at Columbia University under the prominent theatre scholar Frederick Koch, who further encouraged her. Under his guidance she wrote *Scratches* (1929), which was published in the University of North Carolina's *Carolina Magazine*.

Miller's creativity was further stimulated by the lively atmosphere of Georgia Douglas Johnson's S Street Salon, a gathering place for writers to share their works. Miller would commute on weekends to S Street. Here she cultivated an array of friends, among them such writers as Alice Dunbar Nelson, Countee Cullen, Jessie Fauset, Carter G. Woodson, Marita Bonner, and Langston Hughes. During an interview, Miller commented on the S Street gathering:

> Everything Georgia Douglas did was informal. . . . Maybe ten people would attend at a time. Because as I told you, she didn't have too much sitting arrangement. It was a drop-in place. And she just made everybody at home and even, well, Du Bois used to go there too. Langston went, of course. I was with Langston many times when he was there. Owen [Dodson] went too. . . . Well, Richard Wright was there one night too. . . . Well, it wasn't really a membership. She'd just say to two or three people in town, well come on over tonight. It was that informal.[1]

During one of her visits to S Street, Miller was persuaded by historian Carter G. Woodson to collaborate with Willis Richardson on an anthology dramatizing the lives of black heroes and heroines. The result was *Negro History in Thirteen Plays* (1935), written primarily for high school students. For the anthology, Miller contributed the plays *Harriet Tubman, Sojourner Truth, Christophe's Daughters,* and *Samory.* The landmark anthology, which was one of the few publications featuring works by black playwrights, garnered national recognition for Miller and Richardson.

Nails and Thorns is Miller's only piece which focuses on the topic of lynching. Though she did not remember her motivation for writing the play at the time, she entered the one-act in a 1933 contest sponsored by the Association for Southern Women for the Prevention of Lynching (ASWPL), where it became a prize winner. As in two of other Miller plays—*The Bog Guide* and *Stragglers in the Dust*—the main characters are white. There are no known productions of *Nails and Thorns*. The play was first published in *The Roots of African American Drama* (1991), edited by Leo Hamalian and James V. Hatch.

Miller wrote her last play, *Freedom's Children on the March,* in 1943. The following year she retired from the Baltimore public school system, and subsequently moved to Washington, D.C., with her husband, educator John Sullivan, whom she had married in 1940. Feeling that she no longer had a platform for the performance of her plays, Miller began to focus on poetry. Her career as a poet has been as outstanding and expansive as her life as a playwright. In 1986 she won the Mister Brown Award for Excellence in Drama and Poetry,[2] an award sponsored by the National Conference of African American Theatre. The 1990s have seen a resurgence in the production and publication of her plays. Miller died February 9, 1995, in Washington, D.C.

NOTES

1. May Miller (Sullivan) Interview with Kathy Perkins, September 2, 1987.

2. William Brown was manager of The African Company in New York from 1816 to 1823. This was the first professional black theatre.

Nails and Thorns

A PLAY IN ONE ACT   1933

❦

May Miller

PERSONS OF THE PLAY

STEWART LANDERS, *the sheriff of the town*
GLADYS LANDERS, *his wife*
ANNABEL, *a Negro servant*
WILSON, THOMAS, ANDERSON, *aides to the sheriff*
DOCTOR STEELE
CURIOUS TOWNSPEOPLE

Time: *The 1930s.*
Place: *A small town—probably South, probably West—a small town ruled by frenzy.*
Scene: *The comfortable living room of the sheriff's bungalow. The living room is furnished in the mode of the day with radio, tables, reading lamps, and a three-piece suite of overstuffed furniture. There are two windows and two doors in the room. The door to the left leads to the rest of the house; the one to the right, covered with a screen door, leads to the outside. It is early twilight on a warm June day and the windows and doors are open. GLADYS, a slender woman in her late twenties, is standing before the screen door nervously latching and unlatching the catch. Her husband STEWART, a large-shouldered man, is seated in one of the chairs with a paper open before him. He pretends to be reading, but furtively he follows his wife's nervous movements.*

GLADYS: (*bolting the screen door and turning back into the room*) Stewart! (*more urgently*) Stewart!
STEWART: (*laying aside the paper*) Yes—.
GLADYS: I do wish you had notified the Governor this afternoon.
STEWART: I thought I explained to you that the Governor is a busy man and can't be disturbed every time there is a little outburst in a town.
GLADYS: But, Stewart, this isn't any little outburst. You ought to understand your own home town well enough to know that a Negro's assault on a white woman is a pretty serious affair.
STEWART: We don't even know yet that it was a Negro. The Davis girl was pretty hysterical and we couldn't get much straight this afternoon.

GLADYS: But you did arrest a Negro.

STEWART: Yes, simple Lem. Some pretty damaging evidence seemed to point to the half-wit, and we thought we'd better lock him up for safekeeping; that's all. No charges have been placed against him. The girl will be clearer tomorrow and we'll get things straight then.

GLADYS: Tomorrow may be too late.

STEWART: Why? What do you mean?

GLADYS: You know well enough what I mean, but you won't let it pass your lips. Stewart, why can't we be frank with each other? You're sitting there thinking just like I am—what would happen if a mob gathered?

STEWART: (*rising and going to the window*) Come here. Look out there at that quiet street. Does that look like a riot scene?

GLADYS: (*standing beside him*) No, it doesn't.

STEWART: Now listen. Do you hear any sounds of a mob?

GLADYS: Not now, but you can't tell what night will bring. Ugly things move in the dark.

STEWART: Well, if you just must have a mob, we can take care of even that. Didn't I tell you the jail is well protected and I've taken every precaution? Deputies and police are guarding the place and we have enough tear bombs and shotguns to stop any crowd.

GLADYS: You say that to reassure me. Down in your heart you're doubting with me. You're afraid you did wrong not to notify the Governor to have the state militia on hand. Aren't you really?

STEWART: (*indulgently*) The only wrong thing I've done is let you talk yourself into the belief that there is a possibility of a lynching in this town, when there isn't any. (*He walks over to Gladys and leading her to a chair forces her gently into the chair. He pushes a section of the newspaper into her hand.*) Here, read this. The comic will be good for your nerves. I wouldn't miss an evening of "Desperado Joe" for anything. (*enthusiastically bending over her shoulder*) Look here at the pickle he's in. They've just caught Joe who kidnaped Percy's girl. And look at this. It's a wow. (*laughing*) Here the gang's got him, and is he scared!

GLADYS: The gang's got him. Stewart, how can you laugh? (*in a horrified voice*) The gang's got him.

STEWART: Oh, all right—skip it, skip it. Gladys, you're losing your sense of humor. After all, it's only a funny. I do believe this mess is on your nerves.

(*A thin whimper is heard from the next room*)

GLADYS: (*rising and thrusting the paper in Stewart's hand*) You see your loud laughing has wakened Junior.

STEWART: Isn't Annabel with him?

GLADYS: No, she hasn't come yet, but she'll be here almost any time now; she never disappoints.

(*Gladys exits through door to the left. Stewart goes again to the window and looks first to the left and then to the right as if peering up and down the street. He goes to the radio and attempts to dial a station. Disgusted at his failure to clear the static, he returns to the easy chair, snaps on a lamp, and settles to read again. A frantic knock on the screen door breaks the silence. An excited voice calls, "Mis' Landers! Mis' Landers." Stewart goes hurriedly to the door, Gladys comes from the next room.)*

GLADYS: What is it? Who is it, Stewart?

(Stewart opens the door. ANNABEL, *a stout pleasant-looking brown woman, stumbles into the room.)*

STEWART: *(relieved)* See, Gladys, you've worked yourself up to a frenzy about nothing. It's only Annabel.

GLADYS: *(noticing that Annabel, has stood still with her eyes bulging in fear)* Why, Annabel, what's the matter? You knocked on that door hard enough to shake the house. You frightened me.

ANNABEL: *(gasping)* Yes'm. I was scared, too. Mistah Landers, please lock that door.

STEWART: *(latching the screen door)* Sure, I'll lock it, but why?

ANNABEL: Sah, I thought as I'd nevah git heah. I was that scared.

GLADYS: Sit down. Annabel. Now tell us what happened to you.

ANNABEL: *(sinking on a chair)* Ma'm, it's happ'ned to all us cullud folks. Down there beyond the railroad tracks, there's nary a dark face about. They's gone in an' locked their doors an' pushed chairs an' tables up 'gainst 'em so as nobody kin git to 'em. Tomorrer mos' o' 'em what kin fine the money's gonna git way from heah.

GLADYS: Why are they acting like that, Annabel?

ANNABEL: All 'count o' what's happ'ned to po' daffy Lem.

STEWART: Nothing has happened to Lem; they had to lock him up until they find out all about a terrible affair that happened this afternoon.

ANNABEL: That's jes' it, Mistah Landers: them Davises is sich strong people. There's 'nough o' 'em to burn the whole town, an' they kin burn po' Lem easy as that. *(she snaps her fingers)*

STEWART: What a crazy notion, Annabel.

ANNABEL: It ain't crazy. We cullud folks has heard all bout it. Some o' the men uptown done tole their friends an' say foh 'em to git off the streets to keep out o' trouble 'cause they wouldn't lak to hafta burn up all the good cullud folks, too. That's why I was so scared. Mah folks at home tried to keep me, but I knowed you all 'ud be lookin' foh me so I stole out an' kinda bent ovah so as nobody couldn't see mah face an' I sneak on up heah.

STEWART: And you see nothing has happened to you.

ANNABEL: Yes sah, but all along on the streets I seen a li'l bunch o' folks heah an' a li'l bunch there, an' they all was gittin' together talkin', then they'd go jine up wid the other bunch. One time one o' 'em hollered at me an' I started runnin' an' jes' keep right on 'til I got heah.

GLADYS: All right, Annabel, now you're here safe and sound, and you need not worry any more. You go fix the baby's bottle and take it to him. And try to forget all about Lem and the affair.

ANNABEL: (*going offstage through the door to the left*) Yes'm. Yes'm.

(*The door closes behind Annabel and Gladys goes over to Stewart.*)

GLADYS: (*anxiety in her voice*) See, Stewart, what did I tell you?

STEWART: You can't believe everything Annabel says. She's excited and imaginative. She hasn't seen half of what she thinks she's seen.

GLADYS: Annabel has never been one to lie.

STEWART: No. she hasn't, but she's frightened and doesn't know what she's saying. The Negroes are very excitable and I wouldn't be a bit surprised if a number of them didn't leave town suddenly, right here in the midst of crop season. It's too bad. I wish we could have kept Lem's arrest from them. That's one of the bad things about these cursed affairs—the good ones suffer with the bad.

GLADYS: And remember it isn't only the Negroes that suffer. Every time any injustice is done or any disgrace falls, all of us feel it. Our children feel it.

STEWART: (*good-naturedly*) You're one proud mother, aren't you? Ever since Junior drew his first breath, all I have heard is our children.

GLADYS: Seriously, Stewart, before he came, I never had any idea how much you bothered about what your children were going to do, even what they were going to think. Now, all the time I worry about the kind of world Junior will have to live in. That's the reason I didn't like the comic strip you showed me. I hate the thought that he'll be reading about gangs and mobs and enjoy them.

STEWART: I read them, and you don't seem to find me so bad.

GLADYS: You're a man and know the difference between right and wrong. Your ideas are formed and you don't need anything to guide you.

STEWART: (*putting his arm around her shoulders*) But you mustn't get the jitters about it, Gladys, or Junior will have to grow up without a mother to guide him, and that would never do for either Junior or me.

GLADYS: I know, Stewart, I have been a bit nervous, and I'm going to try to keep steady. But I lived in a town once where they lynched a man and I can never forget how the town and the people suffered. It wasn't what they did to the unfortunate man alone. He was out of his misery. It was what they did to every soul in that town. They crucified everything that was worthwhile—justice and pride and self-respect. For generations to come the children will be gathering the nails and thorns from the scene of that crucifixion.

STEWART: Don't misunderstand me, Gladys. I agree with you that a lynching is a horrible thing and even more than you I would hate to have one happen here. Besides, I don't want my son to grow up in a lawless town. This place has never been guilty of a lynching and I would feel terribly responsible at this late date to blot our record.

GLADYS: That's the reason I think you'd better go on out and take a look about town, even though you don't believe all Annabel said. Maybe you'd better have that call to the Governor put through, too, just to be on the safe side.

STEWART: I'll take a look around. I don't believe much in Annabel's vision, but it can't hurt and youll be satisfied.

(*He takes his hat from the table, kisses Gladys and goes out. Gladys stands looking down the street after him. Finally, as if satisfied, she turns back into the room.*)

GLADYS: Annabel, Annabel, come in here.

(*Annabel standing in the doorway, a nursing bottle in her hand*)

GLADYS: Come in here, Annabel. I want you to tell me something.

ANNABEL: I ain't finished feedin' the baby, Ma'm.

GLADYS:You can bring him in here.

ANNABEL: Yes'm. (*She goes offstage and returns with the baby wrapped in a light blanket. She takes the rocking chair indicated by Gladys.*)

GLADYS: Does he seem restless? I heard him whimper earlier this evening.

ANNABEL: No'm; he was jes' hungry, I gis, 'cause he's sartinly makin' way wid this bottle.

GLADYS: Now tell me while you're feeding him—who told your folks about what the people were going to do to Lem?

ANNABEL: I doan 'xactly 'member, Ma'm.

GLADYS: Now try to remember. If you tell me, I can tell Mr. Landers when he comes back and he'll stop all that talk.

ANNABEL: Now let me see. I b'lieve Ruby tole me an' she had it from Josh's Sarah an' Sarah got it from Josh from the store where he works on Main Street. His boss had lots o' men a-comin' an' a-goin' all evenin'. He tole Josh that the folks was gonna give Lem a li'l necktie party so as others would 'member that even if they ain't got sense, they gotta know a white woman; an' if they's crazy 'nough not to, they gotta go to the crazy house.

GLADYS: I wonder why they never sent Lem upstate to the asylum.

ANNABEL: His ma did wanta ask Mistah Landers 'bout sendin' him long time ago, but Mistah Joe what owns the farm say their crops wasn't no good nohow an' they wasn't payin' nothin' an' they bes' keep Lem to help make out, 'cause Lem was strong an' could work.

GLADYS: It's too bad.

ANNABEL: Yes'm, it sho is; I doan know what Lem done 'xactly but the whole town's gone plumb crazy, an' Josh's boss say they's gonna burn Lem.

GLADYS: Now, Annabel, you mustn't believe all that. Lem will have a fair trial. They'll keep him locked up safe until then.

ANNABEL: But they can't.

GLADYS: They can't—what do you mean?

ANNABEL:Josh say the man what hole the keys is the Davis girl's cousin an' he's mad lak all the res'. He come in the store, too, an' plan wid the men.

GLADYS: That's probably wrong. I don't think that's true.

ANNABEL: (*looking up quickly*) What ain't, Ma'm?

GLADYS: About the keeper's being the girl's cousin and planning with the rest.

ANNABEL: Yes'm, 'tis, too. I knows mo' 'bout this town n' you does, Mis' Landers, 'cause mah mammy nursed mos' o' these folks. She say one haf them's related an' those what ain't has got relatives what is. An' I 'members the Davises an' the Miltons is all mixed up there way back. Anyhow, he's gonna let 'em in tonight. Josh heard 'im promise.

GLADYS: (*excited*) Annabel, why did you let Mr. Landers go without telling him that?

ANNABEL: I was that scared, Ma'm, I forgit some things. Mistah Landers didn't b'lieve me nohow; he jes' kinda laff at what I said.

GLADYS: (*going to the door and looking out*) It's so dark now. I'm afraid I'll have trouble finding him but he ought to know. I wish he'd come back by here. (*suddenly thrusting her head further out in a startled gesture*) Annabel, did you hear anything?

ANNABEL: Only you talkin', Ma'm, an' the quiet breathin' o' this blessed angel.

GLADYS: (*excitedly*) Annabel, listen, listen! (*Annabel stops rocking. In the silence, a slight roaring is heard. The sounds grow louder and the jeering of a mob can be heard. The sounds grow louder. Annabel lays the baby on the divan and goes to the door and stands beside Gladys in the doorway.*) I was so afraid and now it's happened; it's happened.

ANNABEL: Don't git upset yit, Ma'm. You doan know what's happ'ned.

GLADYS: Yes, I do. I've felt it coming all the time.

ANNABEL: Didn't Mistah Landers go down to the jail? Ain't he the sheriff an' couldn't he take them keys from Mistah Milton? Maybe that's what he done.

GLADYS: No. I'm afraid he couldn't do anything against a crowd.

ANNABEL: He's got mah prayers to help him out.

GLADYS: It's more than my prayers he's got. I am there with him, helping him fight back the mob. I'm fighting to save all of us from sorrow—the torture to that crazy boy, the disgrace to our town and against all the evil they're building for our children and our children's children to bear. (*Gladys shudders and buries her head in her hands*)

ANNABEL: (*alarmed by the mounting hysteria in Gladys's voice, she looks at Gladys solicitously. Gently touching her arm*) Doan take on so, Mis' Landers. You's shakin' all ovah. You bes' go on in, Mis' Landers, an' lay down.

(*Gladys turns back into the room and walks back and forth. Annabel remains at the door.*)

GLADYS: Lie down, lie down—I can't lie down not knowing what's happening.

(*Hurried footsteps pass. Voices are heard calling, "Lynch him," "String him up," "They got him." The sound of general rioting grows louder and nearer. Annabel latches the screen door and starts to shut the house door.*)

ANNABEL: (*covering her face and sobbing*) Po' crazy Lem—po' Lem. Please, Good Lawd, save 'im.

GLADYS: There's no use closing that door, Annabel. You can't shut it out. I heard. They've got him; haven't they?

ANNABEL: Yes'm, that's what they's hollering.

GLADYS: And they're passing up Greene Street; aren't they?

ANNABEL: Yes'm, I think so.

GLADYS: Right to the town hall to make mockery of all we ought to be. (*growing more excited*) They can't do this. They mustn't.

ANNABEL: And so they's really gonna burn him!

GLADYS: (*in a horrified whisper*) Burn a human being, oh no! There must be some way to stop it.

ANNABEL: You jes' hafta leave it to the Lawd now, Mis' Landers. Oh Jesus, help us.

GLADYS: If only I could make them listen to me. They don't know what they're doing.

ANNABEL: They ain't got no ears now, Ma'm.

GLADYS: If I could make them forget this afternoon, forget the poor crazy fellow and look at themselves and their children.

ANNABEL: They ain't forgot 'em. They's got chillun wid 'em. I seen some o' 'em pass down by the corner.

GLADYS: The children too! They can't do that to our children. They're all we have. They're our promise—our future.

ANNABEL: Yes'm, mah chillun's all I got, too. If 'twasn't foh 'em, I wouldn't be a-workin' all the time 'til I's ready to drap. Then come a time lak tonight an' I git to thinkin' that mah sons has gotta grow up in this town, too, an' 'sposin' aftah all mah work they ends lak that. (*she makes a futile gesture toward the door*)

GLADYS: Surely, your sons will grow up in this town and so will my son and probably their sons' sons. I'll tell that mob how I feel. I'll tell them how you feel. I'll show them my baby—he is this town's tomorrow. (*snatching her baby from the divan*)

ANNABEL: Where you goin', Ma'm?

GLADYS: Out to tell them.

ANNABEL: But you can't do that; you can't take no baby out in that crowd.

GLADYS: My son will show them the way.

ANNABEL: I's hid mah sons an' you'd bes' hide your'n till those folks git some sense.

GLADYS: (*going to the door*) When they hear my plea, when they see my son, they'll understand.

ANNABEL: (*puts out a restraining arm*) They won't lissen. They's wors 'n po' Lem. They's plumb crazy.

(*Gladys breaks past Annabel and, baby in arm, rushes out. Annabel stands stunned, looking after her. She watches for a while and then, as the sounds of the riot grow close, she turns away, closing the house door. She snaps out the large lamp and, leaving the light only from the next room, peeks cautiously out the window from the side. A thundering knock is heard on the door Annabel crouches in fear. The knock is repeated. A voice calls, "Mrs. Landers, Mrs. Landers. Anybody home?")*

ANNABEL: (*looking from window*) Who is you? What you want here? Mistah Landers ain't home.

THOMAS: We ain't lookin' for the sheriff. We're his men an' he sent us here.

(*Annabel opens the door.* WILSON, THOMAS, *and* ANDERSON *enter. They are ordinary white men in rough pants and shirtsleeves.*)

ANDERSON: What you doin' here?

WILSON: She's awright; she the Landers' Annabel.

ANNABEL: Evenin', Mistah Wilson, I didn't know it was you, an' you can't blame me none foh not wantin' to open that do' wid me heah all by mah lone self.

ANDERSON: Where's the missus? The sheriff sent us here to look out for things.

ANNABEL: She got a notion in her head to stop that mob an' ran out wid the baby.

THOMAS: Ran out with the baby! Where?

ANNABEL: Out there where the mob is.

ANDERSON: Good Gawd, Tom, the sheriff'll raise the devil. We was supposed to guard her an' the house.

THOMAS: We'd been here if we hadn't had to stop for you, Wilson.

WILSON: Got any notion which way she went, Annabel?

ANNABEL: She say somethin' 'bout goin' up Greene Street way.

ANDERSON: Say, fellows. you stay here an' look out for things. I'll see if I see anything o' her. She ain't got no business out in that mob with no baby. (*he goes out*)

WILSON: (*sinking in a chair*) Annabel, gimme some water.

ANNABEL: Yes, sah. (*she goes offstage*)

THOMAS: (*going to the porch door*) I think I'll stand here on the porch an' see whether I can hear anything from up the street.

WILSON: Can you?

THOMAS: Nope. Seems to have quieted down. Wonder what's goin' on.

WILSON: You know, I'm glad the boss put me on duty down here. I guess now that they've got the fellow, they'll lynch him an' I ain't much on stomachin' the likes o' that.

THOMAS: Say, Wilson. the boss sure knew what he was doin' when he sent us up here. What fool notion do you think made the missus take a baby out in that crowd? Sure hope Andy finds her. I wouldn't know what to tell the boss.

WILSON: Say, Tom, what happ'ned down to the jail?

THOMAS: The sheriff fought like a hell cat but wasn't no use. Them folks were plumb mad.

WILSON: How'd they get to the jail?

THOMAS: You know haf the deputies were the Davis kin an' I heard Milton give 'em the key.

WILSON: Milton 'll sure be in hot water.

THOMAS: Gee, they're quiet. Wonder if the sheriff finally got 'em to change their minds. You know once down there at the jail I thought he had won 'em over. He stood in front o' Lem's cell pleadin' an' some o' 'em was half listenin'. Then somebody yelled, "'Spose it was your wife!"

WILSON: I know that ended it.

THOMAS: Yeah, 'Course mos' o' the staff stood by the sheriff but I wonder what I'd do if it was my women folk.

WILSON: Dunno, Tom; but then the poor rascal was daffy.

THOMAS: They're so damned quiet up there, I—

ANNABEL: (*coming back with glass of water and handing it to Wilson*) Mistah Wilson, has they burned Lem?

WILSON: I dunno.

ANNABEL: But they got him; didn't they?

WILSON: Yeah.

ANNABEL: An' they took him on up to Town Square to burn him, didn't they?

WILSON: I guess so, Annabel.

ANNABEL: (*sobbing aloud*) Yeah, I know they burnt him, too, jes' lak they said they'd do. Oh, Lawd, have mercy on is po' daffy soul.

THOMAS: (*calling from the porch*) Say, Wilson, here comes the boss.

WILSON: Hey, Annabel, quit that fuss. The boss's had a pretty bad night an' he don't want to come home to no wailin' an' moanin'.

(*Annabel dries her eyes and looks up as Stewart enters. Stewart has a tired, hopeless expression on his face and his shoulders are drooped. Thomas follows him in from the porch.*)

STEWART: Well, boys, we didn't save him.

(*Annabel goes out of the room sobbing.*)

WILSON: (*standing*) Sorry, sheriff. I know you don't want to say
nothin' bout it now.

STEWART: (*taking a seat and dropping his forehead in his hands*) Thank you, Thomas and Wilson.

THOMAS: Any other orders, sir?

STEWART:Nothing right now. The Square is guarded. Thomas, you might go down to the jail and see whether Ogden wants you for anything—he's in Milton's place. I'll be down in a little while. We expect the state militia in about half an hour.

THOMAS: Yes, sir. (*he goes out*)

WILSON: Will they stay? We don't need them now, do we?

STEWART: You can't tell. But we'll be on hand to welcome them. (*looking around*) Where's Mrs. Landers?

WILSON: I dunno, sir, but when we got here she had gone.

STEWART: Gone—gone where?

WILSON: We couldn't 'xactly find out, sir, but Annabel says she took the baby an' went out in the crowd. Tom and I stayed here, an' Anderson went out to look for 'em.

STEWART: My God, Wilson, what are you saying. Took the baby and went out in that crowd! Annabel! Annabel!

ANNABEL: (*drying her eyes as she comes from the next room*) Yes, sah.

STEWART: Annabel, what's this you told Mr. Wilson? Where's Mrs. Landers?

ANNABEL: She went out lak I tole Mistah Wilson.

STEWART: Went out with the baby?

ANNABEL: Yes, sah. She did, sah.

STEWART: Where? When? What did she say?

ANNABEL: Somethin' 'bout when they seen her baby an' heard her plea, they'd lissen.

STEWART: (*grabbing his hat*) Wilson, you stay here 'til I come back. If Mrs. Landers— (*a loud hub-bub is heard on the steps, and Anderson, half-leading, half-carrying the disheveled and hysterical Gladys, enters. They are followed by a small crowd of people who group themselves near the door. Stewart goes quickly and takes Gladys from Anderson's arms*) Where's the baby, Gladys? (*Gladys sobs hysterically*) Gladys, it's Stewart. Tell me, where is the baby?

ANDERSON: Sir, I— (*his voice is drowned by the concert voices of the group and the hysterical sobbing of Gladys*)

STEWART: Can't I get an answer from some of you folks? Where is my son?

(*A loud chorus answers.*)

ANDERSON: (*pushing the people out of the room*) Hey, you folks, git out. The sheriff can't git nothin' straight. (*Wilson aids him in heading the curious people toward the door. One man steps aside from the crowd*) Wilson, don't you see that's the doctor?

WILSON: 'Scuse me, Doc, I didn't know what I was doing. (*he succeeds in getting the others out and closes the door, shutting out their grumbling*)

STEWART: What is it, Gladys? Where's the baby?

GLADYS: Dead—dead! Didn't they tell you? The mob lynched your son along with crazy Lem. They knocked him down—they stamped on him. Oh, Stewart, they won't listen—they can't even see me—they're killing my baby.

STEWART: Gladys, my God, Gladys, you don't know what you're saying. It's the baby. Where did you take the baby?

GLADYS: He's dead, dead, I tell you, and I'm glad. (*laughing hysterically*) He'll never have to see a lynching.

STEWART: Gladys, you are hysterical. Try to think. I must understand you.

GLADYS: I said it. He's dead. He'll never—never— (*she crumples up in Stewart's arms*)

DOCTOR: It is the truth, Sheriff. You'd better let me have her, sir. We'll have to put her to bed. I wouldn't try to question her any further. Your man will tell you. (*he takes Gladys from Stewart's arms*)

STEWART: The truth, truth! (*he opens the door and half-dazed, leads the Doctor carrying Gladys from the room. The Doctor follows*)

WILSON: Annabel, you better go with the doctor to help with Mrs. Landers.

ANNABEL: Yes, sah. (*she follows the Doctor offstage*)

WILSON: Andy, was the Missus tellin' the truth or was she out of her head?

ANDERSON: It was God's gospel. Ain't this a night for the boss?

(*Stewart stumbles back into the room and takes the chair which Wilson has just risen from and pushed toward him. He sits there with his head buried, groaning.*)

STEWART: My God, my God, my son dead! I don't understand.

ANDERSON: Sir, there wasn't no use in lyin' to you. The baby is dead. We picked up the doctor, but when the doctor took one look he knew. He said we'd better leave the poor little thing at his house, an' he come on with us.

STEWART: (*brokenly*) How did it happen, Andy?

ANDERSON: When we got here she had gone, so Tom an' Wilson stayed to watch the house an' I went to look for her. When I got in the thick o' that crowd I looked right an' left an' couldn't find her nowhere. 'Til finally I heard someone say a woman was screamin' 'cause they'd knocked her an' the baby down, an' the baby got trampled in the crowd. I beat my way to her an' sure 'nough it was Mrs. Landers. She was clutchin' the baby an' screamin'. Somebody had her, but I explained you'd sent me to git her. The poor little baby was dead then. Then I got Mrs. Landers down by the doctor's an' we come on here. Somebody yelled they killed the Landers baby—that's how those folks come to follow us.

STEWART: I see. Thank you, Andy.

WILSON: Anything we can do, Mr. Landers?

STEWART: The militia'll be here any minute now. You'd better get on down there and tell them I'll be down as soon as I get things straight here.

ANDERSON AND WILSON: Yes, sir. (*they go out*)

STEWART: (*going to the door of the room*) May I speak to you, Doctor? (*Doctor comes out, closing door behind him*) How is she?

DOCTOR: I've given her a needle and she has quieted down nicely.

STEWART: May I see her?

DOCTOR: I don't advise it. Talking will only excite her more. She has had the severest type of shock. She should see no one until she has had some sleep.

STEWART: And my— my—

DOCTOR: I'm awfully sorry, Sheriff, but he'd been dead when I got him. We left him in my operating room for the night. You can make arrangements in the morning.

STEWART: My son—it all happened so quickly—so quickly. I can't make myself realize it.

DOCTOR: If there's anything I can do—

STEWART: Thanks, Doctor. Will you stay with her until I return?

DOCTOR: Yes. The colored woman says she is staying, too, an' she's very helpful. She seems to be able to quiet her.

STEWART: Yes. Annabel's a very good woman—a very, very wise woman. Now I've got to be getting down to the jail to meet the state militia. They're arriving at nine. (*Stewart takes his hat and goes slowly toward the door. The screen door closes behind him and the Doctor starts back to the room.*)

CURTAIN

Ann Seymour Link
(1906–1984)

In 1936 Ann Seymour's one-act play, *Lawd, Does You Undahstan'?* was awarded second place in a contest for plays on the theme of lynching sponsored by the Association of Southern Women for the Prevention of Lynching (ASWPL). Miss Seymour was encouraged to submit her play by Mrs. Alex W. Spence of Dallas, an ASWPL member and member of the play contest committee. In a letter notifying Seymour that her play had won second place, ASWPL founder Jessie Daniel Ames wrote: "Your play has distinct value in our contest in that it presents the effects of lynching upon a Negro woman and this is something that we want to emphasize in our future programs."[1] The second place award consisted of $35 and publication of the play by ASWPL and Samuel French. *Lawd, Does You Undahstan'?* was published in French's *Twenty Short Plays on a Royalty Holiday* (1937) and in *Representative One-Act Plays By American Authors,* edited by Margaret Mayorga (1937).

Lawd, Does You Undahstan'? was produced at Paine College in Augusta, Georgia, in December 1936 and at the Peachtree Christian Church in Atlanta in 1937. Both productions were directed by Miss Emma C. Gray, an African American faculty member at Paine. Educator Joseph T. Lacy (1915–1994) was a Paine College student and cast member in both productions. Dr. Lacy remembered the cast was selected for their attitudes on the issue of lynching as well as their acting ability. He recalled Miss Gray as "an outstanding educator with a strong interest in civil rights."[2] He also recalled the overwhelmingly positive response to the play by the predominantly black Paine College audience as well as the tension created by performing for the all-white audience at the Peachtree Christian Church. Dr. Lacy also stressed the important contribution dramas written in the anti-lynching tradition made to the anti-lynching movement:

> I believe the philosophy adhered to by such organizations as the KKK and others are actually the acting out of an attitude that says, "if you

cross this line, we'll kill you." These plays brought to the attention of many people the evils of this attitude. . . . They made you see just how easy it was to kill a person. . . . They were like seed fallen on good ground.[3]

Ann Seymour was born and raised in Strawn, Texas, a small coal mining town approximately 90 miles west of Dallas. Ann and her sister were raised by their mother, a devout Southern Baptist. Their father left the family when Ann was an infant. Ann attended Texas State College for Women, graduating in 1927 with a major in Speech Arts and English. While in college she wrote two one-act plays, one of which was awarded the Texas Intercollegiate Press Association Prize. She began her lifetime career of teaching in the public (white) schools of Palestine, Texas, where segregation was strictly observed. In Palestine, she was active in local productions spawned by the Little Theatre movement. She married Edwin William Link, with whom she had two sons, and continued to teach until her retirement. She was active in women's groups in the Presbyterian Church for many years. Throughout her life, Ann Seymour Link continued to write plays and submit them for publication but found little success.[4]

In a 1993 interview Mr. Henry Link, son of Ann Seymour Link, stated that he does not remember his mother ever speaking of this play, but he confirmed that lynchings did take place in Palestine in the 1930s. He described his mother as a humanitarian, explaining, "She was not active in pushing any cause, but a firm believer in racial equality, and in treating all people with respect."[5] Mr. Link remembers the close relationship that developed between his mother and Katie Butler, a black domestic worker in their home. He described Mrs. Butler as "a second mother" to him and his brother.

NOTES

1. ASWPL Papers, Penn State University, Pattee Library, Microfilm Collection, ASWPL File, A218 Reel 4.

2. Dr. Joseph Lacy, telephone conversation with Judith Stephens, November 1991.

3. Dr. Joseph Lacy, letter to Judith Stephens, June 1992.

4. Margaret Mayorga, ed., *Representative One-Act Plays by American Authors* (Boston: Little, Brown, and Company, 1937); Mr. Henry Link, telephone conversation with Judith Stephens, February 1993.

5. Mr. Henry Link, telephone conversation with Judith Stephens, Feburary 1993.

Lawd, Does You Undahstan'?

1936

✿✿✿

Ann Seymour Link

CAST

Aunt Doady, *an old negro woman*
Jim, *her grandson*
Fruit Cake, *negro boy about six years old*
Epsie Lee, *girl whom Jim is going to marry*
Lucy, *Fruit Cake's mother*
Miles Chambers ⎫
Tom Moore   ⎬ *white men*
Man   ⎭
Minor Negro Characters

Scene: *Southern negro cabin.*
Time: *The present.*
The scene is laid in front of a negro cabin. The door is open, as is the one window. Through the door can be seen a table with a lamp on it; and through the window, a bed. Outside it is bright moonlight. To the right, under the window is a wash bench with wash pan, bucket and dipper, and fruit jar with some cyanide in the bottom of it. There is a small wood pile to the extreme left and a wash pot downstage at the right. A cane-bottom chair leans against the house. The only lights are the yellow light of the lamp and the moonlight.
Aunt Doady, *an old negro woman, is sitting on the doorstep, leaning forward, elbows resting on knees. Her black, wrinkled face has the rather mournful tranquility found on so many black faces: a calm acceptance of fate.*

The night is very still until from the shadowy woods close by a whippoorwill calls plaintively.

The dialect is only suggested. The voices are soft and melodious, and the vowels are much plainer than the consonants.

AUNT DOADY: Listen to dat bird! Soun' lak he heart done broke in two. (*The whippoorwill calls again.*) What de mattah, whippoorwill? Why you cryin', hunh? Is youah wife done gone and left you, or is you jus' lonesome cause you ain' got no wife? Ain' no use takin' on lak dat.

(*A little negro boy runs on the stage. He has been running hard and is panting so that he finds it hard to speak. Aunt Doady peers at him.*)

AUNT DOADY: Is dat you, Fruit Cake?

FRUIT CAKE: Yes'm, Aunt Doady, I jus' been . . .

AUNT DOADY: Wheah's youah ma?

FRUIT CAKE: She's a-comin' up de road. I took a short cut through de woods an' when . . .

AUNT DOADY: Who with yo' ma?

FRUIT CAKE: Epsie Lee, pappy an' 'em. Dey's goin' to church, and when I gits to dat ole dead tree stump down in de slough, ole screech owl a-settin' up dere, jus' yell lak evahthing. Hit scah me an' I run as hahd as I kin. Bet I was goin' fastah'n anything. Bet I was goin' fastah'n ole win' could go.

AUNT DOADY: Boy, how many times dat owl screech?

FRUIT CAKE: T'ree times, Aunt Doady.

AUNT DOADY: Is you suah?

FRUIT CAKE: Yes'm, I'se suah! T'ree times, jes' lak dis: Hoo! Hoo! Hoo!

AUNT DOADY: Hush yo' mouf! Dat's soun' I doan lak. Screech owl mean death. Fruit Cake, you ain't got no business comin' through dem woods. Ef'n you hadn', you wouldn' a heard no screech owl.

(*From offstage at the right comes the sound of voices of negroes, laughing and calling to each other, walking down the moonlit road to church. EPSIE LEE, a young negro girl, finely built, with an intelligent, sympathetic face, enters a little ahead of the others. LUCY, Fruit Cake's mother, follows closely. She is good natured and lazy, with an ever ready laugh. Three men and two other women complete the group. They seat themselves easily about the stage, Lucy dropping on the wash bench at the right. One of the men sits on the ground and leans against the wash bench, another sits on the wood pile at extreme left and faces the house; the other man leans against the house in a cane-bottom chair, just to the left of an overturned box where one of the women sits. As they come in, they call greetings to Aunt Doady.*)

ALL: Good evening, Aunt Doady!

AUNT DOADY: I'se fine. How's you dis evenin'?

EPSIE LEE: (*going toward the doorstep where Aunt Doady sits*) M'hunh, cotch you a talkin' to youahself, didn' we, Aunt Doady? Mighty good sign you's gittin' old.

AUNT DOADY: What if I does talk to myself? I'se suah somebody's listenin' den, and dat's mo' dan I kin say ef'n I talks to somebody else. But I'se been talkin' to Fruit Cake.

LUCY: He been heah, has he? I been wonderin' wheah dat chile shisted off to.

AUNT DOADY: He were heah, jus' a moment ago. Fruit Cake, wheah you go? (*Fruit Cake, who hid in the wash pot when he first heard the voices, pops up his grinning head.*) Git outa dat wash pot fo' I skin you. Lawd! You so black I cain' tell wheah you staht an' de wash pot leave off.

FRUIT CAKE: (*hops out*) Aunt Doady, why I so black anyhow?

EPSIE LEE: (*chanting*)

> God made de dahkey
> Made him in de night
> Made him in a hurry
> And fo'got to paint him white!

Dat's what Aunt Doady use to tell me an' Jim. Who learn it to you, Aunt Doady?

AUNT DOADY: My ole mammy learn it to me. Dunno wheah she got it.

FRUIT CAKE: "God made de dahkey." What come nex', Epsie Lee?

EPSIE LEE: "Made him in de night."

FRUIT CAKE:

> "God made de dahkey,
> Made him in de night."

EPSIE LEE:

> "Made him in a hurry
> And fo'got to paint him white!"

FRUIT CAKE:

> "Made him in a hurry
> And fo'got to paint him white!"

LUCY: Night lak dis make me jes' want to sit an' sit.

AUNT DOADY: Seem lak any kin' night make you wan' to sit. Any kin' day, too.

LUCY: (*she laughs with the others*) Reck'n you's right about dat. But when I knows I oughta be up an' doin' sumpin', seem lak I cain' jus' sit without worryin' a mite.

LUCY'S HUSBAND: Worryin' ain't gonna tiah you out none.

EPSIE LEE: Look, ol' moon done got hisself hung in a tree.

FRUIT CAKE: Wan' a drink.

LUCY: Go lif' dat dippah an' git one den.

(*Fruit Cake goes to wash bench and gets a drink of water. After he drinks, he picks up the fruit jar on the bench.*)

AUNT DOADY: Fruit Cake, put dat jah down! Take yo' han's of'n it, I say. Hit's pizen!

FRUIT CAKE: Pizen? Why's it pizen, Aunt Doady?

LUCY: Git away from dere, Fruit Cake! Does you wan' to drop daid?

ONE OF THE WOMEN: Lucy, ain' dat chile got anuthah name?

LUCY: (*laughs*) Lawd, I doan know. Fruit Cake, is you got anuthah name?

FRUIT CAKE: No'm, jes' Fruit Cake.

AUNT DOADY: Humph! Doan even know whethah youah own youngun got anuthah name.

LUCY: Reck'n we kinda run out when he come along. Aunt Doady, what you got pizen in dat jah for?

AUNT DOADY: Dat's wheah Jim keep he buttahflies and bugs. He jes' drop 'em in an' hit doan huht none. Dey jes' sorta goes to sleep.

EPSIE LEE: Jim, he couldn' stan' to huht nothin', not even a little bug.

ONE OF THE MEN: Mighty funny work fo' a man, catchin' 'em buttahflies.

ANOTHER: You ain' gonna catch dat Jim doin' no man's wuhk. He doan lak dat plowin' an' choppin' cotton. No suh! He gotta catch hisself some buttahflies.

EPSIE LEE: (*heatedly*): Jim jus' smart, dat's all. He make a whole lot more money catchin' buttahflies an' sellin' 'em to Professah Brown, dan you does, Reely Watson.

AUNT DOADY: Hit's what he laks to do. Ef'n he'd ruthah catch bugs dan chop cotton, dat's he business, I reck'n. Evahbody be a sight happier ef'n he doin' what he laks.

REELY: What dey do with bugs, anyhow? Wish dey'd come and git some dem boll weevils off'n my cotton.

EPSIE LEE: Jim say Professah Brown stick pins in 'em and put 'em on a card. Dey use 'em in dey studies at de college.

REELY: Still say hit's funny wuhk fo' a man!

EPSIE LEE: I ain' nevah notice you collapsin' from too much work!

REELY: Anyway ef'n I had a gran'son . . .

AUNT DOADY: Well, you ain' got one yet, an' Lawd pity him does you evah have one!

LUCY: Hol' youah mouths, all of you. Epsie Lee, sing somethin' fo' us: "Dat's Why Darkeys Were Born."

AUNT DOADY: Dat's white folks' song. Sing "The Old Hen Cackle."

(*Epsie Lee smiles and starts the familiar old song, moving downstage toward the wash pot. The other darkeys join in. Gradually they get up, and in response to the lively tune, that works into organic melody the notes of the hen cackling, pat their feet and sway their bodies. As the music grows faster, Fruit Cake breaks into a cake walk.*)

THE OLD HEN CACKLE

The old hen she cackle, she cackle in the corn;
The next time she cackle, she cackle in the barn.

CHORUS:

Well, the old hen she cackle, she sholy gwain to lay.
The old hen she cackle, she cackle in the loft;
The next time she cackle, she cackle further off.

CHORUS:

Well, the old hen she cackle, she sholy must-a laid.

The old hen she cackle, she cackle in the lot;

Well, the next time she cackle, she'll cackle in the pot.

CHORUS:

The old hen she cackle, well, she sholy ought to lay.

(*At last, Lucy, the only one, besides Aunt Doady, who has remained seated, rises and interrupts the merriment.*)

LUCY: It's time we git to church, ef'n dey's gonna be any.

AUNT DOADY: You's powerful late gittin' dere.

LUCY: Brothah Hawkins went ovah to Stormy Hill fo' a funeral, so church is late tonight. Bettah come along with us.

AUNT DOADY: Nope. I'se too old fo' dat shoutin' religion now. When you gits as old as I is, an' has known God as long as I has, you doan have to go to church; you can jes' set on youah do'step an' talk to Him. You doan have to say words even. He jus' sorta knows what's on youah min'.

REELY: (*facetiously*): Wish I knowed I stood in with de Lawd lak dat.

LUCY: Ef'n you'd been as good as Aunt Doady all youah life, you wouldn't have to worry no more than she do.

REELY: I vow Aunt Doady's a good woman all right. I ain' nevah knowed her to do nothin' that wasn't right, 'cept run off at de mouth powerful hahd.

EPSIE LEE: Sometime I think Aunt Doady ain' quite lak de res' of us. She's mo' lak a saint, dat's what!

AUNT DOADY: Git out! Doan be makin' no saint out of me. It's jus' dat I'se lived my life, an' it's been a long one, an' in all dose yeahs I'se known de Lawd an' He's known me. We jus' undahstan's each othah, dat's all. I ain' nevah stole, no' lied no mo' that I had to, nor killed nobody. I'se kept as right as I could. And now dat I'se almost ready to go, I feels kinda peaceful lak—without nothin' to worry about.

LUCY: Come on, or we's gonna be late fo' meetin' sho.

(*Epsie Lee lags behind, as the others call good-byes and start off the stage at left.*)

EPSIE LEE: Aunt Doady, ain' Jim comin' to church tonight?

AUNT DOADY: I'se jus' wonderin' wheah Jim at. He stay gone mos' all day, catchin' bugs. Den, dis evenin' jus' befo' suppah time, he go down to de Crossroad Store, an' he ain' come back yet. (*Aunt Doady gets up very slowly and walks to the right as though she is looking down the road.*) I put his tuhnip greens and cawn bread on the back of de stove to wahm, but de stove gonna be stone cold fo' he gits heah, ef'n he doan hurry.

(*Epsie Lee follows her and then turns and goes to the left as she talks. Aunt Doady, listening to her, moves back to the wash bench, gets a drink of water, and then goes to the wood pile, and gathers a few chips, which she drops in her apron.*)

EPSIE LEE: You know, Aunt Doady, it's funny how folks think Jim is lazy and sorta queer 'cause he doan git out and chop cotton or plow lak all de rest ob 'em does. Dere ain' a lazy bone in Jim's body. Us two, we know him; we's de only two what does, I reck'n. Jim, he's jus' different from de othah niggehs aroun' heah, dat's all. He stay in de woods cause he lak 'em. He lak de stillness, de trees, all de birds an' frogs. An' he learn me to like 'em too. I lissen to old bull bats all my life; but one evenin' Jim and me was watchin' 'em swoop around, and hollerin' ovah de lake, an' somehow, jus' de way Jim stood so still-like, a-lookin' at 'em, made me see 'em different; I doan know how. Now I allus gits a little shivery when I sees 'em, jus' lak I does when I sees de mist rise off de lake about sun-up, or de first dogwood in de spring, or heahs a mocking bird singing jus' like he gonna bus' hisself wide open!

AUNT DOADY: Yessuh, Epsie Lee, dere's a whole lot out dere (*she gestures vaguely toward the woods*) ef'n you can jus' stop to see it or lissen to it. Jim, he know how to do it.

(*From a distance Lucy calls Epsie Lee's name.*)

EPSIE LEE: I'se comin'. Good night, Aunt Doady. See you in de mawnin'!

AUNT DOADY: Good night, Epsie Lee. Jim got hisself a mighty fine gal. (*Epsie Lee goes off, left, and Aunt Doady gathers chips. The whippoorwill calls, startlingly close.*) Still grievin', is you? Body'd think you was mou'nin' fo' de whole worl'. (*She stops suddenly and peers to the right.*) What's dat? Who dat out there?

(*Jim, a young negro, comes from the right hurriedly. He is nervous; but even the terror which he tries to hide cannot take away the simplicity and fineness that are naturally his. He tries to assume an air of indifference, even swaggering a little.*)

JIM: It's me, Aunt Doady.

AUNT DOADY: How come you slip through de woods lak dat? You scah a body to death! I been listenin' fo' youah whistle fo' an houh. Come on while I gits youah suppah out fo' you.

JIM: No'm, I don' want it. I ain' got time!

AUNT DOADY: Ain't got time? (*She goes toward him and looks at him closely. His eyes evade hers.*) Fo' why? What you gotta do? Wheah's you goin'? What's de mattah with you, Jim? You's powerful jumpy.

JIM: Ain' a thing, Aunt Doady. Honest!

AUNT DOADY: What you listenin' to?

(*Dogs bark in the distance. At the sound, Aunt Doady lets the chips drop from her lap, and stands still, suddenly fearful.*)

AUNT DOADY: Ain' dem dawgs I heah?

JIM: Yes'm, reck'n so. Maybe deys coon dawgs. Somebody huntin' coons, I reck'n, or maybe deys fox houn's. White folks is a huntin' fox. Good night fo' fox huntin'. Scent easy to pick up.

(*The sound of the barking dogs grows louder.*)

AUNT DOADY: Are you suah dem's fox houn's, Jim? (*Aunt Doady's voice is ominous.*) Jim! Look at me! Dem ain' fox houn's; dem's blood houn's! Gawd!

I cain' nebah fo'git dat soun'! De night dey come an' got yo' pappy. You could heah dem blood houn's, gittin' closuh, and closuh, an' closuh all de time. An' yo' pappy, he was gray as a grave stone. He didn't know what to do, wheah to go, thinkin' dey couldn' fin' him in de lof'. But when white folks staht out lynchin', dey ain' no hidin', no runnin', no talkin' 'em out of it. Dey go up, and dey drag him out, an' he scream! Gawd! I cain' nevah fo'git his screams! (*She is living again the terrible night when her son had been taken by a mob and lynched.*) Dey didn' say much. None o' 'em did, an' dey wouldn' let us. Dey tie him onto a horse an' drag him, drag him ovah de groun', ovah de rocks and weeds. Den dey hang him to a tree an' dey shot him, shot him plum full o' holes! An' dey wouldn' let me or youah mammy go neah him! Dey wouldn't let us take him down! We, we could see him up dere, dangling . . .

JIM: For God's sake, Aunt Doady, stop!

AUNT DOADY: (*brokenly*) Jim, baby. Aunt Doady's sorry! Only I wakes up at night sometime an' I heahs him sayin', "I didn' mean to kill him, I jus' twisted he gun, so he wouldn' shoot me!" An' he wouldn', Jim. Youah pappy wouldn' ha haht nothin'! But de white folks, dey didn' know dat . . .

JIM: I tell you, I can't stand it!

AUNT DOADY: Jim, who dey aftah, dem blood houn's? (*Jim stares at her and the truth finally dawns on her.*) Dey's aftah you!

JIM: I ain' done nothin'! I sweahs I ain'! (*They listen fearfully to the distant barking of the dogs.*) I was comin' along de road from de sto' when I sees Mr. Watkins a layin' in a little huddle ovah to one side. I went ovah to him, an' he was bleedin'. He'd been shot. I stahted runnin' off to git help an' a cah full of white men drove up an' see me a runnin off, an' dey take in aftah me. I knowed den dey think I done it an' it scah me, Aunt Doady. It scah me so I didn' know what I'se doin', so I jus' go fastah'n evah! I heahs one of 'em yell, "Catch him!" An' anothah one say, "Who was it?" An' somebody else say, "I doan know what niggeh it was!"

AUNT DOADY: Why didn' you stop an' tell 'em you ain' done nothin'?

JIM: I'se scahed, I tell you! I couldn' think. I couldn' do nothin' but run! I lights out to'd de ribbah bottom an' dey chases me. Dey almos' had me once. I'se hidin' hin' a little holly tree, an' dey was as close as you is to me now, so close I could ha' teched em. I couldn' even breathe. I heahs one of 'em say he'll go git de sheriff an' blood houn's. I waits till dey leaves an' den I wades across de ribbah wheah it's shallow, so's dey cain't fin' my trail.

AUNT DOADY: Jim baby, you's all wet!

JIM: Ef'n I hurries, mebbe I kin make it to de Louisiana bordah. I'll stay till dey fin's who done it. I ain' gonna face 'em now, Aunt Doady, I cain't!

AUNT DOADY: Yes, I knows, son. I rembah youah pappy. He couldn' splain, he couldn' hide. Heah, go roun' an' look undah dat rock by de hen house doah. I done put a li'l buryin' money in a can dere. You take em. Spec you'll need 'em in Louisiana.

JIM: Thanks, Aunt Doady! I oughta git a lettah from Professah Brown with some money fo' de bugs nex' week. You jes open it an' keep dat.

AUNT DOADY: I go in an' fix a cup of coffee for you. You gonna need it.

(*Jim goes around the house to the back and Aunt Doady goes inside. You can hear her mumbling to herself as she warms the coffee and pours it in a cup. The dogs get closer. She comes to the door and listens; then gets the cup of coffee and brings it outside.*)

JIM: (*coming around the house*): I foun' it. I kin cut through.

AUNT DOADY: (*listening*): Jim, dey's ovah dere too. Dey's split de pack! Listen to 'em ovah dere, and ovah youndah. Dey musta foun' out it was you, an' now dey's aroun', and gittin' closeh. (*They look at each other in terror.*)

JIM: I gotta git out! I hotta hurry! I gotta make it!

AUNT DOADY: No, Jim! You cain' nevah git away from 'em! You cain' nevah now. Heah, run to de shed room an' git de shot gun! (*He disappears into the house.*) God, dey cain't take my Jim! Dey cain't drag him ovah de rocks and weeds, drag him till he's skinned an' bleedin', hang him, put a rope aroun' his neck' and pull it till dey ain' no life lef' in 'em, see him danglin' from a tree! Jim what's so gentle he wouldn' even huht a buttahfly! (*When she says "buttahfly," she stands stock still, struck by a sudden thought. Then she moves slowly toward the wash bench and fearfully picks up the fruit jar containing cyanide. She puts it down quickly, but the dogs sound closer than ever; so hurriedly she takes the lid off the jar, empties some of the cyanide into the coffee and replaces the jar on the bench.*) Lawd, he say it doan huht de li'l wil' things. They just takes a sniff an' goes to sleep. Dey doan evah know what happen to 'em. But ef'n I gives him pizen, I kills him. I kills him myself. Blood on my soul! . . . An' ef'n I doan, dey git him. Dey drag him, dey hang him from a lim'. I goes to Hell, Lawd, not Jim, not Jim!

(*Jim returns carrying the gun.*)

AUNT DOADY: Jim baby, you knows Aunt Doady loves you, doan you, son?

JIM: 'Cose I does, Aunt Doady. Why you ask dat? You been both mammy and pappy to me.

AUNT DOADY: Epsie Lee, she heah dis evenin'.

JIM: You tell Epsie Lee, Aunt Doady, tell huh why I didn' see huh befo' I lef', tell huh I be back fo' long.

AUNT DOADY: Sho, baby, you be back fo' long.

JIM: Lissen! Dey's comin' closuh! Dey's heah almos'. I'se goin', Aunt Doady. I'se gotta' go!

AUNT DOADY: (*talking almost to herself*): Hit's a terrible thing I'se doin'. De pearly gates is gittin' dimmah an' dimmah, furdah an' furdah away. But I'se got to! I'se got to do it fo' Jim!

JIM: What you say, Aunt Doady?

AUNT DOADY: (*hands him the coffee*): Heah. Drink it down. It ain' so hot now. Drink it all at once!

(*Aunt Doady, with horror and misery written on her black face, watches him take a huge gulp of coffee, seeming to swallow most of it at once. He gasps and chokes.*)

JIM: It tastes funny. Aunt Doady, I'se . . . sick.

AUNT DOADY: Hit's cause you'se upset an' nervous, Jim. Heah, come in an' lie down a minute fo' you goes.

(*Jim staggers into the house and drops on the bed. Aunt Doady stands in the door, stunned, looking at him. Then she moves the lamp to a table near the narrow bed so that the lamplight shines on him. You can see his body stretched out on the bed, through the window. She comes back to the door and drops on the doorstep. Her face is tragic in the realization of what she has done.*)

AUNT DOADY: Lawd, I wondah, does you undahstan' . . .

(*The dogs are in the woods near at hand now and men are heard, trying to quiet them. One voice is heard above the others.*)

VOICE: Circle the house and see that he don't slip out! (*Two men enter from the right. Tom Moore is a stalwart, slow-moving, slow-talking man. Miles Chambers is a younger man, thoughtless and arrogant.*)

TOM MOORE: Good evening, Aunt Doady.

AUNT DOADY: (*answering as though she is in a stupor*): Awright, thank you. How's you?

TOM MOORE: Is Jim here?

AUNT DOADY: Yessuh, Jim's heah.

MILES CHAMBERS: Well, tell him to get himself out here and not try any funny business, or else he'll wish he hadn't.

AUNT DOADY: Musta been youah dogs I heahd bahkin' ovah dere. Is you been coon huntin'?

MILES CHAMBERS: (*facetiously*): Oh, we're hunting coon right enough.

TOM MOORE: Aunt Doady, Jim just killed a white man and we're here to get him. You can't let niggers get away with things like that, and you'd better tell him not to try to run.

AUNT DOADY: No, suh, Mr. Moore, he won't run away.

MILES CHAMBERS: Well, stop palaverin' and tell us where he is. (*He grabs Aunt Doady's shoulder and shakes her.*)

TOM MOORE: Cut it out, Miles. Aunt Doady ain't done nothing.

MILES CHAMBERS: You've got to put the fear of God in these damn niggers or they'll take the country. Where is he?

AUNT DOADY: (*pointing to window*): Dere he is. He's daid.

MILES CHAMBERS: Well, I'll be a . . .

(*A man enters from the left. He has been running.*)

MAN: Tom, you haven't done nothin' yet, have you?

TOM MOORE: No, why?

MAN: You're on the wrong track! Jim didn't do it. Henry Watts' brother-in-law killed him. He went over to the county seat and turned himself in. The sheriff caught us at the Catfish Bridge.

TOM MOORE: His brother-in-law! Well! They've been on bad terms for years.

MILES CHAMBERS: Well, old Jim here kicked the bucket before we got him anyway. Couldn't lynch a dead nigger.

TOM MOORE: Shut up, Miles! We're sorry, Aunt Doady. We shouldn't have bothered you. I feel kinda bad about Jim. He allus seemed like a good nigger. He musta had a bad heart.

(*The men, greatly subdued, go quietly and rather awkwardly off the stage. Aunt Doady's face is pitiful to see as she realizes she has needlessly given him poison.*)

AUNT DOADY: Dey wouldn' a took him. Dey wouldn' ha' took him. Lawd, you gotta undahstan'. I didn' know it. I thought dey kill him. I thought dey hang 'em up on a tree lak dey done his pappy. Jesus, I done kill my own gran'son. De owl he hoot t'ree times! Wish it ud been me, Lawd, 'stead uh Jim!

(*Epsie Lee runs in from the left.*)

EPSIE LEE: It ain' so, Aunt Doady. Jim ain' dead. Men down de road say Jim dead. Wheah is he, Aunt Doady?

AUNT DOADY: (*motions toward window*): Dere he is.

EPSIE LEE: Oh, Lawd!

(*Epsie Lee goes into the house. You can see her standing, looking at Jim for a few moments. Then she drops to her knees and sobs.*)

AUNT DOADY: He was standin' right dere talkin' to me jus' a moment ago. An' now he's gone. He ain' heah. I won' nevah heah him come whistlin' home in de evenin'. His cawn bread an' tuhnip greens is still a settin' on de back uh de stove a waitin' for 'em jus' wheah I put 'em myself. Oh, God! Ef'n he could only git up and eat 'em! Dere's all his bugs jes' lak he lef' 'em. Ef'n it hadn' been fo' de bugs, I never would a thought uh de jah! Ef'n I only hadn' ... God, I wondah why us has to do such things! I lose my Jim ... Won' nevah know peace no mo'.

(*The whippoorwill calls, low and mournfully. Lucy and the other negroes, come from the left. They are silent and sympathetic. Lucy goes to Aunt Doady. The others stand about looking in the window, saying nothing. Fruit Cake stays close to his mother, his eyes round with wonder and fear.*)

LUCY: Dere, Aunt Doady. Doan look lak dat. Ef'n you could jus' break down, you feel so much bettah. What happen', Aunt Doady? I see 'em dis mawnin' an' he look jes' es peart, goin' along whis'lin'.

AUNT DOADY: (*unaware that anyone has spoken to her*): He was funny li'l boy. He wa'n't no mo' dan seben when he went out an' catch a fish. He brung him home, dip him in cawn meal, an' fry 'em, jes' so he could surprise me. Bless his haht! He done fo'got to take de fish's insides out ... An' he brung me a new cap jes' las' week. Epsie Lee! Come heah!

(*Lucy calls to Epsie Lee and the girl comes out. She drops to the ground and puts her head in Aunt Doady's lap.*)

AUNT DOADY: He say he sorry he couldn't see you fo' he lef' . . . (*After a moment's silence.*) You'se jus' gonna miss him . . . Fo' God! Wish dat's all my mournin' gonna be!

EPSIE LEE: Ain' it cruel, Aunt Doady? Ain' death cruel?

AUNT DOADY: They's things crueller than death, Epsie Lee. They's things crueller than death.

(*The other negroes start singing very low at first, gradually growing louder, the weird old song, "What Is Dis?"*)

> What is dis dat steals, dat steals
> Across my brow?
> Is it death? Is it death?
> What is dis dat steals
> My breath away?
> Is it death? Is it death?
>
> CHORUS:
>
> If dis is death, I soon shall be
> From ebry pain an' trouble free.
> I shall the King of Glory see,
> All is well. All is well!
> What is dis dat make, dat make
> My pulse beat feeble and slow?
> Is it death? Is it death?
> What is dis dat creeps, dat creeps
> Across my frame?
> Is it death? Is it death?

The curtain falls.

Evelyn Keller Caldwell
(1919–)

Evelyn Keller Caldwell was not raised in an environment that encouraged any type of social consciousness. In fact, she describes her stepfather as "a bigot—against all blacks and Jews" and her mother as being specifically "anti-black."[1] Caldwell drew on her own childhood experiences instead of adopting the racial views of her parents: "There was a little black girl in my class at school. We were partners whenever we had to line up by twos. Her name was Faith and I always liked her."[2] Caldwell attended high school when she was eleven years old and graduated at fifteen as valedictorian. She was awarded a scholarship to Slippery Rock State Teachers College, but her stepfather forbade her to accept it because "he didn't believe in college" and expected her to remain at home and work on the family farm.

Caldwell remembers frequently seeking shelter from the violent nature of her stepfather: "When I was desolate, I used to crawl into a kennel with one of the German Shepherds. I could hide there for hours . . . the dogs never gave away my presence."[3]

Caldwell eventually found the courage to resist her stepfather's violence and domination. One night, when she was eighteen years old, she climbed out of a bedroom window (which she refers to as her "Houdini act") and left the farm forever.

Caldwell built a life for herself in writing and broadcasting, later marrying Larry Caldwell, a radio news director, in Pueblo, Colorado. The issue of race continued to be a divisive factor in her family life. In the 1960s, Caldwell and her husband became godparents to Gary Johnson, a twelve-year-old African American in Pueblo, Colorado. Caldwell's mother never accepted Gary, and Caldwell remembers the strong resentment her mother showed "because Gary and I sat side by side at my husband's funeral."[4]

Caldwell was in her early twenties when she wrote *Voice in the Wilderness*, a radio drama which aired over Sharon Broadcasting, WPIC, in the early 1940s.[5] In addition to writing *Voice in the Wilderness*, which was published in a 1944 collection of her radio plays, Caldwell also dramatized the novels of Charles Dickens.[6] Her adaptations ran as a series over WPIC which was reviewed in *Billboard* as "an ambitious undertaking" but "not quite up to network caliber."[7] Caldwell is credited with being the producer-director-adapter, but the male bias of the reviewer is evident when he describes her as "a gal who took on a man sized job." Caldwell also wrote *The Quality of Mercy*, which was produced by CBS in 1944 starring Akim Tamiroff, and *The Man Who Knew How*, an adaptation of a Dorothy Sayers novel, which also aired over CBS in 1944. She also wrote "Jeremiah XIII, 23," an unpublished short story dealing with segregation in the South in 1958.

Caldwell remembers John Fahnline, former president and manager of WPIC, as "the Father Figure that had been missing in my life . . . never preaching, never criticizing, always seeing both sides of the coin in any disagreement. His teaching was never overt, never obvious. If I was ahead of my time in any of my writing or attitudes, I owe it to him."[8] Another important influence on Caldwell's life was Sara Tarr, a teacher during her junior and senior high school years who encouraged her to write. "We maintained a friendship after I graduated and it was she who offered me asylum in her home for a few weeks following my "midnight Houdini" out the window. This was no idle gesture . . . she was married, with a young child at the time. My stepfather tracked me there, pounded on the front door (while I escaped out the back) and he continued to harass those poor people long after I had moved elsewhere. Sara was proud of the work I did with WPIC, we were never out of touch, and we have continued to be good friends to this day."[9]

According to Caldwell, she cannot recall any specific incident that motivated her to write *Voice in the Wilderness*, but suggests it could have been a news story from around the country because she was monitoring the news all the time. In addition to writing and directing the drama, Caldwell also read the role of Sandy, the secretary. One unusual aspect of the play is that the lynching takes place in the North, accentuating the fact that mob violence was not limited to the South. One of the characters remarks, "I can't believe it! This isn't the South! This is Pine County. Things like that just don't happen here." By drawing on her experience as a "career woman" in the 1940s, Caldwell offered the public workplace within the white community as an additional setting for lynching drama and showed that white individuals who took a stand against lynching were a small minority.

Another unique quality of the play is that it contains a white character presenting the view that members of any lynch mob are criminals and should be tried in the courts for murder. This view was the essence of the NAACP's antilynch bill, introduced during the Truman years, which sought punitive action directly against members of a lynch mob.[10] The play also emphasizes the deepseated racism of the white community, revealing mob members to be men who are well known in the community and accepted as "good law abiding citizens."

This was a strong challenge to the complacency of the white community; many whites believed they could distance themselves from the lynch mob by saying the lynchers were transients or young rowdies who got out of hand.

Voice in the Wilderness is representative of many lynching dramas by white playwrights in that it both exposes and reproduces the racism of white culture. One character refers to the lynching as "a necktie party," and even the district attorney, who is ostensibly trying to bring the mob members to justice, states that under different circumstances the mob might have acted with "some justification." Furthermore, it portrays the white district attorney as the active fighter for justice, whereas the character of Mrs. Jackson, mother of the lynching victim, appears passive and accepting of what has happened to her son. In one scene she appears more concerned for the district attorney's career than for seeing that justice is carried out: "Youah a young man . . . you got youh whole life ahead of you. Don' spoil it, boy. Eff you do what you plannin' to do, dese men ain't neveh goin' to fo'give you." The white district attorney responds to the mother's appeal with a speech on how he must enforce the laws of the land equally for all people.

Answering this criticism, Caldwell points out that she never intended for the white district attorney to be seen as the "hero" of the play. She notes that it is ironic that he loses his fight for justice and that her play was intended to criticize local governments all across the nation that permitted lynchings to continue. Caldwell intended the mother's actions to be seen as very courageous and stressed that the play was written before the ideas of the civil rights movement were widely adopted. In Caldwell's view, the mother's actions show that she is protecting what is left of her family from persecution. Other lynching dramas such as Angelina Grimké's *Rachel* (1916), Myrtle Smith Livingston's *For Unborn Children* (1926), and May Miller's *Nails and Thorns* (1933) incorporate an awareness that overt resistance against a lynch mob put all family members, even entire neighborhoods, in danger.

Evelyn Keller Caldwell currently lives in Englewood, Colorado. She enjoys a continuing relationship with her godson, Gary, and she is also godmother to his children. Although retired for many years, Caldwell continues to enjoy reading and writing: "It was writing that took me to the radio station, and the ability to write that kept me constantly employed for a lot of years thereafter. I will probably go on reading and TRYING to write until I can no longer see the page or find the keyboard. . . . It is where I live."[11]

NOTES

1. Evelyn Keller Caldwell, telephone conversation with Judith Stephens, November 12, 1991.
2. Ibid.

3. Evelyn Keller Caldwell, letter to Judith Stephens, November 15, 1991.

4. Ibid.

5. Evelyn Keller (Caldwell) was born in Akron, Ohio, and raised near Sharon, Pennsylvania. She worked at the Sharon radio station WPIC for fourteen years (1940 to 1954), serving as administrative assistant and, for the final four years, as "Acting Manager" when the president of the station suffered a stroke.

6. Evelyn Keller, *Voice in the Wilderness* in *Eleven Radio Plays by Evelyn Keller* (Boston: Christopher Publishing House, 1944).

7. Sam Chase, "David Copperfield," *The Billboard,* May 28, 1949, n.p.

8. Caldwell, letter to Stephens, 1991.

9. Ibid.

10. Albert P. Blaustein and Robert Zangrando, *Civil Rights and the Black American: A Documentary History* (New York: Simon and Shuster, 1968), 351.

11. Caldwell, letter to Stephens, 1991.

Voice in the Wilderness

A RADIO DRAMA   1944

✻✻✻

Evelyn Keller Caldwell

CHARACTERS

KEITH JAMISON, *district attorney*
SANDY NELSON, *secretary*
MR. GRIMES, *sheriff*
LEE JACKSON, *a hired hand, accused of assault and battery*
MRS. JACKSON, *Lee's mother*
GEORGE STEWART, *jury member*
LAWYER

EFFECTS: *Buzzer. Door opens*

KEITH: Meet the new District Attorney of Pine County!
SANDY: Hello, sucker.
KEITH: Hey!
SANDY: Come on in.

EFFECTS: *Door closes*

SANDY: I just heard it over the radio.
KEITH: You don't sound very pleased.
SANDY: What am I supposed to do, bump my head on the floor?
KEITH: You didn't want me to run, did you? I'll bet you didn't even vote for me.
SANDY: I'm sorry, Keith, I'm just being nasty. I'm proud of you, honestly. I'm . . . I'm awfully glad you won.
KEITH: What's wrong?
SANDY: Oh . . . jealousy, I suppose.
KEITH: Jealousy!
SANDY: Sure. A small-town lawyer is one thing. District Attorney is another.
KEITH: You mean you thought this would make a difference . . . between us?
SANDY: Well, won't it?
KEITH: Goose! I came to offer you a job.
SANDY: You mean . . .

KEITH: As secretary to the District Attorney.

SANDY: (*disappointed*) Oh.

KEITH: I'll need a right hand man, Sandy. The D.A.'s job, even in a place as quiet as Pine County, is no cinch. Not for a novice, anyway. Will you help me?

SANDY: Is that an appeal to my girlish sympathies?

KEITH: Certainly.

SANDY: I have a job, thanks.

KEITH: Please, Sandy?

SANDY: How many babies did you have to kiss to get elected?

KEITH: Sandy!

SANDY: Wouldn't people talk, seeing us together day and night?

KEITH: Well, if it ever became necessary, I suppose I *could marry you.*

MUSIC: *Bridge*

SANDY: Hey . . .

KEITH: What?

SANDY: Stop looking so pleased with yourself. The buttons on your vest are going to pop any minute.

KEITH: Stop speaking so disrespectfully to your superiors.

SANDY: You like this cops and robbers business, don't you!

KEITH: Don't you?

SANDY: Nothing very exciting has happened so far. You've tried a liquor violation case and a couple of juvenile delinquents.

KEITH: What do you want me to do, stage a gang war or a bank robbery?

SANDY: Pine County's too law-abiding for you, Keith. Your talents don't have any scope. How can you get to be another Thomas E. Dewey over a couple of juvenile delinquents?

KEITH: Just for that you can buy your own lunch, my girl.

SANDY: On Wednesday!!! That's . . .

EFFECTS: *Phone rings*

SANDY: Ah! Business is picking up . . . I hope.

EFFECTS: *Receiver up*

SANDY: District Attorney's Office. Oh, yes, Sheriff. . . . Yes, he's here, just a minute . . . (*to Keith*) It's Grimes.

KEITH: Hello. Yes. Oh? . . . I see. (*long pause*) Did she identify . . . Oh. Yes. Yes. I'll come down right away.

EFFECTS: *Phone on cradle*

SANDY: A murder?

KEITH: Almost.

SANDY: Wonderful!

KEITH: Sandy!

SANDY: Who?

KEITH: Old Mrs. Cartwright.

SANDY: Oh. Gee!

KEITH: Do you know her?

SANDY: Yes. She lives on the Mill Run Road. Raises herbs.

KEITH: That's the one.

SANDY: Who did it, do they know?

KEITH: The Sheriff thinks it was a negro they've picked up.

SANDY: Can't the old lady identify him?

KEITH: She's still unconscious. I'm going down to the jail. You skip over to the hospital, Sandy, and if she regains consciousness, call me right away.

MUSIC: *Bridge*

KEITH: Hello, Grimes.

SHERIFF: Hello, Keith.

KEITH: Where's this fellow you picked up?

SHERIFF: Back in a cell.

KEITH: What does he say?

SHERIFF: Nothing, yet. I haven't tried to make him talk. I put him away by himself, give him time to think it over. That works better.

KEITH: But . . .

SHERIFF: I know his kind. I've dealt with 'em before. You get rough and they get stubborn.

KEITH: Who is he?

SHERIFF: Name's Lee Jackson.

KEITH: Who says he did it?

SHERIFF: Nobody for sure. He's been working for Mrs. Cartwright, now and then, doing odd jobs. Hoes the garden, cuts the grass . . .

KEITH: Mmmmhmmm.

SHERIFF: Jennie Bassett, lives down the road a piece, found the old lady layin' in the yard. Bassetts are the closest neighbors. They said they hadn't seen anybody around the place all day except Jackson. They saw him out back cutting wood early this morning.

KEITH: Let's get him in, see what he says.

SHERIFF: (*yells off mike*) Hey, Jerry . . . bring Jackson in here.

KEITH: How badly is the old lady hurt?

SHERIFF: Fractured skull, one arm broken.

KEITH: What sort of weapon was used?

SHERIFF: Club or a stick of some sort.

KEITH: How old is Mrs. Cartwright?

SHERIFF: Around 65, I think. She's just a little thing.

KEITH: Does she live alone?

SHERIFF: Yeah. She's a widow, no children. This Jackson's been doing odd jobs outside, and she gets Jennie Bassett in to do the cleaning.

KEITH: That's how the girl happened to find her?

SHERIFF: Yes, she . . . Oh, all right, Jerry. Sit down, Jackson.

LEE: Yassuh.

SHERIFF: This is the District Attorney.

LEE: I didn't do nothin'!

KEITH: What's your name?

LEE: Lee Jackson.

KEITH: Where do you live?

LEE: Cross de river, by Big Bend.

KEITH: Do you work for a lady by the name of Mrs. Cartwright?

LEE: No, suh.

KEITH: You don't?

SHERIFF: There's no use lying, Jackson. You'll just get yourself in more trouble than you're in right now.

LEE: (*bursts out*) I didn't mean to hurt the old lady, honest I didn't! But she come at me wid a broom . . .

KEITH: Why?

LEE: On . . . on account de pie, I reckon.

KEITH: Pie?

LEE: I was hungry. Ain't much to eat at our house, and I didn't have no breakfast. Old Miz Cartwright had a pie settin' on de bench out back, an' . . .

KEITH: You took it?

LEE: Yassuh.

KEITH: Then what?

LEE: She see me. She yell, "Put down dat pie, you dirty nigger." She come at me wid a broom, aswingin' it at me. I grab de broom away fum her an' she start hittin' at me wid her hands.

KEITH: And?

LEE: I guess I musta hit her wif de broom. Den I got scared an' went off home.

KEITH: I see.

LEE: She ain't hurt bad, is she? I didn't mean to hurt de old lady, boss, she jus' got me mad comin' at me dat way, callin' me names.

KEITH: You shouldn't have left her lying there. Why didn't you call a doctor?

LEE: I 'uz scared, mistuh.

KEITH: Yes, of course. Well . . . that's that, Sheriff.

LEE: What you goin' do to me?

KEITH: You'll have to stand trial for assault and battery.

LEE: I gotta stay in jail?

KEITH: I'm afraid so.

SHERIFF: Take him back, Jerry.

KEITH: And give him something to eat.

LEE: (*fade*) Thank yuh, boss.

KEITH: Poor devil.

SHERIFF: That, if you'll pardon my saying so, is the wrong sentiment for the District Attorney to be expressing.

KEITH: Is it?

SANDY: (*fade in*) Keith . . .

KEITH: Sandy! Why didn't you call me instead of coming over? Is she conscious?

SANDY: No, Keith, she's . . . she died.

MUSIC: *Bridge*

KEITH: Did you make my hotel reservations?

SANDY: Yes, it's all set.

KEITH: Good. You know where to reach me, then, if anything comes up.

SANDY: Nothing's very apt to.

KEITH: No. Take care of these briefs, will you?

SANDY: Sure. Here, you'd better sign these letters before you go.

KEITH: Yes.

EFFECTS: *Phone rings*

SANDY: Are you in?

KEITH: No, tell them I've left.

EFFECTS: *Phone up*

SANDY: District Attorney's office. No, I'm sorry, he's not here. Oh, yes . . . He's out of town, will be until Monday. Shall I have him call you? All right, thank you.

EFFECTS: *Phone on cradle*

KEITH: Who was it?

SANDY: Joe Morrison, of the *Bugle*.

KEITH: Important?

SANDY: I don't think so. Just the usual news snoop.

KEITH: Oh.

SANDY: You know . . . you've got an enemy there.

KEITH: Who, Morrison?

SANDY: Not just Morrison. The paper itself.

KEITH: Why do you say that?

SANDY: Oh . . . just a hunch. They backed the opposition candidate in the election, you know.

KEITH: Yes, it's always been a strong party paper. But I don't think they have any personal animosity towards me.

SANDY: I don't know . . . it's a ratty paper, anyway.

KEITH: What do you mean?

SANDY: They print the dirty side of everything. When they can't find anything shady, they insinuate. Yellow journalism.

KEITH: Well, you can't blame them for inventing a scandal once in a while. There aren't many real ones in Pine County.

MUSIC: *Bridge*

KEITH: Hello, Sandy, you're down early.

SANDY: I thought you'd be in pretty soon.

KEITH: What's new, anything?

SANDY: Let's go in your office.

EFFECTS: *Pause, then door closes*

SANDY: Have you been home yet?

KEITH: No, I just got into town.

SANDY: Seen anybody?

KEITH: No. What's the matter with you?

SANDY: We . . . had a necktie party last night.

KEITH: A . . . what?

SANDY: A lynching.

KEITH: You're *crazy!*

SANDY: Keith . . .

KEITH: Here, sit down. You're . . . kidding, aren't you?

SANDY: No.

KEITH: Who was it?

SANDY: Lee Jackson.

KEITH: Jackson! The Colored fellow that . . .

SANDY: Yes.

KEITH: But . . . Why????????

SANDY: Feeling's been running pretty high for the past couple of days. I didn't think anything like this would happen or I'd have called you. I did try to get you last night, but you'd checked out.

KEITH: Was it because the old lady died?

SANDY: Not just that. The story got around that she'd been . . . criminally assaulted.

KEITH: That's not true!!

SANDY: I know it isn't, but a lot of people believe it. The *Bugle* printed it.

KEITH: The *Bugle!*

SANDY: Saturday night.

KEITH: I can't . . . I can't believe it, Sandy! This isn't the South! This is Pine County. Things like that just don't happen here.

SANDY: Well, they did! I saw it!

KEITH: Sandy! Oh, you poor kid . . .

SANDY: (*struggling to control her voice*) I was . . . just driving home from the farm . . .

KEITH: Take it easy. Want a cigarette?

SANDY: No.

KEITH: Was there any resistance? Didn't the sheriff . . .

SANDY: He wasn't at the jail. Somebody tricked him, got him over to Weston with a fake phone call. There . . . must have been seventy or eighty men. They caught Jerry napping . . . tied him up . . . and dragged Jackson out.

KEITH: You didn't see that part!

SANDY: No. I talked to Jerry and he told me. When I saw them, they had taken Jackson up to that big oak tree on the hill near the reservoir. You know the one I mean?

KEITH: On Furnace Hill?

SANDY: Yes. They stripped him. They stood him on a barrel and tied the rope. Then they kicked the barrel out from under him . . .

KEITH: Don't. You don't have to go on. Why don't you go home for a while?

SANDY: No, I . . .

EFFECTS: *Knock on door*

KEITH: Come in!

EFFECTS: *Door opens*

KEITH: Oh, it's you, Grimes.

SHERIFF: Yeah, I heard you were back.

EFFECTS: *Door closes*

SHERIFF: Sandy tell you?

KEITH: She's just telling me now.

SHERIFF: I couldn't help it, Keith. I knew a lot of people were stirred up about it, but I didn't think it would come to lynching.

KEITH: There's no excuse for it! If the man had been scot-free and it looked as though he weren't going to be punished, then they might have taken matters into their own hands with some justication. But the man was in jail, the law was dealing with him in its own way.

SHERIFF: Hasn't been a lynching in Pine County for thirty-five years.

KEITH: The days of the Vigilantes are over!

SHERIFF: You know the rumor that was going around?

KEITH: That wasn't true.

SHERIFF: That's not the point, Keith. People believed it.

KEITH: Sandy says the *Bugle* printed it.

SHERIFF: Yes. I think that's what touched things off. Till then, it had been just a rumor. But when people saw it in print, it became a fact.

KEITH: They ought to be horsewhipped!

SHERIFF: I don't suppose they meant any real harm, Keith. They were just looking for something to print . . .

KEITH: Sandy says the *Bugle* has it in for me. I wonder . . .

SHERIFF: That's kind of far-fetched, isn't it? I mean . . . it was Jackson that got hung, not you.

KEITH: Yes, but . . .

SHERIFF: No, I think it's just a case of accidentally getting a lot of people riled up. It's too bad, but . . . it's done and there's no help for it.

KEITH: Has there been any trouble across the river, in the negro section?

SHERIFF: Yeah, they're plenty mad about it. I swore in a couple of extra deputies and sent them over. That's where I'm going now.

KEITH: If you go back by the jail, send Jerry up to see me, will you?

EFFECTS: *Door opens*

SHERIFF: Sure, Keith. And . . . don't worry too much about this.

EFFECTS: *Door closes*

KEITH: Don't worry about it! Sandy . . . how do you feel now?

SANDY: Better. I'll be all right.

KEITH: Do you think there was anything personal in what the *Bugle* did?

SANDY: Not . . . exactly, Keith. I mean they didn't do it with you in mind. But if they can turn this lynching into a weapon to discredit you, I think they'll do it.

KEITH: Mmm-hmm.

SANDY: The most horrible part of the whole thing, Keith, was that they brought a bunch of the negroes from across the river and made them watch.

KEITH: Watch the *lynching*?

SANDY: Yes. They were tied, they couldn't get away or do anything for Jackson. They just stood there as though they were hypnotized, and watched him sob and beg for help. They never looked away once . . . just stared, even after the barrel was kicked away and he hung there, kicking.

KEITH: They'll make trouble over this, or try to. And I'll be expected to arrest them for it. I won't do it, Sandy! I won't do it!

SANDY: What makes men such beasts, Keith . . . men who're normally good, law-abiding citizens . . . like Mr. Colby, the druggist?

KEITH: Was he in the mob?

SANDY: Yes.

KEITH: They didn't wear masks?

SANDY: Most of them had handkerchiefs tied around their faces, but it wasn't difficult to recognize them.

KEITH: I see. Who else was there?

SANDY: Oh . . . Joe Racini, the shoemaker, Bill Bradley, Al Somers, Mr. Horvath.

KEITH: Wait a minute . . . get a pencil and make a list of those names.

SANDY: Why?

KEITH: Lynching is a crime, Sandy . . . it constitutes first degree murder. I intend to prosecute every man who helped to kill Lee Jackson!

MUSIC: *Bridge*

SHERIFF: Get out of here, Sandy, I want to talk to Keith.

KEITH: Stay here, Sandy. Anything you've got to say you can say in front of her, Grimes.

SHERIFF: Have you lost your mind?

KEITH: Not that I know of. Why, have you found one?

SHERIFF: You . . . you can't go through with it!

KEITH: Why not?

SHERIFF: I . . . I won't, serve warrants on these men, Keith! I absolutely refuse!

KEITH: What's the matter, afraid you might not get elected next term?

SHERIFF: You don't know what you're doing! Some of these people are the most respected men in the county . . . doctors, merchants . . .

KEITH: And all voters, hmm? Listen, Sheriff . . . I was elected to protect the citizens of this county and to enforce its laws . . . not *part* of the citizens, nor *part* of the laws, but *all* of them. And that's what I intend to do.

SHERIFF: You don't understand what you're getting into, boy! There were seventy or eighty men. You can't prosecute every one of them. You don't even know their names.

KEITH: I've identified twenty-seven of them.

SHERIFF: Even if you arrest them . . . you'll never get a jury to convict them.

KEITH: I'm going to try.

SHERIFF: Keith . . . you're just going off the deep end because you're all riled up. A man was killed . . . I'm as sorry about that as you are, but no good will come of trying to prosecute the mob that did it. Why don't you think it over for a while? When you calm down . . .

KEITH: Look, Sheriff . . . if Lee Jackson had been walking down Elm Street, and Joe Racini, the shoemaker, had suddenly fired a gun and killed him . . . you'd have arrested Racini for murder, wouldn't you?

SHERIFF: That's different!

KEITH: No, it isn't. Just because Racini had seventy or eighty accomplices, and just because Jackson was hanged instead of shot . . . that doesn't alter the situation one iota. Joe Racini and every man who was with him is guilty of murder. So long as I am District Attorney of Pine County, they will not go unpunished!

SHERIFF: I won't help you, Keith! I won't have anything to do with it!

KEITH: Oh, yes, you will! You'll either help me or you'll resign. And another thing . . . Jerry knows the names of the men who broke into the jail that night. So far, he won't talk. You tell him he'll either give me a list of those names, or I'll arrest him as an accessory.

MUSIC: *Bridge*

SANDY: Keith . . . there's someone waiting to see you. An old colored woman.

KEITH: Oh? Who is she?

SANDY: She wouldn't give me her name.

KEITH: All right.

SANDY: Be careful, Keith. Leave the door open.

KEITH: (*laughs*) O.K.

EFFECTS: *Door opens*

KEITH: Hello. Were you waiting to see me?

MRS. JACKSON: You Mr. Jamison?

KEITH: Yes. Don't get up.

MRS. JACKSON: I'm Miz Jackson.

KEITH: What can I do for you?

Mrs. Jackson: Lee Jackson was my son.

Keith: Oh.

Mrs. Jackson: I done heerd what youah aimin' t'do, Mr. Jamison . . .

Keith: You mean . . . arresting the men who lynched your son?

Mrs. Jackson: Yassuh. An' I come to ax you not to do it.

Keith: Not to do it!

Mrs. Jackson: I 'preshiate what you tryin' to do, Mr. Jamison, but it ain't no use. It won't bring my boy back.

Keith: I know that, Mrs. Jackson.

Mrs. Jackson: Youah a young man . . . you got youah whole life ahaid of you. Don' spoil it, boy. Eff you do what you plannin' to do, dese men ain't nevah goin' to fo'give you.

Keith: That's not important.

Mrs. Jackson: Son, it ain't no use you fightin' de debbil all alone. You only get hurt yo'sef.

Keith: Mrs. Jackson . . . the people of this county have had a hand . . . either directly or indirectly . . . in making their own laws. I can't . . . I won't . . . shape my enforcement so as not to tread on their toes. They can't build up an institution and then ignore it. Your son was guilty of a crime. He'd have received a fitting punishment. These men interfered and took from him what they could not give back . . . his life. Their crime was ten times worse than his. And they must pay for it.

Mrs. Jackson: Don't do it, Mr. Jamison . . . please don' do it.

Keith: I've got to! But I'm glad you came, Mrs. Jackson. If I had any doubts before . . . they're gone now.

Music: *Bridge*

Effects: *Shade flops*

Sandy: (*gasps*) Oh . . . it was just the window shade!

Keith: What's the matter with you?

Sandy: I'm sorry. I'm getting so jumpy I have heart-failure at the drop of a pin. The nearer it gets to the date of the trial, the more fluid my knees become.

Keith: Want to resign?

Sandy: It's . . . not for myself, Keith. I'm afraid for you.

Keith: There's no need to be.

Sandy: Yes, there is. You've indicted thirty-three men for murder. They're all out on bail, and every last one of them hates you.

Keith: So you think all thirty-three of them are going to gang up and tar and feather me!

Sandy: When we go home at night, I can feel eyes following us. I expect something to pop out of every alley. It's a horrible feeling, Keith.

Keith: Try to get your mind off it. Hysterics won't help.

Sandy: Keith . . . give it up.

Keith: It's too late for that.

SANDY: No, it isn't. You could fix it . . . have the indictments quashed.

KEITH: No.

SANDY: Mrs. Jackson was right, Keith. This will spoil your whole career. You can't go on. Even if you managed to finish out your term here, you'd never be re-elected.

KEITH: One term will probably be all I can stand, anyway.

SANDY: You had such a nice start . . . people liked you. If things had gone well, you could have run for State Senator, perhaps for Governor eventually.

KEITH: There's no use baiting me, Sandy.

SANDY: You're not thinking about the future at all! You're just blinded by a sudden splurge of heroics!

KEITH: Do you really believe that?

SANDY: Oh, I don't know what to believe!

KEITH: I'm setting a precedent, apparently. The papers are playing up this thing in a big way, all over the country.

SANDY: Is that what you're doing it for . . . the publicity?

KEITH: Sandy . . . I've as little stomach for what's coming as you have. Thirty-three men, most of whom I know intimately, I shall have to try separately for their lives. Something may happen to stop it, of course. I may never get beyond the first trial. That remains to be seen. But even if it should be only one trial, it will be an ordeal such as I have never faced in my life.

SANDY: Then step out, Keith! Resign!

KEITH: No. I got into this, as you say, on an impulse, but I'm going through with it only after a lot of hard, sober thinking. It sounds silly, but . . . it's a principle I'm fighting for, a principle of justice. I honestly believe these men are guilty of murder and that they should be punished. I know that if I don't try them myself, no one else will.

SANDY: It seems so senseless, Keith, demanding the deaths of thirty-three men in payment for one!

KEITH: I probably won't get a death penalty, Sandy.

SANDY: You won't even get a jury!

KEITH: That's what worries me most. After, all the furor that's been raised, where am I going to get twelve unbiased men and women in Pine County? (*sighs*) I wish Darrow were alive.

SANDY: Clarence Darrow would never have stuck his neck out on a case like this!

KEITH: Oh, yes, he would. This is just the sort of fight he loved . . . a battle from start to finish, with all the odds against him.

SANDY: All my common sense tells me that I ought to shake the dust of Pine County from my feet immediately, if not sooner . . . or at least get out of the D.A.'s office.

KEITH: Well, why don't you?

SANDY: Oh . . . somebody's got to be around to throw in the towel for you when the time comes.

Music: *Bridge*

Effects: *Rustle of paper*

Sandy: Open the window, will you, Keith?

Keith: Why? It's cold outside.

Sandy: I know, but I'm reading the *Bugle,* and I need air.

Keith: (*laughs*) Oh! What am I tonight?

Sandy: A pariah, my boy, a despoiler of homes. They're working a nice angle now . . . they've got a letter here, supposedly written by little Jimmy Colby . . . Please don't send my Dad to prison, and that sort of thing. The trouble is, there's a lot of truth in it, Keith.

Keith: Of course there is.

Sandy: Colby has two children, hasn't he? A boy and a girl. His wife is an invalid. How would she manage, Keith, if Colby were convicted?

Keith: How will Mrs. Jackson manage? Lee was her sole support.

Sandy: An eye for an eye, hm?

Keith: I don't pretend to be an avenging God, no.

Sandy: Everybody's against you, can you feel it? Everybody from the judge down to the tipstaff.

Keith: N-no . . . the judge isn't against me, Sandy. But he isn't *for me,* either. I'm afraid he looks on this as a sort of social experiment. The jury, though . . . the most I can say is that I'm pretty confident none of them were in the mob that did the lynching. But they're a dead weight, they've shut their minds against me. Whether I can pry them open and let in a little light, I don't know. George Stewart is the only one who is sympathetic. He was a great friend of my father. Maybe I can use him as a wedge.

Sandy: If you don't start eating and sleeping regularly pretty soon, you'll need more than a wedge. Just lose a little more weight and you can wear your vest for an overcoat.

Keith: Well, Sandy, no matter how the thing comes out, I know one thing . . . I'll have had my baptism of fire . . . I'll be a better lawyer. I think . . .

Sandy: Listen!

Keith: What?

Sandy: I thought I heard somebody in the outer office.

Keith: You're just nervous.

Sandy: No, I . . .

Effects: *Knock on door*

Sandy: Keith!

Keith: Sit still.

Effects: *Pause, then door is opened*

Keith: Oh . . . Hello, George!

George: (*slightly off mike*) Hello, Keith. Could I . . . see you for a minute?

Keith: Sure thing. Come on in.

GEORGE: (*on mike*) Evenin', Miss Nelson.

SANDY: Hello, Mr. Stewart. I'll be outside if you want me, Keith.

EFFECTS: *Door closes*

KEITH: Sit down, George. Anything I can do for you?

GEORGE: (*slowly*): It's . . . kind of personal. I hate to ask it of you, Keith, but I don't know where else to turn.

KEITH: What's wrong?

GEORGE: I need money, Keith. I can't go to the bank again, and it's something that has to be taken care of right away.

KEITH: I see.

GEORGE: It's a . . . personal debt. I don't like having to ask you, but . . . there's nobody else I'd care to . . .

KEITH: I'm glad you came to me, George. How much do you need?

GEORGE: A hundred and fifty dollars.

KEITH: Tonight?

GEORGE: I . . . can come back if you want.

KEITH: Wait a minute, I might have enough here in the safe . . .

GEORGE: This is . . . mighty decent of you, Keith.

KEITH: Forget it, you'd do as much for me. Yes, I think I can make it. Here's fifty, seventy, ninety, a hundred and ten, a hundred and twenty, thirty, forty, forty-five, a hundred and fifty.

GEORGE: Do you . . . want me to sign . . .

KEITH: No. Your word's good enough for me, George.

GEORGE: You sure you can spare this much? I'll pay it back as soon as I can.

KEITH: Don't worry about it.

GEORGE: Thanks a lot, Keith. You . . . won't mention this to anyone, will you?

KEITH: It's between me and thee. It won't go any further.

GEORGE: Thanks, Keith, I . . . thanks. G'night.

EFFECTS: *Door opens*

KEITH: Good night, George.

EFFECTS: *Door closes. Pause. Door opens*

SANDY: (*fade in*) What did Stewart want, Keith?

KEITH: It was . . . private, Sandy.

SANDY: Oh, pardon *me!* Isn't . . . isn't he on the jury?

KEITH: Yes, he is.

SANDY: Uh-huh. That's . . . what I thought.

MUSIC: *Bridge*

KEITH: (*fade in*) I cannot help but feel . . . and I believe you will agree . . . that Lee Jackson died primarily because he was a negro. Had a white man sat in his place in the Pine County jail that night, the law could have taken its course unmolested. There is still in this country a violent and vituperative resentment of the negro race. John Colby would be the first to tell you that he is a tolerant man . . . that above all he believes in racial tolerance. Yet when he and the men with him tied a rope around Lee Jackson's neck, they were no better than the Nazis who tortured and killed their Jewish countrymen. This country has gone to war in behalf of racial tolerance. If you free John Colby, you make a mockery of the ideals for which your own sons and brothers are dying. In the cause of humanity and justice, I ask you to find John Colby guilty of murder.

LAWYER: Just a moment! Your Honor, I ask that you declare this a mistrial! Evidence has just been placed in my hands showing that one of the jurors has been bribed!

EFFECTS: *Excited murmur of voices*

LAWYER: Juror Number Seven . . . George Stewart!

MUSIC: *Bridge*

KEITH: You don't believe me, do you, Sandy!

SANDY: I know why you did it, Keith but . . .

KEITH: Sandy, if you say that just once more, I'll throw you out of here bodily!

SANDY: But Keith . . .

KEITH: I did not bribe George Stewart, regardless of what he says. I gave him money, yes. I did not have him sign a note. But I didn't bribe him. I simply . . .

EFFECTS: *Knock on door, door opens almost simultaneously*

KEITH: What do you want!!?

SHERIFF: (*fade in*) I'm representing a delegation, Keith. A committee, you might say.

KEITH: Why don't you just arrest me and get it over with?

SHERIFF: That's . . . what I came about. We're willing to drop the charge . . . provided you're out of town within twenty-four hours.

KEITH: And if I don't go?

SHERIFF: You'll be prosecuted for bribery.

KEITH: I didn't bribe Stewart, I tell you! Simply loaned him some money!

SHERIFF: Can you prove that? Did you get a note? Did anybody hear the conversation?

KEITH: You know I can't prove it.

SHERIFF: Well?

KEITH: (*sighs*) All right. Call off your dogs. I'll be on the 10:25 tonight.

MUSIC: *Bridge*

KEITH: Chicago, one way, please.

SANDY: (*fade in*) Hello, Keith.

KEITH: Well! Nice of you to come down to see me off, Sandy . . . especially since you think I'm a heel.

SANDY: You mean that bribery business!

KEITH: Yes.

SANDY: Oh, I've changed my mind about that.

KEITH: What!

SANDY: Sure. If you'd really been guilty of bribery, you'd have stayed and fought the thing tooth and nail.

KEITH: That's nice reasoning. You must send me a diagram of it sometime.

EFFECTS: *Train whistle*

SANDY: Well, there she comes. Take my bag, too, will you Keith?

KEITH: Your bag!

SANDY: Sure. I'm going with you.

KEITH: Sandy . . .

SANDY: I like a fighter, Keith. Even when he loses.

MUSIC

Lillian Smith

(1897–1966)

L illian Smith's southern upbringing in Jasper, Florida, and Clayton, Georgia, provided the foundation for her anti-segregationist views. Early in her childhood her parents took in Julie, an orphan girl who had been living with a black family. Lillian enjoyed a close relationship with Julie until it was discovered she was "part black" and hastily removed from the household. This experience left Smith confronting "the paradox of a culture that teaches hospitality, democracy, and Christian charity at the same time that it violently denies the humanity of blacks."[1]

Smith's education included Piedmont College, Baltimore's Peabody Conservatory of Music, and Columbia University's Teachers College. She taught one year in an isolated mountain school in Georgia and spent three years teaching music at a Methodist Mission school in Huchow, China. She returned to Georgia to run the Laurel Falls Camp for Girls, which her father had founded at their Georgia home. With her companion, Paula Snelling, Smith ran the camp and edited a magazine (eventually known as *South Today*) which espoused their anti-segregationist views. During the 1930s Smith and Snelling established a tradition of hosting biracial gatherings and dinners at the camp where southern intellectuals, artists, and political activists could socialize and exchange ideas. In her recent collection of Smith's letters, Margaret Rose Gladney reveals the importance of Snelling's companionship to Smith's creativity and writing.

Through her novels such as *Strange Fruit* (1944) and *Killers of the Dream* (1949), along with numerous articles, reviews, and speaking engagements, Smith became nationally known as a southern writer, civil rights activist, and major contributor to the cause of racial justice in the 1940s and 1950s. During this period, she was awarded honorary degrees from Oberlin College and Howard University. Although battling cancer, Smith remained active in the civil rights movement of the early 1960s, becoming involved with organizations actively fighting for desegregation such as the Congress of Racial Equality (CORE) and the Student Non-Violent Coordinating Committee (SNCC). On July 4, 1966, she received the Charles S. Johnson Award, named in honor of the noted social scientist and former president of Fisk University. Smith died of cancer on September 28, 1966.

Published February 29, 1944, Smith's novel *Strange Fruit* moved to the top of the best seller list of the *New York Times Book Review* by May 14. The novel sold a million copies in hardcover, over three million in Smith's lifetime, and was translated into fifteen languages. The 1993 republication of the novel was accompanied by Alice Walker's comment that "the South can hardly be said to recognize itself without this book."[2] In 1944 Smith signed a contract with director Jose Ferrer and producer Arthur Friend to turn her highly successful and controversial novel into a play. Set in a racially segregated southern town, the novel and play focus on the interracial love affair between a white man and black woman that culminates in a lynching. Although Smith insisted in 1944 that *Strange Fruit* was not about racial prejudice and lynchings but about "human beings and their relationships with each other," she had written to anti-lynching activist Walter White in 1942, while she was still working on the novel, that her theme was "the effect of the southern concept of race upon not only lives but minds and emotions."[3]

Smith's distinctive approach in fighting racial prejudice was to place emphasis on the harm segregation and the notion of white superiority did to whites. In her view such practices and beliefs produced "stunted, crippled, emotionally immature people who were not able to become fully human (or to view Negroes as fully human) because they cut themselves off from human relationships and therefore from human growth."[4] She became known as one of the most liberal and outspoken of white southern writers on issues of racial injustice by declaring the white man as "one of the world's most urgent problems today" and for urging other whites to shift their attention from the so-called "Negro problem" to the white man's "deep-rooted needs that have caused him to seek those strange, regressive satisfactions that are derived from worshipping his own skin color."[5]

As a Broadway play *Strange Fruit* was not successful, but historically it remains one of the most controversial plays in the anti-lynching tradition. The heavily staged production, involving many large sets (twelve scenes, thirty-four actors, and thirty-five stagehands) won praise for the actors and designer George Jenkins, but the play was characterized by New York critics as "episodic" or "too long, too jumbled, too straggling."[6] According to Lillian's sister, Esther Smith, this was not the original version of the play which was preferred by Lillian but unfortunately destroyed, along with other manuscripts and letters, in a 1955 house fire.[7]

Both the novel and the play were surrounded by controversy relating to the language, meaning of the title, and theme of interracial relationships. The banning of the novel in Boston was upheld by the Massachusetts Supreme Court which declared *Strange Fruit* to be "obscene, indecent and impure," and a ban by the United States Post Office Department, barring the book from the mails, was lifted only after the intervention of President Roosevelt, via the influence of his wife, Eleanor.[8] Controversy also surrounded the source and meaning of the title, *Strange Fruit,* which most people (as well as the book's copyright page) attributed to the 1939 Lewis Allan–Billie Holiday song about lynching in the South. In her autobiography, Billie Holiday claimed Lillian Smith told her that "the song inspired her to write the novel and the play about a lynching," but Smith insisted her meaning of the phrase "Strange Fruit" referred to the damaged, twisted people (both black and white) who are the products or results of our racist culture.[9]

The racial controversy over *Strange Fruit* was never strictly divided along racial lines. While W. E. B. Du Bois and Theophilus Lewis praised the book, Dean Gordon B. Hancock, a contributing editor of the Associated Negro Press, saw it as a scathing indictment against the Negro race in general and Negro womanhood in particular. Much of the controversy focused on the character of Nonnie Anderson, the young black woman involved in a love affair with a white man (Tracy Deen). Hancock wrote of the relationship, "When Miss Smith portrays in Nonnie Anderson, a young Negro college graduate, no higher ambitions than to be the mistress and concubine of a dissolute poor white man, she stabs at the very heart and hopes of the Negro race."[10]

The role of Nonnie was played by Jane White, daughter of civil rights activist and anti-lynching crusader Walter White.[11] Jane White received excellent reviews for her acting debut and remembers she was suggested for the role of Nonnie by Paul Robeson. According to White, "other actresses had read for the part but Ferrer was still looking, and there were not that many young black actresses working in the Broadway theatre then because there were hardly any parts for them."[12] White remembers Nonnie as a character representing "innocence" and "purity," and *Strange Fruit* as "a play that dealt with territory that both black and white people needed to know." Abram Hill, producer-director of the American Negro Theatre, publicly debated Smith on the merits of *Strange Fruit,* saying he was moved by her missionary zeal but bored by the play.[13] Paul Robeson demonstrated his support for the play by meeting with the cast backstage and by publicly expressing his wish that "every American could see this moving and prophetic play."[14] Loften Mitchell included *Strange Fruit* in his history of black theatre and described the play as a "totally sincere effort," but a "disaster."[15]

When the play closed in January 1946, Smith wrote of it as "a bitter and terrible fiasco," but by April she described the experience as "fascinating and exhausting."[16] Twenty years later she wrote:

> You see, the play was from the beginning MORE THAN A PLAY. Never was it just a play. There were 35 or 36 in it; about half were white, half (or about that) were Negro; half were northern, half southern. Imagine that mixture! Caught up in that play and under the pressures. . . . It was really like casting and producing and rehearsing in a boiling cauldron.[17]

The final result was that Lillian Smith decided the play would never be produced again. The editors are grateful to Esther Smith for granting us permission to include the play in this volume. The play (based on production assistant George Greenburg's typescript at Lincoln Center) is published here for the first time and is for reading purposes only. Any production of the script is prohibited.

NOTES

1. Anne C. Loveland, *Lillian Smith, A Southerner Confronting the South: A Biography* (Baton Rouge: Louisiana State University Press, 1986). Also see Suzanne Allen, "Lillian Smith" in *American Women Writers: A Critical Reference Guide from Colonial Times to the Present*, vol. 4, ed. Lina Mainiero (New York: Frederick Ungar, 1982), 114–116.

2. In Harcourt Brace Jovanovich's recent (1993) republication of the novel.

3. Loveland, *Lillian Smith*, 64.

4. Loveland, *Lillian Smith*, 50.

5. Will Brantley, *Feminine Sense in Southern Memoir: Smith, Glasgow, Welty, Hellman, Porter, and Hurston* (Jackson: University Press of Mississippi, 1993), 47.

6. John Chapman, "*Strange Fruit* Splendidly Staged, Honestly Written—But Episodic," *Daily News*, November 30, 1945; Ward Morehouse, "'*Strange Fruit*' Offers Good Acting in an Awkward and Disjointed Drama," *The Sun*, November 30, 1945. These and other reviews of the play, from major New York papers, are in *New York Theatre Critics' Reviews*, vol. 6 (1945), 82–85.

7. Esther Smith, letter to Judith Stephens, March 31, 1993.

8. Loveland, *Lillian Smith*, 71.

9. Billie Holiday, with William Duffy, *Lady Sings the Blues* (New York: Lance Books, Inc., 1956), 83–84; Margaret Rose Gladney, *How Am I to Be Heard? Letters of Lillian Smith* (Chapel Hill: University of North Carolina Press, 1993), 71.

10. Hancock, quoted in Loveland, *Lillian Smith*, 69.

11. Walter White was a distinguished leader in the struggle for racial justice. Because of his light complexion, he often traveled throughout the South, passing for white, while investigating lynchings for the NAACP. See *A Man Called White: The Autobiography of Walter White* (Bloomington: Indiana University Press, 1948), and *Rope and Faggot* (New York: Arno Press, 1969).

12. Jane White, interview with Kathy Perkins and Judith Stephens, New York City, June 22, 1993.

13. "Abram Hill writes again on Strange Fruit: Lillian Smith Declines Offer," *Amsterdam News*, January 19, 1946, p. 24.

14. Loveland, *Lillian Smith*, 78.

15. Loften Mitchell, *Black Drama: The Story of the American Negro in the Theatre* (New York: Hawthorn Books, 1967), 126.

16. Gladney, *How Am I to Be Heard?* 101.

17. Gladney, *How Am I to Be Heard?* 95.

Strange Fruit

1945

❈

Lillian Smith

CAST

(in the order in which they speak)

A MILL HAND
ANOTHER MILL HAND
ED ANDERSON
LITTLE SOMEBODY
2ND GIRL
PREACHER DUNWOODIE
TOM HARRIS
DEE CASSIDY
GABE
DOUG
HARRIET HARRIS
CHARLIE HARRIS
TRACY DEEN
CRAZY CARL
SAM PERRY
ALMA DEEN
LAURA DEEN
TUT DEEN
NONNIE ANDERSON
BESS ANDERSON
JACKIE (*Bess's child*)
HENRY MCINTOSH
SALAMANDER
CHUCK

Miss Sadie
Miss Belle
Mamie McIntosh
Tracy Deen (*as a child*)
Henry McIntosh (*as a child*)
A Little Girl
Laura Deen (*as a child*)
Ten McIntosh
A Colored Man
A Maid

SYNOPSIS OF SCENES

The action of the play takes place in Maxwell, Georgia, in your time and mine.

ACT I

Scene 1. Deen's Drugstore. Late afternoon
Scene 2. Anderson home. Early evening
Scene 3. Deens' sun porch. Early afternoon. Two days later
Scene 4. The ridge. Same evening
Scene 5. Deen's Drugstore. The following night

ACT II

Scene 1. Deens' yard. Three days later
Scene 2. The same. Next morning
Scene 3. Salamander's Cafe. Evening of following day
Scene 4. Andersons' gate. Half hour later
Scene 5. Deens' sun porch. Next evening
Scene 6. Anderson's gate. Same evening
*Scene 7. Tom Harris's mill office. Next day. Early evening (The curtain will be
lowered in Scene 7 to indicate the passing of four hours.)*

ACT ONE, SCENE I

*Street Scene: It is early evening, just after sunset; the cool of the day when long thin
shadows stretch across buildings and corners darken an hour before the lights fade.
Where College Street meets Back Street, people pass to and fro on the sidewalk going
into Deen's Corner Drugstore, coming out again. The main entrance to the drugstore
opens on College Street where the offices are: Tom Harris's lumber office, the printing
office of the Maxwell News, and beyond them, the post office and the hardware store.
Up College Street beyond the business section are the homes of the wealthier people of*

Maxwell; and it is from this direction that many of the characters come, white and colored. Beyond the side entrance of the drugstore are the barber shop (and pressing club), fruit store (and hot dog stand), poolroom, ice company, and Salamander's Lunch Counter (colored). Large plate glass windows, filled with the usual display of cosmetics and drugs, front College Street, a smaller display window opens on Back Street. A drinking fountain is at the curb where College Street and Back Street meet. On it is a sign, "FOR WHITES ONLY."

One mill worker in overalls is sitting on a bench; another comes up, dressed for the revival. He is chewing tobacco. CRAZY CARL *is standing, watching them; sometimes Carl is watching Ed Anderson who is standing near the Back Street entrance to the drugstore, waiting for Dr. Sam Perry, who is inside. Ed is thin, restless in his movements, with heavy black hair brushed slick to his head, hands pale as fresh pine. He is a little cocky in his Palm Beach suit and white straw hat. Alert, quick, his temper and sense of humor often tangle with each other. He is clean, neat, good looking, gentle with his sisters, affectionate in his relationship with Sam, though often irritable too. He is impatient now and shows it. Is lighting a fresh cigarette. One knows he has been there a long time. Two young colored girls, pert and high spirited, appear on College Street, self-conscious too, for they are walking near white folks. They are scampering along zig-zagging across the sidewalk, almost falling over each other, giggling, hushing, giggling. One of them is a Little Somebody in a bright pink waist and black skirt, with rundown high-heel pumps and a hat with red roses on it. The other has on a cotton summer dress that once belonged to white folks. Talking, laughing, saying nothing much, saying whatever comes into their heads, laughing so white folks will hear, but easy enough for them not to be offended by the sound. They stop in front of the drugstore and look in each window as they continue to move toward Back Street.*

(Lights go up on Street Scene)

1ST MILL LABORER: Well what you know?

2ND MILL LABORER: Not much.

1ST MILL LABORER: Folks say the preaching's good. How about going to the meetin?

2ND MILL LABORER: My old woman and the kids aim to go. Reckon I'll just let em tell me what it's about.

1ST MILL LABORER: Reckon it's about what it's always about. (*He laughs.*)

(The two colored girls are now passing ED *and as they walk along the white men follow with their eyes the movements of young hips and legs, as does Ed Anderson. It is almost too much for the Little Somebody with red roses and in her excitement she runs into Ed, stops with a stumble of her high-heel pumps and a twist of her torso. The two are now giggling hilariously, one pushing the other.)*

ED: (*amused by all this foolery*) Hi, kid!

LITTLE SOMEBODY: Hi, Mr. City Man. (*stretching her eyes*)

ED: (*looks her up and down*) See you later, kid. (*enjoying her now*)

LITTLE SOMEBODY: (*laughing much*) You don eben know ma name.

ED: It doesn't matter. (*grins, raises eyebrow*) I'll find you. I have ways, you know.

(She switches her little tail in answer and runs over to the other side of the walk where the other girl awaits her. They are still pushing each other in their excitement.)

2ND GIRL: Why you, ain you shamed?

LITTLE SOMEBODY: Is ah done somep'n bad?

2ND GIRL: *(in jealous voice)* Is you? You know you is!

(Ed laughs, watches them, as they go on down the street, looks at his watch suddenly as if tired of this long wait, for he has been leaning against the building or moving around restlessly throughout the scene.

(As Ed is talking to Little Somebody, TOM HARRIS *and* PREACHER DUN-WOODIE *are walking in front of the drugstore. They now stand on the sidewalk talking. Tom Harris is the town's big mill owner, red-faced, bald-headed, easy in manner, sure of himself. He has a big family, is of the Methodist Board of Stewards, and owner of most of the town's basic industries. Preacher Dunwoodie is a big hard muscled man who looks more like a baseball player than a preacher. He is lithe, relaxed, easy moving, with strength and resilience behind the ease. His emotional power, his athletic and high skilled body, his warm easy humorous way with men combine to give him an almost irresistible power over men and women. He has a habit of shaking his heavy hair out of his eyes, and smiling suddenly at you.)*

DUNWOODIE: Well, I've been here nearly a week and not much has happened, except big crowds. Mostly folks from the mill. *(smiles quickly)* What do you think is the matter?

HARRIS: I believe you ought to work more on the business men. They're the folks who have influence. Of course, I'm proud of the way my people from the mill have responded. They're good people.

(As they are speaking, DEE CASSIDY *comes toward them from across the square.)*

DEE CASSIDY: Howdy, Mr. Harris.

HARRIS: Howdy, Dee. Brother Dunwoodie, I'd like you to meet one of our county citizens, Mr. Dee Cassidy. Brother Dunwoodie's holding a revival in town, Dee.

DEE: Howdy-do, Mr. Dunwoodie.

DUNWOODIE: Glad to know you Mr. Cassidy. *(shakes hands)*

HARRIS: Cassidy is foreman of the Talley Farm—biggest cotton farm we have in our county.

DUNWOODIE: Well— *(addressing his remarks to Dee)* I reckon this is your busy time now.

DEE: Will be in a week or two when we begin picking—that is, if there's any niggers left in the county to do the picking.

DUNWOODIE: Many gone?

DEE: By the drove. Flocking up north—like black buzzards circling a carcass. *(The men laugh.)* Mr. Harris, I brought a bill of lumber in. Reckon your truck might bring it out tomorrow?

HARRIS: Sure. Better let me check it over. (*He takes slip, looks over it quickly.*) That's okay. It'll be out tomorrow, Dee.

DUNWOODIE: I hope you and Mr. Talley will find time to come to the services.

DEE: Thank you sir. Much obliged, Mr. Harris. Glad to have met you, Mr. Dunwoodie. (*Dee goes around the corner, stopping for a drink at the fountain, and on to Back Street where he sits on the bench talking to the mill hands.*)

DUNWOODIE: Be fine if we could get some publicity. . . . How about your editor? Miss Belle Taylor was telling me that she heard him in the drugstore with the young people yesterday making fun of the revival.

HARRIS: Well now, Miss Belle is a nice old maid who sort of gets things mixed up. I'll speak to him about it. Think he'll be glad to give you as much as you want. Tell you Brother Dunwoodie, I wish you'd preach a sermon on Christian Stewardship. That's what our business men need to hear. . . .

(GABE *has been standing near, waiting for a chance to speak to his boss. Now he edges up, addresses him softly, tentatively.*)

GABE: Mr. Harris . . .

HARRIS: All right, Gabe.

GABE: I put the express package in your office, suh.

HARRIS: Good.

GABE: Mr. Eller say he's going to need fo' mo' hands on the flat cars in the mornin'.

HARRIS: All right, tell Jim to get them for him.

GABE: Yassir, thanky Boss. (*Gabe turns away, moves around the corner of the drugstore.*)

(*In the drugstore: While street scene is being played,* DOUG *the soda-jerker brings a tray in from the street, fixes another tray and takes it out. Horns blow now and then for curb service; not too often as this is nearing the supper hour for most people and there is not too much activity on the street.*

(*The interior of the drugstore is viewed from the rear, as if the audience is almost inside it. There are double doors opening out upon the street and now and then passers-by can be seen, pausing to look at the displays in the windows. The soda fountain, cigarette counter, and portion of shelves can be seen. There is a telephone near the soda fountain.*

(*The men at the cigarette counter go out as the telephone rings.*)

DOUG: (*picking up the receiver*) Deen's Drugstore. Yes, Mrs. Reid. Dr. Deen's been out all afternoon. I'll tell him when he comes in. Yes ma'm I won't forget. (*hangs up, writes the memo down, goes over to the cigarette counter*)

(*Tom Harris and Preacher Dunwoodie come in from the street as Doug is talking over the telephone. They sit down, order drinks when Doug comes over.*)

DOUG: Howdy, Brother Dunwoodie. Howdy Mr. Harris.

HARRIS: What will you have?

DUNWOODIE: A Coca-Cola, I believe.

HARRIS: Make it two, Doug. Excuse me a moment. Oh Sam . . .

SAM: Yes sir. (*The two men walk toward each other. Up to this time,* SAM *has been in the background, standing as unobtrusively as possible, shifting a little now and then, or looking at the display counter, or wiping his face off. He has been patient and relaxed, unlike his friend out on the street who is growing more and more impatient at this long waiting "on white folks".*)

HARRIS: How are you, Sam?

SAM: All right, thank you sir. (*smiles quietly and in friendliness, for Tom Harris is his good friend*)

HARRIS: Hear there's a lot of fever out at the turpentine still.

SAM: Yes sir.

HARRIS: Pretty bad?

SAM: Well sir, four are pretty sick. One's going to die, it seems. There'll be others, I'm afraid. (*Sighs. He's tired and things are bad on a lot of the farms this summer.*)

HARRIS: What you think it is?

SAM: Two are typhoid. I've heard from the State Board of Health. I'm making tests on the others. They may be malaria. Plenty mosquitoes and flies for it to be both. (*smiles at Harris and seems to mean it*)

HARRIS: (*looks at Sam with respect and almost man to man*) Think we're in for trouble?

SAM: Yes sir. If you'll give me permission, I'd like to go out there in the morning and inoculate them all while they're at work. It's easier to get them that way.

HARRIS: Sure, if you think it's necessary. (*turns to go back to the table, suddenly turns back to Sam*) You look mighty tired, Sam. Things keeping you pretty busy?

SAM: (*forgetting his manners, now speaking simply as one human to another*) I'm afraid so.

HARRIS: You're doing things for your people that nobody else can do. But you're human, remember. Why don't you ease up a bit? Can't keep everybody well, you know. (*smiles at Sam*)

SAM: Yessir, I know. But sometimes . . . you—sort of lose your sense and keep trying. (*He smiles quickly. Sam has a sense of humor about himself.*)

HARRIS: (*puts his hand on Sam's arm in sudden warmth*) You're all right, Sam. Any time I can help out, let me know.

SAM: Thank you, sir.

(*Harris goes over to the tables, sits down, begins to drink his cola. Sam steps back a little, glances at his watch, goes out the side door.*)

HARRIS: Sorry I took so long, Brother Dunwoodie.

(*Street: Sam walks out of the side door, sees Ed waiting there for him, smiles quickly at his impatient friend.*)

ED: Well, it's about time! Thought you must be playing checkers, or something. (*smiling bitterly over his own joke*)

SAM: (*laughs easily, warmly*) No, Dr. Deen hasn't come in yet. Have to sort of wait around, you know, until he comes. How about a bottle of coke? I'll get you one inside.

ED: And drink it out here? Oh no . . .

SAM: (*touches his arm in half warning, half sympathy*) I don't think I'll have to wait much longer. If I do, I'll just see him tomorrow.

ED: Take your time. I'm enjoying Maxwell! (*suddenly grins at Sam, and you see an Ed who can be gay and light-hearted, if given half a chance. Ed offers Sam a cigarette and they stand there smoking. After his cigarette, Sam goes inside. In the meantime, Dunwoodie and Harris are talking.*)

DUNWOODIE: Who's that nigger you call "Sam"? Seems different from most.

HARRIS: Well, he is different. Used to work at my saw mill. One day we had a bad accident—man got caught in the saw. Sam took charge . . . handled it fine.

DUNWOODIE: Talks like he has sense.

HARRIS: Has plenty. I found out he'd been to college.

DUNWOODIE: Don't believe I ever saw one before who was educated.

HARRIS: Well to make a long story short, I sent him to medical school. Now he doctors all the colored folks in the county. We'd find it mighty hard to do without him.

(HARRIET *and* CHARLIE *come in drugstore. Harriet's looking for her father.*)

HARRIET: Hello, Brother Dunwoodie. Dad . . . (*smiles at her father ingratiatingly. As she does so, Charlie and Doug speak to each other*) Mind if I use the car a little while?

HARRIS: Not if you'll drive your mother to the service—and yourself.

HARRIET: Yes, Dad. Good evening, Brother Dunwoodie. (*He hands her the keys. She takes them, goes out of the drugstore as Harris speaks to Charlie.*)

HARRIS: Did you check on those flat cars, Charlie?

CHARLIE: Yes sir. I'm going out to the logging camp in the morning, Dad.

HARRIS: Good!

(*Charlie and Harriet go out.*)

HARRIS: Don't know what I'd do without that boy of mine.
Street:

CHARLIE: You going to the service?

HARRIET: Not if I can get out of it.

CHARLIE: (*grinning*) Tell you what—you go and I'll stay home. Have some reading I'd like to do.

HARRIET: Aren't you funny! I must hurry—left my racquet out at the club. (*turns away, turns back*) Charlie . . . (*voice tentative, a little soft and pleading*) I was hoping you'd take that job in Baltimore. It sounds as if it has a future.

CHARLIE: You don't think the mill has? It's done pretty well for the Harris family.

HARRIET: I know—but—if you stay here . . . what you going to do when they try to organize the mill? You know Dad isn't going to put up with a union. What you going to do then—side with the union or with Dad?

CHARLIE: (*smiles*) We'll see . . . Dad needs me.

HARRIET: (*looks at him wistfully, doesn't say anything*) Bye— (*turns away, meets* TRACY *who is coming around the corner*) Hi, Trace. (*Tracy is tall, thin and stooped, with tired eyes and tired lines around his mouth, quick to smile, quick to see absurdities in other folks. Tenderhearted toward the weak, the failures, usually shows great courtesy to women.*)

TRACY: Hello there.

(*Crazy Carl, who has been all this time watching the others on the street, now drags himself nearer to Tracy, whom he adores.*)

HARRIET: (*voice low, paying no attention to Crazy Carl*) How about you and Dorothy coming over after church? We might ride out to the river, or something.

TRACY: Suit me better to come during the service.

HARRIET: Oh yeah? I've got to take Mother. You know Dorothy isn't missing church and she won't like it if you do. (*Tracy laughs*)

(*Crazy Carl smiles at Tracy now, trying to get his attention; pulls on his coat.*)

CRAZY CARL: Acy . . . Acy . . .

TRACY: Hi, Carl, want a Coca-Cola?

(*Carl nods his head vigorously.*)

CARL: AR . . .

TRACY: Come on in. I'll get it for you—See you later, Harriet. (*He smiles at her affectionately—for they've been lifelong friends and he likes her adoration.*)

HARRIET: All right, Trace.

(*Drugstore: Tracy and Carl go inside drugstore to the counter. Tracy gives Carl a Coca-Cola, goes over to the window display, rearranges it. Carl sits at the counter drinking. Stares at everyone who crosses his line of vision. Carl spends most of his life standing around, looking at Maxwell. As this is taking place,* ALMA DEEN *walks in.*)

DOUG: Howdy, Mrs. Deen.

ALMA: Hello, Doug. Has Laura been in?

DOUG: She was in about four o'clock. Think she's out painting.

TRACY: Hello, Mother.

ALMA: Hello, dear.

TRACY: Here's the mail. (*hands it to her*)

ALMA: Thank you. (*Alma turns, goes over to speak to the preacher and Harris. The two men stand.*)

DUNWOODIE: Mrs. Deen . . . I didn't have a chance after the service to thank you for helping with the children.

ALMA: I was glad to do what I could. (*looks at Harris*) How are you, Tom?

HARRIS: Fine, Alma. Won't you sit down?

ALMA: Thank you. (*Alma sits down with the men.*)

HARRIS: Can I get you something to drink?

ALMA: No thank you. Brother Dunwoodie, I think the revival is going to mean a great deal to our town, especially to our young people. I'd like for you to meet my son. (*She glances over at her son, who is busy fixing a display in the window.*)

DUNWOODIE: Yes, I'd like to.

ALMA: Tracy—will you come over a moment? (*Tracy comes over.*) Brother Dunwoodie, this is my son.

DUNWOODIE: Howdy, Deen.

TRACY: Brother Dunwoodie—Hello, Mr. Harris.

DUNWOODIE: I believe I met you when I was here three years ago, didn't I?

TRACY: No sir. I was in the army then.

DUNWOODIE: I hope you'll be able to get to the meeting.

TRACY: Thank you sir.

HARRIS: I think we'd better move along, Brother Dunwoodie. Good afternoon, Alma.

DUNWOODIE: Glad to have seen you, Mrs. Deen.

ALMA: Thank you. (*smiles at Harris*)

(*Tom Harris touches her on the shoulder as he leaves the table. Harris and Dunwoodie start out of the drugstore as* LAURA *comes in.*)

LAURA: Hello, Mr. Harris . . . How do you do, Brother Dunwoodie? (*she touches Harris's arm affectionately as she passes him, stops at her mother's table*) Hello, Mother. (*kisses her mother on the forehead*)

ALMA: Laura, have you looked in a mirror? (*half frowns, half smiles affectionately*)

LAURA: (*laughs*) I know. I'm a disgrace but it's so comfortable. (*Laura is wearing a mussed up cotton summer dress, play style with moccasins. She has her portfolio of drawings and water colors in her hand. Her hair, tied with a ribbon, looks as it might after four or five hours of painting and her face has a smudge of water color on it. She is attractive even in her untidiness.*)

ALMA: (*as Laura sits down*) I was beginning to be a little worried. (*looks at Laura with affection*)

LAURA: Why, darling? (*Tracy goes out of the front door.*)

ALMA: (*lowers her voice*) There's so much restlessness among the colored folks. I was afraid you were at the river.

LAURA: We were, but we were in Jane's car. (*She holds her portfolio.*) I did some good water colors.

ALMA: I had hoped you were working on your thesis. You have only five weeks before you go back to the university.

LAURA: Yes, I know. I'm afraid I've gone a little stale on it. I was in a painting mood—painted all afternoon. (*Her face lights up suddenly, as she thinks of her work and her pleasure in it.*) Are you ready to go?

ALMA: In just a moment.

LAURA: I'll be in the car. (*She goes out. Alma speaks to Doug who comes over to the table and clears the glasses.*)

ALMA: (*as he turns away.*) Oh Doug . . . (*She lowers her voice a little.*) Yesterday I was looking over Dr. Deen's accounts. I haven't been able to help him as much as I should lately. (*slight pause*) I noticed that Mrs. Corn hasn't had a bill in three months.

DOUG: No ma'm. Dr. Deen told me not to send her a bill until Joe found a job.

ALMA: I see. (*pauses, looks up at him a moment*) That is right, of course. (*voice pleasant*) Has Joe found work yet?

DOUG: He got a foreman's job last week at Harris's mill.

ALMA: Then suppose you send her a bill in a few days. (*voice quiet, pleasantly composed, certain of her fairness to Mrs. Corn and Mr. Deen and to herself*)

DOUG: Yes'm. (TUT *comes in, lays his bag on the counter. He does not, at first, notice Sam, who is still waiting.*)

TUT: Any calls, Doug?

DOUG: Yes sir, five or six. Mrs. Purviance is worse. Martha wants you to come as soon as you can.

TUT: Much obliged.

SAM: Dr. Deen.

TUT: Yes, Sam . . . What can I do for you? (*He smiles at his fellow physician. Their attitude toward each other is that of friendliness and mutual respect. While Tut is white gentleman to colored man in his manner, it is softened by his very real feeling of respect and admiration for this Negro who has worked so hard for his people.*)

SAM: I would like as much typhoid antitoxin as you can spare, sir. And I need some morphine for old Aunt Sue.

TUT: She's the one with cancer, isn't she?

SAM: Yes sir. There's two new cases of fever on the Talley farm. I believe it's malaria. I sent specimens off yesterday.

TUT: Let me know when you hear. I have a case that looks more like undulant fever. Doug . . . give Sam all the antitoxin in the refrigerator except one ampule. I have the morphine here. (*Doug fixes up the antitoxin.*)

SAM: Thank you, sir.

TUT: (*opens his bag, looks at a bottle, hands it to Sam*) This will last you for a while, I think. (*He smiles at Sam, turns away, goes into the pharmacy room where his wife is.*)

SAM: Much obliged. (*After thanking Dr. Deen, Sam waits until Doug can fix up the package for him, then goes outside.*)

TUT: (*comes back to where Alma is*) Well dear, been busy?

ALMA: About as usual. There always seems a lot to do. (*She smiles at her husband.*) Tut, the old Hearn farm is up for sale, $15,000. Quite cheap, don't you think?

TUT: Yes, I do.

ALMA: It would be a fine investment for us. There's some good land . . . (*She looks at her husband.*) It might be just the thing we are looking for, for Tracy.

TUT: Sounds good. I have the feeling though that Tracy might not like to farm.

ALMA: He has to decide on something, Tut. I wish you would talk to him about it. I hate for him to be wasting his time with machinery. He's been working at Adams' cotton gin all day.

TUT: (*chuckles*) Nothing he likes better than to put on a pair of coveralls and take an engine apart. Maybe we should have sent him to Georgia Tech. After all he didn't take easily to law school.

ALMA: I know. But no one in our family has ever done that kind of thing. You'll talk to him about the farm?

TUT: I'll try to, dear.

ALMA: Laura's waiting in the car. Will you be able to come to supper now?

TUT: No. I think I should go to Mrs. Purviance's first.

ALMA: I'll have Henry keep your supper warm for you. Try not to be too late.

(*Tut smiles at her, keeps on with his work. Alma goes out, meets Tracy on street*)

ALMA: Did you get Dorothy's call? She's telephoned the house twice this afternoon.

TRACY: Thanks, Mother. I'll call her later.

ALMA: Don't you think you should call her now?

TRACY: I believe I'll wait.

TUT: Hello, Trace.

TRACY: Hello, Dad.

(*Sam comes out to Ed, who has been standing all this time, waiting. He has smoked, he has walked up and down, has put on his hat and taken it off, but has hung around. As the time has passed he has shown more and more nervousness and impatience.*)

SAM: Sorry it's taken so long. Things do, you know. (*smiles easily*)

ED: You ought to have your own drugstore. (*voice sharp, resentful*)

SAM: I'd settle for an office or a refrigerator. (*easy still, smiling at his restless friend*) Maybe I'll get both.

ED: Yeah? When?

SAM: Oh, one of these days. (*laughs affectionately at his restless friend*) I'm about through, Ed. Let's go over to Salamander's. I'm hungry.

ED: O.K.

(*Dee Cassidy gets up from the bench where he has been talking to the mill hands, saunters over toward Sam, as the two colored men are talking*)

DEE: (*to Sam*) Well, Sam, hear you've been out to our farm again.

SAM: Yes sir. (*You feel that Sam doesn't like this white man. Gabe, who has been talking, goes into drugstore through side entrance.*)

DEE: Whassa matter out there? B'lieve you make my niggers sick a-purpose to git their money. (*Dee laughs here and the white men sitting on the bench laugh, though they don't sound amused.*)

SAM: (*trying to laugh at white man's joke*) Yes sir. This time, it's the fever, Mr. Cassidy. It's right bad among the folks.

DEE: And what can you do for the fever?

SAM: Well sir, maybe a little something. Make like I'm helping anyway. (*There is profound sadness in Sam's smile.*)

DEE: Who's that with you?

SAM: (*hesitates, decides to lie*) It's Aunt Dessie Turnbull's great-nephew, sir.

(*Ed is obviously growing restless over what seems to him Sam's bending to white folks.*)

DEE: Looks like a city nigger to me. (*spitting his tobacco juice now on sidewalk. Ed draws in his breath sharply, beginning to show the resentment which up to now he has managed carefully to conceal.*)

SAM: (*quickly, feeling Ed's near explosion*) No Sir. Just got on his Sunday clothes. (*Sam smiles quickly at Ed, hoping Ed will understand that this kind of double talk has to be.*)

DEE: Well, all I want is to get 'em in the fields next week. See you don't put any of 'em in bed. Need every nigger on the place and then some.

(*A colored soldier in uniform walks around the corner, crosses over toward the drugstore. Dee Cassidy stands there watching him.*)

SAM: Yes sir, I'll do my best. (*Sam walks back to where Ed is standing, a few steps away.*)

ED: (*stops, turns abruptly to Sam, face twisted with fury*) Lord God! How do you take it! Why in hell you think you have to take—

SAM: (*puts his hand on Ed's arm*) Easy boy. (*voice soft and urgent*) Easy . . . Let's go to Salamander's. (*He hurries Ed off of white folk's street into the safety of the lunch counter. The colored soldier turns, walks toward Salamander's also.*)

DEE: (*glances at the white men on the bench*) It makes me plumb want to puke to see a black coon in a uniform. (*The men on the bench laugh, enjoying this. Dee turns, walks around toward the front of the drugstore and on down the street. Inside the drugstore, Tut looks up from his bag which he has been rearranging.*)

TRACY: (*brings a glass bottle to his father. Tut looks at its label, pours out two or three dozen tablets, puts them in his smaller bottle which he keeps in his medicine bag.*)

TUT: Been able to attend the services any, Son?

TRACY: No sir. Afraid I haven't.

TUT: (*busy with the medicine, a little reluctant to say this but feeling that he should*) It would make your mother feel mighty good if you would try to go. You know how she feels about— those things.

TRACY: Yes sir, I know. She talked to me this morning. I halfway promised her I would go, tonight. (*He smiles at his father.*)

TUT: Good. The preacher's a pretty fine man, I think. Intelligent.

TRACY: Take a look at the window, Dad, on your way out, will you? (*lights a cigarette, starts out*)

TUT: O.K. Trace.

TRACY: So long. (*around the corner he meets* HENRY, *who is whistling softly as he walks along*)

TRACY: Hello, Henry. Did you get my laundry?

HENRY: Yassuh.

TRACY: (*grins*) Go by the press club and pick up my suit, will you? And tell Mother I won't be home for supper.

HENRY: Yassuh.

TRACY: You look right happy.

HENRY: Yassuh. I heard the funniest story. I went out to Snooks to see if she had got you any scotch and she told me the doggonest story. Seems somebody— (*they disappear, slowly*)

(*One of the men on the bench stands, stretches a little.*)

2ND MILL LABORER: Nope, no goddam meeting for me. Don' aim to listen to Tom Harris thank the Lord another time for being so good to him. How about me? Why ain't God good to me? What we need in this town is a union, not a revival meeting.

1ST MILL LABORER: (*laughing a little uncomfortably*) Well, don't know about them unions. I hear most of them are run by communist folks. Better change your mind. They say the singing's good.

2ND MILL LABORER: Not for me. (*spits on the sidewalk*) Not if the preacher was to climb the tent pole like that other preacher done before, I'd not go. (*He turns in the other direction as his friend starts toward the revival tent. Then he turns back, raises his voice a little*) Not if he set up there a week, I'd not go.

(*The street corner is deserted except for Crazy Carl. Doug the soda-jerker comes to the door to cool off; a horn toots, and there is laughter in the streets. Crazy Carl has been standing watching the mill hands, watching everybody. Now he pulls himself clumsily over to the drinking fountain, laps and gurgles and slobbers up the water. The lights slowly dim now so that only Crazy Carl and the "FOR WHITES ONLY" sign can be seen clearly. All the rest of the street corner is in darkness, a dim light showing through Salamander's window. Lights dim on the street scene.*)

ACT ONE, SCENE 2

NONNIE *stands at the gate, waiting; behind her the swamp, in front of her Colored Town, beyond it, all Maxwell. Tall and slim and white in the dusk, the girl stands there, hands on the picket gate. You can hear the revival song backwashing against the town: "Whiter than snow, yes, whiter than snow . . . Oh wash me and I shall be whiter than snow."*

It is twilight, and a feeling of quietness and peace surrounds her. This quietness is like an island on which Non stands completely separated from Maxwell and all that Maxwell means. She is like a quiet, vague tune to which each person sets his own words. Remote, yes—but warmly mothering those she loves. Not "looking after them" but giving them love. She has a dignity that comes from deep within, a reticence too, and gentleness. She loves very much all her family and Tracy. As for the world, she rejected it with quiet passion long ago, and refuses to accept it again. She is withdrawn and has done all her growing inside, sending out no faults or virtues, like most folks—whose growth has reached out toward and become part of their world. She has few mannerisms, only the one of pushing her hair from her forehead. She is the sister of Bess and Ed Anderson, Negroes, all three of whom are college graduates. She sighs. Around the row of old cedars from Miss Ada's where the trees open up clearing the path, she sees him coming. Out of the dusk, Tracy appears before her. He takes her hands from the gate, holds them. His eyes search her face, move from her hair, to her eyes, to her throat.

TRACY: You all right?

NONNIE: Of course. (*laughs softly, intimately, showing her love*)

TRACY: Cool, your hands are cool, and it's hot as hell. (*He smiles at her gently.*)

NONNIE: I know. The heat has made Boysie so restless. Mrs. Brown was out of town and so—well, I've been busy.

TRACY: How do you stand nursing him day after day— (*He breaks off suddenly. Stares beyond her, as if forgetting what he has begun to say.*)

NONNIE: (*after a moment of silence, gently answers*) I don't mind. He's so pitiful, Tracy. And sweet. It's a good job—as jobs go. (*She smiles at him, but Tracy does not smile.*) It would be cooler on the ridge. Shall we go there?

TRACY: No, I can't stay but a minute. (*He smiles at her again, showing his love.*) I haven't seen you in days.

NONNIE: What have you been doing?

TRACY: They're installing a new cotton seed press at Adam's warehouse. I've been helping.

NONNIE: You like that sort of thing, don't you? (*smiles*)

TRACY: (*laughs*) Yes, I'm afraid I do. Mother's always wanted me to do something that would keep my shirt clean.

NONNIE: I think you are very good with—machinery. You'll make a great success with it, someday.

TRACY: You're the only one, honey, who thinks so. Mechanical engineering might not be a bad idea. God knows, I ought to settle down—to something.

NONNIE: I know no one is better than you. (*Her voice is deep now as if it had roots in a million years of knowing.*)

TRACY: Always believing in me. Huh? (*he laughs, takes her hand, rubs it across his lips*)

(*They listen to the singing as it softly backwashes against the edge of the swamp. Non and Tracy smile at each other.*)

TRACY: Revival over in town.

NONNIE: Yes, Mrs. Brown told me. Good preacher, she said.

TRACY: I haven't heard him. None of them good for me. Had too much of it when I was a kid.

NONNIE: I know. I remember once when you were fifteen—you got—converted.

TRACY: (*smiles*) I wonder what the word means. All I remember is I was scared out of my skin—until Grandmother straightened me out. She had so much sense. (*He pauses, looks away, saddened by the memory, looks at Nonnie.*) You remember that? Seems strange.

NONNIE: Sometimes I think I remember—everything.

TRACY: (*draws her near to him, whispers the word*) Non! (*pushes her away, looks at a her a long time. Her face now is full of her news, and her fear suddenly of how he will accept it*)

NONNIE: Tracy—I have something to tell you.

TRACY: All right, tell me quick. What is it?

NONNIE: (*looks up at him steadily*) I'm going to have a baby. (*She feels his hand tremble on her arm. Whispers now.*) And I'm glad.

TRACY: Glad! You can't be!

NONNIE: I'm glad.

TRACY: But—

NONNIE: You see, I want it. I'll have something they can't take away from me.

TRACY: (*voice low, hard to catch the words*) What do you mean?

NONNIE: It's like thinking something for a long time . . . One day you write it down . . . you always have it after that. (*She looks at him with a half humorous smile.*)

TRACY: Writing it down—would have been simpler. (*stares out toward the swamp—God! what a mess!—then his face eases. He runs his fingers slowly over the fence pickets.*) Let's don't think about it. (*smiles at her quickly*)

NONNIE: All right. (*She looks at him and smiles back steadily, and he stares into her eyes as if he has not heard a word that she has said.*) I wish you were glad. (*She speaks softly, feels her body shaking against his in sudden betrayal of calm.*)

TRACY: Reckon we ought to talk about it, or something— (*He looks out toward the swamp, again forgetting his words. In the dusk she's as white as Laura! Lord God!*)

NONNIE: No, we don't need to talk about it.

TRACY: I must go, honey. (*He touches her hair, turns away, faces her again*) It's Mother! (*laughs abruptly*) That damned revival's got her worked up. I don't know why. Got everyone worked up. (*laughs again—hesitates*) Now I've promised to go to the service tonight. Had to. (*stares into the evening. Turns suddenly, opens the picket gate, closes it*) I may come back late. All right? (*Through this talk, Tracy shows his conflict between his love and his race and family.*)

NONNIE: All right. (*a door slams*) I'll walk with you to Miss Ada's—Let's go—

TRACY: Something the matter?

NONNIE: No—let's go. (*Nonnie whispers the words now and walks hurriedly down the path.*)

(*Ed comes out on the porch, sits on the steps, lights a cigarette. In the darkness only the glow from the cigarette can be seen. The revival singing can be heard. The song "What a Friend We Have in Jesus" now grows more clear. One can almost hear the words. After a little while, BESS comes up the path with JACKIE.*)

ED: Non . . .

BESS: It's me, Eddie.

ED: Is Non with you?

BESS: No, only Jackie.

ED: (*walks out to meet her*) She oughtn't to go places at night by herself, Bess! (*as if it were Bess's fault*)

BESS: (*a little angrily, feeling the blame in his voice*) She's grown, Ed. She can go where she wants to. She probably went the back way to meet Jackie and me. Don't worry so!

ED: I'm not worrying. Just wondered where the kid had gone. This place is so lonely out here—Hate to think of you and her going around by yourself at night. Lot of rough white men, Bess!

BESS: Maxwell's safer than your city streets—stop griping about your home town.

ED: She was here talking to me, I went in the kitchen—

BESS: Eddie, don't be silly! She'll be back. She's talking to Miss Ada right now. She often sits with her and talks.

JACKIE: I'se sleepy. I'se sleepy.

BESS: Ssh—baby.

(*Sam comes in the gate, lays his bag down, puts his hat on a convenient post.*)

ED: Hello, there.

SAM: Meant to get here earlier, Ed. Hello, Bess.

BESS: You look tired. Haven't had any supper, have you?

SAM: No. So late getting in, thought I'd come right over.

BESS: I'll see what I can find for you.

(*Sam smiles his thanks; Bess goes into the house.*)

ED: Where have you been today?

SAM: Out at Talley's farm all afternoon.

ED: That's one white man I'd keep away from.

SAM: Well, there're folks on his place that have to be doctored, you know. (*He sighs, stretches his feet out.*) Ed, I'm tired.

ED: Fever pretty bad?

SAM: Yeah, right bad. Talley put his foot down on my inoculating them. (*Sam chuckles.*) Well I did it, today.

ED: I'd as soon play with a rattler as argue with Bill Talley.

SAM: I never have arguments. (*He laughs.*) Went out to the field and stuck my needle in every last one of them. Kept my mouth shut. (*Sam looks at Ed and grins.*) Then I went by his house, laughed at a couple of his jokes. Everything O.K.

ED: (*laughs too. Quickly sobers*) And you go like that day after day.

SAM: It's my life.

ED: It's a hell of a life, if you're asking me!

SAM: I see it different. Got my work—got to do it way white folks will work with me. If it takes a little lying and hand licking, what difference?

ED: Difference is—I'd rather die first. (*Bess brings out a tray. Sam takes it, puts it on the step by him.*)

SAM: This is mighty nice, Bess. Looks good. (*He takes a drink of milk, breaks open the sweet potato as his two friends watch him with affectionate amusement.*)

JACKIE: Let's go to bed, Uncle Eddie. (*Ed laughs, gives Jackie a rough hug, plays with his hair*)

BESS: I'll take you, honey—

SAM: Night, boy—

JACKIE: Night. (*They go in the house.*)

SAM: (*puts his hand on Ed's shoulder, speaks seriously now*) Ed, you're butting your brains out on that stone wall. It's easier to climb over it.

ED: What you mean?

SAM: I mean, clear out! You don't belong any more in Georgia. Not even for a week. Stay out! Things worrying you may settle themselves. Things do, sometimes . . . if they don't, you can't help them any, God knows!

ED: Sam . . . (*laughs a little to make his words easy. Finds it hard to go on*) You know a lot about people—ever hear of anybody except crazy folks getting an idea they couldn't get out of their heads?

SAM: Sure. Guess doctoring's mine. (*laughs*) You mean—like a tune that stays in your mind?

ED: Something like that. (*pauses*) No, I'll tell you. (*hesitates, draws in a breath— speaks in a tight voice which he tries to make casual*) I was walking in the park one day, two or three months ago. (*Make a joke of it. He's likely to think you need a straightjacket.*) There were some ants on a stone. Just plain damned ants. I stepped on one . . . mashed it flat. Not thinking, see, one way or another. Minute I did it, something flashed through my mind! "You killed Nonnie!" Had no sense to it, but it kept coming back. At first it was so crazy, it didn't bother me. But it kept coming back in my mind . . . sort of . . . gets . . . on . . . your . . . nerves . . . after a while . . . (*wipes his face, blows cigarette smoke hard*)

SAM: (*voice still easy*) Funny . . . way people think their mind is something different from their body. You don't get nervous when you have a pain in your belly for a second. Goes away. That's the end of it. Let a little gas pain come in your mind, you get to worrying.

ED: (*yeah . . . sound fine. He doesn't understand it any more than I do*) As I said, it didn't bother me at first. Then it began to come back. At night. Or at work. I'd be in the middle of something. I'd hear it. Got so lately it keeps on—

(*breaks off his words, wipes his face*) Crazy thing about it, Sam, of all the people in the world, Nonnie is the one I wouldn't want *anything* to happen to. You know that.

SAM: Everybody has notions at times. Like a tune on a record. It's O.K. unless the needle gets stuck and plays it over and over. Some folks get mad then and break the record. Be easier to lift the needle off.

ED: (*smokes a moment before he speaks again*) Sam—I want to take Non back with me.

(*Sam looks at him quickly*)

SAM: And what would she do up there?

ED: She could get work that wouldn't shame her. At least she wouldn't have to nurse for white folks! Maybe meet someone—and marry—live decently . . .

SAM: (*speaks slowly and with deep feeling*) Nothing Non does can—lower her. She can go through all—kinds of things—and come out of them, the same Non.

ED: (*Now what did he mean by that?*) If you could help me to persuade her to go back— (*trying to get in a lighter mood now*) She's a sister a man would be proud to take to Washington with him.

SAM: Yes . . . (*His face shows his deep feeling for Non.*) She's a sister a man would be proud to take—anywhere. (*pauses, voice soft now, almost a whisper*)

(*Another silence, hard to break—Sam stands.*)

SAM: Well—I promised to meet Mr. Harris down at his office. I'm trying to get the Board of Health to set up a clinic for tuberculosis. And we need it. (*Ed walks with him to the gate. As they get near it, they meet Non coming home from work.*)

ED: 'Lo Biddy. (*holds gate ajar*)

NONNIE: Hello, Eddie. Sam . . . (*She smiles at their old friend.*) Do you have to go?

SAM: Afraid so. (*He looks at Non as if reading a book he has wanted to get to for a long time.*)

SAM: Non . . . are things all right with you?

NONNIE: I'm always all right.

SAM: Good! (*He puts his hand on her shoulder, looks at her a long time, turns to Ed.*) See you tomorrow, Ed. (*Sister and brother stand there.*)

NONNIE: What have you done today?

ED: Not nearly enough! Hung around the tent this afternoon and watched that white man save souls. He's damned good at it.

NONNIE: (*voice betrays her anxiety*) Is it— fun, to watch?

ED: Sort of . . . I reckon. Tickles me to see those white folks— (*seems to forget to finish*) telling the world things they'll be sorry as hell they told after the preacher leaves town.

NONNIE: Why do they do it?

ED: Why do we do anything we do? (*They stand, each staring out into the night, following their own thoughts.*) He didn't make me run to the altar—what

you reckon would happen if I had done that? But all the talk of hell . . .
death . . . sin . . .

NONNIE: How did it make you feel? (*voice anxious*)

ED: Oh I don't know.

NONNIE: Tell me, Eddie . . .

ED: Non, I'm no good at saying things. (*pauses*) Just tears you up . . . like a bad
fuss . . . like liquor does you sometimes . . . kind of like when Mama . . . used
to make us feel we'd lost out with her . . . (*smiles, grows silent—speaks softly*)
Hell would never get a chance at her, would it, kid?

(*Non shakes her head. As he is speaking, Bess comes out, joins them quietly.*)

ED: She worshipped you, Non . . .

NONNIE: She worshipped us all.

ED: But you especially. (*His voice is full of deep feeling now, full of jealous memories
and subtle rebuke.*) Bess and I just filled out the empty spots you left. (*He
laughs a little bitterly. Bess smiles, none too happily herself.*)

NONNIE: Don't say that, Eddie.

ED: I wish she could have lived. (*wistful, but anger rising here*)

NONNIE: We all wish it. (*whispers*)

ED: (*voice harsh*) Because you've changed since she died. You're not the same
person. (*smiles quickly but voice grows angry again as he continues*) Here you
are—you made good grades at college, (*voice grows more belligerent*) everybody thought you were smart. And yet you seem unwilling to *use* your brains.
To *be* anything! We've got to get somewhere! We're colored people, Nonnie!
Sometimes, seems to me— (*pauses, as his fingers pick at the old fence*) you
pretend—you're not. (*Non looks as if she is close to tears.*)

BESS: (*turns quickly and touches his arm*) Don't fuss so much, Eddie . . . Where
did you eat today?

ED: At Salamander's.

BESS: Not so much to eat there.

ED: Swell place! (*sits on steps. Lights a cigarette*) Same old dirt—same old
benches—same old Coca-Cola signs—same old spit—same old stink—
same old rag in Salamander's hand that was there five years ago! Made me
feel I was right back in Maxwell. (*They laugh. There is a pause as they look down
the path. You can hear the singing from the revival. "Beulah Land" is the song
white folks seem enthusiastic about tonight.*)

ED: (*speaks softly and suddenly*) When I came out of Salamander's, I looked
down the street—to Deen's Drugstore. White girls sitting in cars—drinking
cokes, laughing. Crossing their legs, uncrossing them, staring through
me . . . till I began to feel I wasn't there on the sidewalk . . . never had been
there! Black digit marked out with white chalk. That's what it does to you.

BESS: (*keeps her voice light*) If Mama were here, she'd say you ought to get out
and chop cotton a while. Remember how she used to send you out to the farm
when you'd be restless?

ED: (*laughs*) Funny thing, I kind of liked it. (*voice quiet, changes mood*) I keep expecting her to come down that path . . . walking slow, on the edges of her feet, to ease her bunions . . . Was always about this time she'd get home from work . . . (*pauses*) Everything is so empty—and so goddam full of things! How you get used to it?

BESS: It's harder on you, coming back. Non and I have our work, seven days a week, you know. We don't have much time to think.

ED: How about going somewhere with me? Isn't there something we can do?

BESS: Picture show, Eddie?

ED: And sit in that goddam loft?

NONNIE: (*smiles*) We might walk over to see Roseanna and the twins.

ED: Couldn't take Roseanna tonight. Got anything to read?

BESS: I think so. Plenty of magazines—I'm coming home early tomorrow, Ed, and fix you a good supper—

ED: (*smiles his thanks*) Well . . . believe I'll see if I can sleep it off— (*Ed goes into the house. The two girls sit on the steps a few moments in silence.*)

BESS: Non— (*doesn't look at her as she speaks*) I wish Ed hadn't come back. (*Non doesn't answer.*) Let's don't do anything to bother him while he's here. (*Non still doesn't speak. Bess goes on, her voice on edge.*) Ed wants you to go to Washington with him. I wish you would!

NONNIE: Bess . . . I'm going to have a baby.

BESS: (*stares at her*) I don't believe you. (*The girls are silent. Beyond them comes the faint sound of the singing of "Jesus Is Tenderly Calling Us Home," etc.*)

BESS: Tracy?

NONNIE: Yes.

BESS: I knew it. I believe I knew before you told me. I've always known he'd ruin you.

NONNIE: I'm not ruined. I'm happy. (*voice soft*)

BESS: (*stares at Non—whispers.*) I believe you think he loves you.

NONNIE: Yes.

BESS: But Nonnie— (*pauses*) You're such a fool! How *could* you be such a fool! You *know* no white man loves a— And I've tried so hard to look after you— (*voice breaks*)

NONNIE: You have looked after me, honey.

BESS: A fine mess I've made of it! Oh Nonnie, how *could* you! After all Mama tried to do for us—Even if he loved you and respected you, what good'd it do! What *good*, tell me that!

NONNIE: Bess . . . I know Tracy lives in a white world. I know what that means and I've accepted it. It was hard— (*voice falters—grows more certain*) at first . . . but . . . (*pauses*) I understand. It won't change things for us. It can't. (*Suddenly she begins to tremble.*)

BESS: It can't! God Jesus, you say it can't! What do you think love is—a charm you wear around your neck? You don't know what's ahead of you. You haven't any idea! Trouble is, Non, you won't admit this world!

NONNIE: I know what's ahead.

BESS: You'd make me laugh, if I weren't so sick. You won't have the courage to see it through. (*Girls look off into darkness.*)

NONNIE: (*voice soft*) Tracy and I'll work it out.

BESS: Tracy! All my life I've worried! I've seen him at the gate. Of course I've seen him! I just hope to God Ed hasn't. He was there this evening, wasn't he? Where was Ed?

NONNIE: He was in the back yard.

BESS: Oh Non, you're such a fool.

NONNIE: (*softly*) Bess . . .

BESS: (*she doesn't let Non talk now*) We're respectable, Non. Our folks were decent people—fine, good people! What are you doing to us? (*Nonnie's unyielding silence whips Bess on to more words.*) Why can't you be satisfied— Guess that's why— (*pauses as a great wave of song from the big tent sweeps over the town, backwashing against the swamp edge*) I guess you want something you think's better than the rest of us have. Well, it isn't better! (*looks at Non fiercely*) Always, Nonnie, you've wanted better than you could have—

NONNIE: (*touches Bess's arm*) I don't think anyone could be better than Jack, Bess.

BESS: Better than a Pullman porter! (*laughs unhappily*) But you wouldn't want your man emptying spittoons, making up berths, would you? Well, let me tell you, I don't want mine doing it either, but there's nothing else for him to do! (*pauses*) God knows it's better than being a white do-nothing like—

NONNIE: Don't let's fuss, honey. You know what I think of Jack. I've always thought him the finest—

BESS: Oh God, I wish I did. (*groans, speaks quietly after a moment*) When he's away I see it. When he comes home I don't do a thing but give him the devil. (*laughs tremulously, gets up restlessly, walks to the porch railing*)

NONNIE: He understands you. (*Across town the music has grown mournful. The two girls listen a moment.*)

BESS: Non, tell me how long.

NONNIE: Nine weeks.

BESS: We'll get rid of it. Sam—if he'll do it. If not, Aunt Mag. We'll manage it, Biddy. (*pressing the back of her neck in the old gesture of strain*)

NONNIE: I've got to have my baby, Bess. (*Bess does not answer and Non knows she has turned her face toward the clump of cannas because she can't keep her chin still. She watches the fingers move in the old rubbing gesture against her neck. Finally Bess goes to the door, starts in.*)

BESS: Are you coming in?

NONNIE: Not now.

(*Bess sighs, picks up her shoes, goes in. Non slowly goes to the gate and waits.*)

ACT ONE, SCENE 3

Time: *Two days later, shortly after lunch.*

Setting: *The Deens' sun porch with steps leading to the back yard. There are two French doors leading into the house, and a wide whitewashed brick chimney. One door leads into the living room, the other into the hall. The sun porch is used as a summer living room and informal dining room. There are pots of flowers in the windows and hanging ivies and vines. The windows are open as the day is hot and bright. It is a gracious room which shows evidence of moderate wealth and social position. The kind of room one associates very easily with a southern accent.*

Laura is sitting near a window, reading. She is quiet, reserved, a little withdrawn. One has the feeling from the way she reads, the way she handles a book that much of her life has been spent within their pages.

In the rear of this house where the kitchen is, one can hear EENIE *singing, her voice swelling out, dying away to a melancholy humming. Henry is clearing the table. The family has finished their lunch.*

EENIE'S VOICE: Henry . . . Henry . . . (*voice trails out*)

(*Henry glances toward the kitchen but does not answer her. He slowly puts the glasses on the tray, whistling softly, half under his breath.*)

EENIE'S VOICE: (*nearer now, as if she is standing in the hallway just beyond the corner of the living room*) Come heah dis minute and wring dis chicken's neck foh me. I told you to do it, dis mawning. How you expect me to have smothered chicken fo supper when—

HENRY: (*voice low and muttering for Laura is in the room and his manners are too good to carry on his feud with Eenie before white eyes*) She think she boss this whole place—big mouf old— (*he picks up his tray, the telephone rings, lays down the tray, answers it*) Yas'm . . . I'll tell him to come right over. Yes'm, I will. Thank you ma'm. (*As he is talking, Alma walks in. Henry looks at her.*) It's Mrs. Reid again. She say she has a new pain under her shoulder. (*Mrs. Reid is Dr. Deen's ever-flowing well of misery.*)

ALMA: Make a note of it, Henry. Dr. Deen will be in soon.

HENRY: Yas'm. (*Henry writes it down on the telephone pad.*)

ALMA: Henry, Dr. Deen will want a glass of buttermilk when he come in. Will you see that it is ready?

HENRY: Yas'm.

ALMA: (*smiles at Laura, sits down, picks up her knitting*) It's nice to have a chance to see you, dear. We have so little time together any more.

LAURA: I know.

ALMA: (*there is real affection in her voice, and softness. Her love for Laura is the one tender, warm spot in Alma's life*) I miss the little Laura, who used to come running to me with everything.

LAURA: You'd want me to grow up, wouldn't you?

ALMA: Yes, of course. But you must think and feel even if you are grown. There was a time when we talked about such things. (*She smiles a little sadly for she feels an ever-widening chasm between her and Laura.*)

LAURA: I suppose being away at college makes a difference. If there's ever anything important, Mumsie, I'll come running quick to tell you. (*She smiles affectionately at her mother.*) What have you done today?

ALMA: Well . . . I made my talk on India at the missionary society. The ladies said a great many nice things about you. It made me feel very proud of my daughter.

(*Tracy comes in from work at Adams' gin while his mother is talking.*)

LAURA: Thank you, dear.

TRACY: Hello, Mother. Hi, Sis. (*looks quizzically at his sister*) What's your book? Fun—or work?

LAURA: Work, this time, I'm afraid.

TRACY: Degree business?

LAURA: Yes.

TRACY: You want it, Laura?

LAURA: (*smiles at him, raises her eyebrows*) I haven't decided.

(*Alma watches them both, a little annoyed at the sudden cheapening her son has given her pride in Laura's achievement. Laura looks at her wristwatch, stands, still holding the book.*)

LAURA: Mother, have you seen my dark glasses?

ALMA: They're in the table drawer. Are you going out again? Will you be back in time for the service?

LAURA: I—don't know, Mother.

ALMA: I feel that it is our duty to support this revival.

LAURA: But why, Mother? It all seems so crude—those mill people at the altar . . .

(*Tracy has picked up a magazine. He glances now at his mother, then at his sister, half smiles.*)

ALMA: This revival is a community project, Laura. We all are concerned about the lack of spiritual life in Maxwell . . . our young people . . . drinking . . . As for the mill people—they are the ones who especially need God.

(*The telephone is ringing as this is said. Henry comes in and answers it.*)

HENRY: Dr. Deen's residence . . . Yas'm . . . Jes one minute, please ma'm. (*turns from phone*) Hit's Miss Dorothy, Mr. Tracy. (*He grins at Tracy, quickly sobers.*)

TRACY: Tell her I'll call later.

HENRY: Hello Miss Dorothy . . . No'm . . . he ain't here . . . no ma'm . . . Yes'm . . . I'll tell him the minute he gits in. (*As Henry is talking, Alma shows her disapproval while Laura quietly shares Tracy's amusement. Henry goes out. Tracy goes inside the house.*)

ALMA: I'm troubled by what you said, Laura. It doesn't sound like you. Of course Tracy has never shown interest in the church, since he was grown. But then, he's always been a disappointment to us . . .

LAURA: I don't think that we really know him.

ALMA: He has never let us know him—even when he was little. He always went to Mamie with everything—or to his grandmother. And they both spoiled him so! Sometimes I have the strangest feeling that he will always fail . . . I don't see how two children could be so different. (*her voice is sad and weary*)

LAURA: If he could have gone to Georgia Tech and studied engineering as he wanted to, perhaps things would have been different. I don't think we should be too hard on him.

ALMA: You're very loyal to your brother, aren't you?

LAURA: I'm loyal to all my family, darling. (*she goes over, plays affectionately with her mother's hair*) I just think you worry too much about us. (*Alma sighs, looks out of the window, back again. Laura picks up her book. Tut comes in from the garden.*)

TUT: Alma, hello Sugar. Any calls, dear?

ALMA: (*trying to get herself together*) Yes, two or three. (*He hands her four or five roses.*)

ALMA: Thank you, dear. Mrs. Purviance's heart has been very weak. Martha seems alarmed. (*Laura smiles affectionately at both of them, goes out of the room*)

TUT: I'll call her. (*ring*) Miss Sadie . . . get me the Purviance residence, please. (*picks up the phone memo pad*) What is this? What is this, Henry?

HENRY: Yassir. Dat's Mr. Harris. He wants you to check with— (*hesitates, not sure of the etiquette here*) the colored doctor about the fever out at his farm.

ALMA: Henry, get me a bowl, please.

TUT: Hello, Martha . . . what is her pulse? Yes, I know . . . Keep on giving her digitalis . . . and plenty of fluid . . . That's right . . . That's fine, Martha . . . you're a good little nurse . . . Goodbye, Honey.

(*Tut comes back, sits down, picks up a paper. Henry brings in small bowl. Alma begins arranging the roses. Henry dashes out, almost overturns the telephone table.*)

TUT: (*chuckling*) That boy belongs in this house about as much as one of Tom Harris's turpentine mules.

ALMA: I know. Really, Tut, I wonder why we continue to put up with him.

TUT: (*smiles*) Well I suppose because he's been here all his life.

ALMA: I sent Mamie a check for fifteen dollars this morning.

TUT: That's fine. No children ever had a better nurse. We mustn't neglect her.

ALMA: Sometimes I think we should make Henry go and look after Mamie and Ten. He could farm that piece of land for them and take good care of them. Ten is getting so helpless.

TUT: Be mighty hard to get him out of this back yard—and maybe hard for us to do without him. Well . . . believe I'll take a five-minute nap. (*He turns, smiles at his wife.*)

ALMA: Tut, did you remember to talk to Tracy about the farm? I feel that we should not wait too long. Someone may snap it up.

TUT: I will, dear. I haven't been able to get around to it yet.

ALMA: Maybe if he took the farm, he might decide to get married. He hasn't been fair to Dorothy.

TUT: I know. (*voice soothing Alma rather than criticizing his son*) She's been mighty loyal to him.

(*Tracy comes in while Tut is speaking.*)

TRACY: Hello, Dad . . .

TUT: Trace . . .

ALMA: I'll get your buttermilk, Tut. (*She goes out.*)

TUT: How's the seed press coming along?

TRACY: Fine. I came home for my slide rule. There're some calculations I need to make.

TUT: It's good to see you now and then. (*He smiles, hesitates.*) Been kind of wanting to talk to you.

TRACY: (*lights a cigarette*) What's on our minds, Dad?

TUT: (*reluctant to begin, and doing it only because Alma has urged him so strongly*) Lately, I've been realizing how old I'm getting. (*He looks a little guilty as he takes refuge in this time-honored cliché, aware that he is using a big gun with which to batter down his son's defense.*) If anything were to happen to me, I'd feel a lot better to know you were settled . . . in a position to see after your mother. You know, Son, she wants us all to be useful, successful people.

TRACY: I know, Dad.

TUT: She was mighty disappointed when you gave up the drugstore. (*pauses, speaks gently*) You had your reasons for giving it up, I know. (*Tracy doesn't answer. Tut stops, goes on finally.*) Maybe your old dad meddled too much.

TRACY: It wasn't you, Dad. (*He continues smoking for a little, turns suddenly*) It was—Mother! (*Neither man speaks for a moment. Tracy finds it hard to talk to his father like this.*) I liked the drugstore all right—if she had just let—me alone! One day I found her in the office checking my account. (*tries to laugh*) I know she didn't mean it but—checking my accounts as if I wouldn't pay my bills.

TUT: (*gropes along with this one*) She was doing what she thought would help you.

TRACY: If she would just let me work things out in my own way! I've got a little sense, Dad!

TUT: I know . . . You see, she's always handled my bookkeeping. She likes that kind of thing, and I don't.

TRACY: Well, I can't take it!

TUT: Maybe not . . . there's other things you might like better anyway. We have in mind the Hearn farm—it'd make you a good living and you could run it the way you want to. We'd like to buy it, Tracy, and turn it over to you.

(*Alma comes in with buttermilk.*)

TUT: Thank you dear, it looks good. (*He drinks it, as Tracy smokes.*)

ALMA: I hope you will consider it, dear. I was out there looking it over last week. There's some fine acreage for cotton and the house is in excellent condition. There are quite a few things you could do out there. Some of the land is good for a pecan grove.

TRACY: I've never had the slightest desire to farm, Mother.

ALMA: I know you haven't had experience but the tenants living out there are good farm hands. And your father and I both can advise about things. (*Tracy turns away impatiently.*)

TUT: Think it over, Trace.

TRACY: O.K., Dad.

TUT: (*puts down the glass and turns to go*) If the phone rings, take the message, dear. I'm going to catch forty winks. (*Exits*)

ALMA: Tracy—I was with Brother Dunwoodie today, after the service. (*Tracy says nothing.*) He would like very much to talk to you.

TRACY: What about?

ALMA: About everything. He could give you real help.

TRACY: But I don't want his help!

ALMA: I told him (*her face grows determined now*) that I—felt you would be willing to have a talk with him.

TRACY: But Mother—I wouldn't be caught dead talking to a preacher! (*His mother does not answer.*) Of all the damned foolishness . . . (*his voice very low now*)

ALMA: Tracy!

TRACY: I beg your pardon, Mother.

ALMA: I've never heard you use such words before. I have grown to expect quite a few surprises, but never did I think my son would speak—it seems as if you're deliberately ruining your life— (*pauses, convinced now that she is being persecuted by her own son, that Tracy is trying to make a failure out of Laura, trying to take away from Alma her success as a mother. Her eyes travel slowly across her son's face. Suddenly she weeps a little very quietly, then her voice steadies*) I've wanted more than anything else in the world to be a good mother to you and Laura. I've tried to give you both all the love and care that my own mother failed to give me, I've asked little of you in return.

TRACY: (*draws in a breath—trying to keep himself under control*) But Mother, what does all this have to do with the preacher?

ALMA: You seem to destroy everything I try to do for you! We wanted you to go to law school and you left after a few months.

TRACY: I didn't want to study law, Mother.

ALMA: Then the drugstore—you could have made a great success of that, but you threw the chance away— (*Tracy stares at his mother, does not try to answer*) And Dorothy—you know how I've wanted that— (*She is cherishing her feeling of persecution as a child would hold on to her doll. She is silent a moment, weeps very quietly*) What I ask now is such a small thing. (*As Tracy watches,*

Alma's face looks old, hurt and unprotected. He goes over, touches her gently and affectionately.)

ALMA: It's the heat, I think—I haven't been feeling well lately. (*Tracy walks to the edge of the porch, looks away for a little while, turns back, speaks to his mother quietly, knowing now that she has won, yet feeling that he has to say it.*)

TRACY: Mother . . . I'll go see the preacher if you want me to. (*She cannot answer until she gets herself a little under control.*) Mother—I said I'd see Mr. Dunwoodie if you want me to.

ALMA: Thank you dear. (*Tracy has the feeling that his capitulation has not helped much, after all.*)

ALMA: (*stands, picks up her knitting, turns to go out*) Did Laura say when she would be back?

TRACY: No, she didn't say. (*Henry comes in for Dr. Deen's glasses.*)

ALMA: Henry . . . Did Miss Laura say when she would be back?

HENRY: No'm . . . she didn't say.

ALMA: Henry—tell Eenie to make Miss Laura some fig ice cream for supper. (*Exits*)

HENRY: Yas'm . . . (*he looks at Tracy*) Mr. Tracy . . . a jug of good stuff waiting out back. Snooks charged a dollar mo dis time. She says it's the best corn in Georgia. It's in the cabin, Mr. Tracy. (*Tracy doesn't answer—his thoughts still on his talk with his mother, on all that has been happening during these past days. Finally he turns.*)

TRACY: Henry!

HENRY: Yessuh.

TRACY: What you think about—God . . . that kind of thing? (*Henry blinks, shakes his head*) Everybody must have some idea about God. What's yours?

HENRY: Mr. Tracy, you knows I don't no mo know about dat stuff—

TRACY: Does God mean anything to you? You have any feeling about him? (*Henry wipes his mouth with the back of his hand, then pulls at his pants.*) Like for instance—you have . . . for me?

HENRY: Nossuh. Nothin' lak dat—sho.

TRACY: Then why you go to church?

HENRY: (*he works his mouth as if reading a book in which all the words were new. Then sighs, cuts his eyes, chuckles, thinking the white boss was being funny*) Most time to git me a girl.

TRACY: I see. But there's no—

HENRY: Now ain't dat de Gawd's truf! Dis town plumb run dry of girls. Lemme tell you— I'm—

TRACY: Oh for cripes sake, cut it out. We're not talking women. (*Tracy laughs, looks out of the window, turns back*) We're talking about—getting converted. What they mean by it, you reckon?

HENRY: Dog ef I know. (*Tracy is silent now while Henry waits*)

TRACY: Henry—

HENRY: Yassuh.

TRACY: (*slowly*) Are you, afraid of— (*laughs with sudden embarrassment now*) hell . . . things like that?

HENRY: (*voice low*) Sweet Jesus, now you said it! What you reckon hell is like, sho enough? How it gon burn you forever—how it gon do dat, Mr. Tracy?

TRACY: There's no such place, so why all the worry?

HENRY: You mean—

TRACY: You heard me.

HENRY: But da Bible, hit say it, don it—and sho yo ma and pa. We'se bound to go somewheres, Mr. Tracy. Bound to! How come you say dat? How come?

TRACY: Because it's a goddamn lie! Thought up by folks who want you to do their way. That's all! You know it's that. (*voice is quieter now*) And then they give you the works . . . (*He smiles unhappily, seeing himself trapped, knowing he doesn't cut a brave figure in his struggles*) and you end up joining the church— or something. (*looks out of the window*) Two weeks ago we talking about fishing. Things like that. Now—

HENRY: Let's go, Mr. Tracy. Hit'd do us a sight of good to go fish a little. (*he looks out of the door*) They bitin' fine today—

TRACY: (*laughs suddenly, showing his enjoyment of Henry's foolishness*) Whatever else . . . boy . . . (*softly*) Whatever else . . . (*face sober now*)

HENRY: Yassuh.

TRACY: I don't reckon, you damned jackass, I could—do without you. (*he stands*)

HENRY: Nosuh. (*voice soft now*) I knowed dat since I kin remember.

TRACY: Well—how about that drink? (*He goes out of the side door toward the cabin, and Henry follows him slowly, bowed down, though he doesn't know why, by his white friend's trouble.*)

ACT ONE, SCENE 4

The ridge. A few minutes later. It is a bare, open sand ridge, edged with long leaf yellow pines. Behind it the swamp. They later sit down on the sand, but now Non turns, walks a few steps away. Pauses, her back to Tracy. Tracy stands there watching her. The moonlight sifts through the trees, showing clearly the palmetto bushes, a few prickly pears, sand, yet not enough light to show the difference in their color. Now Non turns slowly pushes the hair off her face, smiles. It is a little thing, a quick turn of her body, the slow pushing of hair from her face, but it recalls to Tracy's mind all the good and lovely nights they have had together. She seems a sweet lovely thing to him there in the moonlight. He moves to her quickly and pulls her to him, shamed, somehow, about everything, and deeply touched. He slips his hand back of her head as he holds her, kisses her face tenderly. She turns away, takes his hand. And when he pulls her around he sees that her chin is shaking and there are tears on her face.

TRACY: It's a damned mess! (*hushes abruptly*)

(*Non shakes her head, tries to smile, wipes her eyes. For a little neither tries to talk much. Both staring out into the night. Each staring down a different path that leads to different childhoods.*)

NONNIE: (*shakily*) Don't quite know what's the matter with me. (*He draws her to him and runs his hand across her hair, not knowing what to say. Not knowing in this damned devilish world what to say. He knows from the trembling through her body that she is crying, but there is no sound.*)

TRACY: Would you like to talk to me, Non, about it? (*though God knows he couldn't bear to hear her. After a while she wipes her eyes, pushes her dark hair back, speaks in a low voice*)

NONNIE: I can't talk much about things. (*she smiles at him, pauses a long time, goes on quietly*) You see, it's like this . . . I've always known what I wanted. You. And Mummie, when I was little. I know people are supposed to want other things. I don't seem to . . . I think maybe I feel a little like I used to when Mother was away at work and I'd be playing on the edge of the swamp all by myself. Something would rattle and I'd begin to run . . . not knowing where to run . . . (*she laughs softly, wipes her eyes again*)

TRACY: (*deep tenderness in his voice*) You were a lonely little thing.

NONNIE: (*touches him gently, showing her love*) Yes . . . You used to come to see me after school and bring me tea cakes or cold biscuit and ham. It tasted so good . . . You seemed to know that I was hungry.

TRACY: Don't be silly! I was hungry too. It was just more fun to eat it with you than by myself.

NONNIE: And after we'd eaten, you'd do my arithmetic for me. I thought you were so smart—I still think so.

TRACY: (*his voice shows his torn feelings, tenderness for her, the pull back to his family and to whiteness*) Nonnie . . .

NONNIE: (*arm behind her head now, breast rising and falling in the clear light*) The way things have to be . . . I don't see much of you. It has to be that way. But tonight . . . I think maybe I'm scared. (*She looks out into the night while Tracy watches her closely.*) If we were—the same—color— (*words very low*) we could play together—tonight—drive places in the car, play tennis, maybe . . . I know it sounds funny. (*laughs and her breath catches sharply*) But I've never played except by myself. It would be—nice to play with you. It's been so hot today—Boysie's cried so much—maybe all of it together has made me— (*she tries to laugh*)

TRACY: (*sits up*) God . . .

NONNIE: It's all right, Tracy. I want you to know that. (*speaks earnestly now*) I like having you come out to me . . . just as you do . . . I like being here—whenever you need me. Things that mean so much to Eddie and Bess, and meant so much to Mummie, don't mean the same to me. I decided that when I was a little thing—playing by myself. I had to decide things. Maybe that doesn't make sense to you. But one day when I was a little girl, a white boy tried to take off my clothes in a gallberry patch, and you stopped him. You remember? It was the first time I ever saw you. You were twelve—I was six. (*She turns to him, smiling at her memories.*) I gave you a bunch of honeysuckle. Pink honeysuckle . . . It embarrassed you. You threw it away. Sounds funny, saying it out loud, like this, but there you were, and I knew I was all right. (*Tracy stares out into the dark. It's a voice talking, another voice, talking to Tracy.*) I've felt that way . . . ever since. (*pauses. Suddenly she turns, still speaking softly but urgently*) All those things people think matter, don't matter. They don't matter, Tracy. (*her voice like a whisper. She puts her hand on his knee. It lies there against his white trousers, a shadow. He turns now, looks into her eyes. Her face is strong, sure of its decision*)

TRACY: I'm so damned tired!

(*Nonnie draws his head down to her lap. He settles against her body, closes his eyes. Softly her fingers press temples, move along the nerve back of his ear and down into his neck. Again, again, again.*)

TRACY: Your hands are cool—like the keys on Grandma's piano . . . I'd go—lay my face against them—when I was a little fellow—and they'd make me feel . . . like this . . . Funny, how she always took up for me . . . (*he smiles quietly*) even when I was in the wrong . . . (*again, again, again, Non's fingers press gently*)

NONNIE: She loved you.

TRACY: Yes. (*laughs*) Grandma thought I was all right . . . It was when Mother had got me for something, and I'd be crazy mad—wanting to bawl . . . I'd go and it'd be dim in there . . . and the keys cool . . . like this . . . Have I ever told you that before? Guess I have.

NONNIE: (*leans over and kisses him*) Yes, many times.

TRACY: Reckon so . . .

NONNIE: Do you remember the first time? (*low voice falters suddenly*)

TRACY: First? No, don't believe I do.

NONNIE: Try. (*Tracy can't remember. Nonnie goes on.*) It was at Christmas, and you had come home from college—and—didn't want to go back . . .

TRACY: Sure. I'd flunked my exams. Every damn one!

NONNIE: And we were in the hollow back of the big cypress, and the sun was warm, not a bit like Christmas weather. You remember? (*she is talking swiftly now*) And you talked a while—and then you said, "Nonnie, you've grown up. You're not a kid any more. It made me very proud—for I was only fourteen.

TRACY: Did you? You were a funny little thing.

NONNIE: And then I got tongue-tied and shy—as if I'd never seen you before. You seemed so grown up yourself. You stretched out on the grass and put your head in my lap—and that's when you told me about the piano keys . . .

TRACY: Then what?

NONNIE: (*kisses him again*) I think maybe you remember.

TRACY: You were scared.

NONNIE: Not much.

TRACY: But a little.

NONNIE: Yes. (*fingers following the path of pain along his temples. Tracy laughs softly—at ease*) Happy though, every time since. (*they are quiet as she continues to rub his head*) We have so many memories . . . so many days, hours . . . When you came home from France—you'd been away two years. You remember? You drove out in your mother's car. I heard the sound before you turned the curve at Miss Ada's. And then, there you were standing at the gate. I couldn't say a word! (*her voice soft, on the edge of tears, yet half laughing at herself*) Mother was sick—I couldn't leave until Bess came home. So you drove up one road and down another until it was late and you could come again. Remember? (*Tracy's face is in great pain as he struggles with his strong love for this girl and with the pull of his mother and his white culture. He does not answer her.*) We went to Aunt Tyse's little cabin—we'd been going there since we were kids—we didn't say a word . . . we just went . . . You had a phonograph with you and you played a record—a silly waltz, I think. We danced.

TRACY: Non! (*He seems to want to stop her.*)

NONNIE: And you talked about our going to France to live . . . Sometimes I wonder why we—didn't— (*her voice is lost in a whisper*)

TRACY: Because I couldn't, damn it! I don't know how! (*He stares out in the darkness a long time before he speaks again. When he says the words they come out of a profound embarrassment of spirit and yet there is a strange unawareness of their full significance, else he could not have said them.*) The family is going to buy the Hearn farm. They want me to run it. I drove out there yesterday and looked around. There's a little cottage on the place, about half a mile from the old brick house. (*hesitates, then goes on*) If I put plumbing in and had a good paint job done on it, it would be in nice shape. (*he finds it hard to say the words that white men for centuries have shaped their tongues to*) Would you be willing to—live out there, Non?

NONNIE: (*long silence*) I love you . . .

TRACY: God . . . (*buries his face in his hands*)

TRACY: There's not a girl in this town who can touch you! (*words low, tumbling out under great pressure*) You make them all look like— (*he draws in his breath sharply*) It's a fine old home, that brick house . . . made for you and for our children . . . Why can't I— (*buries his face in his hands*) What's the matter with me, tell me that! What's the matter with me that I can't—

NONNIE: Tracy . . . (*voice full of anguish, and tenderness. Her love is so deep, so all pervasive that she pushes her own pain away now and becomes mature and womanly and protective as she tries to help him with his*)

TRACY: It's Mother. (*stops*) You know what it would do to her.

NONNIE: I know.

TRACY: It—seems everything I want is—something Mother can't understand.

She would never understand this, Non. She would—it would kill her—you see she thinks a thing like this is a terrible sin against God and man. She was brought up that way. Oh, I don't know. (*he stops, tries to go on*) It's all so— Non, everything I have that is good, you have given to me. All my life I've been coming to you and every time I have found what I—came for. I couldn't live without you.

NONNIE: If we could go away—

TRACY: God knows I'd like to leave Maxwell and never come back to it. I hate the place! But if we went, like that . . . Mother would . . . (*He sighs, fatigued by words that seem only to make things worse.*) I don't—seem able to do that to her.

NONNIE: (*does not try to talk now. Softly caresses him, wanting only to ease a suffering for both of them that she knows he has little to do with*) I know.

(*They sit without talking now. Then Tracy turns restlessly.*)

TRACY: Dorothy tried to save my soul tonight. Again. Mother's tried, now Dorothy. Preacher's going to try tomorrow. They evidently think I've got a soul. (*rises, crosses left, and up a few steps*) If Mother weren't so—oh I don't know—because I don't come up to something she expects of me, I'm a failure. Plastered on their faces—big as road signs. Laura—Oh God, I like the kid all right. Nice girl, if they'd leave her alone . . . what's it all about! I just don't know.

TRACY: You like me just as I am—don't you? (*she smiles softly*) I wonder what would happen if we did go away— Maybe we— Trouble with me, I never know how to quit anything! Get started—keep on—

NONNIE: Tracy—

TRACY: Lord! It's late. We'd better be going, hadn't we? (*Scene fades as they turn away.*)

ACT ONE, SCENE 5

Time: *Next evening.*

Setting: *Deen's Drugstore, after the evening service. Laura, Harriet, Charlie are seated at a table, drinking their cokes. Tracy is behind the counter. There is tension among the young people, for however sophisticated and informed they have not come through Brother Dunwoodie's sermon untouched. The whole town is quivering under the impact of these services like a hollow bowl struck by its guilty conscience. All their lives they have sung the old songs. . . . Hearing them now is like flinging a net into your past, dragging back memories of old helpless fears and dreads and failures. Tracy is behind the counter waiting on* SALAMANDER, *old, dried like a tobacco leaf, always ailing. He is buying some pain medicine. Salamander is proprietor of Salamander's Cafe (colored). He has on his old apron and a brown paper bag is on his head, like a cap.*

TRACY: (*wrapping the medicine*) This ought to help your legs a little. Pain much?

SALAMANDER: Yes sir. All night long. Much obliged, Mr. Tracy. (*turns to go, stops, turns back*) Have you got somep'n to help my old liver? Hit never feels right no more.

TRACY: How about a box of Liver Regulator?

SALAMANDER: Yassuh.

HARRIET: Charlie, make Laura show you the water colors she's done. You'll be impressed.

CHARLIE: You holding out on me, honey?

LAURA: Oh, they're not—very good, I'm afraid. I've been out at the river a lot lately. That stretch of sand, the prickly pears . . . (*she smiles half at herself*) I'd thought I'd see what I could do with it.

CHARLIE: How about showing them to me tonight?

(*As the young people are talking Tracy wraps up Salamander's package, hands it to him, takes his money. Salamander goes out,* CHUCK *comes in.*)

DOUG: (*behind the soda fountain*) Hi, Chuck.

CHUCK: Doug, the druggist! (*turns to Harriet*) Sorry Harriet, I had to drive Mother home.

HARRIET: It's all right. Laura and Charlie picked me up.

CHUCK: Have a coke?

HARRIET: No, thanks, Chuck.

CHUCK: Will you, Laura? (*Laura smiles, shakes her head. Chuck goes over for his coke, comes back, sits down by Harriet. While he is getting his coke,* MISS BELLE *and* MISS SADIE *come in, sit down at one of the tables. Miss Belle is one of Maxwell's self-supporting old maids. She is soft and white, plump and pretty, in a way. Wears fussy clothes and bright colors. Miss Belle is easily moved to tears over the trivia of her friends' lives and as quick to claw at any exposed portion of their personality. Inquisitive, gossipy, she lives off of people's private lives nibbling at the morsels their indiscretions dump in her path. Her best friends are the other old maids who work downtown: Miss Sadie, the telephone operator and the women who clerk in the dry-goods stores. Miss Sadie is middle-aged and bright like a bird, with pompadoured red hair, and eyes that see about all that there is to see. She is Maxwell's fever thermometer. One can measure the town's excitement by the busyness of Miss Sadie. All her life is spent crossing other lives and uncrossing them as she plugs one number to another.*)

DOUG: Miss Sadie, what will you and Miss Belle have?

MISS SADIE: A coke, please, Doug.

MISS BELLE: Don't forget to put the cherry in, Doug.

DOUG: I never have in five years, have I?

MISS BELLE: Not but once, Doug.

CHUCK: Who's the guy, Charlie, who stayed at the altar so long? Was he from Milltown?

CHARLIE: (*quietly*) Think so. Don't believe I know his name.

CHUCK: He sure was suffering. Everybody was suffering tonight. You know, that man can really preach. (*The group laughs.*)

HARRIET: Just the same, I think it's immoral. All that weeping, weeping, talk about hell—with every child in town listening. Poor little things will stay awake all night, the way I used to. I wonder why preachers can't talk quietly about Jesus? He knew a lot it wouldn't hurt us to know. So silly of course, when you say it out loud. (*She laughs a little, embarrassed at her previous mood of seriousness. She looks at Tracy. He winks at her, laughs easily, amused at his little firebrand friend. Tracy comes over, sits with the old maids, flatters them with a little attention.*)

TRACY: You're having drinks with me, this time.

CHUCK: I suppose he's trying to appeal to the mill folks. They seem to like it anyway.

HARRIET: Funny . . . he hasn't said a word about all the problems the whole world is worrying over.

LAURA: I suppose all they really want us to do is sponsor religion, not practice it. Or maybe they don't know what they want.

HARRIET: Well, some day, I'm going to begin practicing it—just to see what will happen. They'll think I'm a communist.

CHUCK: Ssh, honey—drink your coke.

MISS BELLE: Harriet, your mother would be shocked if she heard you going on like this.

HARRIET: Yes'm, I know. (*The young people exchange grins with each other.*)

MISS BELLE: I'm shocked a little myself. I think it's about time Maxwell did have a revival.

HARRIET: Let's go for a swim, everybody.

CHUCK: Sure! Get you under water, maybe you'll stop talking.

HARRIET: Tracy, let's pick up Dot—

TRACY: Her mother isn't well. She can't go. (*smiles*) I can't either. Have some work to do. (*The young men pay for the drinks and go out with the girls.*)

HARRIET: Saw you at the service tonight. Remember you said once you'd never go again.

TRACY: No harm going, is there? (*smiles at her, keeps his voice teasing*)

HARRIET: Yes, I think there is. (*hesitates, goes on*) I wish I have more sense to prove I'm right. (*pauses, goes on*) I remember when I was little, I used to worry so when I heard the preacher talk about . . . hell . . . death . . . things like that. I always thought I had committed the unpardonable sin. (*laughs a little shakily*) Used to cry myself to sleep about it. Didn't know what it was . . . just knew I had committed it.

TRACY: Oh well—you're grown now. You don't let it bother you any more, do you?

HARRIET: I wonder if you ever get over it. (*pause, full of her memories*) We worry so much about the wrong sins, don't we? (*turns back to Tracy*) I have to attend the services—with Brother Dunwoodie staying at our house, Mother would have a fit if I didn't. (*looks hard at her old childhood friend*) You don't have to. Why go and listen to all that stuff—those old songs . . . (*she suddenly smiles, making good-natured fun of him*) Do you know, it would be like you to get converted.

TRACY: (*laughing with her now*) If I did—what you reckon would happen? (*Harriet doesn't answer*) The family bought the Hearn farm, Harriet. I'm going to run it for them.

HARRIET: (*glances at him questioningly*) Lonely place.

TRACY: (*looking straight at her*) I like to be alone.

HARRIET: Will Dot?

TRACY: I haven't asked her. (*Tracy goes outside with Harriet, stands there as they leave, smoking. Over to the side, stands Ed waiting for Sam, smoking also.*)

MISS SADIE: (*voice cheerful, unperturbed*) Belle, it's late.

MISS BELLE: Doug, may I speak to you for a moment? (*Doug goes over to the counter where she stands.*) The calomel you gave me last week didn't do me near as much good as it ought to. Don't you think I'd better take a little more.

DOUG: Well, I don't reckon it would hurt you much, Miss Belle. About half a grain?

MISS BELLE: I think you better give me a grain.

DOUG: I'll give it to you in tenth grain tablets. Be sure to take a laxative afterward. It might salivate you, taking so much.

MISS BELLE: Now Doug, I was taking calomel before you were born. So don't tell me.

MISS BELLE: I think I need some vitamins. What would you take, Doug?

DOUG: Most folks take vitamin B or B complex.

MISS SADIE: I'll take the B complex. Charge it, Doug.

DOUG: O.K. Miss Sadie.

MISS BELLE: I reckon you had better give me a package of Epsom Salts, Doug.(*Doug hands the ladies the packages and they go out, Miss Belle paying for hers.*)

TRACY: H'lo Ed.

ED: (*be goddam if you'd call him mister*) H'lo, Tracy.

TRACY: Didn't know you were in town.

ED: Came in last week.

TRACY: Here long?

ED: Week or so.

TRACY: Still in Washington, I suppose?

ED: Still there. (*They look blandly at each other, having exhausted all but one conversational possibility.*)

TRACY: Damn hot weather.

ED: You're right.

TRACY: Well, so long.

ED: So long.

(*Outside the drugstore, Tut Deen meets Tom Harris and Dunwoodie.*)

HARRIS: Howdy, Tut. (*easy casual greetings of old friends*)

TUT: Tom . . . Good evening, Brother Dunwoodie. Sorry I couldn't get out to hear you tonight. Better crowd, I understand.

DUNWOODIE: Yes. Things are better. Fine service tonight.

TUT: (*cheerfully*) I'm glad to hear it. Coming in?

HARRIS: No, it's late. You ever sleep, Tut?

TUT: I sleep fine.

DUNWOODIE: Don't wait up for me, Mr. Harris, I'll be along later.

TUT: Just a minute, Tom. I'll go with you. (*He sticks his head in the door, calls to Doug.*)

TUT: Any calls, Doug?

DOUG: No sir.

TRACY: Good evening, sir.

DUNWOODIE: Hello.

TRACY: Shall we—stay here? Or would you like to go out in the car?

DUNWOODIE: Suits me fine right here.

TRACY: Doug, you can go if you like, I'll close up.

DOUG: O.K. (*Doug wipes off counter, pulls off his white apron, puts on his street coat, and goes out.*) Night, Brother Dunwoodie. Night, Tracy.

TRACY: Night, Doug. (*Tracy closes the front door, turns out all the lights except one, pulls a shade in the big window*) Believe we'll be more comfortable over here, sir. (*They move to another table. The drugstore is now dim except for the light on Tracy and Preacher Dunwoodie.*)

TRACY: Must be a pretty tough job—preaching three times a day. (*feels for a cigarette, goes over to counter for a package*)

DUNWOODIE: Yeah . . . hot work. Your grandfather could take it better than any preacher I ever saw. You remind me of him a little. Only you're leaner, harder. (*he looks at Tracy closely*) More like your grandmother. Quieter though.

TRACY: (*laughs softly*) Grandmother had energy, all right.

DUNWOODIE: She was a great little woman.

TRACY: In a way, you're different from most preachers. Mind telling me how you happened to—be one.

DUNWOODIE: Well, it's pretty easy to answer that. God convicted me of sin and called me to preach the Gospel. Laid a burden on me that I couldn't shake off.

(*Tracy watches the preacher closely, curious and interested. Tracy remains poised, at ease as a host, but perturbed by this whole affair, betraying his restlessness by smoking too many cigarettes.*)

DUNWOODIE: Funny . . . way I tried. Joined the Marines . . . then took up ball playing—got in minor league—looked I was headed for big league stuff—

TRACY: (*real interested now*) What you play?

DUNWOODIE: Third. Yeah . . . Nothing helped. Be on the train—be playing ball even, and I hear the voice whispering: "what you going to do about it?" (*pauses*) After a while I gave in. You can't keep struggling against God, Deen. I learned that. (*Tracy turns away a bit impatiently*)

DUNWOODIE: (*smiles quickly*) I know you're saying, maybe you don't believe in God. Said it myself once. But I lied. You may not believe there's oxygen in the air, but you can't live more'n a minute or so without it. It's that way with God. You can't live in Maxwell without God. Got to have Him to lean on. Man's a funny critter. Seems like the minute he lets go his mother's hand, got to have something else to hold to.

TRACY: (*lights another cigarette. He is restless*) Won't you have a coke, Mr. Dunwoodie?

DUNWOODIE: Believe I will. (*Tracy gets it, preacher thanks him*) You know, when you're preaching . . . going around from place to place on the Lord's business, you run into a sight of sin! Yes sir! All kinds. Some of 'em make you tremble to think of. Makes you wonder how God in His wisdom could've made a creature who could think up as many ways of doing wrong as man has studied up. You wonder why He couldn't have done a little better—I say it in all reverence. But God gave us Jesus, His only begotten Son—I can't forget that, and you can't forget that, Deen—to help us poor stumbling creatures find salvation . . . This business of sin—strange how each man has his own way of sinning. I don't know what your way is but I know about sin. (*He pauses here as if about to choose his words carefully.*) Now there's one sin that causes a lot of trouble . . . (*voice drops confidentially, man-to-man talk now. Very sympathetic: This-is-a-sin-we-white-men-in-the-South-know all-about. Completely identifies himself with Tracy so that he will not feel he's being criticized harshly*) Some men, when they're young, sneak off to Colored Town. Let their passions run clean away with them. Get to lusting—burning up! And they get to thinking . . . they'd rather have that kind of thing than marriage. Lot rather! Scared of white girls. Scared nice white girls can't satisfy them. And they're right. Course no decent, fine white woman can satisfy you when you let your mind out like a team of wild mules racing straight to— (*voice has risen shrilly. Suddenly he stops. Speaks more quietly*) Well . . . that's youth. (*wipes his face with his big handkerchief*) That's youth—the devil . . . (*softly now*) Every time a white man does that, he's doing something unnatural, and unclean. Sinning against his own blood . . . (*He pauses, goes on with his words, voice, tense, low, sure of himself for the preacher honestly sees no other way to solve this problem. Yet underneath his certainty there is a suffering, for he is not without human kindness.*) But—if he does get into—trouble with a colored girl, there's just one thing to do! (*he pauses*) Stop it, and stop it quick . . . Give the girl some money to see her through . . . Or better still, find some good darkie to marry her . . . Give him some money to light a fire under him and get him moving fast. Fix things. There's no other way. (*sighs*) You see, Deen, you have to keep pushing them right back across that line. Keep pushing! That's right. Kind of like it is with a dog. You have a dog, seems right human. You'd a lot rather be around that dog than anybody you ever knew. But it's still a dog. You don't forget that. And you don't forget the other . . . it's the same. God made the white race for a great purpose. Sometimes I've wondered what the purpose is. Between you and I, I've wondered—with all reverence—when God is going to divulge that purpose, for up to now, seems like we have been marking time, or making a mess of things! Well . . . (*smiles suddenly, draws his brows close, and quickly relaxes them, throws back his heavy black hair*) I've done all the talking.

TRACY: I appreciate your taking time with me. To tell you the truth, I'm hardly worth it. (*smiles quickly*)

DUNWOODIE: There's people who think you are. That little Dorothy Pusey . . . your own fine mother. (*continues soberly*) You know Deen, most men learn to love God because their women love him. Same way they begin to love their own children. Ever thought of that? Or because they're scared . . . not to. You're not the easy scared kind.

TRACY: I don't know . . . Sometimes I think I am. (*speaks gravely, slowly*) Trouble with me, I don't believe all that.

DUNWOODIE: Most men don't believe when they start. Most of us have to take some things on faith—like our children, for instance. (*chuckles*) You take things that matter on faith, Deen. There's no way of proving them! You see, on this earth there're two worlds, man's and woman's. Man's has to do with work. Women teach us to love the Lord, and our children. But *we* build the churches, keep 'em going. (*turns and looks at Tracy*) Now when a man gets over into a woman's world, he gets into bad trouble. He don't belong there. God wants your soul where it belongs, for then He'll be surer of getting it than if it was on the other side—where some woman'll get it all. Some men have a deep feeling for God. Comes to 'em easy. Others get it slow. The hard way. But a man makes a living and feeds those young'uns his wife *says* are his even if he ain't sure he loves them yet, don't he? And a man gets on the Lord's side and joins the church, supports it and his town's affairs, even when his heart's not in it much . . . at first. But this is what happens after a time. After a time God begins to seem real to you. Yeah! Not something your mother loved and told you to love! But your own kind. I mean that in a holy and sacred way. And what men are doing begins to seem more important to you and satisfying than anything in a woman's world. So when I say, get on the Lord's side, Deen, I mean one thing when I talk to the ladies and another when I talk to men. (*Tracy's teeth flash again in a quick smile*)

DUNWOODIE: (*draws his heavy brows together, and quickly relaxes them, speaks softly as his face eases into a warm smile.*) Well, how about it? How about trying it on the Lord's side and man's, for a while?

TRACY: I'll think about it. (*speaks quickly*)

DUNWOODIE: (*lays his big warm hand on Tracy's shoulder, sighs.*) God bless you.

TRACY: I don't have much of a feeling for God, and all it seems to stand for in

folks' minds. As for the church, it's not important to me. I don't know that
I even believe in God.

DUNWOODIE: (*silent a moment*) If I didn't believe in God—in a personal God—
not just some theory, Deen—if I didn't believe in God the Father watching
over me day and night, I'd be the meanest man in Georgia. I'd go on such a
rampage . . . (*suddenly sighs. Rubs his hands over his face*) You know, some men
have the devil in them from the day they're born. And I'm one of them. Broke
my poor mother's heart before I gave in. God help me, I put her in an early
grave with my wild ways. Sometimes now when I get to thinking about it, I
wonder how God has been so merciful to me.

(*Tracy is looking straight ahead.*)

DUNWOODIE: You haven't got that on your conscience. Don't get it there, boy,
it's a hard thing to bear.

TRACY: I don't believe—anything. (*laughs, hands tremble as he lights another
cigarette*) But if you did believe—how does a man get going?

DUNWOODIE: For you, seems to me would be like this, join the church, marry
that fine little Dot Pusey, set up housekeeping and make her a good living.
That would be your way to begin. For other folks it might be different. You
see—when you marry, you begin a new life, Deen. A new life, with the pages
bare . . . There can't be anything written on them. If there is, you'd better tear
it out, quick!

TRACY: (*half smiles*) That the way you figure things?

DUNWOODIE: That's the way, Deen. And get going. (*speaks brusquely, turns
quickly and smiles at Tracy and now his voice is rich and firm for he believes what
he is saying*) There's a lot of important folks on your side— (*stands. It is late
and he must be leaving*) And God's among them. Don't forget that. (*For a
moment he seems unable to pull himself out of the troubled mood his own words
have driven him in. Then he achieves a lightness as he turns back to Tracy.*) Well
. . . it's late.

TRACY: I'm much obliged to you, Brother Dunwoodie. Can I drive you home?
(*speaks courteously*)

DUNWOODIE: No, do me good to walk. Good night, Deen.

(*Tracy bows in friendly gesture of good night, opens the door for Dunwoodie who
goes out into the street. Tracy turns, feels in his pocket for cigarettes, goes over to the
counter for a package, leaving the door open. Beyond it the street is silent and empty.
He lights a cigarette, pulls himself up on the counter and sits there, thinking.*)

ACT TWO, SCENE I

Time: *Three days later.*
Place: *The back terrace. The terrace is near the corner of the house, facing the back
yard. There is a trellis, and beyond it is the kitchen, which cannot be seen. A few*

outdoor chairs and a table. The family often have their breakfast there, or sit there in the evenings when they wish more privacy than the sun porch affords.

Tracy sits smoking, watching as Henry collects his fishing tackle on the cabin shed. Henry is going out to the river with some of his friends. He has a pole and his gig knife. Has on khaki pants (or jeans). Tracy is laughing at something Henry has said as the curtain goes up.

TRACY: Well, if you don't get a move on you, they'll be back from the river before you get started.

HENRY: Yassir. They frying them fish right now, I reckon. They tell me they went seining this afternoon. Should of got plenty.

TRACY: That's no kind of fishing. That's plain murder.

HENRY: Yassir. But you got to have somep'n to fry. The women'd be mighty disappointed if they didn't have nothing to cook along with them good old cornmeal fritters tonight. (*Tracy grins. He wishes he could "forget his troubles" and go fishing too.*) Me and some of the boys going gigging. And at daybreak I'm gwine catch you a mess of the prettiest perch— (*he laughs*)

TRACY: You better not come back without 'em. Tell Eenie to fry two for my breakfast, with plenty of grits and butter.

HENRY: Yassuh! I'll be bringing back a string of 'em— (*Henry goes out whistling, with his pole.*)

(*Alma comes down the side path which leads from the sun porch around to the back terrace. She has on a summer dress, a small casual hat, and holds a summer handbag. She has just come from the evening service, having lingered to talk to a few of her friends.*)

TRACY: Hello, Mother. (*he comes over, sits down*) Dad with you?

ALMA: No. He was to go to Mrs. Reid's. I don't know whether he has come back or not.

TRACY: You'd think he'd give her a little extra in that hypo one of these nights, wouldn't you? (*sits on the arm of a chair*)

ALMA: (*smiles*) Dorothy didn't come over? Eenie made a chocolate cake, especially for her.

TRACY: She felt she shouldn't leave her mother. Mrs. Pusey had another spell today.

ALMA: Yes, I know. It hasn't been easy for Dot to have an invalid mother on her hands. Perhaps you'll take some cake over to her later.

TRACY: If you would like for me to. (*he laughs*) Mr. Pug Pusey welcomed me into the family this morning. It got to be a serious affair. (*Tracy eyes his mother quizzically.*) Don't know how much of the Puseys I can take.

ALMA: (*laughs, enjoying this bit of snobbery. Pauses*) Dorothy is superior to her family. They're really quite nice people, Tracy. (*They sit a moment in silence.*)

TRACY: Oh, I haven't anything against them. They're the salt of the earth, I suppose. I've decided, Mother, to join the church. (*He says it with no pleasure in his voice.*)

ALMA: Brother Dunwoodie told me. We are all glad, Tracy—Dorothy especially.

TRACY: (*restless again, irritated too, by his mother's composure and lack of enthusiasm. Somehow he had thought she'd be pleased, really pleased, and maybe surprised*) Dot was telling me about the spool bed and other things of Grandmother's. It's nice of you to give them to us.

ALMA: Your grandmother wanted you to have them.

TRACY: We were out at the Hearn place today. It's a beautiful old house.

ALMA: Yes. One of the best in this country.

TRACY: Dot likes the idea of living there. She's planning all kinds of things to do. Dot likes to change things. (*Me especially, he is thinking, and laughs restlessly.*)

ALMA: She's a wonderful girl but Pusey taste is—a little— (*she stops, goes on*) I'd use only hooked rugs if I were you, with your grandmother's furniture. Dorothy should keep it simple. I'll help her all I can.

TRACY: I'd like to have the portrait of Grandmother, if you don't mind. She said once, I could. Where is it, Mother?

ALMA: I believe it is in my closet. (*as if half-forgotten*)

TRACY: You've never hung it—

ALMA: No . . . there never seemed a place for it.

TRACY: Wish we could have kept the old house in Macon. (*almost to himself*)

ALMA: It was better to have sold it. The street's going down so fast.

TRACY: Suppose so. Grandmother loved it. (*sits down again on the arm of the chair*)

TRACY: Mother— (*He is feeling uncomfortable now and wishes he did not have to say the rest of his sentence.*) Could you let me have some money?

ALMA: (*turns to her son, searches his face. The situation is no longer relaxed and easy*) How much, Tracy?

TRACY: Three hundred.

ALMA: That's quite a lot of money.

TRACY: I know. I hate to ask you . . . Maybe I can pay it back a little later.

ALMA: Why do you need it? (*Tracy does not answer.*) For Dot's ring?

TRACY: Dad gave me money for that.

ALMA: Then why do you need it?

TRACY: I'd rather not say.

ALMA: Have you asked your father for it?

TRACY: No.

ALMA: Why don't you take it up with him? Why, Tracy? (*Tracy does not reply. Shows his restlessness*)

TRACY: I'd rather not bother Dad.

ALMA: You've been gambling?

TRACY: (*looks at his mother: Sure I've been gambling!*) You can call it that. (*He lights a cigarette, tosses the match to the water pitcher tray.*)

ALMA: Have you—told Dorothy?

TRACY: It's none of her business.

ALMA: Everything that concerns you is Dorothy's business now.

TRACY: If you can't let me have it, just say so, Mother. Let's don't argue about it.

ALMA: I can let you have it, Tracy. But I don't understand why you are—so secretive. (*She opens her bag, takes out her checkbook and pen. Looks up again*) I've wanted to say this to you for a long time— (*writes the date on the check, pauses, looks up at her son*) but somehow we don't seem to—have time for talks. Dorothy is a fine girl with fine ideals and we are all happy that you are going to marry her. But you will make her life miserable if you continue the kind of relationship with her that you have with your family. You have never given us your confidence, Tracy. (*She tries to soften the words with a smile.*) You know that . . . and it has made it hard for all of us. (*finishes the check*)

(*Tracy stares at his mother. Here she is finding new faults to pick on. Always disappointed . . . When he had thought she would be glad about Dorothy, about the farm, about the church. Alma looks up now.*)

ALMA: Dorothy wants her marriage to be a success. She is the kind of girl who will put her home above everything else in her life. She wants to be a real wife to you, Tracy. And you will always find her a person who can—forgive things. Whatever you've done, she'll forgive. (*Tracy stares at his mother. His mind is full now of a life of misunderstanding. A life that he cannot bear any longer. Suddenly in his mind he sees Nonnie at the gate waiting and he knows that when he gets there everything will be all right again. He knows suddenly that he'll never give her up, and for a moment the pressures are lifted and he feels strong enough to walk the old path that leads to her and to keep walking it. He hands the check back to his mother.*)

TRACY: I've changed my mind, Mother. I won't need the money. (*Alma doesn't say a word. Slowly puts the check in her handbag. Stands, turns and goes around to the front of the house.*)

ALMA: Good night, Tracy.

(*Tracy sits there. His father comes in from the garden.*)

TUT: Howdy, Trace.

TRACY: Hello, Dad. Thought you were out.

TUT: No—I've been in the garden.

TRACY: Too dark to work much, wasn't it?

TUT: Yes. (*sighs a little*) I've been sitting. (*smiles, he holds two roses in his hand*) Thought your mother might like these. (*looks at one of the roses closely. Pauses. The two men sit there. Tut at ease, blind to his son's perturbed feelings; Tracy, torn by his conflict, smoking nervously*) She's mighty pleased, son, about you and Dorothy. We both think Dorothy's as fine a girl as we could want for a daughter. I was over to see her mother today. We had a good talk about you— (*He looks up at his son, smiles gently.*) She's mighty loyal to you, Trace.

(*Neither speaks for a moment. Tracy is staring out into the darkness, the old fatigue in his eyes.*)

TRACY: How is Mrs. Pusey?

TUT: Well, I don't know. When you got one of these malignant cases, there's not much to do but ease pain, and wait . . . Dorothy was telling me about the boxwood, out at the farm. Says it must be at least fifty years old.

TRACY: She told me. She'd like you to help her with the garden, if you will, Dad.

TUT: All this— (*he smiles at his son*) kind of makes me want to go back to the country myself . . . (*he sits there thinking about his childhood on the old Deen farm*) What I'd like to do would be to get me an old place and build it back up. Get me plenty of stock—

TRACY: I guess it will have to be cotton for me. It's all I know.

TUT: Well . . . I think you'd like that better. But there's nothing I'd like more than being around cows and horses. Even pigs have sense if you watch them close. (*chuckles*) It's done your mother so much good to know you're sort of settled, Son. (*looks at his son with deep affection now*) She's at the time of life when it's mighty easy to worry about things. I don't know how much you know about it, but women go through a hard time at your mother's age— glands get upset—some women get depressed— (*sighs*) Everything we can take off of her now we ought to take. (*He is silent for a little now. Looks at his roses, pulls a dead petal. Looks up at Tracy who is not looking at his father.*) I don't suppose any two children ever had a better mother, do you?

TRACY: I suppose not, Dad.

TUT: Nor any man a better wife. (*sighs*) Well . . . believe I'll go in. This Mareschal Neil is as fine a rose as is grown. I want her to see it. (*stands up. Puts his hand on his son's shoulder as he tells him goodnight*) Night, Son.

TRACY: Night, Dad. (*Tracy sits on the steps thinking. Struggling with a lifelong conflict. He thought he had made up his mind in there—now he doesn't know. He doesn't know any more what path he's walking on.*)

(*As scene changes light, Tracy turns, lost in his conflict. Standing there, he can be seen dimly throughout the following flashback . . . An experience unremembered by him. A vague hazy light shows the backyard 18 years ago. MAMIE, his old nurse, comes out of the kitchen. She is big and dark and strong and full-bosomed. There is a strength in her, and patience, and the ability to do work, but she is warm too and gentle and loves all children. She now has in her hand a saucer containing cookies.*)

MAMIE: Who wants a tea cake? (*Nine-year-old Tracy and Henry rush up from behind the cabin.*)

TRACY: Me . . . Me . . . Oh boy—

HENRY: I do . . . I do . . . Goody—

TRACY: Can I have two, please ma'm.

HENRY: I want two, please ma'm.

(*She gives each of them two, or starts to give them, looks at their hands, shakes her head.*)

MAMIE: Them hands! You can't eat with those hands, can you?
TRACY: No ma'm.

(*Henry looks at his, grins at his mother.*)

MAMIE: Run wash 'em, quick now. (*She walks over to the steps of her cabin, sits down, sighs. She looks sweet and mature and wise in the ways of childhood. The two little boys rush over to the yard spigot, turn it on, wash their hands, a little, just enough to get the top layer off, wipe them on their pants, come running to her.*) Two to each. (*She hands them two. They sit down by her, eat. They lean against her, looking into the sky, looking far away in complete content. Henry on the other side leans against her knee.*)
MAMIE: You bof so hot! Been running?
TRACY: Yes'm.
HENRY: Give us another, Mama.
TRACY: Give us another, Mamie. Please, Mamie, honey. (*patting her face now*) Please Mamie.
MAMIE: No more. Ruin your supper. (*She looks at Tracy.*) Your face is scratched. Heah, lemme see. Lemme see, sugar. (*She pulls him close, looks at it.*) Ain't nothin' to bother wif. Musta breshed by a leaf. (*She laughs at him a little, rumples his hair. He reaches up, catches her arm, hugs her, and suddenly kisses her. And then suddenly Henry on the other side is hugging her and kissing her, and they almost pull her over in their affectionate play. Finally she pushes them away.*) You bof is too big to act lak babies. Run along wid you. Run along.
TRACY: Mamie, honey, Mamie, please give us one tea cake. (*nuzzling up to her now, begging in his best little manner*)
MAMIE: A half a one. A half is more'n you need. Go on and play now.
TRACY: Thank you, ma'm. (*He leans against Mamie again and she pats him a little as if she has done it all her life, rubbing her hand lightly over his hair.*)
HENRY: Thank you, ma'm. (*The boys run back to their game. Henry begins his counting with his mouth full of tea cake.*) One for the money, two for the show, three to make ready, and four to go! (*They run hard across the line. Tracy wins.*) (*smiling*) You beat.
TRACY: Yeah. Let's race around the corner, to the front of the house, and around the big oak tree and back here.

(*A* LITTLE WHITE GIRL *comes around the Deens' house, pushing her bicycle along, stands there watching the boys.*)

LITTLE WHITE GIRL: Hey, Tracy—
TRACY: Hey.
LITTLE WHITE GIRL: Daddy bought me a new bike.
TRACY: I see.
LITTLE WHITE GIRL: Watch me ride it. Come out to the sidewalk and watch me ride it. (*voice soft and begging*)

TRACY: We can't. We're busy.

LITTLE WHITE GIRL: I bet you a nickel I can ride faster than anybody on College Street.

TRACY: (*draws a line*) Come on, Henry, let's race.

LITTLE WHITE GIRL: I bet you two nickels.

TRACY: (*takes the chalk and marks another line*) You can't. No girl can. We're busy, run along.

LITTLE WHITE GIRL: Yan, yan, yan. You scared you can't beat me. I can ride faster— (*She turns and disappears as she is talking.*)

TRACY: C'mon, Henry. Let's race to the corner and around the oak tree and back here to the steps. Ready?

HENRY: Yeah. On the mark—get set—go— (*And off they go, as fast as they can around the house and out of sight.*)

LITTLE WHITE GIRL: (*offstage*) Move, move, move!

HENRY: (*offstage*) Move, move, move yourself! (*There is the sound of a falling bicycle.*)

LITTLE WHITE GIRL: (*offstage, speaking low, voice full of feeling*) How dare you! How dare you get in my way!

HENRY: (*offstage. Knowing nothing else to do*) Ha ha ha ha ha ha!

TRACY: (*offstage*) Ha ha ha ha ha! (*glad to see her fall, after all her bragging*)

LITTLE WHITE GIRL: Stop laughing at me! *Stop it, you little black nigger!*

(*There is a sudden silence now.*)

TRACY: You stop calling him—

LITTLE WHITE GIRL: Chocolate drop, chocolate—

HENRY: White trash, dat's what—

LITTLE WHITE GIRL: Chocolate drop, chocolate drop, dark brown chocolate drop—

(*Mamie stands, face quickened suddenly*)

HENRY: White trash, dat's what—dirty white trash—white— white trash—

MAMIE: You—Henry McIntosh, come here!

HENRY: White trash—

LITTLE WHITE GIRL: Nigger, nigger, nigger.

TRACY: (*offstage*) You ride on your own side of the street, don't come over here—

MAMIE: Come here dis minute. (*She is standing, ease gone from her placid face.*) Come here dis minute. (*There is silence, then Henry and Tracy appear, coming reluctantly unused to the sound in Mamie's voice. She looks hard at Henry.*) I got to whup you. (*The two children stand there in the backyard and watch as Mamie reaches up to the limb of a tree, breaks off a switch. They stand there and watch her as she takes Henry's arm, bends his body over and whips him as she stands there. Tracy stands there, his face full of distress.*) I got to learn it to you, you heah! I got to. You can't look at a white girl like dat, you can't tech one, you can't speak to one cep'n to say, yes ma'm, thanky ma'm. Say it after me! Say it!

(*giving him a hard tap with her switch. Henry begins to cry, frightened by all these things not yet physically hurt*) I can't look at a white girl like dat!

HENRY: (*squalling and catching his breath in strangling gasps*) I can't tech one. (*whipping his legs as she says it*) I can't tech one . . .

(*Tracy bursts into tears at the sight and yet stays through it.*)

MAMIE: I can't speak to one cep'n to say "Yes ma'm and thanky ma'm." (*Henry sobbing breathlessly, but can't say the words*) Say it! Say it! I can't speak to one cep'n to say "Yes ma'm and thanky ma'm."

HENRY: I can't speak to one cep'n to say—yes ma'm—thanky ma'm . . .

(*Henry, sniffing and dazed, runs like a shamed dog into a cabin. Mamie follows him stands at the steps. Tracy watches her. He too has been crying a little, sniffing, hurt to see his playmate hurt; hurt to see Mamie acting strangely. Why didn't she whip him too? What was it all about? He didn't know. Mamie's big brown hands take the switch and slowly break it to pieces, and the sound of the breaking is something hard to listen to. Then she hurls the pieces with sudden fury away from her. Her hands fall to her side. She stands there staring across the roof of the big house in front of her. Stares so long that the small white boy watching her thinks she must not be able to find what she looks for. Slowly she sits down on the steps . . . wraps her hands in her apron . . . lips pull down with the weight of her thinking . . . slowly she lays her face in her lap.*)

TRACY: Mamie . . . (*he says the word with no idea behind it, but goes up to her and as he calls her name the third time, he touches her*) Mamie . . . (*Mamie does not answer*) Mamie . . . (*looks up, brown face wet with her crying, and twisted*)

MAMIE: Go! Go to your *own folks.*

(*He stares at her a moment and then turns, cut to the bone by the new strange words. But though he turns away, he finds it hard to leave her, and moves away slowly and without direction. Down the path come Alma and the five-year-old Laura. They have been out walking. Little Laura has a doll in her arms. He sees them and walks toward them.*)

LAURA: What was the puppy's name, Mummie?

ALMA: I don't know, dear.

LAURA: I want a puppy—

TRACY: Mummie—

ALMA: Hello Tracy.

TRACY: Where have you been?

ALMA: We were taking a walk— (*Tracy draws closer to her*) Don't lean so hard, dear. You're so hot and sticky. And smelly! When have you had a bath?

TRACY: This morning.

ALMA: I don't see how you and Henry get so dirty! Did you take a bath yourself or did Mamie give it to you?

TRACY: Me and Henry—

ALMA: Henry and I—

TRACY: Henry and I took it—we got under the hose in the backyard.

ALMA: That isn't a real bath. Tell Mamie to bathe you before supper. You'll make me think you're a little colored child if you keep so dirty— (*she smiles at him half-humorously*)

LAURA: He dirty boy— (*She nods her head in solemn disapproval. Alma laughs softly at the childish prattle. Tracy jerks Laura's doll out of her arms and throws it on ground.*)

TRACY: I hate dolls! And I don't like her either. (*He gives Laura a hard push which nearly knocks her over.*)

ALMA: Tracy! Pick up the doll and give it back to your sister.

TRACY: I won't.

ALMA: Pick it up, Tracy.

TRACY: No, I won't I won't.

ALMA: I'm waiting.

TRACY: I won't. (*But as he says it, he slowly picks it up and hands it to his mother.*)

LAURA: We don't like bad boys.

ALMA: No, we don't like little boys when they are naughty. (*She takes Laura's hand and they turn away. Tracy watches them. He sits down on the steps crying softly in bewildered misery. Mamie is still sitting on her porch steps, a great distance between them now, suddenly strange and measureless. After a little, Tracy stands, walks slowly around the corner of the house toward his nurse's cabin. Words form in the back of his mind and he opens his mouth to say them.*)

TRACY: Mamie . . . (*is all he can whisper. She turns toward him, looks, finally takes a slow step. And now he is running. He buries his face against her, trying to keep the sound of his trouble in the apron. Through dress and petticoat he feels her leg and holds on to it. He sobs miserably, saying her name over and over.*) Mamie . . . Mamie . . .

MAMIE: It's all right. Everything is all right. Go git him, and make him play. Go git him.

TRACY: (*he is glad to be told what to do; he runs to the door*) Henry, we going to play. Henry . . . Come on, Henry, we going to play.

(*Henry comes out of the cabin. Swollen-faced and bleary-eyed and stiff-jointed. He joins his little white playmate.*)

HENRY: What we goin' to play?

TRACY: Let's play—oh let's play anything. Here—

(*TEN MCINTOSH, Mamie's husband, is just coming from work at the mill, in overalls, looking tired after a twelve-hour workday.*)

TEN: Howdy, chillen. (*looks at Henry. Voice a little heavy with fatigue*) Fall down?

HENRY: No suh.

TEN: Whassa matter? (*Henry hangs his head, doesn't answer*) What's happened, Mamie?

MAMIE: I had to whup him. (*her words are heavy, like lead*)

TEN: (*looks at his son affectionately, cheerfully. Turns away; turns back*) What'd he do?

MAMIE: He sassed a white gal.

TEN: (*pauses, speaks slowly*) Come heah! (*Henry walks over slowly. His father looks a long time at his legs, looks up at Mamie—all his hate for white folks blazes suddenly in his face.*) So you beats your boy half to death cause you think white folks like dat.

MAMIE: I learn him how to behave.

TEN: You beats yo boy like he trash to please white folks.

MAMIE: I learn him how to behave, Ten. He got to learn. You know dat. (*her voice pleading for understanding*)

(*Tracy draws near the words like bits of steel to a magnet.*)

TEN: You beat da spirit out'n him. He won't be a man fit fo nothin'.

MAMIE: Ten—our boy sassed a white gal.

TEN: What ef he did! She sassed him first, I reckon. He's a good boy, good as any white gal in this goddam town. Say a word folks beat you to death. Gawd help us, his own Ma turns on him an—

MAMIE: Ten—I wants my boy to live till he's grown! (*Mamie's voice does not rise against the high brittle sound of Ten's words.*) I want him to *live!* (*voice soft, urgent*) He got to learn. He got to learn how to git along. He got to learn. What he can't do. He got to learn there's white folks and colored folks and things you can't do ef you wants to live. Jesus help me, I'm going to learn it to him.

TEN: You goin to keep yo hands off him! You hear! . . . You tetch him again count of white folks and I'll beat you till yo can't git off'n da floor. He good as anybody, you hear! Good as anybody!

MAMIE: He ain' good as white folks. I got to learn him dat. I gotta do it, Ten.

TEN: Gawd Jesus. I hate the sight of one! Hate livin in Deen's backyard! Told you a hundred time it'd be better in the quarter where we'd be free to do as we like. I don want ma boy brung up with no white boy—don want none of it!

MAMIE: They's good to us, Ten. It don help us none to hate 'em.

TEN: Good to us!

MAMIE: Good as they know how to be.

TEN: Tell you, I hate the sight of one! (*Ten quickly picks up a potted plant in a fancy jardiniere that once had been in the Deens' house and was now Mamie's one fine ornament, and hurls it to the ground, smashing it into a hundred fragments. You can hear the ring of the broken pieces clashing as they roll on the ground.*)

MAMIE: Lawd, Lawd. (*She hushes quickly, and now her hands seek her apron, twisting it in a tight knot as she stands there, looking at her husband. Ten, satisfied a little, eased a little, now walks over to the steps and squats there, staring into the dark yard.*) Hit's easy to break things, Ten, mighty easy to break things. Ain't easy to mend em up again. Dat what I want my boy to learn early. Want him to learn early dat no matter what white folks is always right! And you treats 'em *always respectful.*

(*Lights come on Tracy. He gets up, goes in cabin*)

CURTAIN

ACT TWO, SCENE 2

Time: *Next morning.*

Setting: *Same as evening before. On the table there is a bowl of roses. Henry is standing in the cabin door. Back in the kitchen, Eenie is banging pots and pans in ill temper. Now, she calls out to him, across the hallway.*

EENIE'S VOICE: You Henry! Henry. (*Henry looks toward kitchen, refuses to answer her.*) Where you think you is?

HENRY: I's in New York. (*turns, faces the kitchen*)

EENIE'S VOICE: Bring the rest of yo dishes in heah from the dining room. Right this minute! Hit's near on to eleven by the clock.

HENRY: Listen, big gal—spose you could shut yo mouf?

EENIE'S VOICE: Big gal . . . big—is you crazy! Me and Miz Deen done put up with a Gawd-sight of triflin on count of yo ma and pa. And we's thro'.

HENRY: You and Miz Deen, huh? You know who my boss is? Mr. Tracy is my boss. You ever heard of him befo? (*As he is talking to his unseen enemy, Alma comes on the porch. Stands there—immaculate in white linen, her cool composed face half shadowed by her large hat. She listens to her servants a moment before she speaks.*)

ALMA: Henry . . .

HENRY: Yas'm— (*He comes over to her.*)

ALMA: There will be sherbet for dinner today. You should freeze it early.

HENRY: Yas ma'm.

ALMA: Have you mint in the garden?

HENRY: Yas ma'm.

ALMA: Henry, where is Mr. Tracy?

HENRY: (*puts his tray under his arm*) He's out wid Miss Dorothy, ma'm. (*voice curved in deep obeisance*)

ALMA: (*looking hard at Henry*) His bed—was not slept in last night. He hasn't come to breakfast.

HENRY: (*with cheerful skill*) He got up early, ma'm, and I cleaned it up fo' you all was awake. He drank his coffee in the kitchen, ma'm.

ALMA: (*not believing a word he says*) Please tell Miss Laura when she comes in that I am at church and that Brother Dunwoodie will be our guest today. I should like for her to be here.

HENRY: Yas'm. Anything else ma'm?

ALMA: (*takes envelope out of her handbag*) Please give this to Mr. Tracy when he comes in. (*She goes down the path.*)

(*Henry looks toward the cabin. No whistling now. Goes to the kitchen, brings out a tray. Tracy comes out of the cabin, clothes wrinkled, eyes bloodshot, showing signs of the night's turmoil. He has been asleep in Henry's cabin since dawn.*)

HENRY: Your Ma asked me if I seen you dis morning. I said I seed you out walking with Miss Dorothy. Was scared she was going straight to the cabin to see for herself.

TRACY: How about a drink?

HENRY: Better eat your breakfast, Mr. Tracy.

TRACY: How about a drink!

HENRY: Mr. Tracy, yo better go back to the cabin. Yo Ma won't like you drinkin out heah.

TRACY: Where is she.

HENRY: She gone to church.

TRACY: Then for God's sake, get me a drink!

HENRY: You ain't never done this befo. You ain't never drunk out here. Please come on back to the cabin.

TRACY: Do as you are told.

HENRY: Yassuh. She say give you dis envelope. (*Tracy takes it. Henry goes out to the cabin, quickly returns with a bottle. While he is gone, Tracy picks up the envelope, looks at it. He looks worn and confused. Puts bottle on table.*) Eat yo breakfast, first, Mr. Tracy. (*Tracy motions peremptorily toward the bottle. Henry pours a drink.*) Now eat yo breakfast.

TRACY: (*pushes tray aside*) What time is it?

HENRY: Goin' on eleven.

TRACY: I had a date with Miss Dorothy at ten. (*laughs*)

HENRY: You want me to call her and say you was called suddenly to help Mr. Adams?

TRACY: Never mind. Pour me a drink. (*Henry pours a small drink in the glass.*) Henry—

HENRY: Yassuh.

TRACY: You ever thought of getting married?

HENRY: Gawd no!

TRACY: (*stares out the window. Picks up glass, drains it, pushes it slowly across the tablecloth.*) I'm marrying Miss Dorothy. (*He stops.*) I'm joining the church, too.

HENRY: Gawd Jesus—you jokin! (*Tracy does not seem to hear Henry's words, continues to push the glass slowly up and down the table. Up and back—up and back. It is a long silence. Henry scratches his head, studies the face of this white man he has known and played with all his life. Like a shadow that disappears as it changes direction in the sun, his black sycophancy drops from him.*) Tracy— whassa matter? Tell yo Henry, whassa matter?

(*Tracy turns and looks at his friend. White face twisted, despairing. Black face bulging with sympathy, lips pouting with affection, eyes batting dismay.*)

TRACY: (*whispers*) I wish to God I knew. (*Tracy covers his face with his hands. Henry squats down by him, his big hands hanging idle. He listens to the tearing of Tracy's sobs and makes a futile movement with his tongue while sweat pours from his armpits. And in a frantic gush of sympathy, half falling over his feet he kneels beside his friend and puts his arms around him, grunting out inarticulate comfort. After a time, Tracy raises his head, stares.*) Well, I be damned. What are we doing—having a love feast? (*He laughs, pushes the negro away from him.*) Henry, for Christ's sake, you stink like a polecat! Don't you ever wash?

HENRY: Yessuh. I washes. I sho does. Mebee not so sufficient.

TRACY: I say not so sufficient! Pour me a drink and get a move on you to the kitchen.

HENRY: (*pours another drink. Speaks quietly*) Hit's yo third one, Mr. Tracy.

TRACY: What the hell if it is?

HENRY: You Ma will smell it sho.

TRACY: Tell her I won't be in for dinner.

HENRY: Yassuh.

TRACY: And use a little bar soap before—you go in or you'll turn her stomach. (*then, half to himself*) God—how tired I am of niggers. (*Tracy stands, picks up the envelope, opens it, takes out the check, stares at it, walks slowly down the path.*) Henry, I want to talk to you tonight in the cabin.

HENRY: (*in a whisper*) Yassuh. (*Tracy goes into the house. Henry picks up the tray and glass, mechanically brushes off the table. Stands there, just holding the tray. Sobs—*) Dey got im plumb crazy!

ACT TWO, SCENE 3

One day later. Evening, Salamander's lunch counter. Salamander, slow moving, saying little, wipes the counter. Gabe sits on the counter, hunched up like a light 'ood knot. He is just finishing one of his "lies." He has been telling "lies" in Maxwell all his life, weaving them in and out, making a bright design of black man outwitting white man. Never raising his voice, in a soft, placating drawl, with a bland air of inno-cence. Gabe ties the threads of black shrewdness into such strength that they snap Mr. White Man's power half in two. Around him are Salamander's customers, sitting on their stools, or at tables, listening. At a table apart from the others sit Ed Anderson and Sam Perry, eating their supper, occasionally looking up, laughing at Gabe as they half listen.

SAM: My! I'm glad to get some food in me! (*looks at Ed's plate*) You're not eating!

ED: Don't seem to be hungry. I don't see how you stand all those sick people! That rag of Salamander's keeps reminding me of them. (*looks up at Sam*) I reckon I just can't take Bill Talley and Cap'n Rushton in one afternoon.

SAM: (*laughs, continues his eating . . . Looks up after a moment*) You see, Ed, seems to me— (*voice is soothing now*) We gotta remember there're a few decent white folks here in Maxwell. It helps to remember that.

ED: I've never met one.

SAM: (*smiles*) They're not all Bill Talleys nor Cap'n Rushtons. There're a few others who are different. You know how I feel about Tom Harris. I couldn't have done my work here without him, Ed. He's always willing to do things for our people. Never turns you down.

ED: Uh-huh. You've always liked him. I still don't see why.

SAM: Well . . . maybe because he's done so much for me. He's done things for other folks too. Every good thing this town has, Tom Harris has brought here. He's mighty fair to folks, Ed—makes you feel he's your friend. (*Sam betrays his deep admiration and affection for Harris.*)

ED: And got rich doing it.

SAM: Maybe so.

ED: But he wouldn't call you or me, "Mister."

SAM: No. (*pauses*) Maybe. (*quietly*) If we were white and in his place we wouldn't call Negroes "Mister" either. I say *maybe*. When things get in the mess they're in now and long before anybody living was born. Mind you, I'm not excusing anybody, Ed—just trying not to waste my time hating white folks when there's so much to be done for our people. (*changes mood, speaks cheerfully, more casually*) How about forgetting our troubles and going fishing tomorrow?

ED: Sure.

SAM: Well . . . (*smiling affectionately at Ed*) I better be moving along, Sally Mason's expecting her baby tonight. Time I was making myself handy. She may need me. See you later?

SALAMANDER: How dat white folks' meetin' comin'?

VOICE: Whole town gittin' converted. Whole town. Say dat white preacher he got de Lawd in his show. I heard him last night—man, man! He grabbed old Satan and twist his tail until—

ANOTHER VOICE: Won't be no fun in Maxwell fo a month after dat preacher leave town. Dey say even Tracy Deen done got converted, and jined the church. (*Ed looks up, listening*) Jined the church and my old woman who cooks for the Puseys say he gwine tuh marry dat Dorothy Pusey next month. My old woman say— Dey say old man Brown went into Supply Sto and paid up two years of back bills he owed.

GABE: I went into the meat market and bought a pound of cheese Sad'dy. Gus Rainey, he cut it off, laid it down onto the scale, put his hand on it like he always do—then you know what dat white man done? Jerked his hand off dat scale so fast you thought a snake bit him, turned aroun', put another sliver of cheese on it. Yeah, man—it's gettin' 'em. (*much laughter*)

ANOTHER VOICE: Ain't don' nothin' for Cap'n Harris. Cap'n put same six dollah in my pay envelope that he been puttin' in last ten years.

ED: (*finishes the mullet, takes a swallow of coffee from the thick, hot cup Salamander has just brought over to him, mops his face. Lays a quarter on the table, leans toward Salamander, shouts in his ear*) How are things?

SALAMANDER: Tol'able. (*He puts the quarter in his pocket. Blue lips puckered, he sniffs, lays his rag down, sniffs again.*) Who it be?

ED: Same as yesterday. (*grins, then says kindly*) It's Ed Anderson. Remember, I'm home for a while, with my sisters.

SALAMANDER: Sho, sho. (*rubs his grey-wooled head, goes back to the counter. He stands there, compulsively wiping off the counter as he has spent his life doing. There is a little confusion at the door, the door slams, a loud voice is heard.)*

HENRY: Let a big boy in, yo! (*Henry strides into the room, his wide shoulders pushing aside the human impediments in his path; big Henry, bigger tonight than he has ever been in his life. He slaps a bill on the counter, big mouth bellows.*) How about some food, old man!

VOICE: Look at 'im! He done broke open the Nashnal Bank, sho. Where'd you git ten bucks, boy?

HENRY: (*laughs deep in his belly*) Ten? Look here, man. Look here! (*Henry waves a wad of bills above the shining sweaty black faces.*) Ever see a hundred bucks?

MAN: My Gawd, no!

2ND MAN: An' don' aim to, hit'd kill me sho to look at um—

3RD MAN: Don worry—ain' no chanct of you dyin' fum dat, dat ain a way none of us'll die. Ain' none of us'll die dat sweet . . . no . . . baby.

4TH MAN: Count 'um, boy, while our moufs waters . . . (*his feminine voice pipes high above the others*)

3RD MAN: Sho, count 'um!

4TH MAN: Betch dey's countfitten.

MAN: Betcha he robbed old Mrs. Jones of her pappy's trunk, Ma uster say hit was full of confedit bills, and day ain' worth spit— (*Ed smiles. Feels good to smile and mean it. To sit here like this, waiting for a cup of coffee and wanting it when it comes.*)

HENRY: Spit—well, git dat spit outen yo own eye and maybe you can see. (*Henry slouches over and holds a bill close to the speaker's face.*) How dat, huh, how dat?

MAN: Hit's good as Jesus. (*The voice was awestruck. For a moment there is reverent silence as the still room worships this vision of actual wealth. But soon—*)

MAN: You gon set us up, sho, ain't you, Henry?

HENRY: Sho. Fill um up, Salamander! Fill um all up. (*Henry is near about bursting with hospitality.*)

MAN: How come you got um, Henry.

2ND MAN: Wherever day comes fum, he got um all. No use to pry aroun' lookin' for scraps, is deah, Henry?

3RD MAN: Ain' none lef' aroun' nowheres, is dey, Henry?

HENRY: (*smiles, swells like a toad*) Not a scrap.

GABE: I knows how he got um— (*Every head turns toward Gabe who until now has sat on the counter in silence.*) He go up to Mr. Hahi's down at da mill. And he says Mr. Hahi's, you makes a sight of money outen dis here sawmill, a-cuttin' all dem million feet o' lumber, and wif dem barrels of turpentine a-settin' out deah, gwine up to Savanny ever week, don't yo? An' Mr. Hahi's say, "sho, boy. I makes a mighty lot of money. What kin I do fuh you?" And den Henry say, "Well, Boss, kin you let me have a hundard bucks till Saddy night? I plum run outa change and I needs a liddle snuff fuh ma old woman and a new automobile and a few other liddle things . . ." (*Gabe is at his lifetime role of story telling and the crowd, mouth open, eyes on his face, are following every word in contented identification.*) And den Mr. Hahi's he retches in his pocket and pulls out a roll of bills and wets his finger and counts off a hundard and say, "Reckon a hundard'll do, Henry?" And Henry say—

HENRY: (*in a half-drunken loyalty*) Dis money come fum da Deen family. I works for the Deens. I don work at no sawmill fo no Hahi's white man. I'se de Deens' houseboy . . .

MAN: Sho, hit's a liddle extry they thowed in fo good measure dis week—dat it, ain't it, buddy?

(*Henry's lips swell out, as his liquor swells his loyalty. Mutters stubbornly.*)

HENRY: Tracy Deen give me dis money.

MAN: Ain't yo birfday, is it, Henry?

HENRY: Tracy Deen give me—

MAN: No, hit's Christmus. (*somebody guffaws*)

HENRY: Tracy—

MAN: Sho, Christmus gif, Henry— (*everybody is yelling now, "Christmus gif—Christmus gif"*)

4TH MAN: Sho, Christmus gif.

(*Into Henry's muddled brain enters the necessity to defend his dignity and his employers. He slowly wipes his mouth on his sleeve, and faces the crowd.*)

HENRY: All right, smartcats. Put dis in yo bellies and watch um swell an' bust. Mr. Tracy Deen done gimme dis money cause he and me, we friends, and we'se made a bargain.

2ND MAN: What kind of bargain? (*Henry turns to the counter, swallows the remainder of his third cup of whiskey.*)

HENRY: Hit's a private bargain. (*He giggles drunkenly.*) About a girl. (*He is rolling his eyes now, trying to leer.*)

MAN: What girl?

HENRY: (*rolling his eyes*) Oh, jes' a girl. Hit's a secret! (*He giggles.*)

4TH MAN: What girl? Come on—what girl?

HENRY: Just a purty girl what he done git into trouble. (*Ed sits up as if a knife has been shoved through him.*)

3RD MAN: What's yo bargain?

HENRY: Ah'm to marry her. (*Henry laughs*) Yeah, man, he give me a hundard bucks, and dis big boy gwine to marry Nonnie Anderson too— (*they try to stop him for someone has seen Ed, but it is no use. It is no use to do anything but back out of the way as brown man comes striding across the little room to black man, brown man's face like the wrath of God.*)

ED: You godamn son-of-a-bitch! (*his breath sucking in and out in great sobs*) You damned black nigger!

(*Ed drives into Henry's jaw once, twice. Henry, off his guard and utterly dumb-*

founded to see Ed Anderston standing before him, stumbles back, hits the side of the counter and falls to the floor. Ed turns away from the still man, stumbles out of the cafe. He has no more time to waste on Henry McIntosh. No more time to waste on niggers. Only Tracy Deen's face can he see, only Deen's slow, tired, sarcastic voice rings in his ears. In the cafe there is a silence which comes only when men know that something has begun which they are powerless to end. Big Henry lies as he fell. Salamander looks hard at the door, the window, fearing as he always fears, white eyes. Others follow his look, turn around uneasily. No one has spoken yet, all in cafe surge forward quickly as Henry falls, and then seem to freeze where they are. The thought in everyone's mind is white folks—the town marshal. One by one they fade out of the cafe, except Gabe and Salamander. Now Gabe eases over to Henry, turns his big body. Henry moves. Slowly he sits up, rubs his hands over his head feeling the bones. Breathes deeply and hard. Salamander hands Gabe a wet cloth. Gabe wipes off Henry's face and head, lays cloth back on counter. Henry stands. Salamander is still behind the counter. Gabe, tough as a cypress root, used to turpentine camps and white men's ways, stands there, studying Henry's face. Scene fades out.)

ACT TWO, SCENE 4

The Andersons' gate and steps half hour later.

BESS: Well, we've told the twins everything about college—teachers, courses, what clothes they'll need. When they get there, they'll both think everything we said was wrong.

NONNIE: They're so thrilled.

BESS: (*soberly, half-bitterly*) Poor little fools.

JACKIE: Where day goin, Mama?

BESS: To college, Sugar.

JACKIE: Am I goin to college? (*The two women smile at the child, with no answer. They stand at the gate a moment.*)

BESS: I know it's no use for me to say it, but—if you'd go to bed now, Non . . . you look so tired.

JACKIE: (*pulling at Bess*) Come on, Mummy. Come on.

NONNIE: Not quite yet. (*Bess and little Jackie go inside; Nonnie sits down on the bench. Her face betrays her deeply perturbed spirit and her physical fatigue as she sits there. But one has the feeling that Nonnie has found no words for her inner distress. Tracy appears at the gate, Non sees him, and walks out to meet him.*)

TRACY: Hello. (*he stands there, doesn't open the gate*)

NONNIE: Hello.

TRACY: I've come to tell you— (*he stops, seems unable to go on*)

NONNIE: Yes, Tracy.

TRACY: Guess you heard I'd joined the church. (*Nonnie nods*) Well, (*he laughs a little self-consciously*) I meant it. I mean—it wasn't just something I did, as a matter of form. Like some people. (*he takes out his handkerchief, wipes his face*) I've never felt like this before ... (*he pauses*) As I see it— (*his voice grows a little strident*) My whole life's been wrong. All wrong!

NONNIE: Wrong?

TRACY: Yeah. Things like— (*he doesn't look at her*) like this. All my life I've felt a sense of—I reckon you'd call it sin, maybe the way I've been living—I've changed ... don't know how to tell you ... no so called respectable men keep on doing things like— (*he pauses*)

NONNIE: Like— (*voice is barely a whisper*)

TRACY: Like this—you know what I mean ... Like—but I'm through! If I'm going straight, gotta go straight. Can't do it half way. Thought once—maybe I could—but I see it different now. Yesterday I joined the church and I meant it. Lately I've begun to see things—way I've done the family ... Mother ... ruining her whole—life—Made me realize time comes when a man must face things—see what he's doing to other people— (*Nonnie is pressing her hands together until the bones ache. He stops, begins again.*) Mother's glad, it's kind of—you see, I've always failed her. I've never been the kind of son she—always managed to do the wrong thing. There's Dorothy ... nobody thinks I've been decent to her— Well, to cut it short— (*he draws a deep breath*) Today I gave her a ring. We're to be married next month. That means—means—I can't—I can't keep on like this— (*he is breathing fast now and finds it hard to say his words—words composed for him by three hundred years of white men. A lesson he had learned at last ... after studying it all his life. Now he had it memorized, now he would say it to the end.*)

(*Nonnie tries to say something, anything. But no words will come. This is a lesson that she will never learn. She will not even try. All that is left now is her memory of a life that has suddenly been rammed down her throat so hard that she cannot get her breath.*)

TRACY: (*voice is now low, now high, no longer under control, driven by words that his culture has put in his mouth*) I can't keep on—about the baby—I've fixed that—I've fixed it— (*He seems waiting for her to say something. Her voice cannot break through a whisper.*)

NONNIE: Fixed?

TRACY: Been a damn fool to get you in trouble like this—I never thought—I never thought you'd— (*He breaks off suddenly, looks straight at her. She hopes for one agonizing moment that he's drunk, that this is something he does not mean, does not even know he is doing; he looks so strange wetting his lips again and again as he talks, staring through her and beyond her as if he is saying words for his own ears to hear.*) Well ... no use to talk about it—no use to—thing to do now is to—thing to do now is to— (*He is breathing heavily. Stares away as if he has forgot what he is saying, as if he does not even remember where he is. Turns back, looks at her as if slowly recognizing her, as if slowly dimly remembering what he is to say.*) Get it arranged—It's arranged.

NONNIE: Arranged?

TRACY: Yeah, it's arranged—everything's arranged—it's arranged—what's the matter? (*Nonnie shakes her head.*) Henry's going to look after you—Henry's going—I told him about it—he's going to look after you—give you a name—he's going to—he's— (*draws in his breath, pauses, stares away, continues his words*) Thought it might keep down talk for you and him to— (*For Non, the ground tilts, and everything on it—the swamp, the old house, the graveyard, Miss Ada's, the cedars, a bunch of pink honeysuckle, the old cypress, ridge, all her life swirls around her in slow circles. She catches hold of the fence.*)

TRACY: Knew you'd understand—you have to understand—you—if he dares touch you—he wouldn't dare—he wouldn't—he— (*He can scarcely breathe now as his old feeling for Nonnie almost emerges for a brief moment. He conquers it, goes on with his speech.*) I hate like hell . . . I—here, I almost forgot the damned thing—the money—two hundred—ought to help you through—if you ever need more—if you ever need— (*He holds the package out, but Nonnie's hands are motionless on the picket fence.*) Damn sorry—hoped you would—hoped you'd— (*There is nothing in her empty face, nothing in her body pressing hard against the fence that would give him hope . . . And suddenly it is as if he has begun to see the thing through her eyes, as always she has been able to make him see. He begins to see what he could never have borne . . .*) Nonnie! God in heaven, I can't leave you like this . . . I can't leave you—I can't leave you—I can't— (*He makes a last desperate effort to take her in his arms. Between his hands and the white splotch that is Nonnie, is a great emptiness. He touches her rigid shoulder, touches her hair, her cheek, drops his hand quickly. He lays the money on the fence rail, turns, goes. Nonnie stands unmoving at the gate. Stands there, holding to the picket fence, looking across—White Town. Sharply, lunging two holes through the night, shots ring out. It is as if they go through her body, cutting her nerves awake. Now she is hearing every little sound, but somehow she can't move. It is as if she has no capacity for making the decision to move.*)

BESS: (*comes out quickly, followed by Jackie in his pajamas*) What's the matter? (*Bess's voice grows sharp before the words are finished as she runs down the path. Non shakes her head.*) But what were those shots, Nonnie? (*Nonnie shakes her head. Bess, in her fear, shakes her hard.*) Nonnie, you do know. (*Nonnie slides quietly to the ground. With quick, sharp words, Bess tells Jackie to bring her some water. There are footsteps on the path. Turning quickly she sees Eddie. He comes up to her, as empty-faced as the girl lying beside her knee.*) Get some water, Jackie, hurry.

ED: Well I've done it. (*He sucks in his breath with a little nervous laugh. Bess lets Nonnie's head slip to the ground. She knows with quick nausea that the time has come for whispers. She draws Eddie half behind a bush.*)

BESS: Now what have you done?

ED: Killed him.

BESS: Who?

ED: Deen. (*They stand in darkness, blur facing blur, breathing heavily.*)

BESS: Anyone see you?

ED: No. Don't think so.

BESS: But you don't know. Anyway, they'd know it was you . . . I've got to get you out of town. (*Bess does not hear herself say this.*)

ED: I'll swing the freight.

BESS: And get caught before you're halfway to the tracks! Somebody'll find him. Where— (*She finds it hard to say.*)

ED: Where he dropped.

BESS: But *where?*

ED: Near Miss Ada's.

BESS: They'll find you—they'll come straight here. (*She is shaking all over. Her mind is shut fast. If she could just think, she would know what to do. It was as if all her race's knowledge of how to escape the hands of white man would offer itself to her, only for the thinking. An old hound barks. Its shrill cry trickles down her body like ice water. She beats frantically on a door that will not open. Ed speaks stubbornly.*)

ED: I don't give a damn.

BESS: Oh you're such a fool! (*Jackie comes running out with water.*)

BESS: (*she is hating him, and hating, grows sane. She takes the water mechanically.*) Sam, if he's home—he'll drive you to Macon or—come on.

ED: I've gotta explain to Nonnie—

BESS: Explain your foot! Come—you must go—

ED: I can't leave without— (*Nonnie sits up slowly without speaking. Bess turns, speaks quickly.*)

BESS: He's killed a white man. You know what that means. (*Bess watches Nonnie's face. Around them the black night presses with its dread weight of three hundred years. Against that heaviness they had little strength to breathe. To the brother and sister nothing seems important that moment except to know how Nonnie feels. They wait, each groping toward her through a thick fog of a lifetime of hating and loving and sharing.*)

NONNIE: You must go— (*Bess and Ed cannot hear any feeling in her voice.*)

BESS: (*takes Jackie's hand, whispers to the others*) Come! (*This is addressed to Nonnie and Ed and she turns to go. Suddenly she stops.*) Money. (*They look at her blankly.*) How much have you?

ED: Don't know—five, six. (*As if it didn't matter; as if nothing mattered. Everything left to her. There are faint sounds from White Town.*)

BESS: Nonnie, you'll find my money back of Mama's picture. Get yours. Hurry Nonnie! (*Nonnie's running feet to Bess's straining eyes move through the night as you run in a nightmare. Bess calls after her.*) Get Jackie's bank too.

JACKIE: No, no! Nonnie tan't hav my pennies.

BESS: Ssssh, baby, it's for Uncle Eddie.

JACKIE: He tan't hev um—he tan't— (*Jackie screams this as he begins to kick his way out of Bess's arms.*)

BESS: Hush! I'll whip you! (*Jackie screams in steady crescendo.*)

JACKIE: He tan't hav um, he tan't hav um, he tan't—

BESS: (*moans*) Oh God, make him hush—make him—they'll hear him—

ED: I won't take your pennies, old boy, pipe down. (*Nonnie comes back, breathing hard from her running.*)

BESS: How much?

NONNIE: I—haven't—

BESS: Count it, Non, quick?

NONNIE: (*counts the money*) Twelve—it is nearly twelve dollars.

BESS: Won't take you to Washington, Ed.

ED: No.

(*Nonnie stops. She points to the fence. Unknowing to what she points, Bess turns cold, as if all the cottonmouths of civilization are coiled there to strike them.*)

NONNIE: (*whispers*) There.

BESS: What?

NONNIE: The money. (*Bess follows her gesture, feels along the rail until her fingers find the package. She turns slowly, looks at her sister.*)

BESS: Here, Ed. (*Ed puts it in his pocket. Takes a step toward Non*)

ED: Non . . . I . . . hope you'll forgive me—Non . . . you— (*They watch her as she swallows and swallows again in her effort to answer him. Then she takes his hand and rubs it softly with her fingers, suddenly turns away, stands against a tree, her back to the road and them. Sobs.*) Non, you've got to understand— you've—

BESS: Ed—you have no time—you—

ED: Non, you've—

BESS: Come on, you fool! (*Bess pulls Ed toward the gate. Compulsively she looks toward the place where she knows Ed must have done it. The moon is rising now behind the dark row of tall old trees, it will soon disclose the body as clearly as would daylight. She makes herself stop staring at the trees, makes herself stop wanting to go there, as she feels compelled to do, to see this thing close, this trouble that has been in their lives so long with no naming of it by anyone. It is as if something has prowled through the woods close to you ever since you can remember, sometimes crashing hard against a tree, sometimes just cracking a twig, but you never quite saw it, or were able to name it. And now it lay there before you—dead. Dead . . . And you want, or something deep down in you wants, to look at it a long time . . . She turns quickly, takes the back path which threads its way down through a stretch of dense woods and on to open ground back of the cemetery. Nonnie is left standing there.*

(*Nonnie's eyes are not following the two hurrying people but are turned down the path that leads to Miss Ada's. She stands there a long time as if unable ever to move away.*

(*Jackie sits there watching her, walks to her, pulls her hand. She turns, goes in with him.*)

ACT TWO, SCENE 5

Time: *That same evening. Several hours later.*

Scene: *The Deens' sun porch. In the unseen living room is the casket, and friends are there. Sounds drift out, enough to make one aware that the house has neighbors in it. Harriet Harris comes into the sun porch, moves a chair, empties an ash tray. A maid brings flowers to the door, knocks softly. Harriet goes to the door.*

MAID: Mrs. Rushton sent these roses, Miss Harriet. She says, please ma'm, call her if there's anything she can do.

HARRIET: They are lovely! Will you thank Mrs. Rushton?

MAID: Yes ma'm. (*She leaves. Henry appears from the kitchen with a bowl of custard and a bunch of white and red carnations.*)

HENRY: Mrs. Reid sent the flowers and a custard, please ma'm.

HARRIET: Put the custard in the pantry, Henry, please. (*She takes the flowers and goes out and Henry goes out with the custard as Miss Belle and Miss Sadie come up the side path each carrying flowers. Miss Belle has a spray of white lilies tied with a big bow of ribbon and Miss Sadie a wreath of cape jasmine tied with tulle. They are busy talking to each other in hushed tones as they come up the path, and pause just beyond the steps until they finish their little argument with each other.*)

MISS SADIE: But Belle, you can't believe everything Crazy Carl says!

MISS BELLE: Well, I'm just telling you what I heard. He told Dee Cassidy he saw Henry McIntosh out in the palmettos at daybreak and—

MISS SADIE: What was Carl doing out there?

MISS BELLE: Digging fishing worms. He said he saw a big black out in the—

MISS SADIE: You can see niggers anywhere, Belle. Henry would no more have killed Tracy than you would. Why, I've talked to him all his life over the telephone. He was crazy about Tracy.

MISS BELLE: You never can tell what a darkie will do, Sadie. They're so uppity. Course I said when they put them in uniform we were bound to have trouble! Wait a minute, let me fix this bow. Did many people order flowers?

MISS SADIE: Oh yes! Dozens of them! Dorothy ordered a blanket of yellow roses from Jacksonville.

MISS BELLE: Oh, how beautiful!

MISS SADIE: Poor child—she only wore her ring one day.

MISS BELLE: What kind of casket did they get?

MISS SADIE: A grey one. Very plain and terribly expensive.

MISS BELLE: Such a sweet boy! I don't see how anyone could have killed him. I wonder if it was suicide.

MISS SADIE: It just couldn't have been—from the way he was shot. Most folks think someone wanted his money. (*She stops, arranges a flower or two in her wreath.*) Cassidy took the bloodhounds over to Colored Town this afternoon. They say they're searching every house.

MISS BELLE: Oh my . . . it gives me the creeps.

(*Harriet comes out on the porch just as they walk up the steps.*)

MISS BELLE: Oh Harriet, I knew you'd be here helping poor Laura. It was just awful, wasn't it? I don't see how the family is holding up under it. I wanted to get here earlier with my flowers.

HARRIET: They're lovely, Miss Belle. And yours are too, Miss Sadie.

MISS SADIE: Thank you.

MISS BELLE: I was too nervous to come by myself, so I waited for Sadie. It's dark under the oak trees and with the niggers so upset—you never can tell what might—

(*Henry comes in with a tray, covered by a napkin.*)

HENRY: Miss Harriet, Mrs. Brown sent over a baked ham. She says if there's anything she can do to help—

HARRIET: Just put it in the refrigerator, please, Henry.

MISS BELLE: Oh, Maxwell is the sweetest town . . . Everyone so kind and neighborly . . . aren't they?

MISS SADIE: Let's take our flowers in, Belle.

(*Phone rings as Sadie is speaking. Henry is on his way out. Henry answers it before Harriet gets to it. Belle and Sadie go inside.*)

HENRY: Dr. Deen's residence. No ma'm . . . he ain't in right now. Yes'm . . . (*He lays the receiver down. Tom Harris can be seen coming up the path.*)

HARRIET: Henry . . .

HENRY: Yes'm.

HARRIET: There should be coffee for the gentlemen sitting up tonight. Did Eenie make sandwiches?

HENRY: Yas'm.

HARRIET: Watch out a little for the front door bell, will you?

HENRY: Yas'm.

HARRIET: (*rises, picks up the pad off telephone table, as Tom Harris comes on porch with Charlie*) Dad, Laura gave me the list of pallbearers. She thought you would see about them. (*takes the list from the pad and gives it to him*)

HARRIS: Yes, of course. Where is Tut?

HARRIET: Out on a call, I think. He went out before supper. (*Miss Belle and Miss Sadie return*)

HARRIS: I'd like to know when he comes in.

HARRIET: Yes sir. (*As he turns, Miss Belle, weeping, turns to speak to him.*)

HARRIS: How do you do, Miss Belle? (*he exits*)

MISS BELLE: Hello, Mr. Harris.

MISS SADIE: (*Miss Sadie is weeping too, but more quietly than Miss Belle*) What can we do to help, Harriet? There must be so much that needs to be done.

HARRIET: Miss Sadie, if you'll make a list of names from the cards, before they get lost . . . and Miss Belle, if you'll help answer the front door, that will be a great help.

MISS BELLE: I'll be glad to. (*They go inside as Charlie crosses over to Harriet.*)

CHARLIE: Anything I can do? (*sits in arm chair. Henry enters from kitchen*)

HARRIET: No, or if there is, I can't think of it. (*turns, sees Henry*) I believe that's all, Henry?

HENRY: Yas'm. (*He exits into the kitchen.*)

HARRIET: (*sits on the settee*) It's been like this for hours! This living room is full of people who have never been in this house before! (*rises*) They might at least let him alone . . . now. (*looks off to left*) You remember when we were little, how the four of us used to climb those trees together? We were all happy . . . or we thought we were. (*Her voice is sad. One feels the intimacy of her feeling for the Deens.*)

CHARLIE: I know.

HARRIET: It might have been better had he not come back from the war . . .

CHARLIE: (*rises, crosses to her*) You'd better go home now. Whatever's to be done, I can finish it up. And get rid of Miss Belle and the others!

HARRIET: Are you staying tonight? I thought I'd send Henry to bed early. He must be dead tired.

CHARLIE: Yes. I think somebody close to the family ought to be around. Have you seen Doug?

HARRIET: He's inside.

(*Henry comes in from the kitchen carrying two boxes of flowers.*)

HENRY: They came on the ten o'clock train, Miss Harriet.

HARRIET: Yes, Henry. Put them in the big refrigerator. I think there's room. And while you're there, see about Coca-Colas, will you? They should be on ice. And check on the sandwiches and the coffee.

HENRY: Yas'm. (*Henry picks up the box, holds it a moment, suddenly lays it down, turns, tears rolling down his face.*)

HENRY: I never done it! I never done it! Honest to Gawd, Miss Harriet—

(*Tom Harris comes out as they are talking, listens a moment before he speaks.*)

HARRIET: (*voice low*) Now what is it?

HENRY: (*swallowing hard, trying low and under control*) I saw somep'n—when I come near—hit was my boy! (*sobs as he tries to speak*)

HARRIS: What is all this, Henry?

HENRY: (*not waiting for the sentence to be finished*) I never done it! I never done it—Honest to Gawd—

HARRIS: Just a minute, take it easy. Now what is it?

HENRY: When I came near—he was dead!

HARRIS: Where was he?

HENRY: (*swallows hard*) In the path by Miss Ada's. (*sobs*)

HARRIS: What did you do?

HENRY: (*voice barely above a whisper*) Drug him off in the bushes.

HARRIS: Why?

HENRY: I don't know, suh. I knowed they'd git me sho.

HARRIS: What were you doing out there?

HENRY: I went to wake him up early this mornin. He wasn't in his bed and no place around here. I went out to find him—he ain't been lak hisself lately.

HARRIS: Why didn't you tell somebody?

HENRY: I don't know, suh.

HARRIS: Just a minute, Charlie. Now, Henry—go back to the kitchen, and stay there. Don't go to your cabin.

HENRY: Yassuh. (*Henry leaves the room.*)

HARRIS: Sister, suppose you keep an eye on him, until I talk to Charlie. Then I want you to go home. I'll drop you by the house. (*Harriet goes out.*)

HARRIS: Well, Son—

CHARLIE: Dad . . . the town's gone crazy!

HARRIS: I know. Don't mean anything—just want excitement. Fools stopped me twice coming from the mill tonight—flashing their lights in my face—lost their heads.

CHARLIE: Plenty of guns, Dad.

HARRIS: (*sighs*) I know. Looks as if it takes one dead nigger a year to keep Bill Talley's liver regulated!

CHARLIE: I can't see why the Negroes and God take it lying down!

HARRIS: Son! Talk easy! (*rubs his pink bald head*) It's not so simple as that. Not so simple. (*sighs again*) Keep out of it, and keep your eye on Henry until I get back.

CHARLIE: And what are you up to? (*smiles at his father, realizing that he's planning a way out. Turns to leave the room*)

HARRIS: (*chuckles*) Well, I tell you. (*voice drops low*) I'm going to hide him in the jail. Nobody but the sheriff will know he's there.

CHARLIE: Can you trust Lem?

HARRIS: He knows who made him sheriff—I think. I don't expect him to forget it tonight. When things quiet down, we'll carry Henry over to another county and give him a trial.

CHARLIE: Dad—Henry didn't kill Trace.

HARRIS: I know, Son . . .

CHARLIE: It was bound to be one of the Andersons.

HARRIS: Easy . . . now—if that kind of talk gets started it will break Alma's heart.

CHARLIE: It's easier to take the first innocent Negro you can get your hands on, isn't it?

HARRIS: I know. (*sighs*) We'll send Henry away. If they force a trial we'll clear him. Better still we'll hush it up—won't have a trial. See you later, Son. (*He goes out steps leading to the path.*)

CHARLIE: O.K., Dad.

(*Harriet comes in, crosses to center.*)

HARRIET: Will they—hurt him, Charlie?

CHARLIE: I don't think so. Dad is taking him where he'll be safe.

HARRIET: Do you suppose this is going on forever and ever?

CHARLIE: It will so long as we want it this way.

HARRIET: Dad's so optimistic! You're sure Henry will be all right? He never thinks anything bad can happen.

CHARLIE: I think so. Dad gets what he wants.

HARRIET: I know. Keep an eye out, Charlie.

CHARLIE: Run along now and go to bed.

HARRIET: (*starts toward steps*) You know where everything is. Dr. Deen has never come in. Maybe you can persuade him to go to bed, when he comes.

CHARLIE: (*crosses to Harriet*) Run along. I'll see about everything.

(*Doug walks out as Charlie is talking. Harriet goes down the steps. Charlie stands for a moment, deep in his own thoughts. Turns, as Doug speaks to him.*)

DOUG: Seems cooler.

CHARLIE: Believe so.

DOUG: They say the hounds picked up a scent on the edge of the swamp this afternoon—then lost it—

CHARLIE: Are they back?

DOUG: Came in late. (*He stops at the steps and stands there smoking. Crazy Carl comes up the walk, pauses, blinks at the bright light, pulls himself slowly into the porch.*)

CARL: Acy . . . Acy . . .

DOUG: He wants to look at Tracy.

CHARLIE: You mind taking him in, Doug? (*He turns, goes to the kitchen.*)

DOUG: Come on Carl, I'll show you Tracy. (*Carl and Doug go inside the living room.*)

(*As Charlie goes into the kitchen, Alma, Laura, and Preacher Dunwoodie walk out.*)

DUNWOODIE: I'll be over in the morning a little before ten. Is there anything else I can do for you tonight?

ALMA: No, thank you, Brother Dunwoodie.

DUNWOODIE: Then I will go. Good night, Mrs. Deen. May God bless you and comfort you. Miss Laura . . .

LAURA: Thank you for coming. (*Dunwoodie goes down path*) Mother— (*Laura goes up, touches her arm*) Won't you go to bed now?

ALMA: About the hymns . . . I would like for them to sing "Asleep in Jesus" and "Lead Kindly Light" at the church. At the cemetery I would like for the quartet to sing "Abide with Me."

LAURA: Yes, Mother, I'll tell Mr. Pusey.

ALMA: Laura, have Henry close the west windows, in case it rains.

ACT TWO, SCENE 6

At Rise: *Light comes up on Gabe and Sam at the Andersons. Gabe is sitting on the bench. Sam is standing near. They look as if they have been talking for some time.*

SAM: What did he say, Gabe?

GABE: Said—a lot of things.

SAM: What did he say, Gabe?

GABE: Said— (*draws in his breath, finds it hard to go on*) Said—he was so drunk he didn't know what he was sayin— (*pauses*) Said—Tracy Deen gave it to him—to marry—Nonnie Anderson. (*voice hardly more than a whisper now*) Ed come over, knocked him flat. (*The two men now sit without talking. Sam's face shows his deep suffering and shame.*) Sam . . . they're saying round town that Henry killed that Deen boy. Seems white folks saw him wid money too. (*Sam does not answer.*) They got to git somebody. They'll git im fo' morning if they keep on. Dee Cassidy got a bunch of white men now goin aroun' folks' houses. Jus waitin till he gits his chance.

SAM: (*looks at Gabe a long time*) What you want me to do, Gabe? (*voice a little angry now under this new pressure, but still quiet*)

GABE: Sam, Ten McIntosh and me was out at the camp more'n twelve years together. Henry ain't much count, but it's Ten's boy. And he never kilt Tracy Deen. You know it well as me.

SAM: Yeah, I know. But what do you want me to do, Gabe?

GABE: Cain't let a wrong man die when you know who's done it. Can't do that, Sam.

SAM: (*waits before replying*) What do they care about innocence, that mob? White man dead. Nigger must die.

GABE: Cain't do it, Sam.

SAM: Who are we to decide who killed Tracy Deen? He killed himself. Ed just carried out his orders—that's all he did! And Henry furnished the bullets. Somebody's gotta die . . . might as well be that damned fool as another. God knows he ought to die! Lord God, how can we help ourselves. (*Bess comes through the gate, walks up to the men, hesitates as she sees Gabe, looks quickly at Sam.*) Hello, Bess.

BESS: Hello, Sam. (*voice very low*)

GABE: Howdy. Mrs. Lowe. (*Bess bows her head slightly. Looks as Sam waits*) Well, Sam, I better be going. Good evening, Mrs. Lowe.

(*Gabe goes down the path. Bess turns quickly to Sam, looks at him.*)

SAM: How are you?

BESS: All right, I reckon. I'm glad you're back. Where's Eddie?

SAM: He's all right. Should be. I put him on the train in Macon, told him to go straight to New York. Gave him a friend's address. If he keeps his mouth shut, he's safe.

BESS: If he keeps his mouth shut . . . Sam—what's happened to us? I feel it's the end.

SAM: (*smiles*) Not quite, maybe, I hope not. (*They sit there staring past each other. Sam pauses, goes on after a moment*) For the time being, Eddie is safe. Later— it won't be easy . . .

BESS: (*back in the present now and worried*) Have you heard anything—since you got back?

SAM: No. But then I wouldn't.

BESS: Sam, Ed said he left him on the path. They found him in the palmettos, fifty yards from the path.

SAM: Maybe Ed moved him.

BESS: He said he didn't touch him. I don't believe he would. It's worried me . . . If they don't get Ed, they'll . . . what'll they do?

SAM: (*does not answer until he has to*) I don't know.

BESS: They'll get . . . somebody else?

SAM: (*another silence*) I don't know.

BESS: (*her voice breaks in sudden panic as she realizes the moral implication*) Would we . . . let them?

SAM: (*he doesn't answer, then turns to Bess, tries to smile, tries to speak cheerfully*) Don't cross that bridge. Let's just wait.

(*Bess says no more, and Sam does not answer her. They stare out into the night. White singing from the revival is heard.*)

BESS: God—they're still singing. I wish Non would come. She's so late.

SAM: She'll be coming. (*A pause. Then Bess suddenly turns and faces Sam . . . Anger in her voice now for anger is Bess's best friend and helps her through her troubles.*)

BESS: What's the matter with us? Is it Negro? Is it Anderson? What is it? Sometimes I wonder if there *is* something—Ed killing, Nonnie— (*she almost says it*) so crazy. (*She stops. Sam does not answer.*) God knows Eddie's a fool. (*She turns to Sam.*) But he wouldn't have killed a man if it hadn't been for his color! (*Now she is pleading with her conscience.*) He'd have found some other way. It wouldn't have been killing. You know that, Sam. He was too tender-hearted as a kid to hurt a bug. You know that, Sam . . .

SAM: Yes, I know. (*They don't talk for a little.*) They may come out here, Bess. (*Bess nods her head.*) Take it easy—if they come.

BESS: Yes.

SAM: Don't talk—about—anything.

BESS: No. (*in a whisper. The gate opens and Nonnie walks down the path. The two stand on the steps, watching her, left now without words. Quickly*) Eddie's all right, Non. He's safe. Almost in New York now. Everything's all right, Non. (*Non stands looking at them. Swallows hard, tries to speak, can find no words. Sam lays his hand on her shoulder.*)

SAM: Yes. Everything's all right. (*turns to Bess*) I'd better go now. Goodnight, Bess. (*turns to Non, looks at her, a long time, his face gentle and in pain for her. Wanting to say what he has never been able to say to her*) Goodnight, Non.

NONNIE: (*turns*) Thank you, Sam. (*Sam leaves. They stand there watching him go through the gate. He disappears in the dark. The women are motionless as though carved out of stone.*)

BESS: (*finally turns to Non. The sisters look at each other*) You must be tired, Non. It's so hot.

NONNIE: (*her eyes are on the path to Miss Ada's.*) Yes. Boysie's cried all day.

BESS: (*in a whisper*) I'll go get Jackie. (*She disappears around the house.*)

(*Nonnie stands on the steps, looking, and you feel she will never take her eyes off what she sees there.*)

ACT TWO, SCENE 7

Time: *Next day. Early evening.*

A corner of Tom Harris's office showing his old roll-top desk and chair, a steel file, a straight chair, a calendar advertising fertilizer, a telephone on the wall. It is an old-fashioned office which has adequately met Tom Harris's needs for thirty years. A set of box folders is on a shelf. An old gooseneck electric lamp is on the desk. A ledger is open and a loose-leaf order book is lying nearby.

HARRIS: (*sits there working at the ledger. There is a knock at the door. Harris looks up, calls out*) Come in. (*Sam Perry walks in, stands there, hat in hand. Looks tired as if he has had no rest since he left the Andersons, though he has washed up and changed his shirt.*)

SAM: Howdy, Mr. Harris.

HARRIS: Howdy, Sam. Be with you in a minute. (*Harris jots down a figure or two, looks up.*) Sit down. (*Bends over the ledger on the desk. Sam is relieved to see that there is no one else in the office. He waits, not easy and relaxed as he usually is, though he remains quiet but tense with his anxiety for Ed and his conflict about Henry. Sick with the knowledge so recently learned about Non. Harris looks up from copying figures in his notebook, laughs.*) Bookkeeper has a way of putting everything in the wrong colum. (*Sam smiles politely. Waits. Is restless, tense. There is a contrast between Harris, going casually about his routine work, and Perry, anxious, tired from his journey and the struggle that is going on in him. Harris copies down another figure or two. Looks up at Sam.*) All right—now what can I do for you?

SAM: Well, I've come for some advice, as usual. (*smiles at his white friend*) Seems Mr. Deen's death got folks mighty upset— about things—wondering who killed him. Some are saying one thing, some another. But more and more are saying it was Henry McIntosh. If they keep saying it, they may believe it. (*smiles at his friend*) All day there've been men searching the quarters . . . seems to be a little worked up . . . I'm afraid they may start something. Heard a little while ago they've been watching the Deens' backyard. (*pauses*) Now I happen to know that Henry was over at Gabe's house shooting craps the night Mr. Deen was killed. Boys played late so he stayed all night there. Never left the house until seven o'clock next morning. Reason I know this, I had to see Gabe's wife about daybreak, she's had another of her attacks, and I brought Henry back to town myself and left him at the Deens'. (*Sam speaks under stress, knowing he lies, knowing also he is risking Ed's safety by this, yet feeling compelled to do it.*) Mr. Harris, he's as innocent as I am. If you could do something—we'd all be much obliged to you.

HARRIS: Who's after him, Sam?

SAM: I'm not sure I know. Mostly county folks, I hear . . . and some from town—some of the hands from the mill are out in our section. Mr. Talley and Mr. Cassidy are out there too. (*looks at Harris, smiles grimly*)

HARRIS: (*speaks slowly*) Sam, that's a good story you told, gives Henry a clean slate. Only trouble is, it's a lie. (*Sam's face does not move a muscle. Harris frowns.*) Wish you hadn't told it.

SAM: (*looks steadily at the white man*) I had to tell it.

HARRIS: Why?

SAM: (*looks at Harris a long time*) Because I don't know all the truth. But I know enough to know Henry McIntosh didn't kill Mr. Deen.

HARRIS: Do you have any idea who did kill him?

SAM: No sir. I don't know who Mr. Deen's enemies are. (*Neither man speaks for a long moment.*) I'm mighty afraid, from all I've heard, Mr. Harris, that they'll get Henry McIntosh before morning and if they get him like that, they won't wait to find out who killed Mr. Deen.

HARRIS: We haven't had a lynching here in ten years—we're not having one now. Sheriff Taylor did send a posse out to the swamp. They thought for a while that the hounds had picked up a scent but it was soon lost. They've come back—given that up. Things are settling down now, I think. By morning everything will be all right. It's just that folks get excited when something like this happens—lot of hot heads around—

SAM: Excuse me, sir, if I keep on. But things don't seem to be settling, yet. Every colored house in town is being searched right now. It's mighty easy, when folks get like this—for us to have trouble.

HARRIS: Sam, you know well as me who does the lynching! Riff-raff! no-counts. No decent white man takes part in a lynching. (*pauses, smiling*) Well, the riff-raff can't get at Henry. You know where he is? (*Harris's worried red face eases into a broad smile.*) In jail. Yeah . . . behind bars! Letting the law look after him. Law ought to protect innocent well as guilty—if nobody knows it's doing it. (*chuckles*)

SAM: (*speaks slowly now*) It ought to, Mr. Harris, but bars break right easy when a black man's behind them . . .

HARRIS: Nobody knows he's there! That's the point! They don't know it! They'll be giving up soon now and going home if we sit easy. Things'll cool in a few days, then we can let the law take its course.

SAM: When folks go out on a hunt, they don't like to come back without something.

HARRIS: Funny thing . . . how folks let their imaginations run away with them. Now my wife always believes the worst is going to happen. Of course it *could*, Sam. But there's every chance in the world that it won't.

SAM: That's the way lynchings come about, Mr. Harris. It's believing they won't happen.

HARRIS: I know they do—sometimes. Now if there'd been a raping . . . (*says the word softly, as if hating to say it*) or something like that . . . it'd be different.

(*It'd be different . . . Sam suddenly leans forward. It is somebody else speaking now. Another Sam Perry has stepped in front of him, taken hold of things. You feel that all the time Sam is talking now, he is looking at Nonnie's face, seeing the shreds that are left of her life.*)

SAM: You know who's lynching him? (*Pauses. It is as if Sam is discovering something in himself and Harris for the first time.*) It's me and you! Respectable white folks don't like to get mixed up in things like this. Well, respectable colored folks don't either. You shut your eyes, I shut my eyes and—

HARRIS: You're losing your head, Sam.

SAM: No . . . I've lost my soul! Traded it out in the white man's commissary . . . (*stops, goes on*) Maybe he's nothing much to get excited about. No-count . . . but he's alive— (*Sam has clenched his fist now and is softly beating on the table, brown fist catching the light as it pounds the wood. His voice is hardly above a whisper.*)—stands for something . . . his living stands for something! And they'll get him. Bound to! Got to hate something and kill it. Got to!

HARRIS: Sam, I want you to stop. You're talking too much . . . (*pauses*) I know it's hard for an educated colored man to live in the South. Told you that before. Told you when you finished college you were going to find it hard to come back here and live.

SAM: (*half smiles, begins softly*) I came back because my people need me. I came back— (*looks up into his white friend's face and tries to smile*) because it's my home . . . it's my home . . . born here . . . family born here . . . grandparents born here . . . (*pauses, draws a deep breath. Brown fist beats the table softly, fist moving slowly up and down*) It's the little things that drive us crazy . . . you can kill a man so easy . . . slit a piece of skin at his wrist or the side of his neck, give him one tap at the back of the head . . . you can kill his soul easy as that— (*voice drops almost to a whisper*) God . . . (*brown hand beating softly*) you take it and take it and take it . . . day comes . . . you can't take it any more . . . (*stares out the window*) And you turn on somebody white, or on your own kind maybe . . . somebody blacker or dumber than you, or poorer . . . and tear him to pieces . . . You go crazy as hell and tear him to pieces and tear your own soul and those you love, destroying everything on earth you prize . . . every good . . .

HARRIS: I want you to stop talking! You've lost control. I want you—

SAM: Mr. Harris— (*voice is quiet*) first time in my life I interrupted a white man. Yes, I've lost control. Got to say it. All my life I've bowed and scraped, for the sake of others who needed help. I'd do it the white way, I'd say . . . for them.

It's worth licking a few hands for—I'd say—God! ... God! ... (*You can hardly hear him now. He looks across the room as if he has stopped, has long ago forgot to go on. When he speaks again his voice is low, and he's looking, not at the man he is talking to but across 300 years of suffering.*) It's you white men ... sucked dry as your land ... taking our women ... yes, taking them as ... manure, that's all they are to you ... to make something grow green in your life ... that's all they mean to you ... my own mother ... the woman I love ... white man took her ... used her ... threw her aside like ... something filthy and stinking ... why can't you leave them alone! God Jesus, why do we have to bear this!

(*Tom Harris stands, strikes the table hard with his hand.*)

HARRIS: Hush ... you black— (*stops as if a hand has caught his arm, begins again*) You've forgot, Sam, there're things no nigger on earth can say to a white man! (*Sam stares at him, keeps staring as the room rocks with those words spoken by the best friend he has ever had in the white race. And then slowly he buries his face on the table. His sobs are like somebody tearing a shirt to pieces. Harris sits down, moves the inkwell, opens a drawer of his desk, closes it. Looks at the Negro's bowed head.*) Sam. (*voice quiet now, feeling its way*) I wouldn't have thought it of you—always steady—able to keep your eyes on the middle of the road. Buck up, boy ... (*the black head on the table does not move*) It's hard, for black ... and white. If you try to be decent ... anywhere ... (*sighs, taps his finger on the desk. Does not talk for a minute or two*) I'll see Talley and have it out with him. Don't think it's as bad as you think—he's just trying to scare folks a little. I'll check with Sheriff Taylor anyhow—have him keep an eye on the Deen house. Now Sam ... you go home ... pull yourself together ... Thing a man can't do, black or white, is to lose control. You gotta hold on ... never saw you lose your head before. (*Sam wipes his face, stands up, wipes his face again; the telephone rings.*) Want you to know, Sam, I'm the colored man's friend. A man who tries to be a Christian has to be as fair to colored as white. I believe that. But I've got to work in the set-up we got down here. (*Phone continues to ring.*) I'm no radical, no addle-brained red trying— to— (*finishes the sentence as he takes the receiver down*) turn a hundred years upside down in a minute. (*Sam's face shows that he feels it's been a long minute for the Negro.*)

HARRIS: Hello ... Yes Charlie ... Are you sure? How long? Where did they go? You meet me at home. We'll go together. I'm coming now. (*Harris places the receiver on the hook and looks at Sam. Speaks slowly.*) They got him.

(*White man, brown man, stare across the shadows of the room, across three centuries of the same old shadows.*)

(*Lights dim to show the passing of time.*)

(*Harris's office. Four hours later. Tom Harris is in his office, working. He stops after a little and stares at the wall as if unable to keep his mind off of the afternoon's happenings. You can hear the last song of the service, in the tent across the park. Charlie comes in, speaks quietly, touches his father affectionately. Salamander passes by from the cafe, goes down the street.*)

CHARLIE: Hello, Dad . . .

HARRIS: (*voice soft and weary*) Howdy, Son.

CHARLIE: (*concerned, knowing his father's discouragement*) Mother was worried about you staying downtown so long. Harriet and I brought the car.

HARRIS: (*looks at his watch*) Much obliged, Son.

CHARLIE: Dad . . . (*voice full of deep affection now, anxious to give back to his father the self-confidence that the recent events have taken away*) You were right— reckless with that mob.

HARRIS: Well . . . I don't know. (*worries, knowing that his effort to stop the mob has done no good*)

CHARLIE: I don't think many men would have done what you did.

HARRIS: It didn't do any good.

CHARLIE: Ugly crowd. They might have killed you.

HARRIS: I don't know, Charlie. (*sighs*) I'm too old to know anything.

CHARLIE: (*smiling at his father*) You're younger than any child you've got. And a better man.

HARRIS: Too old to figure out things like this. (*The singing creeps between their sentences—casting a shadow across every thought: "Praise God from whom all blessings flow, praise Him, all creatures here below."*)

HARRIS: Some of the men doing that burning were our hands from the mill. Hard working, good to their families. Two of them stewards in our chapel at the mill. (*"Praise Him above, ye heavenly—"*) I can't understand it. (*Harris sighs deeply. He is hurt, his mind, his heart: his life's philosophy shaken to its roots.*)

CHARLIE: Sometimes, Dad, when I think of things down here, all I can see is a white man kneeling on a Negro's stomach. Every time he raises his arms in prayer, he pushes a little deeper in the black man's belly.

HARRIS: It's your saying things like that, Son, that worries your mother. Know you don't mean it the way it sounds. Know you mean something else . . . I've lived a long time, Charlie . . . I can't live without God, can't live without him. (*Harris's voice has sunk to a whisper. The two men sit there a moment staring away into the darkness. As Charlie begins to speak, Harriet comes in quietly, stands behind her father's chair.*)

CHARLIE: But Dad, no matter how much we want to, we can't be Christians down here with things as they are—

HARRIS: We can keep trying, Son.

HARRIET: (*her voice is quiet too and troubled*) I don't know why we're so shocked. After all, we lynch the Negro's soul every day of our lives. (*The men do not answer her.*) It hurts though to think there wasn't one person in this town with enough courage to stop it.

CHARLIE: Except your own Dad! He tried. Went straight into that mob with their guns and sticks.

HARRIS: I'd rather you'd not tell your sister, Charlie. It's not the kind of thing I want her to hear.

HARRIET: (*softly*) Oh Dad . . . don't be silly! You couldn't (*voice very low*) stop it . . . (*Outside in the street Cassidy and two mill hands pass by.*)

HARRIS: I was too late. (*Harriet looks at him, bends down and kisses his bald head.*) I hope some day you young folks will find the answer. (*The street is quiet outside. Salamander goes trudging along toward his cafe.*) Hope some day you'll find how it all started and what can be done about it. Well . . . I'm kinda tired . . . We'd better go. Your mother will be worrying about all of us.

CHARLIE: I'll lock up, Dad.

(*Harris goes out, meets Preacher Dunwoodie at the corner of the street*)
(*The sister and brother close the desk and get ready to lock up. Charlie opens a box file and takes out some papers.*)

HARRIET: Everybody's scared. (*voice soft now. Harriet is feeling too serious to show much of her old fighting spirit*) White man's blown himself up to such a size, now his own shadow scares him.
Street:

HARRIS: Howdy, Brother Dunwoodie.

DUNWOODIE: Sorry you couldn't get to the service tonight. There wasn't much of a crowd.

HARRIS: Maybe things will be better tomorrow night, after folks settle down.

DUNWOODIE: I can't condone a thing like what happened this afternoon. Terrible to think about.

HARRIS: Yes, it was mighty bad.

DUNWOODIE: Still it doesn't do any good, you know, to criticize people at a time like this. Seems to make things worse. It's always been my policy to keep out of controversies and politics. A servant of God has no business mixing in such matters. Our job is the winning of souls to Christ . . .

(*Sam comes by with his bag.*)

HARRIS: Howdy, Sam.

SAM: Howdy, Mr. Harris. (*He walks on. Harris looks at him as he goes down the street, turns back to Dunwoodie.*)

HARRIS: The children have the car. Would you ride home with us? It's across the square.

DUNWOODIE: Much obliged. (*They disappear around the corner.*)

HARRIET: Did you see it, Charlie?

CHARLIE: From the edge.

HARRIET: Who did it?

CHARLIE: Mill folks—farm folks—Dee Cassidy and his crowd got it going.

HARRIET: Was it—pretty bad?

CHARLIE: Yes.

(*Dee Cassidy and the two mill hands come down the street, pause and speak in undertones.*)

HARRIET: Henry and Tracy . . . we lynched them both.

CHARLIE: Yes . . .

HARRIET: We can't keep on—like this . . . would you have enough courage to change things?

CHARLIE: Right now, I'm more scared not to.

HARRIET: But—tomorrow.

CHARLIE: (*smiles at her, touches her arm affectionately*) Let's go. Dad's waiting.

(*Lights dim in office as the young people go out.*)

Street:

CASSIDY: Well, I better be gettin back to the farm. We want to start picking on Monday.

ONE MILL WORKER: Reckon the niggers will all be there. (*laughs*)

CASSIDY: (*laughs*) They'll be there, bright and early. (*They laugh as they pass out of sight.*)

(*As Sam comes from down the street, Gabe meets him on the corner. Doug comes down the street with coat under his arm.*)

GABE: Howdy, Sam. (*Gabe's voice sounds tired too and not as full of its old spirit as formerly.*)

SAM: (*the same quiet Sam*) Gabe.

GABE: Sam . . . my old woman's had another spell. She's feeling right poorly. Reckon you could come over to see her?

SAM: I'll be over in a little while, Gabe.

GABE: Much obliged.

(*The street is deserted now. Only Crazy Carl is seen, slowly walking around to the fountain. Lights dim as he bends down over it.*)

Endesha Ida Mae Holland
(1944–)

The November 1994 issue of *American Theatre Magazine* recognized Endesha Holland as one of the most produced contemporary playwrights of the 1994–1995 season with her acclaimed play *From the Mississippi Delta,* an autobiographical drama chronicling the author's life from Mississippi prostitute to award-winning playwright and college professor. The play garnered national attention when it was first produced at the New Federal Theatre and the Negro Ensemble Company in New York City in 1987. Since that time, *From the Mississippi Delta* has played to capacity houses throughout the United States. Holland has been featured in numerous national magazines and newspapers and has appeared on national television to discuss her work.

Holland has written six other plays: *Second Doctor Lady, Requiem for a Snake, The Autobiography of a Parader Without a Permit, Homebound,* and *Miss Ida B. Wells,* a dramatic biography. She is one of several contemporary playwrights whose works focus on the topic of lynching. Written as part of her thesis for the master's degree in American Studies at the University of Minnesota during the 1980s, *Miss Ida B. Wells* powerfully depicts the life and times of the civil rights activist and journalist. In a series of monologues, the characters "Wells One" and "Wells Two," who are amalgams of historical fact and creative imagination, take us through Wells's childhood in Mississippi where she was orphaned and on to her life as a crusader and organizer of the anti-lynching movement. Also dramatized are Wells's meeting with Susan B. Anthony, her 1894 attempt to ride in the white train section out of Memphis, her reacting to the lynching of three close friends in this same city, and her subsequent uncompromising campaign against the atrocities of lynching.

Miss Ida B. Wells was first produced in 1982 by At the Foot of the Mountain Theatre in Minneapolis. It has had subsequent productions at other Minnesota theaters and in the Buffalo, New York, area where Holland later resided. The play is currently part of the touring repertory of New WORLD Theater, located at the University of Massachusetts (Amherst) and directed by New WORLD artistic director Roberta Uno. The touring production often sparks an array of discussion on topics including the history of lynching, racial violence in America, Reconstruction, African American women, and the suffrage movement.

Like Ida B. Wells, Holland views herself as a race woman. A former thief and teenage prostitute turned college professor and award winning writer, Ida Mae Holland, the youngest of four children, was born in poverty and segregation on August 29, 1944, in Greenwood, Mississippi. Her mother ran a house of prostitution and later became a midwife. Holland never knew her father. At the age of eleven, Holland was raped by the white man whose children she cared for. By age twelve she was a prostitute, and at sixteen she had a police record for soliciting, shoplifting and fighting. While attempting to turn a quick trick she followed a young civil rights volunteer who would lead her to a new world. Through her involvement in the Civil Rights Movement, Holland was able to gain access to education, which she feels paved the way to her phenomenal success as a playwright and a professor. In a June 1992 *Ebony* interview, Holland states, "I saw and heard things in that office I had never seen or heard before . . . I had never seen Black people sitting down using typewriters or heard Black people talking about civil rights or voter registration."

Through the Civil Rights Movement, Holland discovered her talents as a writer and speaker at rallies and marches. But it wasn't until the firebombing of her home, which tragically killed her mother, that the Movement gained its true meaning. To this day, Holland is convinced that the bombing was the work of the Ku Klux Klan and that she was the actual target.

By age twenty, Holland had been married and divorced and become a single mother. She was encouraged by friends to complete her high school equivalency exam and attend college. In 1966 Holland was awarded a full scholarship to the University of Minnesota, where she majored in Afro-American Studies. While in Minneapolis, she worked with female ex-offenders, helping them acquire job skills. Due to her tireless commitment to the black community, Holland took thirteen years to complete her bachelor's degree, which she acquired in 1979. During this period, she was given the name Endesha, a Swahili word meaning "one who drives others forward," for her persistence in the promotion of education and self-improvement. In 1984 she earned a master's degree from the University of Minnesota, and in 1986 she was awarded her Ph.D.

Holland accepted a position at the State University of New York at Buffalo in the Department of American Studies in 1985, where she was instrumental in recruiting African American students, especially women. She had an equal impact in the Buffalo community, where her Victorian home became a haven for artists, students, faculty, and staff. In 1994, she accepted a position as professor and playwright in the school of theatre at the University of Southern

California in Los Angeles. She is also affiliated with the University's Institute for the Study of Women and Men in Society. Holland is currently working on a new play, *Parader Without a Permit,* and an untitled autobiography for Simon & Schuster.

SOURCES

Dr. Holland, telephone interview with Kathy Perkins, 1995.
Roberta Uno, New WORLD Theater, interview with Kathy Perkins, 1995.

Miss Ida B. Wells

A DRAMATIC BIOGRAPHY   1983

Endesha Ida Mae Holland

THE PLAYERS:

WELLS ONE, *sixty-six-year-old woman with a sense of humor and not a tragic heroine.*

WELLS TWO, *must be able to play a range of characters and ages from early teens to old age.*

Chicago. The late 1920s. Early afternoon in the late fall. Ida B. Wells-Barnett walks through the Loop. WELLS ONE *is sixty-six years old with graying hair and determined shoulders. Her step is spry. She carries several packages and a half-dead potted plant. A young woman,* WELLS TWO, *approaches Wells One.*

WELLS TWO/YOUNG GIRL: Excuse me lady . . . ain't you Miss Ida B. Wells?

WELLS ONE: (*surprised but pleased*) Yes my dear, I am . . .

WELLS TWO/YOUNG GIRL: Oh Miss Wells, in my history class at the Y . . . we was talking about Miss Joan of Arc, the great lady who lived in France . . .

WELLS ONE: (*kindly*) I know of her work well, my dear.

WELLS TWO/YOUNG GIRL: Well, our teacher asked each one of us to name someone we know—who's as great as this lady soldier.

WELLS ONE: Yes my dear . . .

WELLS TWO/YOUNG GIRL: I was the only Colored person there and I had to name another Colored lady.

WELLS ONE: That's right smart of you.

WELLS TWO/YOUNG GIRL: I named you!

WELLS ONE: Me . . .

WELLS TWO/YOUNG GIRL: I stood up real bold-like and said "The greatest Colored lady I know is Miss Ida B. Wells."

WELLS ONE: That was very kind of you.

WELLS TWO/YOUNG GIRL: Every eye in the room turned to me. Our teacher asked me to tell the class what you've done.

WELLS ONE: What did you tell them my dear?

WELLS TWO/YOUNG GIRL: I don't know what you did. But I do know it must be something mighty important—because I hear your name everywhere. (*She falters in embarrassment.*)

WELLS ONE: You did just fine.

WELLS TWO/YOUNG GIRL: Please tell me what you did, so the next time I'm asked—I'll know.

WELLS ONE: My dear young woman, we'll be standing here till doomsday, if I tried to tell you about the things that I've done. But as soon as I get home, I'm going to start writing about my life. I'm going to write a book about my life.

WELLS TWO/YOUNG GIRL: You're going to write a whole book, Miss Wells?

WELLS ONE: Yes my dear, I'm going to write a whole book. I'm going to send you the first copy.

WELLS TWO/YOUNG GIRL: Oh thank you Miss Wells. Then I can read all about the things that you did. Just wait until I tell Mama who I saw. Just wait.

(*Lights up on Wells' workroom. Wells One enters with same spry step.*)

WELLS ONE: (*hollering into other room*) Is the tea just about ready, Ida B?

WELLS TWO/IDA B.: Just about, Mama.

WELLS ONE: Is the tea ready, Ida B? You know, I started drinking tea in England. There we sat:

WELLS TWO/YOUNG IDA B.: Miss Impey, Sir John Gorst, a member of Parliament, and right to my left (*name drops*) Lady Henry Somerset, the Countess of Aberdeen. The butler brought in the tea, he said something to Lady Somerset, she lifted the teapot up . . . and Lady Somerset poured the tea . . . But I tell you, I was ready for them: Miss Impey picked her cup up, and kinda crooked her little finger . . . Sir John Gorst crooked his little finger a bit more than Miss Impey's . . . and Lady Somerset, hers was really crooked. And they were all looking at my cup, even the butler. But I was ready for them. Mr. Douglass had got me ready for them, because he had been to England before. I took a deep breath. I take a deep breath when I'm nervous. I picked up my cup—it felt like tissue paper in my hand. I picked it up and crooked my little finger—more than Lady Somerset could ever hope to crook hers . . . I could've told them that Ida B. Wells—once I take a deep breath, you're going to get some kinda action.

WELLS ONE: I always did want to be named "Iola." I remember Miss Iola McSwine, she would walk up and down the streets, so proud and tall. She was the smartest woman in town. I used to make all my playmates call me Iola. When I got the job writing for the *Living Way*, our church newspaper, all the people said I was too young to be writing for the paper. But I fooled a lot of people. Cause they didn't know who Iola was. A lot of people still don't know that I'm Iola. Writing for the paper gave me the chance to speak out. I wrote about the Pastor's Aid Board one time, and the board got mad enough to try and find out who Iola was. (*laughs*) I even wrote for T. Thomas Fortune's paper, the *New York Age*. You may have read some of my columns.

WELLS TWO: Colored folks from Mississippi can't read or write.

WELLS ONE: I attended Shaw University. My daddy and mama was one of the founding board members of that University. . . . My daddy and mama made sure that I kept my head in some kinda book. As for my writing, I'm real adept with the pen. My mother and father were slaves. I was born on July 16, 1862, in Holly Springs, Mississippi. There were eight of us children and I'm the oldest. My daddy, Jim Wells, was the best carpenter in the county, if not the whole South. Daddy always talked about how he built a lot of the slave owners' houses. And a lot of slave cabins too. "The Civil War was over and we was free, I started rebuilding homes, I even helped the Union Government rebuild plants and factories. I even now built dis house. We done got de freedom; now us gots to keep hit." Daddy took part in just about everything the Freedman's Bureau did in Holly Springs. Many's the time I'd hear mama fussing at him about being too sassy and spending too much time with the Bureau. She always left things in God's hands. She went to church just about every night. Mama was such a Christian, that I was scared to think bad thoughts around her. When I was sixteen years old, the yellow fever epidemic in Holly Springs killed my mama and papa. I knew then that I wouldn't be able to continue going to school. But I had studied real hard and read a lot, so I was well ahead of most of the other students. So I just took a deep breath . . . and started taking care of my other brothers and sisters. Times are hardest when there is no mama or papa in a family. The thirty-third degree Masons helped me put food on the table for the children. They even spoke up in my favor when some of the busybodies wanted to take the children and put them in homes. (*with great force*) Can't nobody say that Ida B. Wells can't take care of her kin. I was looking for work as a schoolteacher in '84. I got on the train in Memphis, going to the country to take a job . . .

WELLS ONE/WELLS TWO: I was minding my own business . . .

WELLS TWO: I brought a first-class ticket on the C-O&S railroad. I took my seat. All of a sudden, a couple of the people who worked on the train—and the conductor—tried to drag me into the "smokers car." For a minute there I didn't know what was happening: the conductor was dragging me by the arm; somebody else, with a lot of medals on his uniform, had me in such a tight grip, till my whole side was numb. Two of the women passengers grabbed ahold of my legs and pulled me off my feet. It was rough going for a minute or two. Then I started to participate—with teeth and feet! If I hada had pyreah gums really bad—there'd been a lot of dead first class passengers. But I can guarantee you that a lot of the ones I kicked—wish they hada been bit.

WELLS ONE: My sense of justice was outraged. There was no way that I was going to let the 14th and 15th Amendments take low to Jim Crow. Not through me, they weren't. (*She laughs at the memory.*) The ticket agent, poor man, when he saw all the first class passengers, running and holding their behinds—he ran and hid.

WELLS TWO: (*bruised and holding her side, she searches for the ticket agent*) You may as well come on out. I know you saw everything that happened—and I'm going to have my lawyer call you for a witness. Come on out, I know you're here.

WELLS ONE: I rode back home on the back of a dray-wagon. A few days later I went to Memphis and hired a Colored lawyer to file suit against the railroad. After months and months of waiting around, one delay after the other . . .

WELLS TWO: (*in lawyer's office*) I brought my case to you, sir, because you're the only Colored lawyer in town. And now you sit here and tell me that the railroad wants to pay me twenty dollars for taking away my rights. Sir, it's not for me by myself that I'm trying to fight to keep our power. I know that if we give up or give into the railroad, we'll pass up the chance to help change things for our people. And you tell me that unless I accept the twenty-dollar offer, you'll be too busy to work on the case anymore. Seems to me that you been bought off by the railroad.

WELLS ONE: I had to get a White lawyer to go to court with me. The courtroom was full; every seat was taken. All the White women was sitting there fanning; and all the Colored women was sitting there holding the White women's babies. Judge Pierce, an ex-Union soldier from Minnesota, rapped three times with his gavel. His voice rung out over the courtroom as clear as a bell—even the babies stopped crying.

WELLS TWO/JUDGE PIERCE: I find in behalf of the plaintiff, Ida B. Wells, damages owed her of $500.

WELLS ONE: The White people in the courtroom were stunned. The Colored people were shamed. My own people felt that I had stepped out of line by suing the railroad. I can see to this day the headline in the *Memphis Appeal* announcing, "Darkie Damsel Gets Damages."

WELLS TWO: (*in the classroom*) Now class, don't carry on so; T.C. was right to ask the question . . . No matter how silly it may sound to us: The answer to your question, T.C., is "no." $500 doesn't make you the richest person in the world. So you see class, even if the Supreme Court of Tennessee hadn't overturned Judge Pierce's decision yesterday—I still wouldn't be the richest person in the world.

WELLS ONE: I may have lost the war, but I was set on taking Jim Crow into battle. My struggle against the railroad was the first of many times that I defied the system. During my fight with the road, none of my people seemed to feel that it was a race matter, nobody would help me in the fight, and a lot of my friends stopped speaking to me. So I trod the wine press alone. I was determined that, if need be, I would be the sole sentinel for my race.

WELLS TWO: (*in the classroom*) So you see boys and girls, instead of being rich, I am the sentry . . . ever-watching, ever on guard—for our nineteen-year-old freedom.

WELLS ONE: I was only five years old when they passed the Reconstruction Act, putting the South under military rule. It's a good thing they did because after the war, the South was still mad at us Colored people, as though we had freed ourselves. A Colored person's life was about as much good as Confederate money. I remember the soldiers riding up and down the road in Holly Springs. All the boys played Rebel soldiers and us girls were the Union nurses. Everybody was talking about the state conventions, held in 1867 and '68. They was praising the high level that the South was reaching for. A level the South had never known before or since. There was one lady, the undertaker's wife, she never missed going to the convention. Miss McDonald, Miss McDonald . . . Who did you see today?

WELLS TWO/MISS McDONALD: There now Ida, quit hollering and I'll tell you. Aw little girl, I tell you; those Colored men, they're some dignified, sitting there in the lawmakers' seats, carrying on and talking all legal-like and all. I said to myself, "Ada Mae McDonald, here you's setting here in the heart of the Confederacy, looking at the Colored men knocking down the barriers on voting and holding office . . . doing away with debtors' prisons and making the White folks put up a law that they can't never own human beings . . . Never. Aw Ida B., I tell you, it's a sight to behold.

WELLS ONE: When they counted up the votes, Louisiana and Mississippi had roughly 97,000 White voters and 224,000 Colored voters.

WELLS TWO/MISS McDONALD: The bottom rail is on the top . . .

WELLS ONE: The truth is that Colored people could affect the laws of the South, but we were never in control of the government. Around about this time, White people started losing their control over us, so they got together in secret groups. The worst of these secret groups were the Knights of the Ku Klux Klan. All the Colored people was afraid of the Klan—some of the White people was scared of them too.

WELLS TWO: Everywhere they ride, they bring death and destruction. They can just ride all times of night, killing and burning up Colored people who "get out of line." The Klan won't stand for us to have nothing to do with voting. They've even started hiding the voting places.

WELLS ONE: We sharecrop their land and trade at their stores.

WELLS TWO: The South is charting its own course.

WELLS ONE: The Hayes Compromise of 1876 shaped our future.

WELLS TWO: The South is charting its own course.

WELLS ONE: No more federal intervention; the South can now instigate Home Rule.

WELLS TWO: The South is charting its own course.

WELLS ONE: We must look to the North for help.

WELLS TWO: Chile, we're picking in low cotton.

WELLS ONE: Our rights are now in the hands of southern Whites.

WELLS TWO: Chile, we're picking in low cotton.

WELLS ONE: We got to get on the defense for survival.

WELLS TWO: Chile, we're picking in low cotton.

WELLS ONE: If we had only been able to foresee the future.

WELLS TWO: The bottom rail is back on the bottom.

WELLS ONE: The men who owns the Colored newspaper here—*The Free Speech and Headlight*—is trying to sell part ownership of the paper.

WELLS TWO: At last I've found—what I truly want to be in life. A newspaper writer.

WELLS ONE: They should just sell the whole paper because they're too scared to print a lot of the news. The only news they print is—who got married, who had a baby—but never any news that's crucial to our safety and progress.

WELLS TWO: Ninety-seven, ninety-eight, ninety-nine, one hundred dollars. Thank you Jesus—thank you Lord. I'm going to march right down to the *Free Speech* office and buy me a third interest in the newspaper. I can hear the people talking now: "dere goes Miss Ida B. Wells, she owns the *Free Speech* newspaper."

WELLS ONE: I knew that I could make the paper work. I sold subscriptions all over the South. I knocked on a lot of doors. I visited every Colored church in the county. I can speak freely and truthfully—now that I got some say so over the paper.

WELLS TWO: The school where I teach, it's not fit for dogs to attend lessen human beings.

WELLS ONE: I complained to the school board.

WELLS TWO: Mr. Superintendent, members of the school board, and parents: thank you for allowing me to speak. My name is Ida B. Wells. I'm certain that most of you know me; I'm part owner of the *Free Speech* newspaper, and I've taught school here for the past two years. This school is ready to fall in: The floors and walls are full of holes. Rats from the levee overrun the classrooms. When it rains we may as well be outside—we get just as wet. We don't have enough books; the ones we have are so old until we can't make out the words. Sir: I demand that you and the board get us some new books—and fix up this school immediately—so that we can get on with the business of teaching and learning.

WELLS ONE: The school board voted—to dismiss me. I hoped that the parents would come to my aid. T.C.'s mother said: "Miss Ida, you ought not to done it, talk like you did to them White folks. You mighta knowed that they would fire you." I think it's right to strike a blow against evil and I don't regret it. It distresses me that a fight made in the interest of the Race—doesn't have the support of the Race.

WELLS TWO: Now I don't have a job. I've got to survive somehow on the money I make from the *Free Speech*. Lord, if you help me through this, I'm willing to walk every road in Mississippi, Tennessee, and Arkansas to sell my paper. I'm willing to help myself, Lord—but I need you.

WELLS ONE: Thank the Lord, that things went well for me. My newspaper was being sold in four states and I was making a difference in the way people think.

WELLS TWO: (*screams in horror*) Will somebody stop them! Oh, my God, somebody do something! (*implores bystanders*) Sheriff . . . banker Matthews . . . Rev Hale . . . oh please somebody, Miss May . . . Miss Goldberg . . . oh, my God—they're burning him. (*She recoils from the stench of burning flesh.*)

WELLS ONE: Three of our leading Colored businessmen died today. The White mob lynched them. We Colored people have got to do something. We got to put a stop to these murders. I've heard about lynching taking place in other parts of the South. But today, right here in Memphis, my friends were killed. Nobody, not even me, lifted a hand to help them. Before he died today—Mr. Brown—he said for us to go North. (*breaks down*)

WELLS TWO: There is no justice for us here. I can truthfully say that—three of us are missing from this meeting tonight. I can truthfully say that—because I saw with my own eyes the hot fire eating into Mr. Montgomery's body. I can truthfully say that—because I heard Mr. James begging for somebody to help him. I can truthfully say that—I saw the very life leave Mr. Brown. Nobody went forward. Nobody. We were scared. We were scared of the White people of Memphis, who got together in a mob . . . and went on a rampage in our section; all on the word of a White storekeeper—who don't want no Colored competition. The only thing we can do is to save our money and leave Memphis. Let's make Memphis a ghost-town. Memphis won't protect our lives, nor give us a fair trial in the courts. What Memphis does is allow us to be taken out and murdered—on the word of *any* White person. I vow to you, right here and now, and those of you that want to tell the White people what I said, hear me good: Me . . . Ida B. Wells, is this day taking up the banner to put a stop against lynching. I'll use my newspaper and whatever else I can—to indict the people of Memphis, or anywhere—I'm going to do battle against lynching.

WELLS ONE: His spirit in smoke ascended to high heaven / his father by the cruelest way of pain / had bidden him to his bosom once again / The awful sin still remained unforgiven / All night a bright and solitary star / Perchance the one that guided him / Yet gave him up at last to fate's wild whim / Hung pitifully over the swinging char / Day dawned, and soon the mixed crowds came to view / the ghastly body swaying in the sun / The women thronged to look, but never a one / Showed sorrow in her eyes of steely blue / And little lads, lynchers that were to be . . .

WELLS ONE/TWO: Danced around the dreadful thing in fiendish glee.*

WELLS TWO: It's a vile and criminal act to lynch somebody. Now the mob usually come at night, leaning on each other for support while they murder. Any Colored person can be lynched. I ask you: Where is the North? I don't believe that the North knows about these murders. Surely it wouldn't ignore our call for help.

WELLS ONE: The mob had their excuses alright. One excuse was to put a stop

---

* Claude McKay's poem, "The Lynching."

to race riots. (*with disdain*) Several Colored people congregating is a race riot to them. Another excuse is that if Colored people try to vote—they're trying to take over. But the excuse the mob use most of the time is that Colored men commit "outrages"—which is rape—against White women. In a twenty-year period, two thousand sixty-odd Colored people was lynched on account of these threadbare lies.

WELLS TWO: Nobody in this section believes the old threadbare lies that all these Colored men assault White women. If southern White men aren't careful they'll over-reach themselves and a conclusion will be reached which will be very damaging to the moral reputation of their women.

WELLS ONE: My editorial enraged the White community. I dared to speak out against the so-called virtue of White women. When I challenged White women's morals, I challenged a very dear symbol of White supremacy, The White people of Memphis—you better know it—accepted my challenge. I was away on business when a "committee" of White businessmen called on me. When they couldn't find me—they wrecked my office. Destroyed my press. So with my paper ruined and my life in danger, I saw no reason to return to Memphis.

WELLS TWO: Well Lord, they don't want me to come back to Memphis, for sure. I got to keep speaking against lynch-law. I guess I'll just head on to the North. I got to protect myself too. I'm going to buy me a gun.

WELLS ONE: Two guns.

WELLS TWO: And a razor.

WELLS ONE: I just wasn't satisfied with writing about lynching in the Colored press. I wanted to present our case before the world. So with the help of the eminent Frederick Douglass—

WELLS TWO: I want to thank Mr. Douglass for allowing me the opportunity to bring the plight of Colored people in America, before you international visitors to Chicago. To those of you who traveled across America, to those of you who traveled from across the waters, I, Ida B. Wells, welcome you to this grand Columbian Exposition—this world showplace for the progress of man. All around you here, America is showing its industrial progress. Indeed, you visitors from other countries are seeing, for the first time: gadgets, all kinds of machines and ideas—such as you've never seen before. Us Americans, including us Colored Americans, are seeing our progress and feeling pride. For some Americans, this lifestyle is the very best. (*takes a deep breath*) But behind this facade—there is problem on top of problem. Colored men are being dragged from their homes in the middle of the night. They're taken and hung from trees—they're burned to death. Crowds of people . . . I hope not none of you . . . stand around and say not one word to stop the lynching. I have here a pamphlet that I wrote and financed. If you'd care to help in the fight against lynch-law in America, then pick up one of my anti-lynch pamphlets. That gentleman over there, Mr. Paul Laurence Dunbar, is handing them out.

WELLS ONE: A lot of the visitors to the 1893 Expo never went back home.

These immigrants just went across town, rented a room, or moved in with kinfolk and stayed. In the early '90s a lot of Colored people migrated to Chicago from the South. Chicago made a difference between us 15,000 Colored people and the swarms of immigrants. They tabled our rights. Colored people could only do housework or unskilled labor. We sure couldn't belong to the organized labor groups. None of the people from across the water had to fight for their legal rights. (*Music is Lohengrin's Wedding March. She recognizes the music and giggles like a young woman who is in her first love affair. She catches herself.*) Well, uh, uh, that didn't happen for another five years. Sometimes my memory runs ahead of me—especially when I think of Mr. Barnett. (*composed*) In 1892 and '93, I wrote regularly for Mr. Fortune's paper, the *New York Age*. When I went on the lecture circuit I had the figures on lynching from the *New York Age*, which Mr. Fortune had put on the front page, to back me up.

WELLS TWO: I have come face to face with the truth concerning the North's feeling on lynchings. I've always wondered why the North was silent. I thought the North didn't really know what was happening in the South. But the North knows what's happening.

WELLS ONE: They accepted the South's threadbare lies.

WELLS TWO: I know that the North knows. I've told them about the horrors I have seen. No word—no comment have I heard from the North. But in spite of your inaction, I shall continue to tell the truth freely.

WELLS ONE: On one of my lectures I met . . .

WELLS TWO: Mr. William Lloyd Garrison. So you're the son and namesake of our famous abolitionist.

WELLS ONE: He used his influence with the businessmen to turn down a loan solicited by Memphis.

WELLS TWO: Somebody heard me because White sympathizers have agreed to bring economic pressures against lynch-law.

WELLS ONE: (*with great pride*) Two Negro women from New York took up my crusade. They called together the leading Negro women of the northeast. They gave me a grand testimonial dinner. All the old-timers say they have never seen anything like it before. (*The name "Iola" is projected in brilliant lights.*)

WELLS TWO: Your magnanimous recognition of my struggle is the signal that Negroes will no longer let lynch-law control our lives. The more I see the situation the more I'm convinced that the South still holds a grudge against us. The laws say that we are no longer slaves. But the South is determined to control us politically, economically and spiritually. Even if they have to lynch us. Oh, but the South has convinced the world that the lynchings are justified in order to stop Negro men from raping White women. I have found that White men, whose seeds have brought forth a race of mulattoes by raping and consorting with Negro women—are the very same men—who make up the lynch mobs.

WELLS ONE: It's my duty to give the facts I have collected to the world. The invitation to visit England came like an open door in a stone wall. Miss Impey of England, editor of the *Anti-Caste*, a magazine that advocated equal rights for the natives of India, invited me to visit Europe after she heard me speak at my testimonial.

WELLS TWO: (*in England, having tea with the notables as before*) Thank you for asking, Lady Somerset. Yes, I'm having a grand time in England. Mr. Douglass (*she sips with little finger crooked*) assured me that I would love your country and I do. Mr. Axom, in your capacity as editor of the *Manchester Guardian*, I'm sure you realize how important it is that the British people know the whole truth. Now the plan that you propose, Sir John, is excellent. I agree that the South will be forced to listen to world opinion. But the committee must go to America soon—before more Negro men are lynched.

WELLS ONE: I was sure that the figures they collected would bear me out to be telling the truth. But the South rose with such a clatter that the English committee never came. The idea of them coming alerted Memphis to the power of foreign public opinion.

WELLS TWO: (*still in conversation with the notables*) No, Rev. Asked, the Christians haven't condemned lynch-law. You ask me if Rev. Dwight Moody or Miss Frances Willard have taken a stand. My answer is emphatically no. Now I know that the British people see Rev. Moody as a zealous exponent of Christianity. He is influential and preaches all over the United States and abroad. Miss Willard, in her position as President of the Women's Christian Temperance Union, is well-known and influential too. They have the ear of the people. (*takes a deep breath*) But I'm compelled in the name of truth to say that they have given the weight of their influences to the South's racism. Rev. Moody encourages the drawing of the color-line in churches. He preaches on separate days to the Negroes on his tours throughout the South. Now Lady Somerset, I hate to say this because I know you have a deep respect for Miss Willard. But she has gone even further. She put herself on record by approving the South's methods. At a meeting in the South where they were defying the Constitution by suppressing the Negro vote, she went on record saying . . .

WELLS ONE: (*in Miss Willard's voice*) "When I go North—there will be no word wafted to you from pen or voice that is not loyal to what we're saying here and now."

WELLS TWO: I can see that you're trying to hold on to your temper, Lady Somerset. But Miss Willard is broadcasting a slander against the Negro race in order to stay in favor with the very people who are shooting, hanging and burning Negroes alive. (*listens to Lady Somerset*) No, Lady Somerset, I'm not over-reacting.

WELLS ONE: The year-old Ida B. Wells club laid out the welcome for me when I returned to Chicago. They made me feel so good. As I approached the entrance to the auditorium, I was stopped by a Mr. Slayton of the speakers bureau.

WELLS TWO: What's that you say, Mr. Slayton . . . the bureau will pay me to speak . . . on issues other than lynching . . . such as? . . . Oh, such as temperance and suffrage . . . Mr. Slayton, I positively refuse. It would be sacrilegious for me to turn aside in a money-making effort for myself. Let me tell you right now and you tell all the others that'll be following after you: You tell them that Ida B. Wells can't be bought—I'm not for sale!

WELLS ONE: Lord, I sure was something. When I finished glaring at Mr. Slayton he scurried off real quick. Of course, I saw him a lot down through the years. He always nodded his head, but he never said another word to me. Lord, I sure was something. I was in Rochester, New York, making a speech, when one of the women handed me a note. (*Unfolds note and reads*) "My dear Miss Wells: Would you do me the honor of being my house guest for as long as you're in the city? Susan B. Anthony."

WELLS TWO/ANTHONY: I gave her her bonnet, and told her to leave my home at once—and never return.

WELLS ONE: Who?

WELLS TWO/ANTHONY: The stenographer. I let her go.

WELLS ONE: You didn't have to do that, Miss Anthony.

WELLS TWO/ANTHONY: My dear Miss Wells, that young woman refused to take dictation from you. You're my guest. I will not allow her to insult you or me. So my dear, you feel that Miss Willard is wrong, even if for the sake of expediency—in order to conquer?

WELLS ONE: Yes, Miss Anthony, I still feel that Miss Willard is wrong. You would have me believe . . .

WELLS TWO/ANTHONY: Listen, my dear, let me tell you of a time when I had to use expediency in order to conquer: As you know, Frederick Douglass has befriended our campaign like no other man—White or Negro. Whenever he comes to our conventions, he is an honored platform guest. Most of our conventions have been held in Washington, D.C.

WELLS ONE: Go on, Miss Anthony.

WELLS TWO/ANTHONY: When the convention was held in Atlanta, Georgia, I asked Mr. Douglass not to attend. I was afraid that the southern White suffragettes wouldn't attend—if they had to sit on the same platform with Mr. Douglass—a former slave. Was I wrong to do so my dear . . . ?

WELLS ONE: Yes, Miss Anthony, I think you were wrong. Although you may have made gains for suffrage—you also confirmed White women in their attitude on segregation and racism.

WELLS TWO/ANTHONY: I have dedicated my life to women getting the ballot. I have never strayed from that goal.

WELLS ONE: Yours, like mine, is often the sole voice raised against glaring injustices—whether it's women's rights or lynch-law.

WELLS TWO/ANTHONY: Unlike you my dear, I could never think of marriage and children. My mission is clear. I must devote all my efforts to the cause. I must keep on my course.

WELLS ONE: Miss Anthony, I know that you have high hopes that the wrongs toward my people will undergo a change—once women get the ballot . . .

WELLS/ANTHONY: What your people need, Miss Wells, is someone who will carry the banner for them. Someone who doesn't have other obligations. But my dear, I'm sure that when we women get the ballot . . .

WELLS ONE: My hopes aren't so high, Miss Anthony. Now I do believe that it's right that women should be able to vote. But knowing White women as I do, and their petty outlook on life, I don't believe that getting the vote is going to change their nature—nor the political position of my people.

WELLS TWO/ANTHONY: That, my dear, is quite unfair . . .

WELLS ONE: You've taken issue with my forthcoming marriage. But you know as well as I do that White women have set precedents of being powerless. They have remained mute in determining social policies. If you, Miss Susan B. Anthony, the backbone of the women's rights crusade, will give in to racism—Lord, we got a long way to go.

WELLS TWO/ANTHONY: More tea, Miss Wells?

WELLS ONE: Yes, thank you, my dear.

WELLS TWO: Who . . . who, who did you say? Frederick Douglass! You sure? They say that Mr. Frederick Douglass is dead . . .

WELLS ONE: Who did you say was dead . . . did I hear you say that Mr. Douglass is dead . . . ? Oh no, my Lord, Mr. Douglass can't be gone. We need Mr. Douglass. He was my mentor, my guide, my leader . . . (*We hear Lohengrin's Wedding March. Trying to fasten gown*) Ida B., uh Ida B., wake up, child, and come help me fasten my wedding dress.

WELLS TWO/IDA B.: (*familiar and tired of the ritual*) Alright mama, but you know it's too small for you.

WELLS ONE: (*adamant*) Fasten it. (*They struggle, but Wells One is never quite able to get the gown fastened.*)

WELLS TWO/IDA B.: Mama, you better not try to sit down. (*She exits, giggling all the way.*)

WELLS ONE: (*relents*) I know this dress is too small. But every time I think of 1895, I think of my wedding day. It was the happiest day of my life. Me and Mr. Barnett did a lot of courting.

WELLS TWO: Every seat in the church is taken.

WELLS ONE: Mr. Barnett is a real Race man.

WELLS TWO: My bridesmaids are so lovely.

WELLS ONE: Everybody is here.

WELLS TWO: There's my love, Mr. Barnett. He's so handsome.

WELLS ONE: Lordy, I was so happy.

WELLS TWO: I, Ida B. Wells, take thee, Ferdinand Lee Barnett.

WELLS ONE: Mr. Barnett was a good catch too.

WELLS TWO: Til death do we part. (*She marches to the Wedding March.*)

WELLS ONE: When I married Mr. Barnett, I bought his paper, the *Conservator*. It was the first Negro newspaper in Chicago. I owned two newspapers and they said that Colored people from Mississippi can't read or write.

WELLS TWO: (*sees cards from well-wishers. As she reads, her face becomes angry*) Letters of protest against my marriage. I've begged a lot of yall to write letters in support of my crusade. You wouldn't do it. On the happiest day of my life, you dare to censor me because I got married. You're more outspoken because you think my marriage will mean loss to the cause than you've been in upholding my hand—while I'm trying to carry the banner.

WELLS ONE: I guess I can't be too hard on people. You expect a woman who gets married to settle down to raising children and being a full-time wife. But the very next week I continued my work. I bet you that I'm the only mother, Negro or White, that made the rounds of the lecture circuit with a new born baby.

WELLS TWO: (*cradling and comforting baby*) Hush now baby, don't cry. Hush now, mama's little ole bitty baby. Mama gone go give talk 'bout some real bad people and she don't want her precious baby to be crying. Hush now baby. (*Wells One takes off gown.*)

WELLS ONE: I carried my baby, Charles, everywhere I spoke. Sometimes I had a nurse. One time the baby hollered so loud, until we heard him in the lecture hall. You met Ida B. She's my namesake. Alfreda is my youngest. A lot of people still call me Miss Wells. You should see them when they find out that I have children. They start asking right off about my husband. My last name is Barnett. It doesn't bother Mr. Barnett when people still call me Miss Wells. In 1901, at an anti-lynch rally, Mr. Barnett introduced me to Miss Jane Addams. He said: Miss Addams, I want you to meet my wife, Miss Wells. (*Wells One and Wells Two/Addams extend hands.*)

WELLS TWO/ADDAMS: My dear Mrs. Wells-Barnett, I'm very happy to meet you.

WELLS ONE: I'm honored to meet you, Miss Addams.

WELLS TWO/ADDAMS: Thank you, my dear.

WELLS ONE: Hull House is doing so much for the immigrants.

WELLS TWO/ADDAMS: We're both trying, in our own way, to change America. My dear, we must work together to reform injustices because, my dear Mrs. Wells-Barnett, my interests are far broader then Hull House.

WELLS ONE: People will listen to you, Miss Addams.

WELLS TWO/ADDAMS: We will send this message to our fellow citizens of the South. Who are once more trying to suppress vice by violence. The bestial in man, which leaves him to pillage and rape—can never be controlled by public cruelty and dramatic punishment—which too often cover fury and revenge . . .

WELLS ONE: Oh Miss Addams, just a minute please.

WELLS TWO/ADDAMS: Yes, Mrs. Wells-Barnett . . .

WELLS ONE: (*goes to Addams*) Now Miss Addams, you know that I think you're the greatest woman in the United States.

WELLS TWO/ADDAMS: Yes my dear, I know that you hold me in the highest of esteem.

WELLS ONE: From your remarks, it seems to me that you've accepted the

South's threadbare lies that Negro men are being lynched for raping White women . . .

WELLS TWO/ADDAMS: My dear . . .

WELLS ONE: Rape is a charge that allows White mobs to kill Negro men. (*unfolds newspaper*) The figures here in the *Chicago Tribune* on lynchings shows that 504 Negroes have been lynched between 1896 and 1900.

WELLS TWO/ADDAMS: Mrs. Wells-Barnett, rape is a heinous crime.

WELLS ONE: It is to be sure, Miss Addams. Can't you see that the South is using the excuse of rape to influence northerners—like you—to understand, even if you don't condone their actions.

WELLS TWO/ADDAMS: I can assure you, Mrs. Wells-Barnett, and everyone here, that I have done my homework on this matter. So my dear, my understanding of this matter is very well thought out. (*She exits in a huff.*)

WELLS ONE: We Negroes looked forward to the coming of the new 20th century. I'll never forget that Sunday, the last day of the 19th century. I kept wanting the day to hurry and be over. I was looking forward to the next day—the first day of the new year.

WELLS TWO: Honey chile, we gone be sweeping wit a brand new broom.

WELLS ONE: My new found hope was soon dampened. The beginning of the 20th century was a sad time for us. In the South, state after state wrote Jim Crow laws into their Constitutions. Here in Chicago and the rest of the North, as the Negro population grew, discrimination ran wild. Us Negro leaders had to re-examine our goals and methods for reaching them.

WELLS TWO: Dis here new broom, hit aint sweeping clean atall.

WELLS ONE: Since I was a leader I had to take action on issues outside of my anti-lynch fight. Lord, I got so mad at some of our people. Sometimes I felt like I was losing my mind. (*Calls into other room*) Ida B., come in here, child.

WELLS TWO/IDA B.: Here I am, mama.

WELLS ONE: Say Mr. Dunbar's poem for me. The one about the mask.

WELLS TWO/IDA B.: We wear the mask that grins and lies / It hides our cheek and shades our eyes / This debt we pay to human guile / with torn and bleeding hearts we smile / and mouth with myriad subtleties / Why should the world be overwise / In counting all our tears and sighs? / Nay, let them only see us, while / We wear the mask / We smile, but oh great Christ, our cries / To thee from tortured souls arise / We sing, but oh the clay is vile / Beneath our feet, and long the mile / But let the world dream otherwise / We wear the mask.*

WELLS ONE: Ida B., you're beginning to sound more and more like Miss Frances E. W. Harper. She had the same carriage about her shoulders like you had just now.

WELLS TWO/IDA B.: Thank you mama, you always say that.

WELLS ONE: It's the truth . . . shh shhh. Listen. Sh shh. You hear the drum, Ida B.?

---

* Paul Laurence Dunbar's poem "We Wear the Mask."

WELLS TWO/IDA B.: No, mama, I don't hear it . . . Wait a minute, I think I hear . . .

WELLS ONE: It's alright, child, you don't have to hear the drum. Whenever I hear Mr. Dunbar's words, I get so shook up. Now where was I . . . Oh yea, at the beginning of this century, I started working closely with other Negro leaders. Our goal was full equality for the Negro. We no longer had Mr. Douglass, he was dead. He led us as far as he could in the 19th century.

WELLS TWO: Mr. Booker T. Washington set us on the wrong course with his industrial education.

WELLS ONE: Mr. Du Bois realized early on that color would be our major problem in this century.

WELLS TWO: Miss Mary McLeod Bethune travels across the South setting up schools and talking about higher education for Negroes.

WELLS ONE: Mary Church Terrell got to be the best educated woman among us. But she let selfish ambition kill her influence.

WELLS TWO/TERRELL: Ida, I hope you're not considering running for the Presidency.

WELLS ONE: I hadn't thought about it, but why shouldn't I run, Molly?

WELLS TWO/TERRELL: I'm going to run again. And I don't want a fight on the floor between us.

WELLS ONE: You listen here, Molly Terrell, you can't run again. The club's by-laws makes you ineligible to serve a third term.

WELLS TWO/TERRELL: What if one of the women move to suspend the by-laws?

WELLS ONE: Why don't you give some of the other women a turn?

WELLS TWO/TERRELL: But who—who among us is better qualified to be President than me?

WELLS ONE: Pretty soon, Molly, the women'll find out about you. Then you won't be able to get elected dog-catcher. All of your money won't be able to help you then.

WELLS TWO/TERRELL: Why, Ida, I never thought I would live to see the day that you talked to me like this. We've known each other since we were children. I never thought I'd see this day.

WELLS ONE: (*following Wells Two/Terrell she shouts after her*) I'm concerned about the Race, Molly, not myself. (*slowly calms herself*) In 1910, I started the Negro Fellowship League. The league was a social service organization for Negroes. I hoped that it would turn out as good as Hull House.

WELLS TWO: The Negro vote is crucial to our survival.

WELLS ONE: In 1914, I started the Alpha Suffrage Club, so that I could mobilize Negro women of Illinois to work for voter registration.

WELLS TWO: I'm wearing so many hats.

WELLS ONE: I still believe that America intends to correct the wrongs against us.

WELLS TWO: I feel like I want to go way back and sit down.

WELLS ONE: My people, Lord, we're so divided.

WELLS TWO: I feel like I want to go way back and sit down.

WELLS ONE: Somebody got to come forward to take up my crusade.

WELLS TWO: I feel like I want to go way back and sit down.

WELLS ONE: I can't go back and sit down—because our lives would never change.

WELLS TWO: I'm a radical.

WELLS ONE: White America must put aside the notion that Negroes are irresponsible. The South must stop telling their threadbare lies. The federal government must assure us of equal rights. Most of all, for us Negroes, we must protect our lives, spend our money where it's appreciated—and stand one with the other.

WELLS TWO: I will leave a record of my resistance.

WELLS ONE: I must inspire future generations.

WELLS TWO: I will state my position.

WELLS ONE: That drum . . . I hear it all the time. Seems like nobody else hears it. Lord, I hope I'm not losing my mind . . .

WELLS TWO: I hear it, Ida B. . . . .

WELLS ONE: You hear the drum???

WELLS TWO: I sure do. Somebody's doing some kinda drumming . . .

WELLS ONE: Well, I declare—you hear the drum. Don't ever give up. Thank you, my dear, thank you.

THE END

Sandra Seaton
(1942–)

S andra Seaton's first play, *The Bridge Party*, was inspired by stories family members told her while she was growing up in the South. The lynching and the subsequent house-to-house search of the African American community that in *The Bridge Party* occur in the fictional Delphi, Tennessee are based on actual events. Seaton emphasizes, however, that the play is not a "docudrama" but rather a presentation of a part of the African American experience that has been often overlooked, the way of life of middle-class blacks in the South before the modern civil rights era. Seaton says that on one level the play is a response to the presentation, in contemporary films and television, of black women as either sex objects or earth mothers. In a 1993 interview, Seaton states:

> I'm frustrated by the one-dimensional portrayal of black people by the media today. Over and over again black people are seen only in relation to whites, as though the whole identity of individual African Americans can be reduced to their reactions to racism. White people can be presented as complex human beings with unique personal identities, but all too often, sometimes with the best of intentions, black people are portrayed as though they had no private lives, no past, no inner depth—rootless in the strongest sense, not geographically but spiritually.[1]

The Bridge Party takes place in the home of Emma Edwards in the summer of 1942, during the weekly bridge party organized by the "Bridgettes," a black women's club. The Edwards men are absent, either in the army or at work. Seaton reveals she wrote the play as "an act of faith and an experiment. I was unsure whether other people would be interested in a play that deals with a lynching through the prism of a group of middle-class African American women playing bridge."[2] While the women play cards, another "bridge party"— the lynching of a black youth on a nearby bridge—is taking place. Fearing the reaction of the black community to the lynching, hastily deputized whites search for guns in the houses of the black community, including the Edwards house. The play dramatizes the ways in which the black women respond to the crisis in the absence of their menfolk and continues a rich tradition of plays by African American women that deal with lynching.

The Bridge Party parallels the work of many early black women writers in its domestic setting and also in the absence of the men of the household. The only men in the play are two white deputies whom Emma and the other women must confront. The presence of the men would have made for a very different dramatic logic, according to Seaton. She was determined to deal with the evils of lynching and segregation without relying on violence and melodrama. The play's evocation of the importance of religion in African American life also links it to earlier works. Although Seaton was not attempting to imitate other black women playwrights, her recognition that "the play would not be the same had the men been present" holds true for earlier plays as well.[3] It was important for her "to show these women as survivors and not victims."[4]

While acknowledging the play's parallels to works by earlier black women playwrights and its origins in family stories, Seaton notes that her dramatic style has been influenced by the poetic understatement and slow tempo of many European movies of the 1950s and 1960s. Seaton remembers how deeply she was affected by the way *The Shop on Main Street*, a Czech film about the Nazi occupation of Czechoslovakia, powerfully conveyed the impact of Nazism not by images of brutality but instead through close attention to seemingly trivial details of everyday life. Seaton states, "If the action of *The Bridge Party* moves at what might at times seem to be a snail's pace, it is because I want the audience to experience the characters as full human beings, not as abstractions or stereotypes. I believe slow pacing allows for a depth of impact more meaningful than the most impressive stunts or special effects can achieve."[5] American films and television, she argues, often glamorize the very evils they purport to condemn. It is rare, she points out, for African American life to be presented without a focus on violence and/or sensationalized sexuality.

Seaton began writing the first version of *The Bridge Party* in a playwriting class taught by Webster Smalley at the University of Illinois (Urbana) in the 1960s and took up the project again in 1988 as a graduate student with Robert A. Martin of Michigan State University. *The Bridge Party* has been given staged readings at Columbia College in Chicago (March 23, 1990, directed by Paul Carter Harrison) and at the Complex Theater in Hollywood (May 11, 1993, directed by Adilah Barnes). The play was a winner of the Theodore Ward Playwriting Prize for New Works by African American Playwrights awarded by Columbia College. Pulitzer Prize–winning composer William Bolcon has supplied music for stage productions of *The Bridge Party*.

Sandra Cecelia Browne Seaton was born on July 10, 1942 in Columbia, Tennessee to Albert Browne and Hattye Evans, both teachers. While her mother was away at school, Seaton delighted in listening to her grandmother's stories of the old days, always told with great flair. Although a career as an entertainer was considered disreputable by many blacks of her era, Seaton's grandmother, Emma Louish Evans, often performed as an endman in local amateur minstrel shows, and even as an elderly woman she was more than willing to demonstrate her routines. Her stories remain an important influence on Seaton's writing. Grandma Emma also instilled in her granddaughter great pride in the work of their relative Flournoy Miller, who wrote the book and starred in *Shuffle Along*, a musical that preceded *Show Boat* in integrating songs and story into an artistic whole, and, according to Arna Bontemps, inaugurated the Harlem Renaissance.

Seaton is presently working on a number of projects that, like *The Bridge Party*, explore and celebrate the experience of African Americans before the modern civil rights era. These include a play, *The Will*, and a scholarly edition of the writings of J. H. Kelly, an African American educator. Her work has appeared in journals such as *Shooting Star, Obsidian II: Black Literature in Review*, and *Midwest Miscellany*. Presently an Associate Professor of English at Central Michigan University, she is married to James Seaton and is the mother of four children. Sandra Seaton resides in East Lansing, Michigan.

NOTES

1. Interview with Sandra Seaton by Kathy Perkins, Lansing, Michigan, April 14, 1993.
2. Sandra Seaton, "How I Came to Write *The Bridge Party*." Presented at the Association for Theatre in Higher Education (ATHE) Conference, New York City, August 7, 1996.
3. Seaton interview.
4. Seaton interview.
5. Seaton, "How I Came to Write *The Bridge Party*."

The Bridge Party

1989

❁

Sandra Seaton

CHARACTERS

EMMA EDWARDS, *59, mother of Leona, Marietta, and Theodora*
LEONA EDWARDS BARNES, *29*
MARIETTA EDWARDS, *27*
THEODORA EDWARDS NICHOLSON, *22*
MARY JANE BARNES, *58, Leona's mother-in-law*
PETT MAE, *39, guest*
RUTH, *34, guest*
EVA ZOE, *23, guest*
SAMUELLA, *39, guest*
TOWNSEND, *58, temporary sheriff's deputy*
FRANK BYRD, *24, temporary sheriff's deputy*

The play attempts to recreate the speech and atmosphere of southern black middle-class life in the 1940s. Today the language might seem mannered and slightly artificial. The pace is slow, creating an effect of formality.

Setting: *The sitting room of the Edwards home on East End Street in Delphi, a small town in middle Tennessee. The house, built by the parents of Emma Webster Edwards before the Civil War, sits at the top of East Hill on a large plot of land. It is a typical middle-class Southern black home of the time: immaculate, well-maintained, with handed-down furnishings and mementos. The room expresses a sensibility influenced by both Southern gentility and an African sense of design. This African American eclecticism reveals a special flair, an artistic touch that resists definition. Although there is no hint of garishness, the crowded quality of the sitting room suggests that interior decoration has relieved a pent-up need for self-expression when few other avenues were possible.*

As the play opens, we see a suite of Victorian furniture—a settee trimmed with delicately carved mahogany and two matching chairs, all of well-worn, faded bottle-green velvet. The high ceilings in the sitting room serve to offset the large scale of the pieces. A low marble table in front of the settee holds a Bible, a Tennessee A&I yearbook, and two small fans. On either side of the table, the two matching chairs face each other. To the left of the settee is a tile fireplace—white with tiny green flecks—handmade by the father, Will. Family photographs, ornately framed, an occasional tintype, and a small mirror have been grouped on the wall over the fireplace. On our right, two straight-back oak chairs with padded leather seats stand behind the settee, next to a tall curtained window that looks onto the front porch. Across the room to our left, another window, identical in height, stands next to a bookcase. A doorway to the left of the fireplace leads to a bedroom. Next to the bedroom door is an entrance leading to a long hallway and the kitchen. Off to the right side of the living room stands a player piano stacked high with boxes of piano rolls. A doorway to the right of the piano leads to the front door. A phone without a dial rests on a small wall shelf near the piano. Paul Laurence Dunbar's Lyrics of Lowly Life has been tucked away in an opening under the shelf. A walnut victrola sits on a table covered with a fringed commemorative armed forces scarf of deep blue satin; beside the victrola is a stack of records. The usual crocheted doilies are absent, but two large velvet tapestry pillows on a window seat, behind and to the left of the settee, are perfectly arranged and unsoiled. Next to the window stands a barrister's bookcase filled with newspapers and books, among them copies of the Nashville Globe, college texts, old A&I yearbooks, American Negro Songs by J. W. Work, The Complete Poems of Paul Laurence Dunbar, James Weldon Johnson's God's Trombones, and a pocket Longfellow.

Three tables are set up in the living room for the weekly meeting of "the Saturday Afternoon Bridgettes." Because of the segregation laws enforced in public places, African Americans have developed their own social system, in which clubs like the Bridgettes play an important role. Most of the women in the club are school teachers. One, Pett Mae, is the wife of a prominent black doctor. Two others, Ruth and Agnes, are morticians who have continued the family business after the death of their husbands. Leona, Theodora, and four guests, all club members, are playing three-handed bridge. The Edwards sisters are the hosts; the guests are Pett Mae, Eva Zoe, Samuella, and Ruth. Two tables positioned in the foreground are in use. Theodora, Eva Zoe, and Samuella are seated at the table on our right. Leona, Pett Mae, and Ruth are seated at the table on the left. Players at one table respond, sometimes with quiet laughter, to the conversation at another table. The third table is set off a little from the others and is empty.

Time: 1942—A Saturday afternoon in July. A number of local men are away in the armed services. Will and Emma Edwards's two sons, Morris and Leon, are serving in the Army Air Corps. Randolph Nicholson, Theodora's husband, is at an Army base in California.

ACT ONE

(LEONA, *who appears to be uncomfortable, is arching her back away from the spine of the chair. Her hair is freshly done in croquignole curls, a style popular with black women of her generation. She wears a print crepe dress, muted in color with lace at the bodice, one she would never wear when she is teaching at Macedonia Hill School. A pretty young woman with light brown skin, she is the only one of the sisters who has to straighten her hair. Although she is in the eighth month of pregnancy, she wears her usual clothes, with only the slightest adjustment; few would suspect she is about to have a child. Lately she has been high-strung and occasionally quick-tempered, in contrast to the relaxed manner of other women at club meetings. Since childhood her comments have more often reflected what one should say rather than what she really feels. In her mind the line between her own feelings and the feelings of others has become so blurred that she has little awareness of any conflict; a sense of unexplained tension is evidence that the line remains. Her only jewelry, a diamond ring on a gold chain, hangs around her neck. A paper fan of the sort passed out by funeral homes is beside her.*)

LEONA: Pett Mae, where's Marietta and those sandwiches? I told her . . . (*she stops to catch her breath, looks at the door*) shrimp salad sandwiches and spiced tea. Shrimp salad and tea. (*She plays out the words with her hands, then pushes a curl off her forehead.*)

(PETT MAE, *a large woman with very light skin and short, bobbed hair, is the wife of the more prominent of the two local black doctors and a teacher at the black elementary school. Stately rather than blatantly sensual, she could not be described as either an "earth mother" or a "big fine mama." She laughs to herself often and hums constantly as she plays cards. Pett Mae has a high lilting voice; she likes to trill her words. Occasionally, she gestures with a white linen handkerchief. As she listens to Leona, she fumbles with the cards, organizing them in her hand.*)

PETT MAE: Be sweet now, Leona. You look real cool and pretty. Real sweet. Anybody'd think you carried on this way all the time.

(RUTH, *who is seated on the right side of Leona, places her hand firmly under Leona's arm. A mortician who has continued the family business after the death of her husband, Ruth still retains all the vitality and freshness of a new bride. She can be playful one moment, serious and plain-spoken the next. Ruth is tall and sturdily built, with deep brown skin, even and rich in color, and startlingly white teeth. Since an illness in her early twenties, she sits with one leg pulled up and walks with a limp, which at times becomes a dance. She is dressed in a white tea length gown with long full sleeves, single-pleated from shoulder to the wrist on both sides; the skirt drapes to allow her to sit gracefully.*)

RUTH: Now Pett, she can't help it.
PETT MAE: (*after thought*) Just be sweet, real sweet.

(EVA ZOE, *who is seated with Theodora and Samuella at the opposite table, calls out to Leona. Eva Zoe, also a teacher, was Theodora's college roommate at Tennessee*

A&I. She wears a dress of vermillion red, small pearl earrings, and thin gold bracelets that slide back and forth when she moves. A raffia purse, tightly woven with strips of bright cotton, is beside her at the table. Unlike the other women, Eva Zoe wears rouge, but not so much as to appear excessive. A three-cornered, veiled Mr. John hat is perched at an angle to one side of her full bangs.)

EVA ZOE: Listen to Pett, Leona.

RUTH: Right now she just can't.

LEONA: You know those little tea sandwiches . . . you take a sharp knife right across the edge, takes the crust right off. You hold them like little diamonds, then you cut them down the middle into teeniny diamonds. (*She gently twines the gold chain at her neck.*)

(THEODORA, *after trying without success to concentrate on the bridge game, examines her cards again, then, like a teacher starting the first morning class, raps them against her open hand. Tall, statuesque, light-skinned, with long slender limbs, she has the looks of a movie star of the forties. All the sisters are considered attractive, but Theodora is thought to be the most beautiful. Although she tries hard to give an image of coolness and restraint, she is nervous and jittery underneath. Theodora has a new teacher's energy and a new wife's dreams about a future after the war when everything will go according to plan.*)

THEODORA: Two tables of three-handed bridge. (*pause*) When's the rest of the bunch gonna get here?

LEONA: You hold them like little diamonds, then you cut them down the middle. (*She continues to finger the gold chain at her neck.*)

THEODORA: Leona— (*fidgeting with her hand, slightly exasperated*) Marietta's been making shrimp salad sandwiches for years. (*looks over at the empty table*) Somebody, hurry up. Bid so I can get up and help serve.

RUTH: Whoa now, Theodora. You're just like one of those thoroughbred race horses. I swear you Edwards all race around. (*pause*) Cleanest house I've ever seen. You all must sweep and clean all day.

PETT MAE: Oh my! Will you look at this hand? (*rearranges cards, shakes her head*)

LEONA: Theodora's been up since five this morning sweeping and washing.

RUTH: That Theodora. She's a fast one.

THEODORA: (*feels forehead, as if trying to hold back some mounting pain*) Getting ready for my trip.

LEONA: Theodora gets up sweepin'. I used to sweep all the time myself . . . couldn't stand to see anything on the floor.

PETT MAE: Slam! (*proudly spreads hand on the table*) We don't need to play this one out, ladies. (*tickled*) All that carryin' on. (*Pett Mae laughs to herself. Theodora, disgusted, picks up cards and shuffles the deck.*) Spades—ace, king, queen . . .

LEONA: If Marietta doesn't hurry up, I'll start sweeping myself. (*sighs and reaches for the paper fan*)

EVA ZOE: (*leaning over from the second table*) That's a pretty dress, Leona.

LEONA: (*ignores Eva Zoe*) I used to sweep all the time . . . just don't feel like it lately.

EVA ZOE: Your dress, Leona, it sure is nice.

LEONA: (*turns sharply to Eva Zoe*) Willie C. gave it to me. (*loudly, quickly*) Said they wouldn't let her wear it to teach. Said they wouldn't let me teach in it either. She told me to keep it, wear it to club meeting. Before Willie C. went out West, remember, Eva Zoe, how she used to sit at that piano over there, beaux crowded all around? Willie C. always did have beautiful clothes.

EVA ZOE: Well, it sure looks pretty on you.

LEONA: (*looks down, smiles faintly and tries to place the chain properly at her bodice*) Pretty or not, Professor Samson Barnes don't 'low no dresses with lace at his school.

RUTH: (*to the air*) Yes, Professor Barnes.

PETT MAE: Well, we're bidding this afternoon, ladies, not teaching. Better leave the professor out of the game. (*The women laugh.*)

LEONA: Leave him out? If he saw me teaching in this, lace all around the neck— he'd leave school, march right home and tell it: "Mary Jane, oh, Mary Jane." It's a good thing my mother-in-law can't see me. She'd be carryin' on right now. (*pulls at her necklace*)

PETT MAE: Little bird . . .

LEONA: I tell you, it's a good thing.

PETT MAE: Little bird, you married Samson and Mary Jane's son . . .

LEONA: Married. That's right, married.

PETT MAE: (*holds Leona's hand*) You married Mary Jane's son, not the whole family.

THEODORA: Pett . . . (*fumbling with her cards too*) shoot, pass me that box of talcum powder.

RUTH: (*to Theodora*) You're as jittery as a little bug. (*begins to hum "Pony Boy" up and under*)

LEONA: (*sadly*) Randy, handsome as he is, away from home.(*Ruth continues to hum.*)

THEODORA: I'm gonna sprinkle these cards. Get 'em to shuffle a little.

PETT MAE: I bet Randy boy's late with his letter.

(SAMUELLA, *a teacher and an Oberlin graduate, is an elegant woman who seems a little more formal than the rest. She wears glasses on a chain and has a thin silver streak in her hair. Her mauve gown, with its short fitted sleeves and set of three diagonal pleats across the bodice, flatters her coloring.*)

SAMUELLA: A young husband all the way out in California.

LEONA: Theodora sweeps and sweeps.

RUTH: (*begins to sing "Pony Boy." continues to sing while the women are talking*) Pony boy, pony boy won't you be my pony boy, giddiup, giddiup, giddiup, whoa, my pony boy. (*pause*) She's a thoroughbred alright.

LEONA: You can tell when Theodora's worried.

PETT MAE: She tries to look real cool, but we all know better.

LEONA: You can tell by how hard she sweeps.

RUTH: Don't tell Theodora that.

(*Theodora sticks out her tongue at Pett Mae. Music fades out.*)

PETT MAE: I'm an old bird, can't fool me. Give Theodora— (*pause*) Miss Thoroughbred—the powder.

THEODORA: *Mrs.* Thoroughbred.

SAMUELLA: Correction noted. (*Her glasses slip and dangle on their chain.*)

PETT MAE: Mrs. Thoroughbred. (*calls out to Theodora*) Theodora, Doctor's first wife used to put powder on a handkerchief.

(*"A Tisket, A Tasket" up and under*)

RUTH: What'd she do that for?

PETT MAE: (*still trying to get Theodora's attention*) She'd put it on the handkerchief and slide it down her girdle.

THEODORA: Her girdle?

PETT MAE: That's right, Theodora.

THEODORA: I'd never wear one of those.

PETT MAE: She sure did . . . (*pauses*) in her girdle, so she wouldn't stick to herself when she played whist.

(*Theodora laughs.*)

RUTH: (*pulls at her dress, adjusts herself in her seat*) The heat'll do that.

(*All the women laugh except Leona, who twists uncomfortably. Music fades out.*)

SAMUELLA: Leona, where's that letter everyone's been going on about?

THEODORA: It wasn't a letter, Sam. (*pause*) The boys sent us that tablecover over there.

SAMUELLA: (*points to the table with the scarf*) The blue one, the one with the Army Air Corps insignia?

EVA ZOE: Look at that fringe.

SAMUELLA: I heard your papa had Morris and Leon placed in the same colored troop.

LEONA: Me and Leon, we're the look-alikes all right. Of course, Leon . . . Remember that time up town . . . Leon's so high strung.

SAMUELLA: The twins.

LEONA: Morris and Theodora too. They're twins. Seems like half the town, everybody we know's going to war. Theodora, when you go out there with Randy, you think you'll see Morris and Leon?

THEODORA: I've got the worst headache.

SAMUELLA: (*covers her mouth with her hand and straightens up.*) Lord knows, Leona, if you don't stop all this carrying on . . . Pett—how did Doctor put it . . . about nerves in the summertime?

EVA ZOE: Miss Samuella, so proper, you know it's more than that.

PETT MAE: Cool down now, ladies. Remember, you don't have to bid if you don't have anything.

LEONA: Marietta! Oh, Marietta . . .

EVA ZOE: I bet she's out there singing to the radio.

PETT MAE: Warblin' like a bird.

(*Eva Zoe hums a country tune.*)

LEONA: Singing to the radio? I don't know why. The opera won't start till nightfall. Marietta! She sure does love that Grand Ole Opry.

EVA ZOE: (*continues to hum*) Singin' along with Mr. Deford Bailey.

THEODORA: Eva Zoe—bid!

PETT MAE: Ladies, ladies. Tend to your hands. (*in a lilting voice*) Too early for the Opry.

LEONA: Well, I wish Marietta would come on. (*fans herself, looks at her watch*) You know I have to keep her straight. The last time she made those little sandwiches she used tongue.

PETT MAE: (*titters to herself*) Oh ho.

SAMUELLA: Used to be that's all people fixed.

LEONA: Chopped it so fine you couldn't tell. (*straightens necklace again*)

THEODORA: You didn't know the difference, Leona.

LEONA: That's not the point.

RUTH: Marietta can fix anything. Bet she coulda used my old shoe.

THEODORA: And Leona can eat anything.

LEONA: Should've been shamed of herself, said "Oh you're gonna love this, Leona. It'll melt in your mouth."

RUTH: I bet it tasted like your Papa's catfish.

LEONA: Well, if that's the kind of fish he catches, Papa can keep it.

THEODORA: Leona, shh! (*looks around*) Papa's gone to Nashville, taking President Hale and the doctors from Meharry fishing, (*exaggerated manner*) just to help put food on the table.

LEONA: Well, he can. Ate that stuff Marietta fixed like a little baby eating pablum . . . every bit. Then she tips in and says "Oh, by the way, Leona, it's tongue." (*draws her shoulders in and shivers*) I could have died. (*Theodora and Ruth laugh.*) Papa spoils us, brings us whatever we want. No man will ever be like him.

THEODORA: I'll miss him when I leave.

LEONA: Don't say that, Theodora. (*pauses*) Not now.

RUTH: You all are grown. Not many can outdo the Edwards . . . Theodora and Leona teaching. Marietta and Emma working too.

PETT MAE: All living under the same roof. (*eyes Theodora cautiously*) That's a fortune.

EVA ZOE: No wonder Leona bought that beaver coat last Christmas.

LEONA: Eva Zoe, you bought one too . . . all the gang did, just like follow the leader. (*pauses*) Theodora . . . you looked like a starlet in yours.

EVA ZOE: Like one of those Dandridge sisters. What's her name?

RUTH: Just like I said, Leona, we're grown women, taking care of ourselves.

LEONA: (*stops suddenly. Startled expression, as if she is thinking of the idea for the first time*) I'm on my own. (*Women all stop talking. Total silence*)

PETT MAE: You'll get by, little bird.

LEONA: Not when it's like this . . . it's hard . . . (*looks at empty table*) Poor Agnes, she's by herself too. . . . Ever since Bailey passed . . . I guess that's why she's not here.

PETT MAE: Doctor did all he could.

RUTH: Don't tell a soul—I paid for Bailey's suit myself.

PETT MAE: (*visibly upset, glances at Ruth*) Ruth had it hard.

RUTH: Now, Pett . . .

PETT MAE: Didn't have Jim around to help with the bodies.

RUTH: When the call comes I go out, middle of the night, doesn't matter. I go right over to the family. This leg of mine aches so . . . sometimes I take a cane. Last Friday, I went from home to home. They're always waiting, with a cup of coffee, to sit, talk things over.

LEONA: I know you had to work hard on the body, Ruth. You and Jim . . .

PETT MAE: Jim's gone, Leona.

LEONA: (*not listening to Pett, turns to Ruth*) Now your husband's gone. Randy in the army out in California. Morris and Leon overseas. You have to do all the business yourself . . . take care of it, call on the families . . .

THEODORA: Ruth always did dress the bodies, Leona.

(*The women are unselfconsciously keeping alive bits of the culture of their old world.*)

PETT MAE: And washed and pressed the hair. She styles it the same way they always wore it, even picks their favorite color (*pause*) makeup and all.

SAMUELLA: I can still picture my mother's gown.

LEONA: You all, you all, remember last New Year's Day, how it snowed and snowed and snowed and all you all came by in Doctor's brand-new Buick? Poor Pett, got stuck in that little bitty curve out front, had to turn around, couldn't even come in the house. Well, that very morning, an undertaker came all the way from Spring Hill, right here to East End Street, just to court Theodora.

SAMUELLA: Spring Hill? Callie Morton's grandson—Mrs. A. J. Morton and Sons Funeral Home? Theodora never told me that.

PETT MAE: An undertaker's high up—can't go much higher.

EVA ZOE: Except for doctors and preachers. If my child married one . . .

RUTH: (*soothingly to Leona*) We didn't have much time together . . . not like some folks. After I married Jim his mother took me aside . . . like so. (*gestures with one hand*) "Girl"—she always called me "Ruth girl"—"close your eyes and picture it . . . Jim . . . white gloves, fine linen suit, a gold watch chain spilling out. You'll belong to the town. Like one of the family. When the call comes, you'll go to the sick bed, hold a hand. At the church you'll lead the way. The Lord's own shepherd . . . standing by the aisle, ushering the kinfolk to their seats. The smell of fresh gardenias, so many you can't count them all. Back from the cemetery you'll be served with the family, chicken, baked ham. Press your hair on Saturday morning, tie it up and sweat all day over a hot stove—never! (*pause*) Not as long as you live."

LEONA: You didn't have much time together . . .

RUTH: Not like some . . .

LEONA: Jim's gone. V. K., Mary's husband, he's gone too. Two funeral parlors in town and both run by women—And me and Calvin . . . (*throws down her hand*) married a year and already separated.

(*Samuella shakes her head, as if embarrassed by Leona's directness.*)

PETT MAE: (*feels the cards lovingly*) These cards are playing real nice, Leona. You better pick up your hand so we can whip these . . . (*touches her mouth coquettishly with a lace handkerchief*) 'n's (*mumbles something under her breath and leans back tittering*)

RUTH: (*looking at Leona*) She'll be all right. She tires out these days.

PETT MAE: Just stay real cool and pretty. (*touches her face*) In the pink. (*winks*)

(*The women laugh, even Leona.*)

RUTH: That gold necklace sure looks lovely with your dress, Leona.

(*Leona pulls the necklace out of her dress and holds the small diamond ring attached to its chain in the palm of her hand. Meanwhile,* MARIETTA *enters from the kitchen carrying a tray of beverages. Ruth and Pett Mae examine the ring as Marietta approaches the table. Soft-spoken and gentle, she wears a plain, crisply starched shirtwaist dress of faded spring colors, flat sandals with stockings, and a full white apron with pockets across the front. The darkest of all the four sisters, she has deep brown skin, fine features, straight black hair from her mother's Indian heritage, and dimples—not as deep as Theodora's. Marietta is profoundly religious, but she does not expect others to share her beliefs or follow her example. Her faith in God underlies both a sweet, girlish quality and a firm matter-of-factness about everyday life. Interested in everything but reluctant to judge others, she rarely argues or keeps up a discussion any longer than necessary.*)

LEONA: (*thoughtful*) Lovely.

RUTH: And that's not all . . . land sakes, look at that ring.

PETT MAE: That's a big one, all right.

RUTH: I'll say.

LEONA: It shines just like a star, an evening star, even in the daytime.

PETT MAE: If push comes to shove, you can pawn it.

(*Marietta carries a tray with sandwiches and a pitcher of spiced tea. Leona fidgets in her seat. The other women set their hands aside and wait patiently. An aroma of oranges and cinnamon fills the air.*)

SAMUELLA: (*stops short, grabs glasses and holds them in the air. Sniffs aroma*) Oranges and cinnamon!

PETT MAE: (*gestures to Marietta, then speaks happily, melodiously*) Here she is, just as sweet as she can be. Our own Sunday School superintendent.

RUTH: Miss Saint Paul AME.

EVA ZOE: When you gonna learn how to play bridge, Marietta?

MARIETTA: I learned all I'm gonna learn, thank you. (*Marietta's speech is old-fashioned and reminiscent of her mother's. She is a bridge between Emma and the other daughters.*)

THEODORA: Bridge doesn't agree with Marietta's religion.

LEONA: Takes after Grandma . . . When Grandma was alive, we used to have to lock ourselves in our room just to play cards.

THEODORA: We cut our teeth on cards.

LEONA: Remember the first time Willie C. came home from A&I? We used to hide in her room so she could teach us bridge.

PETT MAE: Marietta thinks church-going folks shouldn't play cards.

MARIETTA: I said no such thing. Suit yourself. Do what you want. (*laughs*) Makes me no never mind.

EVA ZOE: There's not a woman in this room that plays cards on Sunday. (*All the women nod.*)

PETT MAE: Sometimes me and Leona, Doctor and Doctor's new helper, Tommy, play cards till midnight on Saturday, then we lay our hands down.

SAMUELLA: Many a slam was ruined by the strike of the clock.

(*Women agree in unison, nodding heads.*)

RUTH: Marietta just has those ways. She promised the Lord she wouldn't play cards.

LEONA: Finger sandwiches! (*pause*) Marietta—little olives on the side, Oriental pickles, (*pause*) and chicken bouillon.

PETT MAE: Be sure and save a little room for Miss Estelle's cake now, Leona.

LEONA: It's so hot. (*to Marietta*) Just stir the tea and pour it on the ice. That's all I need. Please hurry, Marietta. (*fans herself*)

MARIETTA: As many folks as I've cooked for, I guess I know how to make iced tea.

(*A car can be heard passing by.*)

LEONA: All that noise.

(*Cars go by again.*)

THEODORA: That has to be the boys on their way back from Nashville.

LEONA: (*deep in thought, only half-hearing the conversation*) I heard Cordie Cheek was coming back today. If he is . . . I heard his trial was over. (*nervously glances at door*)

MARIETTA: Didn't have a trial. Grand jury up at Nashville—all white, every last one of them—they let Cordie Cheek go.

PETT MAE: A colored child.

RUTH: Saved.

SAMUELLA: Case dismissed for lack of evidence. (*removes glasses*) Deliberated and refused to indict.

MARIETTA: They'll be whoopin' and hollerin' when Cordie Cheek gets to town. Mr. Saul Blanton'll be doin' plenty of business . . . sellin' plenty of liquor tonight.

PETT MAE: Not just to his own bunch, either.

MARIETTA: (*pours more tea for Leona*) When the law comes back, they'll want what he's sellin'. Come morning, Mr. Saul Blanton'll know all *their* business.

(*Cars go by.*)

RUTH: Every Jim and Mandy, they'll be headin' up to ol' King Saul's, fiddlin' till the sun comes up.

EVA ZOE: Colored and white.

MARIETTA: White folks go to a colored bootlegger, they leave their money and a whole lot more. A bootlegger, he stays real quiet. Sits up all hours of the night. Hardly rests at all. Anytime folks need a loan, somebody to go outa town, you better find him. He'll make the folks up to the courthouse understand what you need, the only way they know to, with the dollar. You in trouble, you best to ask Mr. Saul.

LEONA: (*startled, as if hearing the conversation for the first time*) Marietta, what about the Lord?

(*Samuella leans forward in her seat.*)

MARIETTA: The Lord helps those who help themselves.

LEONA: Marietta . . .

MARIETTA: Oh, hush and drink your tea.

LEONA: I can't.

MARIETTA: Oh, go on, gal.

LEONA: I can't. I can't just sit here. I won't be still till that boy Cordie Cheek comes back to town. (*fans herself*)

THEODORA: I bet it's the Alphas. (*flustered*) Randy's an Alpha.

MARIETTA: Didn't say a thing about no Alphas.

(*More cars go by.*)

RUTH: I didn't know the Alphas made all that commotion.

PETT MAE: Ask the fraternity sweetheart.

EVA ZOE: Little Miss Ivy.

THEODORA: It's after the game. (*pause*) You know how everybody gets . . . (*pauses*) after the game.

LEONA: If Cordie Cheek comes back today all the folks'll be out to see him. (*pause*) All of Macedonia School.

(*The screen door starts to open slightly. The women look up.*)

THEODORA: Maybe that's the rest of the bunch. (*looks at back table*) The game's over by now. If Punk and Mrs. Hawthorne get back from Nashville in time, we can still get the prize for attendance.

(*Marietta sets the empty tray next to Leona and walks past the piano to the front door to investigate.* MARY JANE BARNES, *Leona's mother-in-law, enters. Consciously old-fashioned, she wears a plain dress, drab purple in color, with a high collar and tiny buttons up to her neck—a style she considers appropriate for the wife of the principal of Macedonia Hill School. She does not conceal her hostility to the group. When Mary Jane glares disapprovingly at Leona, Leona begins to fan herself more rapidly. The women at the tables look at Mary Jane, then Leona. Mary Jane doesn't speak.*)

MARIETTA: Make yourself comfortable, Miss Mary Jane. Rest a spell. How you and Professor Barnes gettin' along? (*Mary Jane doesn't answer. She was angry when she arrived, but now her anger is increased by the sight of the women playing cards.*) Every Saturday afternoon, you know, the "Bridgettes," they meet at a different house, every Saturday. (*Mary Jane shakes her head in disbelief. Marietta points to the empty table.*) Didn't get the crowd we usually do. (*turns to the first table. gestures to Pett and Ruth proudly. They nod as each of their names is called.*) You know Pett Mae, your doctor's wife, and Ruth, Jim passed away. She's the mortician now herself. They're sittin' at the front table.

MARY JANE: (*waves them away*) Hush up! Been knowin' that one since I taught her in first grade. (*points to Eva Zoe*) And that one and that one over there. Every last one of you.

EVA ZOE: (*stands up*) Miss Mary Jane, I just love your dress. (*sits down slowly*) Never will be a teacher like Miss Mary Jane.

(*Leona arches her back and pulls away from the chair. She clutches her necklace tightly. The women arrange their hands. Mary Jane stands for a minute, then moves toward the straight-backed oak chair off to the corner.*)

MARIETTA: Mama'll be home t'rectly, Miss Mary Jane.

(*Mary Jane sits down in the chair. Leona stares intently at Theodora until Theodora becomes uncomfortable. Theodora gets up, goes to victrola and picks a record from a stack. She plays "Take the A-Train" by the Duke Ellington Orchestra.*)

SAMUELLA: Theodora would come up with that one. (*pause*) The theme for the club dance.

EVA ZOE: Remember our last formal . . .

SAMUELLA: Presenting the "Bridgettes" of Delphi, Tennessee . . .

EVA ZOE: We were dressed to kill.

(*The women applaud and laugh. Mary Jane watches them closely, twisting nervously in her seat. She picks up a book and raps it on the side of her chair.*)

MARY JANE: Eva Zoe, wipe that red mess off your face. You can see it all the way through the window.

(*Eva Zoe reaches for her purse, pulls out a compact, and checks her makeup.*)

PETT MAE: Better have something cool, Mary Jane. Doctor wouldn't want you all hot and . . . (*gestures in the air with her hands*)

(*Mary Jane looks over at the tables. Frustrated because she feels she is being overlooked, Mary Jane tries to control her anger. The other women cast furtive glances at her and then look away.*)

PETT MAE: Theodora always did pick the latest.

RUTH: She's a thoroughbred all right. (*gestures to Theodora, hums and snaps her fingers*) "Take the A-Train" . . . that's Ellington's song.

EVA ZOE: Leona can sing it for our summer dance . . . for the Bridgettes.

SAMUELLA: Takes after Mother Emma, the finest songstress in middle Tennessee.

(*Mary Jane looks on disapprovingly.*)

RUTH: Go on over to the piano, Pett. Leona, you sing.

PETT MAE: That's a hard one . . . how does that go? (*Pett Mae hums to herself, but remains in her seat, arranging her bridge hand.*)

RUTH: Oh, Leona can sing anything.

EVA ZOE: And eat anything too.

(*All the women laugh except for Leona and Mary Jane.*)

PETT MAE: Remember when Leona sang at the club dance? She was wearing that blue crepe dress, the one with the gold hobnails across the front . . . so cool looking.

(*Women all rush to speak.*)

EVA ZOE: Like a dream.

RUTH: Hello, Nashville.

SAMUELLA: Our regional meeting.

RUTH: President P. M. Crosley-Gaines behind the motor, pullin' up in Doctor's big Buick.

(*Fadeout "A-Train." "A Tisket, A Tasket" up and under*)

SAMUELLA: The majordomo of the clan.

RUTH: All of you, the whole gang piled in. Leona, me and Miss—Mrs. Jitterbug up front, Eva Zoe, Sam, Punk.

EVA ZOE: We were doin' some scootin', weren't we, Pett?

PETT MAE: Old Harry Gorman, Doctor's best patient . . . went all the way to New York for those dresses . . . I woke him up bright and early that Saturday morning.

THEODORA: Before the rooster crowed.

PETT MAE: (*pretends to hold phone to ear*) "Rise on up. Open that store so we can pick up that girl's dress on the way to Nashville."

EVA ZOE: It sure did fit her nice.

LEONA: Nice is right. I bet you I couldn't teach in it. What you wanna bet?

THEODORA: Leona . . .

(*Music stops. Mary Jane turns sharply and looks at Leona, then turns away, wringing her hands nervously.*)

MARIETTA: (*looks over at Mary Jane*) Rheumatism flaring up, Miss Mary Jane?

(*Marietta leaves room and enters again with glasses of iced tea. Theodora rises and helps serve the tea. The other women murmur approval as they drink.*)

PETT MAE: (*motions to Theodora to give a glass to Mary Jane*) Doctor's orders, Mary Jane.

LEONA: (*waves hands in the air, stiffly*) This tea sure does cool me off. Keeps my hair from going back. (*glances worriedly at Mary Jane*) Always did wish I had your hair, Theodora.

(*Theodora smiles. Leona mouths words silently and fumbles with her necklace. The necklace with its ring comes loose and falls to the floor. Mary Jane stands up and tries to see what's going on. Marietta serves tea to the second table, then sets a tray with four glasses at the empty table.*)

MARIETTA: (*walks to the front, picks up the necklace. She speaks loudly, as if to distract attention from her actions.*) Mama always said you were marked.

THEODORA: Who was marked?

MARIETTA: Leona. Leona was.

THEODORA: Oh, Marietta.

MARIETTA: She was. Mama said when she was carrying Leona, she used to go across the street over where Miss Cora used to live. Went there all the time. Said Miss Cora's little girl was real dark, had real nappy hair. Mama said the little girl marked her.

LEONA: Marietta, you oughta be shot.

(*Marietta laughs.*)

EVA ZOE: Miss Mary Jane fixes hair right out of her house. She's heard of it too, haven't you, Miss Mary Jane?

(*Mary Jane strains to hear every word.*)

MARY JANE: Eva Zoe Walker, look at you—face greased, like somebody threw a bucket of paint all over you!

PETT MAE: Stay cool now, Mary Jane.

MARY JANE: (*takes a long sip of tea*) Hair all curled up, fried . . . it's bad for the nerves. (*waves her hand, as if to dismiss the question*) Women come to me, they get nothing but a warm comb.

(*Eva Zoe looks embarrassed. She hides her face with cards, then sits straight up as if in school.*)

MARIETTA: (*walks over to Leona to hand her the ring. Mary Jane gets up and follows Marietta. When Marietta turns around abruptly, Mary Jane goes back to her seat. Mary Jane watches Marietta but isn't able to see what she is handing Leona.*) Leona, when you were born, Mama said you had the nappiest hair she'd ever seen.

(*Women at both tables giggle to themselves.*)

LEONA: Everybody's heard that.

RUTH: Oh hush, Marietta.

THEODORA: Marietta always did like to tell stories.

RUTH: No tellin' what she'll come up with.

MARIETTA: I mind my own business, thank you.

THEODORA: Marietta always did tell things.

MARIETTA: *Did,* Miss Ivy.

LEONA: (*laughs in spite of herself*) Like that one about Papa stealin' a pig and hidin' it up on Professor Kelly's roof.

MARIETTA: I wadn't but twelve.

LEONA: Don't matter. You told it.

MARIETTA: Nappy or not, the professor used to chase all us home.

LEONA: Mother always did have beautiful hair. Papa has that (*waves her hand as if to smooth the air*) fine soft hair. Mother never could figure out how I got this hair.

MARIETTA: They say when you're carryin' a child and certain folks get too near you, they mark you ... (*pauses*) for life. (*raises her voice so Mary Jane will be sure to hear*) Said when she was carrying you, used to go over to Miss Cora's all the time. They say you have to be careful when you're carrying a child. Don't they, Pett?

(*When Mary Jane stands up abruptly, her glass slips from her hand and shatters on the floor. She starts to pick up the pieces, then straightens up and marches out of the room. The front door can be heard slamming. Theodora rushes to sweep up the broken glass. Eva Zoe goes over to Leona, alternately whispering and laughing nervously. The women calmly begin to play cards again. Marietta busies herself removing the dishes and straightening the room.*)

PETT MAE: That bird was movin'. (*titters*)

MARIETTA: Miss Mary Jane's one of those old-timey folks.

EVA ZOE: That's right, don't mess with Miss Mary Jane.

PETT MAE: Never saw one fly off the handle like that.

SAMUELLA: I don't think Miss Mary Jane approves of you ladies.

EVA ZOE: Speak for yourself, Sam.

PETT MAE: That bird wanted something from one of Emma Edwards' high yellow daughters.

MARIETTA: "Wanted" is right. Miss Mary Jane woulda been singin' all the way to Happy Hollow if that ring Leona dropped on the floor was in her pocketbook right now.

SAMUELLA: (*leans over to Theodora*) Mother Emma better not hear about you all running Miss Mary Jane out.

THEODORA: (*does not answer but picks up her cards and studies her hand. Mischievously, she holds her cards close to her chest, away from Samuella and Eva Zoe.*) I'm bidding two hearts. (*Restless*) Her son oughta keep her home.

LEONA: (*Refusing to comment about Mary Jane, she tries to concentrate on the game at her own table with Ruth and Pett Mae.*) Three diamonds. (*turns to Ruth*)

RUTH: (*with finality*) Pass.

(*Eva Zoe is looking into space, still thinking about Mary Jane's visit. Theodora glances at her sideways.*)

PETT MAE: Look at these cards! Come on ladies . . . the honeymoon's over. (*arranging her cards*)

RUTH: Used to be Miss Mary Jane didn't worry so much about other folks.

THEODORA: Eva Zoe!

(*Theodora nudges Eva Zoe. Eva Zoe seems to be daydreaming.*)

MARIETTA: Hasn't been the same since she left teaching, started doin' hair out of her house. (*gathers and arranges dishes on tray*)

THEODORA: Well, she didn't get what she came for. (*pause*) Eva Zoe—I said two hearts.

(*Eva Zoe laughs out loud, snaps to attention, and throws hands in air dramatically, as if to surrender.*)

RUTH: (*over shoulder to Theodora*) All right, Miss Jitterbug. Leona— (*turns to Leona*) Leona, what you gonna do?

LEONA: I already bid.

RUTH: I don't mean that.

LEONA: Everybody has to run sometimes.

MARIETTA: (*comes forward*) When I ran off with Joe Harlan I didn't have a thing in my suitcase but Grandma's old hymnal book . . . (*pauses*) and that satin nightgown from Sears, Roebuck, four sizes too big. Grandma couldn't stand Joe, so we ran off.

RUTH: The superintendent of the Sunday School.

LEONA: (*responds enthusiastically, eager to avoid Ruth's question. Looks in her hand and looks up*) I still can't imagine Marietta running off with anybody.

SAMUELLA: Running off. I wouldn't say that . . . no, I wouldn't say that. Eloping, that's better.

MARIETTA: Papa told me to go to college, to A&I. I had to go off and get married. Didn't last either. (*pauses*) I've been working as a cook and a nurse ever since.

LEONA: You never look back, Marietta.

MARIETTA: Well, it's done. No use talking 'bout it now. Should of thought about it then. You make your bed hard, you lie in it. Too late now.

LEONA: Too late.

THEODORA: It's never too late for a Barnes to get her way.

MARIETTA: Go on back with him. Might as well. He makes a good living.

THEODORA: Leona could leave town—go off somewhere else.

MARIETTA: He's a teacher. You'd have whatever you wanted. Might as well stay. Some things just meant to be. Lord might want it that way.

THEODORA: But Marietta . . . (*raises voice*) What if they can't get along?

PETT MAE: Married to a big-shot Kappa. Look at that ring. (*covers mouth lightly with handkerchief*) Anything I got while I was married, I'd keep.

LEONA: (*clutching necklace*) I never said a thing about giving anything up.

THEODORA: Sometimes women just have to leave anyway. (*stares at Leona's stomach*)

MARIETTA: Used to be you couldn't teach after you got married.

SAMUELLA: Just like Mother Emma.

EVA ZOE: And Miss Mary Jane too.

LEONA: If Mary Jane comes back here again, I swear I'll . . . (*pauses*) She sure does wear me out.

THEODORA: She can't bother you as long as we're here.

SAMUELLA: Mother Emma won't let her.

LEONA: Doctor's gonna want to see me before the end of the week. The way I'm feeling, it might be time. (*guards her stomach with her hands*)

PETT MAE: (*sprinkles more powder on the cards*) You little birds have to be careful. Doctor wouldn't have it any other way.

RUTH: Right after Eugene was born they had a dance over to the Elks. Doctor told me not to go. Went out wearing a real thin chiffon dress, caught the flu. They had to put me to bed for a month. When I got out the bed, this leg here, it didn't have a bit of feeling. Just started to draw up. (*hits leg*) I been limping ever since.

PETT MAE: (*touches Leona's hand*) Always say to B. F., "Doctor, what must that one do?" He'll always say "Care, just a little care."

THEODORA: Hear that, Leona? You have to be careful. Can't go having a taste for everything, then acting fretful just because you can't have it. Look at you whinin' and carryin' on . . . by the time the rest of the gang gets here . . . you won't be worth a dime.

(*Theodora gets up and starts to tidy room. Marietta adjusts chairs at empty table and walks to the front. Leaves room. Theodora walks to spotlight. Fadeout on other lights*)

THEODORA: All that old furniture in the living room . . . (*shakes her head*) every time we have club meeting, there's hardly room to put up the card tables, there's so much furniture. Grandma's folks—out at the Thatcher Plantation—when she first got married, they sent all this old furniture out here. You know how velvet gets when it's old and faded. Just like the inside of a casket. Willie C.—that's my oldest sister—she used to teach over at Macedonia Hill. When she got her first paycheck, she went right out and put the money down on that player piano over in the corner. She always did know how to have a high time. Said she was tired of all this small town stuff. Everybody out in California has that new Spanish style, at least that's what Willie C. says.

About Leona—I'll take care of things if Mother lets me. I'll take care of Leona. Marietta's cooked for half the town, Leona oughta know that. That's not it.

Both our brothers, Morris and Leon, they're gone, overseas. (*raises her voice*) That's part of it . . . they put the thing about Cordie Cheek in the *Nashville Globe*. Leona keeps the whole paper, the one about that boy, right by her bed. She's taking it real hard. (*fidgets, wrings her hands. Squeezes hands together and forces a pleasant expression*)

If Papa was here, she'd settle down . . . Papa . . . When he takes the white sportsmen out on his boat, they toe the line. No drinking, smoking, and not a bit of swearing. "Mr. Edwards," that's what they call him—and he'll leave you if you're a minute late. 1939—the year I went to A&I—Papa sent me this yellow raincoat—the one he used to wear on his boat. (*Theodora's music, "Take the A-Train," begins.*) All the bands that came to Nashville signed it. Erskine Hawkins and the 'Bama State Collegians, Jimmie Lunceford, Count Basie. I had those big city boys signing all over the back of that coat. I'd turn around like this. (*Turns around*) They'd write their names right here. (*points to back of coat*) Me, Willie C., Leona, Eva Zoe—half the town went to A&I, our half the town, that is. I was the fraternity sweetheart, too. All the Alphas said it was because I had the deepest dimples . . . (*pauses, slows down for emphasis*) and the straightest teeth they'd ever seen. They're always saying I look like somebody. Now it's one of the Dandridge sisters. Dorothy . . . that's it, Dorothy Dandridge. The club dance is two nights before I leave. If I can get those new records for the club dance. What's that one? If Saul Blanton's shop gets it in time . . . (*touches forehead. more resolved*) This headache, it's been comin' on for days. I've never been late for anything in my life. And I don't plan to be late leaving. (*pauses. music up, then under*) I've been up since five this morning sweeping and washing. Getting ready for my trip. I've never been any farther than Nashville, Tennessee in my whole life, and now I'm going out West. Willie C. and Ray, that's her husband, they'll show me and Randy the town: picture shows, big bands, tall trees— (*sways from side to side*) palm trees—not the kind you see out back. (*proudly*) Los Angeles, California. I hear they jitterbug all night. (*pauses*) Willie C., she knows everything about the apple . . . (*aside*) that's what everybody calls the big city.

(*Spotlight fades, music fades. Bring up lights on bridge players. The women in the room continue their bridge game. Emma enters from the front door, clutching a white apron tightly in one hand. Emma is the mother of four daughters, Leona, Marietta, Theodora, and Willie C., and two sons, Leon and Morris. Like many African American women of her generation, she is a mixture of African, Indian and white. A slender, elegant woman with medium-brown skin and heavy black straight hair, Emma wears a breezy looking summer dress, the skirt just full enough to move easily as she walks. With a cameo brooch at the neck and her hair pulled back into a chignon, she could be coming from an afternoon tea. Emma is a polestar; the women of the town look to her for guidance. She speaks and gestures with a dramatic flair that becomes a weapon in difficult situations.*)

WOMEN: Howdy, Mama Emma. (*They murmur respectfully in unison. The conversation has the quality of call and response used in the black church.*)

EMMA: (*laughs*) Mary Jane's after me. I was walking up the hill, when lo and behold if Mary Jane didn't come walking right up behind me. (*mischievous expression, as if starting to tell a wicked story*) I was walking along, (*looks up, moves right hand across the air*) kicking up the dust . . .

(*Mary Jane enters suddenly.*)

MARY JANE: Just the one I was lookin' for.

EMMA: (*turns, looks at audience*) What did I tell you? (*eyes are knowing*) She was right behind me.

MARY JANE: I was right behind her.

EMMA: Sure was hot out there. (*looks at Mary Jane out of the corner of her eye*)

RUTH: Up to the white Methodist church, Mama Emma?

EMMA: There too.

MARY JANE: I followed her every step.

EMMA: (*ignoring Mary Jane*) So I turned and whipped around the corner. I said to myself, I'm goin' to see how my Leona's doing.

MARY JANE: That's where I was going too.

LEONA: Mother does the work of ten.

THEODORA: And she gave birth to ten.

(*Women murmur in approval.*)

PETT MAE: Oh yes.

EVA ZOE: And doctor delivered all ten. Six living.

EMMA: It was mighty hot . . . (*pauses*) down at that kitchen.

MARY JANE: (*negatively*) The Methodist church.

EMMA: (*ignoring Mary Jane*) You girls know Viola McCoy?

RUTH: The judge's wife?

EMMA: Well, Viola McCoy up and starts with me: "Now Emma, this here is a book on how to set the table. I 'spects you would enjoy it."

LEONA: Everybody knows about women like Mrs. McCoy. (*glances at Mary Jane*)

EMMA: (*laughing*) She told me just the other day (*aside*) you know I just listened, didn't say a word—"Now Emma, if you just come down and cook us our meal, you won't have to wash nary a dish." (*stops short. Hands on hips, theatrically*) Biggest liar I've ever seen.

THEODORA: Now, mother.

LEONA: Calling Mrs. McCoy a liar . . . (*pauses*) Mother.

THEODORA: Mother sure does like to perform.

LEONA: Mother always has wanted to be on the stage.

RUTH: Have some iced tea, Mama Emma.

EMMA: That's all right, darlin'. (*pats Ruth on hand*) Your mama'll be all right. (*graciously*) Have some iced tea, Mary Jane. (*takes glass and hands it to Mary Jane*)

MARY JANE: Emma, there's a thing or two . . .

EMMA: Mind your glass, Mary Jane. (*begins to sip tea, gradually assuming a strong, fixed stare*) Will's gone fishing with the doctors from Meharry. I got Leona. Don't know what I can do for you.

(*The sound of cars going by can be heard. The women all look towards the window.*)

LEONA: Sure is a lot of commotion around here. (*sighs and sips tea*) When it's hot . . . in the summer when the screens are in . . . you can hear everything in the world . . .

MARY JANE: Everything.

LEONA: It was spring the last time I saw Cordie Cheek.

THEODORA: It's those boys from out of town racin' up and down the hill again.

MARIETTA: Thought it was the Alphas.

THEODORA: It's that old bunch from out of town.

PETT MAE: Every time Tuskegee plays A&I they run through here. Bad as poor . . . (*trails off*)

(*Mary Jane begins to fidget.*)

LEONA: That's where everybody goes, over to Tuskegee to get married.

MARY JANE: That's where you went with my son.

LEONA: (*off in her own world*) The day before Easter.

MARY JANE: It was wet and cold.

LEONA: (*responds but doesn't argue with Mary Jane*) When we went to Tuskegee, I had to wrap a coat around myself. I wore my silk crepe dress. (*looks off*) The one Aunt Ellen sent from Detroit, a peach color, soft, draped.

THEODORA: Sure did. You got all those clothes. The same size as that lady Aunt Ellen works for.

MARY JANE: It's been six months since you talked to my boy.

LEONA: (*stands up*) In front of all these people.

MARY JANE: In a small town, everybody finds out anyway.

LEONA: All right, it's been six months since he went home to your house. I moved my things out first. We didn't live at Miss Estelle's a year.

SAMUELLA: Mother Emma, don't let her come in here . . .

EMMA: (*wheels around, addresses women playing bridge. She speaks in an exaggerated way, as though she is performing a role.*) Girl hardly grown trying to sass our guest. (*turns to Mary Jane*) Now Mary Jane darlin', don't carry on so. (*Emma is quiet, dignified. She lets Mary Jane take the floor. Her manner is deferring; to a stranger she might seem weak.*)

MARY JANE: What did you expect? Her not knowing how to take care of a house. Calvin was used to having everything kept up.

LEONA: I was good to your boy.

MARY JANE: Girl . . . (*moves closer*) did you or did you not bring him down here every day?

(*Emma looks from Mary Jane to Leona as the mother-in-law and the daughter-in-law talk.*)

LEONA: This is my house, too, Miss Mary Jane.

MARY JANE: To your mother's house to eat his dinner?

LEONA: I was a grown woman teaching out at Morning Star, out in the country. Miss Smith drove me into town late. When I got home . . .

EMMA: (*steps forward*) My daughter's not on trial.

MARY JANE: To your mother's house to eat his evening meal.

LEONA: Mother always had the dinner ready.

MARY JANE: A wife's place is at home. Not out in the country somewhere. (*pause*) Is this the way you brought her up? Is this how you raised this girl?

SAMUELLA: Mother Emma . . .

EMMA: Be still, girl. (*toughly, then glancing sweetly to Mary Jane*) Give a visiting mother-in-law her due.

LEONA: (*roused to attention*) A wife's place? He never complained about that. I taught out at Theta, Morning Star . . . when we lived at Miss Estelle's, I paid my part . . . four rooms, half the house. Was that my place? Things were fine when I was out in the country. The little school children, they hung on my every word. Every night, when I got home, Calvin was there waiting. Then I came back to town. People started meddlin', talkin' behind my back . . . some people, that is . . . I've heard things—horrible things, gossip, lies . . . (*throws cards down*) Who'll take my hand? (*Leona walks by the front table. She goes off through the darkened side of the stage. A record begins to play—"Until the Real Thing Comes Along," by Andy Kirk and the Clouds of Joy.*)

RUTH: Lay Leona's hand down. Somebody'll bid for it.

MARY JANE: I'll tell you how it oughta be: my boy comes home, marks his school papers, maybe has a good hot cup of tea, all the while your girl's there making sure of everything. He only has to look up, give a nod . . . (*softly*) that's all . . .

EMMA: Lie low, catch a meddler. (*crouches down, as if listening for an intruder*)

MARY JANE: Don't you know a man gets tired, just thinkin'?

EMMA: Well, I'm thinkin' I'm a Christian, so I can't say what's on my mind. (*moves head around, imitating Mary Jane. Stops suddenly and looks around*)

MARY JANE: Any other woman around here . . . (*eyes the other women. Emma looks around for Leona.*) have my boy to come home to, sweet heaven, she'd be there now.

THEODORA: She's lyin' down, Mother.

EMMA: (*nods, takes off her apron*) Now let me tell you something. (*turns to Mary Jane*) If you want to judge, judge me. I'm proud (*touches her chest*) of my children.

MARY JANE: Proud that you cooked her husband's meals?

EMMA: Good and proud. (*pause*) Mary Jane, the two of us, we taught together—you and me. My daughter's a teacher and I was a teacher before her. Your boy knew that when he married her.

MARY JANE: Teacher! I wish Samson could see the way she's fixed up right now. Hair all curled up and greased, dress open at the neck.

EMMA: The child's entertaining her club.

MARY JANE: Entertaining, all right. A songstress, that's what you raised. You brought her up to perform and go on . . .

EMMA: That's right! I brought her up to perform and go on.

MARY JANE: Emma Edwards . . .

EMMA: I brought her up to be gracious and refined, to bring sunshine to any gathering. (*switches around the stage*)

MARY JANE: Emma Edwards, I come to see if your daughter's going to do the right thing.

EMMA: My daughter's not on trial. (*struts up to Mary Jane*) If you want to judge, judge me.

MARY JANE: All right, I'll say it then. I heard you singing and playing over to the school . . . Songstress—that's what they called you! . . . Playin' that ragtime piano, right there at the school dance. (*Emma puts her hands on her hips and squints at Mary Jane.*) Playin' the piano. You call that Christian? I been knowin' you all my life. Why, I remember the day you and Will Edwards was walkin' home from school . . . the ninth grade. He dared you to take your hair loose, down over by that bridge—halfway to kingdom come. I saw your mother come lookin' for you. Saw her pull out a switch 'bout the size of this finger. She whipped you all the way home.

EMMA: Judge me, Mary Jane— (*reaches up and undoes the bun in the back of her head. She shakes her head and her long, heavy hair falls over her shoulders.*)

MARY JANE: (*While Mary Jane speaks, Emma sways from side to side, as if dancing.*) Alright. I've seen you put on dresses all done in satin and silk, all sorts of finery, wastin' hard-earned money. I've seen you sit out on the front porch with all your children, your hair piled up on your head posing for pictures every time that old man comes by in the wagon. They say you put on fancy clothes and shawls with fringes just to sit in the house at night. When that ol' show comes to town you run off and follow 'em, up to the school. For what?

EMMA: We hid from my ma! (*pause*) I paid three dollars when *Shuffle Along* came to town . . . two nights at the old Macedonia School. Me and my chum Olivia we dreamed—went on for days about dressing in silk. We shined our shoes with biscuits and painted our eyes just to sit and watch . . .

MARY JANE: *Shuffle Along!* (*scornfully*) Silas Green!

EMMA: My cousin, the one wore tie and tails to supper . . . he was in all those shows that came through here . . . *Shuffle Along, Brownskin Models* . . . all those shows. (*Mimicking a gesture she has seen in the traveling shows, Emma brings hands up simultaneously in clockwise and counter-clockwise circles.*)

MARY JANE: *Brownskin Models*? Hair all plastered with grease, skirts up to the neck. You call that Christian?

EMMA: I'll tell you Christian—go up yonder to St. Paul's A.M.E. Church up on Macedonia Hill. Look by the front of the church. My pappy's name is right on the cornerstone. (*pauses*) He helped build that church.

MARY JANE: A.M.E.? (*pause*) African Methodist. Well, that's about the only African thing about you. When your mammy switched you with that black willow she was tellin you somethin'. Son, I said go on down to Mt. Lebanon, find a nice lookin' Baptist girl—no sirree, not him, he had to run all the way cross town . . . A.M.E . . . You an' your high yellow daughters. African Methodist. I told him, I said, marry a Baptist. You and your high yellow . . .

EMMA: Now let me tell you something. Go on down to Mt. Lebanon Missionary Baptist Church. You said it—Mt. Lebanon Baptist Church. Tiptoe around the altar and climb up in the pulpit. Open up the Old Settlers' Bible, the one that's been sittin' there one hundred and some odd years. Turn to the first page. Run your fingers down the list of the founders: my grandma, Liza, my great-grandpappy, Demps; they set the first stone. Every which a way I turn—I got it on both sides. Baptist this a way, A.M.E. that a way . . . high is right. Look up high—that's where you'll see Emma Edwards. (*hands on hip; switches around*) I never made a difference between light and dark. I never made a thing about color. Why, my own pappy was the blackest man you've ever seen. My mother loved him and married him. (*takes her hair and throws it over her shoulder.*)

MARY JANE: Injun hair—I can see who you come from. (*pause*) Well, I think your daughter's too high falutin', that's her problem. I guess she thinks she's too light. (*struts around the stage*) . . . carryin' on . . . hair all curled up. (*Mary Jane hears noise, turns to see Marietta entering the room carrying a stack of hymnals.*)

EMMA: If you think my daughter's so high falutin', then why you here askin' about her? My daughter's carryin' a child, your son's child. She's the ma, he's the pa. Don't nobody care about whether your son's light or dark. I got four girls, and they all have the same father. I nursed them all, raised them all, never said, well, this one's first, this one's lighter. (*walks along gesturing low, from side to side*) Next time you're huntin' for a switch, Mary Jane, go on down to the Duck River, where Will keeps his boats; you'll see a Black Willow, real light brown, but you keep walking and you come to one nearly black. You feel that wood and you say to yourself, this wood's too soft, but lo-and-behold, the real light one and the black one, both of 'em, they keep the mud and dirt from falling down the banks . . . (*pats her side*)

(*Marietta drops her stack of hymnals.*)

MARY JANE: (*hears the noise and looks around, hoping to see Leona*) Where's your daughter?

EMMA: Which one, Mary Jane? The real bright one? Leona? Didn't you see her walk out?

MARY JANE: (*watches doorway for a minute, then turns to Emma*) The reason she's not goin' back with my boy . . .

EMMA: You're the reason.

MARY JANE: The reason she's not goin' back with my boy . . . I don't think he's the father in the first place. (*Emma moves closer, glaring at Mary Jane. They confront one another, staring.*) You heard me.

EMMA: And just who do you think the father might be, Sister Jane?

MARY JANE: You know that's Wallace Mitchell's child.

EMMA: Lord ha' mercy.

MARY JANE: Emma Edwards. Don't you take the Lord's name in vain.

EMMA: All my girls, Mary Jane, and get this straight— (*tenderly*) every one of my girls will always know— (*angrily*) the father of her children.

MARY JANE: Dark as Calvin is? Why, that child'll be light enough to pass.

EMMA: Pass? Pass for what? Why Marietta Edwards, my own newborn, was as white as a bedsheet the day I gave birth to her. (*gestures to Marietta*) Look at how dark the child is now.

(*Marietta suppresses a grin and covers her face.*)

MARY JANE: There's only one thing Calvin wants.

EMMA: (*hands on her hips*) And what's that?

MARY JANE: He wants his gold. He wants it back.

(*Stage is dark. Leona walks to spotlight. Fadeout on other lights*)

LEONA: (*holds up the chain with the ring on it*) He wants this back. Why should I give it to him? That day when we ran off to get married, I wore flowers in my hair. I was teaching school out at Morning Star. Of course, I taught a long time before I got married. He was living down at Miss Estelle's—that's how we met. That night after we came back from Tuskegee, we went back to Miss Estelle's. I didn't go out much at A&I. Me and Wallace Mitchell courted. We weren't 'lowed off campus on school nights. Had to go in groups on Saturdays. Of course I went to the formal dances. (*Leona's music starts. "Until the Real Thing Comes Along," by Andy Kirk's Orchestra*) Wore beautiful clothes from Aunt Ellen. She worked for this rich white lady in Detroit. Everybody at Hale wanted to wear my clothes. I just wanted to get good grades, that's all. Be invited into the honorary. Oh yes, about Mrs. Viola McCoy . . . Papa knows her husband; Mama knows him too. I sassed him that first summer I was home from college. He slapped me on the face. Said "It's a good thing you're Emma and Will's child."

When I came back home from A&I after I got my teaching diploma, I taught out at Morning Star. Taught a long time before I got married. One of the teachers over to the school said to me "Calvin, you remember Calvin Barnes, from A&I, sharp as a tack, went to Fisk too. He's stayin' over to Miss Estelle's and teaching at Macedonia Hill. He's a Kappa. You didn't know him at A&I, did you?" I thought and I thought. No, I didn't know him . . . tall, a quick little smile, broad shoulders, suits straight from New York, fitted just so at the waist—neat as a band box. You should have seen us at the Elks. I can still wear my clothes. If I go to the club dance in Pett and Doctor's basement, I'll wear one of Aunt Ellen's dresses. I won't even show. My mother-in-law says I'm carrying Wallace Mitchell's child. It's a lie and she knows it. One thing, I will always know the father of my children. I know it'll be a girl. I know how she'll be, not too light and not too dark, the same color all over. Of course as soon as they find out you're expecting you have to stop teaching. I don't know why. This saleslady uptown didn't even notice. Am I foolish, vain? Don't I have a right to be? It's my ring. Why should I give it back? Theodora thinks I ought to leave the baby with Mother, go off somewhere else. She says a teacher with a divorce . . . says they'll never hire me back. She thinks I oughta go away, leave the baby right here. Marietta says I ought to go back to him, that a wife's place is with her husband. No matter how bad things get. She says she learned her lesson . . . (*softly*) and I believe her, but she doesn't know about that Saturday night after club meeting when Calvin drove me home. I put my purse down on the seat. Tucked my gloves inside the strap. Said "Calvin . . . I'm going to have our child." (*imitates man's voice*) "A child . . . whose child? (*mimics Calvin's laugh*) That's no child of mine." That's why I left. That night—I cried and cried—went running home to Mother. All right—I'm sorry— (*little sobs and whimpers*) if you're looking for a big hero— I never was that brave. Was I supposed to sit there like a dummy? If you don't whine, who'll know you're alive? If you can't stand things, don't you have to let somebody in this world know? Mary Jane Barnes . . . (*turns to look at women*) she sure makes me hot. It's a good thing Morris and Leon aren't here. They'd put her out.

(*Spotlight fades; bring up lights on bridge players. Music stops*)

EMMA: My Leona never did rip and run like some girls. I sent her to Hale Dormitory at A&I. Miss Bea Gordon from home was housemother to the girls. All my girls lived at Hale.

MARY JANE: You know there's something odd about a woman who waits till she's twenty-nine to marry and have a family.

EMMA: My Leona. She taught right there at Macedonia. Just like all the rest of your husband's teachers.

MARY JANE: Being principal never meant watching every move.

EMMA: Samson Barnes does.

MARY JANE: Gettin' late. (*looks at watch*) I'm a real busy woman, too busy to get all dolled up just to play Miss La Dee Da, sit up in the house and eat folks' food all day. Why, I never in my life held a card.

EMMA: Lie low, catch meddler.

MARY JANE: I'm not meddlin'. You hear me—my son wants his own.

EVA ZOE: (*jumps up from her seat*) A girl would have to be crazy to give up all that gold.

(*Theodora stands up and pushes Eva Zoe down.*)

MARY JANE: My boy wants his ring.

EMMA: (*lowers her head, taking in the words, then looks up abruptly*) Well, maybe he'd better come and get it.

MARY JANE: Either the ring goes back or she comes back. (*turns to door where Leona exited. Yells loudly in direction of the door*) My boy needs a wife waitin' for him when he comes home at night. Either come back to my boy or give me that ring. If you want to stay, I can't stop you. But the ring goes back.

(*Lights fade.*)

ACT TWO

A record begins to play "Until the Real Thing Comes Along." The time is early Saturday evening. Normally the club meeting would be over by now, but the women are still together.

THEODORA: Everybody oughta be back from Nashville by now. The rest of the gang'll be tippin' in. (*to Eva Zoe*) Leona sure does love that old record.

EVA ZOE: Bet you're thinking about the club dance.

THEODORA: That old song. (*pause*) Not for our dance.

MARIETTA: They didn't bring that boy Cordie Cheek back from Nashville.

(*Music stops. Women look at Marietta.*)

LEONA: (*enters, walks to her table and steadies herself on a chair*) I thought his trial was over . . .

MARIETTA: It was over, all right.

LEONA: When school let out, he came up and said, "Miss Leona, we're leavin' the country, comin' to town. I'll be at Macedonia Hill before you can say Jack Robinson. You'll be my teacher." He didn't know I wouldn't be there.

RUTH: Hair combed, shoes all shined. I can see him now.

THEODORA: You know how people talk. He'll be all right.

MARIETTA: They didn't bring him back, Theodora.

THEODORA: Listen to the superintendent. You all—Marietta's tellin' those tales again. (*keeps eyes on cards*)

SAMUELLA: He went before the grand jury.

PETT MAE: The paper said they freed him on that charge of messing with a white girl. (*keeps arranging cards*)

MARIETTA: After the girl's own ma died, Miss Sadie, the Cheek boy's mother, she raised that girl, all her brothers and sisters . . . cooked and cleaned, worked for the family her whole life.

LEONA: Cordie played out there, right along with the rest of those children.

MARIETTA: I'm telling you now, and this ain't no tall tale. Mr Saul told me. They had a party on that old bridge over there.

LEONA: He was a little boy out in the country at Theta. That's where I taught him.

MARIETTA: They really had a party on that old bridge.

LEONA: I brushed his teeth, showed him how to lace his shoes. Out in the country you teach everything . . .

MARIETTA: Cordie Cheek's gone. I'm tellin' you now and this ain't no tale. Mr. Saul told me. They hung him on the way back. You know, by the Murfreesboro Pike. A bunch of them. Got together right there, on that old bridge that goes over the Duck River. They stopped the car and . . .

(*Several women stand up at their seats. Others hold bridge hands to their chests. Leona grasps the chain at her neck.*)

PETT MAE: He was a marked man.

EMMA: A man (*pause*)that boy wadn't but fourteen years old.

MARIETTA: After the grand jury freed the boy, the same ones that took him down for the trial, they picked him up again, turned off the road by that old bridge.

(*Women murmur quietly.*)

EMMA: They were waitin' for the boy, the girl's brother and his gang.

MARIETTA: Mr. Saul Blanton . . . he's the first to know . . . knows everything. What he told me . . . after they stopped the car—said the Cheek boy tried to run off. The brother, the whole gang, they went right after him, grabbed the boy, held him down, with him screamin' and hollerin' the whole time. They kept him out there two hours, wanted the boy to write a confession—but his hands . . . (*Leona moans. Marietta holds her right hand up to the light and turns it slowly.*) they were burned so bad—he couldn't even move. (*Leona moans again.*) I heard they shot him close up, that's what Mr. Saul said, said you could see the powder burns, then they hung him before he died.

(*Pett Mae knocks talcum powder off cards. The cars come by again, but this time they stop. A car door can be heard closing. There are footsteps, and then a man's voice calls through the screen door.*)

MAN'S VOICE: Anybody home?

(*The door opens suddenly.* TOWNSEND, *a large, middle-aged white man, hatless with thinning hair, is standing there wearing a deputy's badge pinned to the lapel of his open-collared shirt. Townsend looks around the room, then scowls at the player piano.*)

TOWNSEND: (*looks around again*) Y'all tryin' to hide somethin'? (*goes over to piano and bangs the keys*) Where'd you get this? (*walks over to Pett Mae, looks at her dress. Goes back to the door and yells outside*) Hey Byrd! (*pause*) Byrd! (*louder*) Come on, hurry up, they raisin' hell in here. (*turns back to women quickly. Looks around but doesn't speak*)

EMMA: (*feigning respect. Eyes him mischievously*) And what might we do for you this fine afternoon, sir? (*Emma says everything graciously, as though to the manner born, but with an air of pretense.*)

(FRANK BYRD, *the younger deputy, steps in quickly, looks around, then glares at Townsend. At first glance, Byrd seems confident, assured, adult, but one senses there is a young boy just underneath the surface. He is thin and wiry with light-brown hair. Wearing a white shirt, tie and expensive gold cufflinks, he seems to be dressed for a social occasion, as though his appearance here is the result of a last-minute decision. His temporary deputy's badge is stuffed in his pocket.*)

BYRD: Townsend, will you stop all that infernal yellin'?

TOWNSEND: Hey Byrd! Look here. (*points to Pett Mae*) This darkie been playin' poker for money.

BYRD: (*ignores Emma and points to Pett Mae nervously, then yells*) Townsend, (*pause*) over here's the wife of our colored doctor and that one over there, she's a colored undertaker.

TOWNSEND: Undertaker! (*jumps, nudges Byrd, laughs, then tries to hide. Townsend has turned away from Pett Mae. Rests his hand nervously against his side*) Lord, I'm tired. Been all over town. I was up on Main Street, heard this gunshot, like to went right through me. (*holds side*) Right here. (*goes over to piano and bangs on the keys*) Lord, if I told my pa about this . . .

BYRD: Maybe you better go see a doctor, Townsend.

TOWNSEND: Doctor . . . college boy, you got all the answers . . . all the answers. (*spits*) Byrd, I ain't never been to no doctor in my life.

BYRD: Got one . . . call him up for you.

TOWNSEND: Well, I ain't goin'. My mammy, two my brothers, they all died of the pox. The doc, he never came out to the Hollow but once; too busy treatin' the rich folk. (*whispers, laughing*) Say, you ever hear the one about the undertaker and the farmer's widow?

BYRD: (*pulls away*) Maybe we'll send you to the colored doc. He treats a heap of our folks.

TOWNSEND: A nigger. (*shakes his fist*) Look here, college boy.

BYRD: No, you look here. I told you, Townsend, you're not in Alabama. And furthermore the name's Byrd. Byrd, that's what you call me, understand?

TOWNSEND: College boy. All slicked up. Tie, shirt shining all around the cuff. (*Holds up Byrd's arm to show cufflink*) Like he's goin' to the Opry. How you gone play the law, dressin' up like a choir boy? (*laughs, walks around*)

BYRD: (*turns away and then back to Townsend*) Know where you are, Townsend? (*pause*) Well, do you? You're in Will Edwards' house. We don't say that in here.

TOWNSEND: I tell you what I know— (*gets in Byrd's face*) know trouble when I see it. Gamblin', sittin' up holdin' hands fulla cards, no tellin' what they fixin' to do. Lord, if I tole my pa about this . . . a piano. Come on y'all, it's time for Grand Ole Opry . . . (*starts humming loudly*) That's right, ain't it, Byrd? (*leans against tables and talks to Byrd as if women aren't there. Bumps into Pett Mae and then jumps away, feigning fear*)

BYRD: (*teasingly*) The colored doctor—fellow named B. F.—my uncle, aunt, four cousins, whole family goes down there.

TOWNSEND: He ain't no real doctor, is he, college boy? (*goes over to piano and rubs his hands across it*)

(*Samuella raps hand on table, looks insulted.*)

BYRD: Most of the town says he is, and if he isn't, I'm gonna turn you over to the undertaker, one in the white dress over there.

(*They stand talking as if they are alone.*)

TOWNSEND: Where? Undertaker where?

BYRD: (*Byrd points to Ruth*) Your kind . . . you don't listen, do you, Townsend?

TOWNSEND: Her? Uh, uh, no sir. (*moves away from Ruth*) No sir—I'm 'fraid 'a undertakers. That's bad luck . . . bad bad luck and a female undertaker . . . colored one—that's double, triple bad. You ever hear the one about the undertaker? (*whispers to Byrd*) Him and the widow, see, they're at the wake . . .

BYRD: (*pushes Townsend away*) Better get you to the doc quick.

TOWNSEND: If I let him cut on me . . . (*rubs hands on piano, starts to daydream*)

BYRD: My Uncle Ashley had a big knot on his hand. Doc B. F. took him in on a Sunday and took the blame thing off.

TOWNSEND: If I let him cut on me, I'd sleep three, four days good an' get up early an' stay up the whole time he was cutting on me.

BYRD: You'd keep him honest.

TOWNSEND: No liquor or nothin'. (*yells at Pett Mae, then walks around taking note of things. Dusts off vase, looks it over carefully, then puts it down and picks up handful of cards*) I wouldn't close my eyes.

(*They both laugh and circle the tables.*)

TOWNSEND: Where I come from, if you see a whole lot of women livin' in a big ol' house playin' card games . . . strange men in and out all day and half the night, first one then the other . . . a piano . . . entertainin' they call it (*waves hand at group*) a bunch of us, we get together with the Klan, ride in, and make 'em stop.

BYRD: And if they don't?

TOWNSEND: If they don't stop, we run 'em out of town.

BYRD: (*dryly*) Alabama style.

TOWNSEND: Go on, just try it . . . start a cathouse in Farley, gamblin'—shoot . . . I seen 'em beat the mayor for stealin' tax money . . . The Klan, they come through one night, burn down every cathouse in Lima County. Heap o' folks, the colored, they don't understand the Klan.

(*Samuella spreads her cards in front of her face.*)

BYRD: (*nervously*) Don't know any . . . (*looks at Townsend*) Worse than the poorest trash.

TOWNSEND: (*nudges him*) Who, the colored? (*laughs*)

BYRD: (*Seriously*) A man I know said once he belonged to it.

TOWNSEND: They ask me, you a member? I say, I ain't sayin' yes and I ain't sayin' no.

BYRD: Wouldn't know.

TOWNSEND: (*nudges Byrd*) Why, I saw a picture show once—a man ridin' this horse all done up like a hero in white and everything.

BYRD: I know the one you mean.

TOWNSEND: Pretty as hell—I like to cried. (*loudly*) If a man lets his goats and horses go from one yard to the next and don't keep 'um home, why, I know the Klan to go after him and whip his tail.

BYRD: Worse than the low-downest colored . . . Lord knows I met more than a few white men that were.

TOWNSEND: Boy— (*pause*) what you say? You see this pistol here? I call it ol' D. W., an' you know I ain't shot but two men in my whole life. Ask D. W. (*starts to pull a revolver out of his pocket*) Me and all the boys back home, we tryin' to keep 'em pure. My pa always said if you treat your ladies right, make sure everybody else does, too . . . (*yells, grabs at pocket*)

BYRD: This here's the wife of Will Edwards, takes the white sportsmen fishin'.

TOWNSEND: D. W., say hi to the colored lady. (*Starts to reach in his pocket. Byrd grabs his hand and holds him back.*)

BYRD: I thought I told you, Townsend. (*pause*) I thought I told you. (*turns quickly*) Howdy, *Miss* Emma.

EMMA: Afternoon. (*turns to him quickly, as if seeing him for the first time. Mock excitement*) Why, if it isn't young Mr. Frank, Judge Jordan Cooper's grandbaby home from Vanderbilt.

(*Byrd clutches his hat, hesitates for a moment, then throws it on the piano bench.*)

TOWNSEND: Howdy. (*bows in an exaggerated manner to Emma, then turns to Byrd*) Howdy, Vandy.

EMMA: Home from law school.

TOWNSEND: Vandy!

BYRD: Howdy, Aunt Emma. Don't mind him. I know you folks. Been knowing you since I was a little boy.

EMMA: Yes sir. (*bows slightly, shifts feet a little*)

TOWNSEND: They got a bunch of us to come here . . . take care of things. 'Cause a all the trouble that boy caused.

EMMA: We wouldn't be causing any trouble. (*smiles beatifically*)

TOWNSEND: Well, we ain't lookin' for none either. We been told to go to every colored (*pauses*) in town, every house. Had to come to yours too. (*looks around*) Collect all the guns.

EMMA: (*in mock disbelief*) Why sir . . .

BYRD: (*turns to Emma*) Emma . . . We know Will has a gun. (*then turns to Townsend*) Best damn guide around. Ask anybody.

TOWNSEND: Guide? Vandy, what you know about guidin'? Ain't hardly used a razor.

BYRD: They say he's a cousin to Davy Crockett. Ask anybody.

TOWNSEND: Davy Crockett? (*pause*) Can he wrastle a bear?

BYRD: Yep, and that's not all. If you go out with him, Townsend, you can't drink or swear. He's got rules . . . not one bird over the limit . . . Why, I was out on the Duck River one day, saw him fishing with Cordell Hull. Sure enough, Mr. Cordell Hull, the Secretary of State. Will Edwards was paddlin' a boat with one hand, (*Townsend starts to pay closer attention*) reached up, shot a duck out of the air with the other. And you know, the water didn't even move. (*Townsend laughs and moves closer.*) Last October, first day of huntin' season, pourin' down rain, my Uncle Ashley took a party, three cars, all the way to Brentwood just to go shootin' with Mr. Will Edwards, that's what they call him—best shot in Middle Tennessee, white or colored. Next time we go, I'll call you . . . (*motions Townsend closer*) Only five dollars a man for the whole day.

TOWNSEND: (*jerks away angrily. Looking around*) We been all up and down the hill, all over Mink Slide, all the way to the bottom. We got every gun. (*Pett Mae and Ruth huddle around Leona, murmuring words of comfort. Townsend sits down at their table. Pett Mae starts to chatter nervously.*) You, (*points at Pett*) the doc's wife, the one gon' sew me up, shut your mouth. (*Pett Mae continues to chatter.*) I said shut your mouth! (*turns sharply*) Damn it, I said shut up. (*looks at Byrd and then at Pett Mae. Townsend slaps his knee. Pett Mae starts to cry. Leona stares at Pett Mae unbelievingly, then covers face with hands.*) Do I have to tell you again?

BYRD: (*steps in front of Townsend*) Told my pa, Aunt Emma. Said don't go pickin' up any old piece of trash off the road. (*motions to Townsend*) Aunt Emma, we know Mr. Will's got a gun. We're going to Saul Blanton's house up the street. (*to Townsend*) Bootlegger's bound to keep guns in the house. Cock fights, gamblin' half the night . . . got to keep order over all that. (*turns to Emma*) Emma, when we come back, we want that gun.

TOWNSEND: (*Townsend and Byrd walk toward door.*) We goin' up to that bootlegger. Me and Vandy gon' have us a party all night.

BYRD: Gamblin'? Klan hear that, they might not want you . . . run you out of Farley. (*goes over to piano bench and picks up hat.*) Sorry, Townsend, I'm busy.

TOWNSEND: (*Townsend whispers to Byrd, then starts walking around the room*) Bet you are, school boy. I bet you are.

(*Townsend and Byrd exit.*)

MARIETTA: Half the white folks in town buy their liquor from Saul Blanton. 'Course he bootlegs something stronger than that. (*stands by the door, looking out. Talks to women from this spot.*) Well, I 'spect they'll be comin' back down here t'rectly— (*passes sideways glance at Emma*) Byrd and his deputy.

THEODORA: Deputy, my foot.

RUTH: (*holds Pett Mae's hand. Tries to comfort her*) Who in the world sent for that old deputy showed up here with Frank Byrd? Never seen hide nor hair of him in my life.

MARIETTA: (*looks out window*) No tellin'. They line 'em up, hand 'em a gun and a badge. Reckon that's all the schoolin' they need.

(*As the women talk, Emma stares at the window. She pats her foot angrily.*)

LEONA: Poor little Pett Mae. Are you scared? They didn't hurt you, did they? (*pause*) Did they, Pett honey?

PETT MAE: (*attempting to regain composure*) Let's see. I went up town, paid the light bill. Did I remember to pick up that dress from Gorman's? I'll have Doctor's helper go by there this evening.

(*Emma seems annoyed, as if she has been interrupted in the middle of deep thought. She shakes her head, then waves her hand understandingly at Pett.*)

EVA ZOE: College of Physicians and Surgeons—that's where Doctor went, didn't he, Pett?

SAMUELLA: A real doctor—the nerve.

PETT MAE: (*gives Ruth a reassuring hug*) Ol' Samuella. Always rufflin' up.

THEODORA: What's a cathouse?

SAMUELLA: (*coughs. There is a long silence. Rises from her seat*) Ladies, I speak to you now as your parliamentarian. We will not dignify the various and sundry vulgar comments made in our presence by addressing them directly.

EVA ZOE: Amen.

THEODORA: If that old man's a deputy my little schoolchildren might as well be.

MARIETTA: Don't matter what you think. If he puts that gun to your head you'll be gone just the same.

(*Emma walks to spotlight. Fadeout on other lights. Emma addresses audience. She acts out sequence, alternating between mocking tone and an overly gracious tone.*)

EMMA: (*mocking, imitating the deputy's surly tone*) "What you all doin' up there playin' poker for money?" (*answers graciously*) "Why sir, we wouldn't be doing a thing like that." (*pauses, seriously*) You know I always wanted to be on the stage. Judge Cooper's grandbaby couldn't match that. (*laughs*) My mother always said "Lie low, catch meddler." (*loudly*) That's "lie low, catch a meddler." The law's known for putting its nose in other folks' business. One night they drove right up to the house. Said (*menacing tone, acting role*) "What you darkies doin' up there on that porch?" I said, (*graciously*) "Why, sir, we're just out getting a spot of evening air." (*loudly, angry*) So they said to me, (*menacing*) "Well, you better get on in the house." And I said (*graciously*) "Why sir, this is just Emma Edwards up here on the porch with her family." And he says (*shocked*) "Will Edwards' wife? Doggone." And I said, (*graciously*) "Why, yes sir." And off he drove. (*starts laughing*)

I'm a performin' woman. (*hand on one hip*) You know when I was comin' up you weren't allowed to sing and go on for a living. Me and my chum Olivia, we performed over to the old Macedonia school. I used to be the end man for the minstrel show. Oh, I was something in my time. (*starts to strut across stage*) I walked for the cake. (*demonstrates step*) Did the real Charleston—not the way they try to do it now. After I was grown, Mama couldn't say a thing then, I would get up on the stage and do the Charleston. (*laughs*) Played the piano for all my girls, right over there at old Macedonia school, for every last one of their dances. (*sings out loud, first line of song only*) "There'll be a Hot Time in the Old Town Tonight." All the songs didn't go fast, either. Sometimes I'd go slow (*moves slowly, gesturing with hands, sings to waltz time first few lines of "I'm Just Wild About Harry." Continue instrumental of "I'm Just Wild About Harry" up and under*)

I sang and played so till one night Will Harold came up and got me, that's his real name, William Harold Edwards, always called him Will, he said "Woman, come from over there—they can hear you singin' all the way to Nashville." Will Edwards always thought he could boss me. (*puts both hands on hips*) He was the one told me to take my hair down. (*tension rises in voice*) The day Mama whipped me all the way home . . . I had great long braids, way down my back—Will said, "Emma, put your school books down and let me see if that's real hair. The teacher at school says you got those braids from an old Injun man. Go on, I dare you." (*aside*) When I was a little girl over at old Macedonia, they used to tease me, they'd say "Emma, who's that old Injun man ridin' around in back of your house?" Well, when Will started teasin' me too, I got mad as the dickens. Said, "Why that old Injun man's my Grandpa." And I took down every last braid.

Theodora's running around 'bout to get one of her headaches. Thinks she knows everything. Leona's in one of her nice-nasty spells. I wish she'd hurry up and have that child. Marietta, she won't say a word, busy openin' and closin' the church. When my girls start tryin' to tell me what to do, I just tell them (*soothingly, proper*) "Darlin', why your mother's forgotten more than you'll ever know." If my heirs ever try to sell this piece of land . . . well, I'm telling you—they'd better look for some real aristocrats. Nobody except aristocrats. (*uppity, proper*) This land was given to me by my mother's grandpa. (*raises voice*) My mother was John Thatcher's daughter and Judge Thatcher's niece . . . the sons of the biggest plantation owner in middle Tennessee. They let my mother get married right there at the Thatcher place. She wore a red velvet dress, little sleeves puffed up like so . . . (*aside*) a real aristocrat. (*quietly*) When mama was alive they used to come and get her for all the funerals. Sent me to Fisk, too. They gave us all this furniture. That velvet settee, those two chairs over there, everything you see. (*pause*) I've given birth to ten children. (*angrily*)

Leona's going to have a child, and the baby . . . There's never been an argument like that in this house before. But I can't condemn Mary Jane. She's just trying to do right by her son. I've been knowin' her all my life. She's just not an aristocrat. Mary Jane's an honest-to-goodness talker. The way she goes on you'd think people ought to go to jail just for playin' cards. (*laughs*) She's as bad as the law. I'm only speakin' for Emma Edwards, but I've been goin' to church on Sunday and to the meeting of the Phyllis Wheatley Circle and to my lodge (*hands on hips*) longer than I care to remember. You can't fault Emma Edwards there. I'm used to people talkin'. I just let her talk. Just talk herself out. Won't change my mind. Furthermore, won't get her anywhere, either. If I had to count the times Mary Jane and Samson have stopped here and stayed for dinner . . . the two of them . . . and about half of the rest of the town, too. I remember the time I baked chicken, made those teeniny little rolls, real light and that charlotte russe. Wish I had some teeniny little rolls about now. I never have closed my door to folks, (*turns to one side*) specially meddlers. Meddlers, (*holds her hands together as if cupping something precious*) they're real sly—you won't catch one (*reaches in the air and brings hand down empty*)—don't even say hello when they pass (*looks over her shoulder quickly, then turns back*) unless they've got a reason. I've never fought with one, don't get mad either. (*lifts finger in air*) I just let them talk, then I strut around, sing a little, smile and send them on their way—they're halfway down the road before they figure anything's wrong. (*laughs*) I never have closed my door— specially to meddlers.

(*Continue music to end. Music fades. Spotlight fades. Bring up lights on bridge players. It's getting dark outside. None of the women at the bridge party have left, although the club meeting has been over for some time. On the surface, the women are relaxed and sociable. An atmosphere of underlying tension, however, has been created by the news of Cordie Cheek's lynching.*)

THEODORA: Mother sure loves to perform.

(*Emma eyes Theodora sheepishly. Emma sits still, not moving; thoughtful pose. Marietta enters, stepping lightly. She goes over to the phone on the wall and places a call.*)

MARIETTA: (*talks for a minute quietly*) Yes sir, Mr. Saul. I thank you kindly. (*hangs up phone, turns to Emma and women*) Well, Mr. Saul says he's been entertaining Frank Byrd and his deputy.

(*Women laugh nervously.*)

PETT MAE: If anybody can cut a rug, it's ol' Saul.

(*Leona enters room. Sits down in chair. No music*)

RUTH: How you feelin', Leona?

LEONA: I'll pass, I guess.

RUTH: It's the weather. When I was carryin' Gene, got so bad one night, had to sleep out on the porch. (*fans herself*)

LEONA: I keep thinkin' about Cordie Cheek. That child. I taught that child one year . . . seems like I been knowin' him all my life. (*crying, turns to Emma*) Mother, I can't help myself.

EMMA: Help yourself! Help yourself to bed. That's all you need to do right now.

LEONA: It's a good thing Morris and Leon aren't here. Hot as they are, they'd have the whole lot of us up to the courthouse . . . we'd all be on trial.

(*Theodora looks uncomfortable. Emma shakes her head and closes her eyes as if to cancel out Leona's words.*)

RUTH: Look at Mama Emma.

PETT MAE: She's not about to let them mess with her. (*trying to change subject*) Didn't the boys mail you that scarf over there, Mama Emma?

(*Theodora is looking off into space, trying not to listen to the conversation. Emma is still deep in thought.*)

LEONA: (*points to the scarf*) Every time I see that scarf, it makes me think about Leon and Morris.

THEODORA: I can feel one of my headaches comin' on . . . Don't start all that stuff (*glares at Leona*) just when I'm getting ready for California.

PETT MAE: Now Theodora, that's no way to talk about your own.

LEONA: I'm trying, Theodora. I'm trying.

RUTH: Mary Jane's as bad as the law.

PETT MAE: That bird's after one of Emma Edwards' high-yellow daughters. (*looks at Leona with a mischievous smile and touches handkerchief to her face*)

MARIETTA: I know one thing—I sure don't have time to go round worryin' about what shade a brown I am. (*laughs, then looks straight ahead*) I'll tell you that right now.

LEONA: If I'd lived that long I'd know better than to go on like that.

EMMA: How long?

LEONA: As long as Mary Jane Barnes.

EMMA: (*turns to Leona*) Many an old bird shat in the nest. (*All the women laugh except Samuella, who slides down in her seat.*) Go on back to bed, Leona. Nothin' for you to do runnin' around here.

LEONA: You all won't let me do a thing. I'm older than Theodora. You let her go off to California, and she's only 22 years old . . . just got her teaching certificate last June. Theodora goes everywhere.

EMMA: Theodora's not the one that's going to have a child. (*strains voice*) I don't have to tell you that. (*rubs hands hard on dress, then, soothingly to Leona*) Now darling . . . (*moves closer*) Leona . . . you know you're just a baby to me. That's all you'll ever be to your mother.

LEONA: Mother, I've been teaching almost eight years now. I can take care of myself.

EMMA: You think I'd let Theodora go runnin' off to California by herself if her husband wasn't out there in the army?

THEODORA: (*turns to Emma*) Mother, Willie C.'ll be out there waiting . . . the oldest sister I got. You know she's grown.

EMMA: That's right, waiting—where's Willie C. gonna be on that long train ride out yonder? No tellin' what's out there. (*pause*) How long they say it was?

(*"Take the A-Train" up and under*)

PETT MAE: Six days.

THEODORA: I don't have to go by myself.

EMMA: You don't have to go at all.

THEODORA: Leona could go with me.

(*Music stops.*)

EMMA: Leona?

THEODORA: Leona (*pause*) me and Leona—could make the trip together.

EMMA: Leona who? . . . Leona's having a child this month. How's Leona going all the way out to California?

RUTH: Leona? Her insides never would take a trip like that. After a baby it takes months to get yourself straightened out.

SAMUELLA: Ladies, please! We're at club meeting.

MARIETTA: Sometimes you mess yourself up for life.

RUTH: Pett . . .

EVA ZOE: Pett girl . . .

RUTH: Bring on the major-domo.

PETT MAE: Doctor wouldn't have it. A train trip could start the worst hemorrhaging. I knew of this one girl . . . (*titters nervously*) she started right on the train . . . and it's even worse for the baby.

SAMUELLA: If my mother could hear this . . .

THEODORA: Well that's not what they say now.

PETT MAE: They? Who's "they"?

THEODORA: Pett, it's all the latest.

EVA ZOE: Listen to the expert.

MARIETTA: Can't even stand the sight of blood.

THEODORA: Hush, Marietta! Everybody up at Meharry's heard it.

MARIETTA: Up at Meharry . . . girl won't even clean a chicken. Fainted only time she ever tried it, talkin' about Meharry.

THEODORA: Why, I've heard of women getting up and walking the next day. Eating whatever they want.

EVA ZOE: Leona can do that now. (*Women laugh.*)

PETT MAE: With her stomach all torn up, why it would be a crime. If Doctor . . . (*Pett Mae and Samuella take deep breaths.*) A woman could drive herself half-crazy carryin' on that way. (*starts to cry*) Why, our Leona never would recover.

(*Ruth comforts Pett. Samuella nods her head repeatedly.*)

THEODORA: Maybe she could leave the baby here, start a new life.

(*Marietta listens to the conversation from the doorway near the piano; she continues to look towards the front door at frequent intervals.*)

EMMA: A new life? Now, let me tell you something, Theodora Edwards Nicholson, and you get this straight—no daughter of mine's gonna leave a child and go runnin' off somewhere.

(*Leona is not responding. She is watching Theodora and Emma's faces. There is a ray of hope in her expression, as if perhaps a solution for her will come out of all this.*)

THEODORA: Oh mother, it's nothing like that.

LEONA: The whole town'll be talkin'.

EMMA: The whole town's already talkin'.

LEONA: Folks say . . .

EMMA: What folks? Don't tell me about "folks."

LEONA: They say having a baby without a father . . .

(*Samuella's hands fly up to her mouth.*)

EMMA: (*hands on hips*) Who's "they"? You always talkin' about "they." (*pauses*) Girl, if you have to go runnin' in every direction every time this one says that way and the other says this way . . . you'll be runnin' all your life. They . . . (*thinks for a second as if toying with the word*) Who's "they"? . . . nice-nasty, that's what it is . . . as long as I can remember, Leona, I've been tellin' you . . . if you do what everybody says just to be doing it even if it's wrong and then you turn your nose up when things get a little dirty even if it's for a good reason, you'll be an old bird up in a nest and you still won't know which way to turn—you won't know which way is right and which way is wrong. You remember what I called it—I said "nice-nasty." You hold your head up, Leona Edwards, even if you're the only one who thinks you ought to, even if the whole town's preachin' and moanin'.

LEONA: Sometimes they won't hire you back teaching after you have a baby.

EMMA: My daughter wouldn't worry about that, even if she had to wash and iron—day and night.

THEODORA: Now, Mother. (*tries to humor her*) Leona's a school teacher. She shouldn't . . . (*The rest of the sentence is inaudible.*)

EMMA: (*pats her foot up and down to her own words, speaks loudly to drown out Theodora*) And never see that child awake. She'd work her fingers to the bone . . . (*stops rhythm suddenly and stomps her foot emphatically*)

LEONA: Mother, I don't know if I can do it on my own.

EMMA: You're Emma Edwards' daughter. You're not on your own—and don't you forget it.

LEONA: But what about a father?

EMMA: (*slaps her hands hard on her skirt*) No use goin' on over somethin' you can't change. Life wasn't meant to fit your purpose or anybody else's, (*pauses*) for that matter. (*narrows eyes. Looks directly at Leona*)

LEONA: (*sheepishly*) Maybe I can get some money from the Thatchers.

THEODORA: O Lord, there Leona goes talking about that mess again.

EMMA: (*to Theodora*) Don't you talk about your forefathers, young lady. Now, you listen to me, my mama was John Thatcher's own daughter . . . Why I remember, I wodden't but so high. My ma would take me down to the courthouse . . . Saturday after Saturday. (*starts to walk*)

THEODORA: Mother and those stories.

MARIETTA: Used to say Fridays.

EMMA: Woman, don't you know I was a school girl (*slaps her thighs*) writing out lessons all day Friday? (*stops abruptly and checks herself*) Don't you get ol' Injun riled up. (*Women laugh politely.*) Saturday after Saturday we'd go up the stairs, way up top of the courthouse, great big desk, a white man, long silver hair, fell in a wave. (*waves hand in the air*) He'd reach in his pocket like so, (*Emma beckons. Marietta leans over and looks in Emma's apron pocket.*) say "Ellen, here take this for the children, buy the little ones some shoes." My ma, she never said one word. After while, I just couldn't stand it. One day, one morning, bright and early we were halfway down the stairs . . . I turned round, looked back up, said "Ma, who was that old white man?" She looked down at me. Like so. "Why Emma darling, (*sweetly*) that old white man was your own uncle . . . (*fiercely, hands on hips*) Judge Hamilton Thatcher."

THEODORA: Next thing you know she'll have her old Injun grandpa struttin' right up to the courthouse.

EMMA: Look at you. Injun yourself.

LEONA: Theodora, don't you sass now.

EMMA: She always did sass me. Sasses her own ma. But I'll tell you darkies one thing . . . half the town's sittin' on Emma Edwards' land.

LEONA: The biggest plantation in middle Tennessee.

MARIETTA: Used to be the biggest. They're not that grand anymore.

EMMA: Why, they sent a car out to get me for every one of their funerals.

(*Cars go by.*)

MARIETTA: Ain't seen them since you finished Fisk. (*walks to the door and looks out*)

THEODORA: And she won't either.

MARIETTA: Sure won't. (*opens the door. Mary Jane rushes in, pushing past Marietta.*)

MARY JANE: Cars runnin' up and down the street. Keeping a woman on foot from going back to her own house. Couldn't get home—Had to walk all the way back up the hill.

EMMA: The law's out everywhere these days.

MARY JANE: Well, I don't want them asking me—trying to find out where I'm going. They'll pay for killing Cordie Cheek. They took that boy's life. When people take things that don't belong to them, they ought to pay.

EMMA: The law knows what they did.

MARY JANE: When somebody takes somethin' . . . Better not lay a hand on my boy.

LEONA: Mother, I swear I think I'm 'bout to pass out.

RUTH: Poor child, must be the flu.

EVA ZOE: Don't get your pretty dress all rumpled, Leona. (*Leona carefully follows Eva Zoe's instructions.*) Press the lace down around the collar. There, that's better. Now stand up and smooth your skirt.

(*Leona stands up, then collapses into the chair.*)

EMMA: Marietta—Look in yonder in that cabinet behind the stove. Fetch me
   that bottle of tonic. Get a move on. (*goes over to Marietta and whispers*)
LEONA: Mother, I can feel it coming on . . . (*fanning*) This teeniny little pain,
   started right here, it's going all the way up my arm.
EMMA: (*loudly to Marietta*) Tie an assifidity bag around her neck. (*softly*) Rest
   yourself, Mary Jane.
MARY JANE: When somebody takes something that doesn't belong to them in
   the first place, you never forget. (*Emma sits on edge of straight-backed chair,
   silently rocking back and forth, staring straight ahead.*) I had to come back. I
   wodden't a been nothin' out there by myself . . . Not that I was leaving the
   whole thing for good. I planned to come back to East Hill anyway.
LEONA: (*gets up and starts walking around. Calls out to Marietta*) Marietta,
   Marietta, you gettin' ready to serve that vanilla cream and a little piece of
   Miss Estelle's cake?

(*Marietta comes out carrying a bottle and a teaspoon. After some coaxing, she gets
Leona to sit down and open her mouth. Mary Jane is embarrassed that she had to
come back to the house so soon. She looks over at Leona and shakes her head. Still
looking at Leona, Mary Jane pulls up a chair and accidentally bangs into the table as
she sits down.*)

EMMA: (*loudly, mischievously*) Mary Jane, was that you, or the chair broke?
MARY JANE: I'm back here because of what they did to that boy—Cordie
   Cheek. (*starts to sweat. Wipes face on sleeve*) My feet—my whole body's 'bout
   to give way. My throat's dry as that wind out there. Took all I had to come
   back here. (*looks startled, as if finally realizing what has happened*) I was driven
   back . . . all because of what they did to that boy on the way from Nashville.
   Bunch of thieves. Next thing you know they'll be saying we started this mess.
   (*gradually raises voice higher and higher*) I circled back, turned all the way
   around; my mind's just a spinnin' and spinnin'. But I want you to know I
   didn't forget. I'm still gonna get it back. I still want my ring.

(*Silence can be heard in the room. No one responds. Finally Theodora heaves a
dejected sigh.*)

THEODORA: Some people sure do have a lot of nerve.
EMMA: (*half-humorously*) Folks need to rest . . . walked all the way up East
   Hill—a glass of water for our guest.

(*Emma steps forward and motions to Theodora. Theodora gets up and hands Mary
Jane Barnes a glass of water. Women murmur in unison. Mary Jane watches from her
chair.*

EMMA: (*half-humorously again*) Give this traveler, weary that she might be, a
   drink of water. (*Women murmur again. Room darkens a little.*) Mary Jane, rest
   yourself.

(*Mary Jane sips water. Laughing and talking can be heard outside the house. Men's voices are heard. A voice calls out at the screen door.*)

VOICE: Sheriff's deputy.

(*Theodora goes to the door. Ushers in Townsend. He is red-faced. Walks up to Theodora. Room becomes darker. Lights down, then gradually up*)

TOWNSEND: Think college boy's tired of me. (*staggering drunk*) I think he's looking for hisself a little starlet. (*leans over Theodora*)

MARY JANE: Well, he better keep lookin'.

TOWNSEND: You wanna know somethin'? You ain't got no hospitality. (*turns to Theodora again. Laughs. Moves in closer. She doesn't look right at him. Scratches his head*) Ain't I seen you somewhere before?—That's right. Somethin' at the picture show. Yeah, you look real familiar . . . (*scratches his head again. Theodora's expression freezes. Deputy looks around. Surveys women sitting at table*) Where's the gun?

EMMA: I looked, sir. I looked high and low. (*exaggerates, looks up and down, waving hands and feigning bewilderment*) I do believe Will took all his guns, sir. He's gone off hunting with the colored doctors from Meharry (*lowers eyes*) . . . and with President Hale.

TOWNSEND: (*hesitates, as if trying to make sure he's hearing right*) President who?

EMMA: Yes sir, President Hale from A&I. (*looks sideways*) A&I, sir. That's the colored college up at Nashville.

TOWNSEND: (*still looking around*) Hale—hell! (*Theodora smiles, covers mouth with hand. Women turn faces down to hide laughter. Townsend looks at women, then starts to stagger.*) Do you or do you not have a gun? That's what Reilly P. Townsend wants to know.

(*Marietta steps forward. Stands next to Theodora*)

EMMA: I'm doin' poorly right now.

TOWNSEND: You keep this up, I'm tellin you now . . . they gon' close you down.

EMMA: And my daughter . . . (*gestures to the left and to the right at all the women in the room. Townsend follows her as she gestures. He staggers, then stands erect.*) You know, she ain't quite . . . well. Her Pa ain't here either. My daughter, she ain't well, you know. (*lowers her head sheepishly. Townsend stares coldly at Emma.*) Will's gone off hunting with the colored doctors from Nashville. (*glances knowingly at Marietta*) And where is young Mr. Frank, Judge Cooper's grandbaby? (*Townsend does not respond.*) Young Mr. Frank, Judge Cooper's grandboy, home from school . . .

TOWNSEND: The grandbaby's held up down there at Blanton's house. (*walks around*) Sittin' over in a corner like he's too good or somethin'. (*stands still and sways slightly. It is clear that Townsend has been drinking heavily.*) Saturday night. Damned if that Blanton don't have everything made and put in a bottle. (*laughs*) He sure does know how to make a fella feel at home. (*walks around, then stands in one spot*) Never mind the college boy. I'm the law around here now.

(Mary Jane stands up, puts her hands on her hips. She disapproves but restrains herself from interrupting.)

EMMA: Will's gone off hunting, sir . . . *(women eye each other knowingly)* with all his colored gentlemen from Nashville.

TOWNSEND: *(screams)* I heard that already. *(Pett Mae starts giggling nervously. Townsend speaks to group.)* "Gents," huh? *(gestures mockingly)* Well . . . Ain't you never heard of hospitality? Hell, *(pause)* it's the middle of July. This ain't the North Pole. Fella don't mind a woman puttin' on the dog. You, the one gon' operate, you goin' down the street. *(Pett Mae holds onto the chair. Townsend grabs Pett Mae and shoves her toward the door.)* Gon' need a undertaker too. *(points to Ruth)*

MARY JANE: When somebody takes something that's not theirs in the first place, they ought to be tried . . . they ought to pay.

TOWNSEND: *(pulls Mary Jane closer)* What's wrong with this darkie? She crazy or somethin'?

(Mary Jane looks frightened. She stutters. She suddenly realizes that she is in danger of being arrested and possibly even lynched or killed herself.)

EMMA: *(touches Mary Jane's shoulder. Turns to deputy)* We're all doin' poorly right now. *(turns to Mary Jane)* Bless your heart, Mary Jane. *(to Townsend)* You know how a woman is when she wants her own. *(to Mary Jane)* That boy of yours worked from sun up to sun down . . . *(Mary Jane glares at Emma and jerks away.)* . . . till his legs gave way under him. *(Mary Jane looks skeptically at Emma. Emma reaches toward her.)* To give my girl that stone. I can see it shining . . . all the way over here. Great big pretty stone. *(Emma gestures towards Leona. Townsend strains and stretches to look across the room.)*

MARY JANE: All the way over here. *(points to the palm of her hand and laughs sarcastically)*

EMMA: You knew I'd come around.

MARY JANE: So, you finally took to using that head your Maker put up on your shoulders. Well, well, it's about time. *(to the women)* She's seen the light.

EMMA: Strong light. Almost blinds my eyes.

MARY JANE: *(to women)* She can see good when she wants to, *(laughs, nudges Eva Zoe)* can't she?

EMMA: Your boy worked his fingers to the bone to give my girl *(waves her hands)* that gold. *(Townsend looks more and more interested.)* Leona's got your ring and bless the Pete . . . you're sick and tired of goin' on about it. *(Townsend perks up when he hears about the jewelry.)* I know what you want—everybody in town's heard you—you want your ring. You want it back.

MARY JANE: Anything to give that boy his own. Lord, I love that boy. I'd wear rags to church, anything to give that boy his own. *(Townsend goes over to Leona and looks her over carefully. She clasps her necklace to her. Mary Jane struts over to Leona, ignoring Townsend.)* When somebody takes something that's not theirs in the first place . . . *(Mary Jane has forgotten the danger of the situation; Townsend wheels around angrily, assuming that Mary Jane is speaking to him.*)

EMMA: (*to Townsend*) You know she's just a heartbroken woman goin' on about our folks' foolishness.

TOWNSEND: (*to Emma*) Good thing she ain't talkin' 'bout a white man.

EMMA: Mary Jane, don't bother this fine gentleman with all our mess. (*pause*) Thank Mr. Townsend for all his protection . . .

MARY JANE: (*glares at Townsend*) One of these days, if that Saul Blanton keeps up all this carryin' on, they gonna pack him up and run him outta Delphi on a rail.

EMMA: (*quickly turns to the deputy and begins to walk towards door. Mary Jane follows her*) . . . and all your help and great concern . . . but you know that Frank Byrd's just a college boy. He's liable to get into deep trouble what with all the rowdies and unpredictables Blanton lets in down there.

MARY JANE: They oughta run him out of town this very hour.

TOWNSEND: (*jumps to attention*) If there's any runnin' to do, Reilly P. Townsend gonna do it, you hear?

EMMA: Have mercy, have mercy! All this runnin' around, folks up to Blanton's all night, raisin' Cain, got the poor woman half-sick. That's the truth, sir.

TOWNSEND: Runnin'—I'll run it . . . Gotta mind to call my boys: "Git on down here and take care of this mess."

EMMA: Run, Mr. Townsend! Go on—you need to head up there and deal with all that carryin' on . . . Lord knows young Mr. Frank needs you more than we do. All those folks from out of town roamin' around, keepin' up the devil all night . . . cockfightin' and who knows what all.

TOWNSEND: (*looks at Emma and grins. Hesitates for a minute, then walks swiftly toward door. Stops, turns around. Leans over to piano; bangs a little*) Been a long time since I felt so good . . . Bring on the Opry. It's Saturday night. (*Goes over to stacks of boxes containing piano rolls. Picks up one of the rolls*) This a player piano? (*laughs hysterically, then yells*) I got business. Ain't got all night, you hear?

EMMA: You're right again, Mr. Townsend, sure 'nough . . . You need to help the boy out . . . give the child some peace of mind. Things go on down there at Saul Blanton's folks never dreamed of in Farley.

(*Emma guides Townsend towards the door. Marietta follows behind.*)

TOWNSEND: Soon as I go back to Blanton's and play wet nurse to the college boy, I'll be back . . . you hear?

(*Emma opens door and ushers Townsend out. When the deputy goes out, Marietta falls against the door in relief. For a moment, everyone is still. When Emma returns, the room fills with talking and strained laughter, expressing both mourning and relief.*)

SAMUELLA: The nerve of that man. (*Women laugh again.*)

MARIETTA: White folks think we can't own pianos. (*Emma looks on innocently, then turns away grinning, as if she is hiding a secret.*) Lord have mercy, look at Mother.

PETT MAE: (*admiringly imitates Emma. Holds handkerchief to her mouth*) "All those rowdies and unpredictables . . . folks from out of town, keepin' up the devil half the night . . ."

RUTH: Mama Emma, you plum forgot that old deputy's from out of town too.

EMMA: Darling, you know your mother knows that.

THEODORA: Mother, you ought to be shot . . . Will Edwards huntin' in the middle of July!

(*Women laugh.*)

LEONA: Mother, I thought you told us Papa went fishin' . . .

PETT MAE: With Doctor's good old buddies from Meharry.

MARIETTA: Might as well ask her 'bout the guns Papa left in the cellar when he went off fishing with the doctors from Meharry. Go on.

EMMA: Meddler! (*mock disgust*) Thought she was out there listening to the Opry.

MARIETTA: And while you're on it, ask her about that old mahogany cabinet with the double lock. See if she'll show you that key stuffed in her apron pocket.

EMMA: (*pretends to ignore Marietta and begins fussing with her hair*) That Marietta Edwards sure is one nosy child. Wonder she's got time to bother other folks so much. Better tend to her own messy self. Find all those Sunday School books she's been lookin' for all week.

MARIETTA: Go on, ask her.

PETT MAE: Not while that old deputy's down the street.

EMMA: That ol' meddler? I sent him on his way.

LEONA: Mother sure does like to perform.

RUTH: Mama Emma, it sure is too bad you couldn't have been in the traveling shows.

EMMA: Mama Emma's danced and sang all she wants to, darling. (*looks up serenely*) Your Mama Emma has lived her life.

THEODORA: Oh Mother, you'll be here after I'm dead and gone.

MARY JANE: (*has been sitting in the corner with her hands folded. Stands up, a determined look on her face*) I'll be goin' now. (*silence*)

RUTH: Evenin', Miss Mary Jane.

(*Women murmur.*)

PETT MAE: Nighty night, Mary Jane.

EVA ZOE: Miss Mary Jane . . . (*stands quickly*) bye now.

RUTH: Save me and Gene a seat at sunrise service . . . like you always do.

MARY JANE: (*waves women away*) And if you don't mind, I'll take my diamond. Got to be seein' about my supper. (*waits, but Emma does not respond*) I said,

I'll be taking my ring. Right here, if you please. (*Mary Jane pats the palm of her hand.*)

(*Leona folds her arms.*)

EMMA: Mary Jane, you oughta know I was just performin' for that old deputy.

MARY JANE: Performin' or not, the ring's mine.

EMMA: Sister Jane, you oughta know by now, that ring's not mine to give away. Never has been.

MARY JANE: I'll call the law down here right now.

EMMA: The old deputy mighta come to your aid, but he won't be back this night. When Marietta called Saul Blanton on the phone, said the law's on the way, I know Saul was waitin' when they got there . . . (*laughs*) We've dealt with the law up here on East Hill many a day. (*looks at Mary Jane*)

MARY JANE: You mighta dealt with the law, but you won't put me off. (*Emma grabs her own hair and brings it forward over her shoulder.*) Your girl can come back, but she'll have to mind her manners, do for my boy the way she ought to.

LEONA: Miss Mary Jane . . .

MARY JANE: Lay a fresh doily behind his head every evening—do whatever.

LEONA: Miss Mary Jane . . .

MARY JANE: Buttermilk dumplings rolled *this* thin, summer peaches, the kind I put up.

LEONA: Ma'am, I'm stayin'. I'm going to raise the baby right here. That ring belongs to me and I'm keeping it. When something belongs to you, you have a right to keep it.

(*Mary Jane plants her feet firmly on the floor, as though determined to have her way.*)

EMMA: (*grabs Mary Jane by the arm*) You're welcome here, Mary Jane, always will be. (*motions to Marietta to bring over a chair. Mary Jane picks up chair and carries chair over to Leona and sits down next to her. Leona stares straight ahead.*) We're not about to put anybody out. I guess Cordie Cheek's mother'll be coming to see you about the wake. She'll be picking out the suit.

PETT MAE: My own pappy wore the loveliest shade of blue.

LEONA: He'll look fine in his suit. He'll look fine, won't he, Ruth?

RUTH: A young boy's suit. (*pause*) I'll be going by Miss Sadie's. (*looks at door*) Sometime this evening.

(*Emma starts to arrange her hair. She reaches in her apron pocket and takes out a few hair pins. Taking out one pin at a time, she slowly pins her hair up at the top of her head.*)

PETT MAE: (*high-voiced*) Look who's gettin' fixed up.

MARIETTA: Mother's gone and found herself a party.

EVA ZOE: Where's the party, Mama Emma? Up there at Saul Blanton's?

EMMA: Never you mind about a party . . . (*teasing back*) I'll party you.

(Women laugh nervously. A few of them absentmindedly begin to arrange their hair and clothes as if preparing for the evening. Emma takes off her apron and throws it on the sofa, then smooths out her dress. She reaches in her pocket for another pin and puts it in her hair. Mary Jane smooths her skirt and adjusts the collar of her dress.)

SAMUELLA: Look at Mother Emma—dressing up.

EVA ZOE: Remember, Mama Emma, when you used to get all fixed up and play for our high school dance?

THEODORA: Mother doesn't need a party to get dressed up and step out.

MARIETTA: She never did.

LEONA: She'll start gettin' ready at the drop of a hat.

RUTH: *(to the other table)* Theodora, Eva Zoe, Sam, all you all . . . *(Ruth struggles to stand.)* I've got a body to pick up.

(There is a long silence.)

PETT MAE: The law's acting real ugly tonight.

THEODORA: I wouldn't set foot out there if you paid me.

(Emma walks to the door, opens it slightly and starts out.)

RUTH: Where you goin', Mama Emma?

EMMA: *(turns and addresses women)* Why, I remember one night I put on everything I owned. Shawls, everything. *(hands on hips)* Will said, "Lord have mercy, Emma, where you think you're going?" I turned around just like this, said "Just going out to look at the stars."

(Leona goes to the bedroom. She returns holding a silk crepe dinner dress to her body. She seems to be deep in thought, then turns towards Emma.)

EMMA: *(walks over to a chair and picks up a shawl)* It's dark now . . . a beautiful night and the stars are all out . . . I guess I'll go out on the porch. The stars'll be out right about now.

(Ruth struggles, stands up and walks a few steps toward the door. Emma walks out the door while Mary Jane and the women watch.)

(Stage is dark. Spotlight on Marietta.)

MARIETTA: I don't know why things had to turn out the way they did with Cordie Cheek. God tests your faith. Sometimes there's no point in tryin' to blame anybody. Maybe it had to be this way. No point in trying to talk about how things could have been different. I just have to believe that.

Leona's been goin' on about havin' that baby without a husband . . . about what the town'll say . . . lots worse things been said about folks. If that's all anybody ever says about you, you've done pretty well, I'd say. By the time she gets through nursin' that baby, she won't have time to worry about what folks think.

I try to be real quiet, real nice and not worry folks with a whole lot of mess. When Leona and Mother start that talk about the Thatchers, I just let them go right on. Don't say a word. Makes me no never mind. I wouldn't be surprised if Leona told that same story to the baby . . . that baby . . . I'll tell you one thing . . . it'll be a talkin' one. You know Leona's the one that always listened to Mama's stories when she was comin' up. Mother likes to tell folks that Grandma got married up to the Thatcher house in a red velvet dress. She did no such thing. (*slowly explaining*) Grandma ran off and got married, same as me. When her own Papa died they sent for Grandma in a big black car. She wouldn't even go. Said she was mad—at the Thatchers. Why? (*Laughs*) That's somethin' you'd have to ask Grandma. I couldn't tell you that. You see, Mother likes a good story. And she knew Leona would eat up whatever she told her.

Let other folks live in peace. That's all I know to say. Leave other folks alone. I try to help when I can, otherwise I leave them alone. Mary Jane goes on about card playin'. (*pause, with emphasis*) She's performin' herself. Card playin'? If that's all anybody ever says about you, you've done pretty well, and that's the truth.

Like I said, I don't know why things had to turn out the way they did with Cordie Cheek. Folks'll go on for days . . . doin' a whole lot of whoopin' and hollerin'. But it won't amount to much. Saul Blanton. They think he's just a performer. Somebody to laugh at. They think he's a gambler, a bootlegger, just somebody interested in money. They come runnin' through here . . . all the time lookin' for this old gun and that one. Saul Blanton can get 100 guns from Chicago, just like that. Now I don't believe in gamblin' . . . (*aside*) That's how Saul Blanton got rich, that and bootleggin'. (*faces audience again*) But sometimes you gotta fight evil with evil. They take us for a bunch of fools. They think they know where all the guns are?

Like I said, I don't approve of gamblin'—or guns either—but I don't judge people. I hope it never comes to guns—but it might have to. I'll tell you this—if it does they'll be pullin' the white folks out of the Duck River, buryin' them at night. Folks'll be on the roofs down in the Bottom, on top of Ruth and Jim's business, Saul Blanton's barber shop, Curtis' cafeteria, the Elks' lodge, with rifles aimed, just a waitin'. And when they come through— (*pauses, looks off*) They're busy lookin' for one gun. Time may come. I ain't sayin' it will come, but I'm tellin' you . . . Saul Blanton can get guns from Chicago any time he wants.

Now I hope it never comes to that—but the Lord works in mysterious ways. Folks may not believe this, but the whole world's lookin' right here. If you think what we say don't count, just watch. I'm not sayin' I'd fight, but we're going to get justice sometime. We're gonna get it, sure as day and night.

(*Spotlight fades slowly.*)

END

Michon Boston
(1962–)

Michon Boston found a voice in dramatic writing while pursuing other creative endeavors like music, the visual arts, and media. Her desire to write dramatically was long inspired by watching old black and white movies on television with her mother, observing her sister's activities as a theater major at Howard University, and hearing stories—truth or fiction—from the extended family.

A native of Washington, D.C., Michon Boston was born September 16, 1962, to Theodore W. and Caroline Long Boston. She attended the Duke Ellington School of the Arts, graduating in June 1980, and continued her education at Oberlin College in Ohio, where she completed her B.A. degree in English in 1984. Inspired by outstanding black alumnae of Oberlin, like Anna Julia Cooper and Mary Church Terrell, Boston received a grant from the National Endowment for the Humanities (NEH) for her research on the history of black women students who attended the college from the 19th century to 1979.

"Iola's Letter" received 2nd prize for drama in the Larry Neal Writer's Competition Awards sponsored by the D.C. Commission on the Arts and Humanities in 1994; and was a finalist for a Chesterfield Film Company fellowship at Universal Studios in Los Angeles. Readings of "Iola's Letter" have been sponsored by Playwrights Forum, The Capital Hill Arts Workshop and the Source Theatre (1994 Summer Theatre Festival).

It is 1893, in New York City. Ida B. Wells, in exile from the South, poses for a publicity photo to take on her voyage to England where she will rally support against lynching in the U.S. She reflects on the events that brought her to this moment, a crusade launched in Memphis, Tennessee, the scene of the brutal murders of three prominent black businessmen by a lynch mob. As editor and partner of the "colored" newspaper *Free Speech*, Ida uses her only weapon—a column known as "Iola's Letter"—to expose the truth behind the murders and rescue a community from a racially biased and tarnished image.

As to why she wrote *Iola's Letter,* Boston states:

> Vera Katz, professor of drama at Howard University, was looking for plays to direct about outstanding American black women. Her preferences were Georgia Douglas Johnson of the Harlem Renaissance; contemporary poet Gwendolyn Brooks; and Ida B. Wells of the 19th and early 20th centuries.
>
> After studying the lives of black women who attended Oberlin College from the 19th and 20th centuries, I was drawn to writing a drama featuring a thriving, black middle class and intellectual community existing in 19th century America. Much attention is focused on the 1960s as the pivotal era for an African-American initiated movement for civil and voting rights; and the 1920s or Harlem Renaissance as the birth of the Black intelligentsia. But the movement for self-determination, human and civil rights, and the building of an intellectual community in this country began when the first Africans stepped on the shores of North America. Both slave and free Black men and women would converse privately and publicly about citizenship and the right to life, liberty and the pursuit of their own well being in a new country. I never intended *Iola's Letter* as a biography of Ida B. Wells. I wanted to explore the ideas and issues of her times, and as a result have found strong parallels between then and today.

The first public staged reading of *Iola's Letter* was produced in 1994 by the Source Theatre in Washington, D.C. The reading was directed by Howard student Jackie Carter, and the role of Ida B. Wells was performed by a talented 15–year-old actor named Yendi Yarborough.

Boston's other plays include *Stained Glass Houses* and *Anthropology,* which premiered at the Source Theatre, Washington, D.C. Boston has served on the board of Women in Film in Washington, D.C., and is a member of Playwrights Forum, Women in Film L.A., and the Dramatists Guild. Boston also designs and makes cloth dolls when she's not writing. Boston resides in Washington, D.C.

SOURCES

Correspondence between Michon Boston and Kathy Perkins, 1995.

Iola's Letter
1994

❧

Michon Boston

CAST OF CHARACTERS

IDA B. WELLS, *"Iola." Partner and editor of the* Free Speech *newspaper in Memphis. Age 29.*

REV. NIGHTINGALE, *founder of the* Free Speech *and former partner. Minister of the largest Black congregation in Memphis.*

MR. FLEMING, *partner with Ida at the* Free Speech *and business manager.*

ISAAC, *the* Free Speech's *young assistant. Runs the printing press.*

THOMAS "TOMMIE" MOSS, *Ida's best friend and owner of the People's Grocery, which was financed from Tommie's letter carrier job.*

BETTY MOSS, *Ida's best friend and Tommie's wife. Betty is expecting a second child in the first act.*

MAURINE, *Betty and Tommie's young daughter. Ida's goddaughter.*

SHOP OWNER, *ladies' dress shop owner. A white businessman who advertises in the* Free Speech.

MR. CARMACK, *reporter for the* Memphis Commercial.

BLACK JUDAS, *pseudonym for a nameless criminal who stalks the Black community.*

SAM JOHNSON, *an older citizen in the Black community. Robbery victim.*

MRS. JOHNSON, *Sam Johnson's wife. Rev. Nightingale's church secretary.*

PHOTOGRAPHER

WOMAN (*train station, Mississippi*)

MAN (*train station, Mississippi*)

YOUNG MAN (*Mississippi*)

WITNESS

ASSISTANT (*for Thomas Fortune's New York Age newspaper*)

NEWSPAPER BOY

MOURNER

VOICE OF CONDUCTOR (*train stations*)

ACT ONE, PROLOGUE

Photographer's studio, New York City—1893. PHOTOGRAPHER *adjusts the chair and background for a portrait setting.*

PHOTOGRAPHER: Alright, we're just about set up in here. Are you ready? (*no answer*) I said, are you ready, Miss Wells?

(IDA B. WELLS *enters, dressed soberly.*)

PHOTOGRAPHER: Wonderful. Please sit. (*directs Ida to her chair*) Head up. Turn please.

(*Photographer goes to the camera and slips the cover over his head. Unsatisfied, he comes from behind the camera.*)

PHOTOGRAPHER: (*studies Ida*) Perhaps you should stand. You'll look taller . . . like a grand lady.

(*Ida stands. Photographer goes under the cover again. Ida doesn't smile. Her expression remains sober.*)

PHOTOGRAPHER: Head up and tilt a little.

THOMAS FORTUNE: (*offstage*) The princess of the press. She handles a quill with a diamond point.

(*Photographer comes from behind the camera, exasperated.*)

PHOTOGRAPHER: Miss Wells. You look as if you've been to a funeral, not a woman about to take her first steamboat across the Atlantic.

(*Enter* NEWSPAPER BOY.)

NEWSPAPER BOY: (*delivering papers*) "Eight Negroes lynched since last issue of the *Free Speech,* the colored newspaper of Memphis . . . Miss Iola tells the whole story. Read it in the *Free Speech!*"

(*Newspaper Boy sells copies to patrons.*)

IDA: I intend to take this portrait with me to Europe.

MR. CARMACK: The black wretch. The darky damsel who wrote this foul lie should be taken to the corner of Main and Madison streets and burned at a stake.

IDA: Did you know Thomas Moss?

(*Spot on* THOMAS MOSS.)

THOMAS: You know, Ida, we're the first generation—*the first*—not to be brought up in chains. We have the education, our own businesses and with new opportunities out west . . . this is our chance to grab the brass ring. Maybe we can't accomplish all we want for ourselves, but for the next generation and the next . . .

(*Spot down on Thomas.*)

IDA: Thomas Moss was an innocent man. Hinting at the truth put a price on my head.

(BLACK JUDAS *enters.*)

BLACK JUDAS: Every time they see you, they see me. A nigger . . . a black, low-down nigger. All niggas. Always niggas!

PHOTOGRAPHER: Hold the pose per-fect-ly still please.

LIGHTS DOWN *on photographer's studio.*

ACT ONE, SCENE I

The offices of the Free Speech—*1892.* MR. FLEMING *closes an ad deal with a white* SHOP OWNER.

MR. FLEMING: And I'll make sure your two-inch ad goes right next to "Iola's Letter," our most popular column.

SHOP OWNER: Iola. She's the one who runs this paper, right?

MR. FLEMING: She's my partner. You know, among our people she's known as the princess of the press.

SHOP OWNER: Is that so?

MR. FLEMING: That's right.

SHOP OWNER: I've seen her in my shop. Seems like a decent gal.

MR. FLEMING: A credit to her race.

SHOP OWNER: We'll see how this advertising deal goes for a month and then talk about an extension, alright?

(*Shop Owner and Mr. Fleming shake hands.*)

MR. FLEMING: Good, sir. And like I said, you will have a loyal colored clientele just for advertising in the *Free Speech*. I guarantee it.

SHOP OWNER: Good. I'm always pleased with the Negro customers that come in the shop. Let's hope this will keep them coming.

MR. FLEMING: It will, sir. It will.

SHOP OWNER: Afternoon to you, Mr. Fleming.

MR. FLEMING: Thank you, sir.

(*Shop Owner exits. Mr. Fleming counts the cash before putting it away in the strongbox.*)

MR. FLEMING: Isaac!

(*Enter* ISAAC *wearing a printer's apron with ink smeared on the front.*)

ISAAC: Yes, Mr. Fleming.

MR. FLEMING: Copy looks good, son. Now make sure the ink comes out crisp and clear. No splotches especially on the ads. I want to keep that two hundred a month in our cash box.

Isaac: Yes sir, Mr. Fleming.

Mr. Fleming: Oh, and has that new newsprint come in?

Isaac: Yes sir. A ton of it. Not to be disrespectful, Mr. Fleming, but are we really gonna print a newspaper on—

Mr. Fleming: (*interrupts*) Yes, yes, Isaac. I don't know which is worse. Her last Iola's Letter column or this new newsprint. One more thing. Take this advertisement to the mercantile and see if he approves the copy.

Isaac: Yes, sir.

(*As Isaac opens the door, he's stopped by an exasperated* Rev. Nightingale.)

Rev. Nightingale: Boy, can't you see where you're going?

Isaac: Yes sir, Reverend. I mean no. I mean excuse me, I gotta go.

(*Isaac exits.*)

Mr. Fleming: Good morning, Reverend—

Rev. Nightingale: Where is she? Where is the "sapphire of the press"?

(*Rev. Nightingale clutches a newspaper and waves it before Mr. Fleming's face.*)

Mr. Fleming: What's the problem?

Rev. Nightingale: Tell me something, Fleming, do you ever read your own newspaper?

Mr. Fleming: I proof every copy.

Rev. Nightingale: I'm not talking about whether the word scandal ends in a-l or e-l. I mean read!

(*Rev. Nightingale slams the paper on Mr. Fleming's desk. Mr. Fleming reads the newspaper, shielding himself from Rev. Nightingale's piercing glare.*)

Rev. Nightingale: She accused me of using this paper for political purposes. And what has she done since I left the *Free Speech* but discredit my colleagues and anyone else who doesn't measure up to *her* standards of morality and conduct.

Mr. Fleming: Franklin . . . maybe—

Rev. Nightingale: Mr. Fleming, I'm not a partner here any longer, I'm a customer and insist on immediate satisfaction.

Mr. Fleming: Franklin.

(*Rev. Nightingale is quite serious.*)

Mr. Fleming: *Reverend.* It's not so bad. I'm sure no one even paid attention to this . . . this "editorial."

Rev. Nightingale: Mr. Fleming, do you take me for a fool? Everyone reads Iola's Letter. *Everyone.* The preachers' alliance has called a meeting for tomorrow and I've spoken with several of the members already. We see no other choice but to advise our congregations to boycott this newspaper starting next Sunday.

Mr. Fleming: Boycott!? Boycott the only colored paper in town?!

REV. NIGHTINGALE: My Beale Street Baptist brings in five hundred subscriptions alone. It would be hard to make that difference up no matter how many subscriptions she sells in Mississippi. I was the sales manager, remember? But I'm also aware of the importance of this paper as one of its original co-founders. (*takes out a letter from his coat*) Now, I've taken it upon myself to draft a retraction. All you have to do is have her sign it and there will be no further trouble.

MR. FLEMING: (*pauses*) She's not going to sign it.

REV. NIGHTINGALE: Well then, what about you? Aren't you equal partners?

MR. FLEMING: I'm the business manager. I sell the ads.

REV. NIGHTINGALE: I see. Then a boycott is inevitable. When will you see, Fleming? Ida B. Wells is an impatient, self-serving, conceited young woman. If someone doesn't take hold of her and teach her the ways of this world, heaven help us, we'll lose everything we've gained.

MR. FLEMING: But a boycott, Nightingale. How is that going to help us?

(*Enter Ida with* THOMAS *in the middle of one of their friendly debates.*)

THOMAS: My point is land ownership. Without it a man has no say in this country. I'm not waiting for my 40 acres and a mule when there's the opportunity to start our own towns with our own money and labor right out west.

IDA: But your grocery's a success here in Memphis. Why start over in some unknown, untamed territory?

REV. NIGHTINGALE: Miss Wells.

IDA: Rev. Nightingale. What's the pleasure of your visit today?

REV. NIGHTINGALE: No pleasure at all.

(*Rev. Nightingale takes the newspaper he brought and shoves it into Ida's hand. Thomas goes over to Mr. Fleming to get the low-down.*)

IDA: I assume you know this "gentleman"?

REV. NIGHTINGALE: This gentleman *you* accuse of (*reads*) jumping out a woman's bedroom window in his nightclothes when discovered by the harlot's husband happens to be a well-respected colleague of mine.

MR. FLEMING: Wells, the reverend says the preachers' alliance will call for a boycott of the paper. I just sold a new ad for the next four editions this morning.

IDA: Reverend Nightingale, this story isn't new. It appears in newspapers every day. Besides there were at least five witnesses, and the good reverend himself knew he was in the wrong. Thou shalt not commit—

REV. NIGHTINGALE: Don't you dare quote scripture to me, young lady. This newspaper has gone downhill since the day you pushed your way into partnership. Fleming and I believed your name would actually bring some prestige to a modest publication like the *Free Speech*. But look what happened. Numerous stories that make the Negro look ridiculous, careless and morally corrupt.

IDA: Would you rather see Mr. Carmack's view on these matters in the *Memphis Commercial?*

REV. NIGHTINGALE: Of course not. We have yet to convince the rest of Memphis or the world that we are human beings making human errors. Of course your generation wouldn't understand because you haven't struggled like some of us. You expect immediate gratification when it's been nearly thirty years since the day we were freed. Slavery still burns in me.

IDA: It burns in me too, Reverend. I may not have lived as a slave, but I was born one. My mother and father carried those memories to their graves.

REV. NIGHTINGALE: Then why do you deliberately sabotage any and every step we take towards progress? Our colored schools for example. How you attacked them so viciously . . . You remember, Fleming. She knew anything printed in this paper had to be signed off by me and now the few colored schools we have left are in worse shape because of that editorial you published behind my back.

IDA: Someone needed to speak out against the few and utterly inadequate buildings for colored children. How does a child get a good education in a one-room shack and from teachers whose mental and moral character are not the very best? I wrote that in the interest of the children.

REV. NIGHTINGALE: The children?

IDA: And the race.

REV. NIGHTINGALE: Well, don't you think it may have been in the best interest of the children to have one of their more capable teachers teaching now? I don't blame them for firing you.

IDA: I don't regret it.

REV. NIGHTINGALE: No, I suppose not. In some ways, sister Wells, you remind me of the phoenix—falling into the fire then rising again from the ashes. But I fear one day you won't be so fortunate and neither will the rest of us who may perish with you. Good day, Mr. Fleming, Thomas. (*exit Rev. Nightingale*)

THOMAS: Whew! That wasn't the best example of customer relations.

MR. FLEMING: He left this for you. It's a retraction. (*hands Ida the letter*) It's going to make a big difference if they start the boycott.

IDA: If the truth makes people cross, then so be it.

MR. FLEMING: But there is something called discretion.

(*Ida rips the retraction in half.*)

IDA: Nightingale may tell his congregation what to do, but he doesn't have that influence here. Now, Tommie, I'll take my mail.

THOMAS: That's why I make this my last stop. Always something exciting going on. (*passes out letters*) Fleming, Fleming, Miss Iola, Iola, Wells . . . this looks interesting . . . Letter to the Editor.

MR. FLEMING: I sense you're not taking this boycott matter seriously.

IDA: I'm very serious about the running of this paper.

THOMAS: If you're not going to publish Nightingale's letter then why continue to call this paper the *Free Speech*?

IDA: Because Rev. Nightingale for all his talk is in his heart afraid. Afraid that perhaps someone out there might actually try their hand at *thinking* for themselves.

MR. FLEMING: Now, Wells, he's just trying to do what he thinks is right for his people. And that's the God's truth.

THOMAS: You can't deny, Nightingale does like to have his way. I'm sure it doesn't set too well to have a little lady like Ida brushing him off like a firefly. But I understand, Fleming. He was your first partner here.

MR. FLEMING: Speaking of partners, Thomas, you, Calvin or Henry never did get back to me about taking out advertising for the People's Grocery. Let me show you our new paper. (*Fleming takes out a sample sheet of pink newsprint*)

IDA: It's here?

MR. FLEMING: We can say you'll be tickled pink shopping at the People's Grocery.

THOMAS: Pink?

IDA: No one will ever confuse it for the *Memphis Commercial* ever again.

MR. FLEMING: You can be certain of that.

THOMAS: I've been so busy with the store, this postman's job, and you know Betty's due to have the baby soon. And Maurine. Can't forget my daughter.

IDA: My goddaughter.

THOMAS: And just keeping up with these reports I'm getting from the Oklahoma territories, has my mind pretty occupied. Look, Fleming.(*takes out paper*) There are at least a dozen well-established Negro communities out there.

MR. FLEMING: Let me see that. (*reads*) I don't know. Out there you're pretty much on your own.

IDA: The territory's too spread out. It would take months to get supplies into those townships.

THOMAS: The railroad's coming through.

IDA: But there're no colleges, theaters, music halls.

THOMAS: Eventually they'll have all that.

IDA: No newspaper.

THOMAS: You can start one.

MR. FLEMING: How? No mercantiles, no banks . . .

THOMAS: No lynchings. The point is the people out there got fed up with the South. Who's to say what happens in Mississippi won't someday happen here.

MR. FLEMING: It hasn't before. Memphis is a different kind of southern town. It has a certain reputation to protect.

IDA: From what I've read about these incidents I'd like to know what Negro man in his right mind would attack a white man for no reason, unless he was provoked.

THOMAS: Would he be provoked to rape a white woman?

MR. FLEMING: Rape? He'd be crazy.

IDA: No woman provokes a man to such a crime. If the brute they describe is found guilty, perhaps he deserves death.

THOMAS: By a mob? I don't believe anyone deserves to die that way.

IDA: No. That's why we've got to commit ourselves to education and decent character. That will protect us in the end. And put money in our purse. Being wasteful and spendthrift will keep our race poor and the slave of the man with money, never in a position to demand a thing.

THOMAS: Amen. And that's the seed those western townships are planting. Let me tell you . . . out there—

(Enter Isaac, out of breath.)

ISAAC: Mr. Fleming. Oh, Miss Wells, Mr. Moss. Sam Johnson got robbed.

MR. FLEMING: What?

THOMAS: Old Sam Johnson?

ISAAC: Yeah. They say it's Black Judas, again.

MR. FLEMING: My god, is he hurt?

ISAAC: Said, he cut Johnson on the leg pretty bad last night. But the doctor fixed him up.

IDA: Was there an arrest?

ISAAC: No, mam.

THOMAS: As long as Judas stays in the Negro section of town, no lawman's going to waste his time tracking him down.

IDA: There's no reason why we can't insist that these lawmen protect our citizens. I'm going over to see Mr. Johnson and get more details.

MR. FLEMING: Now? This may not be a good time.

THOMAS: Oh, if he's the Sam Johnson I know, I'm sure he's already talking about going after that "nigger" by now.

IDA: I want a description of the man printed in the next issue.

MR. FLEMING: Say, I'm going to the lodge tonight. Why don't I get one of the fellas to do it. You know Johnson. He likes to talk . . .

IDA: Man to man.

MR. FLEMING: You want the story don't you? Besides, the details may be a little unsettling.

THOMAS: Come on, Fleming. Ida's a professional. If she can't handle it, there's no point in her being in the newspaper business.

IDA: Let me check my list.

THOMAS: Ida's list. Everything to buy, things to do, people to see carefully documented.

IDA: It keeps me from wandering off the trail. Goodness, I have an editorial to finish and the subscriptions. Okay Fleming, see who's available. But make sure they get the story by tomorrow at the latest. Isaac, you keep us updated.

ISAAC: *(with enthusiasm)* Yes, mam! *(Isaac exits to the press room.)*

THOMAS: If this man's still about, you shouldn't be alone in this office late at night. Why don't you bring your work to the store tonight. I've got to do our books, Betty's making a cake, and we can all wash it down with some strong coffee.

IDA: That sounds wonderful, Tommie, but I—

MR. FLEMING: And don't forget about the boycott. How are we going to handle that?

THOMAS: That's right.

IDA: (*picks up the two halves of Rev. Nightingale's torn letter and puts them together on the table*) I want the names of every minister belonging to the alliance. These names are going to be printed in my editorial to the effect that these men uphold the immoral conduct of one of their number and are willing to support preachers who would sneak into the homes when their backs were turned and debauch their wives.

MR. FLEMING: That's all we need. The preachers' alliance on our backs.

THOMAS: Don't worry, Mr. Fleming. They're men of God. (*to Ida*) Let's hope they turn the other cheek. Listen, if you don't come for coffee, I insist you come to dinner.

IDA: I don't know.

THOMAS: Come on. When was the last time you had a *real* home-cooked meal? Not at the boarding house.

IDA: True.

THOMAS: Maurine would love to see you. Listen, I bet Betty's setting the table right now. Come on. Maybe we can get there in time to help her. Fleming, how about you?

MR. FLEMING: That's mighty nice of you, Thomas, but I'm going to head to the lodge and get someone on this Johnson story.

IDA: I'll come with you, Fleming.

MR. FLEMING: Sorry, Wells. You know the rules. Men only.

IDA: But this is different.

THOMAS: Trust Fleming, Ida. He'll get you a good man to do the story. You concentrate on those subscriptions after dinner at *my* house. I can smell the sweet potatoes, fried tomatoes, chicken, biscuits and gravy. Mmmm.

IDA: Alright. (*takes out her list and writes*) Dinner.

ACT ONE, SCENE 2

BETTY, *who is seven months pregnant, sets the dinner table. She moves deliberately and slowly. Her daughter* MAURINE *helps.*

BETTY: The fork goes there and the knife goes there.

(*Enter Thomas and Ida.*)

THOMAS: Dear wife, we have one extra for dinner. Let me do that. (*takes the plates*)

BETTY: Ida! I'm so glad. You usually never have time for anything but what the boarding house leaves for you. (*Maurine runs to hug Ida.*)

IDA: Hello sweet pea. I know, Betty, but your husband is a very persuasive salesman.

BETTY: Sweetheart, set another place for your aunt Ida. Tommie, how did you manage to get her away from the *Free Speech?*

THOMAS: (*takes a plate from Betty and sets a place at the table*) She was hungry and so am I. I keep telling Betty, we should open a restaurant in the People's Grocery featuring her famous southern cooking.

BETTY: Famous with this household.

THOMAS: (*pats his belly*) Soon, I'll be as big as you.

(*Betty laughs. She feels the baby kick inside her.*)

THOMAS: Is that . . . ? (*presses his hand against Betty's stomach*) That's my son. That's my Junior. Ida, feel this.

IDA: What?

THOMAS: A future president of the United States.

BETTY: Don't be silly, Tommie.

THOMAS: If you don't expect great things, you don't get them. Come on, Ida.

IDA: Are you sure, Betty?

(*Betty takes Ida's hand and places it on her stomach.*)

IDA: Incredible.

THOMAS: I know it's a boy.

IDA: How?

THOMAS: Because I do. Don't get me wrong. I love Maurine. She's daddy's peach, aren't you, sweetheart?

(*Thomas picks Maurine up and swings her in the air. He sits down with Maurine on his knee.*)

IDA: Do you expect her to be president of the United States?

THOMAS: Let's say I wouldn't be surprised. After all I'm her father. But women don't vote.

IDA: Yet.

BETTY: Show's over, children. Time to eat. Tommie, I want you to take Henry and Calvin a plate when you go to the store tonight.

THOMAS: I'll do that. (*pause*) Are you thinking about shifting your crusade from the race to women and the vote?

IDA: Don't be ridiculous, Tommie. Of course not, but I do see where one can benefit the other.

THOMAS: When it means something. Even with the Negro vote there are some places where it still doesn't count. When Washington said "yes" the rest of the South was busy finding ways to say "no" and still are.

IDA: And eventually that's going to change. I can write but so many editorials and sell but so many subscriptions. I've got to have my say on that ballot.

THOMAS: Well, Ida, there are people out there who wouldn't agree with you. They feel politics isn't the place for women.

IDA: It has to be for Negro women.

(Betty silently indicates to Thomas to cut back on the debating.)

THOMAS: I know, I know. The dinner table is no place for politics if you want to enjoy your food. But one other thing I wanted to talk with you about, Ida. This is something you should definitely write about. There's been a lot of information floating around about Booker T. Washington's Tuskegee Institute in Alabama. We even got a flyer at the store . . .

IDA: Really?

THOMAS: They sure are taking in a lot of donations from mostly white patrons. The whole country seems to think Mr. Washington just might have the answer to the race problem.

IDA: Of course. A school that teaches you how to be a better shoeshine boy or maid—why not?

THOMAS: Don't be so fast. I think this merits Iola's attention. A lot of those students came from nothing and now they're running their own farms, brick works and other businesses, like me.

IDA: You're hardly a product of Washington's cotton gin.

THOMAS: I think there's something to be said for industrial education.

IDA: Is that your great expectation for your children? To learn to pull up radishes or stuff a mattress instead of learning Latin, literature, and mathematics?

BETTY: That's quite a contrast.

THOMAS: It's about putting money in our pockets today.

IDA: With straw in our brains. A solid literary education makes for a superior mind and character.

THOMAS: Still the teacher. It may not be the solution, but it's a choice.

IDA: Which would you choose for your children, Betty? Tuskegee or Fisk?

BETTY: My choice is . . . to let my children make their own decisions.

THOMAS: There. And if it's Tuskegee, I won't say nay.

BETTY: Well, Tuskegee will turn out a fine blacksmith, but we still need teachers, preachers, doctors and journalists to complete the picture.

IDA: Hear, hear.

THOMAS: Letter carriers and businessmen.

IDA: I wish Mr. Washington well, but not at the expense of lowering our higher expectations as you said.

THOMAS: Lower? I'm sure Mr. Washington has very high expectations of his program.

IDA: I mean there are other concerns. Voting rights, for example. Mr. Washington's theory has been that we'd better give attention to trying to be first-class people in a Jim Crow car than insisting that the Jim Crow car be abolished.

THOMAS: (*laughs*) I've heard Washington's such a popular man these days with the white folks that he doesn't have to ride the Jim Crow car anymore.

(*Ida is slightly annoyed. Thomas smiles.*)

BETTY: Let's say grace.

(*All hold hands at the table and bow their heads.*)

ACT ONE, SCENE 3

Next day in Sam Johnson's home. SAM JOHNSON *talks with* MR. CARMACK *of the* Memphis Commercial *newspaper.*

SAM JOHNSON: You need to put up signs in the post office and a good picture of him in the paper.

MR. CARMACK: Sure thing. Don't need his kind around.

SAM JOHNSON: You got that right. I say if you catch him, hang him. Pretty soon he'll kill some one here. Mark my word. Did you get what I told you about him cutting me?

MR. CARMACK: Yep. I got it.

(*Ida is greeted by* MRS. JOHNSON.)

IDA: (*to Mrs. Johnson*) What is Carmack doing here?

MRS. JOHNSON: He called on Mr. Johnson saying he heard about the robbery and wanted to cover it in the *Commercial.*

(*Sam Johnson tries to lift himself out of the chair, but the pain in his leg prevents him.*)

MR. CARMACK: That's okay, uncle. I can show myself out.

(*Mrs. Johnson goes to Sam Johnson. Ida meets Mr. Carmack on his way out.*)

MR. CARMACK: Ida B. Wells. Now what's a little teacher gal like you doing here?

IDA: Making sure people in this town get the truth.

MR. CARMACK: Aw, I think people in this town know enough. They know these Negro districts ain't safe for nobody with hordes of ignorant and dangerous types hanging about. Look at poor old Johnson in there. Can't go outside his own house. Can't blame the white man on that.

IDA: I blame the men who are supposed to uphold the law for not catching this thief.

MR. CARMACK: Don't worry. He's gonna get caught. These niggras get cocky and that's when *we* get 'em. Just like those friends of yours at that People's

Grocery on the curve. That other grocer's about to lose his business because of those boys and he ain't too happy about it.

IDA: Those are some of the finest and most honest men you'll meet in Memphis. They saved their money just like any other businessman in this town. They have a right to open their store anywhere they want.

MR. CARMACK: Mmm hmm. I'm sure. (*exits*)

MRS. JOHNSON: Come in, Miss Wells. Sam, Miss Ida B. Wells wants to talk to you about the robbery.

SAM JOHNSON: Ida B. Wells? Who's she?

IDA: I'm from the *Free Speech*.

MRS. JOHNSON: Can I get you a cup of tea and a biscuit?

IDA: No, thank you, Mrs. Johnson.

SAM JOHNSON: I thought some fella was coming from the *Free Speech*.

IDA: That had to be changed. I'm filling in.

SAM JOHNSON: (*studies Ida*) I don't remember seeing your name in the paper.

IDA: Perhaps it's because I use my pen name, Iola.

MRS. JOHNSON: Iola. Oh we read Iola's Letter all the time, don't we Sam?

SAM JOHNSON: Yeah. But I don't always agree with everything you say in that paper though.

IDA: That's not uncommon.

(*Sam Johnson relaxes.*)

SAM JOHNSON: You say some good things sometimes. Things somebody should be printin'. Damn, my leg is near going to kill me. Fetch me that pillow.

(*Mrs. Johnson takes a pillow from the couch and gently puts it under Sam Johnson's leg.*)

SAM JOHNSON: No good nigger cut me when I took him down.

IDA: Is this what you told Mr. Carmack?

SAM JOHNSON: I sure did.

IDA: Was Mrs. Johnson with you when this happened?

MRS. JOHNSON: No, I wasn't. You see, Sam—

SAM JOHNSON: I can tell my own story. I was coming from the bank after making a fifty-dollar withdrawal. That money was to buy a parlor organ for my wife, see. After a few stops, I'm walking back to the house. It's dark. Then this man jumps from behind this corner. I took him with everything I got, but he had a knife, cut my leg. I'm lying on the ground and he went through my pockets and took every cent I had, including my good pocket watch.

IDA: What did the man look like? Was he colored?

SAM JOHNSON: Was he colored? He was black. Black as coal. Black Judas. That's who it was. Everybody else who's met up with him knows the face. Here, let me show you what he did. (*unwraps his wound*)

MRS. JOHNSON: Sam, you think that's necessary?

SAM JOHNSON: She's a newspaper writer. Look here.

IDA: That is a nasty wound. Have you seen a doctor?

SAM JOHNSON: You women always talking about doctors. Well, one's gonna come by today. But you let that nigger come 'round here again. I got something for him. I'll shoot him to the middle of next week.

IDA: Were there any witnesses, Mr. Johnson?

SAM JOHNSON: I work long and hard for every penny I got. And then here comes one of those no-account Negroes who feels that what's mine should be his.

LIGHTS UP *on a small area of the stage. Black Judas enters carrying a liquor bottle outside the Memphis city limits. He counts the remaining cash he took from Sam Johnson.*

BLACK JUDAS: Stupid niggers. What they doing with this much money. Huh. Hey Toby! Ha! Ha! What you got? Two chickens? Shoot. Listen, I can buy a whole flock of those stupid birds. Shoot. Stupid old nigger, still stealing food. (*drinks from the bottle*)

SAM JOHNSON: Those kind have no respect for the working man. You've seen them, sitting around drinking liquor, chasing women and carrying on around decent folks like us. No sir. They're a disgrace to the race.

BLACK JUDAS: I need something to do with myself tonight. I'm not going to hang around a bunch of bums.

SAM JOHNSON: I remember the old days. I remember when another man could buy and sell me at will. But you don't see me throwing myself away on liquor, cutting people up and stealing. Those that are low life in the free world was low life on the plantation, I guarantee that.

IDA: It wasn't an easy life for anyone. But my concern is how we bring this man to justice. With no justice there's no freedom.

SAM JOHNSON: We've got to stop making excuses for these people, otherwise they'll just drag us all down with them. But you let that dog do the same thing to a white man that he did to me and see what happens. He'll deserve whatever he's got coming to him. No-good nigger. He's just lucky I didn't have my gun.

LIGHT SOFTENS *on Sam Johnson, Ida, and Mrs. Johnson.*

BLACK JUDAS: Whew! Let's see what's going on t'night. Oh looka here. (*opens a* Free Speech) This paper's finally got some color to it. Let's see what the society Negroes are up to. Betcha these bastards wouldn't be half as uppity if it weren't for some white daddy or something. What, Toby? Yeah, I can read. I'm not stupid like you. Stupid nigger. Fisk singers. Niggers trying to sing like white folks. No sir. The Mika-do, a musical set in Ja-pan. What's that doing here? Oops, I don't believe it. I don't believe it. All-black minstrel show, tonight. Damn if I'm gonna miss that. Hey Toby, let's go to the minstrel show tonight. It'll be real funny. Yeah, we'll fry up those chickens and take them with us. (*laughs*)

ACT ONE, SCENE 4

The Moss home—evening. Thomas reads the Free Speech.

THOMAS: What's your pleasure, ladies? There's the theater, literary, music and a minstrel show. Now that sounds like fun. Ida can work on her letter while she cakewalks across the floor.

(*Enter Betty and Ida. Betty carries a small photograph.*)

BETTY: Ida says she doesn't want to go to the dance tonight, Tommie. Besides, it wouldn't be any fun for me to just watch. Ida, I think this picture of you is beautiful.

IDA: I'm not sure. Perhaps I'll just send it to my sisters and aunt in California. At least I look healthy.

THOMAS: What do you mean just watch, Betty? Come here.

(*Thomas grabs a pregnant Betty by the waist and swings her around in a dance.*)

THOMAS: Show me those skinny legs.

(*Ida watches with admiration.*)

BETTY: (*out of breath*) This baby's going to start kicking before I do if we're not careful.

(*Thomas and Betty kiss before Thomas helps his wife to a chair.*)

THOMAS: Let me see this picture. What's wrong with it?

IDA: I'm just not happy with it. I don't look like a newspaper woman. I look like someone's cleaning woman in her Sunday best. Look at my lip.

BETTY: (*to Thomas*) She wants to send it to someone.

THOMAS: Who?

IDA: Three prominent colored newspaper men want my picture to make an engraving for their papers.

THOMAS: I like this picture. Send it and stop worrying about it and enjoy your night off.

IDA: I haven't even started on my next Iola's Letter, and I'm leaving for Mississippi in two days. I shouldn't—

BETTY: Ida, you can write on the train. Tommie and I are worried about you. You spend all your time alone at the *Free Speech*, go home alone to your room at the boarding house and travel from state to state by yourself. Maybe we wouldn't feel this way if you had a husband.

IDA: If I had a husband I wouldn't have a newspaper at all. But I have the kindness of wonderful, dear friends.

BETTY: I remember when you had scads of admirers, went to parties and recitals and were teaching and writing articles all at the same time.

THOMAS: Really. What happened to that, Ida?

IDA: Owning a paper isn't quite the same as writing for one. And many men find the newspaper business an unnatural profession for a woman or a wife except for maybe the ones who write for papers also.

THOMAS: And she keeps a list of those literary Romeos. I deliver the evidence.

IDA: They are well respected journalists and colleagues.

THOMAS: Women of today. You're educated, well spoken, well groomed, you go to the literary societies, concert halls, take elocution lessons. Do you still take those elocution lessons?

IDA: After reciting Lady Macbeth's death scene, I thought it best to leave Shakespeare to the actors and speeches to the lecture halls.

THOMAS: But if you're not interested in getting a husband then can all these accomplishments be for the race?

BETTY: Perhaps these are the things that Ida chooses to make her happy, Tommie. And we shouldn't worry so much.

THOMAS: I'm not worried. I do wonder. Every woman wants to be swept off her feet—

IDA: I do enjoy the society of gentlemen. And if the day comes when I carry orange blossoms down a church aisle, it'll be by my choice made through proper connections and not a broomstick.

THOMAS: Proper connections. You can't fool me. That's why you write those fiery letters. They catch a man's eye. You probably have yours on Nightingale. (*laughs*) Thomas Fortune of the *New York Age*.

IDA: I do not! Stop it! (*laughs*)

THOMAS: Frederick Douglass! You always said you wanted to meet him.

IDA: I'm warning you, Tommie.

BETTY: Tommie, that's ridiculous. Stop teasing. (*laughs*)

THOMAS: I'll stop. All I want is for our good friend to be happy, that's all.

IDA: And I am.

THOMAS: I'll respect that. Now let's get back to our entertainment for the evening.

BETTY: Let me look in the *Memphis Commercial*.

THOMAS: Why?

BETTY: I'm always curious to see how the other half lives.

THOMAS: How's old Johnson, Ida?

IDA: Back to nigger this and nigger that. He's fine. A description of the man they call Black Judas will be in the next *Free Speech*.

BETTY: (*chilly*) Did you read the description in the *Memphis Commercial?* (*gives Ida the paper*)

IDA: This just talks about the Negro section of town. God, these people. Listen. "What would you do if your wife or daughter were so assaulted?"

BETTY: Read what they say about the People's Grocery.

THOMAS: (*reads*) The People's Grocery is the meeting place of the colored illiterates and those who are bereft of moral conduct and character—Damn it!

IDA: Tommie, you should demand an apology and a retraction.

THOMAS: They're not going to print it.

IDA: They know you're the first of our race selected to serve a position in the federal government. They know your record, Tommie, and Henry and Calvin's too. You're the three most decent businessmen in this town.

BETTY: I can't believe some of the things that paper prints. You should stop selling the paper in the store, Tommie.

THOMAS: Henry, Calvin and I had a feeling something was going on. I'm sure the grocer across the curb had something to contribute to this. You'd think it would be a good thing for colored men like us to open this store in our own section of town. You'd think there wouldn't be any trouble about it. I could see if we opened the People's Grocery in the white section. No, they're just upset that the colored people don't have to pay double the price anymore. They're unhappy because we stock everything and more than they do and we're a success. So now they want to intimidate us and find some reason to run us out. Well maybe I should run . . .

IDA: Run where?

THOMAS: West. Ride, run, take the next train west . . . where no newspapers like the *Memphis Commercial* give you free publicity.

IDA: What will going west prove if you can't improve your situation here? If you don't demand your rights here, there's no guarantee you'll have them out there. Remember when I sued the railroad when they threw me off the ladies car. There were no Jim Crow laws then, so what they did was totally improper and illegal.

BETTY: Didn't you bite the conductor on the back of the hand when he grabbed you?

IDA: He ripped my dress and embarassed me in front of the other passengers who encouraged the three men to drag me out to the smoking car. But I went to court and won five hundred dollars in damages.

THOMAS: Two hundred you had to pay back to the railroad when they appealed. Ida, at one time I thought like you, I believed like you. When I got the letter carrier's job I felt by God we're the first generation of free Negro people. It's on our shoulders now. But we've got two set of rules to play by. Their rules and their rules for people like us.

IDA: The rules say we hold these things to be self-evident that all men are created equal.

THOMAS: Do you really believe that?

IDA: Yes, with all my heart, even if the lawmakers don't, that's what I believe. No matter what, Tommie, we've got to live, think and act as free people. And that means we have the right to hold the lawmakers accountable to the laws that protect our freedom. We have to believe we can have a grocery, a newspaper, and our family, friends, children to carry on after us. If you run, you only give the evil room to stretch its arms and eventually find you again.

THOMAS: For a woman whose own life has been an uphill struggle, it amazes me how your spirit never seems to break. Do you really have that much faith in people?

IDA: I have faith in truth and what is just. And when people recognize the two, they will be moved to act fairly and guarantee the best for all of us. You have the right, Tommie, to defend yourself.

THOMAS: (*dryly*) For how long?

BETTY: (*after a beat . . .*) Perhaps we can all use something inspirational this evening. The Fisk Jubilee Singers at Beale Street Baptist.

IDA: I think that's a good idea, though I'm not sure I'll be welcomed at Nightingale's church.

BETTY: Nonsense. If they're true Christians, they won't turn you away. Tommie, what do you think of that? The Fisk Singers. (*Tommie doesn't respond. Betty approaches him gently.*) I'd like to see the concert.

THOMAS: (*after some coaxing*) The Jubilee Singers is good.

IDA: A good bon voyage before I go to Mississippi to sell subscriptions.

THOMAS: (*comes alive*) Well, if the conductor on the train gives you trouble this time, go for the leg.

IDA: Maybe I will.

THOMAS: Oh, Calvin, Henry and I decided to take out ad space in the *Free Speech*.

IDA: Fleming will kiss you for it.

BETTY: Ida, do you need anything to take with you on the trip? I can fix you a lunch box.

IDA: I'll be fine, Betty.

THOMAS: Remember, Ida, Mississippi isn't Memphis. Be careful of what you say and where you say it.

IDA: Tommie, I was born there. I know where I'm going and what to do.

BETTY: Let me get Maurine.

IDA: You're right. She should have an opportunity to see the race at our best. And Fisk Jubilee is definitely our best.

THOMAS: Ida. Sometimes I wish I had your courage.

IDA: Courage?

THOMAS: Madness?

IDA: We need you here, Tommie. I need someone to sell the *Free Speech* in their store. We're making a difference. We really are.

(*Enter Betty with Maurine.*)

THOMAS: Yes, someday we will.

SFX—*Fisk Jubilee Singers performing a Negro Spiritual.*

ACT ONE, SCENE 5

Train platform in Mississippi. A WOMAN *(black) waits and reads the paper. A* MAN *(black) sits next to her. He tips his hat. The Woman inches away. Ida enters with an armful of* Free Speech *papers and her bag. The Man stands, tips his hat, and offers her a seat. Ida sits down on the bench. The Man sits next to her. Ida unfolds a* Free Speech *and starts to read. The Man gets the message and inches away. The Woman lowers her paper, noticing Ida's bright pink paper.*

WOMAN: Are you from Memphis?

IDA: Yes, I am. Actually I was born here in Mississippi.

WOMAN: So was I. I noticed your paper. I live in New York now. I couldn't stand the South anymore. A woman just can't feel free in the South like she can in the North. But when you leave family behind, you do have to pay a visit once in awhile. Is that why you came?

IDA: No, actually I came to sell subscriptions. I'm the editor of the *Free Speech*.

WOMAN: (*pause*) You're Iola. I should've recognized you in an instant. Oh girl, those awful engravings in the paper don't do you justice.

IDA: Let me give you a complimentary copy. You too, sir.

WOMAN: Thank you. I subscribe to Thomas Fortune's paper in New York. You're familiar with it, I'm sure . . . the *New York Age?*

IDA: Yes, I am.

MAN: So you're a newspaper woman?

IDA: That's right.

WOMAN: She's Iola. You've heard of her?

MAN: Can't say I have, but I know now. This must be the only pink paper in the country.

WOMAN: I bet you're anxious to get back to Memphis.

IDA: I sure am. My partner's going to be very happy to see all the new subscriptions.

WOMAN: Oh my, Miss Iola, didn't you read the news about the lynching?

IDA: What lynching?

MAN: Where?

WOMAN: In Memphis. It's in all the papers. (*shows Ida the article*) Three men who ran this store called the People's Grocery were found dead outside the city limits. It was a shock to everyone. One was the first Negro federal employee of that city. Letter carrier named Thomas Moss.

MAN: Shame. God shame. Train's coming.

SFX—*Train approaching. Ida is frozen.*

WOMAN: It's on time for once. Miss Iola, are you alright?

(*Ida tries to let out a sound, but the shock of the news takes control of her body. Finally her voice releases a long . . .*)

IDA: No!!!!!

(*Ida stands, but cannot hold her balance. The steam from the train covers the platform. The Man and the Woman try to steady her.*)

SFX—*The train engine and steam—louder than before.*

WOMAN: Oh my God. I think she's going to faint. Help her.

(*Ida screams again, but the only sound is of the train pulling in.*)

ACT TWO, SCENE I

Grave site—a funeral procession led by Rev. Nightingale enters. Betty is assisted by two men. Ida brings up the rear walking with her goddaughter Maurine. Betty sits. Ida leads Maurine to her mother.

IDA: I've learned to tell this story unimpeded by my own emotions. The first time a panic seized me. Only those in the audience could see the tears dropping. I beckoned for a handkerchief and I wiped my nose and streaming face, but I told the story.

ISAAC: It all started with some colored and white boys fighting over a game of marbles outside the People's Grocery store. Well, the colored boys got the better of the fight, but when the father of the white boys saw what was happening, he came out and whipped one of the colored boys.

MR. FLEMING: Naturally, the father and friends of the colored boy, including Calvin and some others, jumped from the People's Grocery Company porch, and those colored folks got the best of them. But later the men who frequent the white grocery across the road threatened to come in Saturday night to clean out the People's Grocery.

IDA: Several armed men stationed themselves in the rear of the People's Grocery Company, not to attack but to repel a threatened attack. About ten o'clock that night when Tommie was posting his books for the week and Calvin McDowell and Henry Stewart were waiting on customers before closing, shots rang out in the back room of the store.

MR. FLEMING: They said they saw a couple of white men running through the back door. Thomas, Calvin, and Henry fired on them and wounded one of the men, the rest fled and gave the alarm. The next morning some officers came back to the grocery store and arrested Thomas, Calvin, and Henry.

(*Enter Mr. Carmack with his pad and pencil.*)

MR. CARMACK: It's a low dive in which drinking and gambling were carried on: a resort of thieves and thugs. A clean sweep of this section produced their petty thief they've been looking for. But if those officers they shot should die, it'll go hard on the ringleaders.

SAM JOHNSON: Those officers said they were performing their duty, hunting up criminals who they said were harbored in the People's Grocery. Now you know. They raided decent colored folks' homes and dragged people out on suspicion. That's why we got together and went to guard Moss, McDowell, and Stewart at the jail house. But nothing happened for days. We thought maybe this whole thing had passed. We didn't have to stay another night.

(*Spot on Black Judas as he stumbles inside a jail cell where he's provoked by a group of men who've come in to take the prisoners.*)

BLACK JUDAS: I wasn't doing nothing at that grocery store. Get offa me. I'm not one of them! What are you doing?

(*Black Judas' reactions match Ida's descriptions of the events.*)

IDA: A select mob came in one night while they slept and dragged them out of their cells. They carried Calvin, Henry, and Thomas a mile north of the city limits, and horribly shot them to death. When they were found, Calvin McDowell's fingers had been shot to pieces. It seemed he got hold of one of the guns of the lynchers and because they couldn't loosen his grip a shot was fired into his closed fist. His eyes were also gouged out. Henry Stewart had a bullet hole in the neck. And Tommie. . . .

REV. NIGHTINGALE: Thomas Moss, beloved husband, loving father, dear brother and friend. A model man among his people—begged for his life. Thomas Moss begged for his life, not for himself, but for the sake of his wife Betty, and his daughter Maurine and his unborn child. I say to you as Jesus, our lord, our savior said from the cross, as he took our sins upon himself, he said "Daughters of Jerusalem, weep not for me but weep for yourselves and for your children."

BLACK JUDAS: God, oh god! They did that to those men! They ain't gonna do it to me! No, no. They ain't gonna do it!

(LIGHTS DOWN *on Black Judas*)

IDA: When Tommie was asked if he had anything to say he told them "Tell my people to go west. There is no justice for them here." No justice.

REV. NIGHTINGALE: But let not these events lead us astray. If the Negro is to survive in the South, then the Negro must at all costs obey the laws. We mustn't agitate the situation. It will only bring more violence and death.

IDA: The city of Memphis has demonstrated that neither character nor standing avails the Negro.

MR. FLEMING: There's no justice in this city . . .

SAM JOHNSON: No justice.

(*The mourners leave. Ida grows more impassioned.*)

IDA: There is only one thing left to do—save our money and leave a town that will neither protect our lives and property, nor give us a fair trial in court. Ministers, lead your congregations, dispose of your property, abandon your craving for fine clothes, furniture, instruments and good things to eat. Take that money and leave Memphis. Go west! There is no justice for you here! No justice!

MOURNER: (*sings—solo*)

> Why would an innocent man,
> like Tom Moss,
> Be shot in the head.

Oh me, Oh my, Lord have mercy on me!
Oh me, Oh my, Lord have mercy on me!

With a gun in their hand
They'll shoot any one of us
like they shot Tom Moss
Like they shoot an innocent man

All we can do is pray to you Lord,
'Cause there's nothing else we can do but say

Oh me, Oh my, Lord have mercy on me!
Oh me, Oh my, Lord have mercy on me!

ACT TWO, SCENE 2

Free Speech *offices. Mr. Fleming proofs the next issue, but is concerned about Ida, who is completely absorbed in the boycott and other matters related to the lynching, neglecting other significant newspaper business.*

MR. FLEMING: There's a pile of papers waiting to be mailed to our out-of-town subscribers.

IDA: I'll get to it.

MR. FLEMING: We got some new subscriptions in yesterday. You should start adding them to the list. (*no answer from Ida*) You know, mandating a boycott means we're going to lose a lot of advertising dollars so we're going to need those subscriptions and then some to keep us going.

IDA: (*impatient*) I said I'll get to it, Fleming.

(*Isaac enters from the front door with the mail.*)

ISAAC: Here's the mail.

(*Ida snatches the letters but pauses. She gives Isaac a reassuring pat on the back.*)

MR. FLEMING: Wells, you should go home. Give your mind a rest.

IDA: Who can rest in a town like this? For me the nightmare continues whether my eyes are open or shut.

MR. FLEMING: Well what about we get something to eat, the three of us? I know how lonely you must be now that Betty and Maurine's gone too. Where did you say they went?

IDA: Indiana.

MR. FLEMING: Indiana. I guess she must have some family up there. I don't blame her for not wanting to stay here. But it would be good for you to get out. Be with people.

IDA: I—I can't. I've got this boycott to manage and there're these Oklahoma reports . . . Where's my list?

MR. FLEMING: (*frustrated*) Damn it! I can't run this paper by myself. Look at you. Nothing else matters in the world but this boycott, and jumping on and off trains to Mississippi empty handed, and those letters. You think this will avenge Tommie's death? You think this will force a judge's hand? The criminal court judge himself was part of the mob that night. So, let me tell you something, Wells—there isn't going to be any justice. There isn't going to be a trial and if those men stood on the bandstand tomorrow and shouted loud and clear that they were the ones who lynched Tommie, Henry and Calvin, no jury in this country would sentence them to a day in prison. Now we've got a duty to run a colored newspaper here. You and me. We've got readers waiting and a new issue to get off.

IDA: Don't tell me about duty. Have you read any of these letters?

MR. FLEMING: No, I haven't.

IDA: (*takes letters from a folder on her desk*) South Carolina—thirteen lynchings; Georgia—sixteen lynchings; Alabama—twenty-seven lynchings; Mississippi—seventeen; Texas—five. There was a time I thought lynching, though irregular and contrary to law and order, was just an unreasoning anger over the terrible crime of rape, and perhaps in some cases it was deserved. But Thomas Moss, Calvin McDowell, and Henry Stewart were lynched in Memphis, one of the leading cities of the South in which no lynching had taken place before, with just as much brutality, just as much loathing as any other victim of a mob. And they committed no crime against white women.

ISAAC: But why? Why did they do it to them? They caught Black Judas that night. He was there in the jail cell. Why didn't they take him?

IDA: Because, Isaac, they found an excuse to get rid of Negroes who're acquiring wealth and property. It's a way to keep the race terrorized and keep the nigger down.

MR. FLEMING: How many of those reports are you getting?

IDA: Read them for yourself. I intend to investigate every one.

MR. FLEMING: So you're leaving, again.

IDA: Yes. And after that I'm going to the Oklahoma territory to see what our Memphis people are accomplishing out there.

ISAAC: I heard two ministers took their whole congregations out of Memphis to Oklahoma.

MR. FLEMING: You'd think Moses had come through town.

IDA: So you see, Fleming, this is not a time to rest.

MR. FLEMING: What makes you think they're going to allow you to poke around investigating these killings?

IDA: At this point I don't feel I need anyone's permission.

MR. FLEMING: You do need protection and what law is going to give you that?

IDA: If the *Memphis Commercial* can publish every fine detail of Tommie's killing that night without resulting in one arrest including the man who wrote that report, then I don't expect any protection for me under any law. If they can operate by their own rules, then so can I. (*goes into her desk drawer and pulls out a revolver*)

MR. FLEMING: (*surprised*) Where did you get that?

IDA: I was expecting some retaliation from the lynchers. But it'd be better I die fighting against injustice than to die like a dog or a rat in a trap.

MR. FLEMING: Have you lost all your senses? It's against the law for colored people to own guns in Memphis.

IDA: Maybe taking one lyncher with me would even up the score a little bit.

(SFX—*Knock on the door*)

MR. FLEMING: Put that thing away. Now!

(*Ida puts the revolver back in her drawer. Mr. Fleming unlocks the door. Shop Owner enters.*)

MR. FLEMING: Good morning, sir.

SHOP OWNER: Are you closed today?

MR. FLEMING: No sir. We were just having a short business meeting.

SHOP OWNER: Good morning, Miss Wells, Isaac.

MR. FLEMING: I was proofing the next edition. Got your ad on the front page. See.

SHOP OWNER: Oh, I see. Very good, very good. (*pause*) Uh, Mr. Fleming, I hate to say this but I'm going to have to withdraw my advertising. Between your boycott and now this mass colored migration my business is suffering. It wouldn't make sense for me to continue advertising with this paper.

MR. FLEMING: But the boycott isn't going to last forever. (*to Ida*)

(*Ida remains silent and steadfast.*)

MR. FLEMING: What if I give you three free advertisements in addition to the ones you paid for.

(*Shop Owner shakes his head.*)

MR. FLEMING: Two inches for the price of one.

(*Shop Owner shakes his head.*)

MR. FLEMING: Okay, we'll pull it after this edition, but your account stays open until this all blows over.

(*Shop Owner shakes his head.*)

MR. FLEMING: Okay, Isaac. Take it out.

(*Isaac takes the paper to the print room. Mr. Fleming opens the cash box and gives the Shop Owner his refund.*)

SHOP OWNER: Look, I'm just as appalled by the incident as you are. Those were three decent Negro men. But there's a law that says Negroes can't shoot at white people. I mean, it's unfair, I guess, but it's the law. There's nothing you or I can do about that. Listen, I've met with some of the business leadership and said to them that the Negro people have been our best patrons, deserving our very best service, and any discourtesy towards them should be severely punished.

MR. FLEMING: And they agreed?

SHOP OWNER: Well, the representatives from the streetcar company are willing to oblige. But they do feel since a large share of Negro labor was paid to lay down the tracks on the streets then it would be only fair that the Negro people should give patronage in return.

IDA: Did you *know* Thomas Moss?

SHOP OWNER: Never a finer, cleaner man walked the streets of Memphis than Thomas Moss. A credit to his race.

IDA: Yet he was murdered with no more consideration than a dog because he as a man defended his property from attack. What do we owe the streetcar company?

SHOP OWNER: The streetcar company had nothing to do with the lynching. It's owned by northern men.

IDA: And run by southern lynchers.

SHOP OWNER: Not all of us are lynchers.

IDA: But did you know about the plan to murder him? (*Shop Owner looks pensive.*) Did you speak out against it?

SHOP OWNER: I would have. (*pause*) In my store every customer is treated with respect and courtesy. That hasn't changed.

(*Shop Owner exits. Fleming locks the door.*)

MR. FLEMING: How dare you treat an advertiser—

IDA: How dare he come here expecting *us* to feel sorry for him all because he's losing money.

MR. FLEMING: He's not the only one losing money. He made a business decision.

IDA: And you offered him the moon and stars in return.

MR. FLEMING: If there's no newspaper, there's no boycott, no reports from Mississippi, no anything! (*grabs his hat and coat*)

IDA: Where are you going?

MR. FLEMING: To the lodge. Maybe there're some clear thinking people there.

IDA: But I have a train to catch. One of the partners has to be here.

MR. FLEMING: Partners, Wells? Are we really? (*Mr. Fleming opens the door.*)

IDA: Mr. Fleming. (*Mr. Fleming stops.*) In the next edition, about the boycott. Please tell the readers to keep up the good work. (*Mr. Fleming exits.*)

ACT TWO, SCENE 3

In a rural area of the "deep South," Ida waits for a reluctant witness to a crime. Meanwhile at the Free Speech *offices, Rev. Nightingale meets with Mr. Fleming. Mr. Fleming's hands and shirt are stained with printer's ink. He shoves things about in anger. Rev. Nightingale goes to pour himself some coffee, but the pot is empty. The boycott has taken its toll on the simple pleasures.*

REV. NIGHTINGALE: So where is she now?

MR. FLEMING: Back in Mississippi or someplace, I suppose. Meanwhile I'm stuck back here trying to run this paper with no help. Now Isaac's family has picked up and headed for Oklahoma too.

REV. NIGHTINGALE: How long will she be gone this time?

MR. FLEMING: I don't know. She never sends a telegram. But then the kind of stuff she's doing down South, who knows . . .

REV. NIGHTINGALE: What is she doing?

MR. FLEMING: Talking to people. Talking to anybody connected with a lynching.

Back in the "deep South," a YOUNG MAN *approaches Ida followed by a* SECOND YOUNG MAN:

YOUNG MAN: Are you Iola?

IDA: Yes, I am.

Back at the Free Speech:

REV. NIGHTINGALE: What does she expect to gain but more misery, more violence.

MR. FLEMING: A list.

REV. NIGHTINGALE: A list?

MR. FLEMING: A very long list of things unspeakable.

LIGHTS DOWN *on the* Free Speech *offices. Back to* . . .

IDA: (*to Young Man*) You mentioned a picture in the paper.

YOUNG MAN: Yeah. (*reluctantly takes the picture out*)

IDA: They burned your brother alive?

(*Young Man nods his head.*)

IDA: Was the young girl white?

(*Young Man nods his head.*)

IDA: Where is she now?

YOUNG MAN: Nobody knows. But she said herself—he was the wrong man. They didn't care. They just had to hang somebody.

LIGHTS DOWN *on Ida.* LIGHTS UP *on Mr. Carmack with a copy of the* Free Speech *on his writing desk. He prepares his next editorial.*

MR. CARMACK: Ida B. Wells, a known agitator among her own people, wants to protect the life and livelihood of the rapist, the murderer and the thief. So long as such brutes exist and roam abroad to do their devilish work, let a mob of determined men in the heart of the largest city in Tennessee within a few hours of the arrest of the culprit break into the public jail and wreak vengeance on the lecherous villain whose crimes smell to heaven.

LIGHTS DOWN *on Mr. Carmack.*

Sfx—*Train.*

Lights Up—*Ida talks with another* Witness *at the scene of another lynching. Ida retraces the steps.*

Witness: The barrel was found here with nails driven into the sides of it. They rolled it down the hill until she was dead.

(*Ida shows no indication of horror. She takes a deep breath.*)

Ida: Were there any other witnesses?

Witness: There were several. So says the newspaper.

Ida: Does anyone know why this happened?

Witness: She . . . she was the kind who wasn't afraid to say what was on her mind even to white folk. You know the type. But I can't imagine what she did or said to deserve this.

(Lights Down *on Ida, Witness*)

(Sfx—*Train*)

(*Mr. Fleming and Rev. Nightingale enter.*)

Mr. Fleming: I've got to wire this cash.

Rev. Nightingale: Is she dipping into the cash box now?

Mr. Fleming: No. This is the money collected for the people trying to cross the high-water zone on the Mississippi to get to Oklahoma.

Rev. Nightingale: Don't they know there's no promised land in Oklahoma? There's starvation, hostile Indians, no milk and honey.

Mr. Fleming: Where did you read that?

Rev. Nightingale: The *Memphis Commercial.*

(*Mr. Fleming shakes his head and counts the cash.*)

Lights Down *on the* Free Speech

Lights Up—*train platform*

Voice of Conductor: Guthrie, Oklahoma.

(*Ida waits at the station for her ride. Isaac enters.*)

Ida: Isaac! (*gives Isaac a warm hug.*) It's so good to see a familiar face. How did you know I was coming?

Isaac: Everyone knows. When they asked someone to pick you up, I volunteered. Can I take your bag? You must be real tired. The family can't wait to see you.

Ida: I can't wait to see all the good things going on out here.

Isaac: I have to admit, it's a little rough, but most folks say they'll take their chances in the wilderness rather than come back to Memphis.

Ida: Well, it's certainly a place where you can assert your womanhood or your manhood. Gosh you've grown up so.

Isaac: I have? Yes, I have. Miss Wells, I can't wait to show you everything. It may not be Memphis, but you'll like what people have started so far. You know, a lot of people have been asking if you would bring the *Free Speech* out here. They miss having their own newspaper. I thought about starting one myself, but . . . I guess I need help.

IDA: While I'm here, I'll help you.

ISAAC: Really?! Uh, the wagon's over here.

(*Exit Ida and Isaac.*)

ACT TWO, SCENE 4

The Free Speech *offices. Rev. Nightingale enters. The new bell announces him. Mr. Fleming emerges from the back wiping his hands on his printer's apron.*

MR. FLEMING: I'm glad it's you.

REV. NIGHTINGALE: I hear you're leaving Memphis.

MR. FLEMING: What do you mean?

REV. NIGHTINGALE: Read your paper, Fleming. It says so in the *Free Speech.*

MR. FLEMING: Oh that. She wants to move the paper to Oklahoma. I say we're staying right here. Nothing leaves from this office unless both partners are in agreement. Have a seat.

REV. NIGHTINGALE: So she's back in town.

MR. FLEMING: Well, she was. But she's gone again. Gone to visit Betty Moss in Indiana.

(*Rev. Nightingale goes to Ida's desk and sits in her chair.*)

REV. NIGHTINGALE: I guess it's about time she did. (*uncomfortable*)

MR. FLEMING: Wait there. I'll get your chair. She said it was too rigid for her. (*goes to the back and brings out a large ink-stained chair*) Here you go. See, I saved it. Don't worry. The ink's dry.

REV. NIGHTINGALE: I must say, I was surprised to hear from the *Memphis Commercial.*

MR. FLEMING: It was quite a shock to me as well.

REV. NIGHTINGALE: So what does this Carmack fellow want?

MR. FLEMING: He says he's heard about Wells' investigations.

REV. NIGHTINGALE: Is that so. Well, what's one little colored woman asking a few questions.

MR. FLEMING: You know the boycott has put them in a bad way as it is. But now I'm starting to think that this list she's putting together may start something really bad. Have you been reading Thomas Fortune's paper?

REV. NIGHTINGALE: Yes, I have. Very interesting. Very interesting.

MR. FLEMING: A thousand copies of the paper were delivered here. And I'm sure Carmack must've read one.

REV. NIGHTINGALE: If I'm following you correctly, Fleming, it seems to me,

Miss Iola is about to embark on a direct discord with our southern gents with an assault of her own.

MR. FLEMING: Exactly.

REV. NIGHTINGALE: I give her credit. She knows what to aim for. Southern manhood is defined by the purity of his white magnolia blossom—the seed from which southern chivalry flourishes.

MR. FLEMING: And they'll do anything to protect their women's reputations.

REV. NIGHTINGALE: No, Fleming. It's not the woman's reputation he's protecting. (*looks down at his crotch area and passes a knowing glance to Mr. Fleming*)

REV. NIGHTINGALE: (*sarcastically*) Unfortunate circumstance for the colored woman because she has no virtue to be outraged. And her reputation is forever threatened.

MR. FLEMING: Wells is always talking about morality. She knows this isn't the kind of story for printing in a respectable newspaper.

REV. NIGHTINGALE: Maybe. But what other weapon has she got?

MR. FLEMING: She has a gun.

REV. NIGHTINGALE: But it's illegal for a colored person—

MR. FLEMING: Don't you think I know that?

(*Enter Mr. Carmack.*)

MR. CARMACK: Evening, boys.

MR. FLEMING: Mr. Carmack.

MR. CARMACK: I just wanted to stop by and see how this boycott's getting on. I assume it's coming to a close by now.

MR. FLEMING: It's hard to say. Miss Wells hasn't submitted her next editorial yet.

MR. CARMACK: You think she's going to call it off in the next edition.

MR. FLEMING: I don't know.

MR. CARMACK: Or maybe she's going to call for a mob to come get that boy in the jail cell now. What do you all call him? Black Jesus or something.

REV. NIGHTINGALE: Judas. Black Judas.

MR. CARMACK: Hmph. Well, that shows I haven't been to church in awhile.

REV. NIGHTINGALE: Mr. Carmack, so you'll know, Miss Wells does not represent the views of all the colored people in this city.

MR. CARMACK: I hope not. After all this gal bit a train conductor on the hand. (*laughs*)

(*Mr. Carmack sits in Ida's chair.*)

MR. CARMACK: Listen. I'm a newspaper man myself. My job is to get people to read the paper, to get next to what people out there are thinking. And right now they're thinking this *Free Speech* is a big stew of trouble for this town.

REV. NIGHTINGALE: What kind of trouble?

MR. FLEMING: Who's saying this?

MR. CARMACK: Come on, reverend. Men's wives are driving them crazy. Their gals don't come work for them anymore. They all gone to Indian country, living in teepees or something like animals. And look at the streetcar. We're still trying to pay for that thing. It was built for your people. If it wasn't for the streetcar, none of you would ever see downtown Memphis. You expect decent folks to put up with this much longer? Listen. What happened to those three Negroes is long past now. Most folks have already forgotten about it and you all should too.

REV. NIGHTINGALE: Certainly you can't expect people in this section of town to forget just like that.

MR. CARMACK: I don't expect anything. I'm doing you a favor as one newspaper man to another. Stop this boycott and there won't be trouble.

REV. NIGHTINGALE: I suggest you contact the editor.

MR. CARMACK: But wasn't that your job at one time? Or maybe I'm talking to the wrong man.

REV. NIGHTINGALE: As a leader in this community and founding member of this establishment, I feel it's my duty to protect our interests. I'm sure Mr. Fleming would like to see his advertisers come back. Isn't that right, Mr. Fleming?

(*Mr. Fleming is silent.*)

REV. NIGHTINGALE: What's most important is for everyone to obey the law, colored and white. I've preached that from my pulpit. Those who don't are probably on the other side of the Mississippi or locked up like Judas.

MR. CARMACK: Then we can count on some cooperation?

REV. NIGHTINGALE: I'll see to it.

ACT TWO, SCENE 5

LIGHTS UP—*photography studio in Indiana. Betty, Maurine, and Thomas, Jr. sit before a backdrop for a portrait. Ida enters, adjusting her dress and hair. The photographer poses her next to Betty. He goes behind the camera.*

PHOTOGRAPHER: Everyone look this way. Don't move. (*The flash goes off.*)

IDA: This is the first new dress I've worn in a long time.

BETTY: I'm glad you let me convince you.

IDA: However, it does feel strange.

BETTY: Perhaps you're tired from all the traveling.

IDA: Maybe so. Look at Maurine. She's beautiful, and Thomas, Jr.

BETTY: Tommie wanted a son. Not that he didn't love Maurine, but you know how men are. (*Ida smiles.*)

IDA: Betty, I hope you don't mind my visiting. I was concerned I was bringing bad memories to you.

BETTY: No, indeed. I couldn't go another day without seeing you. Every morning Maurine would wake up and say, "Is she coming today, Momma?" If I said "no" one more time, she would've burst into tears.

IDA: It's me who's being selfish in making this a happy escape from Memphis and the *Free Speech*.

BETTY: What do you mean by escape? You love that newspaper.

IDA: I just want to leave that behind me for now. Do more shopping. Perhaps find a hat for this dress.

BETTY: Ida, please. Why don't you tell about what's going on in Memphis? I don't need silence as protection. I want us to talk.

IDA: I haven't been this fearful in a long time, selfishly afraid. I have no father, brother or husband to protect my good name. Mr. Fleming and I had some words before I left. He's probably the closest I have to a friend there now.

BETTY: Are you in trouble?

IDA: I'm not sure.

BETTY: What are you finding down South?

IDA: Men who control all the forces of law and order can easily and legally punish any one of choice in a court of law, especially those who have neither political nor financial power to evade any justly deserved fate.

BETTY: But *we* had the resources. We had the store.

IDA: Having that store was your crime. But if we must be punished in court, I would've preferred seeing Tommie linked to a chain gang and alive.

BETTY: For Tommie, it would be better to be dead than a slave.

IDA: Is death the only path to freedom? Is it always the price? You know, I'm thinking of moving the *Free Speech* to Oklahoma or selling my partnership and just leave Memphis.

BETTY: Sell?

IDA: I've fought all my life, pushed, struggled when maybe what I should've done all along was to find a life and a family like you. But I was too stubborn and hard headed.

BETTY: Ida, what makes you think my life is any happier or easier than yours? I've done my share of pushing. Pushing out those horrible memories of that night. Pushing Thomas to the bank when he wanted to buy property and set up a business. Giving birth to two children.

IDA: I didn't mean to insult you.

BETTY: I know.

IDA: I suppose I'm saying that I admire you, Betty. And in your own way you've always been behind me in everything.

BETTY: You know, for a long time I didn't think you knew I existed apart from Tommie. (*pause*) You know, Rev. Nightingale said our freedom is destined to be a struggle . . .

IDA: Rev. Nightingale?

BETTY: I remember him saying it was necessary for our people because those who are entitled never know the true value of anything whereas those who seek and earn find themselves holding a treasure. (*Ida is silent.*) Well, this is quite new. I was looking forward to a debate especially after mentioning Rev. Nightingale.

IDA: Nightingale's not my enemy. But I'm amazed you're not afraid.

BETTY: I have children to raise on my own. My fears become their fears. My duty is to hope despite everything.

IDA: I remember when my parents died after the yellow fever epidemic and the Masons debated over how to divide my sisters and brothers up among their own families. The unanimous decision, however, among the Masonic brothers was that I, fourteen, was old enough to fend for myself. When all was arranged to their satisfaction, I, who said nothing before and had not even been consulted, calmly announced that they were not going to put any of the children anywhere. My father and mother would turn in their graves to know their children were scattered like that. The Masons scoffed at the idea of me taking over the combined efforts of a mother and father but I held firmly to my position.

BETTY: And were you frightened?

IDA: At every step. What does a fourteen-year-old know of the world?

BETTY: Ida, you know you're welcome to stay with us as long as you want. But I don't think you will.

IDA: I have to go back.

BETTY: I want to give you something. It's a picture of Tommie taken before we were married. (*Betty takes the photo from her purse*)

IDA: You should keep it.

BETTY: No. I don't need it. I have the comfort of good memories. Besides, it'll help you to know we're all pushing behind you.

(*Ida and Betty hug.*)

ACT THREE, SCENE I

Free Speech *offices. Mr. Fleming brings in the copy for Ida.*

IDA: Mr. Fleming, did you proof the copy?

MR. FLEMING: Yes, I did, with the last office pencil.

IDA: Eight Negroes lynched since the last issue of the *Free Speech*. Three were charged with killing white men and five with raping white women. Nobody in this section believes the old threadbare lie that Negro men assault white women. If southern white men are not careful they will overreach themselves and a conclusion will be reached which will be very damaging to the moral reputation of their women. Thank you. I want to sign Ida B. Wells to that letter.

MR. FLEMING: You know, when I was a county clerk back in Marion, Arkansas, I started a harmless little sheet called the *Marion Headlight* for the freeman. We thought we were really moving ahead in those days. Negro senators, congressmen and all. But then someone said there were too many of us and it was time for the niggers to go. And so I was forced out of my county clerk job, my paper destroyed along with everything else I had. And that's when I came to Memphis. I'm not going to lose the *Free Speech* over a stunt like this. I worked too hard to get it where it is today.

IDA: Are you saying you want out of the partnership?

MR. FLEMING: Is that what you want?

IDA: It's a political world and this paper is part of it.

MR. FLEMING: Well, read this. (*points to the copy*) Nightingale felt he had to do something before the whole town breaks out in a race riot.

IDA: I didn't sign on this.

MR. FLEMING: I know. You've been gone so long, I couldn't wait. If we leave your letter as is, Carmack will see it and by God he'll answer. Listen, I reluctantly supported the boycott even though it meant losing nearly every advertisement we had. But you can't follow up with an attack on the moral reputation of white women.

IDA: What I'm intending is to tell the truth.

MR. FLEMING: Newspapers aren't in the business of telling the truth. We're in the business of providing information. How many threats have we torn from our door already? Five? Ten?

IDA: How many more Negroes will have to die? Twenty? One hundred? The list is getting longer, Fleming. What about the Negro farm worker lynched for raping the white seven-year-old daughter of the sheriff, or should I say the grown woman I saw in Mississippi who had to be more than seventeen years old; or the proper society mistress of Natchez who gave birth to a unmistakably dark child and the colored coachman forced to leave town after hearing the news. Here's the sworn statement of a mother whose son was lynched for rape. He left his place of work because of the advances made by the beautiful daughter of the house. Later the boy and the girl met secretly and often until they were discovered and that's where the cry of rape was raised. You know what happened then?

MR. FLEMING: You don't need to tell me.

IDA: Or to Allen Butler, a wealthy Negro man in Indiana, well known in the community, hanged in his own house by an angry mob because his son was having an affair with their white live-in maid. Their lives would mean nothing if not for this newspaper.

MR. FLEMING: Then for the sake of saving more lives, stop this pursuit.

(*Ida takes out Tommie's picture and gives it to Mr. Fleming.*)

IDA: You look at this picture, then tell me to forget.

(*Ida takes the copy and exits. Mr. Fleming sits down, studying Tommie's photo.*)

MR. FLEMING: God, Thomas. How can I forget?

ACT THREE, SCENE 2

Ida barges into Rev. Nightingale's study, followed by Mrs. Johnson.

MRS. JOHNSON: Miss Wells, you can't just go in there.

IDA: No disrespect to you, Mrs. Johnson.

REV. NIGHTINGALE: It's alright. Sit down, Iola.

IDA: Miss Wells.

REV. NIGHTINGALE: But we're not at the *Free Speech,* are we?

IDA: I want to talk about this editorial. Fleming showed it to me before we went to print.

REV. NIGHTINGALE: Yes. So do you have any suggestions on how I can make it better?

IDA: I'm not printing it. How can you tell people to stop the boycotts, return to normal life and obey laws that do not protect them?

REV. NIGHTINGALE: The reason we have laws, Miss Wells, is not to protect but to maintain order and stability.

IDA: I'm doing what's best for all our people.

REV. NIGHTINGALE: Yes, I'm sure. But perhaps if you'd listen to other voices around here . . .

IDA: You mean threats.

REV. NIGHTINGALE: I mean listen to me, Miss Wells. I wouldn't want to see you hanging from the limb of a tree for shooting into an angry mob.

IDA: For what reasons would there be mob violence if I may ask?

REV. NIGHTINGALE: Your recent and so far unpublished letter to the readers. Frankly I'm quite impressed—a young lady like you willing to wrestle with such a sensitive issue. But I'm not willing to sacrifice any more Negro lives for it.

IDA: Neither am I. But the first shot has already been fired. And now someone must be willing to speak out freely on this issue, otherwise lynch law will be law. And then who will suffer for it?

REV. NIGHTINGALE: There are ways we can all avoid unnecessary suffering.

IDA: How? Put us out of our misery through systematic genocide. Reverend, didn't you say the road to freedom is paved through struggle? That the rewards we treasured most were earned along the way. Well, I've struggled with Tommie's death, with lynch law and now I've earned the precious right to speak out. I've been duly provoked to take this course. My path is set.

REV. NIGHTINGALE: To destruction. Ida B. Wells, isn't having the newspaper enough? Isn't being the accomplished woman you are enough? You've come too far to lose everything. And think about Mr. Fleming. He's your partner. Consider him.

IDA: We've already lost too much. When enough people read and realize the motives behind lynch law, there'll be such a moral outcry.

REV. NIGHTINGALE: And are you the one to rally the people and lead them on this crusade?

IDA: Of course not. The finest Negro leadership—Thomas Fortune, Frederick Douglass, Mrs. Josephine St. Pierre Ruffin of Boston— are putting themselves on the line to support us.

REV. NIGHTINGALE: Northerners?

IDA: Prominent northerners.

REV. NIGHTINGALE: And if they're making such a personal sacrifice then why haven't we seen them here in Memphis? You know why? Because they have their little southern errand girl.

IDA: Anything I've done has been of my own initiative.

REV. NIGHTINGALE: Someone your age shows more impetuousness than initiative. Tell me, when you were investigating your lynchings, did you send *every* report to Thomas Fortune no matter what the situation? How many Thomas Mosses did you find among the "innocents"?

IDA: Enough.

REV. NIGHTINGALE: And if you say these consented adulteries were the cause of such foul play, does this mean you're putting aside your moral measurements and judgments?

IDA: Where there's injustice—*yes.*

REV. NIGHTINGALE: And what of the moral reputation of the white woman? This isn't new. You've known of these liaisons for years. Even before your parents' time. Which picture are you painting? One that shields colored manhood or the colored woman's wounded pride?

(*Ida is furious but is silent.*)

REV. NIGHTINGALE: I advise you to map out a new road to freedom, young lady. We have a whole generation trying to get solid footing on this ground we have right here. And some can't even do that.

IDA: I suppose that's why you have the largest congregation in Memphis. As long as there are no expectations then an important man such as you becomes more important. You have all the answers.

REV. NIGHTINGALE: Now you listen here, young lady . . .

IDA: No, Nightingale. You're the most powerful colored man in Memphis now. The Negro people think so, the white people. Mr. Carmack even thinks so I'm sure.

REV. NIGHTINGALE: Don't talk to me like this is the *Free Speech.*

IDA: Oh, but it is. It's a little colored gal pushing her way into your world. My god, if Harriet Tubman herself attracted attention, you'd try to push her into the dust. Alright. Have it your way. You be the Negro in charge. I've got a paper to run.

(*Ida leaves Rev. Nightingale in a huff, leaving the* Free Speech *proof behind. Rev. Nightingale picks up the paper. He reads it then crumples it tightly between his hands.*)

ACT THREE, SCENE 3

The Free Speech *offices—night. Ida unlocks the front door.*

IDA: Mr. Fleming.

The offices are quiet. Ida goes to her desk and notices a fresh copy of the next Free Speech. *She reads the note attached.*

IDA: "To silence envious tongues: be just, and fear not." Shakespeare.

(*Ida looks at the new proof.*)

IDA: Nightingale's letter is gone.

(*Ida writes another note, tacks it to the copy, and puts it on Mr. Fleming's desk. She adds . . .*)

IDA: Leaving for Philadelphia and New York. Will wire back. Ida.

(*Ida goes back to her desk and opens her drawer where she keeps the revolver, but it's missing.*)

IDA: Oh my lord.

(*Ida looks in other drawers, then gets up from her desk trying to figure out where she may have put it. But Ida doesn't notice Black Judas enter from the print room with the gun. He silently approaches her, then covers her mouth with his hand.* IDA *doesn't have time to scream. He puts the gun to her head.*)

BLACK JUDAS: Don't scream and nothing will happen. Now where do you keep your cash box? Huh? Where do you keep it?

(*Black Judas slowly removes his hand from her mouth, but keeps the gun pointed. Ida tries not to panic.*)

IDA: In that drawer.
BLACK JUDAS: Which drawer?
IDA: (*nods her head towards Mr. Fleming's desk*) Over there.
BLACK JUDAS: Go get it.

(*Black Judas follows Ida to the drawer.*)

BLACK JUDAS: Take it out. Slowly.

(*Ida follows his instructions, mindful of the gun in his hand.*)

IDA: You know there's been a boycott. We don't have as much money as we usually do.
BLACK JUDAS: Hush up and just give me what you got in there.

(*Ida scoops the few bills and change from the box. Black Judas puts it in his pocket.*)

BLACK JUDAS: Now sit down over there.

(*Ida goes back to her desk and sits down.*)

BLACK JUDAS: Is that your desk and chair?

IDA: Yes, it is.

BLACK JUDAS: (*laughs*) A little lady like you hiding a pistol in her desk drawer. You know it's illegal for niggers to carry guns in this town.

IDA: Yes, I know.

BLACK JUDAS: (*mocks*) Yes, I know. Talk like a white woman. Naw. You talk like one of those northern school teachers used to come down here trying to straighten little nigger boys like me out. Look at cha.

IDA: You have your money, now why don't you go away.

BLACK JUDAS: Go away. For what? You know I kinda like it here. Beats that jail cell I was in. I was back there readin' when you came in. I betcha thought I couldn't do that. Betcha thought I couldn't read all the things you said about me. Give me a name and everything. Black Judas. Hmph. You got a name, too. Princess of the Press. Huh. Is that what them white folks call you, too? Hmph. You know you do kinda look like a princess and I guess I'm the ugly old bull frog. (*laughs*) What kinda perfume do you wear?

(*Ida leans away from Black Judas.*)

BLACK JUDAS: You too good for a nigger like me ain't cha. Well I don't want cha. I don't want none of y'all. The sooner I leave this town the better. Where's your purse?

IDA: Right there.

BLACK JUDAS: Empty it. Take everything out.

(*Ida empties her purse.*)

BLACK JUDAS: Just give me the money. Come on.

(*Ida takes the few coins she has.*)

BLACK JUDAS: You don't make much here, do you?

IDA: A newspaper requires money.

BLACK JUDAS: It makes money, too.

IDA: Did they release you from jail?

BLACK JUDAS: Release me? Hell no. I released myself. Shoot. Wasn't gonna be long before they did to me what they did to them three men I was with. Scared the hell outta me that night. I just knew they was gonna take me with 'em.

IDA: You were there?

BLACK JUDAS: You wanna know don't you? I guess they was friends of yours. They talked about you enough. But they wasn't like most of them uppity type niggers around here. They seemed like good kinda men. Shoot. Not many of them around. I remember that night real good. They was sleep but I wasn't. One of them men had the key to the jail and then a bunch of them came in and grabbed all of us. I must've gone crazy 'cause all I can remember was them saying, "This one of those crazy niggers. Crazy. We don't want him." They tied the other three up and dragged them out. Left me. That was the scariest thing ever happened to me. Shoot.

IDA: They left you?

BLACK JUDAS: What, you wishin they took me 'stead of them. I'm not one of them. I'm not even half a man. I'm just another low-life nigger. I know some of these niggers 'round here would lynch me just as fast as they can. You people always talkin about how much you love the race. How much you do for the race. Well I'm the race. Whatcha do for me? Naw, you do for folks like ya'selves. You know why? Because I'm the part of you you want to forget about. I'm the part of you them white folks love to hate. Cause every time they see you, they see me. A nigger. A black, low-down nigger. All niggas. Always niggas!

(*Black Judas is more aggressive.*)

IDA: I see no nigger.

BLACK JUDAS: You see no nigger? Then what do you see?

IDA: Someone who wants much and gets little; who expects more from others than himself. An angry man who hates the conditions in which he lives but feels powerless to change them.

BLACK JUDAS: That's enough! You see this gun. That's power. I can pull this trigger and shut your mouth for good. I'll shut them all up. Just pull the trigger, just pull the trigger.

IDA: But why Negro people?

BLACK JUDAS: Because nobody's gonna hang a man for attacking a nigger. And because I don't like most of the colored people in this town and they don't like me. Ain't that right?

IDA: They don't like what you do.

BLACK JUDAS: What's the difference? That's who I am. Tell me. If I was lynched instead of them men, would you boycott for me? (*Ida thinks.*)

(*Black Judas puts the gun down. Ida eyes it.*)

BLACK JUDAS: Would you boycott for me?

(*Ida looks up into Black Judas's eyes.*)

IDA: I'd rather you rot in jail.

BLACK JUDAS: (*pause*) Hmph. Rot in jail. Like a piece of old fruit. Well I ain't gonna rot in nobody's jail, ya hear.

BLACK JUDAS: (*picks up the gun and goes to the window*) I thought I saw somebody out there. Lookin for me. They're lookin for me, ain't they. Or maybe not. Maybe they're lookin for you. Maybe I should wave them over. Hey, we're in here! Come get the niggers!

IDA: You have what you want. Why don't you just leave.

BLACK JUDAS: Why don't I leave. I never leave. I just pass through like the wind. (*laughs, then seriously*) I scare you.

(*Black Judas finds a mirror in the* Free Speech *office. He grabs Ida's face, pressing it close to his.*)

BLACK JUDAS: You're scared of me!!! aren't you! Got a name for it. Black Judas. Well you know what they say, the Blacker the Berry, the sweeter the traitor.

(*Black Judas releases Ida.*)

BLACK JUDAS: This your gun? (*puts it in Ida's hand*) Shut 'em up for good. Go ahead. Pull the trigger. (*Ida cocks the hammer.*)

(*Newspaper Boy enters.*)

NEWSPAPER BOY: (*holding up newspapers*) Eight Negroes lynched since last issue of the *Free Speech*, the colored newspaper of Memphis . . . Miss Iola tells the whole story. Read it in *Free Speech*!

(LIGHTS UP *on Mr. Carmack.*)

MR. CARMACK: (*quoting Ida's editorial*) If southern white men are not careful they will overreach themselves and a conclusion will be reached which will be very damaging to the moral reputation of their women. (*writes*) "The black wretch who wrote that foul lie should be tied to a stake at the corner of Main and Madison streets, a pair of tailor's shears used on her and she should then be burned at a stake."

BLACK JUDAS: I guess I've broken enough laws for the night.

(*Before Black Judas exits he slams a coin down on the desk.*)

BLACK JUDAS: That's for the paper.

(*Black Judas exits. Ida puts the gun down on the table and picks up the coin. She takes a deep breath.* BEAT.)

A red glow consumes the stage followed by the sound of a crackling fire burning out of control. Shouts of looters and an angry mob are heard.

ACT THREE, SCENE 4

SFX—*Train coming to a stop.*

VOICE OF CONDUCTOR: Jersey City!

Train station—Jersey City. Ida stands next to her trunk on the train platform looking for a familiar face. She opens her hand slowly and purchases a newspaper with the coin. Mr. Thomas Fortune's ASSISTANT *enters—a very professional, northern and formal individual.*

ASSISTANT: Miss Wells.

IDA: Yes.

ASSISTANT: I'm from the *New York Age*. Mr. Thomas Fortune asked me to meet your train.

IDA: That's very kind of him.

ASSISTANT: (*indicates trunk*) Is this all you brought with you?

IDA: Yes it is.

ASSISTANT: We were very concerned after learning about the destruction of the *Free Speech* offices. It's a miracle you got out of town alive.

IDA: The *Free Speech* gone? I don't understand.

ASSISTANT: Sorry. I thought you knew. We got a dispatch first thing. (*takes the newspaper*) Here it is.

IDA: (*reads the article*) Mr. Fleming. Where's the nearest telegraph office? I need to make sure Mr. Fleming—

ASSISTANT: His wire came this morning. He managed to get out of Memphis safely but says your home is being watched and it's best you stay here rather than go back.

IDA: But everything I own is there, everything except . . . what's in that trunk.

ASSISTANT: Your hotel room's available until we can arrange more permanent lodging, and Mr. Fortune has taken the liberty of setting up a desk for you at the *Age* office. It's terrible having to lose your own newspaper but I believe you'll have a greater advantage working from New York. Already, we're getting requests from women's clubs and suffragist groups asking for you to speak to their membership. We'll arrange your transportation from here. Mr. Fortune says Frederick Douglass has admired your work and would like for you to meet with him in Washington. And there's also a possibility for you to go abroad. It's always effective to have someone who's fairly known, educated, eloquent to speak from personal experiences to the Europeans. It was very successful for the anti-slavery movement and many of the British abolitionist groups are still active. I'll give you the list of issues Mr. Fortune wants to cover in—

IDA: Thank you. But I can manage a list on my own.

ASSISTANT: (*impressed*) Yes, mam. If you'll excuse me, I'll have a porter take your trunk to the cab. (*exit*)

IDA: North. Sometimes a reluctant gateway to justice, but nevertheless a steadfast one. The southern public mind is so hardened that it doesn't object to the coarsest language and obscene vulgarity in its leading journals so long as it's directed against a Negro. Their only reply to my statements about lynching is not proof of their falsity, but insults to me personally.

(*As Ida makes her plea, Thomas joins her on stage—and other shadows of her past.*)

IDA: (*continues*) This abuse cannot alter the fact that three respectable men named Henry Stewart, Calvin McDowell and Thomas Moss were taken out of jail and horribly shot to death for firing on white men in self-defense. The *Commercial*'s inflammatory editorials were greatly responsible for that lynching and the authorities carried it out. They also openly advised that I too be lynched for protesting against mobs and their false charges against their Negro victims. To that I owe the destruction of my newspaper and my exile from home.

(*As Ida continues, Black Judas, Rev. Nightingale, Issac, Mr. Fleming, Betty and*

Maurine, Mr. and Mrs. Johnson, et al. enter and take their places on stage, composing a portrait of a community.

IDA: (*continues*) A single picture of the Negro has been drawn for the world. . . . a picture which triggers the person who sees it to withdraw and remain silent, when he means to condemn hanging, burning-alive and injustice. That is why I am forced to show another.

PHOTOGRAPHER: Hold it.

Flash goes off.

THE END

THE WRITERS' LEAGUE AGAINST LYNCHING

69 FIFTH AVENUE
NEW YORK CITY

Telephone: ALgonquin 4-6548

Harry Hansen, *Chairman*
Suzanne La Follette, *Secretary*
Nella Larsen, *Assistant Secretary*
Lenore Marshall, *Treasurer*

January
16th
1934

EXECUTIVE COMMITTEE
John Chamberlain
Clifton Fadiman
Lewis Gannett
Harry Hansen
Inez Haynes Irwin
Suzanne La Follette
Lenore Marshall
Dorothy Parker
George S. Schuyler
Harrison Smith
Benjamin Stolberg
Walter White
Helen Woodward

LEAGUE MEMBERS
Louis Adamic
Frederick Lewis Allen
Sherwood Anderson
Philip Barry
Ernest Sutherland Bates
Carlton Beals
Robert Benchley
Stephen Vincent Benét
Bruce Bliven
Harry Block
Roark Bradford
George Britt
Louis Bromfield
Heywood Broun
Sterling Brown
James Branch Cabell
Erskine Caldwell
V. F. Calverton
Stuart Chase
Countee Cullen
Virginius Dabney
James H. Dillard
Edward Donohoe
W. E. B. Du Bois
Morris L. Ernst
John Farrar
Edna Ferber
Rudolph Fisher
E. Franklin Frazier
C. Hartley Grattan
Horace Gregory
Ernest H. Gruening
Harold Guinzburg
Louis M. Hacker
Alfred Harcourt
Abram L. Harris
Jessie Fauset Harris
Arthur Garfield Hays
Henry Hazlitt
Du Bose Heyward
B. W. Huebsch
Sheila Hibben
Fannie Hurst
Will Irwin
James Weldon Johnson
Alfred A. Knopf
Joseph Wood Krutch
Newman Levy
George Milburn
Christopher Morley
Lewis Mumford
George Jean Nathan
Mary White Ovington
Gretta Palmer
Drew Pearson
William Pickens
Elmer Rice
William Soskin
J. E. Spingarn
Geroid Tanquary Robinson
Carl Van Doren
Irita Van Doren
Mark Van Doren
Richard Van Gelder
Carl Van Vechten
Oswald Garrison Villard
Roy Wilkins
W. E. Woodward

My dear Mrs. Meyer:

The Writers' League Against Lynching extends to you a cordial invitation to become a member.

Stirred by the recent increase in the number and viciousness of lynchings and the growing spirit of mob violence throughout the country, a group of us met to determine in what way we writers could best help to formulate public opinion against such lawlessness. It was out of this meeting that the Writers' League Against Lynching developed and during its short life it already has done notable work. Among its accomplishments is the telegram sent in the name of the League to President Roosevelt asking a public pronouncement against lynching. We have been informed that the President's unequivocal statement in December over a national hook-up in which he termed lynch law as "that vile form of collective murder" was in part due to the Writers' League's telegram.

One of the immediate activities planned by the League is the appearance of several of its members to speak against lynching before a Senate committee in Washington.

We very much hope that you will join us. The annual membership dues are two ($2.00) dollars, payable to Lenore Marshall, treasurer, 69 Fifth Avenue, New York City.

Sincerely,

Harry Hansen
Chairman.

Mrs. Annie Nathan Meyer
1225 Park Avenue
New York City.

Suzanne La Follette
Secretary.

SL:CTF

Appendix 2. Table of Lynching Dramas*

Lynching Dramas by African American Women

DATE	PLAY	PLAYWRIGHT	PUBLISHED	FIRST PRODUCED
1916	*Rachel*	Angelina Grimké	Cornhill, 1920 (self-subsidized)	March 3, 4, 1916, Myrtilla Miner Normal School, Washington, DC, by the local branch of the NAACP (Drama Committee)
1918	*Mine Eyes Have Seen*	Alice Dunbar Nelson	*The Crisis,* April 1918	April 10, 1918, Howard High School, Wilmington, DE
1919	*Aftermath*	Mary Burrill	*The Liberator,* 1919	New York Krigwa Players, 1928, David Belasco Little Theatre Tournament
c. 1920–25	*Mara*	Angelina Grimké	MS. at Moorland-Spingarn Res. Ctr., Howard Univ.	—
1925	*A Sunday Morning in the South*	Georgia Douglas Johnson	Hatch and Shine, eds., *Black Theatre USA,* 1974	—
1926	*For Unborn Children*	Myrtle Smith Livingston	*The Crisis,* July 1926	—
c. 1929	*Safe*	Georgia Douglas Johnson	Brown-Guillory, ed., *Wines in the Wilderness,* 1990	—
c. 1930	*Blue-Eyed Black Boy*	Georgia Douglas Johnson	Perkins, ed., *Black Female Playwrights,* 1989	—
—	*A Bill to Be Passed*	Georgia Douglas Johnson	—	—
—	*And Still They Paused*	Georgia Douglas Johnson	—	—

*These lists are works in progress and are not intended to be exhaustive. (FTP = Federal Theatre Project; NEC= Negro Ensemble Company.)

DATE	PLAY	PLAYWRIGHT	PUBLISHED	FIRST PRODUCED
1931	*Climbing Jacob's Ladder*	Regina Andrews	Perkins and Stephens, eds., *Strange Fruit*, 1998	Harlem Exp. Theatre, 1931
1933	*Nails and Thorns*	May Miller	Hamalian and Hatch, eds., *Roots of African American Drama*, 1991	—
1955	*Trouble in Mind*	Alice Childress	Patterson, ed., *Black Theatre*, 1971	Greenwich Mews Theatre, NYC, 1955
1962	*Incident in a Southern Town*	Gertrude Greenidge	Peterson, ed., *Contemporary Black American Playwrights*, 1988	—
1983	*Ida B. Wells*	Endesha Mae Holland	Perkins and Stephens, eds., *Strange Fruit*, 1998	At the Foot of the Mountain, MN, 1982
1985	*Dreaming Emmett*	Toni Morrison	—	Capital Rep. (Market Theatre), Albany, NY, 1986
1989	*The Bridge Party*	Sandra Seaton	Perkins and Stephens, eds., *Strange Fruit*, 1998	—
1989	*The Death of the Last Black Man in the Whole Entire World*	Suzan-Lori Parks	Lamont, ed., *Women on the Verge*, 1993	BACA Downtown (Brooklyn Arts Council)
1994	*Iola's Letter*	Michon Boston	Perkins and Stephens, eds., *Strange Fruit*, 1998	—
1994	*Wake Up Lou Riser*	Kia Corthron	—	Circle Rep. Lab., NYC, July 1994

LYNCHING DRAMAS BY WHITE AMERICAN WOMEN

DATE	PLAY	PLAYWRIGHT	PUBLISHED	FIRST PRODUCED
1919	*The Noose*	Tracy Mygatt	Alain Locke Collection, Howard University	Neighborhood Playhouse, NYC, 1919
1923	*The Awakening*	Mary White Ovington	1923; repr. Books for Libraries Press, 1972	—
1925	*The Forfeit*	Corrie Crandall Howell	*Poet Lore* 36, Jan.-Dec. 1925	—

DATE	PLAY	PLAYWRIGHT	PUBLISHED	FIRST PRODUCED
1932	*Black Souls*	Annie Nathan Meyer	Reynolds Press, 1932	Provincetown Play-house, NY, March 1932
1936	*Lawd, Does You Undahstan'?*	Ann Seymour	Samuel French, 1937; Mayorga, ed., *Twenty Short Plays on a Royalty Holiday,* 1937	Paine College, Augusta, GA, Dec. 12, 1936
1936	*Youth Challenges Justice*	Mrs. M. A. Salvo	ASWPL, Sept. 1936	Institute for the Prevention of Lynching, Jacksonville, FL, May 5, 1936
1938	*Mourners to Glory*	Rietta Winn Bailey	Koch, ed., *American Folk Plays,* 1939	Carolina Playmakers, Chapel Hill, NC, Mar. 3, 1938
1944	*Voice in the Wilderness*	Evelyn Keller	*Eleven Radio Plays by Evelyn Keller,* 1944	Aired over WPIC, Sharon, PA, early 40s
1945	*Strange Fruit*	Lillian Smith	Perkins and Stephens, eds., *Strange Fruit,* 1998	Royale Theatre, NYC, Nov. 29, 1945–Jan. 19, 1946

LYNCHING DRAMAS BY AFRICAN AMERICAN MEN

DATE	PLAY	PLAYWRIGHT	PUBLISHED	FIRST PRODUCED
1925	*Frances*	G. D. Lipscomb	*Opportunity,* May 1925	—
1928	*Son Boy*	Joseph Mitchell	*Sat. Eve. Quill* June 1928	—
1931	*Scottsboro Limited*	Langston Hughes	*New Masses,* Nov. 1931	—
1932	*Bad Man*	Randolph Edmonds	*Six Plays for a Negro Theatre,* 1934	Morgan Players of Baltimore–Negro Intercollegiate Dramatic Assoc., Richmond, VA, 1932
1934	*A Sign*	George Streator	*The Crisis,* Jan. 1934	—
1935	*Brothers —American Drama (A Verse Drama)*	James Weldon Johnson	*Saint Peter Relates an Incident: Selected Poems by James Weldon Johnson.* New York: Viking, 1935	—

DATE	PLAY	PLAYWRIGHT	PUBLISHED	FIRST PRODUCED
1935	*The Call of Jubah*	Randolph Edmonds	synopsis in Peterson, *Early Black American Playwrights and Dramatic Writers*, 1990	—
1935	*Mulatto*	Langston Hughes	*Five Plays by Langston Hughes*, 1963	Vanderbilt Theatre, NYC, 1935
1935	*Sweet Land*	Conrad Seiler	typescript in Hatch-Billops Coll.	Lafayette Theatre, NYC, WPA/FTP, 1937
1937	*A Bitter Pill*	Lew Payton	*Did Adam Sin? And Stories of Negro Life*, 1937	—
1937	*Swing Song*	Ralph Coleman	typescript in Hatch-Billops Coll.	Negro Federal Theatre of Mass., Boston, 1937–39
1937	*Don't You Want to Be Free?*	Langston Hughes	*One-Act Play Mag.* Oct. 1938	Suitcase Theatre, NYC, 1937
1938	*Liberty Deferred*	John Silvera and Abram Hill	Hatch and Shine, eds., *Black Theatre USA*, 1974	—
1937	*Darker Brother: A Satirical Fantasy*	Conrad Seiler	*Lost Plays of the Harlem Renaissance*, 1996	Gilpin Players, 1937
1937	*Sick and Tired*	Theodore Ward	typescript in Hatch-Billops Coll.	Abraham Lincoln Center, Chicago, 1938
1938	*Smokey*	Thomas Desire Pawley	—	Univ. of Iowa, 1939
1938	*Hell's Half Acre*	Abram Hill	FTP typescript	Unity Players, Bronx, 1938
1964	*Blues for Mr. Charlie*	James Baldwin	Dial Press, 1964	ANTA Theatre, NYC, 1964
1975	*Waiting for Mongo*	Silas Jones	synopsis in Peterson, *Contemporary Black American Playwrights*, 1988	NEC, NYC, 1975
1983	*Sons and Fathers of Sons*	Ray Aranha	synopsis in Peterson, *Contemporary Black American Playwrights*, 1988	NEC, NYC, 1983

DATE	PLAY	PLAYWRIGHT	PUBLISHED	FIRST PRODUCED
1990	*Dat Great Long Time*	Cedric Turner	—	Univ. of Louisville, 1990
1991	*The Little Tommy Parker Celebrated Colored Minstrel Show*	Carlyle Brown	Elam and Alexander, eds., *Colored Contradictions*, 1996	Negro Ensemble Co., NYC, 1991
1995	*Coming of the Hurricane*	Keith Glover	Dramatists Play Service, 1994	Denver Theatre Co., 1995

LYNCHING DRAMAS BY WHITE AMERICAN MEN

DATE	PLAY	PLAYWRIGHT	PUBLISHED	FIRST PRODUCED
1906	*The Clansman*	Thomas Dixon	typescript at Library of Congress	Liberty Theatre, NYC, 1906
1909	*The Nigger*	Edward Sheldon	Macmillan, 1910	New Theatre, NYC, 1909
1914	*Granny Maumee*	Ridgely Torrence	*Three Plays for a Negro Theatre,* NYC, 1917	Stage Society, NYC, 1914 (white cast); Garden Theatre, Madison Square Garden, NYC, 1917 (black cast)
1923	*Judge Lynch*	John Wm. Rogers	*One-Act Plays for Stage & Study,* Samuel French, 1925	1924 Nat. Little Thea. Tournament (won Belasco Cup)
1926	*In Abraham's Bosom*	Paul Green	Samuel French, 1927	Garrick Theatre, NYC, 1926
1932	*Never No More*	James Knox Miller	Plot summary in Burns Mantle, *Best Plays of 1931–32*	Hudson Theater, NYC, 1932
1932	*"Lynch Him"*	Fred St. Amant	*The Epworth Highroad,* July 1932	—
1934	*They Shall Not Die*	John Wexley	Knopf, 1934	Royale Theatre, NYC, 1934
1934	*Stevedore*	Paul Peters and George Sklar	Covici, 1934	Civic Repertory Theatre, NYC (Theatre Union), 1934
1935	*Necktie Party*	Randolph F. Blackford	*Southern Churchman,*1935	—

DATE	PLAY	PLAYWRIGHT	PUBLISHED	FIRST PRODUCED
1936	*Country Sunday*	Walter Spearman	ASWPL, 1936	—
1936	*Mob Tide*	John Walker	—	Carolina Playmakers, NC, 1936
1936	*New Nigger*	Fred Howard	—	Carolina Playmakers, NC, 1936
1936	*Kids Learn Fast*	A. B. Shiffrin	*New Theatre* 3 (Nov. 1936)	—
1936	*Lynchtown*	George Sklar and Paul Peters	*New Masses*, 1936	—
1960	*To Kill a Mockingbird* (based on the novel by Harper Lee)	Christopher Sergel	Dramatic Publishers, 1960	—

International Lynching Dramas

1946	*The Respectful Prostitute*	Jean-Paul Sartre	*Art and Action,* New York: Twice a Year Press, 1948; Alfred Knopf, 1949	Theatre Antoine, Paris, 1946

BIBLIOGRAPHY

BOOKS

Aptheker, Bettina. *Woman's Legacy: Essays on Race, Sex, and Class in American History.* Amherst: University of Massachusetts Press, 1982.

Barlow, Judith. *Plays by American Women: 1900–1930.* New York: Applause Books, 1985.

Blaustein, Albert P., and Robert Zangrando, eds. *Civil Rights and the Black American: A Documentary History.* New York: Simon and Schuster, 1968.

Brantley, Will. *Feminine Sense in Southern Memoir: Smith, Glasgow, Welty, Hellman, and Hurston.* Jackson: University Press of Mississippi, 1993.

Braxton, Joanne M., and Andree Nicola McLaughlin, eds. *Wild Women in the Whirl-wind: Afra-American Culture and the Contemporary Literary Renaissance.* New Brunswick: Rutgers University Press, 1990.

Brown-Guillory, Elizabeth, ed. *Their Place on the Stage: Black Women Playwrights in America.* New York: Praeger, 1988, 1990.

Brown-Guillory, Elizabeth, ed. *Wines in the Wilderness: Plays by African American Women from the Harlem Renaissance to the Present.* New York: Praeger, 1990.

Brown, Sterling. *Negro Poetry and Drama and the Negro in American Fiction.* New York: Atheneum, 1978.

Brundage, W. Fitzhugh. *Lynching in the New South: Georgia and Virginia, 1880–1930.* Urbana: University of Illinois Press, 1993.

Bzowski, Frances Diodato, comp. *American Women Playwrights, 1900–1930.* Westport: Greenwood, 1992.

Cameron, James. *A Time of Terror: A Survivor's Story.* Baltimore: Black Classic Press, 1994.

Collins, Winfield H. *The Truth about Lynching and the Negro in the South.* New York: Neale, 1918.

Cutler, James Elbert. *Lynch Law: An Investigation into the History of Lynching in the United States.* Montclair: Patterson Smith, 1969.

Decosta-Willis, Miriam, ed. *The Memphis Diary of Ida B. Wells.* Boston: Beacon Press, 1995.

Dolan, Jill. *The Feminist Spectator as Critic.* Ann Arbor: UMI Research Press, 1988.

Downey, Dennis, and Raymond Hyser. *No Crooked Death: The Lynching of Zachariah Walker.* Chicago: University of Illinois Press, 1991.

Duster, Alfreda M., ed. *Crusade for Justice: The Autobiography of Ida B. Wells.* Chicago, University of Chicago Press, 1970.

Edmonds, Randolph. *Six Plays for a Negro Theatre.* Boston: Walter Bacon, 1934.

Evans, Mari, ed. *Black Women Writers (1959–1980).* New York: Anchor Books, 1984.

Giddings, Paula. *When and Where I Enter: The Impact of Black Women on Race and Sex in America.* New York: Morrow, 1984.

Ginzburg, Ralph. *100 Years of Lynching.* New York: Lancer Books, 1976.

Gladney, Margaret Rose. *How Am I to Be Heard? Letters of Lillian Smith.* Chapel Hill: University of North Carolina Press, 1993.

Grant, Donald L. *The Anti-Lynching Movement: 1888–1932.* San Francisco: R and E Research Associates, 1975.

Hall, Jacquelyn Dowd. *Revolt Against Chivalry: Jessie Daniel Ames and the Women's Campaign Against Lynching.* New York: Columbia University Press, 1979.

Hamalian, Leo, and James V. Hatch, eds. *The Roots of African American Drama.* Detroit: Wayne State University Press, 1991.

Harris, Trudier, ed. *Dictionary of Literary Biography: Afro-American Writers from the Harlem Renaissance to 1940,* vol. 51. Detroit: Gale Research, 1987.

Harris, Trudier. *Exorcising Blackness: Historical and Literary Lynching and Burning Rituals.* Bloomington: Indiana University Press, 1984.

Harris, Trudier, ed. *Dictionary of Literary Biography: Afro-American Writers before the Harlem Renaissance,* vol. 50. Detroit: Gale Research, 1986.

Hart, Lynda, ed. *Making a Spectacle: Feminist Essays on Contemporary Women's Theatre.* Ann Arbor: University of Michigan Press, 1989.

Hatch, James V., and Leo Hamalian, eds. *Lost Plays of the Harlem Renaissance, 1920–1940.* Detroit: Wayne State University Press, 1996.

Hatch, James V., and Ted Shine, eds. *Black Theatre USA: Plays by African Americans: The Early Period, 1847–1938,* 2nd ed., rev. and enl. New York: Free Press, 1996.

Hay, Samuel A. *African American Theatre: An Historical and Critical Analysis.* New York: Cambridge University Press, 1994.

Herron, Carolivia, ed. *Selected Works of Angelina Grimké.* New York: Oxford University Press, 1991.

Hill, Errol, ed. *The Theatre of Black Americans: A Collection of Critical Essays.* New York: Applause, 1980, 1987.

Hine, Darlene Clark, ed. *Black Women in America: An Historical Encyclopedia.* Brooklyn: Carlson Publishing, 1993.

Holiday, Billie, with William Duffy. *Lady Sings the Blues.* New York: Lance Books, 1956.

hooks, bell. *Ain't I a Woman: Black Women and Feminism.* Boston: South End Press, 1981.

hooks, bell, *Talking Back: thinking feminist, thinking black.* Boston: South End Press, 1989.

Hull, Gloria T. *Color, Sex and Poetry: Three Women Writers of the Harlem Renaissance.* Bloomington: Indiana University Press, 1987.

Hull, Gloria T., Patricia Bell Scott, and Barbara Smith, eds. *All the Women Are White, All the Blacks Are Men, But Some of Us Are Brave: Black Women's Studies.* Old Westbury, N.Y.: Feminist Press, 1982.

Jones, Jacquelin. *Labor of Love, Labor of Sorrow: Black Women, Work, and the Family, from Slavery to the Present.* New York: Vintage Books, 1985.

Joseph, Gloria I., and Jill Lewis, eds. *Common Differences: Conflicts in Black & White Feminist Perspectives.* Boston: South End Press, 1981.

Keller, Evelyn. *Eleven Radio Plays by Evelyn Keller.* Boston: Christopher Publishing House, 1944.

Koch, Frederick, ed. *American Folk Plays*. New York and London: Appleton Century, 1939.

Lamont, Rosette C., ed. *Women on the Verge: 7 Avant-garde American Plays*. New York: Applause Theatre Books, 1993.

Lerner, Gerda, ed. *Black Women in White America: A Documentary History*. New York: Vintage Books, 1973.

Locke, Alain, and Montgomery Gregory, eds. *Plays of Negro Life: A Source-Book of Native American Drama*. 1927. Reprint, Westport, Conn.: Negro Universities Press, 1970.

Loveland, Anne C. *Lillian Smith: A Southerner Confronting the South*. Baton Rouge: Louisiana University Press, 1986.

MacLean, Nancy. *Behind the Mask of Chivalry: The Making of the Second Ku Klux Klan*. New York: Oxford University Press, 1994.

Mainiero, Lina, ed. *American Women Writers: A Critical Reference Guide from Colonial Times to the Present*. New York: Frederick Ungar, 1982.

Mayorga, Margaret, ed. *Representative One-Act Plays by American Authors*. Boston: Little, Brown, 1937.

Mayorga, Margaret, ed., *Twenty Short Plays on a Royalty Holiday*. New York: Samuel French, 1937.

McDowell, John Patrick. *The Social Gospel in the South: The Women's Home Mission Movement in the Methodist Episcopal Church, South, 1886–1939*. Baton Rouge: Louisiana State University Press, 1982.

McGovern, James. *Anatomy of a Lynching: The Killing of Claude Neal*. Baton Rouge: Louisiana State University Press, 1982.

Meyer, Annie Nathan. *It's Been Fun: An Autobiography*. New York: Henry Shuman, 1951.

Meyer, Annie Nathan. *Black Souls: A Play in Six Scenes*. New Bedford, Mass.: Reynolds Press, 1932.

Mitchell, Loften. *Black Drama: The Story of the American Negro in the Theatre*. New York: Hawthorne Books, 1967.

Molette, Carlton W., and Barbara J. Molette. *Black Theatre: Premise and Presentation*. Bristol, Ind.: Wyndham Hall Press, 1986.

Moses, Wilson Jeremiah. *The Golden Age of Black Nationalism, 1850–1925*. New York: Oxford University Press, 1978.

Murphy, Brenda. *American Realism and American Drama, 1880–1940*. New York: Cambridge University Press, 1987.

NAACP. *Thirty Years of Lynching in the United States, 1889–1918*. New York: Arno Press and the New York Times, 1969.

Newton, Judith, and Deborah Rosenfelt, eds. *Feminist Criticism and Social Change: Sex, Class and Race in Literature and Culture*. New York: Methuen, 1985.

Ovington, Mary White, *The Awakening: A Play*. Reprint, Freeport, NY: Books for Libraries Press, 1972.

Patterson, Lindsay, comp. *Black Theater: A 20th-Century Collection of the Work of Its Best Playwrights*. New York: Dodd, Mead, 1971.

Perkins, Kathy A., ed. *Black Female Playwrights: An Anthology of Plays before 1950*. Bloomington: Indiana University Press, 1989.

Peterson, Bernard L., Jr. *Early Black American Playwrights and Dramatic Writers: A Biographical Directory and Catalog of Plays, Films, and Broadcasting Scripts*. New York: Greenwood Press, 1990.

Peterson, Bernard, *Contemporary Black American Playwrights and Their Plays*. New York: Greenwood Press, 1988.

Raper, Arthur. *The Tragedy of Lynching*. Chapel Hill: University of North Carolina Press, 1933.

Richardson, Willis, and May Miller, eds. *Negro History in Thirteen Plays.* Washington, D.C.: Associated Publishers, 1935.

Saunders, Leslie Catherine. *The Development of Black Theatre in America.* Baton Rouge: Louisiana State University Press, 1988.

Scharine, Richard G. *From Class to Caste in American Drama: Political and Social Themes Since the 1930s.* New York: Greenwood Press, 1991.

Smead, Howard. *Blood Justice: The Lynching of Mack Charles Parker.* New York: Oxford University Press, 1986.

Smith, Jessie Carney, ed. *Notable Black American Women.* Detroit: Gale Research, 1992.

Tate, Claudia. *Allegories of Political Desire: The Black Heroine's Text at the Turn of the Century.* New York: Oxford University Press, 1992.

Thompson, Mildred I. *Ida B. Wells-Barnett: An Exploratory Study of an American Black Woman, 1893–1930.* Brooklyn: Carlson Publishing, 1990.

Tolnay, Stewart E., and E. M. Beck. *A Festival of Violence: An Analysis of Southern Lynchings, 1882–1930.* Chicago: University of Illinois Press, 1995.

Walden, Daniel, ed. *W. E. B. Du Bois: The Crisis Writings.* Greenwich, Conn.: Fawcett, 1972.

Walker, Alice. *In Search of Our Mothers' Gardens.* San Diego: Harcourt Brace Jovanovich, 1983.

Wells-Barnett, Ida B. *On Lynchings: Southern Horrors, a Red Record, and Mob Rule in New Orleans.* New York: Arno Press and the New York Times, 1969.

White, Walter. *A Man Called White: The Autobiography of Walter White.* Bloomington: Indiana University Press, 1948.

White, Walter. *Rope and Faggot: A Biography of Judge Lynch.* New York: Alfred A. Knopf, 1929; Arno Press, 1969.

Wilkerson, Margaret B., ed. *9 Plays by Black Women.* New York: Mentor, 1986.

Williamson, Joel. *The Crucible of Race: Black-White Relations in the American South since Emancipation.* New York: Oxford University Press, 1984.

Wilson, Garff B. *Three Hundred Years of American Drama and Theatre: from Ye Bare and Ye Cubb to Hair.* Englewood Cliffs: Prentice Hall, 1973.

Wright, George C. *Racial Violence in Kentucky, 1865–1940: Lynchings, Mob Rule, and Legal Lynchings.* Baton Rouge: Louisiana University Press, 1990.

Yellin, Jean Fagan. *Women and Sisters: The Anti-Slavery Feminists in American Culture.* New Haven: Yale University Press, 1989.

Zangrando, Robert. *The NAACP Crusade Against Lynching 1909–1950.* Philadelphia: Temple University Press, 1980.

ARTICLES

Barrett, Michele. "Ideology and the Cultural Production of Gender," in Judith Newton and Deborah Rosenfelt, eds., *Feminist Criticism and Social Change.* New York: Methuen, 1985, 65–85.

Boyce Davies, Carole and Elaine Savory Fido. "Talking It Over: Women Writing and Feminism," *Out of the Kumbla: Caribbean Women and Literature.* Trenton: Africa World Press, 1990, ix–xix.

Braxton, Joanne M. "Ancestral Presence: The Outraged Mother Figure in Contemporary Afra-American Writing," in Braxton and McLaughlin, 299–315.

Carby, Hazel. "'On the Threshold of Women's Era': Lynching, Empire, and Sexuality," in Henry Louis Gates, Jr., ed., *Black Feminist Theory: "Race," Writing, and Difference.* Chicago: University of Chicago Press, 1985, 301–616.

Dickerson, Glenda. "The Cult of True Womanhood: Toward a Womanist Attitude in African-American Theatre," in Sue Ellen Case, ed., *Performing Feminisms:*

Feminist Critical Theory and Theatre. Baltimore: Johns Hopkins University Press, 1990, 109–118.

Donlon, Jocelyn Hazelwood. "Georgia Douglas Johnson," in Hine, *Black Women in America,* 640–642.

Du Bois, W. E. B., "Triumph," *Crisis* 2 (September 1911), 195. For additional *Crisis* writings on lynching see "We Are a Nation of Murderers" in Walden.

Edmonds, Randolph. "Black Drama in the American Theatre: 1700–1970," *The American Theatre: A Sum of Its Parts.* New York: Samuel French, 1971, 379–424.

Esonwanne, Uzo. "Race and Hermeneutics: Paradigm Shift—From Scientific to Hermeneutic Understanding of Race," *African American Review* 26, no. 4 (1992), 565–582.

Fehrenbach, Robert J. "An Early Twentieth Century Problem Play of Life in Black America: Angelina Grimké's Rachel," in Braxton and McLaughlin, eds., *Wild Women in the Whirlwind,* 89–106.

Fletcher, Winona. "From Genteel Poet to Revolutionary Playwright: Georgia Douglas Johnson," *Theatre Annual* 30 (1985): 41–64.

Fletcher, Winona. "Georgia Douglas Johnson," in Alice Robinson, Vera M. Roberts, and Millie Barranger, eds., *Notable Women in the American Theatre: A Biographical Dictionary.* New York: Greenwood, 1989, 473–477.

Fletcher, Winona. "Georgia Douglas Johnson" in Harris, ed., *Dictionary of Literary Biography,* vol. 51, 153–164.

Gorden, Lynn. "Annie Nathan Meyer and Barnard College: Mission and Identity in Women's Higher Education, 1880–1950," *Higher Education Quarterly* 26 (1986): 503–522.

Greene, Michael. "Angelina Weld Grimké," in Harris, ed., *Dictionary of Literary Biography,* vol. 50, 149–155.

Gregory, Montgomery. "A Chronology of Negro Theatre," Alain Locke, *Plays of Negro Life,* Westport, Conn.: Negro Universities, 1970, 409–422.

Grimké, Angelina. "'Rachel' The Play of the Month: The Reason and Synopsis by the Author," *The Competitor* 1, no. 1 (1920), 51–52.

Hatch, James. "Some African Influences on the Afro-American Theatre," in Hill, ed., *The Theatre of Black Americans,* 13–28.

Height, Dorothy, "Self Help—A Black Tradition," *The Nation,* July 24–31, 1989.

Johnson, Guion Griffis. "The Ideology of White Supremacy, 1876–1910," in Fletcher Melvin Green, ed., *Essays in Southern History: The James Sprunt Studies in History and Political Science,* vol. 31. Chapel Hill: University of North Carolina, 1949, 124–156.

Kline, Herbert. "Drama of Negro Life," *New Theatre* 3, no. 2 (February 1936), 26–27.

McKay, Nellie. "What Were They Saying?: Black Women Playwrights of the Harlem Renaissance," in Victor A. Kramer, ed., *The Harlem Renaissance Re-examined.* New York: AMS Press, 1987.

Miller, Jean Marie. "Angelina Weld Grimké: Playwright and Poet," *CLA Journal* 21 (1978): 513–24.

Molette, Barbara. "They Speak: Who Listens? Black Women Playwrights," *Black World,* April 1976, 28–34.

Morrison, Toni. "Rootedness: The Ancestor as Foundation," in Mari Evans, ed., *Black Women Writers (1950–1980): A Critical Evaluation.* New York: Anchor Books, 1984, 339–345.

Murray, Pauli. "The Liberation of Black Women," *Women: A Feminist Perspective.* Palo Alto: Mayfield, 1975.

Nordyke, Lewis T. "Ladies and Lynchings," *Survey Graphic,* November 1939, 683–686.

Ogunyemi, Chikwenye Okonjo. "Womanism: The Dynamics of the Contemporary Black Female Novel in English," *Signs,* 1985, 64–89.

Smith, Barbara. "Toward a Black Feminist Criticism," in Newton and Rosenfelt, eds., *Feminist Criticism and Social Change*, 3–18.

Smith, Valerie. "Black Feminist Theory and the Representation of the 'Other,'" in Cheryl Wall, ed., *Changing Our Own Words: Essays on Criticism, Theory and Writing by Black Women*. New Brunswick: Rutgers University Press, 1989, 38–57.

Smith, Valerie. "Split Affinities: The Case of Interracial Rape," in Marianne Hirsch and Evelyn Fox Keller, eds., *Conflicts in Feminism*. New York: Routledge, 1990, 271–287.

Stephens, Judith. "Anti-Lynch Plays by African American Women: Race, Gender, and Social Protest in American Drama," *African American Review* 26, no. 2 (Summer 1992), 329–339.

Stephens, Judith. "The Anti-Lynch Play: Toward an Interracial Feminist Dialogue in Theatre," *Journal of American Drama and Theatre* 2, no. 3 (Fall 1990), 59–66.

Stephens, Judith. "Lynching, American Theatre History, and the Preservation of a Tradition," *Journal of American Drama and Theatre* 9 (Winter 1997), 54–65.

Storm, William. "Reactions of a 'Highly Strung Girl': Psychology and Dramatic Representation in Angelina W. Grimké's *Rachel*," *African American Review* 27, no. 3 (1993), 461–471.

Terborg-Penn, Rosalyn. "Discontented Black Feminists: Prelude and Postscript to the Passage of the Nineteenth Amendment," in Lois Scharf and Joan Jensen, eds., *Decades of Discontent: The Women's Movement, 1920–1940* Westport, Conn.: Greenwood, 1983.

Terborg-Penn, Rosalyn. "African American Women's Networks in the Anti-Lynching Crusade," in Noralee Frankel and Nancy S. Dye, eds., *Gender, Class, Race, and Reform in the Progressive Era*. Lexington: University of Kentucky Press, 1991.

Terrell, Mary Church. "Lynching from a Negro's Point of View," *North Atlantic Review*, June 1904, 853–868.

Walker, Ethel Pitts. "The American Negro Theatre," in Hill, 247–260.

THESES AND DISSERTATIONS

Austin, Addell. "Pioneering Black Authored Dramas: 1924–27," Michigan State University, 1986.

Dyrda, Cynthia Ann. "Lynching as a Social Effect of Modernization in Early Twentieth Century America," Penn State University, 1983.

Elam, Harry Justin, Jr. "Theatre for Social Change: The Artistic and Social Vision in Revolutionary Theatre in America, 1930–1970," University of California at Berkeley, 1984.

Goldenberg, Myrna Gallant. "Annie Nathan Meyer: Barnard Godmother and Gotham Gadfly," University of Maryland, 1987.

Hay, Samuel Arthur. "The Image of the Black Man as Projected by Representative White American Dramatists, 1900–1963," Cornell University, 1971.

Hicklin, Fannie E. "The American Negro Playwright, 1920–1964," University of Wisconsin, 1965.

Tanner, Jo Ann. "The Emergence and Development of the Black Dramatic Actress, 1890–1917," City University of New York, 1989.

Thomas, Marjorie Ann. "An Overview of Miss Anne: White Women as Seen by Black Playwrights," Florida State University, 1973.

Udosen, Willye Bell. "Image of the Black Woman in Black American Drama, 1900–1970," East Texas State University, 1979.

Young, Patricia. "Female Pioneers in Afro-American Drama," Bowling Green University, 1986.

INTERVIEWS

Evelyn Keller Caldwell. Playwright, *Voice in the Wilderness*, 1944 (October 1991).

James, Cameron. Founder, Black Holocaust Museum, Milwaukee (1994).

Joseph Lacy. Actor, *Lawd, Does You Undahstan'?* by Ann Seymour, Paine College, 1936. (November 1991).

Henry Link, son of Ann Seymour, playwright, *Lawd Does You Undahstan?* (February 1993).

Sandra Seaton. Playwright, *The Bridge Party* (1993).

Esther Smith, sister of Lillian Smith, playwright, *Strange Fruit*, 1945 (correspondence, May, June 1993).

Jane White, actor, *Strange Fruit*, Theatre Royale, New York, 1945. (June 1993).

COLLECTIONS

America's Black Holocaust Museum, Milwaukee

American Jewish Archives, Cincinnati, Ohio

Association of Southern Women for the Prevention of Lynching Papers, Microfilm Edition, Pattee Library, Penn State University

Barnard College Archives, New York City

Billy Rose Theatre Collection, New York Public Library at Lincoln Center

Federal Theatre Project, George Mason University

Fisk University

Hatch-Billops Collection, New York City

James Weldon Johnson Collection, Yale University

Manuscript Division of the Library of Congress

Moorland-Spingarn Research Center, Howard University

Schomburg Center for Research in Black Culture

WEB SITE

Plaines, Milford F. http://www.tnp.com./holocaust

Kathy A. Perkins *is Associate Professor of Theatre at the University of Illinois, where she heads the Lighting Design Program. She is the editor of* Black Female Playwrights: An Anthology of Plays before 1950, *and co-editor with Roberta Uno of* Contemporary Plays by Women of Color.

———————◆———————

Judith L. Stephens *is Associate Professor of Speech Communication at Penn State University, Schuylkill Campus, where she teaches theater, women's studies, and speech communication. She serves on the Executive Board of the Black Theater Network (BTN) and has published articles on women in American theatre in* African American Review, Theatre Journal, Theatre Annual, Text and Performance, *and* The Journal of American Drama and Theater, *among other publications.*